Ultimate Guide to Medical Schools

Fourth Edition

Josh Fischman and the staff of *U.S.News & World Report*

Foreword by Bernadine Healy, M.D.

Anne McGrath, Editor

Robert Morse, Director of Data Research

Brian Kelly, Series Editor

Published by Sourcebooks, Inc.

P.O. Box 4410

Naperville, Illinois 60567-4410

(630) 961-3900 FAX: (630) 961-2168

www.sourcebooks.com

Fourth Edition

Printed and bound in the United States of America

DR 10 9 8 7 6 5 4 3 2 1

Table of Contents

On Being a Doctor

Medicine is a way of life. It is a way of knowing and thinking, of seeing the world, and of feeling about people. No one
is born a doctor, and the long road to becoming one requires
unrelenting study, discipline, and the cultivation of unique
talents and skills. But whatever the domain of medical pursuit and however removed from the bedside one's work may
ultimately be, its ethos and raison d'être stem from that one
enduring relationship: physician and patient.

In our time, this most personal of human services has
burgeoned into a $2.5 trillion enterprise employing 1 in 10
Americans. It is a growth propelled by the endless frontier
of medical discovery, translating into better ways to care for
people. In that sense, a medical career is the intellectual

journey of a lifetime. In a field where the sands shift so quickly and one technology is swept away by another, medical school is not about teaching you all the facts you'll ever need to know. Rather, it is the place in which students are slowly converted from laypeople into doctors.

This conversion takes time, with and beyond the books, journals, and professorial pronouncements. Ultimately, one becomes a doctor from an immersion in the unpredictable, varied, and complex ways in which patients fall ill and the momentous efforts of people and technology to make them well. It comes from learning the secrets of the body, the passages of life from birth to death, the tortured times and the peaceful times of human souls, and the uplifting (and carefully harnessed) power of the physician to make a difference every step along the way. For the best of students, by the time they walk across the stage and accept their medical diploma, doctorhood has seeped into the marrow of their bones, the depth of their hearts. Whatever their chosen line of work, they will always see the world through the lens of a doctor.

That lens is broad. Medicine embraces a continuum of knowledge and practice from the micro to the macro level—from the medical scientist in the laboratory, to the doctor at the bedside, to the public health specialist tracking down the latest epidemic anywhere in the world. And along that broad spectrum, one can carve out a professional life of research, teaching, practice or administration—or some combination of all four. There is a place for generalists and specialists, writers and policy wonks, computer jocks and business gurus—all part of a medical community doing something that is in its ultimate purpose about helping another human being.

That the profession helps human beings in a profound and measurable way is in fact why young people dream of being a doctor, and it is the single most common reason medical school applicants give for pursing a medical career. Indeed, it is that perspective that ultimately overrides some of the negative sides of a career in medicine, which in today's world can discourage even the strongest-hearted premed. For medicine as we know it today brings its own set of hassles: managed care, increasing government regulations, and malpractice premiums (and massive malpractice awards), on top of discouraging medical school debt averaging more than $156,000 at a time when physicians' incomes are relatively stagnant.

Although there are two applicants for every medical school slot, and the quality of prospective students is thought to be as good as ever, there is widespread belief among medical school educators that because of these strains, fewer students are interested in applying to medical school now than a decade ago, a phenomenon masked by the dramatic increase in female applicants. But the reality is that no profession—and nothing worth pursuing in life—is free from its own set of hassles. The reward-to-hassle ratio is what counts. It is something each prospective doctor must sort out for himself or herself.

And the rewards of today's medicine are many. The expanding knowledge base is truly compelling and ever changing to the betterment of patient and doctor. There is virtually no illness we cannot make better, if not cure, and with improved drugs and technology and emerging knowledge of human genomes, we see more tailored treatment of individual patients with better results. As for the doctor's personal life, the hours today are more reasonable and controllable than in the past. The solo doc is becoming a rare breed; large group practices and clinics enable medical practitioners to escape the direct brunt of administrative hassles while at the same time gaining camaraderie and an enriched practice environment. Medicine is a tough and fulfilling career, immutably purpose driven, value laden, intellectually stimulating, and emotionally gratifying. But it is a profession that demands the right stuff of those who serve.

Certain deeply held personal qualities are essential; without them, from my perspective as a former medical school dean, students quite simply need not apply. Think hard about them, for they are the essence of the art and the science of being a doctor.

Compassion and generosity. Kindness goes beyond "bedside manner." It is reflected in generosity of time and self, and sensitivity to the unique circumstance of any given situation. Making an extra stop by the room of a lonely patient; giving a worried family member your home phone number; being calm and measured with an ornery, angry, or noncompliant patient. Sickness can bring out the best in people but also the worst, and a physician can lighten a patient's load by being a source of hope, caring, and cheerleading—along with providing technical expertise.

Hard work and grit. It takes a lot of stamina to be part of a world that is always on call in some fashion. The stress might come from a rather mundane struggle with an insurance company for an extra day in the hospital or a needed MRI, or from perseverance against an engulfing bureaucracy. But stress most especially comes from the challenge of caring for the very sick. This demands the courage to make tough medical decisions and, in the face of risk and uncertainty, to proceed with

a risky operation or embark on a drastic course of medical therapy. It takes grit to confront one's inevitable failures and learn from them—without becoming timid because of them. In their hearts, doctors must live with the confidence that at the end of the day, they did the best they could, and tirelessly so.

Scholarship and good sense. With medical practice reborn almost every day in new knowledge and emerging technology, new approaches are an essential part of medicine, disseminated in hospital corridors, medical rounds, mortality and morbidity conferences, journal clubs, and national medical gatherings. The wise and learned physicians are those who can sift through the flood of new knowledge and the latest evidence to make it apply to any given patient. That's why we teach medicine at the bedside and through individual case studies of real people. And that's why we respect reasoned judgment that often comes out with different advice. Should that 30-year-old woman with a newly discovered benign heart tumor have prompt heart surgery, as is the practice? Of course—but she is six months pregnant and, with surgery, risks losing the baby, so dare we wait? The PSA is intermittently elevated in a 55-year-old man. Do you watch, or do you biopsy? Yes, a lumpectomy is the conventional wisdom for this precancerous change detected by mammogram, but this patient wants a mastectomy as an alternative because she has a breast cancer gene running through her family. Do we go along? The hyperactive child is driving his family to distraction with behaviors that another family could manage better. Do you medicate?

Medical wisdom is about knowing when conventional practice guidelines apply, particularly in the context of the unlimited variables that confound any given patient's illness or circumstance.

The best decisions come from the marriage of scholarship and good sense.

Integrity and trust. Despite the variability of human illness, one of the great insights of medicine is that with regard to reaction to their disease, all patients are fundamentally the same. Though they may show it differently, they share the same fears and vulnerabilities; and have the same needs for comfort, support, and trust. The physician is the focus of that trust, and that is a heavy responsibility. Never give advice that you yourself would not take—or you would not recommend to a loved one. Imagine you are the patient, particularly when the going gets tough. Matters of privacy, conflicts of interest, participation of patients in research trials—these are all issues of trust. Underpinning this essential quality of being a doctor is a quiet reverence for what it means to be a doctor and what it feels like to care—in the deepest sense—for a patient in your charge. The late Dr. George Crile, Jr., a pioneering Cleveland surgeon and son of one of the founders of the Cleveland Clinic, wrote a short passage in his book on cancer back in 1955 that captures the quiet reverence of a profession that has the ability to restore health or even life, and always to relieve human suffering. His words mean as much now as they did then:

No physician, sleepless and worried about a patient, can return to the hospital in the midnight hours without feeling the importance of his faith. The dim corridor is silent; the doors are closed. At the end of the corridor in the glow of the desk lamp, the nurse watches over those who sleep or lie lonely and wait behind closed doors. No physician entering the hospital in these quiet hours can help feeling that the medical institution of which he is a part is in essence religious, that it is built on trust. No physician can fail to be proud that he is part of his patient's faith.

The student who understands that faith is the one who is ready to embark on life as a doctor.

Dr. Healy graduated from Harvard Medical School and spent much of her career caring for patients and teaching and researching at the Johns Hopkins School of Medicine and the Cleveland Clinic Foundation. She served as the dean of the College of Medicine and Public Health at Ohio State University, served as the president of the American Red Cross, and was the first woman to be the director of the National Institutes of Health. Currently, she writes health and medical columns for U.S.News & World Report, where she speaks to some 20 million "patients."

Introduction

There are certainly easier careers than medicine. You'll struggle through difficult science courses, indenture yourself for a *long* decade of school and training, and lose countless hours of sleep. The reward? You may end up owing $150,000, being mired in paperwork that robs you of time for patients (or for a life outside of work), and holding a job that leaves you a ripe target for malpractice lawsuits.

And in spite of it all, medicine could be the best choice you ever make. You could be the person who turns pain and suffering into relief and hope. You might solve the mystery of an illness that has stumped generations of doctors. Your colleagues will be extraordinary people. You will see babies safely born, and you will save people's lives.

"I think I have the best job on Earth," said Ronald Drusin, a doctor and vice dean for education at Columbia University's College of Physicians and Surgeons. "Half of my time, I deal with students and help make sure they get the best education. And half the time I'm in practice as a cardiologist, working at our heart transplant center. So I get to see miracles every day."

"I can't put into words how wonderful this job is," said Cynthia Romero, a family practice doctor in Virginia Beach, Virginia. "I spend my time seeing my patients as people, not just handing out medications. I get to know them, see them again and again, and help them to live a healthy lifestyle. And I can see that it makes a big difference in my community."

It sounds ideal—and idyllic. But before you rush into medical school, stop and think about whether the vision of the profession you carry in your head matches today's reality. Medicine has always demanded a lot of physicians, even in the pre-HMO days of small practices and house calls. For many years, however, it has been changing in ways that doctors simply don't like. Lawrence Klein, an internist who enjoys his private practice in Washington, D.C., feels frustrated that increasing bureaucracy and financial pressures steal time from his patients. After all, seeing patients and giving them good care is what drew him to medicine in the first place. Would he go to medical school today? "Yes, but I'd think about it a bit more."

He'd consider, for example, the skyrocketing malpractice insurance premiums now hitting doctors—price hikes that insurers blame on outrageous jury awards in malpractice cases. "It's a dangerous situation for everyone," said Donald Palmisano, former president of the American Medical Association. "The costs are forcing doctors to close practices." Indeed, physicians in Pennsylvania, West Virginia, Connecticut, and many other states have held protest marches to plead for relief.

Klein would also factor in the pressure that hospitals, practice groups, and HMOs exert on doctors to bring in more revenue by seeing more patients and seeing them faster. And he would certainly think about one unfortunate consequence of rising healthcare costs: Employers, looking for the best deals, are switching health plans frequently—every two years, in many cases—and that means that patients have to switch doctors, too. As a result of these switches and the hurried patient visits, many physicians find it impossible to build the long-term relationships they feel are so essential to effective patient care. Indeed, fewer med school graduates are even going into primary care, opting instead for specialties such as radiology where they believe they will be insulated from these forces.

Because of the time, vast sums of money, and effort involved, it's important to take a hard look at yourself—your motives, your goals, your personality—before embarking on this course. One undergrad at the University of Virginia, after slogging through organic chemistry and other premed courses, getting top marks, and prepping for and acing the all-important Medical College Admissions Test (MCAT), began collecting school applications. Then, she remembers, she was sitting in the school library one night and looking across the table at a bunch of med students hunched over their books. "That's all they ever do: work," she said to her best friend. "That's not a life. It's a huge sacrifice. And I don't think I can do that." She didn't.

At least she realized her mismatch early.

"Sometimes we have alums who stop med school after two or three years," said Carol Baffi-Dugan, director of health professions advising at Tufts University. "It's not often, but when it happens, it's the saddest thing. They've got debt coming out of their ears. And they've devoted an incredible amount of time and energy learning skills that are not really transferable."

So how can you give yourself a reality test before medical school tests you? The Association of American Medical Colleges poses several general questions, such as: Do I care deeply about other people, their problems, and their pain? Do I enjoy helping people with my skills and knowledge? Do I enjoy learning and gaining new understanding? Do I often dig deeper into a subject than my teacher requires? Surely, your response in all cases ought to be a well-considered and resounding "yes" if you're about to start writing tuition checks. But a "yes" could just as easily foreshadow a brilliant career in social work.

So as you go about measuring your reservoir of empathy and intellectual drive, check your motives, too. "People want to go into medicine for all sorts of reasons," said a student at Columbia's College of Physicians and Surgeons. "Sometimes it's money or prestige. And that's just stupid. Look, you'll always make a comfortable living as a doctor. But there's got to be something more for you to be happy." Larry Sullivan, the prehealth professions advisor at Avila University in Kansas City, Kansas, often sees students who "have 'inherited' the idea of being a doctor. It comes from pressure from their family, or their peers." This, said Baffi-Dugan, is "one of the biggest pitfalls: the idea that 'it's going to make my parents happy.'" Still others want to practice because they've always watched *ER* on television and think that medicine is dramatic and exciting. They don't consider how little independence doctors often have in real life and how difficult a workplace the healthcare system can be.

It's also worth considering whether or not you have some specific strengths that seem to stand out in the profession. Admissions directors and advisors agree that good doctors come in a whole range of personality types. "Is every good doctor an extrovert? No," said Baffi-Dugan. But beyond an honest desire to help sick people, good doctors do share some important characteristics, chief among them self-discipline, an ability to think clearly and make decisions in a crisis, and conscientiousness.

A mix of great attention to detail and a desire to strive for high-quality work proves extremely valuable in medical school, too. In an unpublished study of 610 Belgian medical students over six years of their education, across the board, conscientiousness predicted the strongest performance in medical school. This finding mirrors an earlier study of 176 English med students, in which teacher references, student personality statements, and personality scores were all compared to see what factor best predicted med school performance, and the winner was conscientiousness.

Why do care and thoroughness mean so much? "You have to have remarkable perseverance to get through medical school," said Cheryl Weinstein, associate professor of psychiatry at Harvard Medical School, who has studied learning and learning disabilities. "If you are reasonably intelligent and can learn facts, you can get through the MCAT. If you have high intelligence and love science, you are likely to get the references. But once you have to start spending the long hours, once you have to sustain attention and be able to plan and attend, if you don't have [perseverance], you will be found out."

Ask yourself: Are you someone who meticulously proofreads a paper before handing it in, not relying on the caprices of computerized spelling and grammar programs to do your work? Did you work extra hours as a hospital volunteer because there was work that needed to be done? And when former professors or former employers write your recommendations, will they note that assignments and projects were never late?

"You have to have remarkable perseverance to get through medical school."

Perhaps the most practical way to research the depth of your commitment is to actually watch what real doctors do. Marilyn Becker, former director of admissions for the University of Minnesota Medical School, said that her picks usually had some serious experience in a medical setting before med school, often in a community clinic, a doctor's office, or a hospital. Applicants are strongly encouraged to get this sort of exposure, perhaps part time while they're in college or over the summers. Sullivan said that Avila University makes such work a part of a course called Introduction to Health Care Careers. More typically, students arrange it on their own. In college, Virginia Beach doctor Cynthia Romero set herself up with what she calls "mini rotations" by asking different doctors if she could shadow them for a week or more. (And she did this even though she already had more than a passing familiarity with the profession: Her mother is a physician.)

Romero liked what she saw, but for others, work experience can be a jolting reality check. "People volunteered in hospitals and realized they didn't have the patience to see patients," Romero

recalled. "Or they couldn't handle the pressure, or they couldn't stand seeing sick children. Some got really upset at the sight of blood." That's a fairly safe sign that you should bail out.

Those who stay the course but aren't truly enthusiastic are easy to identify when you meet them, said Charles Bardes, associate dean of admissions at Weill Medical College of Cornell University. "That's why you can't get into medical school without an interview," he noted. What are the signs of true commitment to an activity mentioned in an application? "Did they do this work in a perfunctory way, say for just one hour per week? Were they involved in the leadership of this activity, or did they just show up?" he said. "We try and get a feel for all this when we interview the students." Nor was Becker impressed by someone who emphasized his or her family's illustrious medical past as qualification—two doctor-uncles, a grandfather on the faculty of a renowned med school—rather than a personal passion for the profession.

One student at Columbia remembers that he felt it was really important to take time off after college to put to rest any doubts about his career direction. He worked as a chef for a while and then as a high school teacher. Not only did he gain confidence in his decision to go to med school, but "now I have some sense of professionalism," he said. "Being a doctor is a position of responsibility. You need a solid sense of yourself. School won't teach you that."

Assuming that all this soul searching reveals you're meant to be in medicine, this book is your step-by-step guide to getting there. The first chapter offers snapshots of what you'll experience as a first-year med student, followed by a discussion in Chapter 2 of how to choose a medical school that meets your particular needs. Chapter 3 profiles the life and academics at five very different types of medical schools. In Chapter 4, you'll find a firsthand account of what applying to medical school really entails and you'll learn how to fine-tune your application so that your first-choice school chooses you. Chapter 5 is a primer on that all-important topic: financing your education. And Chapter 6 explores second chances, telling you what to do if you don't get accepted the first time.

Beginning on page 83, you'll find a series of exclusive lists that allow you to compare medical schools on all kinds of key attributes: which are the hardest and easiest to get into, for example, and which ones leave graduates with the most and least debt. Finally, in the directory at the back of the book, you'll find detailed information on the country's medical schools, including schools offering the D.O. degree in osteopathy. This alternative medical degree involves a slightly different course of training, which is described in Chapter 2.

As you go through the extensive—some would say excruciating—application process, bear in mind that the interview, recommendation letters, and work experiences act as a final filter. They separate good students who *like* the idea of being a doctor from those who really would *be* a good doctor. Assuming that you possess all of the right qualifications, your best chance of making it through this sieve is to do what Harvard's Weinstein, and several ancient philosophers, suggest: "Know thyself." Perhaps friends, parents, mentors, school counselors, or trusted doctors will be able to ask you all the right questions to help you make this important decision. Regardless, there is only one person who can give the right answer. You.

Chapter One

Q&A: Students Talk about Med School

Yes, medical school is tough, but it is also rewarding, exhilarating, satisfying, and fast-paced. Before you start, you may want to do a little traveling, because you won't have time afterward.

How did *U.S.News & World Report* reach those conclusions? By going to the experts. We sought out a panel of med students and asked them a host of questions about their experiences, choices, and goals.

Here are our panelists:

Nicole Joy, 23, a native of Miami, who earned a B.S. degree in biology from Duke University and attends Duke University School of Medicine.

Justin Kopa, 28, a native of Scranton, Pennsylvania, who received a B.S. degree from Georgetown University and attends the University of Washington School of Medicine.

Erin Miller, 23, a native of Rochester, New York, who has a B.S. in biomedical engineering from Northwestern University and attends Case Western Reserve University School of Medicine.

Why did you decide to go to medical school?

Joy: Though it sounds cliché, I have always known that I wanted to go to medical school. I think that as a physician, I will be able to challenge myself intellectually while also serving others in my community. I love that I can use my education to contribute to the health of others while also contributing to the scientific discoveries that drive improvement in patient care.

Kopa: I had an undergraduate degree in biology and was doing community work in East Coast inner cities. I was seeing a lot of people who were very sick and could not afford care. It seemed like medicine was a way of pursuing my interest in biology in a way that could contribute to a real need.

Miller: I decided to enter medical school because it was the one field that combined my passion for science with direct interactions with people. The way things work has always intrigued me—I love figuring out machines and processes, which is why biomedical engineering initially appealed to me. Pure science didn't hold my interest, though, because it takes so long to see results and you have to think theoretically to see what sort of impact you have on people. Medicine is more immediate: You talk with patients every day, your work is focused on making a tangible difference or improvement, and it comes back to figuring out how a complex machine—the body—is working (or malfunctioning!).

Why did you decide to attend the school where you are?

Joy: During my years as an undergraduate student at Duke, I worked in several laboratories and discovered my love for basic science research. I knew that I wanted to incorporate research into my medical career, and I thought that Duke's unique third year would give me an excellent opportunity to do just that. Also, during my undergraduate years, I was able to work with several faculty members of the medical school, and I was impressed by how much time they devoted to their students and to teaching, which I found very welcoming and appealing.

Kopa: There were three main things, I think. First, UW is one of the few schools of its caliber to stay explicitly committed to training primary care physicians. Having a sense that I wanted to practice in a primary care field, I thought that it would be helpful to have peers with shared interests who could help to shape and encourage my education. Second, UW was the only school I applied to that had an academic track (we call them pathways) that allowed medical students to elect to focus on medical issues unique to underserved communities. Finally, and probably most significantly, when I came for my interview, I felt like the people I met were satisfied with my academic performance but were mostly interested in the experience I had working with underserved communities. They made me feel like UW was a place that would value what I brought to medical school and would help incorporate my experiences into my medical formation.

Miller: Case appealed to me on paper because it stressed independent, integrative, and applicative learning. Half of class time is spent in small groups working through a case—combining physiology with disease processes and tying it back in to the patient's symptoms, with treatment completing the circle to restore normal function. The students lead these sessions and choose the key points in each case, mirroring the actual practice of medicine, by doing our own research and directing our study instead of being spoon-fed material. I believe this method of learning will make me a better physician. In actuality, the final factor that led to my decision to come to Case was the students. When I interviewed here, students were friendly, relaxed, and welcoming. Each person I met had a unique story or something special to share. Everyone was involved beyond simply class work and learning the material—I felt a real sense of community, whether it was fundraising for our free clinic or planning social events. Additionally, this atmosphere is fostered by the administration and program structure—through the elimination of grades and the emphasis on small-group work, students here are taught to help each other, instead of compete for a position in the class. I knew by coming to Case I would be finding a family as well as receiving a great education, and the school has repeatedly gone beyond my expectations.

Is medical school what you expected? Why or why not?

Joy: For the most part, there haven't been many surprises. The only thing that really surprised me was how friendly and noncompetitive the learning environment was during my first year. Before every exam, my email inbox was flooded with detailed outlines and study guides that my classmates had made for themselves and sent out to the entire class. There is a general misconception that medical students are übercompetitive and cutthroat, and that has been proven wrong to me so far.

Kopa: I'm not sure I expected to be as satisfied as I am. Classes are hard, and all the time that we spend in a lecture hall can be pretty overwhelming. We were fortunate in that our class got along very well from the beginning. The camaraderie helps us to bear the monotony and the struggle to stay on top of the textbook learning. At the same time, clinical skills and patient care are a major part of our preclinical curriculum. In addition to our classes, we spend time every week practicing interviewing and physical exam skills.

Miller: Medical school is not what I expected after hearing horror stories from doctors about impossible tests where the footnote on page 548 is the subject of an entire essay and endless hours of grueling memorizing. My experience at Case has been exactly the opposite: I have plenty of independence in what I learn and am not forced to memorize useless details. Instead of the detail focus, we are expected to build conceptual models and apply processes to actual situations. The focus has really been on the application of big-picture ideas.

Choose one word to describe your first year, and explain it.

Joy: Intense. Whereas most medical schools have two years dedicated to classroom learning, Duke covers all of the basic sciences in 11 months. Because of the condensed nature of the first year, we move through material very quickly, have a lot of exams, and go to school through July. Though first year was tough academically, it is worth it because we start our clinical rotations during our second year, which is earlier than most other medical schools.

Kopa: Fast. Everything in medical school feels fast. Classes move fast, you learn to move fast, the people around you feel like they can move really fast, and by the time you get to the end of the year, you look back and say, "Wow, that went by fast."

Miller: Involved. On a superficial level, medical school requires you to put so much time and effort into learning the material that it can really take over. But further, I found I have had endless opportunities as a medical student to become involved in the community here: I have served on the student committee for admissions, led orientation for the class following mine, attended lectures, produced movies and skits, played intramural sports, researched, and worked independently with physicians. Being a medical student is not simply a daily activity but a lifestyle. It pulls in all aspects of your personality— your communication skills, science knowledge, analytical skills, physical endurance, and empathy. Unlike many other professions, you can't really leave "work" at school when you go home at the end of the day; it's a lifestyle and really involves every aspect of your being.

What is the most memorable experience of your first year? Why?

Joy: The moment that stands out the most in my memory from my first year is my first anatomy lab session. For days before, I was apprehensive about what my cadaver would look like, what the lab would smell like, and how I would react to dissecting a dead human being. I will never forget the pungent smell of the preservative and the unsettling feeling I got when I took the gauze off of our cadaver's face, realizing that he was real and that he too once had a life. This was the first time I really felt like a medical student—having the opportunity to experience things that others never get the chance to experience.

Kopa: I spent the summer working in a clinic in rural Washington. It was my first time spending every day in a clinical setting. I loved the people that I met and the feeling of being a doctor (well, at least, a pseudo doctor).

Miller: During the spring of first year, I was assigned to an 11-session preceptorship in the MetroHealth emergency department. After watching the physician I was shadowing interview two patients, we walked back to pick up the next chart, which she glanced at for only a moment before handing it to me. "Why don't you go see this one?" she said and pointed in the direction of Room 54 as she turned down the opposite hall to drop off a sample at the lab. I must have stood in the hall outside of the patient's room for five minutes reviewing the vitals, practicing how to say the patient's name, how to introduce myself, and coming up with appropriate questions to ask for a chief complaint of "cough and wheezing." I was only a first year! I felt like I knew nothing. Walking into that room alone was probably the scariest part of medical school, but it was also the most rewarding. When someone says "thank you" after you make them feel better (often with a simple Albuterol treatment), it means the world. This made me realize how much I had learned in just under a year of school. It definitely wasn't everything, but that's why we're here, right?

Is the work as hard as you expected, harder, or easier? Why?

Joy: The work is about as difficult as I anticipated. Initially, I felt overwhelmed with the amount of material I had to learn for each exam, but after a while, I got the hang of how to study efficiently, which I think is the key to doing well and enjoying medical school. Our clinical rotations, however, are more difficult than I had anticipated. The amount of time we spend in the hospital is more than I thought we would, but because you are so busy interacting with patients and learning, the days and nights go by pretty fast, which makes it very manageable.

Kopa: I think it's a mix. It has been about five years since I've been in this kind of rigorous classroom setting, so I'm often surprised by how hard the work is. Often, whole weeks will disappear amidst tests and patient write-ups and interviews. I think what surprises me most about it, though, is that I usually get to the other end of that tunnel and look back, only to discover that I actually enjoyed the work.

Miller: The work has been much easier than I expected, not because there isn't a lot of it but simply because I enjoy it. I love going to every small-group session and am excited to begin research on each new disease or system. It doesn't feel like a job or a chore like classes often did in undergrad, because I am not learning information simply to be able to spit it back out onto a piece of paper at the end of the semester, but instead, I am learning processes that I know for a fact I will be using in the future to treat patients. Everything fits together in medical school to put together a big picture of health and disease, and the final goal is always in mind.

What is the best course you have taken, and why?

Joy: My favorite course during first year was Anatomy. The dissection labs were fun, interesting, and very hands-on. Though we had been taught anatomy through lectures and readings, dissection was really the best way to understand the structure and function of the human body. Another aspect of anatomy that made it so much fun were the professors, who were truly amazing. They love to teach, were full of life, had a great sense of humor, and managed to make anatomy lectures fun and entertaining.

Kopa: I think that our Introduction to Clinical Medicine class has been the most engaging for me. It's the big-picture course that tries to tie all of the basic science stuff together into clinical settings. We also spend time having more reflective discussions about patient care. This gets put into practice in patient interviews and practice physical exams.

Miller: We don't really have "courses" at Case, since the curriculum is so integrated, but the best equivalent I can refer to is my community preceptorship. I followed an emergency room attending around every week during spring semester of first year, seeing patients both on my own and with my preceptor. It was the most valuable for me because it reinforced concepts that I had learned in the classroom and really demonstrated the usefulness of basic science knowledge while treating patients. The variety of complaints I saw varied from headaches, lacerations, and colds to heart attacks, strokes, and motor vehicle accidents and exposed me to an immense variety of medicine. It reinforced practical skills and what I do know about medicine as well as highlighting how much I do not know and providing incentive to continue learning.

What course are you most looking forward to, and why?

Joy: Now that I am finished with classes, I am looking forward to starting my third-year research project. This unique aspect of the Duke Med curriculum is why I chose to study here, and I am excited to get started on my project and to learn more about how physician scientists integrate scientific research with clinical practice.

Kopa: I think that I'm most excited about our clerkships next year. While I have a sense that I want to

How med school works

Though schools vary widely in the courses they teach, most of this variation is grafted on top of a basic curriculum: two years of medical science followed by two years of clinical practice. This is followed by an apprenticeship period, or residency, that lasts from three to seven years. Here's a general outline:

Years One and Two: Coursework covers these topics: anatomy and embryology, physiology, biochemistry, histology, neuroscience, medical genetics, pharmacology, microbiology, pathology, and immunology. These first two years may also include courses on sexuality, nutrition, healthcare delivery, ethics, and other subjects.

Years Three and Four: You start clinical rotations in hospitals, usually beginning with surgery, family medicine, pediatrics, neuroscience, and obstetrics and gynecology. As you gain experience in patient care, these are followed by more rotations with advanced responsibility. You can also take elective courses in areas such as end-of-life care, psychiatry, or public and community health. Year four is also when students apply for residencies at various hospitals around the country in particular medical specialties. You graduate at the end of four years, and you can put an M.D. or D.O. after your name.

Year Five Postgraduate: You begin the first year of your residency, sometimes called an internship, taking primary responsibility for patient care while being supervised yourself by experienced doctors. Depending on the program— surgery, for instance, is very time-consuming—residencies can last as long as seven years.

Beyond Year Five: There's a lot of hard work involved in residency programs. After completing them successfully and passing national medical exams and state licensing tests, you are a full-fledged physician.

---

go into primary care, I really don't have a lot of experience in any of the other specialties. It will be great to have a chance to learn about other branches of medicine.

Miller: My surgical rotation is the "course" that I am most looking forward to. One of the main reasons I have chosen medicine is my desire to help people, as cheesy as that may sound. In surgery, you open someone up, fix the problem, and then send them home better. I'm really big on immediate results and see surgery as a venue where I can make serious, tangible differences in people's lives.

What advice would you give to someone thinking about applying to medical school?

Joy: I would tell them to relax and be themselves during medical school interviews! Your grades and MCAT scores are probably pretty good if you are applying to medical school, and I think that your best bet is to let your personality shine during your interview. This will truly make you stand out amongst the many other applicants with good grades and good MCAT scores, and it will allow schools to see you as a person rather than as just a student, which I think is what they are looking for.

Kopa: Hang in there. The application process can be daunting because you have to put yourself out there so much. It takes a long time for interview requests to come back, and usually you don't even hear back from most of the schools you apply to until much later. I found the whole experience to be pretty exhausting. Just be patient, and stay confident in the work you've already done.

Miller: Make sure medicine is what you want to do with the rest of your life, and make sure it is for the right reasons. The right reasons are not having the letters of M.D. after your name, job security, or financial rewards. My classmates who were unsure about medicine have really struggled through first year, not because they could not do the work but because they did not enjoy it. It's very hard to spend your entire day learning about things you aren't interested in, and nearly impossible to deal with the everyday stresses of medicine if you are more passionate about another profession. Pursue medicine not because you just could "see yourself doing it" but because you can't stand not to.

What advice would you give to someone about to begin the first year?

Joy: I would stress the importance of finding a balance between school, friends/family, and personal time. School can sometimes get so busy that it seems like all you are doing is studying, taking tests, and thinking about medicine. Finding time for your favorite hobbies, for your friends, for exercise, or for whatever makes you happy will really help you be a better student. Your personal happiness will be your biggest strength in helping you get through the toughest exams and the most stressful rotations.

Kopa: Stay calm. If you've been accepted to medical school, you've made it over the biggest obstacle.

Much of what you are about to experience will be new, unfamiliar, and challenging, but trust yourself and the people who decided that you were the right person for their school. The road that lies ahead won't be easy, but you're on the right track.

Miller: Look at the big picture. Don't get caught up in the details. The large concepts you are learning are what will stick with you and will create the framework for everything you'll do in the future—for boards, on rotations, and in practice. Details get forgotten or aren't useful in the real world. Sure, they make you look smart, but if you know surfactant comes from lamellar bodies in type II pulmonary alveolar cells yet can't remember why surfactant is important during inspiration, how are you going to treat your patient? The concepts help you build a model you can use to reason through most symptoms and many pathologies and will help you throughout your professional life.

What is the single most valuable thing you did to prepare for medical school?

Joy: The month before starting school, I went on a two-week vacation to Europe with my college roommates. I had a great time traveling and came back to school ready to start work again.

Kopa: I spent about two months working as an orderly in a palliative care hospital. Caring for people's nonmedical physical needs at such a vulnerable time in their lives helped to shape my understanding about the amazing power of medicine as well as its limits.

Miller: The most valuable thing I did in undergrad was to learn how to study independently. This involves time management, focus, and identification of important concepts. Many students rely on lectures and syllabi to direct their learning, but this level of detail is not often given to you in medical school, and you certainly do not get an assigned reading and problem set to go along with every patient. Being able to identify key points and research them on your own is invaluable; it helps you take the next step in learning. Don't rely on being spoon-fed the material by your professors. Medical school is all about thinking through problems, which is learned through practice, not memorization.

What was the most useless?

Joy: Stressing out about what clothes to wear to my interviews!

Kopa: I'm not sure that anything has been useless. I think that medicine is a broad enough field that it can really draw on any experience and make it useful. At least, it has drawn on all of my experience. I'm tempted to say that the stress and anxiety along the way have been useless... they can be if they are unchecked or become distractions, but sometimes, in healthy doses, both stress and anxiety can actually be good motivators to work hard.

Miller: I bought new shoes! I thought I needed a more professional wardrobe to be taken seriously when I see patients, but heels just aren't fun when you're on the wards. OK, I jest, but honestly, nothing is useless. Everything you do is a learning experience. It makes you who you are, and all those experiences add up to determine how you handle school and deal with patients.

What do you wish you had done but didn't do?

Joy: Nothing, really. Things have worked out well so far.

Kopa: I wish I had traveled more before medical school. I've been fortunate to have seen some other parts of the world, but I would have liked to do more traveling before starting this process. It's hard to get away once school starts.

Miller: Taken a year off and traveled. I was so excited about medical school that I didn't want to wait even another month to start. Don't get me wrong; I really love medical school and am happy with my decision. But medicine is a commitment you are making for the rest of your life, and once you start, there is very little time to just drop everything and disappear for an extended period of time. There isn't a need to rush medical school: More than half of my class is nontraditional and has taken time off to go abroad, do research, teach, or pursue other careers. If there's something you've been meaning to do— climb every 14er in Colorado, visit Australia, write a book—now is the time to do it. Medicine will be here when you get back.

With one year down, do you think you made the right choice?

Joy: Definitely! I have made great friends, worked with incredible professors, and have had a great time in school so far.

Kopa: So far, so good.

Miller: Absolutely.

How has med school affected your personal life?

Joy: Being a medical student has taught me to appreciate the small pleasures in life. Getting one free afternoon on a nice day and having time to go for a jog or watch a movie feels like a mini vacation.

Kopa: The rigors of medical school have required me to work much harder at staying in touch with friends and family. I think it's a constant struggle to keep balanced. And the sad truth is that I've had to be a little more selective in which relationships I can actually keep up with.

Miller: Medical school has taught me to take more responsibility in my personal life. There is a distinct switch in attitude from others when you matriculate. They treat you as an adult instead of an undergraduate student. Expectations are higher, and I realize the importance of acting as a professional. I still take plenty of time to go out with my friends, socialize, and have a blast, but at the same time it's not college anymore—no frat parties, no 5 a.m. nights. There are often those hard decisions between staying in and getting caught up on sleep and going out to watch the game with your classmates. It is definitely more of a balancing act than in college, but you learn pretty quickly to juggle both your interpersonal relationships and work. I am still able to keep in contact with the friends I was close to in college, take weekend trips, go out to dinner with classmates, and work out on a regular basis. The structure of my life hasn't changed so much as my approach towards it, which I think is a more mature one.

The popular image of medical school is one of overworked, frantic students. Do you think that is true? Why or why not?

Joy: Long hours of studying and working in the hospital are part of the medical school package. Nobody applies to medical school thinking that they are going to get eight hours of sleep every night and that it will be a breeze. While most medical students are probably overworked and sleep deprived, I think that we expect it and that most of us are happy and thankful to be getting such a great education. Keeping that in mind makes those long work nights worthwhile.

Kopa: There's a fine line between working hard and being overworked. Medical students work hard and are, at times, frantic. Part of the experience, I think, is figuring out how to manage the massive amount of work in a way that doesn't burn you out. Fortunately, you're not doing any of this

alone, and most of your classmates are like you in that they have developed their own ways of coping with hard work. In my experience, it helps to share strategies and capitalize on free time by socializing. Approaching the whole thing with a team mentality minimizes the frantic feelings and keeps you working hard as opposed to overworking.

Miller: This frantic image is not what I see in my classmates. Sometimes, around the time of a big exam, people can get a bit worked up, but that's the Type A personality of med students. I see in my fellow students the ability to work diligently to learn what is necessary but also a talent for relaxation when it's over. For the most part, I believe the line between being frantic/overworked and taking things in stride is created by time management. Those who are able to focus on the important points and study efficiently end up succeeding without the "frantic" image. It's a lot of information, but it's also manageable if you take the right approach. Case has done a great job directing our focus to the big picture and also with independent time management. It creates a relaxed atmosphere rather than a frantic one.

Is there anything in your undergrad work or life that compared to the work during your first year?

Joy: As an undergraduate student, I took Organic Chemistry, Genetics and Molecular Biology, and a research course in the same semester. Though the material was completely different, the amount of studying that I did then was comparable to the amount of studying I did during my first year at medical school.

Kopa: I had a strong academic background and have done some pretty hard work since college. Both have helped me to approach the daunting task of medical school with confidence and patience. I think medical school is unique among my previous experiences because of the volume of material available and the heightened expectations that come along with knowing it.

Miller: The work during first year is completely different from anything I have experienced in life. The application-based learning that takes place at Case is the integration of multiple different skills. For example, one small-group session in medical school combines elements of journal club (having read and analyzed current literature), problem sets (figuring out a solution independently), seminar discussion (constructing and supporting an argument or treatment plan), and independent work (student-led discussion with little faculty intervention). Although many different aspects of learning in medical school are commonplace in undergraduate education and life, putting these skills together creates an entirely new experience, requiring a new approach. Medical school is not solely about learning the material but also about learning the process. Medicine is a field that relies on both independent learning and collaboration.

Has there ever been a moment when you thought you had made a mistake in going to medical school? Explain.

Joy: No. Even though medical school has been difficult at times, I enjoy the challenge, and I know that I am working towards achieving my goals.

Kopa: Fortunately, I have been very happy with my experience at UW so far. Classes are challenging but exciting. More than anything, I love the time that we get to spend meeting patients and learning about the course of their illnesses. It seems like patient exposure always comes at the right time, just when the monotony of classroom work is getting overwhelming.

Miller: No. I spent a lot of time considering my decision to enter medical school. With a physician father and strong ties to the medical community, I heard a lot of backlash from physicians who were not happy with their job. They complain about insurance companies, ineffective resource use, long hours, lawsuits. I was often discouraged from applying to medical schools; thus, I invested a lot of time exploring both medicine and other career options to determine what the right choice for me was. In the end, I realized I am truly drawn to this field and wouldn't be satisfied in another profession. There is nothing else out there I would rather be doing.

Have any of your classmates dropped out? Why did they do so?

Joy: A few classmates have had to retake classes, but nobody that I know of has dropped out.

Kopa: UW is very supportive of its students and very thorough in the selection of candidates who know they want to be doctors. I don't know of anyone who has dropped out, but I know of several people who have chosen to expand. With the support of the faculty and administration, they have taken time off or have elected to take fewer classes than the rest of the class. Almost always it has been because of personal events that come up unexpectedly. Of the three people I know who have chosen to do this, all of them were struggling with the death or illness of close family or friends and felt as though it was better to focus their energy elsewhere. The administration seems very supportive of this and continues to provide free counseling services (which all medical students are entitled to).

Miller: Yes—only two. They were both for personal reasons.

Where do you expect to be in five years?

Joy: Hopefully, I will be in the middle of my residency.

Kopa: I hope to be doing primary care work in American inner cities.

Miller: In five years, I expect to be in a surgical subspecialty residency in a major teaching hospital. I also hope to be involved in research at this institution, which I believe will be assisted by the strong research background I am receiving at Case. Five years seems so far away, but compared to how fast the past year has gone, I know I'll be making some tough choices much sooner than it seems!

Chapter Two

Which Is the Right School for You?

There are essentially two ways to choose a medical school. There's the cynical approach: "You don't really have much choice," said one student. That is, you'll apply to the very few schools that might take you, and if you're lucky "get into one or maybe two. And there you go." This view gets some support from many medical school admissions officers, although they phrase it a little more diplomatically: All schools offer a similarly fine education because of medicine's rigid accreditation requirements. (Still, their own schools are better than most, these officers hasten to add.) So what does it matter where you go, in the end?

Then there's the smarter approach. It won't make getting in any easier, but it greatly improves your odds of thriving if you make it. "Schools really aren't created equal," said Lucy Wall, assistant dean for admissions at the University of Wisconsin Medical School. "There are differences in teaching methods and curriculum, some schools are more research oriented, public schools can be very different environments than private schools.... There are lots of things to consider." A school's location can make a huge difference in the kind of experience you have, both academically and in terms of your quality of life. An institution's

---

"Schools really aren't created equal.... There are lots of things to consider."

---

reputation—whether it's viewed as a topflight research school or the place to go to become a primary care physician—can influence your chances of getting the residency slot you want after graduation. And since the learning environment is greatly affected by the other students and the campus culture, the most important consideration may be "that gut feeling you get about a school, how comfortable you feel there," said Lauren Oshman, a former president of the American Medical Student Association and a graduate of Baylor College of Medicine in Houston.

Take Fernanda Musa's experience as a first-year student at Columbia University's College of Physicians and Surgeons in New York City. Musa wanted to attend a big-city institution doing cutting-edge research ("our teachers are some of the top names in their fields") where she would see the greatest variety of patients and conditions. Columbia was the perfect fit, she said. "The school culture is so happy. We're a really close, supportive group. We study together, and we also go out to concerts and bars. Most first-year students live

together in Bard Hall, and that's where we get this great sense of community." Jessica Vorpahl, when she went to the University of Wisconsin as a student interested in family practice, felt equally thrilled about her Midwestern, primary-care oriented, smaller-town school: "There's absolutely no better place. I'm totally convinced."

The hard numbers—your overall grade point average, your all-important science GPA, and your score on the Medical College Admission Test—will narrow the field considerably by telling you which schools are within your reach. (See Chapter 4 for tips on figuring out the extent of your reach, then check out the directory at the back of this book for a sense of the numbers needed for entry at each school.) But your proper place in the field will depend on more, much more, than collections of statistics. Examining how the school teaches students (Does it rely on huge lectures? Will you get clinical experience early on or not until the latter half of your med school career?), what its curricular strengths are, what specialties graduates go on to practice, and how current students feel about the school will give you the best chance of finding, like Vorpahl, "no better place."

Consider the school culture

At the University of Iowa's Carver College of Medicine, students from all four years are grouped into small "learning communities" and interact both in class and out. First-year students relish the contact with upperclassmen, who are founts of invaluable advice about choosing courses and figuring out ways to fit all your hospital rotations into a tight schedule.

At more traditionally organized schools, such as the University of Chicago Pritzker School of Medicine, older students can disappear from sight once they start their clinical rotations. "Insanely competitive" is the phrase one student from the University of Alabama School of Medicine used to describe class-mates. While the med school at Johns Hopkins University also has a reputation for intense competi-tion, many students there protest that this is a myth—though they concede that, as a group, they tend to drive themselves hard and aren't exactly famous for kicking back and relaxing. At Yale, on the other hand, a policy of optional exams and no grades (students get evaluations from faculty) seems to create a less-pressured atmosphere, aided by the school schedule, which mandates a few weekday afternoons off.

Clearly, getting a feel for the ambience of a school requires some on-the-ground reporting. When you visit campus for your interview—which every med school requires—you'll be taken on a guided tour set up by the admissions office and designed to impress. Figure out how to break away and do some independent poking around. One way to gather information is to visit a school early in the application process—before you're called in. Medical school admission offices aren't set up for drop-in visits the way college admissions offices are, so you may not get a lot of help from them. But you can contact alumni from your college at a particular med school, and they should be able to find you people to talk with and places to stay. Once you're on campus, don't be shy about but-tonholing a few students and asking them some pointed questions:

What is student life like outside the classroom? Columbia students might tell you about the school's P & S Club, a student-run group central to most medical students' social lives that one day is running a wine tasting and another is producing *West Side Story* with students in the starring roles. One student at Iowa reports that in Iowa City, "the world stops for college athletics. This place is overwhelmed by Hawkeye fever, and it's a lot of fun. Everyone goes to football and basketball games. At hospitals, you even see doctors with Hawkeye lapel pins next to their name badges." Hopkins students, in contrast, say they have to work to find extracurricular activities in Baltimore; the fun is there, but you need to dig for it.

How intense is the competition? Often a lot less so than you might think. Sure, there are people at Hopkins who are intensely competitive, said one student, "but it hasn't affected me." Study groups and note-sharing are more the norm. A student at Case Western Reserve University School of Medicine said, "I had heard students at Case were kind of snobby, and I was concerned that might lead to competition, but that's definitely not the case!" At Alabama, too, the "insanity" is more exception than rule. "The students are very helpful if you ask," said an Alabama student. "I think there are really only a few people who don't like to help others, and nobody likes them anyway."

Many new med students may *fear* competition because they remember, all too clearly, how fiercely they fought to get into medical school in the first place. But the reality is that once admitted, students feel a kinship with one another—that they're in this often-grueling, often-exhilarating experience together, said Jack Snarr, former associate dean for student programs at Northwestern. They want to do well so as to get into a good residency program, but they aren't willing to do it by hurting others. "I know what I want to score on an exam, because I know what I'm capable of. But I don't want to get that score by withholding information from another student," said a student at Wright State University School of Medicine in Dayton, Ohio.

How accessible are the professors? Try to get input from a number of people because opinions may differ a lot within schools: Students who hang back may find they have very little contact with faculty, while more assertive students have no complaints. A lecture format, which predominates during the first years of school at the University of Chicago, for example, will probably make it more difficult to get to know faculty, especially if the school and the lectures are large. In the faculty-led small discussion and problem-solving groups that pepper the first years at Cornell University's Weill Medical College in New York City, by contrast, even the shyest students are soon known by name. At the University of Minnesota School of Medicine–Duluth, where entering class sizes hover around 50 rather than the more typical 100 to 150, faculty and administration "really feel more like family," said one student. "People have open-door policies, and you can just walk in and discuss something if you have a problem or are confused by something."

Yet even at schools like Chicago, professors have office hours. Find out whether they keep them and whether those who go up and knock on the door are welcome or treated as nuisances. Keep in mind that even though medical schools list particular faculty members as "course directors" in their catalogs, at some schools you may see that professor only at the first lecture and then spend the rest of the semester dealing with assistants.

How welcoming are the school and the student body to people of different backgrounds? You can often tell a lot by just walking around with your eyes open. How diverse does the population seem to be?

How much a part of things are the minority students? "We do OK on women here," said Philip Farrell, former dean at Wisconsin. "But we don't do so well on minorities."

Nor do a good many other medical schools, but finding and encouraging would-be minority doctors is a goal that some are now getting serious about. Wisconsin has initiated "pipeline" programs to try and remedy the shortage, running summer science and math workshops for disadvantaged and minority high school students. Some med schools, such as Columbia and the University of California–San Francisco, have tried to build special support networks for minority students to reduce feelings of isolation and deal with any academic troubles. At UCSF, for example, the Medical Scholars Program was started because some underrepresented minority students found a few of the science courses to be tough going. Students who want help can meet twice a week in small workshops to discuss coursework, problem-solving skills, and better ways of organizing their study time. The workshops also serve as social hubs, where students meet one another and forge friendships.

If you can't manage to get to a school in person, some virtual exploration might be in order. Student perspectives can be found on the website of the Student Doctor Network (www.studentdoctor.net), a volunteer not-for-profit group that collects questionnaires about medical schools from premed students who have visited them. "Really laid back, friendly and enjoyable. Interviews were conversational. I had to explain my nontraditional stuff, which I expected (I'm 25). Really got me excited about the school," wrote one visitor to the University of Michigan–Ann Arbor. Another visitor to the same school, however, had this to say: "I got the real picture from some of the students. They told me most people are sons of doctors, or their parents are wealthy benefactors of the school. Lots of Ivy Leaguers too over there, not much room for people without money."

Obviously, opinions can differ, and you're sure to get conflicting information. But complaints can clue you in to areas that bear further investigation. The SDN site also features blogs and Twitter updates on topics from admissions interview pitfalls and avoiding burnout to switching medical specialties.

Weigh the location

Beyond student culture, one of the most important features of a school to consider is its address. Location affects the kinds of patients you'll see, the range of diseases you'll be trained in, and the emphasis the school puts on different medical specialties—not to mention whether or not your significant other will have to give up his or her job and follow you out of state.

"An urban setting exposes you to a wide variety of patients, simply because that's the population. And that's going to make you a more well-rounded clinician." said Charles Bardes, associate dean for admissions at Cornell, which sits on the east side of Manhattan. It's important, he said, for applicants comparing schools to get a sense of the patient populations when they're visiting campus. "Walk up and down the hospital halls, and talk to students." If the school has a spectrum of hospitals, he said, there will in all likelihood be a spectrum of patients. A student at Cornell, for instance, might spend time in a hospital where a number of patients are elderly and have brittle bones, then move on to a hospital in a poor neighborhood and see pregnant teenagers and children

affected by lead poisoning. And because the school is affiliated with the world-renowned Memorial Sloan-Kettering Cancer Center, the student might well see more rare cancers than the average medical student—and the latest in treatment.

But don't take this to mean that all noncity schools will offer you an all-white or otherwise one-dimensional experience. Even though the

"An urban setting exposes you to a wide variety of patients, simply because that's the population."

University of Wisconsin School of Medicine and Public Health is located in the small city of Madison, for example, it sends students to training sites across the state. They can spend weeks seeing patients in small towns like Chippewa Falls, where many people have adequate health insurance and are easily available for follow-up care. But they can also go to Milwaukee, which has a large Latino population, and where patient care might involve surmounting language barriers that don't exist in Chippewa Falls. That said, schools like Minnesota–Duluth and Iowa, in rural states, do tend to focus more on family practice medicine because that specialty is much in demand in these areas.

Indeed, public institutions supported by state money generally emphasize medical training targeted to state and local needs. While it's possible to be trained in ophthalmology or oncology at the University of Washington in Seattle, for example, there's a definite push to turn out primary care docs who will stay in the Northwestern corner of the country and practice. Wisconsin offers many more

Connor Shannon was the son of a doctor, and he knew, very early, that he wanted to be an M.D., too. So after graduating from the University of Colorado, he trained as an emergency medical technician, spent a couple of years working, and applied to 25 medical schools. Because his science background was relatively weak, which in turn "made me not do so well on the MCAIs," he was rejected by 23 schools and wait-listed by the remaining two.

In the months that followed, Shannon got to know several doctors with the "other" medical degree—a doctor of osteopathy, or D.O.—and began to suspect he might be chasing the wrong kind of training. "I liked [the D.O.s'] bedside manner better," he said. Shannon went to—and loved—the Chicago College of Osteopathic Medicine at Midwestern University.

Many medical school advisors recommend applying to a combination of D.O. and M.D. schools right from the start. "Both produce well-trained doctors," said Carol Baffi-Dugan,

program director for health professions advising at Tufts University. Curricula at both cover the same basic scientific principles of medicine, and osteopaths are licensed in all 50 states in surgery, internal medicine, and every other medical discipline.

Where the two schools of medicine differ is in philosophy. Doctors of osteopathy "treat people, not just symptoms," says Karen Nichols, dean of the Chicago College of Osteopathic Medicine. "The course list looks exactly the same, but the M.D.'s focus is on discrete organs. The osteopathic focus is that all of those pieces are interrelated. You can't affect one without affecting another." That means more than paying simple lip service to the idea of the "whole" patient: It means examining his or her environment, family, and general situation in life, too. Michael Kuchera, a D.O., described the emphasis as being on health rather than disease. Not surprisingly, more than 65 percent of the 55,000 licensed osteopaths in the United States are primary care

physicians—in family practice or pediatrics, for example. The American Association of Colleges of Osteopathic Medicine provides a description of osteopathic training, as well as links to the 26 schools of osteopathic medicine, on its website (www.aacom.org). The D.O. programs and their contact information are listed in the Directory section of this book.

Beyond their other medical studies, osteopathic students get 200 hours of training in "osteopathic manipulative medicine," a hands-on technique for diagnosis and healing. Limited motion in the lower ribs, for instance, can cause pain in the stomach that seems a lot like irritable bowel syndrome. Identifying the muscle strain in the ribs through manipulation, and then treating it, can relieve the stomach distress. An osteopath learns to apply specific amounts of pressure on a body part, attempting to relax it or stimulate it. While such an approach might have raised eyebrows in the profession a decade or two ago, these days no one—except perhaps the crustiest old M.D.s—dismisses it as New Age nonsense. Manipulative medicine is based on the not-terribly-heretical idea that structures in the body influence function and that a problem in the structure of one body part can cause problems in the function of other parts.

Don't think of applying to D.O. schools as a fallback plan. Some of them accept a greater percentage of applicants than do M.D. schools, but many are just as selective. And all D.O. schools are searching for a particular kind of person. "Students have to understand the osteopathic schools are not looking for people who couldn't get into M.D. schools," said Nichols. "I want them to understand the osteopathic philosophy, to have spent time with a D.O. so they can get a strong letter of recommendation." And as for Connor Shannon, he decided that his rejections were a good thing because they allowed him to land where he was always meant to be.

opportunities to learn about rural healthcare than does Columbia. At SUNY Downstate Medical Center College of Medicine in Brooklyn, students get exposure to a high-risk obstetrics program because there are so many high-risk pregnancies in that community.

Another way state schools fulfill state objectives is by educating their own residents, and doing so relatively cheaply. "The first issue I usually ask students to think about when thinking about schools is where they live," said John Friede, the health professions advisor at Villanova University in Philadelphia. "Staying in-state can often mean real savings and getting out of school with less debt." Pennsylvania residents who choose Pennsylvania State University College of Medicine pay about $33,000 per year in tuition, for instance. The school charges students from out of state an extra $12,000 per year. If Pennsylvania residents go to Duluth to study medicine, they pay more than $38,000 for the first year, while the Minnesota locals pay about $31,000. Likewise, leaving state for a private institution could mean tuition bills of $30,000–40,000 a year. (See Chapter 5 for other strategies for financing your education.)

You'll probably find that staying close to home gives you a better chance of getting in, too. Recently, for example, the University of California–San Diego School of Medicine had about 3,000 in-state applicants and admitted 120; of about 1,100 applicants from out-of-state, it took just 2. Wisconsin's med school is committed to taking 80 to 90 percent of its students from the Badger State. Finally, of course, a school's location can mean a great deal for your personal life. One of the reasons Columbia worked so well for one student is that her family members, who lived in Brazil, found it easy to fly up and visit her on the East Coast; a California school would have called for a longer, more expensive trip.

Put prestige in perspective

You might be tempted to pay any amount of money to get your M.D. from a great medical school—a really, really great school. Someplace you've always heard about, like Harvard, or Stanford, or Cornell, or Johns Hopkins, whose name alone says "first-rate education."

Not so fast, cautions Bardes. As associate dean

"Staying in-state can often mean real savings, and getting out of school with less debt."

---

for admissions at Cornell, he can certainly brag about a top-notch faculty and state-of-the-art facilities. He just can't say that Cornell's strengths add up to a quality of education that's significantly better than most others. "The quality range in medical schools is much narrower than in other types of schools," he said. Andrew Frantz, associate dean of admissions at Columbia, which usually scores near the top in the annual *U.S.News & World Report* ranking of med schools, agreed: "For maybe 90 percent of the schools, the quality seems very tight, and very high." Or as Delores Brown, associate dean for admissions at Northwestern's med school, put it: "For medical training, there is no bad school."

Why would medicine produce such a tight bunch? There are a few reasons. Bardes points out that because the public has a life-and-death interest in highly skilled physicians, the accreditation process for medical schools is unusually elaborate and demanding. That process, overseen by both the Association of American Medical Colleges and the American Medical Association, examines everything from the technology at student clinical sites and the

teaching qualifications of the faculty to the curriculum content, ensuring that it covers not just the scientific basis of medicine but also behavioral and socioeconomic aspects. The resulting accreditation reports for any given school are as bulky as a Los Angeles telephone directory. "They ask a lot of questions and want very specific answers," said one admissions director, hefting his school's report off his desk. "There are about 120 certification standards in here. With us, they liked our faculty development program and our mentoring program for students. But they thought we had too many lectures and not enough self-directed study."

Another equalizer? The national standardized tests students must take during their four years in school. Passing the initial U.S. Medical Licensing Examination, which tests knowledge of basic medical science, is required for promotion from the second to the third year, and students have to pass further stages of the test during their final two years in order to graduate. Obviously, failure doesn't just hurt the student: A pattern of failures reflects badly on the school and may jeopardize its accreditation.

Schools that do enjoy an aura of prestige tend to be the ones with the big research programs, said Thomas Langhorne, the prehealth professions advisor at Binghamton University in New York. "These are schools with lots of Nobel Prize winners, or researchers that make discoveries about diseases, or get big grants, and so they get a lot of press," he said. "You read the names 'Harvard' and 'Stanford' a lot. But these are things that, to me, don't have a lot to do with your training to be a physician."

It's not that a strong and active research program is irrelevant; in fact, the research might well enhance your academic experience. If you find yourself drawn to the study of glaucoma or the genetics of antibiotic resistance, for example, it should be relatively easy at a school pulling in lots of grants In these areas to get funding for a short research project, often working alongside a faculty member. The research may also inform course content—indeed, the experts may be teaching the classes. At a smaller school with less research money—say, a state school focused on primary care—you'll have fewer opportunities to "follow your nose" and go in unexpected directions. And anyone who tells you that having Harvard or Cornell on a résumé won't open a few extra doors simply isn't being honest.

In certain cases, however, a great research reputation might actually be a career handicap, said Phyllis Guze, former president of the Association of Program Directors in Internal Medicine—the people who run residency programs and thus hire med school graduates for their first job. "You can come from a school with a stellar academic reputation, and depending on the residency you're applying for, that's not going to help you," she said. If she were looking at applicants for an inner-city hospital residency without a big research component, a Stanford résumé wouldn't be the top one on her pile. "It's a school noted for great scholarship and academic physicians," she said, "so why would the student be interested in this kind of hospital? Program directors really think about things like this."

Rather than focusing on reputation, advisors and med school faculty suggest taking a hard look at the concrete—and the metal and the electronics. Good facilities are a harbinger of a good educational expe-

rience. Wisconsin's new health sciences building, for instance, has Ethernet jacks at every classroom desk, so if a lecturer is using a PowerPoint presentation, students can download it right onto their laptops. The University of Pittsburgh School of Medicine is going totally wireless, so students can do the same thing even when sprawled out in a hallway.

Pittsburgh also has installed high-resolution

"The quality range in medical schools is much narrower than in other types of schools."

---

cameras and monitors that cover every inch of its anatomy lab. Typically, when new students are dissecting a cadaver and people at one table find something interesting, like the heart, "a buzz goes through the room and 150 students line up to look," said John Mahoney, the school's assistant dean for medical education. "That takes forever, and number 150 probably can't see anything. But with our cameras, an image immediately shows up over every dissecting table, so all students have to do is look up for a great view." Features like these indicate that the school is investing in education and not neglecting students to pay hospital debts.

One aspect of a school's reputation that should matter to you a lot is how well-regarded it is among residency directors who aim to hire the most skilled doctors they can find. Examining the school's record on residency matches will give you a good idea. In general, academic hospitals—those closely affiliated with a university—tend to be more sought after because they are better teaching environments than stand-alone hospitals. And how many of the students get into their top choices? At most schools, 90 percent of graduates get into their first-, second-, or third-choice program. If the school reports a lower number, that should be a warning.

There are other signs of trouble, and they have to do with money. If a school is strapped, count on it: You'll be affected. In the late 1990s, for instance, MCP-Hahnemann University School of Medicine in Philadelphia was in dire straits because its hospitals

---

"You read the names 'Harvard' and 'Stanford' a lot. But these are things that, to me, don't have a lot to do with your training to be a physician."

---

were hemorrhaging money. Morale among faculty was low, and researchers had trouble getting the school to pay their bills on time. Since then, Hahnemann merged with another Philly school to form the Drexel University College of Medicine. With new management, new money flowing in, new technology, and new ownership arrangements for the hospitals, there is much more happiness on campus. So check the local newspapers for stories about financial worries. You might even call a broker. If a school or medical center has floated bond issues, agencies like Moody's rate those bonds based on the financial soundness of the institution issuing them.

What and how you'll learn

A school's curriculum and the style faculty use to teach it are crucial elements of your decision, even though the topics covered during the first and second years are pretty much the same wherever you go. Anatomy and embryology, physiology, biochemistry, histology, neuroscience, genetics, pharmacology, microbiology, pathology, and immunology—all are

basic science areas that every budding doctor needs to cover.

What varies is the way in which they are taught; many schools present the facts in tried-and-true large lectures, while others emphasize small-group discussions that center on solving problems. Some schools use a mix of the two styles. At Harvard and Pittsburgh, two institutions that rely heavily on "problem-based learning," or PBL, a group of first-year students studying anatomy or immunology or microbiology will meet for, say, 90 minutes to discuss a hypothetical patient with specific symptoms—Mr. X has come to his family doctor complaining of fever and chills—and brainstorm ways to figure out what's wrong. If the course is microbiology, someone might suggest an infection. Then the question becomes: What kind of infection? Everyone goes off to research possible conditions and appropriate diagnostic tests, and the group meets again and again during the week, eventually arriving at a solution: Mr. X has a staph infection. The idea is that by teaching themselves how to solve problems, students are better equipped for the real world. "When they present to you one specific disease and you talk about it in PBL, it really sticks with you," noted a Pittsburgh student. A microbiology lecture on staph, in contrast, might present a list of germs, symptoms they can cause, and antibiotics that might kill them.

Not everyone is a believer in PBL. One Columbia student pointed out that while it gives students the needed information, it can also take a lot of extra time. "It's great when everyone in the group comes in with a different knowledge base and can exchange information. But the first year of med school is *not* like that. People actually know very little. So you end up spending an awful lot of time running around to the library, looking up basic things. It's not efficient at all. The Columbia faculty agrees with him for the most part and has emphasized lectures, adopting PBL techniques in just a few courses. One University of Chicago med student added that she got more with less fuss out of the science lectures that dominate at her school: "You need to have the basic sciences down first in order to do something good later. It might not seem interesting, but we can't help patients without it."

Another variation is the way schools serve up the required topics. For example, many are moving away from courses that cover discrete subjects such as microbiology or pharmacology as overviews of the entire body, moving instead toward interdisciplinary "organ-based" courses that examine all aspects of, say, the kidneys. Students learn about kidney anatomy, microbiology, immunology, and the drugs that affect this organ. Next, they might move on to the heart and circulatory system, then go on to the nervous system, and so on throughout the body. "I think it helps you put things together and see how the body actually works," said a Duluth student. Her school, along with Brown, Yale, the University of Texas Medical Branch–Galveston, and many others, has switched to this way of teaching.

The amount of time spent helping patients—or at the very least seeing patients—is an increasingly important variable, too. For a large part of the past century, the basic science courses during the first years of med school kept students in large lecture halls or with their noses buried in textbooks. Then, in the third year, they'd enter the hospital for clinical training and encounter their first real patients. Often they were ill-prepared. "Our faculty was getting worried that students weren't making the connections between science and patient care that they

> *"You need to have the basic sciences down first in order to do something good later."*

could be making," said Donald Innes, associate dean for curriculum at the University of Virginia's medical school. That concern was shared nationwide, said Robert Eaglen, a former member of the Liaison Committee on Medical Education, the curriculum guidance arm of the Association of American Medical Colleges. Medical schools across the country began revamping their first-year curriculum so that student–patient encounters would occur early on.

It's a welcome change for many students. "I want the science backed up by experience," said one student at the University of New Mexico, explaining that the promise of early and plentiful experience with patients drew him to that school. As a supplement to time in class, New Mexico places first-year students in local clinics where they work with supervising physicians in actual practice. "Having a real face behind these medical problems is really helpful," said the student. Moreover, students learn early how to interact with patients—a skill you can't get from a textbook, said Scott Obenshain, New Mexico's former associate dean for undergraduate medical education. The contact is helpful to patients, too—which is why New Mexico originally started making it happen. "We're in a rural area and we have a great call for physicians who have general skills, rather than specialists," said Obenshain. Case Western pairs students in their first month of school with expectant mothers at local clinics. The students work as

---

"Our faculty was getting worried that students weren't making the connections between science and patient care that they could be making."

---

patient advocates until these mothers give birth.

Some schools simulate patient interaction instead. Virginia, for instance, uses "standardized patients" in first-year lecture classes. These are not real patients but people who have been trained to complain of symptoms that are signs of a particular illness. Students learn to take medical histories from working with them and progress to giving them physical exams.

Most schools also now require that first-year students "shadow" practicing physicians on their rounds, perhaps once a week or once a month. But beware: Not all shadowing experiences are equally useful. "Applicants really should ask if shadowing is an active or passive experience," said Cornell's Bardes, who believes that just sitting around watching the doctor work doesn't do much good. A more active role, which Cornell asks of its students, is to function as a patient advocate or a kind of social worker in a medical clinic, talking to the patient and making sure any concerns are addressed by the medical team. "Not only does that get the student

involved with the patient," Bardes said. "It also involves the student with the doctors and nurses directly, and helps the student understand that care is a team effort."

New topics are also shouldering their way into the mix. At Pritzker in Chicago, first-years take a course called Introduction to Clinical Medicine, which gets away from science and into interpersonal relationships and ethics; at Iowa, this course is called Foundations of Clinical Practice. UCSF offers an introduction to pain treatment. And Emory, in Atlanta, teaches Complementary Medical Practices as an elective, in which students visit acupuncture studios and Chinese herbalists. Other schools have added complementary medicine to the curriculum, too, as doctors begin to realize how many of their patients take herbs and supplements.

Finally, although medical students often joke that "C equals M.D." (meaning that you can count on being a doctor as long as you don't flunk out), it's worth considering the way schools on your list handle grades. The traditional "ABC" system may be the most comfortable one for you if you like getting fairly specific feedback about how firm a grasp you have of the material. Some students at Yale, in fact, say that school's relaxed no-grade approach can cause people to slip far behind unless they are highly motivated and disciplined. On the other hand, many students find that simple pass/fail grades relieve some of the pressure that comes with a letter system. One student at Case Western noted that grading policies helped him choose between Case in Cleveland and Ohio State in Columbus. Ohio State was a lot cheaper and "in a town that felt more like home." Yet he decided on Case largely because the first two years of the program are graded pass/fail. To him, that meant the likelihood that Case "might be more humane than the rest" and that there would be more cooperation with other students. Indeed, he reports that his time in school was filled with fun as well as work, and much of the credit goes to his fellow students. "So I'll take my Case Western degree and smile."

Chapter Three

Inside Five Top Schools

There's more than one way to become a doctor—157 ways, in fact, if you count all of the accredited medical schools in the country. (Turn to the Directory for details.) The five top schools profiled in this chapter each typify a different approach to the teaching of medicine. All place highly in the annual *U.S.News & World Report* rankings. Two are public schools, one in a small Midwestern city (the University of Wisconsin in Madison) and the other in a dense, urban West Coast setting (the University of Washington in Seattle). Both of these schools try to meet local needs by turning out world-class primary care doctors, but they do so in very different ways.

The remaining three are private institutions. Duke University, in the Southeast, has an accelerated program of science courses for first-year students, setting them up to do complex research. At Yale University in the Northeast, students don't take exams unless they want to, yet are required to write a thesis. Then there is Johns Hopkins University in the mid-Atlantic, a research power-house whose students serve urban Baltimore when they are not busy in the school's labs.

Of course, each school boasts features that defy the limits of any stereotype: Washington, for instance, creates family doctors while also pulling in more research money than most other schools in the nation. That's why any school you're interested in merits a closer look. To give you a head start, here are profiles, including student and faculty view-points, of each member of this medical Fab Five.

University of Wisconsin School of Medicine and Public Health

- Madison, Wisconsin
- Public
- Enrollment 2009–2010 academic year: 1,700
- Overall rank in the 2011 *U.S. News* medical school rankings (research): 27
- Overall rank in the 2011 *U.S. News* medical school rankings (primary care): 12
- Average MCAT score: 10.4
- Average undergraduate GPA: 3.70

Walk over to the University of Wisconsin School of Medicine and Public Health's anatomy depart-ment and you'll be able to talk to—or take a class from—James Thomson, the scientist who first iso-lated human stem cells from an embryo, a giant breakthrough that has raised hopes for dramatic new medical therapies and embroiled the country in an ethical debate over use of these cells.

Nearly 600 of Wisconsin's almost 1,300 fac-ulty members are involved in leading medical sci-ence programs in cancer, cardiovascular disease, aging, neuroscience, and other key areas. The uni-versity as a whole pulled in $770 million in research money in a recent year, making it one of the top public schools doing this kind of work. So what draws most students to Madison?

"I chose to attend the University of Wisconsin because of its strong sense of community among students and faculty," said one graduating senior. "The commitment to patient care, medical educa-tion, and research is simply outstanding. In terms of the research, I was lucky enough to have spent time working in a lab, where I studied novel drugs to treat neuroendocrine tumors."

Robert Golden, dean of the school, said the school is pioneering a new model of medical edu-cation—fully integrating biomedical science, the care of individual patients, and the health of diverse populations.

"We have launched a revolutionary experi-ment, as we transform into the first-ever school of medicine and public health. The integration of medicine and public health is extremely impor-tant," he said. "When those two approaches are separated by silos, there are missed opportunities for synergies, collaborations, and whole new per-spectives on complex topics ranging from cancer to obesity. We want our medical students to learn how to take the pulse of a community, as well as a patient, and to learn how to prevent, as well as diagnose and treat disease."

Golden said the school is "fortunate to be embed-ded in an incredibly strong research-intensive university," noting that it has great partners in

Madison, including the schools of nursing, pharmacy, and veterinary medicine, as well as fine partners at the school's academic campuses in Milwaukee, Marshfield, and La Crosse.

The med school has about the same number of Ph.D. students as it does M.D. students. Joint M.D./Ph.D. degrees in the Medical Scientist Training Program are also popular, as is the new M.D./M.P.H. program. Pioneering research programs on the connection between cancer and nutrition, and on cardiac electrophysiology, have spawned courses for medical students.

This, then, is the "Wisconsin idea": While the university is tucked away on a narrow isthmus of land, almost cut off by two surrounding beautiful lakes, Mendota and Monona, the medical school itself is a statewide institution. Students do research in Madison at the highly regarded cancer center, for example, but also go to Milwaukee and work with the urban poor or head out to small towns like Eagle River or Ashland, where they learn about rural healthcare issues and everyone around knows their names. Feeling a strong responsibility to make sure Wisconsin has the necessary supply of doctors, the university's Board of Regents presses the school to reserve 75 percent of the spots in each entering class for in-state students, many of whom will stay in the area once they get their M.D.

To fan interest in treating patients, the school pairs first- and second-year students with family practice doctors, internists, or pediatricians for a half-day each month. Students themselves run a program called MEDIC (Medical Information Center), which puts them to work advising patients at clinics in the Madison area. The SMPH benefits from its statewide campus, with students spending an average of 16 weeks during their third year at academic campuses in La Crosse, Marshfield, and Milwaukee. For at least six weeks during the fourth year, the school sends everyone out for rotations in small-town clinics and hospitals throughout the state. "It's not that they absolutely want to push us in that direction, but they definitely want to expose us to that,"

"When I went to get recommendations for residency programs, there was no shortage of people I could talk to."

said one student interested in family practice. And the exposure definitely gets results: Since 1999, about 15 percent of each graduating class has gone into family medicine residencies. Internal medicine has drawn an additional 12 to 20 percent, and the third most popular specialty has been pediatrics. In contrast, about 5 or 6 percent choose surgery, and a fraction of a percent go into neurology. However, it's not all provincial. The school does look beyond the Dairy State borders: It runs a summer medical clinic in Ecuador, for example.

Whatever specialty students explore, they do it in close contact with their professors. Particularly at the small-town sites, there's often just one student rotating through at a time, which translates into a lot of attention from teacher-physicians. That's true on campus, too. Faculty members have a reputation for being very approachable and often come in during the evenings to tutor students. "There's a lot of interaction with professors," one student said. "When I went to get recommendations for residency programs, there was no shortage of people I could talk to. I was on a first-name basis with a lot of them." Indeed, teaching skill, not just the number of publications or amount of grant funding brought in, is weighed more heavily in promotion decisions than at most schools, and junior faculty are assigned a senior faculty mentor to help them along.

The warm, intimate feeling extends to fellow students. "I got into here, and Dartmouth, and Yale," said one third-year student. "This place seemed different. People at Madison take time out of their schedules to stop and discuss the school with you, in the classrooms and in the hallways, because they like it so much. I remember I visited one other school where I didn't see a student all day, and I know they weren't all on vacation."

Students call the culture supportive, not competitive; there are even side bets in each class on how many members will end up marrying one another. Students from each of the four years join "houses," which are learning communities that provide common space for studying and socializing.

"The curriculum at the SMPH has been going through continuous innovation," said Byron Crouse, the interim senior associate dean for academic affairs. "With the transformation from a medical school to a School of Medicine and Public Health, there has been increased use of small groups and community engagement." He explained that the learning communities enabled by the structure of the Health Sciences Learning Center have promoted a sense of shared goals within the school that extends to engagement with the community at large, through service-learning opportunities and programs such as MEDIC. "The Wisconsin Academy for Rural Medicine (WARM) and Training in Urban Medicine and Public Health (TRIUMPH) are new programs now underway to promote future practice in rural and urban underserved communities," he added.

Amenities at the school improved drastically in 2004, when Wisconsin's new Health Sciences Learning Center opened, giving Wisconsin one of the most modern medical school buildings in the country. Numerous classrooms and labs allow for smaller course sections and discussion groups. The school's formerly separate libraries are now consolidated here and equipped with more computer terminals as well as wireless access. The entire building, in fact, is a wireless heaven, with numerous "hot spots" where students can download course materials and medical data out of the ether. The building also houses Wisconsin's nursing and physician assistant programs, allowing for a lot of cross-pollination of ideas and staff.

Parking spaces are still going to be a problem, however. If that's a big issue for you, Madison is not going to make you happy. But everything else—the patient contact, the access to leading research if you want it, the new building, the famously rich university-made ice cream sold at the student center—makes for some of the best-trained (and happiest) future doctors around.

Duke University School of Medicine

■ **Durham, North Carolina**
■ **Private**
■ **Enrollment 2009–2010 academic year: 421**
■ **Overall rank in the 2011** *U.S. News* **medical school rankings (research): 6**
■ **Overall rank in the 2011** *U.S. News* **medical school rankings (primary care): 42**
■ **Average MCAT score: 11.4**
■ **Average undergraduate GPA: 3.72**

Most medical students spend their third year of school in hospitals, shuttling from pediatric wards to cardiology units to emergency rooms and beyond, trying out various clinical specialties.

At Duke, things work a bit differently.

A third-year student might find herself in a microbiology lab, working with a fungus that can cause meningitis in people with weak immune systems, surrounded by fungus-filled petri dishes looking for a gene that helps the fungus become virulent. Or, she could be across town at a Duke clinic examining dozens of patients to determine the reliability of various blood pressure monitors.

Instead of spreading basic science classes across the first two years, Duke packs them into the first 11 months, running August through July. As a result of this acceleration, students get into the hospital sooner—during year two instead of year three. Their third year is devoted full-time to research. In other words, the program is geared toward producing physician-scientists who can easily move between the lab bench and the bedside.

"Medical students of the future will learn to appreciate a complex gray scale of health and un-health," said Nancy Andrews, dean of the school. "We strive to give graduates both the tools and the ethos of lifetime scholarship so they can advance our understanding of those complexities." An M.D./Ph.D. herself, Andrews noted that 25 percent of Duke students go on to pursue dual degrees such as an M.D./Ph.D. or an M.D. combined with a new master's degree in global health, which focuses on the health concerns of poor and marginalized populations.

The early push to cover everything from physiology and neurobiology to pathology in the first year doesn't mean spending all day, every day in a lecture hall. First-year students spend a third of their time in didactic instruction, a third in interactive learning situations, and another third in independent study. "We're learning the essentials, not a lot of fluff, because you don't need it," said one second-year student, adding that she felt extremely well prepared for her clinical rotations.

"We aim to provide graduates with both the tools and the ethos of lifetime scholarship."

In fact, most students are eager to hit the wards. "I came to med school to practice medicine, to put a white coat on and get out into the hospital—not to sit in a classroom for two years," explained a student in the fourth year of a combined M.D./Ph.D. program in medical sociology and health policy.

Edward Buckley, vice dean for education, lauds the concept of a third year for research in part because he's seen that a rigorous scholarly experience in bio-medical-related research trains future physician leaders to be able to interpret constantly advancing research. "Even studies in the Journal of the American Medical Association need to be evaluated for accuracy," he said. "Learning to critically read scientific literature helps graduates more quickly understand when things change from research to therapy. And the best way to assess the value of research is to be involved in research yourself."

The individualized research process requires a lot of initiative and self-motivation—much like the rest of the Duke experience—but gives students exceptional benefits. It provides an opportunity to work closely with a faculty mentor, for one thing, perhaps one of the big names you see on the covers of your textbooks. It can also be an important résumé boost when you start shopping for a residency, particularly if you've published a scientific paper or two.

Recently, Duke revamped its curriculum to better address changes in the field of medicine. The traditional first-year lecture courses were regrouped

---

"There's no better way to assess the value of research than to do it yourself."

---

into four blocks—Molecules and Cells, Normal Body, Brain and Behavior, and Body and Disease— and a Practice Course. The change puts the focus on individual organ systems rather than broad topics, and places more emphasis on interaction and case-based learning. The second year has five weeklong "mini courses" that cover diagnostic exercises and exposure to areas of healthcare such as physical rehabilitation and social work. In addition, the research year was expanded from eight to 10 months and requires a written thesis.

During her third year at Duke, Stephanie Chang received a Sarnoff fellowship that allowed her to pursue cardiothoracic research at Stanford. "This experience was invaluable, not only because of the mentors that I met, but also because it allowed me to truly understand the nature of being a clinician-scientist, which solidified my desire to pursue academic medicine," she said.

Both research and clinical opportunities abound throughout the relatively young and rich Duke University Health System, a $2 billion system closely affiliated with the medical school, encom-passing myriad healthcare providers from the Duke Hospital and Clinics to the Duke HomeCare and Hospice. That range provides chances for students to gain exposure to many different areas of medicine. This is perhaps another reason that the vast majority of students here end up concentrating on competitive specialties and subspecialties like dermatology, pediatrics, plastic surgery, orthopedics, and radiology, as opposed to primary care or family medicine.

A good number obtain coveted residencies in these areas at top institutions, including nearly a quarter at Duke itself. After they graduate, some 20 percent of Duke students go on to hold academic positions; the remaining 80 percent pursue a wide variety of career paths, from running biotech companies to working in government health organizations and serving as physicians in small towns.

Students report that the culture at Duke is overwhelmingly collegial. Many tell tales of sharing notes and study charts with their whole class during the first year. This may partially be the result of a grading system that de-emphasizes competition for A's. At Duke, first-year students are evaluated on a pass, fail, and honors basis.

It also helps that faculty members are very accessible. In the first year, students are assigned to an advisory dean, and they meet with that person and a handful of peers for lunch once a week. These gatherings let students discuss current events and school-wide issues, or simply blow off steam. In the second year, larger groups of 25 congregate to talk about being in the hospital and to share important milestones, such as delivering a baby for the first time.

In addition to its many academic advantages, Duke can also provide a relatively inexpensive medical education. The low cost of living in Durham, combined with typically strong financial aid offers, results in a much lower average debt burden: The average for Duke graduates is $112,792, compared with the national average of slightly more than $156,000. That, students say, relieves a lot of anxiety about the future. The medical school offers some full-tuition merit scholarships and, recently, 37 out of 100 third-year students received research scholarships from sources such as the Howard Hughes Medical Institute. Despite the hard work, students say, there's plenty of time to hang out with friends and enjoy Durham Bulls minor league baseball and the university's nationally ranked basketball teams.

The comprehensive, student-produced *Duke Med School Made Ridiculously Simple* is a favorite resource for information about how you'll spend your free time, in addition to academics.

Duke is, in short, a school of tremendous challenges but also tremendous opportunities. The fearless thrive and go on to push back the current boundaries of medicine. "We're an ambitious institution, and we're proud of how our graduates follow their own big dreams of clinical and research success," said Dean Andrews.

Yale University School of Medicine

- New Haven, Connecticut
- Private
- Enrollment 2009–2010 academic year: 414
- Overall rank in the 2011 *U.S. News* medical school rankings (research): 6
- Overall rank in the 2011 *U.S. News* medical school rankings (primary care): N/A
- Average MCAT score: 11.9
- Average undergraduate GPA: 3.78

At the Yale School of Medicine, many exams are optional, anonymous, online self-evaluations, and preclinical students get two free afternoons each week. San Francisco native Nancy Allen noted that Yale students really enjoy spending time with one another inside and outside the academic setting. "There is also a very fun and creative feel to the campus culture, and this is reflected in the annual Second Year Show, in which the entire second-year class puts on a production involving video, singing, dancing, and acting," the UCLA graduate added.

Jill Rubinstein described the culture on campus as open, friendly, and intellectually stimulating. "There is a great sense of camaraderie among the students," she said. "The association between the medical school and the university as a whole is also a great asset, providing outlets for just about any creative, cultural, or athletic endeavor imaginable. The location in New Haven is another asset, with a wealth of good restaurants and theater, and proximity to great hiking trails, beaches, state parks, etc."

Welcome to the "Yale System." It aims to give med students wide latitude in constructing their own educational experiences, akin to Ph.D. programs in, say, genetics or history. And if this is utopia, it requires plenty of self-discipline. Dean Robert J. Alpern said the Yale System emphasizes collaboration over competition and each student's own initiative and interests over a school-driven curriculum. "It attracts students who are highly self-motivated—students with a passion for learning who have competed very successfully throughout college, often serving in leadership roles in their school and community," he said. "At Yale, because of the atmosphere of common purpose, one student's success does not come at the expense of another's—instead it reinforces it. Students here excel, and they help each other attain new heights."

Ryan Schwarz describes his first two years as "wonderful," adding that they defied the stereotype of what medical school is like. "Yes, we worked and studied quite hard, and yes, there was an enormous amount of information to learn very quickly," he said. "But, because of the Yale System, it was a noncompetitive and friendly environment, and we could go at our own pace. There weren't

---

"Yale really allows students to pursue a project that they are interested in."

---

tests every three weeks, and as a result, everyone was much more relaxed and the quality of living was much better than that of my friends' experiences at other med schools."

The school's size—each class is roughly 100 students—also breeds an intimate, cooperative atmosphere. For second-year students who cycle through a long series of total-immersion modules—a few weeks on the cardiovascular system followed by a few weeks of psychiatry, and so on—classes outside the lectures are invariably tiny. In labs and workshops, class size stays below 20.

What Yale does require is a thesis, an unusual demand among medical schools. This project, usually begun during the first or second year and completed during the fourth and final year of school, may be lab research or an investigation of clinical, epidemiological, or sociological subjects. "The funding for summer research is plentiful, and Yale really allows students to pursue a project that they are interested in, whether it is in humanities, basic science, or clinical research," said student Hao Feng.

Recent papers have examined the stigma attached to AIDS in Africa and the causes of type 2 diabetes, studied in lab mice. Students doing this work can tap into Yale's resources as a leading research institution (it received $341.3 million in National Institutes of Health grants in 2008), funding thesis-related research through grants and getting access to top faculty for thesis advisors.

"One of the most striking of my experiences at Yale is the level of interaction I have with faculty," said Allen. She added that during preclinical years at Yale she had multiple opportunities to work with faculty one-on-one for presentations and that during her surgical rotation, she has had the opportunity to meet with a faculty mentor weekly to discuss topics such as career planning,

Roughly half of each class takes an extra year to graduate, often to devote a full year to the thesis. In these cases, Yale waives fifth-year tuition.

Because of this program, Yale is known for breeding academic physicians. Even students who aren't drawn to Yale for the thesis often wind up getting hooked on research. Many publish their papers in medical journals. "We look for students who are highly intelligent, curious, and committed to excellence," said Dean Alpern. "Many will continue on in academia, either as physician-scientists or biomedical researchers." He added that increasingly, Yale students are interested in global health and policy development as it affects the improved delivery of healthcare and that nearly all want the impact of their work to be broad and meaningful to a large number of people.

Indeed, Yale-New Haven Hospital, the school's main teaching hospital, doesn't count family medicine among the residencies it offers, though a large number of Yale students do take residencies in pediatrics.

Despite the heady academic atmosphere, students are not locked in an ivory research tower. The M.D. program puts students in touch with patients early on. From the first year, all students meet weekly to practice taking medical histories from fellow students, then from actual patients—sometimes within the first few weeks of med school. This is a big help when students hit the hospital wards full time in their third year. One third-year student said he didn't appreciate the weekly meetings until he had to tell a former drug user that he'd need regular kidney dialysis for the rest of his life—a test of interpersonal, rather than medical, skills. "By the time third year rolls around," he said, "you spend time caring for the patient instead of figuring out how to gather information from them." Even during their time in the hospitals, students are encouraged to take control of their learning. "The structure on the wards is flat as opposed to hierarchical," one student said. "There's no objection to saying, 'I don't think that's right' to an attending [physician]. Just because they've had all this training doesn't mean they can't be challenged."

Many spend the time doing volunteer work, like educating local schoolchildren on AIDS/HIV prevention or creating basic medical records for New Haven's homeless population. An auction organized by students raises more than $30,000 annually for the homeless. With plenty of low-income residents, New Haven is flush with volunteer opportunities.

"Students here participate in numerous extracurricular activities," said student Aaron Feinstein, "whether it be volunteering at local clinics, raising money for the community, advocating for local and national health policy changes, pursuing collective interests in a particular aspect of medicine, or simply working to better the lives of medical students on campus."

The medical school is also a short walk from Yale's main campus, which allows students to interact with other university departments. Most of their engagement, however, is at the med school itself, where the administration seems unusually responsive to student input. When a pair of students recently developed a formula that allowed third-year students to schedule their clinical clerkships more easily, administrators agreed to adopt it. And when international students lobbied to extend financial aid to foreign students in 2003, the school obliged.

"We hope [Yale graduates] will be leaders in whatever field they choose after medical school, always seeking to acquire new knowledge and to improve the quality of healthcare," Alpern said. "We also hope they will instill in others the values of a broad education, critical thinking, and innovation."

Johns Hopkins University School of Medicine

- **Baltimore, Maryland**
- **Private**
- **Enrollment 2009–2010 academic year: 480**
- **Overall rank in the 2011 *U.S. News* medical school rankings (research): 3**
- **Overall rank in the 2011 *U.S. News* medical school rankings (primary care): 25**
- **Average MCAT score: 11.9**
- **Average undergraduate GPA: 3.87**

Johns Hopkins University School of Medicine has been at the forefront of medical education since its founding in 1893. In those days, when most schools offered only lectures and students did not deal with live patients, Quaker merchant Johns Hopkins insisted that the medical school bearing his name had to be connected to a hospital with the size and means to train medical students. As a result, Hopkins students learned through hands-on experience. Eventually, this model spread throughout American medical education.

Since its founding, the school has been home to over a century of influential medical educators, such as William Osler and William Halsted, inventors of the modern medical residency. Johns Hopkins researchers invented the implantable pacemaker, discovered restriction enzymes that let geneticists manipulate DNA, and developed CPR.

And Johns Hopkins is committed to continuing innovation. "In this new century, Hopkins is once again transforming medical education with a new curriculum, called Genes to Society, which is no less revolutionary," said Dean Edward D. Miller. "Incorporating new insights gained by the mapping of the human genome and the profound knowledge of how public health affects people's lives, the Genes to Society curriculum will prepare new students for a new age in medicine, the likes of which could scarcely have been envisioned even 25 years ago."

The school views the curriculum as an essential adaptation in the training of new doctors and health-care delivery. The curriculum, which was five years in development, takes "a systems approach to understanding human health and disease, from genes and molecules to organs" and "teaches that care must be based on genetic variation, not a one-size-fits-all view of disease or patients."

"Our Genes to Society curriculum builds on the fundamental insights learned during the past several decades through the study of molecular biology," said David G. Nichols, M.D., vice dean for education and professor of anesthesiology and critical care medicine. "With this new knowledge, and within this beautiful new building, students will begin by studying the basic building blocks of life and progress through higher and higher levels of organization and complexity. Through the use of advanced teaching technologies and collaborative learning, Genes to Society marks a new revolution in medical education." Johns Hopkins has devoted a new facility—the Armstrong Medical Education Building—to accommodate and facilitate the new curriculum. The four-story building features an advanced anatomy lab, digital classrooms, and student lounge space.

With such a focus on the cutting edge, it should be no surprise that more than half of Hopkins graduates spend some part of their career in academic medicine, whether as full professors or as part-timers at local medical schools. Only about 10 percent of graduates concentrate exclusively on primary care.

Most of the teaching in later years happens one-on-one, with a research mentor or on the wards, noted Nichols. "Teaching how to develop a bedside manner—that's really a one-on-one kind of experience," he said. "You can't teach it in a lecture, and you can't read about it in a book."

Even before bedside manners are taught, however, Hopkins students begin feeling the research tug: More than 90 percent do some kind of research as an elective, most often in the summer after their first year. One fourth-year student said she came to school with a strong interest in international health. She'd been an anthropology major in college, and she said there was no way anyone was getting her to sit at a lab bench for months at a stretch. "Then all of a sudden, here I was working in a lab, and, you know, I took a year off to do it." Her research, on how HIV lives in the body even during antiviral treatment, taught her how the lab relates to patient care—in her case, to the international HIV prevention work that she eventually wants to do.

Besides its name for fostering cutting-edge research, Hopkins has a reputation for generating cutthroat competition. Hopkins takes only 120 of its 4,000 or so applicants every year, so its students are among the best in the country academically. Nonetheless, many students say they usually study in groups, helping each other get through the difficult science courses. And during those first few years of school, students spend a great deal of time together, in and out of class.

"In my experience, campus culture is friendly—the administration is open to feedback from students, professors on a whole have been very approachable and open, and faculty love working with students on research projects," said El Paso native Richa Gupta. "Students are highly motivated, brilliant, and passionate, but the best thing about them is that they are always willing to help each other out and collaborate. Students here have packed academic schedules but are still able to pursue their passions—whether it be trying to start a free-care clinic or spending a summer doing research."

Professors also have a reputation for being supportive. Laura Cappelli noted that during her interview she was impressed with not only the clinical training students receive but also the accessibility of the faculty. "The students and faculty were very enthusiastic about their experiences," she added. "I

have always been of the mind-set that people make an institution, so I thought Johns Hopkins would be a great place to train."

Her first impression was correct, and Cappelli reported that she has "found wonderful mentors on the faculty who care about my career and helping me develop my interests."

Hopkins's urban home, Baltimore, may be

"I like being in a hospital that serves an incredible diversity of patients."

known as "Charm City," but those charms are usually not immediately evident to med students. The hospital and school are wedged into a dense urban campus in rough East Baltimore, although the neighborhood has been improving in recent years. Eventually, students learn to navigate Baltimore's diverse neighborhoods, and many fall in love with the city. Washington, D.C., is less than an hour away, and students can get to New York City in a few hours.

The city plays a role in students' education, too. Part of the hospital's mission is to take care of the poor. While students see many unusual cases referred from other hospitals (because Hopkins has so many top specialists), they also tackle the day-to-day health problems of their closest neighbors. Many students work on community health projects: Some teach sex education workshops in Baltimore middle schools, work on a program to introduce local high school kids to health careers, or mentor pregnant teenagers.

"I like being in a hospital that serves an incredible diversity of patients, as well as being in a needy community that students can really make a difference in," said Gupta. "The School of Medicine is located in the heart of East Baltimore, and the hospital and faculty are definitely very much dedicated to serving the population that surrounds it."

University of Washington School of Medicine

- Seattle, Washington
- Public
- Enrollment 2009–2010 academic year: 888
- Overall rank in the 2011 *U.S. News* medical school rankings (research): 6
- Overall rank in the 2011 *U.S. News* medical school rankings (primary care): 1
- Average MCAT score: 10.33
- Average undergraduate GPA: 3.67

In 1971, four states decided that their medical education needs would be best served if they formed a united front behind the University of Washington School of Medicine. Joined by Wyoming in 1996, the consortium is known as WWAMI, the acronym for five northwestern states—Washington, Wyoming, Alaska, Montana, and Idaho—that together make up more than a quarter of the landmass in the United States.

The five pooled far-flung resources, doctors, and science faculty at local colleges to bring WWAMI residents to Seattle—and get them back to WWAMI states once they've graduated. The states each get to designate a number of medical school seats, which are in turn supported by state funds and tuition. The tuition paid by students in Alaska, Idaho, Montana, and Wyoming is the same as that paid by Washington residents.

The results are impressive. Since the founding of the program, 60 percent of the medical school's graduates have chosen to practice within the five-state area, and 41 percent of the medical school's graduates have entered primary care practice—family medicine, general pediatrics, or general internal medicine. This commitment to rural primary care came about, said Paul Ramsey, the school's dean, because 37 percent of the population in the region lives in rural areas.

"Our students have great opportunities to train and care for the underserved throughout our five-state WWAMI region and worldwide," Ramsey said. "Training sites vary from urban clinics and hospitals in Seattle, Spokane, Anchorage, and Boise to small fishing villages in Alaska and ranching towns in Montana and Wyoming—all with outstanding clinical teachers."

The route many of the medical students take can be a bit unusual. Nearly half of a med school class can end up spending the first year taking basic science courses such as physiology and microbiology at one of five Northwestern schools at six locations outside Seattle. More than a hundred UW students can spend their first-year summers working side by side with local doctors in underserved, rural areas.

According to students, primary care "is just part of the culture" that suffuses UW and its affiliated hospitals. In both the first and second years, students take the required course Introduction to Clinical Medicine, where they are tutored in interviewing skills, usually in small groups of six or seven. "Through our Colleges program, all students are assigned a faculty mentor who trains them in clinical skills at the bedside during second year and stays connected with the students throughout their education, wherever they are," Ramsey said.

In their third and fourth years, when a lot of other med students are touring specialty areas in big teaching hospitals, UW students are encouraged to do their rotations outside Seattle, in more than 100 WWAMI towns from Nome, Alaska, to Buffalo, Wyoming, and beyond. "It's just an unbeatable experience out there," said one student who did his family medicine rotation in a five-doctor clinic in eastern Washington. The doctors there had known their patients for years. In some cases, they were delivering the babies of people they'd delivered. "I saw things I'd never see in an urban hospital with a hundred interns running around," he said.

When students do rotations as far away as Alaska, the isolation puts a premium on developing diverse medical skills. "Out there, you have no idea what could walk in the door at any moment," a student reported. "If you can't handle it, the patient gets choppered a hundred miles to someone who can," and the helicopter ride can, for critically injured patients, take too long.

While there certainly is a focus on primary care, the University of Washington School of Medicine is not without options, and many of those come from UW's enormous research presence. In fiscal year 2009, the school's faculty was awarded more than $700 million in grants from the National Institutes of Health. Nearly 2,000 faculty members regularly make their way to the school's medical research labs along Portage Bay of Lake Washington and a new research hub on the shores of Lake Union called UW Medicine at South Lake Union.

"I saw things I'd never see in an urban hospital with a hundred interns running around."

Calling the UW School of Medicine home are 33 members of the Institute of Medicine and 32 members of the National Academy of Sciences. Students have the opportunity to work with UW School of Medicine scientists at the Fred Hutchinson Cancer Research Center and at other notable biomedical research institutions in the city.

One graduate who ended up working as a general internist in Billings, Montana, earned three separate grants at UW to work with the school's collection of human and primate eyeballs, one of the largest in the country, studying ophthalmology and developmental proteins in retinas.

Chapter Four

Getting In

There are lots of good reasons for wanting to be a doctor. Maybe you think you have a healing touch, or you want to serve the community, or there's something about solving the puzzle of an illness that satisfies your mind and your soul. And there are probably some bad reasons, like doing it for the money, or because your family will be disappointed if you don't make medicine a career. But no matter what the motives, everyone has to jump over the same hurdle: medical school admissions.

It's not an easy leap. More than 40,000 people try to get in every year, yet just around 18,000 succeed. And that's only the overall picture. Individual schools can be much more picky. The University of Chicago Pritzker School of Medicine recently received over 7,700 applications for its incoming class of about 170 students. Georgetown University School of Medicine had over 10,600 applicants for about 190 spaces. You do the math.

If you want in, you'd better be *able* to do the math. This is a brainy crowd. Admissions committees are swamped with applications from students whose undergraduate grade point averages hover at 3.4 and who average a score of 27 out of 45 on the Medical College Admission Test (MCAT). Those who attend the most competitive schools consistently score well over 30. "The competition is very intense," said

---

"The competition is very intense. There are a whole bunch of applicants who, in terms of numbers, are all equally qualified."

Greg Goldmakher, a medical school advisor with AdmissionsConsultants, Inc. in Vienna, Virginia. "There are a whole bunch of applicants who, in terms of numbers, are all equally qualified."

To stand out—and get in—applicants must find ways to distinguish themselves from the rest of the premed pack. In this chapter, you'll learn how. *U.S. News* asked admissions directors at the nation's top medical schools to describe what they look for in candidates who get the green light. All of them said good grades and MCATs are a great start. But science smarts are not enough. Admissions committees are looking for unique, highly motivated people who excel in and out of the classroom. "It's a very special segment of the human race," said Andrew Frantz, associate dean of admissions at Columbia University's College of Physicians and Surgeons in New York. "They have to be intelligent, sensitive to others, compassionate, committed to finding joy in their work, and they should want to be of service to others." Here are tips to best let you show those traits, along with ways to get the best test scores and grades that you can.

Making the grades

It all starts in the classroom. Science is the backbone of medicine, and no matter how caring or compassionate you may be, medical schools want to know that you can handle the academic material. You will need to complete certain science courses before you can apply to medical school, and you should start taking them freshman year, if possible. By the time you apply to medical school, you should have completed one year each (including labs) of chemistry, biology, physics, and organic chemistry. In addition, medical schools often want to see a year of English and a year of math, including a semester of calculus. The American Medical Student Association (AMSA) tells premeds to head for their school's preprofessional health advisor, usually found in the career counseling office, and together plot a course for completing all of the classes.

Pace yourself. A heavy load of rigorous courses can drag down your performance in each class, so don't take more than two prerequisites a semester.

If you decide to jump on the premed track a bit later—say, well into your sophomore year—you may need to take summer classes to make up for lost time. Find a summer school that is comparable to the one you attend during the school year; admissions committees do take note of the difference. "We are troubled by someone taking one or two semesters of something like organic chemistry at a community college over the summer," said Robert Witzburg, associate dean and director of admissions at Boston University School of Medicine. But if the course is taken at a school like the one you're already

The "nontraditional" student

There was a time when almost every applicant to medical school came directly from college. No longer. An ever-increasing number are taking time after they graduate to pursue other interests or get some work experience. Called "nontraditional applicants," even though their path is becoming a tradition in itself, these people are often viewed favorably, even prized, by admissions committees. Boston University's medical school admissions office says the school's nontraditional students, many of whom have put off their physician training to work in jobs serving communities without many resources, demonstrate "flexible intelligence" and an ability to interact well with patients. Henry Ralston, who was the associate dean of admissions at the University of California–San Francisco agreed. That's why he encouraged premeds to take a year off and get some experience outside of the school setting. "I prefer older students," he said.

But not all schools feel this way, cautioned Trina Denton, a nontraditional applicant who served as director of premedical affairs at AMSA, the medical student advocacy group. Some medical schools may worry that applicants who have taken time away from studying will find it hard to get back into the habit. Applicants can ask the schools they are interested in if taking time off could harm their chances of getting in—or better yet, ask for the numbers of nontraditional students in the entering class.

Some nontraditional applicants decide after finishing college that they want to apply to medical school but have not taken the prerequisite science courses. Such applicants should consider a premed, postbaccalaureate program. You get the basic courses plus the chance to take some advanced electives. At Georgetown University, the postbaccalaureate program "gives students the courses they need so they will qualify as premed despite the fact that they may have majored in poetry," said Douglas Eagles, a former program director. Programs take one to two years and offer students some valuable structure and help when they get ready to take the MCAT and prepare their school applications. Some people find this much easier than going it all alone. And because postbaccalaureate programs can include some of the same courses a first-year med student would take, they let the admissions office see that you can really do the work—because you have.

The Association of American Medical Colleges offers a searchable database to find these programs nationwide. Go to www.aamc.org and search "postbaccalaureate programs." (For a list of several well-regarded programs, see 354.) An alternative is to take the classes on a full- or part-time basis at a local university under a nondegree-seeking status, and med schools will usually accept them. Some are more restrictive, however, so check with the schools before signing up.

studying at, he said, "no one here is going to be bothered by that."

If you plan on using Advanced Placement courses taken during high school to fulfill these requirements, be wary. Many med schools won't accept them, and whether they do or not can depend on your other science courses.

"The ideal candidate has strong performance in science, but also has taken humanities."

Remember, schools want to see that you can handle the material. So college students who major in science and also received AP credit can demonstrate they know the basics by performing well in their upper-level science courses. Med schools are more likely to let their AP work count for a college course. But applicants who do not take more advanced college science classes may not be able to use their AP scores. If you already have an idea about the med schools you want to apply to, check with those admissions offices about their AP credit policies.

This focus on science doesn't mean you have to major in biology or physics. In fact, admissions committees look for students who have challenged themselves academically and taken a broad range of classes throughout their undergraduate years. "The ideal candidate has strong performance in science but also has taken humanities," said Albert Kirby, former associate dean for admissions at Case Western Reserve University School of Medicine in Cleveland, Ohio. "We love students who are nonscience majors," said William Eley, executive associate dean for education and former director of admissions at Emory University School of Medicine in Atlanta. "We are looking for that breadth because it indicates involvement in the human side of medicine."

Indeed, majoring in something nonscientific might actually help you. In a crowd of biology and physics students, that history degree stands out. According to the Association of American Medical Colleges (AAMC), 52 percent of humanities and social science majors who applied were accepted to medical school in 2001. That's actually a little better than the 48 percent of successful applicants who majored in biology.

Take some humanities courses. Applicants who focus solely on science can be viewed as weaker candidates than those who have performed well across many fields.

Testing, testing

In addition to science classes, undergraduates must take the MCAT, an eight-hour standardized test given by the AAMC. Typically, applicants take the test in April of their junior year, although the MCAT is also given in August. You must preregister at www.aamc.org/mcat. Registration usually begins on February 1 for the April test and on June 1 for the August test. Aim for the April date because then you have August as a fallback if your scores aren't as high as you want. Try to register early because space can be limited at certain testing sites and slots are filled in the order in which they are received. The fee can be paid by credit card or by an electronic money transfer.

Unlike other standardized tests that attempt to predict a student's ability (such as the SAT), the MCAT is content driven, testing your mastery of the basic science material covered in premed courses. The test consists of four sections: physical sciences, which includes physics and chemistry; biological sciences, which includes biology and organic chemistry; verbal reasoning; and the writing sample. You can score up to 15 points in each of the two science sections and in verbal reasoning, for a possible total score of 45. (Most med school applicants, successful and unsuccessful, score in the high 20s and low 30s.) The writing sample is graded according to an eleven-letter system that goes alphabetically from "J" (lowest) to "T" (highest).

Obviously, it's best to have completed all of the science prerequisites before you take the test. Even so, to adequately prepare, you should plan to devote between 200 and 300 hours to studying. Many applicants, perhaps as many as three-quarters, choose to take a preparatory class to help them structure their studying and to ensure that they cover all of the material. Princeton Review and Kaplan, Inc., offer widely available courses. You get multiple classroom sessions, prep materials, and practice tests. The courses are expensive, running well over $1,000, but if you are not satisfied with your score, the companies will refund your fee or let you take the course again. (That's not going to help you, however, if you're not satisfied with your score and not satisfied with the course itself.) There are many local prep companies, too. But prep courses certainly aren't a must; if you feel you can be both disciplined and organized in your studying, you can purchase practice tests from the AAMC and a study guide from a bookstore, and prepare on your own.

Consider prepping. Prep classes can particularly help because they provide proctored practice tests to get you used to the grueling task of sitting and answering questions for eight hours straight.

Taken together, your GPA and MCAT score form the basis of the initial cut medical schools make in their applicant pool. Why? Studies have shown that performance on the MCAT and in undergraduate courses is a reliable predictor of how well an applicant will do during the first two years of medical school.

It takes about two months to get your scores back. If your April MCAT score falls well below what you expected, consider taking the test again in August. Medical schools vary on whether they will use your highest or your most recent score, with some averaging the two. Call admissions offices to find out how they handle the second set. But be warned: Waiting for the August score to come in could slow down the admissions committee's review of your application, and when schools offer admissions on a rolling basis, that may reduce your chances of getting a spot.

Apply yourself

Once you have completed the MCAT in April, it is time to start thinking about assembling your application. This is one-stop shopping: Most medical schools use the American Medical College Application Service (AMCAS), a division of the AAMC, to process all the paperwork. You submit one completed application online, and that includes an application form, a personal statement, transcripts from all the undergraduate schools you have attended, and other paperwork, as well as a list of schools you want to apply to. For a fee, AMCAS assembles your application file,

So you want to apply to medical school

Applying to medical school is not for the faint of heart. It is a long, hard, and expensive journey that requires planning, dedication, and perseverance.

For Matthew Shulman, who graduated from Stanford University in 2005, it even involved walking away from a job. Shulman, 27, was working as a writer in the Health and Medicine section of *U.S.News & World Report* when he decided to go to medical school.

"I knew I wanted a career that was collaborative, constantly advancing, and, most importantly, focused on helping people," he explained.

His first step was to enroll in a yearlong post-baccalaureate program to take some prerequisite science classes. He also began working as a research assistant at the Wilmer Eye Institute at Johns Hopkins University.

"Applying to medical schools is a very involved process and requires a lot of time, patience, attention, and commitment," he said.

Shulman enrolled in an MCAT prep class while taking the science courses he needed. He found that because the "material was complementary and fresh in my mind, tackling the test seemed less daunting." Getting an actual test score before beginning the application process allowed him to gauge the schools where he would be competitive before starting on the applications.

Once he had determined which schools he wanted to apply to, he began funneling the information to the American Medical College Application Service, or AMCAS.

All personal statements, essays, transcripts, and letters of recommendation are sent either electronically or by mail to AMCAS, which then provides the information to the medical schools an applicant has selected.

Shulman said that getting started early is essential because applicants have to coordinate transcripts, line up recommendations, and often work with a premed advisor.

"I devoted around a month and a half to writing the personal statement—making sure I had time to edit it—and to compiling all the necessary paperwork either to be uploaded through the AMCAS website or sent, via my premedical advising office, through the mail directly to AMCAS."

Once the medical schools receive the applications, the hard work begins. Schools send out invitations to students they are interested in, asking them to complete a secondary application. This application typically involves writing a number of different essays designed to provide a more in-depth portrait of the student and the student's reasons for applying to the particular school.

"The secondary applications, I found, took even longer than the primary AMCAS application because each school required many essays," Shulman said. "On the positive side, this allows the applicant to learn a lot more about the schools to which he or she has applied and how, for example, a particular school's research opportunities, curriculum, and faculty mentorship may suit the candidate."

With each step, the time and cost involved grows. Each AMCAS application costs about $35, and the secondary applications are $75 to $130. This doesn't factor in the cost of MCAT test prep, which can run from a low of around $2,000 to over $7,000 for intensive summer programs that make the $230 for the actual test look modest.

At this point, however, the worst is over. Once the schools review the secondary applications, they decide whether to arrange an interview. The invitation is, by no means, a guarantee of admission. However, the schools interview only a small percentage of applicants, and an invitation shows you are in the home stretch.

Shulman described the interview as an "exciting opportunity to meet with the admissions committee, faculty members, and students, and to see the medical schools up close. It also allows you the chance to put a more personal touch to the application and to give the admissions committee a more clear sense of your personality, background, and motivations."

Shulman recommended doing some prep work before meeting with the admissions committee. He cautioned against having a prepared script but instead advised focusing on topics you would like to highlight, past research experiences, or why you are excited about the school. "It's also a good idea to prepare some questions that you may have about the school to ask the interviewer," he said.

All told, Shulman estimated he spent about two months and about $3,500 applying to medical school.

"The application process is long, expensive, and requires a good deal of endurance," he said. "But it's a necessary part of the journey to fulfill one's dreams and aspirations to become a physician."

Matt Shulman has been accepted to medical school for the academic year beginning fall 2010.

verifies it, and forwards it to the schools you have designated. The service also sends along your MCAT scores if you tell it to do so. (If you plan on retaking the test, you have the option to withhold your scores.)

The application, along with timelines, resources, and worksheets, is available at www.aamc.org/amcas. You should be able to get the application about mid-March, and the service begins accepting completed applications on June 1. It stops accepting applications two weeks before whatever deadline is set by the medical schools you are applying to, and that's generally from October to mid-December. It is your responsibility to meet these deadlines.

Double-check. Some schools do not use the AMCAS application and rely on some other form instead. Contact the schools you are interested in to see if you need other application materials.

After AMCAS, there's still more application paperwork to deal with. Once the service has sent a copy of your application to each of your chosen medical schools, the schools themselves may send you a "secondary application." Some schools send secondary applications to all applicants, others send them only to those who make the initial cut after a review of GPAs and MCATs. The secondary application usually asks for additional personal essays, letters of recommendation, and an application fee. AMSA recommends that applicants fill out and return secondary applications no later than two weeks after they are received to avoid paperwork pileup.

Because the competition is so steep, plan to send out about 10 to 15 applications, maximizing your chances of success. Include three or four "reach" schools—where you just might have good enough credentials to get in—two backup schools, and five to 10 schools that you have a reasonable chance of getting into. What's a reach and what's a backup? Look at the mean GPA and MCAT scores for the incoming class of each medical school, which you can find in the directory section of this book. If your numbers are higher, you can think of the school as a backup. If they are lower, consider the school a reach—and the greater the gap, the longer the reach. Close matches are just that: By the numbers, you're a good fit. (See Chapter 2 for details about other important factors—things to consider before you worry about your chances for successful admission—in choosing schools.) Of course, the rest of your application has to be strong: Good numbers are ultimately no substitute for a poor essay or lackluster recommendations.

Getting personal

The next phase of application review, if you have the grades and MCAT scores to make it past a school's cutoff points, is when the school tries to get to know you as more than a set of numbers. Admissions committees are keenly interested in learning who you are, based on what you have done and how you express yourself. Here is where your written statements, recommendation letters, and interview come into play.

Keep in mind that medical schools receive thousands of applications from people who appear to be pretty much the same as one another. They have good grades, good MCATs, and experience working in a research lab for a summer or two. They have worked in a hospital shadowing a physician and have volunteered with a community organization delivering food to homeless people. These are strong candidates, said Goldmakher—but they are not distinctive. If you want to get into an ultraselective school, you will need to be all this and more. That could mean demonstrating a longer commitment to one of these extracurricular activities or to the pursuit of something that is entirely unrelated to medicine but is challenging nonetheless. The depth of your involvement in a project will indicate to medical schools how important that activity was to you.

Schools really are not looking for any one type of person or set of experiences. They want individuals with traits such as leadership, compassion, commitment, enthusiasm, and competence. For example, athletics can be an excellent way to show that you can work with a team—an important trait in many fields of medicine—as well as demonstrate that you have leadership skills and the ability to make quick decisions. Athletics also demonstrates physical stamina, which can be important in certain fields, such as surgery. Admissions committees will consider all of these traits, so include in your application hobbies and talents that you are passionate about even if you think they are not relevant to your interest in becoming a doctor. These outside interests reveal a lot to admissions committees about who you are and what you are capable of. Andrew Frantz from Columbia University said he is drawn to applicants with an interest in theater because acting "forces you to put yourself in another person's shoes. It is very important in medicine to be able to extend yourself emotionally."

Countdown to med school

WHEN	WHAT YOU SHOULD DO
College freshman year and sophomore year	Get some medical experience
	Contact your premed advisor about planning coursework
	Do some community work
	Check out the nonmedical world—don't be one-dimensional
Junior year	
Sept. through Dec.	Take an MCAT prep course if you can afford it
Jan./Feb.	Register for the April MCAT
	Take a prep course if you still need it
March	Last chance to register for April MCAT
April	MCAT test date
May	Start writing your personal statement
June	Turn in AMCAS application; register for August MCAT if you're taking the test again
August	MCAT test date
Senior year	
Sept./Oct./Nov.	Fill out secondary applications and send them in
	Go on interviews
Oct.	Early decision applicants receive admission letters
Jan.	Another chance to register for an MCAT, if you plan to start med school more than a year from now
April	MCAT test date
	Regular admission applicants receive admission letters
May/June	Graduate and start packing for med school

Of course, actors and lacrosse goalies still must know something about taking care of people, in sickness and in health. "Applicants need to show that they can deal with illness," said Henry Ralston, former associate dean of admissions at the University of California–San Francisco School of Medicine. Volunteering at a hospital or nursing home, shadowing a physician, or even having personal exposure to serious illness, such as a terminally ill family member, are all avenues to gain such experience.

But even here you can find ways to set yourself apart from the typical medical school applicant and further bolster your application. Gaye Sheffler, director of admissions at the University of Pennsylvania School of Medicine, recalled one student who, along with his wife, developed a program for Hispanic residents in his community who were having difficulty accessing healthcare. That showed inner strength, she said, and an ability to take a project to its end, in addition to hands-on experience in the medical field.

Recommendation letter 101

Letters of recommendation should speak to these experiences or personality traits, and they should be written by people who know you well. It is better to have a letter from someone who can provide details about how you work and what kind of a person you are than one from some well-known professor who only taught you in a 250-student lecture and cannot say very much about you as an individual. If you have been engaged in a variety of activities outside of the classroom, it should not be hard to find people who can write about you in detail. Athletic coaches, employers, and volunteer work supervisors are all good sources of letters.

Choose wisely. Avoid asking for letters from people like your minister or congressman unless they can speak directly to your ability to lead, teach others, put forth the extra effort, or learn new skills.

Medical schools will want to see letters of recommendation from your college professors. Students who attend large universities may have a harder time establishing a close relationship with their teachers, especially in basic science classes with 100 or more students. The folks at AMSA

suggest a way around this problem: Approach professors of larger classes near the beginning of the term to let them know that you will be applying to medical school and may ask them for a letter of recommendation at the end of the semester. Throughout the semester, attend the professor's office hours to ask questions about the material. After the class has ended and your grade has been determined, then make the request for the letter. Bring a copy of your résumé and perhaps your personal statement and be ready to sit down to discuss your interests and desire to become a doctor. Make sure you ask the professor if she or he can write a *strong* letter of recommendation on your behalf. If the answer is no, look elsewhere. If it is yes, send a thank-you note two weeks after you ask for the letter, both to be polite and as a gentle reminder to finish the letter in time to meet your application deadlines. (And don't forget to send along a stamped, addressed envelope.)

Your undergraduate school may have a pre-professional committee, generally made up of faculty members from different academic departments and a preprofessional advisor. They will ask you for your academic record, personal statement, letters of recommendation, employment and volunteer experience, and extracurricular activities. You may be called in for an interview as well. Using this information, the committee will write a single letter of recommendation, which you then send to all of the medical schools you are applying to.

Making a statement

The personal statement is your chance to show that you can express a point of view clearly while also explaining a little bit about yourself. It's also probably the hardest part of the application process, prompting a lot of staring at a blank computer screen, multiple drafts, and much anxiety. Here are strategies to make things easier.

Pick a topic that reveals something about you that admissions committee members would not otherwise have known. It should come from your life experiences, such as an event or person that has made a deep impression on you. And it should reflect you and your life in an honest, thoughtful way. "Tell me something I don't know, not just 'I love science and I want to help people,'" said Emory's Eley. "There are moments in life that teach. Tell us about them. It could be about being sick, or a special grandparent, or climbing a mountain."

Structure the personal statement either around a theme or as a chronology, advised Goldmakher. A thematic essay about being sick, for example, might focus on shepherding a friend or family member through illness. Admissions committees want to see that you can write and express yourself well, but they also want to get to know something about your insights and attributes. A chronological essay might focus more on a series of events or activities and how you grew or changed as a result. One example might be an essay about a year spent abroad.

Gimmicks are not impressive. Although you want your essay to stand out, avoid tricks that fall flat, such as poems, plays, or mock press releases.

Face to faces

If your written application sparks enough interest, the admissions committee will invite you to visit the school for an interview. At some schools, this will be a one-on-one with a faculty member, but at others you may sit down with a group of senior medical students and professors. Whatever the configuration, interviews have some things in common. Someone is probably going to ask you to elaborate on some experience you wrote about or ask you to talk about your interests in medicine or your background.

> "If they have followed their heart, their eyes will light up, and that's what we look for."

Some typical questions: Why do you want to be a doctor? What makes you think you'll make a good one? What experiences in your life led to this decision? What weaknesses do you struggle against in yourself? The committee is looking for signs that you are mature, confident without being arrogant, and able to communicate well.

You can write passionately about many things in your application, but in an interview, applicants often reveal how truly meaningful an experience was. "If they are doing all of these things because they think it's what they are supposed to do, it will be a boring interview," said Eley. "If they have followed their heart, their eyes will light up, and that's what we look for."

To prepare for the interview, brush up on current events, especially those related to medicine as well as some issues like medical ethics. Goldmakher said that admissions committees generally aren't looking for one particular answer when they ask you these less personal kinds of questions. They are interested in how you think and whether you can see different points of view. He advises his clients to take a deep breath, come up with a few points they want to make, and try to express them clearly. Don't rehearse your answers too much: Admissions directors say canned answers are a good way for an applicant to get, well, canned.

Be sure to know something about the school before you arrive for the interview. It is a big turn-off to admissions committees if they ask you why you are interested in their program and it becomes clear you don't know very much about the school. Take advantage of the chance to ask about something specific to the school—and not something easily answered in the brochure. It shows you have genuine interest. After the interview, remember to send a thank-you note to the people who interviewed you as well as anyone else who helped you throughout the interview day. This is a good way to get them to remember you.

After all this, what's left? You get to sit back and wait for your acceptance letters.

Chapter Five

Finding the Money

Make no mistake: It costs an arm and a leg to become a doctor. The tab at private medical schools—for tuition, living expenses, and books—easily tops $200,000 over four years. At the George Washington University School of Medicine, for instance, the four-year budget is almost $250,000—and that's before allowing for the inevitable tuition increases. Costs are equally high for out-of-state students at public institutions. A nonresident at the University of North Carolina–Chapel Hill School of Medicine will pay nearly $235,000. Even in-state students at public medical schools can expect to spend $150,000 or more to earn an M.D. degree.

Most medical students borrow heavily to cover the bills. Total debts in excess of $156,000 are typical for new doctors, and that's not counting whatever they may have borrowed as an undergraduate. Not surprisingly, many young docs continue to feel strapped for cash even after their incomes begin to soar.

How can you limit the damage? While financial aid in the form of grants and scholarships is not as plentiful as it is for undergraduates, most schools do make modest need-based or merit-based awards to some medical students. A handful of outside scholarships are available, too—especially for members of minority groups. Uncle Sam's largesse, in the form of tax credits for the cost of higher education, can also free up some extra cash. And students who are willing to serve in the military or commit to practicing medicine in underserved communities can go to medical school practically for free—or at least have a portion of their debts forgiven.

Even if you do have to borrow a bundle, you can take some comfort in the fact that education debt is as cheap as it ever has been because interest rates are relatively low. And through your tax deductions, the federal government will chip in on the interest you do pay. Here's what you need to know to pay for your degree.

Need-based grants might help a little—very little

As you'll probably remember from your undergraduate days, anyone applying for financial aid funds handed out by the federal government has to fill out the Free Application for Federal Student Aid, also known as the FAFSA. That's where you'll start, but the truth is that most medical schools have only a modest amount of money available for need-based grants. They assume that most students will borrow to finance their degrees and will easily be able to repay their debts once they are doctors.

Even schools with more money available generally won't meet your full need with grants: There simply aren't enough funds available at the graduate level to fulfill the requirements of students no longer dependent on their parents. At Johns Hopkins University School of Medicine in Baltimore, for instance, the average need-based grant is $22,513; tuition runs about $42,000 for first-year students, who need an estimated $54,645 to cover everything. (The school offers over 200 endowed scholarships to help meet students' financial need.)

You may find that your eligibility for need-based aid varies dramatically from school to school. That's because medical schools, like undergraduate colleges and universities, use different formulas to calculate how big a discrepancy there is between what med school will cost and what your income and assets are. Under the formula used to hand out federal aid, for example, all graduate students are considered *independent:* supporting themselves, regardless of their age or whether they have financial help from their parents. Bottom line: Full-time students at schools using the federal formula will have significant need.

But most medical schools use their own institutional formulas, which classify many students as *dependent.* You'll provide schools with information about your parents' income and assets on additional needs-analysis forms (GAPS–FAS, CSS, and Need Access are the common ones), and the financial aid office will consider those resources to be available to pay the bills. At Johns Hopkins, parent resources are weighed on a case-by-case basis. "If someone is the son or daughter of elderly parents, we won't expect much," said Paul T. White, former assistant dean for admissions and financial aid. "But there are also children well over

30 whose parents are still supporting them. We consider that," White said.

Parents' income and assets also are used in determining who is eligible for federal Scholarships for Disadvantaged Students. These are need-based awards, specifically for medical students who come from disadvantaged backgrounds, based on family income or ethnicity. The size of the award varies from school to school.

Regardless of which forms are required, be sure to get them in as soon as possible after January. Some aid is awarded on a first-come, first-served basis.

Apply with an eye on the merit money

Harvard Medical School does not award any merit scholarships. At the University of Michigan Medical School, by contrast, about one-third of each entering class receives a renewable scholarship ranging from $1,000 to $30,000 a year. At Vanderbilt School of Medicine in Tennessee, around 16 percent of students receive full-tuition scholarships, some based solely on academic merit and extracurricular record (such as the Canby-Robinson Scholarship), others based on a combination of merit and need.

Schools that do have merit money to dole out usually base their awards on the admission application. High MCAT scores and undergraduate grades are a big factor, but, like Vanderbilt, many schools are also looking to attract people with varied strengths and backgrounds. Many of the awards are endowed scholarships handed out based on the donor's wishes. One award might be reserved for residents of a certain state or county, for example, another for students studying cardiology or pediatrics.

Search for outside scholarships

Scholarships from foundations, associations, and civic organizations are not as plentiful in medicine as they are for other graduate students, and many are reserved for minority students, residents of specific states or counties, or students concentrating in specific areas of medicine. Regardless, it's well worth checking an online search engine for possibilities. (Good search engines include www.fastweb.com and www.collegenet.com. Also try the excellent listing of grants on Michigan State University's website at http://staff.lib.msu.edu/harris23/grants/3gradinf.htm.) Check with any civic, religious, or community groups you or your family members belong to, as well. And be sure to ask your med school's financial aid officer for other leads.

How varied are the opportunities? Here's a sampling of scholarships:

• The Jack Kent Cooke Foundation Graduate Scholarship program (www.jackkentcookefoundation.org) makes approximately 35 awards a year to college seniors or recent grads who are pursuing graduate study. The scholarship pays for full tuition, fees, room, board, and books (up to $50,000 a year) for up to six years of graduate study. Candidates must be nominated by their undergraduate institution.

• The Medical Scientist Training Program (www.nigms.nih.gov/Training/Mechanisms/NRSA/InstPredoc/PredocOverview-MSTP.htm) is for students pursuing a combined M.D./Ph.D. degree at one of 41 participating medical schools, including Harvard, Stanford, Tufts, and the University of Michigan. Students accepted into the program, which is funded by the National Institutes of Health, earn full tuition plus a stipend; $21,000 to $26,000 per year is typical.

• The Nicholas Pisacano Family Practice Scholarship is awarded by the American Board of Family Practice (www.fpleaders.org/prog_leadership.shtml). Five awards of $7,000 per year, up to $28,000, are made to third-year med school students planning to specialize in family medicine.

• National Medical Fellowships (www.nmf-online.org) are awards of up to $10,000 for med students who have financial need and who are African American, mainland Puerto Rican, Mexican American, American Indian, or native Alaskan or Hawaiian. The group also offers numerous other merit-based fellowships and scholarships for minorities.

Get set to borrow

The average medical student borrows roughly $156,000; 58 percent borrow more than $150,000, and almost 30 percent borrow more than $200,000, according to the Association of American Medical Colleges. Ultralow interest rates will help ease the sting. And if you shop around for a lender, you may save a bit more in upfront fees.

Federal loans. Government-guaranteed Stafford loans are a staple for most medical students; a typical full-time student borrows the annual maximum of $8,500 in a "subsidized" Stafford loan plus at least a portion of the additional $30,000 allowed each year in "unsubsidized" loans, for a total of up to $38,500 per year. The federal government pays the interest on a subsidized loan while you're in school and for six months after you graduate or drop below half-time status. Interest accrues on the unsubsidized loan while you're a student, so the grand total mounts, but with both types of loan you can delay making payments until after graduation—

or even until after your residency. In total, you can borrow up to $224,000 in Stafford loans to finance your medical education, including whatever you've already taken on as an undergraduate.

To qualify for a subsidized loan, you have to show on your FAFSA form that you have "need" (a gap between what you've got and the cost of school), which is fairly easy to do with medical school costs being so high. If your school participates in the Federal Direct Student Loan Program, you'll borrow directly from the federal government. Otherwise, you can choose your own funding source using a list of preferred lenders provided by your school. While all lenders offer the same interest rate on Stafford loans, some waive the up-front origination and guarantee fees (which can run up to 4 percent of the loan amount), some reduce the interest rate in repayment if you sign up for automatic payments or make a certain number of payments on time, and some do both. Rates on these variable-rate loans change every summer, but will not exceed a cap of 6.8 percent through 2013.

Students with high financial need—the FAFSA shows that they're expected to contribute very little or nothing to their medical school education—will also qualify for a Perkins loan of up to $8,000 per year. The interest rate is a fixed 5 percent. In addition, there are no up-front origination fees. The Perkins is a subsidized loan, so no interest accrues until nine months after you graduate or drop below half-time status—or until after your residency if you qualify for a deferment (page 57).

The federal government also makes certain loans available specifically to medical students. Federal Loans for Disadvantaged Students are available to needy students from disadvantaged backgrounds, based on family income or ethnicity. The interest rate is a fixed 5 percent, with no loan fees, and interest is subsidized. Primary Care Loans, which have the same rate and no fees, go to students who agree to enter family medicine, internal medicine, pediatrics, or preventive medicine—and to practice primary care until the loan is fully repaid. There's a big catch, though: The interest rate jumps to 18 percent if you change your mind and practice in another specialty.

Private loans. If the federal loan limits leave you short, private lenders stand ready to lend you up to the full cost of your education, less any financial aid. (Some medical schools also have their own loan programs.) Interest rates tend to be only slightly higher than the rates on Stafford loans, but origination fees can be significantly higher—up to 6 percent of the loan amount—and interest begins accruing right away. Some lenders that market specifically to medical students will even lend you up to $13,000 to cover the costs of traveling to your residency interviews.

Some popular programs include Sallie Mae (www.salliemae.com), Medical Access Loan from Access Group, Inc. (www.accessgroup.org), CitiAssist Health Profession Loans from Citibank (www.studentloan.com), and MedAchiever from KeyBank (www.keybank.com/educate).

To qualify for a private loan, you need a clean credit history—or a cosigner. It's a good idea to check your credit reports for errors before you apply.

Home-equity loans. For students who own a home, a home-equity line of credit is another attractive choice. Rates are low, fees are minimal, and the interest on up to $100,000 in debt is tax deductible if you itemize. If you expect to graduate into a high-paying job, home-equity debt may be a better choice than other debt because you won't qualify to deduct the interest on government or private student loans. Interest on student loans will be fully tax deductible only if your income falls below $50,000 if you're a single taxpayer and below $100,000 if you file jointly. Remember, though, that a home-equity line of credit is secured by your home. Will you be able to make the payments when you're a struggling resident?

Find help paying the money back

At 2010 rates, the payment on $100,000 in Stafford loan debt is roughly $1,000 a month over the standard 10-year repayment term. Those payments usually aren't manageable on a typical resident's pay of $40,000 or so a year. But there are ways to ease the burden.

Deferment and forbearance. Most medical residents with high levels of debt will qualify for an economic hardship deferment on their Stafford loans, which allows them to push off making payments for up to three years. Interest continues to accrue on unsubsidized loans (at the "in-school" rate, which is somewhat lower than the "repayment" rate that kicks in when payments are due) but does not accrue on subsidized loans. After three years, residents can continue to have their payments suspended for the remainder of their residency by requesting "forbearance," during which interest accrues on all loans at the repayment rate. You file an application for deferment or forbearance with your lender.

Flexible repayment options. The standard 10-year repayment term for Stafford loans—which for most new doctors begins after residency ends—can be stretched in various ways to reduce your monthly payments. With an extended repayment plan, for instance, you can lengthen the loan term to up to 30 years. Another option, a graduated repayment schedule that extends over 12 to 30 years, starts you off with lower payments than the standard plan would call for and then ratchets them up annually as your paycheck presumably grows. Income-contingent or income-sensitive repayment plans adjust your payment each year based on your income. In the end, you'll pay more interest over the longer payback periods, but you can always boost your payments as your income rises to pay down the loan more quickly than you're asked to.

Loan consolidation. You may also be able to reduce the interest you pay on Stafford loans by consolidating them when interest rates are low. That locks in current interest rates instead of allowing them to fluctuate annually. You may even be able to consolidate your undergraduate and early medical school loans to take advantage of low rates while you're still in school. For more details on student loan consolidation, see www.loancon solidation.ed.gov at the Department of Education's website, or www.federalconsolidation.org, a website sponsored by Access Group, Inc., a private non-profit lender.

Student loan interest deduction. You can deduct up to $2,500 a year in student loan interest if you earn less than $50,000 as a single taxpayer or less than $100,000 if you are married and filing jointly. (You can deduct a lesser amount with income up to $65,000 filing singly or $130,000 filing jointly.)

Note to parents: You get to take this deduction on your own return if you're legally obligated to pay back the debt and you claim the student as a dependent on your tax return.

Loan repayment programs. Doctors who agree to practice certain kinds of medicine where there are shortages or who work in underserved areas of the country can qualify to have significant portions of their debt forgiven. Through the National Health Service Corps, for instance, doctors practicing primary care medicine in underserved areas can have up to $50,000 of their debt repaid by the federal government during a two-year minimum service commitment. An additional $35,000 a year in debt repayment is available to doctors who sign up for a third or fourth year of service.

Many states have similar debt repayment programs for doctors who live or are licensed in the state and who practice primary care medicine in-state. Doctors in Massachusetts, for instance, can earn $25,000 a year in debt payments if they work a minimum of two years in a Massachusetts community health center. A listing of state programs is available at the website of the Association of American Medical Colleges, at services.aamc.org/fed_loan_pub.

The National Institutes of Health offers a debt repayment program for employees engaged in various kinds of research, including AIDS research, pediatric research, and clinical research, whose debt load is at least 20 percent of their annual salary. M.D. researchers can have up to $35,000 per year of debt repaid during a two-year service period.

Get a job

One reason M.D. students tally up so much debt is that most cannot work part time while earning their degree, even during summers. "There is no time to work," said Conway Jones, coordinator of financial aid at the University of Missouri–Columbia School of Medicine. For that reason, most financial aid officers do not include a federal work-study job in financial aid packages for med students. But for students who feel they can handle it, work-study is available and can reduce the need to borrow. An award of $1,500 to $2,000 might typically cover 10 to 15 hours of work a week in the university hospital or in a lab.

In most programs, there is a summer break between the first and second years of med school, after which the academic year runs 11 or 12 months. During the first-year summer break, some students earn extra money assisting faculty with a research project or participating in a summer preceptorship in which they shadow a doctor in exchange for a stipend. At the University of California–San Francisco, for instance, students can earn $3,000 for a four- to six-week full-time summer preceptorship.

Take advantage of Uncle Sam

If your household income is modest, the federal government offers help in the form of a tax credit or tax deduction for educational expenses. Medical students who qualify will want to take advantage of the Lifetime Learning tax credit, worth $2,000 a year (20 percent of the first $10,000 you spend in tuition and fees each year). You qualify for the full credit if you file a single tax return and your income is $43,000 or less, and for a partial credit if you make up to $53,000. If you're married and filing jointly, the full credit is available when income is less than $87,000, and a partial credit is available up to $107,000. (A tax credit reduces your tax bill dollar for dollar.)

Most full-time medical students won't exceed those thresholds. (In fact, those with little or no income won't benefit at all from the credits because they won't owe any taxes to begin with.) But if you do cross the line—perhaps because you

are married and your spouse earns a good income—you may still qualify for a tax deduction for your educational expenses. For 2009, students cannot take a deduction if their adjusted gross income is between $50,000 and $60,000 ($100,000 and $120,000 if they file a joint return). Note: You can't take both the credit and the deduction.

Medical students who are willing to pay for their education with a service commitment to the military or to the National Health Service Corps can start their medical careers with little or no debt. An Armed Forces Health Professions Scholarship, for instance, pays for tuition, fees, books, and supplies, plus a living-expense stipend of about $1,992 a month. After your residency, you repay the armed forces with a year of service for each year of support you received. You can get in touch with an Army, Army Reserve, Navy, or Air Force recruiter for more information. (Anyone who is gay or lesbian will want to keep in mind the military's policy on homosexuality; one website that provides an overview is gaylife.about.com/cs/politicsactivism.)

Students on a National Health Service Corps scholarship also get a free ride that covers tuition, fees, books, and supplies, plus a stipend. The tradeoff: These students agree that, for each year of support, they'll practice a year of primary care medicine in an underserved area, which may be a rural community or even a prison. What if you renege? You'll owe the government the loan amount plus interest, and $7,500 for each month of service that you miss. This is not a commitment to make lightly.

If there's time, plan ahead

If you're looking ahead to medical school in the next couple of years and can set aside some savings, take advantage of the tax benefits of a state-sponsored 529 plan. While most investors use these plans to save for a child's undergraduate expenses, the plans generally allow you to open an account and name yourself as the beneficiary.

The primary benefit is that the earnings on your savings will be tax-free, and your state may throw in a deduction for your contributions. All 529 plans include investments that are appropriate for adults who will need to tap the money soon, such as bonds and money-market accounts.

While many of the broker-sold 529s impose up-front sales fees that would minimize or offset any tax benefits over just a year or two, many of the direct-sold plans, such as those offered by TIAA-CREF and Vanguard, do not. Several are paying a guaranteed 3 percent or so right now. Not a bad parking place for a couple of years, especially when Uncle Sam isn't claiming any of the gains.

Chapter Six

What If You Don't Get In?

Dreams have a predictable way of taking unpredictable turns. For many, the dream of med school started in childhood with a mini doctor's bag molded in black plastic, and continued through grueling college organic chemistry classes and cram sessions for the MCAT. But for all too many, what comes next is a mailbox full of rejection letters—and an uncertain future. These rude awakenings are unavoidable: Many medical schools accept fewer than 1 in 10 or 15 of those who apply.

So what happens next?

Your first priority should be to put things in perspective. "A lot of high-quality kids can't make the cut," said William Harvey, who recently retired after spending years advising aspiring medical students at Earlham College in

Richmond, Indiana. While this sometimes can be the result of unrealistic aspirations, he notes, it may be for reasons as impersonal as that you hail from the same state as a huge number of other applicants that year.

And take heart: You do have options. You can rethink your goals altogether. You can retake your MCATs and get more science courses—perhaps a master's degree—and reapply. Or you can do what thousands of successful doctors have done: study abroad.

Trying again

You might as well start by reassessing your goals. Are you so sure that you belong in medicine that you're really prepared to go through all this again? "The hardest thing about medical school is not getting in, it's getting through," warned Karen Nichols, dean of Midwestern University Chicago College of Osteopathic Medicine. If an honest second look tells you that "you aren't motivated by all the right reasons, you must not come." Added Nancy Nielsen, senior associate dean at the University at Buffalo School of Medicine and Biomedical Sciences: "Ask [yourself] how badly you want to be a doctor, and if the answer is 'more than anything,' consider reapplying."

That's assuming you've got the grades, of course. You may have spent your last four summers working at an inner-city clinic and every scrap of free time reading journal articles about cancer research, but if your college grades are mediocre, "you can apply till the cows come home, but you're not going to get in" to a U.S. school, said Nielsen. Even if you do have a respectable grade point average, statistics from the Association of American Medical Colleges show that repeat applicants are less likely than first-timers to be accepted, so you may have to target less competitive schools this go-round.

Ask admissions officers at the schools that sent rejection letters to explain your shortcomings. Often, they're happy to offer insights. The University of Minnesota Medical School–Twin Cities, in fact, sends out rejections with an explicit offer: "I am very willing to speak with applicants by phone or in a personal interview and give them very, very specific information about what they can do to improve their applications," said the former director of admissions, Marilyn Becker. Good scores may have been overshadowed by weak essays, flat letters of recommendation, or an unimpressive science background. The tell-all post-rejection interview "takes the mystery out of it and gives concrete ideas" about what to do next, Becker said.

If the admissions staff isn't helpful—and even if they are—pose the same question to your undergraduate advisor, said Nichols. "Ask them to be ruthless—and have thick skin." Then apply their answers to the next application. While you're tapping undergrad resources, you might also ask someone in your college admissions office to give you a mock interview. The right answer, expressed in the wrong way, can tank an acceptance. Nichols noted that she once had an applicant say, "I would really like to go to your school because I really don't want to work that hard." She added, "What he meant was, 'Your school really understands the importance of a balanced approach.'" The end result of his poor phrasing: He didn't get in.

It's probably a given that you'll revisit your MCAT scores; taking the test again and raising your numbers will certainly be a big help. So find a study group. Take a prep class. Hire a tutor. And take as many practice tests as you can. Admissions deans further recommend looking critically at your science background and doing whatever you need to do to bolster it. Indeed, one of the best ways to upgrade your application is to get a master's degree in one of the sciences.

It pays to get work or service experience, too; exposure to the healthcare field will enhance an application, admissions deans say. If grades and MCAT scores are equal, "the person who has a history of volunteering has an edge," Nielsen said. Volunteering for a medical facility that interests you, such as a clinic, a pediatric cancer ward, or a nursing home, underscores your commitment to medicine and desire to learn and can also offer evidence that you've got other valued attributes. Leadership, for example, "is one quality that is highly weighted," said Gregory Vercellotti, former senior associate dean for education at the University of Minnesota. So are level-headedness and heart. The admissions committee is on the lookout for "students who have a sense of well-being and balance and can demonstrate compassion," he said.

When your new, improved application is ready to go, don't worry too much that your rejection will taint it. "Given the number of applications and number of students who have to try more than once, there's nothing really adverse about a second application," said Vercellotti. Indeed, it's worth remembering that some people are accepted on the third or occasionally the fourth try.

Looking abroad

During Peter Burke's first two years of college, he was "a student athlete, with more emphasis on 'athlete,'" he said. Though he "got serious" by junior year and worked for a few years as a lab technician after graduation, his early history hurt him when he decided on medical school. "I was always having to explain my first two years in college," he said—and American medical schools were not forgiving. So he joined more than 8,000 Americans currently taking an alternate "offshore" route and went to the American University of the Caribbean School of Medicine, located in St. Maarten.

Many aspiring doctors look at the offshore schools as a poor substitute for U.S. institutions, but the reality is that more than 25 percent of doctors practicing in the United States today got their education outside of the country, according to the American Association of International Medical Graduates. Some 43,000, or 6 percent, of these doctors are United States citizens. "There are a number of international schools that are worth looking at," said former Earlham advisor Harvey. (For a list of foreign schools that educate significant numbers of American students, see page 361.)

Look carefully, though, because the quality of overseas programs varies enormously. Some of the most highly regarded schools in Europe are just as selective as U.S. medical schools and are not known for training Americans who failed to make the cut stateside. Besides AUC, foreign schools that do take large numbers of U.S. citizens—and that have track records for turning out solid doctors—include St. George's University School of Medicine in Grenada, Tel Aviv University Sackler School of Medicine in Israel, and Ross University School of Medicine in Dominica (which is now owned by DeVry University).

How do you determine which schools are worth your time and money? Separating the winners from the losers is a chore made both easier and harder by the Internet, which will probably be your first route to campus. Building an impressive website is much easier than building a high-quality faculty or campus; on the other hand, the Web can be a source of expert advice and an insider's point of view.

Approach your search with a critical eye, advised Harvey. The overseas medical schools that cater to Americans follow a curriculum

---

"There are a number of international schools that are worth looking at."

---

essentially the same as that of U.S. schools—two years of basic sciences followed by two years of clinical rotations in hospitals—in preparation for the same set of licensing exams all U.S. doctors-to-be must pass. But you may find considerable variation in the quality of the faculty (Where did they train? What kind of research are they engaged in? Will you be taught by full-time professors or part-time local practitioners?) and how accessible they are. While a dedicated, permanent staff is ideal, some students note that they have had excellent courses taught by gifted U.S. professors enjoying the adventure of a year in an exotic locale.

The faculty/student ratio will provide a clue as to how likely you are to get professors' attention; in the United States, the Mayo Medical School has 14 faculty members per student. Anyone considering a European or other medical school that doesn't teach in English will want to find out whether there's an English-language program and if foreign students have the same access to faculty as native students do.

To assess how well schools prep students for the U.S. Medical Licensing Examination (USMLE), compare their students' pass rates on "Step 1," the portion of the exam taken after second year, and "Step 2," generally taken during the last clinical year of medical school or around graduation. Pass rates vary. For example, Tel Aviv's Sackler School's recent pass rate for Step 1 was 98 percent; St. George's in Grenada had a 90 percent pass rate. Lesser schools have lower rates—sometimes much lower. As is true for American medical schools, too, you'll want to find out what type of clinical experience you can expect, and how early. Ask what kind of support services students have available: stress management? counseling? help with study skills?

A number of offshore schools have come and gone in the past several years, particularly in Mexico, Central America, and the Caribbean. So focus from the start on schools with a history. Indeed, before you invest in a place, make sure the place has invested in itself. Be wary of a school operating in rented space—some marginal schools have been known to hold classes in hotels or even private homes—because a school that rents classrooms is unlikely to keep its doors open when times are tough.

Make a visit before you commit so you can gauge quality and viability by sitting in on classes, quizzing students, and checking out the library and labs. While a listing in the "World Directory of Medical Schools," published by the World Health Organization, doesn't guarantee that a school is worthy, being included is considered a good sign. Another tip: The U.S. Department of Education Federal School Code Search (www.fafsa.ed.gov/

FOTWWebApp/FSLookupServlet) lets you plug in a foreign institution's code number and find out if it can receive and distribute American financial aid.

Find out, too, who the school considers a worthy candidate. At Ross University School of Medicine in Dominica, the class admitted in January 2004 had an average undergraduate GPA of 3.18. And whereas "most U.S. schools are looking at [MCAT scores of] 27 and above, our average was 21," said Andrew Serenyi, director of marketing for the school. At American University of the Caribbean, the incoming classes often include "people who are nurses, paramedics, and EMTs; career transfers; people who are young, didn't study well in college and didn't get the grades that they needed; and people who are wait-listed," said Susan Atchley, professor of immunology and director of community services. "They judge you based on what you are doing now instead of on what you did as an 18-year-old," said Burke, who was 28 when he arrived at AUC in September 2000. "But then you have to prove yourself. My class started with 180 [students] and is now about 90. If you're not meeting the criteria, you'll get weeded out of the system."

Many students attending offshore schools return to the United States after the second year to do their clinical rotations in U.S. hospitals; before applying to any overseas school, ask if the school is affiliated with clinical sites in the United States. Students often find residencies in the States, too, through the same match system as do their stateside peers (students pick schools and schools pick students and the computer matches them up). The website of the Educational Commission for Foreign Medical Graduates (www.ecfmg.org) walks students through the required steps to a U.S. residency.

The chances of making a match are good for students from reputable international programs who have strong USMLE scores. While some 15,000 students graduate from U.S. medical schools each year, there are about 21,500 postgraduate residency positions available. Among the eligible U.S. citizens attending St. George's University Medical School who applied in a typical recent year, 99 percent landed U.S. residency positions. Students from Ross University School of Medicine have been offered residencies at such noted hospitals as Yale–New Haven Hospital, Loma Linda University Medical Center in California, Georgetown University Medical Center, and UCLA Medical Center. As you shop for a school, ask those that interest you to provide a contact list of graduates who are now practicing in the United States, as well as a history of residency placements.

"The great equalizer is standardized tests," said Burke, who said he scored in the 95th percentile on Step 1 and in the 99th on Step 2. Before he finished his fourth year in a cardiology rotation at Providence Hospital in Southfield, Michigan, he was matched to a residency in internal medicine with the hospital. From there, he planned to move on to a cardiology fellowship.

Finding your Plan B

What do you do if, in the end, your dream is dashed? "You need to think about Plan B: a different career choice," said Harvey.

But Plan B may well be a modification of Plan A: a career in public health or another health-related field, or the pursuit of a Ph.D. in the biological sciences, for example. Carol Baffi-Dugan, who advises undergrads going into health professions at Tufts University in Massachusetts, said the first thing she asks students who have been rejected by a medical school is why they were attracted to medicine in the first place. "Sometimes a student is motivated by an incredible love of science. It may be that that student would be intellectually stimulated and more successful doing a Ph.D.," she said. "But if they say the classic, 'I want to help people and use science,' then I start to talk about the clinical health professions and the area of public health. Other health professions are playing an increasingly important role in healthcare delivery." She has also pointed to physician assistants, who can specialize in cardiology or surgery, or nurse practitioners, who can specialize in pediatrics. (For an introduction to a number of healthcare options, see Chapter 7.)

Baffi-Dugan said she hopes that the students she advises have at least been thinking about other possibilities all along. At a recent freshman orientation, she told the incoming class, "Look at all areas [in medicine], even if you do decide that a M.D. degree is what you want. You will understand that medical care is a team effort [and] you'll be better prepared." You will also be more likely to make a thoughtful and heartfelt choice. No one wants "the dentist who wanted to be a doctor," Baffi-Dugan said.

Chapter Seven

Other Choices, Other Paths

So you like medicine and you like making people feel better, yet you don't want to be a doctor? Good. Though it may surprise many physicians, there are plenty of good health careers that *don't* take you through medical school. Physical therapy, physician assistant, and nursing are among some of the booming fields in the allied health professions. People working in them say the intellectual challenges, emotional rewards, and relationships with patients are often more satisfying than in the doctor's world. "I can see a patient for 10 consecutive weeks, make corrections in their treatment, and see steady progress," said one physical therapist. "How many doctors can do that?"

Here we profile eight such professions, highlighting the pluses and minuses of each, the training needed, and tips on how to get into a program or school. We also list the top three schools in each field (or more in the case of a third-place tie) according to the latest *U.S.News & World Report* rankings, which are based on opinion surveys of faculty and administrators at accredited schools. (Note: There are no rankings for dentistry programs.)

Physician Assistant

Healthcare has changed enormously over the past 20 years, and as a result, the role physician assistants play in medicine has been transformed. Treating acute illnesses is now less important than preventing them. Widespread use of routine screening and an arsenal of new drugs has made managing chronic illness a top priority. Today, there is a premium on controlling costs, and four of five Americans are enrolled in managed care plans. Healthcare is delivered not only by physicians but by a team of medical providers, and physician assistants have become some of the team's most sought-after players.

Physician assistants (PAs) are licensed to practice medicine under the supervision of physicians. They are nationally certified after graduating from an accredited program, usually about two years in length, and passing a certifying exam. More than half of the nation's 74,000 PAs specialize in primary care—family medicine, internal medicine, pediatrics, or obstetrics and gynecology. Over a third specialize either in surgery or emergency medicine. They see patients, take histories, evaluate tests, make diagnoses, prescribe drugs, give advice, suture cuts, perform simple surgeries such as biopsies, and more.

"I love the potpourri of family practice," said Julie Theriault, who has been a physician assistant at the Sutter Medical Group in Elk Grove, California. "I do see some complicated things, and one of the key factors in the job of a PA is knowing when to get the doctor involved. I just had a diabetic patient who was on three medications and yet her blood sugar level was still out of whack. So I called the doctor." Theriault was able to describe the patient's test results and other factors, allowing the physician to make a diagnosis and advise treatment—even though he was located in another office miles away. The ability of one highly paid doctor to supervise a number of PAs who can manage patient care on-site not only cuts costs; it also allows rural and medically vulnerable communities access to care when they may have had none before. A study of primary care providers in two Western states showed that more physician assistants were practicing in rural areas than any other type of provider, and in vulnerable minority and poor communities, physician assistants, along with family physicians and internists, provide the majority of medical services available.

Pluses. PAs end up in much the same place as primary care physicians but spend about half the time in school and probably one-fifth of the money to get there. Salaries are high, and many practices and hospitals work out flexible schedules to allow PAs to have lives outside of work. Women find the PA career—with its high skill levels, good salaries, and flexible hours—particularly rewarding: They make up nearly 60 percent of the profession.

Minuses. Some doctors worry that the huge growth in nonphysician clinicians may lead to competition—rather than cooperation—between doctors and PAs. Physician assistants estimate that they can treat 50 to 75 percent of the complaints that send patients to doctors. The ability of physician assistants to treat so many conditions, coupled with a two- to fourfold increase in the number of PAs and other nonphysician clinicians, has left doctors wondering if there may be less need for M.D.s in the future. Still, Joseph Kaplowe, physician assistant coordinator at New Britain Hospital in New Britain, Connecticut, said that's unlikely. "With so many people in the population getting into their 50s and 60s, and that being the age at which people need more health and hospital care, there will be a need for more docs *and* more PAs."

Training. Many of the first PAs were Navy medical corpsmen who had received training and experience in Vietnam but returned home to find there were no similar positions in the civilian healthcare system. At the same time, the nation faced a shortage of primary care physicians, particularly in rural and inner-city communities, so PA positions were created for these veterans.

Today most PAs are trained not on the battlefield but in programs that offer a master's degree. The coursework is divided into two parts spread over two years. The preclinical curriculum during the first year includes medical science courses—topics such as pharmacology, signs and symptoms of diseases, and primary care aspects of every medical specialty. The second year consists of clinical clerkships where PA students work with physicians treating patients and managing their cases. Many programs now require a thesis or "capstone" project on a medical topic of interest such as obesity or childhood depression. Newly minted PAs must pass a national certifica-

tion exam, and then must acquire 100 hours of continuing medical education every two years and be recertified every six years.

Tips on getting started. Nationally, there are about two applicants for every opening in PA programs, and at some schools the competition is stiffer. Applicants to PA programs must complete at least two years of college-level courses in basic

---

"With so many people in the population getting into their 50s and 60s...there will be a need for more docs and PAs."

---

and behavioral sciences as prerequisites. There are 140 PA programs at various schools across the country, and for about 80 of them applications can be submitted online through a central system, at www.caspaonline.org. At this site, you can click on the schools, look at what their programs offer, and get details on requirements, prerequisites, and more. You can apply to more than one program and add to your list if your application is turned down at your first few choices.

Most PA students already hold undergraduate degrees in a wide variety of fields and have worked in healthcare for four years before beginning training. Kaplowe said, "The most competitive applicant for PA school is 28 or older and this is a second career for them. They have a liberal arts degree, and they understand the way the world works. They'll be able to communicate better to patients, staffs, and to write clearly. The person who has a strong work ethic, who understands they will be part of a team, who understands the boundaries that they work in— he or she will be a successful PA applicant."

Top schools. Master's programs, ranked in 2007: 1) University of Iowa; 2) Duke University, North Carolina; 3) Emory University, Georgia.

To find out more. The American Academy of Physician Assistants (703-836-2272; www. aapa.org) has extensive resources about schools, training, and careers on its site.

"The person who has a strong work ethic, who understands they will be part of a team, will be a successful PA applicant."

Nursing

In Victorian England, nursing was routinely considered "menial employment needing neither study nor intelligence." But then came Florence Nightingale, whose lifesaving work during the Crimean War in the mid-1800s transformed the practice into a respected and highly skilled profession. Today, nurses are witnessing an explosion in demand for their services, from geriatric care in nursing homes to cutting-edge work in high-tech medical facilities. There is now a veritable "candy store" of opportunities in the field, said Patricia Rowell, senior policy fellow at the American Nurses Association. Ruth Corcoran, CEO of the National League for Nursing, concurred: "The job security is amazing, the salaries are very fair, and it's an opportunity to make a difference every day in work that is appreciated and needed."

This is still an intimate career, requiring empathy and close relationships with patients who may be sick or dying. In general, nurses collect and analyze data on patients' physical and psychological situa-

tions, help diagnose ailments, provide continuous care and monitoring, and offer critical support to physicians. But there's more than one kind of nurse, and they are classified by their skill levels.

First come licensed vocational or practical nurses. They are typically high school graduates with a year of nursing training from a vocational school or junior college. They work under the direction of higher-level nurses and focus on the physical care of the patient, such as monitoring vital signs, making beds, and caring for some wounds.

Above LPNs are registered nurses, and they make up the majority of the field. They are state licensed and have earned either an associate degree in nursing from a community college or a bachelor's of science in nursing from a four-year school. Unlike LPNs, they handle medications, complex treatments, patient assessments, and plans for care. RNs can remain generalist nurses and serve in operating rooms, pediatric and maternity wards, rehabilitation centers, or psychiatric units, to name just a few places.

There are more options for students who earn postgraduate degrees, such as a master's in nursing. These are gateways to a variety of specialized paths. Nurse practitioners, for instance, see patients in primary care settings and help set up treatment plans. Clinical nursing specialists provide expert care in fields like oncology. Nurse anesthetists take care of a patient's anesthesia needs during surgery or childbirth. There's also academia: Some highly motivated baccalaureate students go directly into Ph.D. programs that prepare them for teaching and research positions.

Pluses. Many hospitals allow nurses to negotiate their work schedules, which is a boon for working parents. "If you have a child who is in school all day, you may want to work days so you can be home at night," Rowell said. If you want regular hours, you can find them in public health clinics or doctors' offices. Nursing is also a highly mobile profession, with opportunities growing overseas as well. The current nursing shortage means plenty of jobs, and salaries that keep going up.

Minuses. Nurses in some hospitals are asked to work different hours every week, or even every day. As an acute care nurse, Rowell worked three separate shifts: Days were 7 a.m. to 3:30 p.m., for five or 10 days straight, followed by a couple of days off, and then a stretch of night and evening shifts. "You can't really plan anything more than a month ahead of time," she said.

Training. LPNs start with that one-year vocational training program. The first step in the RN path is usually the associate or bachelor's degree. There are 569 such bachelor's degree programs in the United States, which take four years to complete, and 885 associate degree programs, which take from two to three years. Most bachelor's degree programs require students to first apply for general undergrad admissions. After completing the school's required courses, students may then apply to the nursing program. The University of Washington's school of nursing in Seattle is a good example. It requires students to take 90 credits—usually during freshman and sophomore year—in English composition, problem-solving, statistics, art, sociology, and the sciences before they can begin the nursing program. Applicants also must maintain at least a 2.0 GPA and provide a résumé outlining healthcare experience (volunteer and paid), a recommendation from a healthcare provider, and various essays. Once admitted, nursing students take various courses ranging from anatomy to pharmacotherapeutics to ethics. There also are several required clinical practicums. Clinical nurse specialists and other advanced nursing degree candidates take more advanced courses and must do a thesis or research project.

Once students have completed their undergraduate program, there's yet another hurdle: a state license. That means passing a nationally standardized test from the National Council Licensure Examination (NCLEX). Depending on your state nursing board, additional certification may be required for clinical nurse specialists and nurse anesthetists. You can find links to those boards through the National Council of State Boards of Nursing site at www.ncsbn.org.

The cost of a nursing degree varies enormously depending on the program and the school. Community colleges are the least expensive, costing $3,000 to $5,000 per year. At the other end of the spectrum, a private, four-year college can cost more than $20,000 per year.

Tips on getting started. Preparing for a nursing program is no cakewalk. High school students should take the most rigorous college prep courses, especially in biology, chemistry, and math. They must also show excellent writing skills because documentation is a big part of nursing. Clear communication is essential because nurses assess patients and relay information to other healthcare providers. Each undergraduate nursing program has its own set of admission prerequisites, but there are some basic requirements: the SAT or ACT exam and high school courses in math, biology, chemistry, English, and a foreign language. The American Nurses Association also recommends courses in computer science and the behavioral and social sciences. Rowell said volunteer work in a nursing setting is key for students "to see if it's what they really want to do. We see students drop out because they had an idealized notion of what a nurse was. Try it out a bit."

Top schools. Master's, ranked in 2007: 1) University of Washington; 2) University of California–San Francisco; 3) University of Pennsylvania.

To find out more. The National Student Nurses Association (718-210-0705; www.nsna.org/career) has information about the variety of nursing careers. So does the American Nurses Association (800-274-4ANA; www.ana.org). The American Association of Colleges of Nursing (202-463-6930; www.aacn. nche. edu) has details on schools and programs.

Dentistry

Dentists roll up their sleeves, put on their surgical gloves, and get down to work in patients' mouths. They pull out painful wisdom teeth, fill cavities, and fit prosthetics where teeth used to be; some operate on cleft palates or even do cosmetic surgery. Research has linked oral health to general health, so dentists see their work as helping to keep their patients hale and hearty overall. Dentists work with their hands more than most physicians do, said Laura Neumann of the American Dental Association, and that's a stimulating part of the job. "They work in a small space. It requires very fine motor skills," she said. Those skills are applied not only to the mouth's function, but also to its appearance. "We like to say it's an art and a science," said Neumann. "The art that goes into restoring or improving aesthetics can be both challenging and fun, and people always feel good when you've done something like that for them."

Over 80 percent of dentists are general practitioners, and most are in private practice. The rest specialize: Orthodontists correct poorly aligned teeth, for instance, while oral surgeons operate in and around the mouth. Other specialties include prosthodontics (restoring or replacing teeth) and periodontics (treating diseases of gums and other structures around the teeth).

Pluses. Dentistry can drastically improve a patient's life without placing the life-and-death stress of medicine on its practitioners. "Sometimes medical problems can be a little bit depressing," said Neumann. But in dentistry, "you tend to deal with less life-threatening situations." Plus dentists get to treat diseases directly, not just by writing prescriptions, and there's a great deal of satisfaction in that approach. Dentists earn a healthy income, and demands from work don't take over their lives. "Especially if you have your own practice or you're an associate, you can control your hours," Neumann said. That makes it an attractive career for women, she noted. She had three children—one before dental school, one during, and one just after. "I started practicing right away. I'm not going to say it was a piece of cake, but it was doable."

Minuses. In addition to learning how to pull teeth, anyone interested in private practice should be willing to learn how to manage a payroll and a small business. There's also the inescapable fact that people don't like coming to see you. But with improving technology, things have gotten much more pleasant for the patient—although they never seem to get used to the sound of the drill.

Training. Dental schools offer a D.D.S. (doctor of dental surgery) or the equivalent D.M.D. (doctor of dental medicine); both degrees are universally accepted. Like medical school, dental school lasts four years. In the first two years, students take classes in basic sciences—such as anatomy, microbiology, and physiology—concentrated on the head and neck. They try out techniques on synthetic models or extracted teeth. Since most dentists end up in private practice, courses on management are also part of the dental training. Students learn how to lead a dental team—which usually includes a hygienist and a dental assistant—and follow employment and tax laws.

Students may begin to see real, live patients in their second year, or sooner in some cases. That clinical experience accelerates in the third and fourth years, when they treat patients under the supervision of faculty dentists. A few schools have students rotate through community-based clinics or hospitals, but the majority of clinical work is in dental schools' own clinics.

Before they can practice, dentists have to pass a national written exam and a clinical licensing exam that may vary from state to state. In every state but Delaware, you can start practicing as soon as you get your degree, but about 40 percent of graduates go on to a residency for further training. Some residencies are in dental schools, others in hospitals. The length of residency depends on the specialty. Most general practice residencies are one year, while orthodontics and periodontics take three years and oral surgery takes four years. Some oral surgeons earn an M.D. as part of their residency, which takes an additional two years. Having an M.D. can make it easier to get hospital privileges. There are a variety of other programs, such as one- to two-year residencies in public health. A public health dentist might work for a city, running dental education and screening programs.

Tips on getting started. Dentistry isn't a fallback for students who don't have high enough numbers to get into medical school. Recent entering classes of Harvard's medical and dental schools had the same average GPA: 3.8. In addition to great grades, schools usually require students to have had courses in English, biology, chemistry, and physics—these are part of an established predental curriculum, and

---

"Sometimes medical problems can be a little bit depressing," but in dentistry, "you tend to deal with less life-threatening situations."

---

your school's health advisor can fill you in on other details. Remember, too, that aligning teeth and making sure they look good is also an art—admissions offices take that seriously. Students should consider taking studio art classes to help with their spatial skills. And get some experience: schools want applicants to prove they care about dentistry, and part of that proof is spending time with professionals, doing "chairside observation," and shadowing dentists.

Applicants should also decide whether they are most interested in a practice or in doing research: Some dental schools focus on clinical skills, others on scientific research. Schools do try to simplify the application process by using a central service: AADSAS, the Associated American Dental Schools Application Service (www.adea.org), will send your application to all the schools you select. As part of your application, you have to take the computerized DAT, or Dental Admissions Test. The test covers biology and chemistry, perceptual ability (matching shapes and judging distances), reading comprehension, and math. Registration is online at the American Dental Association's website (www.ada.org; look for its Education and Testing section), and you can schedule the test for almost any time at one of a few hundred testing centers across the country. You can spend $1,000 on a DAT prep class, but that's not necessary if you buy practice tests and study on your own. Some schools also require a manual dexterity test, like carving a piece of chalk or soap to specifications.

To find out more. The American Dental Association has information on careers in dentistry and on the DAT test (312-440-2500; www.ada.org). The American Dental Education Association (1-800-353-2237; www.adea.org) publishes the *Official Guide to Dental Schools* ($35), which describes the programs at U.S. and Canadian schools and explains the application process.

Psychology

Psychologists have moved far beyond the "talking cure" during the century since Sigmund Freud set up his couch in Vienna. Therapists still talk, of course, and still try to cure. But the field has broadened significantly. Through a wide variety of psychotherapies—some short term, some long, some directed at modifying behavior, some focused on the thinking behind that behavior—psychologists may work with clients to identify and change unhealthy or irrational attitudes that make people dissatisfied with their lives and, in some cases, utterly miserable. They may also test applicants' fitness for jobs using paper-and-pencil questionnaires, perform IQ tests, and do other kinds of assessments. Some teach and do academic research in different topics, such as a culture's effect on the way people feel. School psychologists work with students' behavior problems and may help teachers learn to manage classrooms. Psychologists may also bring their understanding of the mind to bear on physical illnesses, cooperating with physicians to help patients with stress-related ulcers or others who don't stick with their medications.

One thing all psychologists have in common is that they view distress as a complex problem, not one simply rooted in body chemistry or solved solely by antidepressants. "If you see the solutions to mental illness lying in biology, then I'd probably go to medical school," said George Stricker, a clinical psychologist recently retired from Adelphi University in Garden City, New York. (Unlike psychiatrists, psychologists can't prescribe drugs—except in New Mexico, where they recently won that right.)

Pluses. When clinical psychologist Tom Olkowski worked in a suburban Colorado school system, he evaluated children and helped them, their families, and teachers understand how the kids could learn better. "When you see a kid who's been struggling doing better in school, that's something tangible," he said. Variety is another advantage: Olkowski's psychology Ph.D. gave him the background in research and theory to work in many fields. In his 30-year career, he worked not only in schools but also in a mental health center; wrote a book on the stress of moving with children; and made two videos for a real estate company on the same topic.

Minuses. Psychology can be stressful, especially when you deal with clients who may turn suicidal or violent. Olkowski cautioned that doctoral training doesn't prepare you for running a private practice, when you have to know about things like marketing and cash flow. Insurance restrictions on the number of therapy sessions with a client can add to the hassle factor. And training is expensive: Clinical psychologists often emerge from school $30,000 to $60,000 in debt.

Training. In most states, you need a doctorate in order to practice independently, without a doctorate-level psychologist supervising you. To get that doctorate, Ph.D.s used to be the only option for psychologists. But today, the Psy.D. (doctor of psychology) degree has become popular (although there are still more Ph.D. programs than Psy.D. programs). A Ph.D. has more emphasis on original research and requires an extensive dissertation. Students usually spend five years taking classes, doing research, and learning clinical skills, plus at least another year completing the dissertation. Psy.D. programs concentrate more on clinical practice and therapeutic methods. Students still learn how to do research and how to use the findings but have to write a shorter paper to graduate. The clinical emphasis makes the Psy.D. attractive, but the Ph.D. makes it easier to get an academic job.

All doctoral students also learn the foundations of the discipline, including skills such as assessing patients using a variety of tests and how to practice ethically. Many students study statistics and research design. They also learn the cognitive, social, and biological bases of behavior, which may include classes in neurological and physiological psychology. Many states license only psychologists with doctorates from programs accredited by the American Psychological Association (most programs are APA accredited). Graduates who want to be licensed as psychologists also have to take a national written exam and, in some states, a separate test that may cover the state's ethical codes and mental health laws. Many states also require that psychologists practice under supervision for a while before they can get an independent license.

Are you doctorate phobic? Consider a master's in psychology. Master's programs are short—two or three years—and thus relatively cheap. The degree allows you to do marriage and family counseling, mental health counseling, and social work. Master's programs are accredited by the Masters in Psychology Accreditation Council.

Tips on getting started. You don't have to be a psych major in college to get into graduate school, although it may be tougher to work the classes you'll need into your art history major. Most programs require undergrad courses in statistics and experimental psychology. Stricker also recommends getting some experience with emotionally troubled people to be sure you want to work with them professionally. He suggests volunteering with a peer counseling service, for example. If you plan on going to a Ph.D. program, research experience can be very helpful; try finding a professor who will let you volunteer in his or her lab. About half of the U.S. doctoral programs in psychology require applicants to take the Graduate Record Examinations. Some programs also require the psychology subject GRE, which has multiple-choice questions about experimental and natural sciences, social sciences, and general psychology, including the history of the discipline and research design. Scores on these tests are important, but schools place even more emphasis on the applicant's statement of goals, recommendations from professors, and research experience.

Doctoral students who responded to a 1999 survey funded by the Pew Charitable Trusts said one extremely important factor in picking a school was choosing an advisor you can work with. A Ph.D. student and her advisor may work together closely or meet a few times a year, depending on the school and the person, so it's important to choose someone whose style fits your own. It's also a good idea to ask about funding when you're looking at schools to find out how students there are financially supported. Ph.D. students can be carried on an advisor's research grant. But because Psy.D.s are usually offered by smaller schools that don't have a lot of research money, most Psy.D. students have to come up with loans, which means more postgrad debt.

Top schools. Doctorate programs in clinical psychology, ranked in 2008: 1) (tie) University of California–Los Angeles, University of Washington, University of Wisconsin–Madison.

To find out more. The American Psychological Association (800-374-2721; www.apa.org) has information on psychology careers and education. The APA's *Graduate Study in Psychology* (www.apa.org/books; $28.95) lists psychology programs in the United States and Canada, and is updated yearly. The Pew-funded survey on Ph.D. student experiences (www.phd-survey.org) has a valuable section devoted to psychology.

Physical Therapy

The human body is pretty good at self-repair, knitting torn muscles and fractured bones together after an injury. But sometimes it can't handle the workload alone. Physical therapists help the healing process by flexing stiffened muscles, stretching limbs, and teaching balance to people who have been off their feet for a while. "It's the study of movement and its application, but it's more than that," said Sue Schafer, associate director of the School of Physical Therapy at Texas Woman's University in Dallas. It's understanding individual needs, she said, and matching them to individual capabilities. When assessing a patient—from a hulking football player to a stroke survivor to a tiny

infant—the therapist determines what structures are damaged and what a patient needs to do to recover—given his or her particular physical limits—and then oversees the appropriate rehabilitation therapy. Techniques include exercise, massage, ultrasound, and heat therapy.

Sports medicine is one of the better known PT subfields, but therapists don't just rehab athletes. Today, for example, they are often called on to work with breast cancer patients, advising them on how to remain active while undergoing chemotherapy and radiation treatments, and also working to reduce postsurgery side effects such as painful swelling of the arms. Although they often work in tandem with occupational therapists, physical therapists focus on increasing mobility and strength and decreasing pain, while occupational therapists tackle the ability to perform specific tasks.

Pluses. Hanging out with professional sports teams and mixing with world-famous ballerinas isn't too shabby, but in reality, very few physical therapists have celeb-studded jobs. The rest relish the opportunity to work extensively one-on-one with patients and see the fruits of their labor in every step that patients make. PTs also have the flexibility to work in either a hospital or private practice, and the range of patients—from kids with cerebral palsy to senior citizens recovering from hip replacement surgery—keeps them on their toes.

Minuses. The work takes a toll on therapists' own bodies. The job can require heavy lifting—moving around large patients or large equipment—and standing or crouching for long periods of time. "It's a physical profession and eventually we have personal limitations," Schafer said. "I don't do well getting on the ground anymore, and that's what you have to do when you work with children." Other therapists say that the greatest frustration is patients who are not willing to do the work needed for recovery. Physical therapy often demands that patients be not only cooperative but determined.

Training. Either a master's or doctorate is required to practice. (The Commission on Accreditation in Physical Therapy stopped recognizing baccalaureate professional degrees a few years ago, and by 2020, the American Physical Therapy Association hopes to make the profession an all-doctorate field.) Master's programs usually take two years and teach students basic sciences such as chemistry and biology as well as the psychosocial aspects of disease, intervention and treatment options, and current PT research directions. In addition to classroom work, students receive an average of 15 weeks of field training at hospitals, rehab centers, schools, or outpatient clinics.

Doctorates, which take about three years, supplement this training with expanded work in areas like pharmacology, radiology, healthcare management, and pathology. They also insist on more field training—as long as a year. Graduates must pass a national exam as well as fulfill any individual state requirements, which may include additional training to maintain licensure.

Tips for getting started. To get into a PT program, applicants need some prerequisite undergrad courses, which include psychology, biology, physics, chemistry, statistics, and the humanities. A high GPA in these courses is important, as is performance on the GRE. But program directors warn that numbers alone won't get you in. Applicants need to show a knack for working with people. Work as a physical therapy assistant (an accredited aide who has completed a two-year program) or volunteer experience at a nursing home or hospital can also make an application shine.

Top schools. Master's and doctorate programs, ranked in 2008: 1) University of Southern California; 2) (tie) University of Pittsburgh, Washington University in St. Louis.

To find out more. The American Physical Therapy Association (703-684-2782; www.apta.org) lists accredited programs and residency and fellowship information and offers financial aid advice.

Occupational Therapy

Most people view occupations as that thing they do from 9 to 5. Occupational therapists don't. While OTs most often help patients with temporary or permanent disabilities function smoothly in the workplace, they handle every aspect of the business of life, from inventing ways for handicapped parents to make lunches for their kids to teaching premature babies the proper movements for nursing. Retired folks don't stare into computer monitors or punch time cards every day, but they can call on occupational therapists to help them relearn how to dress and bathe themselves after a hip replacement or stroke.

As in physical therapy, the long-term goal of occupational therapy is to increase independence. But while physical therapists focus on overall strength and movement, OTs tackle obstacles to particular activities. When consulting with a patient, a therapist must break down an activity into each of its components, whether they are physical, environmental, mental, or behavioral. "Bowling isn't just picking up a ball and rolling it," explained Janet Falk-Kessler, director of Columbia University's occupational therapy programs. "It involves everything from posture, bilateral motor coordination, aspects of vision, sound, and strength. It also has social components, like how one behaves in a bowling alley."

It's a field that requires a lot of creative problem-solving. When some of Falk-Kessler's students were working with the homebound elderly, they discovered that the Meals on Wheels packaging was too difficult to open. So the therapists created a tool specifically designed to cut the boxes.

Pluses. Not bound to hospitals, occupational therapists can ply their trade in a range of industries. Some work with architects—helping design accessible homes and buildings—while others, who are interested in mental health, can work with children and teenagers who have anxiety disorders or substance abuse problems, improving their ability to stay on task and interact better with peers and adults.

Minuses. Sometimes patients have difficulty understanding the purpose of therapy. "We're not here to take away the pain. You have to feed your dog and we have to figure out how to do that," explained one therapist. Dealing with insurance companies that offer patients only limited therapy coverage can also be frustrating.

Training. Undergraduate degrees for OT are on their way out: As of January 2007, the Accreditation Council for Occupational Therapy Education recognizes only those programs that confer a master's or doctorate. The new emphasis is on the master's degree, which requires two years of classroom study, including courses in anatomy, sociology, psychology, and biology. This is followed by six to nine months of fieldwork under the guidance of a licensed therapist. Some combined baccalaureate/master's programs can shorten the amount of schooling by a year. A national certification exam is required to practice.

Tips for getting started. Proof of a commitment to community service looks stellar on any kind of application, but for almost all occupational therapy programs, it is required. To impress admissions officers, work beyond the minimum number of hours and try to volunteer in hospitals that will allow you to shadow members of the occupational therapy unit. Experience in varied settings, like homeless shelters or schools, helps demonstrate your dedication as well. There are some required undergrad courses, including biology, physiology, and psychology. Programs also examine GPAs and scores on the Graduate Record Exam.

Top schools. Master's and doctorate programs, ranked in 2008: 1) (tie) Boston University, Sargent College of Health & Rehabilitation Sciences; Washington University in St. Louis; 2) University of Southern California.

To find out more. The American Occupational Therapy Association (301-652-2682; www.aota.org) has resources on education and snagging a job in the field. The American Occupational Therapy Foundation (301-652-6611, ext. 2250; www.aotf.org) has information on financial aid.

Social Work

When life gets tough, social workers get moving. People at high risk for AIDS, or low-income parents who are caught between the demands of work and the need to find decent child care, have traditionally been able to get counseling and practical help from social workers employed by public welfare agencies and hospitals. Today private companies, including HMOs and for-profit health service organizations, have added social workers to their payroll to advise patients and their families. While specialties aren't strictly defined in the field, most social workers build an area of expertise or gain certification in the areas of family care, public health, or mental health.

Pluses. No surprises here—the positive impact you have is a big reason for doing this job. Many social workers also praise the diversity of the work, which can range from grief counseling to supervising a homeless outreach program. Some social work positions also allow for flexible working hours; private firms, in particular, often hire counselors on a part-time basis.

Minuses. The emotional rewards typically are higher than the monetary ones, and the long, intense hours often lead to burnout.

Training. Education requirements for social workers vary in each state; the Association of Social Work Boards lists all of them. A master's degree as well as a passing score on a licensing exam are needed for most positions, especially clinical or management ones. However, some entry-level positions, such as child welfare case workers or counseling jobs in the private sector, call for only an undergraduate degree in social work. That degree, offered at many universities, involves the study of social welfare policies and methods. As part of the major, most schools require seminars on dealing with individuals and families, along with an internship where students are placed in a public or private social service organization to get hands-on experience dealing with patients.

The master's degree is similar but more intense. In over 150 programs accredited by the Council on Social Work Education, students take two years of classes in social welfare policy and practice, human behavior, and research methods. Other courses may include applied psychology, sociology, and ethics. Budding social workers also need to take a 900-hour practicum. At the University of Illinois–Urbana-Champaign, for instance, graduate students work Monday through Thursday at anywhere from a school to a nursing home depending on their area of interest; the work typically includes client interviews and case evaluations. On Fridays, students attend a seminar at the school to discuss and learn from their experiences.

An increasing number of graduate schools are offering minors and dual-degree programs for students who want to demonstrate an expertise in a certain area—and get a step ahead in the job market. Columbia University is starting a dual-degree program in social work and international affairs that will help graduates land positions with international organizations like the United Nations. "We know that there isn't a single social problem that requires one profession to intervene," said Jeanette Takamura, dean of the university's School of Social Work. "So why should we offer one single degree?" The program at Columbia takes three years to finish, and students graduate with two master's degrees. The school also offers dual social work degrees in other areas such as urban planning and Jewish studies.

If you want to become a clinical social worker who provides mental health therapy, you need to receive still more training. Clinical social workers who work as psychotherapists, doing in-depth counseling, can receive reimbursement for their services from HMOs. Besides a master's degree, psychotherapists need two years of supervised work experience and a passing score on a clinical licensing test.

Tips on getting started. "You need to have passion if you want to be a social worker. And that passion can't be taught," one social work professor said. The best way to demonstrate this kind of dedication is to show it on your résumé. If you haven't been working in a related field such as teaching or nursing, volunteer experience is very important for an applicant—even as little as spending one evening each week playing cards at a nearby nursing home or one Saturday a month helping mentally ill children. While universities do not require an undergraduate degree in social work, most schools do give preference to students who have performed well in social sciences courses like psychology and sociology. Many graduate schools of social work do not require applicants to take the Graduate Record Exam, but they do want to see a high undergraduate GPA.

> *"Social workers work with some of the most seriously troubled individuals in American culture."*

Top schools. Master's programs, ranked in 2008: 1) Washington University in St. Louis; 2) University of Michigan–Ann Arbor; 3) University of Chicago.

To find out more. The National Association of Social Workers (202-408-8600; www.social workers.org) has general information and career advice The Council on Social Work Education (703-683-8080; www.cswe.org) has complete listings of accredited school programs. The Association of Social Work Boards (800-225-6880; www. aswb.org) administers the licensing exams and maintains information on each state's test and license requirements.

Speech-Language Pathology

Humans need to communicate. It's an essential characteristic of the species. But sometimes it doesn't come easy. That's where speech-language pathologists (SLP) come in. They work in hospi-

tals, clinics, schools, corporate offices, or private practice, diagnosing speaking and communication problems and developing treatment plans. For example, children who have trouble articulating certain words and sounds can learn to talk fluently with proper training. For stroke victims who suffer aphasia—trouble speaking, comprehending, or writing language—early treatment by an SLP can help preserve and improve language skills by using verbal or visual drills and conversational role-playing.

Pluses. Good salaries and opportunities to work in a variety of settings with all kinds of patients keep SLPs happy. Those that tire of working in a hospital, for instance, can easily find another job in a school helping students with speech problems. New SLPs say they are amazed and gratified when they see a struggling student finally turn a corner.

Minuses. "It's not like giving somebody a pill," said Diane Paul-Brown of the American Speech-Language-Hearing Association. Some patients with severe disabilities may never reach normal levels, and their progress can be slow and frustrating. There are also hassles in getting compensation from schools and insurers.

Training. In almost every state, practicing speech-language pathologists must have a master's degree in the field, pass a national licensing exam, and complete a nine-month supervised fellowship. Programs are accredited by a council of the American Speech-Language-Hearing Association, and a typical master's curriculum involves four semesters and a summer of full-time study. Classes focus on specific disorders. For example, at the University of Maryland–College Park, besides a diagnostic methods course and an audiology course, all students must study aphasia, voice disorders, stuttering, child language disorders, and phonological disorders. They can also take electives such as augmentative communications (using technology to enhance innate ability). Once graduate students have a grasp of their field and its tools, they begin clinical rotations where they learn how to evaluate and diagnose actual patients and design customized courses of treatment. Some programs also require a thesis.

Tips on getting started. Aspiring undergrads can major in speech pathology or communication sciences and disorders, which gives them many of the prerequisite courses for grad school. (Some grad programs accept only applicants with these majors.) The prerequisites include anatomy and physiology of speech, anatomy and physiology of hearing, speech science, hearing science, speech and language development, phonetics, psychology of language, and acoustics.

You're not barred from becoming an SLP if you didn't major in it, however. Some students without this background do postbaccalaureate work before applying to grad programs, while others apply anyway and are accepted with the provision that they first take a year of make-up classes. In general, schools are looking for high GPAs and GRE scores. Students with better chances of admission usually have volunteered or worked in nursing homes and preschools.

Top schools. Master's programs, ranked in 2008: 1) University of Iowa; 2) (tie) Northwestern University, Illinois; Purdue University–West Lafayette, Indiana; University of Wisconsin–Madison.

To find out more. The American Speech-Language-Hearing Association (800-498-2071; www.asha.org) has extensive student materials with a guide to accredited programs by state.

The *U.S.News* Insider's Index

How Do the Schools Stack Up?

Which are the hardest and easiest medical schools to get into?

While the number of applications to medical schools has dropped in recent years, it is still extremely hard to get in. Many of the most competitive only accept 1 in 20 of those who apply—or even fewer. Schools are ranked here from most to least selective based on a formula that combines average MCAT scores and undergraduate GPA for the Fall 2009 entering class as well as the school's acceptance rates. Average GPAs and MCATs will give you a sense of the competition.

Most to least selective

	Overall acceptance rate	Acceptance rate (men)	Acceptance rate (women)	Acceptance rate (minorities)	Average undergraduate GPA	Average composite MCAT score (scale: 1-15)	Average MCAT score, verbal reasoning (scale: 1-15)	Average MCAT score, physical sciences (scale: 1-15)	Average MCAT score, biological sciences (scale: 1-15)	Average MCAT score, writing (scale: J-T)
Washington University in St. Louis	11.0%	9.1%	13.8%	9.2%	3.86	12.4	11.4	12.8	12.9	Q
Harvard University (MA)	4.5%	4.1%	5.0%	5.0%	3.86	11.9	10.8	12.5	12.4	R
Johns Hopkins University (MD)	6.7%	6.2%	7.2%	7.5%	3.87	11.9	10.9	12.3	12.5	R
University of Chicago (Pritzker)	3.7%	1.7%	6.2%	5.1%	3.82	11.9	11.1	12.3	12.3	Q
Columbia University (NY)	4.3%	N/A	N/A	N/A	3.80	11.9	11.2	12.1	12.4	Q
University of Pennsylvania	4.8%	4.8%	4.8%	4.8%	3.81	11.9	11.1	12.3	12.4	Q
Yale University (CT)	6.5%	5.8%	7.3%	7.6%	3.78	11.9	10.9	12.2	12.6	R
University of California–Los Angeles (Geffen)	4.1%	4.8%	3.2%	7.8%	3.81	11.6	10.6	11.9	12.2	Q
University of Michigan–Ann Arbor	8.4%	7.4%	9.5%	N/A	3.75	11.8	11.0	11.9	12.4	Q
University of Pittsburgh	7.8%	7.4%	8.2%	8.3%	3.74	11.7	10.8	12.0	12.2	P
Vanderbilt University (TN)	6.1%	5.4%	7.2%	7.3%	3.81	11.3	10.4	11.5	11.8	Q
Case Western Reserve University (OH)	9.0%	8.2%	10.1%	9.7%	3.73	11.6	10.7	11.9	12.1	Q
Cornell University (Weill) (NY)	4.5%	3.2%	5.9%	5.4%	3.75	11.5	10.6	11.7	12.1	Q
Northwestern University (Feinberg) (IL)	7.3%	7.0%	7.6%	8.4%	3.74	11.5	10.5	11.9	12.2	Q
Baylor College of Medicine (TX)	7.4%	7.2%	7.7%	7.9%	3.83	11.1	10.4	11.4	11.7	P
Duke University (NC)	4.3%	4.2%	4.6%	5.1%	3.72	11.4	10.3	11.9	12.0	P
Mount Sinai School of Medicine (NY)	5.9%	5.6%	6.1%	6.4%	3.69	11.6	10.9	12.0	12.0	Q
Stanford University (CA)	3.5%	4.0%	2.9%	4.0%	3.75	11.3	10.5	11.7	11.9	Q
University of California–San Francisco	4.5%	4.0%	5.1%	N/A	3.74	11.3	10.5	11.5	11.9	R
Univ. of Texas Southwestern Medical Center–Dallas	12.3%	12.2%	12.3%	12.1%	3.80	11.2	10.5	11.4	11.8	Q
University of Virginia	14.0%	13.0%	15.0%	16.4%	3.75	11.3	10.5	11.6	11.7	P
University of California–San Diego	6.1%	6.0%	6.2%	5.4%	3.76	11.0	10.1	11.4	11.6	Q
Dartmouth Medical School (NH)	6.2%	5.7%	6.8%	5.6%	3.73	11.1	10.6	11.3	11.5	Q
New York University	6.7%	6.4%	7.0%	8.2%	3.74	11.0	10.3	11.3	11.5	Q
Emory University (GA)	8.0%	7.4%	8.7%	8.3%	3.66	11.2	10.8	11.3	11.6	P
Ohio State University	11.0%	9.4%	13.4%	9.5%	3.72	11.0	10.5	11.0	11.5	P
St. Louis University	8.7%	8.1%	9.5%	8.0%	3.73	10.9	10.5	11.1	10.1	P
University of Florida	9.2%	9.1%	9.3%	7.3%	3.78	10.6	9.9	10.8	11.0	Q
Brown University (Alpert) (RI)	4.1%	4.1%	4.2%	4.0%	3.62	11.1	10.5	11.5	11.3	Q
Yeshiva University (Einstein) (NY)	6.9%	6.2%	7.6%	7.3%	3.72	10.6	9.9	10.8	11.1	P
University of Colorado–Denver	7.3%	6.8%	8.0%	5.6%	3.69	10.7	10.4	10.6	11.2	P
Boston University	4.7%	4.0%	5.4%	4.4%	3.65	10.7	10.0	10.9	11.2	P
University of Connecticut	7.1%	6.1%	8.1%	6.0%	3.71	10.5	9.9	10.3	11.2	Q
University of California–Irvine	6.5%	5.2%	7.8%	6.2%	3.66	10.6	9.7	10.8	11.3	Q
University of Massachusetts–Worcester	22.2%	21.0%	23.5%	N/A	3.67	10.8	10.3	10.8	11.3	Q
University of Minnesota	8.7%	7.6%	10.1%	6.7%	3.71	10.4	10.0	10.3	10.9	P
University of North Carolina–Chapel Hill	5.1%	4.4%	5.9%	4.4%	3.64	10.7	10.4	10.7	11.0	P
University of Rochester (NY)	6.7%	5.5%	8.0%	5.3%	3.66	10.6	10.1	10.6	11.1	Q

	Overall acceptance rate	Acceptance rate (men)	Acceptance rate (women)	Acceptance rate (minorities)	Average undergraduate GPA	Average composite MCAT score (scale: 1-15)	Average MCAT score, verbal reasoning (scale: 1-15)	Average MCAT score, physical sciences (scale: 1-15)	Average MCAT score, biological sciences (scale: 1-15)	Average MCAT score, writing (scale: J-T)
University of Southern California (Keck)	5.5%	4.7%	6.4%	4.9%	3.62	10.8	9.9	11.0	11.5	Q
University of Texas Health Science Center–Houston	11.3%	12.5%	9.9%	9.6%	3.70	10.5	10.1	10.5	11.0	P
University of Wisconsin–Madison	8.8%	6.9%	11.3%	7.4%	3.72	10.4	9.9	10.3	10.9	P
Indiana University–Indianapolis	14.8%	14.3%	15.4%	N/A	3.73	10.3	9.8	10.2	10.7	P
Medical College of Wisconsin	6.6%	5.6%	7.9%	N/A	3.74	10.2	9.6	10.0	10.6	P
University of Iowa (Carver)	9.7%	8.5%	11.3%	11.4%	3.70	10.4	10.0	10.3	10.8	P
University of Maryland	7.5%	6.4%	8.7%	6.1%	3.71	10.3	10.0	10.2	10.6	P
University of Missouri	11.2%	8.1%	15.5%	6.1%	3.77	10.1	9.9	9.8	10.4	P
Jefferson Medical College (PA)	4.8%	4.2%	5.4%	4.9%	3.65	10.5	10.2	10.6	10.8	Q
Stony Brook University (NY)	7.9%	8.1%	7.7%	6.3%	3.60	10.7	10.0	11.0	11.0	P
University of Cincinnati	9.6%	8.3%	11.3%	N/A	3.58	10.8	10.3	10.9	11.2	O
University of Miami (Miller) (FL)	6.9%	6.6%	7.4%	7.5%	3.68	10.4	10.0	10.3	10.8	P
Georgetown University (DC)	4.1%	3.8%	4.4%	N/A	3.62	10.5	9.9	10.6	11.0	Q
University of Alabama–Birmingham	12.2%	12.4%	11.9%	9.9%	3.74	10.1	9.9	9.9	10.5	P
University of Kentucky	9.1%	N/A	N/A	N/A	3.68	10.3	9.8	10.2	11.0	O
University of Washington	6.2%	5.1%	7.5%	4.2%	3.67	10.3	10.1	10.0	10.9	Q
Creighton University (NE)	6.0%	5.0%	7.3%	4.7%	3.72	10.0	9.6	9.7	10.3	P
Tufts University (MA)	7.5%	7.7%	7.4%	6.7%	3.60	10.6	10.1	10.7	11.0	P
Univ. of Med. and Dent. of NJ–New Brunswick (Johnson)	9.8%	8.9%	10.7%	9.0%	3.64	10.4	9.9	10.5	10.9	P
University of Texas Medical Branch–Galveston	18.5%	19.4%	17.4%	33.3%	3.76	10.0	9.2	9.4	9.4	P
Loyola University Chicago (Stritch)	6.6%	5.8%	7.4%	4.8%	3.59	10.5	10.2	10.3	10.9	N/A
Oregon Health and Science University	4.5%	3.9%	5.1%	3.5%	3.66	10.2	9.9	9.8	10.8	P
Temple University (PA)	6.2%	5.1%	7.3%	6.0%	3.63	10.3	9.8	10.3	10.7	Q
University of California–Davis	4.1%	3.4%	4.8%	4.2%	3.57	10.6	9.9	10.7	11.2	Q
University of Nevada–Reno	30.1%	31.2%	28.8%	N/A	3.65	10.5	9.9	9.7	10.4	Q
University of South Florida	8.4%	7.8%	9.1%	12.5%	3.71	10.0	10.0	10.0	11.0	P
University of Vermont	3.9%	3.6%	4.3%	3.4%	3.70	10.0	10.0	10.0	10.0	Q
University at Buffalo–SUNY	10.2%	9.3%	11.1%	N/A	3.65	10.2	9.5	10.2	10.9	P
West Virginia University	6.3%	6.6%	6.0%	6.0%	3.73	9.7	9.5	9.5	10.0	O
Rush University (IL)	4.1%	3.7%	4.6%	4.0%	3.60	10.2	9.9	10.0	10.5	Q
Texas A&M Health Science Center	19.1%	20.2%	18.0%	20.1%	3.68	10.0	10.0	10.0	10.0	Q
Wake Forest University (NC)	4.1%	3.8%	4.5%	N/A	3.60	10.2	10.1	10.0	10.5	Q
SUNY–Syracuse	7.5%	6.9%	8.3%	7.0%	3.61	10.1	9.4	10.5	10.6	P
University of Oklahoma	13.5%	14.4%	12.2%	9.6%	3.72	9.7	9.9	9.3	10.0	Q
Wayne State University (MI)	16.4%	15.6%	17.4%	14.5%	3.64	10.1	9.3	10.3	10.6	P
George Washington University (DC)	3.2%	N/A	N/A	N/A	3.64	9.8	9.6	9.6	10.2	P
New York Medical College	8.2%	7.5%	8.9%	7.1%	3.60	10.1	9.7	10.2	10.6	Q
University of Nebraska Medical Center	11.8%	10.8%	13.3%	6.2%	3.70	9.7	9.5	9.4	10.2	P
University of Toledo	8.9%	7.9%	10.1%	N/A	3.62	10.0	10.0	10.0	10.0	P
Drexel University (PA)	7.6%	6.9%	8.4%	7.2%	3.54	10.2	9.6	10.3	10.8	O
Texas Tech University Health Sciences Center	10.3%	10.7%	9.9%	9.5%	3.68	9.7	9.5	9.5	10.2	R
University of Tennessee Health Science Center	18.6%	20.5%	16.3%	15.4%	3.63	10.0	10.0	10.0	10.0	P
University of Arizona	25.7%	N/A	N/A	N/A	3.68	9.8	9.6	9.6	10.1	Q
University of Louisville (KY)	10.2%	9.6%	10.9%	7.0%	3.63	9.8	9.6	9.5	10.2	N
Virginia Commonwealth University	7.1%	6.5%	7.9%	7.6%	3.62	9.8	9.3	9.7	10.3	P
University of Texas Health Science Center–San Antonio	13.6%	12.2%	15.2%	14.8%	3.58	10.0	10.0	10.0	11.0	Q
Eastern Virginia Medical School	5.6%	5.3%	6.0%	N/A	3.46	10.3	10.0	10.0	11.0	N/A
University of Hawaii–Manoa (Burns)	6.9%	6.8%	7.1%	13.5%	3.62	9.6	9.0	10.0	10.0	P
University of Kansas Medical Center	9.5%	8.1%	11.4%	5.0%	3.65	9.5	9.5	9.0	10.0	Q
University of South Carolina	7.0%	6.3%	7.8%	4.5%	3.68	9.4	9.6	8.9	9.6	O
University of South Dakota (Sanford)	18.5%	21.1%	15.2%	7.7%	3.62	9.8	9.4	9.7	10.4	O

Which are the hardest and easiest medical schools to get into?

	Overall acceptance rate	Acceptance rate (men)	Acceptance rate (women)	Acceptance rate (minorities)	Average undergraduate GPA	Average composite MCAT score (scale: 1-15)	Average MCAT score, verbal reasoning (scale: 1-15)	Average MCAT score, physical sciences (scale: 1-15)	Average MCAT score, biological sciences (scale: 1-15)	Average MCAT score, writing (scale: J-T)
Florida State University	6.7%	5.8%	7.7%	5.4%	3.70	N/A	9.1	9.2	9.9	O
Medical University of South Carolina	13.6%	14.6%	12.4%	15.9%	3.59	9.8	9.7	9.6	10.1	O
Northeastern Ohio Universities College of Medicine	9.3%	8.8%	9.9%	8.9%	3.70	9.2	9.3	8.9	9.3	O
Uniformed Services Univ. of the Health Sci. (Hebert) (MD)	12.2%	14.1%	8.7%	7.4%	3.51	10.1	9.9	10.0	10.4	P
University of Utah	9.1%	7.6%	12.9%	7.8%	3.64	9.5	9.2	9.2	10.2	N/A
University of Arkansas for Medical Sciences	25.6%	N/A	N/A	N/A	3.64	9.5	9.6	9.0	9.9	O
East Tennessee State University (Quillen)	8.8%	8.9%	8.7%	5.9%	3.68	9.1	9.1	8.7	9.4	O
Michigan State University	6.6%	5.9%	7.4%	8.1%	3.54	9.6	9.2	9.3	10.2	O
Des Moines University (IA)	14.6%	13.1%	16.5%	9.1%	3.70	9.0	8.9	8.6	9.6	O
University of North Dakota	30.2%	23.8%	36.0%	33.3%	3.71	9.1	9.1	8.7	9.6	N
East Carolina University (Brody) (NC)	14.0%	12.4%	15.9%	11.5%	3.60	9.3	9.0	9.0	10.0	P
Louisiana State Univ. Health Sciences Center–Shreveport	41.4%	44.7%	37.7%	25.0%	3.70	9.2	9.0	8.6	9.8	P
Southern Illinois University–Springfield	13.4%	13.1%	13.9%	N/A	3.55	9.4	9.4	9.0	9.8	O
University of New Mexico	16.2%	13.9%	18.7%	17.4%	3.57	9.4	9.3	8.8	10.2	N/A
Morehouse School of Medicine (GA)	1.5%	N/A	N/A	N/A	N/A	N/A	N/A	N/A	N/A	N/A
Western University of Health Sciences (CA)	14.2%	14.5%	13.8%	12.4%	3.56	9.3	8.6	9.3	9.9	O
Wright State University (Boonshoft) (OH)	8.4%	N/A	N/A	N/A	3.51	9.4	9.1	9.3	9.9	P
University of North Texas Health Science Center	20.4%	20.1%	20.8%	19.0%	3.57	9.2	9.0	8.9	9.8	P
Mercer University (GA)	15.8%	13.7%	17.9%	10.2%	3.53	9.2	9.1	8.9	9.7	N/A
Nova Southeastern University (FL)	17.3%	18.3%	16.2%	12.3%	3.44	9.6	9.4	9.4	9.4	M
Univ. of Med. and Dent. of NJ–Stratford	6.2%	5.5%	6.8%	6.0%	3.54	9.0	8.7	8.8	9.5	Q
Michigan State University	13.3%	12.2%	14.5%	7.6%	3.57	8.8	8.5	8.6	9.4	O
Touro University (CA)	6.0%	N/A	N/A	N/A	3.42	9.3	8.5	8.9	10.5	P
Ohio University	5.2%	4.7%	5.9%	4.1%	3.63	8.2	7.9	7.9	8.7	P
Lake Erie College of Osteopathic Medicine (PA)	10.3%	10.4%	10.1%	18.5%	3.45	8.9	8.9	8.4	9.4	O
University of New England (ME)	6.3%	5.7%	7.0%	1.8%	3.45	8.9	9.1	8.5	9.2	Q
Oklahoma State University	23.0%	24.1%	21.5%	15.1%	3.59	8.4	8.4	7.9	9.0	N
A.T. Still University of Health Sciences (Kirksville) (MO)	10.9%	11.6%	10.0%	7.6%	3.47	8.7	8.7	8.1	9.2	O
Edward Via Virginia College of Osteopathic Medicine	10.1%	11.1%	9.0%	6.2%	3.53	8.3	8.0	8.0	9.0	Q
West Virginia School of Osteopathic Medicine	14.5%	15.4%	13.4%	N/A	3.44	8.0	8.0	7.6	8.5	M
Pikeville College (KY)	5.1%	5.6%	4.5%	3.0%	3.44	7.4	7.4	7.0	7.9	N

The total cost of an M.D. degree can easily top $200,000 at the most expensive private schools once you factor in living expenses. Private medical schools are ranked here by tuition and fees for the 2009–2010 academic year, with the most expensive at the top. Public institutions follow, sorted by in-state tuition so you can easily see what you might save by sticking close to home.

Private Schools

	Tuition and fees	Room and board
Tufts University (MA)	$50,968	$11,844
Columbia University (NY)	$49,347	$14,652
University of Southern California (Keck)	$49,268	$15,842
New York University	$49,203	$13,500
New York Medical College	$47,790	$19,484
George Washington University (DC)	$47,644	$22,376
Cornell University (Weill) (NY)	$47,455	$11,460
Case Western Reserve University (OH)	$47,290	$17,890
Washington University in St. Louis	$47,150	$10,139
Boston University	$47,088	$12,464
Rush University (IL)	$46,272	$10,100
Georgetown University (DC)	$46,177	$17,060
Creighton University (NE)	$46,086	$13,500
Duke University (NC)	$45,992	$13,740
Harvard University (MA)	$45,833	$12,520
Northwestern University (Feinberg) (IL)	$45,737	$14,958
Stanford University (CA)	$45,639	$23,097
University of Pennsylvania	$45,546	$18,410
Drexel University (PA)	$45,440	$15,888
St. Louis University	$45,315	$11,988
Yeshiva University (Einstein) (NY)	$45,227	$15,000
Jefferson Medical College (PA)	$44,547	$16,005
Yale University (CT)	$44,350	$11,310
Dartmouth Medical School (NH)	$44,285	$10,250
Brown University (Alpert) (RI)	$44,054	$16,500
University of New England (ME)	$43,755	$12,000
Johns Hopkins University (MD)	$43,620	$17,736
University of Rochester (NY)	$43,410	$16,000
Western University of Health Sciences (CA)	$43,340	$12,942
Emory University (GA)	$42,876	$23,664
Loyola University Chicago (Stritch)	$42,755	$17,679
Vanderbilt University (TN)	$42,352	$10,800
University of Chicago (Pritzker)	$42,349	$17,000
Temple University (PA)	$41,936	$11,220
Meharry Medical College (TN)	$41,685	N/A
Mount Sinai School of Medicine (NY)	$41,103	$16,694
A.T. Still University of Health Sciences (Kirksville) (MO)	$41,070	$10,912
Wake Forest University (NC)	$39,395	$20,780
Touro University (CA)	$39,000	$14,798

Who's the priciest? Who's the cheapest?

Private Schools, cont'd.

	Tuition and fees	Room and board
Mercer University (GA)	$38,400	$13,740
Morehouse School of Medicine (GA)	$36,714	N/A
Des Moines University (IA)	$35,840	$14,040
Medical College of Wisconsin	$34,558	$9,000
Edward Via Virginia College of Osteopathic Medicine	$34,386	$26,472
Pikeville College (KY)	$33,450	N/A
Nova Southeastern University (FL)	$32,933	$18,260
University of Miami (Miller) (FL)	$30,188	$24,655
Lake Erie College of Osteopathic Medicine (PA)	$27,500	$11,550
Baylor College of Medicine (TX)	$14,828	$22,649

Public Schools

	In-state tuition and fees	Out-of-state tuition and fees	Room and board
East Carolina University (Brody) (NC)	$10,193	$35,183	$11,162
Texas A&M Health Science Center	$11,394	$24,494	$13,200
Louisiana State University Health Sciences Center–Shreveport	$12,033	$27,630	N/A
University of Texas Health Science Center–Houston	$12,159	$24,384	$15,070
University of North Carolina–Chapel Hill	$13,360	$37,426	$27,426
Texas Tech University Health Sciences Center	$13,461	$26,561	$13,269
University of Texas Medical Branch–Galveston	$14,270	$27,370	N/A
University of Texas Southwestern Medical Center–Dallas	$14,640	$27,740	$17,529
University of North Texas Health Science Center	$14,877	$30,627	$15,125
University of Texas Health Science Center–San Antonio	$15,170	$28,270	$16,463
University of Massachusetts–Worcester	$15,738	N/A	$12,554
University of Nevada–Reno	$17,656	$39,038	$13,590
University of Arkansas for Medical Sciences	$18,032	$35,156	N/A
University of New Mexico	$18,365	$47,105	$11,254
Oklahoma State University	$20,065	$37,987	$7,200
West Virginia School of Osteopathic Medicine	$20,150	$50,150	$14,170
Florida State University	$20,354	$60,546	$15,385
University of Oklahoma	$20,648	$44,766	N/A
University of Alabama–Birmingham	$21,053	$54,307	$18,444
University of South Dakota (Sanford)	$21,099	$43,274	$21,940
West Virginia University	$21,270	$46,018	$7,857
University of Washington	$21,472	$50,512	$15,141
University of Arizona	$22,699	N/A	$11,540
University at Buffalo–SUNY	$22,940	$42,110	$12,423
Stony Brook University (NY)	$24,049	$41,889	$10,855
SUNY–Syracuse	$24,112	$41,952	$17,631
University of Tennessee Health Science Center	$24,219	$45,129	$17,226
East Tennessee State University (Quillen)	$24,457	$48,215	$12,621
University of Wisconsin–Madison	$24,616	$35,740	$17,115
University of Missouri	$24,856	$48,367	$9,380

	In-state tuition and fees	Out-of-state tuition and fees	Room and board
University of North Dakota	$24,893	$44,724	$9,104
University of Utah	$25,139	$46,882	$9,360
University of Hawaii–Manoa (Burns)	$25,215	$51,303	N/A
University of Maryland	$25,604	$45,648	$21,500
University of California–Los Angeles (Geffen)	$26,114	$38,359	$14,600
University of Louisville (KY)	$26,329	$43,425	$8,494
University of Nebraska Medical Center	$26,650	$59,250	$14,400
University of South Florida	$26,833	$54,044	$11,000
Michigan State University	$26,953	$58,175	$13,632
University of California–San Diego	$26,969	$39,214	$12,028
Southern Illinois University–Springfield	$27,262	$75,238	$9,450
University of California–Irvine	$27,336	$39,581	$14,527
University of Toledo	$27,428	$56,234	N/A
University of Michigan–Ann Arbor	$27,473	$43,827	$21,477
Eastern Virginia Medical School	$27,620	$50,380	$12,285
University of California–San Francisco	$27,708	$39,953	$19,636
Ohio University	$27,744	$39,210	$12,992
University of Colorado–Denver	$28,151	$52,977	$16,200
University of Kansas Medical Center	$28,178	$47,626	$11,106
University of Iowa (Carver)	$28,248	$44,062	$0,000
University of South Carolina	$28,278	$61,912	$12,613
Virginia Commonwealth University	$28,566	$42,612	$13,400
University of Florida	$28,652	$56,500	$9,465
Wright State University (Boonshoft) (OH)	$28,867	$43,867	$11,946
University of Medicine and Dentistry of New Jersey–Stratford	$29,178	$43,990	$13,650
Indiana University–Indianapolis	$29,239	$43,075	$15,168
Wayne State University (MI)	$29,275	$59,275	$13,250
University of Kentucky	$29,341	$53,747	$14,850
University of Cincinnati	$29,385	$45,135	$19,188
Ohio State University	$29,423	$33,301	$9,080
University of Connecticut	$29,576	$52,621	N/A
University of Vermont	$29,583	$50,403	$10,923
University of Medicine and Dentistry of New Jersey–New Brunswick (Johnson)	$29,688	$44,500	$13,660
University of California–Davis	$30,256	$42,501	$14,355
Northeastern Ohio Universities College of Medicine	$30,599	$59,212	$10,500
Michigan State University	$32,114	$69,581	$15,792
Medical University of South Carolina	$33,829	$57,161	$13,320
University of Virginia	$35,150	$44,708	$19,818
University of Minnesota	$36,136	$44,044	$12,015
University of Pittsburgh	$37,486	$41,506	$15,110
Oregon Health and Science University	$38,689	$51,845	$18,000

Which schools award the most and the least financial aid?

Compared to what you're going to need, you may be surprised at how little you get: Medical schools assume that their students will borrow to pay the bills because they'll make enough after graduation to manage the loan payments. However, a lucky few with top scores and undergraduate grades may find a merit award on the table. Schools are ranked here by percentage of students receiving aid.

Private Schools

	% receiving aid of any kind	% receiving loans	% receiving grants/ scholarships	% receiving work-study benefits
Vanderbilt University (TN)	100%	68%	100%	0%
Nova Southeastern University (FL)	97%	96%	3%	0%
Pikeville College (KY)	97%	93%	42%	N/A
Medical College of Wisconsin	96%	85%	63%	0%
Des Moines University (IA)	95%	89%	37%	N/A
University of Chicago (Pritzker)	95%	74%	86%	0%
University of New England (ME)	95%	88%	23%	0%
Edward Via Virginia College of Osteopathic Medicine	94%	87%	52%	0%
A.T. Still University of Health Sciences (Kirksville) (MO)	94%	94%	19%	18%
Creighton University (NE)	94%	92%	59%	0%
Loyola University Chicago (Stritch)	94%	85%	73%	0%
Mercer University (GA)	94%	89%	54%	0%
Wake Forest University (NC)	94%	90%	70%	0%
Lake Erie College of Osteopathic Medicine (PA)	93%	89%	31%	0%
New York Medical College	93%	92%	33%	3%
Western University of Health Sciences (CA)	93%	90%	49%	0%
Temple University (PA)	92%	85%	42%	8%
Touro University (CA)	92%	91%	16%	8%
Duke University (NC)	91%	65%	68%	0%
George Washington University (DC)	90%	80%	39%	0%
Rush University (IL)	90%	88%	57%	6%
University of Rochester (NY)	89%	79%	55%	18%
University of Southern California (Keck)	88%	83%	52%	0%
Emory University (GA)	88%	77%	73%	0%
Washington University in St. Louis	88%	52%	73%	0%
Georgetown University (DC)	88%	86%	48%	1%
Baylor College of Medicine (TX)	87%	70%	58%	17%
Case Western Reserve University (OH)	85%	80%	61%	0%
Dartmouth Medical School (NH)	85%	85%	50%	0%
Drexel University (PA)	85%	84%	42%	15%
Stanford University (CA)	85%	60%	82%	11%
St. Louis University	85%	81%	65%	0%
University of Pennsylvania	85%	64%	70%	2%
Yale University (CT)	84%	69%	64%	4%
Morehouse School of Medicine (GA)	83%	79%	46%	1%
Jefferson Medical College (PA)	83%	78%	45%	14%
Columbia University (NY)	82%	69%	58%	10%
Boston University	82%	77%	32%	0%
Cornell University (Weill) (NY)	81%	72%	65%	19%

	% receiving aid of any kind	% receiving loans	% receiving grants/ scholarships	% receiving work-study benefits
Harvard University (MA)	81%	76%	54%	1%
Johns Hopkins University (MD)	80%	77%	60%	14%
Tufts University (MA)	79%	74%	27%	10%
Yeshiva University (Einstein) (NY)	79%	75%	53%	0%
Mount Sinai School of Medicine (NY)	77%	65%	37%	9%
University of Miami (Miller) (FL)	77%	77%	42%	0%
Northwestern University (Feinberg) (IL)	76%	69%	47%	0%
Brown University (Alpert) (RI)	73%	73%	45%	0%
New York University	70%	70%	40%	7%

Public Schools

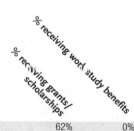

	% receiving aid of any kind	% receiving loans	% receiving grants/ scholarships	% receiving work-study benefits
University of Nebraska Medical Center	99%	91%	62%	0%
University of California–Los Angeles (Geffen)	98%	92%	97%	0%
West Virginia School of Osteopathic Medicine	98%	96%	18%	7%
University of North Dakota	97%	90%	59%	0%
University of South Dakota (Sanford)	97%	90%	88%	0%
Virginia Commonwealth University	96%	91%	51%	0%
University at Buffalo–SUNY	96%	77%	25%	0%
University of Colorado–Denver	96%	91%	76%	5%
University of Kansas Medical Center	95%	82%	90%	0%
University of Wisconsin–Madison	95%	92%	18%	0%
Oklahoma State University	95%	92%	16%	32%
University of Arizona	95%	85%	71%	4%
University of Iowa (Carver)	95%	90%	65%	0%
University of Utah	95%	90%	52%	0%
Wright State University (Boonshoft) (OH)	95%	86%	52%	3%
University of South Carolina	95%	88%	40%	0%
Indiana University–Indianapolis	94%	91%	34%	0%
University of Missouri	94%	88%	70%	0%
West Virginia University	94%	85%	50%	0%
University of Louisville (KY)	94%	90%	35%	0%
Oregon Health and Science University	93%	89%	79%	1%
Southern Illinois University–Springfield	93%	87%	37%	0%
University of California–Davis	93%	84%	93%	0%
University of Massachusetts–Worcester	93%	90%	31%	0%
Michigan State University	92%	86%	48%	N/A
Ohio University	92%	91%	24%	0%
University of California–Irvine	92%	78%	74%	0%
University of Kentucky	92%	82%	48%	16%

Which schools award the most and the least financial aid?

Public Schools, cont'd.

	% receiving aid of any kind	% receiving loans	% receiving grants/scholarships	% receiving work-study benefits
University of Minnesota	92%	83%	73%	1%
University of Pittsburgh	92%	81%	66%	0%
Ohio State University	92%	85%	54%	0%
Michigan State University	91%	88%	40%	0%
University of Arkansas for Medical Sciences	91%	88%	45%	0%
University of New Mexico	91%	86%	66%	0%
University of Virginia	91%	81%	68%	0%
University of Washington	91%	85%	68%	0%
East Carolina University (Brody) (NC)	90%	83%	50%	0%
University of Maryland	90%	85%	81%	0%
University of Nevada–Reno	90%	90%	80%	0%
University of North Texas Health Science Center	90%	88%	53%	2%
University of California–San Francisco	90%	82%	90%	1%
Texas Tech University Health Sciences Center	90%	81%	67%	0%
University of Michigan–Ann Arbor	89%	81%	65%	0%
University of California–San Diego	89%	80%	53%	1%
University of North Carolina–Chapel Hill	89%	79%	80%	0%
University of Oklahoma	89%	87%	33%	0%
University of Tennessee Health Science Center	89%	84%	45%	0%
University of Vermont	89%	83%	48%	0%
University of South Florida	88%	85%	40%	0%
University of Texas Health Science Center–San Antonio	87%	86%	63%	0%
Stony Brook University (NY)	87%	86%	25%	4%
University of Cincinnati	87%	86%	40%	2%
University of Toledo	87%	73%	30%	7%
University of Connecticut	87%	82%	58%	0%
University of Texas Southwestern Medical Center–Dallas	87%	79%	66%	4%
Texas A&M Health Science Center	85%	82%	45%	0%
Wayne State University (MI)	85%	83%	37%	2%
Medical University of South Carolina	85%	83%	16%	0%
SUNY–Syracuse	85%	80%	32%	10%
University of Florida	84%	76%	63%	0%
Louisiana State University Health Sciences Center–Shreveport	83%	79%	18%	0%
Northeastern Ohio Universities College of Medicine	83%	81%	26%	0%
University of Hawaii–Manoa (Burns)	82%	70%	53%	0%
University of Medicine and Dentistry of New Jersey–New Brunswick (Johnson)	82%	81%	23%	5%
University of Texas Health Science Center–Houston	78%	77%	26%	0%
University of Alabama–Birmingham	77%	70%	30%	0%
Eastern Virginia Medical School	76%	76%	43%	0%
Uniformed Services University of the Health Sciences (Hebert) (MD)	0%	0%	0%	0%

Which are the largest and smallest medical schools?

As you compare schools, you'll want to pay attention to the total enrollment, the size of the first-year class, and the faculty-to-student ratio. All will have an impact on the schools' personalities, the availability of professors outside of class, and the extent to which you engage with your classmates.

	Total enrollment	% in-state enrollment	Size of first-year class	Faculty-to-student ratio
Lake Erie College of Osteopathic Medicine (PA)	1,717	29%	543	0.3
Wayne State University (MI)	1,287	85%	322	0.8
Indiana University–Indianapolis	1,257	85%	333	1.2
Drexel University (PA)	1,087	29%	262	0.5
Jefferson Medical College (PA)	1,018	49%	257	2.5
University of Minnesota	984	84%	238	1.7
Michigan State University	959	92%	327	0.2
University of Texas Health Science Center–Houston	944	95%	250	0.9
Nova Southeastern University (FL)	925	49%	235	0.1
University of Texas Medical Branch–Galveston	920	94%	233	1.1
University of Washington	901	78%	221	2.6
University of Texas Health Science Center–San Antonio	900	92%	225	1.2
University of Texas Southwestern Medical Center–Dallas	896	88%	236	2.0
Western University of Health Sciences (CA)	874	61%	226	0.1
Des Moines University (IA)	869	25%	222	0.1
Ohio State University	855	85%	227	3.2
Case Western Reserve University (OH)	817	29%	198	2.5
Medical College of Wisconsin	817	42%	209	1.5
Georgetown University (DC)	804	0%	204	2.3
New York Medical College	792	29%	199	1.7
Yeshiva University (Einstein) (NY)	780	43%	191	3.6
West Virginia School of Osteopathic Medicine	778	28%	215	0.1
Virginia Commonwealth University	760	58%	204	1.6
Tufts University (MA)	748	36%	201	2.5
University of Alabama–Birmingham	747	86%	181	1.6
Temple University (PA)	741	50%	194	0.6
University of North Carolina–Chapel Hill	734	74%	164	1.9
University of Miami (Miller) (FL)	733	69%	194	1.9
University of California–Los Angeles (Geffen)	726	96%	188	3.4
University of Kansas Medical Center	723	87%	181	0.9
George Washington University (DC)	717	0%	187	1.1
St. Louis University	712	52%	182	0.8
Boston University	709	17%	181	1.6
Harvard University (MA)	705	N/A	165	11.7
Northwestern University (Feinberg) (IL)	700	27%	169	3.1
Univ. of Med. and Dent. of New Jersey–New Brunswick (Johnson)	700	99%	163	1.4
A.T. Still University of Health Sciences (Kirksville) (MO)	698	27%	177	0.1
Baylor College of Medicine (TX)	698	90%	189	2.8
Edward Via Virginia College of Osteopathic Medicine	689	35%	193	0.1

	Total enrollment	% in-state enrollment	Size of first-year class	Faculty-to-student ratio
University of North Texas Health Science Center	685	96%	190	0.6
New York University	683	45%	166	2.2
Uniformed Services Univ. of the Health Sciences (Hebert) (MD)	681	5%	171	0.5
Medical University of South Carolina	670	90%	174	1.6
University of Michigan–Ann Arbor	670	43%	170	2.6
University of Southern California (Keck)	670	73%	176	1.8
University of Toledo	666	90%	173	0.4
University of Oklahoma	653	92%	167	1.2
University of Maryland	645	82%	165	1.9
Columbia University (NY)	638	34%	155	3.0
University of Cincinnati	637	91%	169	2.4
University of Wisconsin–Madison	635	80%	169	1.7
SUNY–Syracuse	633	N/A	167	0.7
University of California–San Francisco	631	94%	149	3.0
University of Pennsylvania	622	38%	161	3.9
University of Tennessee Health Science Center	620	96%	170	1.2
University of Arkansas for Medical Sciences	618	88%	174	1.7
University of Colorado–Denver	614	81%	160	3.7
Michigan State University	610	73%	168	1.0
University of Louisville (KY)	610	79%	165	1.2
Texas Tech University Health Sciences Center	581	97%	149	1.0
University of Arizona	577	99%	166	1.8
University of Iowa (Carver)	576	68%	155	1.4
Loyola University Chicago (Stritch)	574	45%	145	N/A
University of Virginia	571	58%	145	1.6
University of Pittsburgh	569	31%	150	3.7
University at Buffalo–SUNY	565	100%	145	0.7
Rush University (IL)	547	79%	144	0.9
Touro University (CA)	540	N/A	135	0.1
Mount Sinai School of Medicine (NY)	534	35%	140	2.1
University of Florida	527	99%	135	2.3
Oregon Health and Science University	523	64%	124	3.3
Emory University (GA)	517	32%	137	3.9
University of California–San Diego	498	98%	126	2.1
Creighton University (NE)	495	11%	127	0.5
University of New England (ME)	495	19%	127	0.1
Stony Brook University (NY)	492	95%	124	1.1
University of Nebraska Medical Center	488	89%	130	1.3
University of South Florida	482	99%	120	2.0
Texas A&M Health Science Center	481	94%	157	2.0
Johns Hopkins University (MD)	480	27%	120	5.1
Wake Forest University (NC)	475	37%	121	2.0
Washington University in St. Louis	475	8%	122	3.5
Northeastern Ohio Universities College of Medicine	472	95%	118	0.7
Stanford University (CA)	470	39%	86	1.8
University of Massachusetts–Worcester	469	98%	125	2.3
University of Medicine and Dentistry of New Jersey–Stratford	463	95%	134	0.4
Louisiana State University Health Sciences Center–Shreveport	461	100%	118	0.8
Ohio University	461	95%	118	0.2
University of Vermont	458	30%	113	1.2
Florida State University	455	99%	117	0.3

	Total enrollment	% in-state enrollment	Size of first-year class	Faculty-to-student ratio
Vanderbilt University (TN)	451	18%	116	4.5
Eastern Virginia Medical School	448	63%	122	0.8
University of Rochester (NY)	440	48%	104	3.3
University of Kentucky	439	78%	121	1.8
West Virginia University	432	68%	112	1.5
University of Chicago (Pritzker)	430	30%	89	2.1
Meharry Medical College (TN)	425	32%	109	N/A
Duke University (NC)	421	11%	101	3.4
University of California–Irvine	420	100%	104	1.1
Wright State University (Boonshoft) (OH)	417	98%	106	0.9
Yale University (CT)	414	10%	99	2.8
Brown University (Alpert) (RI)	412	8%	96	1.7
University of California–Davis	407	100%	93	1.6
Cornell University (Weill) (NY)	406	45%	103	4.5
University of Utah	396	94%	82	3.0
University of Missouri	387	88%	97	1.4
Oklahoma State University	357	85%	98	0.3
University of Connecticut	346	91%	88	2.6
Dartmouth Medical School (NH)	343	9%	86	2.6
Morehouse School of Medicine (GA)	329	N/A	109	0.6
University of South Carolina	329	95%	86	0.7
University of New Mexico	323	100%	80	2.3
Mercer University (GA)	311	100%	94	1.0
East Carolina University (Brody) (NC)	306	100%	86	1.3
Pikeville College (KY)	302	50%	81	0.1
Southern Illinois University–Springfield	293	100%	78	1.2
University of Hawaii–Manoa (Burns)	254	87%	63	1.0
East Tennessee State University (Quillen)	253	92%	66	0.9
University of Nevada–Reno	245	92%	N/A	1.0
University of North Dakota	241	85%	66	0.6
University of South Dakota (Sanford)	214	94%	55	1.4

Which get the most research money? Which get the least?

How much research does the school support? One prime indicator is the amount of grant money the medical school and its affiliated hospitals are awarded by the National Institutes of Health, the federal research department devoted to medicine. Institutions with an asterisk have received grants to the medical school only.

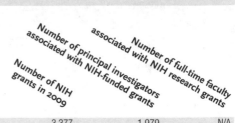

	Amount of NIH grants in 2009, in millions	Number of NIH grants in 2009	Number of principal investigators associated with NIH-funded grants	Number of full-time faculty associated with NIH research grants
Harvard University (MA)	$1,413.1	3,377	1,979	N/A
University of Washington	$713.2	1,399	806	1,307
University of Pennsylvania	$641.6	1,390	745	1,105
University of California–San Francisco	$471.2	960	694	923
University of California–Los Angeles (Geffen)	$468.7	1,412	800	2,016
Columbia University (NY)	$468.3	956	545	946
Johns Hopkins University (MD)	$444.7	943	733	1,339
University of Michigan–Ann Arbor	$443.4	1,088	602	887
University of Pittsburgh	$410.2	1,033	616	1,016
Duke University (NC)	$398.8	672	438	834
Yale University (CT)	$353.9	876	650	555
Washington University in St. Louis	$348.0	653	416	886
Case Western Reserve University (OH)	$329.2	690	415	624
Vanderbilt University (TN)	$315.1	955	486	1,128
University of California–San Diego	$301.1	645	310	477
Emory University (GA)	$282.6	658	368	722
Mount Sinai School of Medicine (NY)	$279.4	649	325	631
Cornell University (Weill) (NY)	$275.2	807	394	832
Stanford University*	$265.0	700	339	380
University of Chicago (Pritzker)	$261.1	839	417	671
University of North Carolina–Chapel Hill	$237.0	547	290	564
Northwestern University (Feinberg) (IL)	$232.6	966	422	464
Baylor College of Medicine (TX)	$221.4	605	386	554
Yeshiva University (Einstein) (NY)	$214.1	503	338	506
Boston University	$205.1	546	281	645
University of Colorado–Denver	$200.8	618	445	529
Ohio State University	$198.8	676	412	595
University of Alabama–Birmingham	$195.1	498	276	588
Oregon Health and Science University	$193.7	612	411	513
University of Cincinnati	$191.4	750	369	N/A
University of Texas Southwestern Medical Center–Dallas	$191.2	641	397	985
University of Wisconsin–Madison	$187.7	556	263	449
New York University	$183.7	472	283	368
University of Southern California (Keck)	$177.5	376	214	469
University of Iowa (Carver)	$166.0	406	235	369
Georgetown University (DC)	$165.4	350	227	347
University of Maryland*	$161.4	341	272	524
University of Rochester (NY)	$161.3	480	315	493
University of Minnesota	$153.8	458	264	264
Brown University (Alpert) (RI)	$148.7	409	252	274
University of Virginia	$145.8	428	245	913
Medical College of Wisconsin	$128.0	221	199	366
University of Massachusetts–Worcester*	$124.8	335	234	473
University of Miami (Miller) (FL)	$122.8	320	200	446
University of Texas Medical Branch–Galveston	$117.5	252	255	N/A

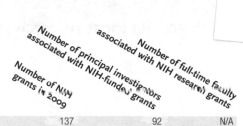

	Amount of NIH grants in 2009, in millions	Number of NIH grants in 2009	Number of principal investigators associated with NIH-funded grants	Number of full-time faculty associated with NIH research grants
University of South Florida	$113.6	137	92	N/A
Wake Forest University*	$110.7	304	172	197
Temple University (PA)	$108.2	326	204	324
Indiana University–Indianapolis*	$102.7	362	229	400
Tufts University (MA)	$101.5	340	179	248
University of Texas Health Science Center–San Antonio	$99.3	281	183	348
University of California–Davis	$94.9	304	176	396
Medical University of South Carolina	$94.2	269	167	366
University of California–Irvine	$91.9	308	135	232
Virginia Commonwealth University	$84.7	275	212	333
University of Utah	$84.4	279	153	N/A
Wayne State University*	$83.6	175	144	254
Dartmouth Medical School (NH)	$83.4	254	148	228
University of Florida	$81.4	418	248	237
Jefferson Medical College (PA)	$73.9	266	158	255
Stony Brook University (NY)	$68.1	319	206	247
University at Buffalo–SUNY	$65.4	299	162	228
University of Arizona	$65.1	164	120	166
University of Kentucky	$65.0	189	125	224
University of Kansas Medical Center	$63.8	209	141	211
University of Arkansas for Medical Sciences	$62.1	166	149	285
University of Texas Health Science Center–Houston*	$61.0	202	103	201
University of New Mexico	$56.6	206	99	194
University of Vermont*	$56.6	152	85	183
University of Connecticut	$54.8	149	149	149
University of Nebraska Medical Center*	$51.0	123	88	146
George Washington University (DC)	$49.0	N/A	110	N/A
Univ. of Med. and Dent. of New Jersey–New Brunswick (Johnson)	$44.8	117	103	203
Rush University (IL)	$44.2	133	96	243
University of Oklahoma*	$42.0	132	83	83
University of Louisville (KY)	$41.7	125	95	161
University of Tennessee Health Science Center*	$38.7	125	107	234
Uniformed Services University of the Health Sciences (Hebert) (MD)	$38.3	53	35	35
University of Hawaii–Manoa (Burns)	$31.2	100	38	80
Morehouse School of Medicine (GA)	$25.1	39	30	N/A
University of Missouri	$24.6	76	50	74
SUNY–Syracuse	$24.2	69	52	87
Michigan State University	$20.9	83	35	73
St. Louis University	$20.6	115	68	127
Drexel University*	$20.4	55	80	82
Loyola University Chicago (Stritch)	$19.4	80	65	86
New York Medical College	$19.4	53	33	95
University of North Texas Health Science Center	$18.9	101	42	56
West Virginia University	$17.8	62	49	98
Louisiana State University Health Sciences Center–Shreveport	$16.6	55	39	44
University of Nevada–Reno*	$16.6	N/A	N/A	N/A
Creighton University (NE)	$12.2	61	31	52
University of Toledo	$11.3	61	39	74
University of South Carolina	$11.3	63	34	51
University of South Dakota (Sanford)	$11.2	23	13	21
Southern Illinois University–Springfield*	$10.5	44	29	29
Texas A&M Health Science Center	$10.4	73	46	49
Wright State University (Boonshoft) (OH)	$7.9	27	19	N/A
Texas Tech University Health Sciences Center	$7.2	28	19	30
Eastern Virginia Medical School*	$6.7	56	36	22

Which get the most research money? Which get the least?

	Amount of NIH grants in 2009, in millions	Number of NIH grants in 2009	Number of principal investigators associated with NIH-funded grants	Number of full-time faculty associated with NIH research grants
East Carolina University (Brody) (NC)	$6.0	28	21	41
University of North Dakota	$5.6	20	12	32
Michigan State University	$5.1	37	25	35
East Tennessee State University (Quillen)*	$4.9	22	15	21
Florida State University	$4.7	9	N/A	N/A
Univ. of Med. and Dent. of New Jersey–Stratford	$3.2	14	11	18
Northeastern Ohio Universities College of Medicine	$3.0	11	12	11
Mercer University (GA)	$2.3	5	13	N/A
Ohio University	$.9	3	11	15
Western University of Health Sciences (CA)	$.7	3	3	3
Nova Southeastern University (FL)	$.6	2	1	3
Oklahoma State University	$.6	9	9	9
A.T. Still University of Health Sciences (Kirksville) (MO)	$.4	2	2	4
Edward Via Virginia College of Osteopathic Medicine	$.3	3	5	10
Des Moines University (IA)	$.1	1	2	2
Lake Erie College of Osteopathic Medicine (PA)	$.0	0	0	0
University of New England (ME)	$.0	0	0	0
West Virginia School of Osteopathic Medicine	$.0	0	0	0

How much should you expect to borrow? The average medical school grads who take out loans start their residencies owing more than $156,000—and that's not counting undergraduate loans. This table shows the average amount of debt incurred by borrowers in the Class of 2009, from highest to lowest.

School	Average medical school debt
University of New England (ME)	$205,014
Creighton University (NE)	$194,548
Tufts University (MA)	$192,162
Western University of Health Sciences (CA)	$191,254
George Washington University (DC)	$188,200
Drexel University (PA)	$182,921
New York Medical College	$181,000
West Virginia School of Osteopathic Medicine	$180,630
A.T. Still University of Health Sciences (Kirksville) (MO)	$176,958
Temple University (PA)	$176,184
University of Chicago (Pritzker)	$175,809
University of Minnesota	$174,964
St. Louis University	$173,346
Michigan State University	$172,697
Georgetown University (DC)	$172,240
Michigan State University	$171,752
University of Southern California (Keck)	$170,870
Boston University	$170,059
Oregon Health and Science University	$170,000
Morehouse School of Medicine (GA)	$168,449
Edward Via Virginia College of Osteopathic Medicine	$165,833
Mercer University (GA)	$165,823
Des Moines University (IA)	$165,220
Medical University of South Carolina	$163,794
Rush University (IL)	$163,472
Indiana University–Indianapolis	$162,964
Jefferson Medical College (PA)	$162,885
Nova Southeastern University (FL)	$162,148
Loyola University Chicago (Stritch)	$161,976
Wright State University (Boonshoft) (OH)	$160,750
Pikeville College (KY)	$158,470
University of Vermont	$158,313
Lake Erie College of Osteopathic Medicine (PA)	$158,000
Touro University (CA)	$156,000
University of Miami (Miller) (FL)	$155,420
Medical College of Wisconsin	$155,390
Virginia Commonwealth University	$153,147
Northwestern University (Feinberg) (IL)	$151,978
Ohio University	$150,868
Wake Forest University (NC)	$149,793
Northeastern Ohio Universities College of Medicine	$148,162
Florida State University	$147,597
University at Buffalo–SUNY	$147,563
Emory University (GA)	$146,824

School	Average medical school debt
Oklahoma State University	$146,359
University of Louisville (KY)	$144,399
Eastern Virginia Medical School	$143,605
University of Rochester (NY)	$142,554
New York University	$142,413
Stony Brook University (NY)	$142,323
West Virginia University	$141,825
Wayne State University (MI)	$141,556
University of Toledo	$141,250
University of Pittsburgh	$141,018
Ohio State University	$140,772
University of Cincinnati	$140,174
University of Colorado–Denver	$138,352
University of Maryland	$138,252
Univ. of Med. and Dent. of NJ–Stratford	$138,227
University of North Dakota	$138,054
University of Oklahoma	$137,543
Case Western Reserve University (OH)	$137,342
University of Utah	$137,289
University of Kentucky	$135,835
Yeshiva University (Einstein) (NY)	$135,350
Mount Sinai School of Medicine (NY)	$133,186
Univ. of Med. and Dent. of NJ–New Brunswick (Johnson)	$132,911
University of Missouri	$131,948
SUNY–Syracuse	$130,894
University of Wisconsin–Madison	$130,507
University of Nebraska Medical Center	$128,337
University of South Dakota (Sanford)	$127,554
Brown University (Alpert) (RI)	$127,408
Southern Illinois University–Springfield	$126,472
Texas Tech University Health Sciences Center	$125,883
University of South Carolina	$125,232
University of Arkansas for Medical Sciences	$124,841
University of Iowa (Carver)	$124,440
Yale University (CT)	$124,135
University of Kansas Medical Center	$123,309
University of Texas Medical Branch–Galveston	$122,556
University of Virginia	$122,369
University of Pennsylvania	$121,389
Vanderbilt University (TN)	$120,000
University of New Mexico	$119,564
Louisiana State Univ. Health Sciences Center–Shreveport	$119,207
University of South Florida	$119,020
University of California–Davis	$118,826

Whose graduates have the most debt? The least?

	Average medical school debt
University of Texas Health Science Center–San Antonio	$118,321
University of Connecticut	$117,410
University of Massachusetts–Worcester	$117,332
University of Texas Health Science Center–Houston	$116,197
Cornell University (Weill) (NY)	$116,024
East Tennessee State University (Quillen)	$115,594
University of North Texas Health Science Center	$114,454
Columbia University (NY)	$113,146
University of California–Irvine	$112,793
University of Washington	$112,530
University of Arizona	$111,894
University of Michigan–Ann Arbor	$111,139
University of Tennessee Health Science Center	$110,041
Dartmouth Medical School (NH)	$109,688
University of Nevada–Reno	$108,224
University of Florida	$107,589

	Average medical school debt
University of California–Los Angeles (Geffen)	$107,081
Texas A&M Health Science Center	$105,144
Harvard University (MA)	$103,663
Duke University (NC)	$103,403
University of Alabama–Birmingham	$101,682
University of California–San Francisco	$101,333
Washington University in St. Louis	$101,191
University of North Carolina–Chapel Hill	$100,090
University of California–San Diego	$98,773
Johns Hopkins University (MD)	$94,717
University of Texas Southwestern Medical Center–Dallas	$94,000
Baylor College of Medicine (TX)	$91,402
Stanford University (CA)	$86,137
East Carolina University (Brody) (NC)	$85,177
University of Hawaii–Manoa (Burns)	$79,872
Uniformed Services Univ. of the Health Sciences (Hebert) (MD)	$0

If you're looking for a medical school culture that is welcoming to students from a wealth of backgrounds, one way to judge is by the percentage of minority students already there.

	% minority	American Indian	Asian-American	Black	Hispanic	White	International	Men	Women
Morehouse School of Medicine (GA)	95%	0.3%	14.6%	78.7%	1.5%	1.5%	2.7%	31%	69%
Meharry Medical College (TN)	94%	0.9%	7.3%	82.1%	4.0%	5.6%	0.0%	41%	59%
University of Hawaii–Manoa (Burns)	71%	0.8%	83.5%	0.0%	0.4%	13.8%	1.6%	47%	53%
Baylor College of Medicine (TX)	59%	1.7%	36.5%	5.4%	15.5%	40.7%	0.1%	49%	51%
University of California–Los Angeles (Geffen)	59%	0.7%	33.9%	9.5%	14.7%	32.1%	0.1%	52%	48%
Stanford University (CA)	57%	0.9%	36.0%	3.6%	13.2%	41.9%	4.5%	54%	46%
University of California–Davis	56%	0.2%	38.3%	4.2%	10.6%	46.4%	0.0%	41%	59%
University of California–San Francisco	55%	2.1%	29.6%	7.9%	15.2%	36.3%	0.0%	45%	55%
Harvard University (MA)	53%	0.9%	29.8%	10.1%	8.2%	38.0%	6.4%	51%	49%
University of Texas Southwestern Medical Center–Dallas	53%	0.1%	32.7%	5.5%	14.1%	40.4%	1.0%	54%	46%
University of California–Irvine	51%	0.2%	36.2%	2.1%	12.6%	47.4%	0.0%	52%	48%
University of Medicine and Dentistry of New Jersey–Stratford	51%	0.0%	22.0%	14.9%	7.1%	48.6%	0.0%	44%	56%
Texas A&M Health Science Center	48%	0.6%	32.0%	4.0%	11.4%	48.6%	1.0%	53%	47%
Duke University (NC)	48%	1.4%	22.1%	18.5%	2.6%	44.9%	3.8%	51%	49%
Northwestern University (Feinberg) (IL)	46%	0.9%	34.6%	5.0%	5.9%	44.0%	3.7%	52%	48%
Stony Brook University (NY)	46%	0.8%	31.5%	7.7%	5.5%	54.1%	0.4%	53%	47%
Johns Hopkins University (MD)	46%	0.6%	33.8%	7.9%	3.3%	51.0%	3.3%	52%	48%
University of California–San Diego	45%	1.6%	34.5%	1.6%	7.2%	43.6%	0.0%	52%	48%
Boston University	45%	0.3%	27.4%	9.6%	7.6%	40.5%	4.7%	47%	53%
Western University of Health Sciences (CA)	45%	0.2%	40.5%	0.7%	3.0%	46.2%	1.8%	53%	47%
University of North Texas Health Science Center	45%	0.6%	31.7%	2.6%	9.6%	53.6%	0.7%	54%	46%
Drexel University (PA)	44%	0.6%	34.8%	4.7%	4.0%	49.4%	0.0%	51%	49%
Yale University (CT)	44%	0.7%	26.8%	9.4%	6.8%	43.7%	9.4%	51%	49%
Brown University (Alpert) (RI)	44%	0.5%	26.5%	8.3%	8.3%	43.0%	1.7%	47%	53%
Univ. of Med. and Dent. of New Jersey–New Brunswick (Johnson)	44%	0.1%	30.7%	8.7%	4.0%	46.6%	0.0%	45%	55%
University of Pittsburgh	43%	0.0%	27.4%	8.6%	5.3%	53.1%	0.0%	55%	45%
University of Texas Medical Branch–Galveston	43%	0.5%	15.9%	10.0%	16.6%	52.2%	0.8%	54%	46%
Cornell University (Weill) (NY)	43%	1.7%	19.5%	10.6%	11.1%	52.7%	1.5%	53%	47%
University of Southern California (Keck)	41%	0.6%	23.9%	4.0%	12.8%	47.2%	1.9%	52%	48%
University of Miami (Miller) (FL)	41%	0.3%	21.0%	7.2%	12.7%	51.3%	0.0%	55%	45%
Virginia Commonwealth University	41%	0.9%	31.4%	5.9%	2.4%	57.6%	0.4%	53%	47%
Case Western Reserve University (OH)	41%	0.5%	27.7%	7.7%	2.8%	49.9%	5.0%	55%	45%
University of South Florida	41%	0.6%	24.5%	5.6%	10.2%	54.8%	0.0%	49%	51%
University of Texas Health Science Center–San Antonio	40%	0.4%	16.9%	5.1%	17.6%	55.2%	0.1%	48%	52%
Mount Sinai School of Medicine (NY)	39%	0.4%	24.3%	7.3%	9.4%	50.2%	4.5%	48%	52%
University of New Mexico	39%	4.6%	5.0%	1.5%	27.6%	53.6%	0.0%	44%	56%
Washington University in St. Louis	39%	0.6%	28.4%	5.5%	4.4%	49.1%	1.5%	51%	49%
Northeastern Ohio Universities College of Medicine	39%	0.0%	33.3%	2.3%	3.2%	57.0%	0.0%	51%	49%
Texas Tech University Health Sciences Center	38%	0.9%	25.1%	2.6%	9.6%	58.2%	0.0%	57%	43%
Columbia University (NY)	38%	0.3%	16.5%	10.0%	7.8%	57.7%	4.4%	52%	48%
Temple University (PA)	37%	0.9%	20.5%	7.3%	8.6%	54.9%	0.0%	53%	47%
New York Medical College	37%	0.1%	33.0%	3.3%	1.0%	53.3%	0.6%	48%	52%
George Washington University (DC)	37%	0.1%	24.0%	11.9%	1.0%	48.7%	2.5%	41%	59%
University of Chicago (Pritzker)	37%	0.5%	21.4%	8.6%	6.3%	50.7%	3.0%	51%	49%
New York University	37%	0.6%	26.4%	3.1%	6.6%	57.4%	0.3%	51%	49%
University of Michigan–Ann Arbor	37%	0.7%	25.1%	5.4%	5.4%	55.8%	0.0%	48%	52%
University of Maryland	36%	0.0%	22.6%	11.2%	2.5%	55.8%	0.2%	42%	58%

Which schools have the most minority students? The fewest?

	% minority	American Indian	Asian	Black	Hispanic	White	International	Men	Women
Jefferson Medical College (PA)	36%	0.2%	23.6%	2.1%	4.8%	63.9%	5.5%	50%	50%
Nova Southeastern University (FL)	36%	0.4%	22.5%	3.2%	9.7%	57.7%	1.7%	54%	46%
University of Rochester (NY)	35%	0.5%	19.1%	10.9%	4.3%	65.2%	0.0%	51%	49%
University at Buffalo–SUNY	34%	0.7%	27.3%	3.2%	0.4%	66.0%	0.0%	50%	50%
East Carolina University (Brody) (NC)	33%	1.3%	10.8%	14.1%	3.6%	66.7%	0.0%	50%	50%
SUNY–Syracuse	33%	0.3%	18.9%	12.5%	0.8%	61.1%	6.3%	50%	50%
Florida State University	33%	0.9%	13.2%	10.1%	8.8%	64.4%	0.0%	43%	57%
University of Florida	32%	0.9%	19.7%	4.6%	7.2%	63.0%	0.0%	52%	48%
University of Connecticut	32%	1.2%	15.0%	11.3%	4.9%	63.9%	1.4%	44%	56%
Tufts University (MA)	32%	0.1%	23.9%	3.3%	4.8%	62.8%	0.7%	55%	45%
University of Pennsylvania	32%	0.6%	16.4%	7.6%	7.6%	59.0%	1.1%	51%	49%
University of Cincinnati	32%	0.0%	23.7%	6.4%	1.9%	68.0%	0.0%	59%	41%
University of Texas Health Science Center–Houston	32%	0.3%	12.6%	5.0%	14.1%	64.1%	0.3%	58%	42%
Michigan State University	32%	1.1%	17.9%	8.5%	4.4%	65.4%	0.8%	49%	51%
University of Arizona	32%	1.2%	17.7%	2.8%	10.1%	68.3%	0.0%	44%	56%
St. Louis University	31%	0.1%	25.3%	2.8%	1.5%	60.8%	2.1%	60%	40%
Ohio State University	31%	0.0%	18.2%	6.3%	5.0%	69.0%	0.1%	57%	43%
University of Virginia	31%	N/A	N/A	N/A	N/A	N/A	N/A	53%	47%
University of Nevada–Reno	31%	N/A	N/A	N/A	N/A	N/A	N/A	51%	49%
Georgetown University (DC)	30%	0.2%	17.8%	7.1%	2.7%	62.8%	1.2%	51%	49%
Wayne State University (MI)	30%	0.3%	18.8%	9.7%	1.6%	55.8%	3.8%	53%	47%
Rush University (IL)	30%	0.7%	23.0%	2.9%	3.3%	68.9%	0.0%	50%	50%
Emory University (GA)	30%	0.2%	17.6%	8.1%	3.7%	62.7%	2.5%	47%	53%
Wake Forest University (NC)	28%	1.1%	13.5%	10.1%	2.9%	58.9%	4.2%	54%	46%
Wright State University (Boonshoft) (OH)	27%	0.2%	16.1%	7.0%	1.4%	72.7%	0.0%	46%	54%
Southern Illinois University–Springfield	27%	1.0%	9.6%	13.3%	3.4%	72.7%	0.0%	50%	50%
Medical College of Wisconsin	27%	0.7%	17.1%	4.5%	4.8%	65.5%	0.6%	52%	48%
Vanderbilt University (TN)	27%	0.4%	17.1%	8.9%	0.7%	57.0%	6.4%	53%	47%
Oklahoma State University	27%	9.5%	7.0%	4.8%	5.6%	71.7%	0.0%	52%	48%
University of North Carolina–Chapel Hill	27%	N/A	N/A	N/A	N/A	N/A	N/A	49%	51%
University of Toledo	27%	0.5%	19.7%	4.7%	2.0%	64.7%	0.2%	56%	44%
Edward Via Virginia College of Osteopathic Medicine	26%	1.2%	11.9%	8.1%	5.2%	67.2%	0.3%	49%	51%
Lake Erie College of Osteopathic Medicine (PA)	26%	0.5%	17.4%	1.5%	3.4%	74.7%	0.1%	54%	46%
Ohio University	25%	1.3%	9.1%	10.6%	4.3%	74.6%	0.0%	47%	53%
Dartmouth Medical School (NH)	25%	0.9%	18.7%	1.5%	4.1%	57.1%	11.7%	50%	50%
University of Wisconsin–Madison	25%	0.0%	17.0%	4.9%	2.8%	75.3%	0.0%	47%	53%
University of Vermont	24%	0.0%	14.2%	1.7%	6.3%	72.9%	2.6%	46%	54%
Medical University of South Carolina	24%	1.0%	7.2%	13.3%	2.7%	70.0%	1.0%	58%	42%
Yeshiva University (Einstein) (NY)	24%	0.1%	15.4%	3.8%	3.1%	40.1%	2.2%	49%	51%
Indiana University–Indianapolis	24%	0.8%	11.9%	5.0%	4.7%	70.0%	1.8%	57%	43%
University of Washington	24%	1.6%	15.8%	2.4%	3.8%	66.4%	0.0%	46%	54%
Oregon Health and Science University	23%	1.7%	18.9%	1.5%	1.1%	76.7%	0.0%	47%	53%
Eastern Virginia Medical School	23%	N/A	N/A	N/A	N/A	N/A	N/A	55%	45%
University of Alabama–Birmingham	23%	0.8%	13.9%	6.8%	1.2%	76.2%	0.0%	59%	41%
University of Tennessee Health Science Center	22%	0.2%	10.0%	10.2%	1.8%	69.7%	0.0%	60%	40%
Loyola University Chicago (Stritch)	22%	0.0%	12.2%	4.5%	4.9%	75.1%	0.0%	48%	52%
University of Massachusetts–Worcester	22%	0.0%	14.7%	4.9%	1.9%	78.5%	0.0%	45%	55%
University of Minnesota	21%	4.2%	9.5%	2.3%	3.5%	78.9%	1.7%	51%	49%
University of Utah	21%	0.3%	14.9%	0.8%	4.8%	74.7%	0.0%	66%	34%
University of Iowa (Carver)	20%	0.7%	10.6%	4.9%	4.7%	78.8%	0.0%	50%	50%
University of Oklahoma	20%	6.1%	12.7%	0.9%	0.2%	59.3%	0.0%	61%	39%

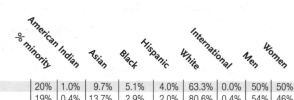

	% minority	American Indian	Asian	Black	Hispanic	White	International	Men	Women
University of Kansas Medical Center	20%	1.0%	9.7%	5.1%	4.0%	63.3%	0.0%	50%	50%
Michigan State University	19%	0.4%	13.7%	2.9%	2.0%	80.6%	0.4%	54%	46%
University of Arkansas for Medical Sciences	19%	0.2%	11.5%	5.5%	2.3%	80.6%	0.0%	59%	41%
Uniformed Services Univ. of the Health Sciences (Hebert) (MD)	19%	0.7%	11.9%	1.5%	5.0%	73.7%	0.0%	71%	29%
West Virginia School of Osteopathic Medicine	19%	0.4%	14.1%	1.4%	3.1%	76.0%	0.0%	53%	47%
University of Louisville (KY)	19%	0.2%	10.5%	7.2%	1.1%	76.6%	0.0%	56%	44%
Creighton University (NE)	19%	1.0%	13.7%	3.2%	0.8%	73.7%	0.4%	52%	48%
University of South Carolina	19%	0.3%	11.9%	5.2%	1.2%	81.5%	0.0%	53%	47%
University of Missouri	18%	1.3%	11.1%	4.4%	1.3%	77.3%	0.0%	50%	50%
University of Kentucky	18%	0.0%	10.9%	4.1%	0.5%	75.9%	3.6%	59%	41%
University of Colorado–Denver	18%	1.0%	9.3%	1.8%	5.2%	79.3%	0.3%	52%	48%
West Virginia University	16%	0.0%	14.1%	0.7%	1.4%	83.8%	0.0%	61%	39%
A.T. Still University of Health Sciences (Kirksville) (MO)	15%	0.0%	10.2%	1.3%	2.0%	79.2%	1.6%	61%	39%
Mercer University (GA)	15%	0.0%	10.6%	2.6%	1.0%	84.9%	0.0%	54%	46%
East Tennessee State University (Quillen)	14%	N/A	8.7%	5.1%	0.4%	85.8%	N/A	53%	47%
University of North Dakota	13%	9.5%	2.9%	0.0%	0.8%	86.7%	0.0%	47%	53%
Louisiana State University Health Sciences Center–Shreveport	12%	0.2%	7.2%	3.9%	1.1%	86.8%	0.0%	57%	43%
University of Nebraska Medical Center	11%	0.4%	4.9%	2.5%	0.4%	91.6%	0.2%	58%	42%
Des Moines University (IA)	10%	0.1%	8.6%	0.5%	1.8%	81.1%	1.8%	52%	48%
University of New England (ME)	8%	0.0%	6.9%	0.8%	0.6%	80.6%	0.4%	47%	53%
Pikeville College (KY)	6%	0.3%	6.3%	2.3%	1.3%	85.8%	1.0%	56%	44%
University of South Dakota (Sanford)	3%	2.8%	2.8%	0.5%	0.5%	93.0%	0.0%	54%	46%

hich schools turn out the most primary care residents? The fewest?

If you are interested in family practice, general pediatrics, or general internal medicine, you probably want to consider schools that send most of their graduates on to primary care residency programs.

	Average % 2007-2009 graduates entering primary care residencies		Average % 2007-2009 graduates entering primary care residencies
Michigan State University	80.5%	University of Kentucky	43.0%
West Virginia School of Osteopathic Medicine	70.3%	Baylor College of Medicine (TX)	42.6%
University of North Texas Health Science Center	68.6%	University of Kansas Medical Center	42.4%
Morehouse School of Medicine (GA)	65.0%	Univ. of Med. and Dent. of NJ–New Brunswick (Johnson)	42.3%
Pikeville College (KY)	64.0%	Georgetown University (DC)	42.0%
University of New England (ME)	63.0%	Loyola University Chicago (Stritch)	42.0%
Lake Erie College of Osteopathic Medicine (PA)	61.0%	Northeastern Ohio Universities College of Medicine	42.0%
University of Nebraska Medical Center	60.0%	University of California–San Diego	42.0%
University of Vermont	58.0%	University of Minnesota	42.0%
Touro University (CA)	56.0%	University of Pennsylvania	42.0%
Edward Via Virginia College of Osteopathic Medicine	55.0%	University of North Dakota	41.7%
University of Massachusetts–Worcester	54.9%	University of Utah	41.6%
East Carolina University (Brody) (NC)	52.3%	Michigan State University	41.4%
University of North Carolina–Chapel Hill	51.3%	University of Louisville (KY)	41.3%
A.T. Still University of Health Sciences (Kirksville) (MO)	51.0%	Rush University (IL)	41.0%
East Tennessee State University (Quillen)	50.9%	Temple University (PA)	41.0%
Texas Tech University Health Sciences Center	50.3%	University of Arizona	41.0%
University of Arkansas for Medical Sciences	50.3%	University of Iowa (Carver)	41.0%
Nova Southeastern University (FL)	50.0%	University of Texas Southwestern Medical Center–Dallas	41.0%
University of Hawaii–Manoa (Burns)	50.0%	University of New Mexico	40.9%
Western University of Health Sciences (CA)	50.0%	St. Louis University	40.7%
West Virginia University	50.0%	Emory University (GA)	40.2%
Univ. of Med. and Dent. of NJ–Stratford	49.5%	University of South Carolina	40.2%
Des Moines University (IA)	48.0%	Medical University of South Carolina	40.1%
Eastern Virginia Medical School	47.0%	Meharry Medical College (TN)	40.0%
Ohio University	47.0%	Ohio State University	40.0%
University of Texas Health Science Center–San Antonio	47.0%	University of California–Los Angeles (Geffen)	40.0%
Oregon Health and Science University	46.6%	University of Maryland	39.4%
University of Missouri	46.3%	New York University	39.3%
University of Washington	46.0%	University of Alabama–Birmingham	39.1%
Wake Forest University (NC)	46.0%	University of California–San Francisco	39.1%
Wright State University (Boonshoft) (OH)	46.0%	Indiana University–Indianapolis	39.0%
Florida State University	45.8%	University of Tennessee Health Science Center	39.0%
Oklahoma State University	45.0%	Mercer University (GA)	38.6%
Tufts University (MA)	45.0%	University of Oklahoma	38.5%
University of Connecticut	45.0%	University of Pittsburgh	38.5%
Yeshiva University (Einstein) (NY)	45.0%	University of Wisconsin–Madison	38.4%
Creighton University (NE)	44.0%	Jefferson Medical College (PA)	38.3%
Texas A&M Health Science Center	44.0%	Louisiana State Univ. Health Sciences Center–Shreveport	38.2%
University of Colorado–Denver	44.0%	University of California–Irvine	38.0%
University of California–Davis	43.9%	New York Medical College	37.9%
George Washington University (DC)	43.0%	University of Texas Medical Branch–Galveston	37.8%
Stony Brook University (NY)	43.0%	University of Miami (Miller) (FL)	37.7%
University of Chicago (Pritzker)	43.0%	Southern Illinois University–Springfield	37.6%

	Average % 2007-2009 graduates entering primary care residencies		Average % 2007-2009 graduates entering primary care residencies
Brown University (Alpert) (RI)	37.3%	Johns Hopkins University (MD)	33.2%
Harvard University (MA)	37.3%	Duke University (NC)	33.0%
University of Toledo	37.2%	Dartmouth Medical School (NH)	32.6%
University of South Dakota (Sanford)	36.9%	Mount Sinai School of Medicine (NY)	32.6%
Virginia Commonwealth University	36.4%	Wayne State University (MI)	32.0%
Drexel University (PA)	36.3%	Case Western Reserve University (OH)	31.0%
University of Cincinnati	36.3%	University of Southern California (Keck)	31.0%
Northwestern University (Feinberg) (IL)	36.2%	Vanderbilt University (TN)	30.7%
Boston University	36.0%	Stanford University (CA)	30.6%
University of South Florida	36.0%	Cornell University (Weill) (NY)	30.0%
University of Rochester (NY)	35.5%	Uniformed Services Univ. of the Health Sciences (Hebert) (MD)	30.0%
University of Michigan–Ann Arbor	35.2%	University of Texas Health Science Center–Houston	30.0%
SUNY–Syracuse	35.0%	University at Buffalo–SUNY	28.4%
University of Florida	35.0%	Columbia University (NY)	28.0%
University of Virginia	35.0%	Yale University (CT)	21.7%
Medical College of Wisconsin	34.0%	University of Nevada–Reno	19.3%
Washington University in St. Louis	33.3%		

Which schools' grads are most likely to stay in state? The least likely?

If you want to stay close to where you study after you graduate, you may want to consider schools whose new doctors choose residencies in-state. Some states also offer incentives to graduates who stay and practice in underserved areas. Doctors in Massachusetts, for instance, can receive as much as $20,000 a year in debt payments if they work at least two years in a Massachusetts community health center.

	Average % 2008-2009 graduates accepting in-state residencies			Average % 2008-2009 graduates accepting in-state residencies
Michigan State University	83%		University of Alabama–Birmingham	45%
University of California–Davis	78%		University of Connecticut	44%
University of California–San Diego	75%		Indiana University–Indianapolis	44%
University of California–Los Angeles (Geffen)	75%		University of Missouri	44%
Ohio University	73%		Louisiana State Univ. Health Sciences Center–Shreveport	44%
University of California–Irvine	72%		Northwestern University (Feinberg) (IL)	44%
University of Southern California (Keck)	69%		University of Tennessee Health Science Center	43%
Stony Brook University (NY)	65%		Ohio State University	42%
University of California–San Francisco	65%		Western University of Health Sciences (CA)	42%
University of North Texas Health Science Center	61%		University of North Carolina–Chapel Hill	42%
Stanford University (CA)	60%		University of Colorado–Denver	42%
Texas Tech University Health Sciences Center	60%		University of Arizona	40%
Wayne State University (MI)	60%		University of Nebraska Medical Center	40%
Northeastern Ohio Universities College of Medicine	59%		West Virginia University	40%
University of Texas Health Science Center–Houston	58%		Univ. of Med. and Dent. of NJ–Stratford	40%
Mount Sinai School of Medicine (NY)	56%		University of Oklahoma	40%
Yeshiva University (Einstein) (NY)	56%		University of South Carolina	39%
University of Massachusetts–Worcester	56%		University of Louisville (KY)	39%
New York University	55%		Medical University of South Carolina	38%
Oklahoma State University	55%		University of Pennsylvania	38%
SUNY–Syracuse	54%		Michigan State University	38%
University of Arkansas for Medical Sciences	54%		Jefferson Medical College (PA)	38%
University of Texas Medical Branch–Galveston	54%		Johns Hopkins University (MD)	37%
Texas A&M Health Science Center	53%		University of Miami (Miller) (FL)	37%
University of Texas Southwestern Medical Center–Dallas	52%		University of Chicago (Pritzker)	37%
University at Buffalo–SUNY	52%		University of Kentucky	37%
University of New Mexico	49%		East Carolina University (Brody) (NC)	36%
Wright State University (Boonshoft) (OH)	49%		University of Washington	36%
University of South Florida	49%		University of Michigan–Ann Arbor	36%
University of Minnesota	48%		Emory University (GA)	35%
New York Medical College	48%		University of Pittsburgh	35%
Baylor College of Medicine (TX)	47%		Drexel University (PA)	35%
Columbia University (NY)	47%		Southern Illinois University–Springfield	34%
Touro University (CA)	47%		Oregon Health and Science University	34%
Florida State University	47%		Wake Forest University (NC)	34%
Rush University (IL)	46%		University of Maryland	33%
University of Cincinnati	46%		University of Toledo	33%
University of Texas Health Science Center–San Antonio	46%		University of Wisconsin–Madison	33%
Cornell University (Weill) (NY)	45%		Boston University	33%
Harvard University (MA)	45%		Eastern Virginia Medical School	33%
Temple University (PA)	45%		Medical College of Wisconsin	33%

	Average % 2008-2009 graduates accepting in-state residencies			Average % 2008-2009 graduates accepting in-state residencies
University of Kansas Medical Center	33%	West Virginia School of Osteopathic Medicine	25%
Mercer University (GA)	33%	University of South Dakota (Sanford)	24%
Duke University (NC)	32%	University of North Dakota	23%
Lake Erie College of Osteopathic Medicine (PA)	32%	Nova Southeastern University (FL)	22%
East Tennessee State University (Quillen)	32%	A.T. Still University of Health Sciences (Kirksville) (MO)	20%
Tufts University (MA)	31%	Yale University (CT)	20%
University of Hawaii–Manoa (Burns)	31%	Creighton University (NE)	19%
Virginia Commonwealth University	31%	University of Vermont	19%
Georgetown University (DC)	30%	Edward Via Virginia College of Osteopathic Medicine	18%
Morehouse School of Medicine (GA)	30%	George Washington University (DC)	17%
Vanderbilt University (TN)	29%	University of New England (ME)	16%
University of Rochester (NY)	28%	Des Moines University (IA)	16%
Washington University in St. Louis	28%	University of Virginia	16%
Univ. of Med. and Dent. of NJ–New Brunswick (Johnson)	27%	Pikeville College (KY)	15%
St. Louis University	27%	Brown University (Alpert) (RI)	15%
University of Florida	25%	Uniformed Services Univ. of the Health Sciences (Hebert) (MD)	13%
University of Utah	25%	Dartmouth Medical School (NH)	10%
Case Western Reserve University (OH)	25%	University of Nevada–Reno	9%
University of Iowa (Carver)	25%		

The *U.S. News & World Report*

Ultimate Medical School Directory

How to use the directory

In the following pages, you'll find in-depth profiles of medical schools fully accredited by the Liaison Committee on Medical Education, plus schools that offer the Doctor of Osteopathy degree accredited by the American Osteopathic Association. The schools are listed alphabetically in two sections: those conferring the M.D. degree, followed by schools of osteopathy.

The data were collected by *U.S. News* from the schools during late 2009 and early 2010. If a medical school did not supply the data requested, or if the data point does not apply to the school, you'll see an N/A, for "not available." Schools that did not return the *U.S. News* questionnaire are listed at the end of the directory.

You may also want to consult the online version of the directory at www.usnews.com, which allows you to do a customized search of our database.

ESSENTIAL STATS: In addition to the medical school's address and the year the school was founded, you'll find the following key facts and figures here:

Tuition: for the 2009-2010 academic year.

Enrollment: full-time students during the 2009-2010 academic year.

Specialty ranking: the school's 2011 *U.S. News* ranking in various specialty areas, where applicable (the possible areas are women's health, geriatrics, internal medicine, AIDS, drug/alcohol abuse, rural medicine, pediatrics, and family medicine).

GPA and MCAT: The undergraduate grade point averages and Medical College Admission Test (MCAT) scores shown are for the fall 2009

entering class. The MCAT score is the average of the scores on the verbal, physical sciences, and biological sciences portions of the test.

Acceptance rate: percentage of applicants accepted for the fall 2009 entering class.

U.S. News ranking: A school's overall rank indicates where it sits among its peers in the 2011 ranking of medical schools published by *U.S. News* (at www.usnews.com) and in its annual guide *America's Best Graduate Schools*. Schools are ranked separately in research and primary care, and the schools in the top 60 are ranked numerically. Schools below the top 60 are listed as "unranked."

ADMISSIONS:

Application website: Many medical schools allow you to complete and submit an application online.

Applicants and acceptees: The acceptance rates for the fall 2009 entering class are broken down by in-state, out-of-state, minority, and international students. The admissions statistics—numbers of applicants and of people interviewed and accepted—are also for the fall 2009 entering class.

Profile of admitted students: Besides the GPA and MCAT scores of fall 2009 entrants, we list the proportion majoring in biological sciences, physical sciences, non-sciences, other health professions, and other disciplines. The percentage who took time off between college and medical school is also shown.

Admission dates and details: We note whether the university uses the American Medical College

Application Service (AMCAS), and whether it asks for a second, school-specific application form. Besides key deadlines for applicants to the 2011-2012 first-year class, you'll find information on whether the school has an Early Decision Plan (EDP), whether a personal interview is required for admission, whether admission can be deferred, and what undergraduate coursework is required.

Admissions policy: The text describing admissions policies was written by the schools. *U.S. News* edited the information for style but did not verify it.

FINANCIAL AID:

Tuition and other expenses: for the 2009-2010 academic year. For public schools, we list both in-state and out-of-state tuition.

Financial aid profile: The data on financial aid awards and the percentage of students receiving grants, loans, and scholarships are for the 2009-2010 academic year. The average debt burden of borrowers who graduated in 2008 does not include their undergraduate debt.

STUDENT BODY STATS: What will your classmates be like? This section supplies the breakdown of male and female students, the in-state enrollments, and the ethnic makeup of the student body during the 2009-2010 academic year (which may not add up to 100 percent due to rounding).

ACADEMIC PROGRAMS: Besides information on areas of specialization, you can look here for a sense of how early in your training you'll have contact with patients.

Joint degrees awarded: Some medical students pursue a second degree in another university department to marry their interests or gain an edge in the job market. One common joint degree, the M.D./M.B.A., combines medicine and business. Another, for those interested in research, is the M.D./Ph.D. degree. Other degree combos include the M.D./J.D. (law) and the M.D./M.P.H. (public health).

Research profile: An indicator of how big a role research plays at the medical school is the amount of grant money the faculty brings in. We list the total amount of National Institutes of Health (NIH) grants awarded to the medical school and affiliated hospitals in fiscal 2009.

CURRICULUM: The text describing the curriculum was provided by the schools. *U.S. News* edited the text for style but did not verify the information.

FACULTY PROFILE: Here, you'll find the number of full-time and part-time teaching faculty during fall 2009, as well as information on whether they teach in the basic sciences or in clinical programs. The full-time faculty/student ratio gives some indication of how accessible your professors are likely to be.

SUPPORT SERVICES: How does the school help students deal with the pressure of medical school?

RESIDENCY PROFILE: This section provides data on the residency placements of graduates—the most popular residency and specialty programs chosen by the 2008 and 2009 graduates, plus the proportion of graduates who enter into primary care specialties (family practice, general pediatrics, or general internal medicine). The latter figures are three-year average percentages from 2007-2009 and the proportion of 2008-2009 graduates who accepted in-state residencies.

Baylor College of Medicine

- 1 Baylor Plaza, Houston, TX 77030
- Private
- **Year Founded:** 1900
- **Tuition, 2009-2010:** $14,828
- **Enrollment 2009-2010 academic year:** 698
- **Website:** http://www.bcm.edu
- **Specialty ranking:** pediatrics: 5

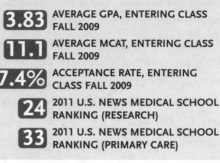

3.83 AVERAGE GPA, ENTERING CLASS FALL 2009

11.1 AVERAGE MCAT, ENTERING CLASS FALL 2009

7.4% ACCEPTANCE RATE, ENTERING CLASS FALL 2009

24 2011 U.S. NEWS MEDICAL SCHOOL RANKING (RESEARCH)

33 2011 U.S. NEWS MEDICAL SCHOOL RANKING (PRIMARY CARE)

ADMISSIONS

Admissions phone number: **(713) 798-4842**
Admissions email address: **admissions@bcm.tmc.edu**
Application web site: **http://www.bcm.edu/admissions/**
Acceptance rate: **7.4%**
In-state acceptance rate: **15.1%**
Out-of-state acceptance rate: **4.1%**
Minority acceptance rate: **7.9%**
International acceptance rate: **1.0%**

Fall 2009 applications and acceptees

Type	Applied	Interviewed	Accepted	Enrolled
Total:	4,588	717	340	186
In-state:	1,390	408	210	148
Out-of-state:	3,198	309	130	38

Profile of admitted students

Average undergraduate grade point average: **3.83**
MCAT averages (scale: 1-15; writing test: J-T):
Composite score: **11.1**
Verbal reasoning score: **10.4**, Physical sciences score: **11.4**,
   Biological score: **11.7**, Writing score: **P**
Proportion with undergraduate majors in: Biological
   sciences: **26%**, Physical sciences: **27%**, Non-sciences:
   21%, Other health professions: **0%**, Mixed disciplines
   and other: **26%**
Percentage of students not coming directly from college
   after graduation: **9%**

Dates and details

The American Medical College Application Service
   (AMCAS) application is accepted.
School asks for a second, school-specific application as part
   of the admissions process.
Oldest MCAT considered for Fall 2011 entry: **2006**
Earliest application date for the 2011-2012 first-year class:
   06/01
Latest application date: **11/01**
Acceptance dates for regular application for the class
   entering in Fall 2011.
Earliest: **16-OCT-10**

Latest: **20-JUL-11**
Applicants have N/A weeks to respond to admissions offer.
The school does consider requests for deferred entrance.
Starting month for the class of 2011–2012: **July**
The school does have an Early Decision Plan (EDP).
A personal interview is required for admission.

Undergraduate coursework required

Medical school requires undergraduate work in these subjects: biology, English, organic chemistry, inorganic (general) chemistry.

ADMISSIONS POLICY
(TEXT PROVIDED BY SCHOOL):

   Most applicants accepted have an overall GPA of 3.5 or
higher. Attention is on the applicant's course selection, academic challenge imposed by the curriculum, and the extent
extracurricular activities/employment limited the opportunity for high academic achievement. Applicants are not
required to major in a scientific field and we actively seek
individuals with broad educational backgrounds.

FINANCIAL AID

Financial aid phone number: **(713) 798-4612**
Tuition, 2009-2010 academic year: **$14,828**
Room and board: **$22,649**
Percentage of students receiving financial aid in 2009-10:
   87%
Percentage of students receiving: Loans: **70%**,
   Grants/scholarships: **58%**, Work-study aid: **17%**
Average medical school debt for the class of 2008: **$91,402**

STUDENT BODY

Fall 2009 full-time enrollment: **698**
Men: **49%**, Women: **51%**, In-state: **90%**, Minorities: **59%**,
   American Indian: **1.7%**, Asian-American: **36.5%**,
   African-American: **5.4%**, Hispanic-American: **15.5%**,
   White: **40.7%**, International: **0.1%**, Unknown: **0.0%**

ACADEMIC PROGRAMS

The school's curriculum frequently give first-year students substantial contact with patients.

There are opportunities for first- or second-year students to work in community health clinics.

Program areas. AIDS, drug/alcohol abuse, family medicine, geriatrics, internal medicine, pediatrics, rural medicine, women's health

Joint degrees awarded: M.D./Ph.D., M.D./M.B.A., M.D./M.P.H., M.D./J.D.

Total National Institutes of Health (NIH) grants awarded to the medical school and affiliated hospitals: **$221.4 million**

CURRICULUM

(TEXT PROVIDED BY MEDICAL SCHOOL):

BCM helps students acquire a foundation of basic & core clinical sciences, & skills & attitudes required to be capable, compassionate physicians. A student-centered learning environment, scholarship & career mentoring, an integrated curriculum of 1.5 years pre-clinical & 2.5 years of individualized clinical experiences provide students with a strong entry into the continuum of medical education.

FALL 2009 FACULTY PROFILE

Total teaching faculty: 1,933 **(full-time)**, 1,556 **(part-time)**

Of full-time faculty, those teaching in basic sciences: 16%; in clinical programs: 84%

Of part-time faculty, those teaching in basic sciences: 7%; in clinical programs: 93%

Full-time faculty/student ratio: 2.8

SUPPORT SERVICES

The school offers students these services for dealing with stress: expanded-hour gym access, peer counseling, professional counseling, support groups.

RESIDENCY PROFILE

Most popular residency and specialty programs chosen by the 2008 and 2009 M.D. graduating classes: anesthesiology, dermatology, emergency medicine, family practice, internal medicine, neurology, ophthalmology, otolaryngology, pediatrics, surgery–general.

WHERE GRADS GO

42.6%

Proportion of 2007-2008 graduates who entered primary care specialties

47.0%

Proportion of 2008-2009 graduates who accepted in-state residencies

Boston University

- 72 E. Concord Street, L-103, Boston, MA 02118
- Private
- Year Founded: 1848
- Tuition, 2009-2010: $47,088
- Enrollment 2009-2010 academic year: 709
- Website: http://www.bumc.bu.edu
- Specialty ranking: geriatrics: 18, women's health: 17

 3.65 AVERAGE GPA, ENTERING CLASS FALL 2009

10.7 AVERAGE MCAT, ENTERING CLASS FALL 2009

 **4.7%** ACCEPTANCE RATE, ENTERING CLASS FALL 2009

34 2011 U.S. NEWS MEDICAL SCHOOL RANKING (RESEARCH)

56 2011 U.S. NEWS MEDICAL SCHOOL RANKING (PRIMARY CARE)

ADMISSIONS
Admissions phone number: **(617) 638-4630**
Admissions email address: **medadms@bu.edu**
Application web site:
https://www.bumc.bu.edu/busm/myapplication/shared/signin.aspx
Acceptance rate: **4.7%**
In-state acceptance rate: **9.0%**
Out-of-state acceptance rate: **4.4%**
Minority acceptance rate: **4.4%**
International acceptance rate: **3.8%**

Fall 2009 applications and acceptees

Type	Applied	Interviewed	Accepted	Enrolled
Total:	10,816	1,124	506	176
In-state:	731	146	66	34
Out-of-state:	10,085	978	440	142

Profile of admitted students
Average undergraduate grade point average: **3.65**
MCAT averages (scale: 1-15; writing test: J-T):
Composite score: **10.7**
Verbal reasoning score: **10.0**, Physical sciences score: **10.9**, Biological score: **11.2**, Writing score: **P**
Proportion with undergraduate majors in: Biological sciences: **36%**, Physical sciences: **20%**, Non-sciences: **15%**, Other health professions: **9%**, Mixed disciplines and other: **20%**
Percentage of students not coming directly from college after graduation: **78%**

Dates and details
The American Medical College Application Service (AMCAS) application is accepted.
School asks for a second, school-specific application as part of the admissions process.
Oldest MCAT considered for Fall 2011 entry: **2006**
Earliest application date for the 2011-2012 first-year class: **06/01**
Latest application date: **11/01**

Acceptance dates for regular application for the class entering in Fall 2011.
Earliest: **11-JAN-11**
Latest: **10-AUG-11**
Applicants have 2 weeks to respond to admissions offer.
The school doesn't consider requests for deferred entrance.
Starting month for the class of 2011–2012: **August**
The school does have an Early Decision Plan (EDP).
A personal interview is required for admission.

Undergraduate coursework required
Medical school requires undergraduate work in these subjects: biology, English, organic chemistry, inorganic (general) chemistry, physics, humanities, demonstration of writing skills.

ADMISSIONS POLICY
(TEXT PROVIDED BY SCHOOL):
We draw upon a large and highly qualified applicant pool, with more than 100 applicants for every seat in the entering class. Our students represent the full range of geographic, cultural, ethnic, and educational diversity of our pluralistic society. We believe that diversity contributes to the strength of the experience for all of us.

FINANCIAL AID
Financial aid phone number: **(617) 638-5130**
Tuition, 2009-2010 academic year: **$47,088**
Room and board: **$12,464**
Percentage of students receiving financial aid in 2009-10: **82%**
Percentage of students receiving: Loans: **77%**, Grants/scholarships: **32%**, Work-study aid: **0%**
Average medical school debt for the class of 2008: **$170,059**

STUDENT BODY
Fall 2009 full-time enrollment: **709**
Men: **47%**, Women: **53%**, In-state: **17%**, Minorities: **45%**, American Indian: **0.3%**, Asian-American: **27.4%**,

African-American: **9.6%**, Hispanic-American: **7.6%**, White: **40.5%**, International: **4.7%**, Unknown: **10.0%**

ACADEMIC PROGRAMS

The school's curriculum frequently give first-year students substantial contact with patients.

There are opportunities for first- or second-year students to work in community health clinics.

Program areas: AIDS, drug/alcohol abuse, family medicine, geriatrics, internal medicine, pediatrics, rural medicine, women's health

Joint degrees awarded: M.D./Ph.D., M.D./M.B.A., M.D./M.P.H.

Total National Institutes of Health (NIH) grants awarded to the medical school and affiliated hospitals: **$205.1 million**

CURRICULUM
(TEXT PROVIDED BY MEDICAL SCHOOL):

A foundation in basic and clinical sciences is enriched by early patient contact, 9 required clerkships, and 20 weeks of 4th year electives. Years 1 & 2 lectures are < 3 hrs/day with most available online. An integrated year-long course is offered in yr 2. Clinical training occurs at Boston Medical Center and community settings with highly diverse patients. >130 electives are available in yr 4.

FALL 2009 FACULTY PROFILE

Total teaching faculty: **1,158 (full-time)**, **1,327 (part-time)**
Of full-time faculty, those teaching in basic sciences: **16%**; in clinical programs: **84%**
Of part-time faculty, those teaching in basic sciences: **8%**; in clinical programs: **92%**
Full-time faculty/student ratio: **1.6**

SUPPORT SERVICES

The school offers students these services for dealing with stress: expanded-hour gym access, peer counseling, professional counseling, religious support, support groups.

RESIDENCY PROFILE

Most popular residency and specialty programs chosen by the 2008 and 2009 M.D. graduating classes: anesthesiology, emergency medicine, family practice, internal medicine, obstetrics and gynecology, otolaryngology, pediatrics, psychiatry, radiology–diagnostic, surgery–general.

WHERE GRADS GO

36.0%

Proportion of 2007-2008 graduates who entered primary care specialties

33.0%

Proportion of 2008-2009 graduates who accepted in-state residencies

Brown University
Alpert

- 97 Waterman Street, Box G-A213, Providence, RI 02912-9706
- Private
- **Year Founded:** 1764
- **Tuition, 2009-2010:** $44,054
- **Enrollment 2009-2010 academic year:** 412
- **Website:** http://med.brown.edu
- **Specialty ranking:** drug/alcohol abuse: 12

3.62 AVERAGE GPA, ENTERING CLASS FALL 2009

11.1 AVERAGE MCAT, ENTERING CLASS FALL 2009

4.1% ACCEPTANCE RATE, ENTERING CLASS FALL 2009

32 2011 U.S. NEWS MEDICAL SCHOOL RANKING (RESEARCH)

49 2011 U.S. NEWS MEDICAL SCHOOL RANKING (PRIMARY CARE)

ADMISSIONS

Admissions phone number: **(401) 863-2149**
Admissions email address:
   medschool_admissions@brown.edu
Application web site:
   http://med.brown.edu/admissions/secondary_forms
Acceptance rate: **4.1%**
In-state acceptance rate: **10.2%**
Out-of-state acceptance rate: **4.0%**
Minority acceptance rate: **4.0%**
International acceptance rate: **0.5%**

Fall 2009 applications and acceptees

Type	Applied	Interviewed	Accepted	Enrolled
Total:	5,257	248	218	94
In-state:	108	17	11	8
Out-of-state:	5,149	231	207	86

Profile of admitted students

Average undergraduate grade point average: **3.62**
MCAT averages (scale: 1-15; writing test: J-T):
Composite score: **11.1**
Verbal reasoning score: **10.5**, Physical sciences score: **11.5**,
   Biological score: **11.3**, Writing score: **Q**
Proportion with undergraduate majors in: Biological
   sciences: **39%**, Physical sciences: **15%**, Non-sciences:
   46%, Other health professions: **0%**, Mixed disciplines
   and other: **1%**
Percentage of students not coming directly from college
   after graduation: **37%**

Dates and details

The American Medical College Application Service
   (AMCAS) application is accepted.
School asks for a second, school-specific application as part
   of the admissions process.
Oldest MCAT considered for Fall 2011 entry: **2006**
Earliest application date for the 2011-2012 first-year class:
   07/01
Latest application date: **11/01**

Acceptance dates for regular application for the class
   entering in Fall 2011.
Earliest: **10-NOV-10**
Latest: **10-AUG-11**
Applicants have 3 weeks to respond to admissions offer.
The school does consider requests for deferred entrance.
Starting month for the class of 2011–2012: **August**
The school doesn't have an Early Decision Plan (EDP).
A personal interview is required for admission.

Undergraduate coursework required

Medical school requires undergraduate work in these subjects: biology, organic chemistry, inorganic (general) chemistry, physics, behavioral science, calculus, social sciences,
general chemistry.

ADMISSIONS POLICY
(TEXT PROVIDED BY SCHOOL):

   Selection criteria are academic achievement, faculty evaluations, and evidence of maturity, leadership, integrity, and
compassion. Eligible candidates present a minimum cumu-
lative grade point average of 3.00 (4.00 scale) in undergraduate courses. Applicants must complete baccalaureate
degree requirements before entry into medical school.

FINANCIAL AID

Financial aid phone number: **(401) 863-1142**
Tuition, 2009-2010 academic year: **$44,054**
Room and board: **$16,500**
Percentage of students receiving financial aid in 2009-10:
   73%
Percentage of students receiving: Loans: **73%**,
   Grants/scholarships: **45%**, Work-study aid: **0%**
Average medical school debt for the class of 2008:
   $127,408

STUDENT BODY

Fall 2009 full-time enrollment: **412**
Men: **47%**, Women: **53%**, In-state: **8%**, Minorities: **44%**,
   American Indian: **0.5%**, Asian-American: **26.5%**,

African-American: **8.3%**, Hispanic-American: **8.3%**, White: **43.0%**, International: **1.7%**, Unknown: **11.9%**

ACADEMIC PROGRAMS

The school's curriculum very frequently give first-year students substantial contact with patients.

There are opportunities for first- or second-year students to work in community health clinics.

Program areas: AIDS, drug/alcohol abuse, family medicine, geriatrics, internal medicine, pediatrics, rural medicine, women's health

Joint degrees awarded: M.D./Ph.D., M.D./M.P.H.

Total National Institutes of Health (NIH) grants awarded to the medical school and affiliated hospitals: **$148.7 million**

CURRICULUM

(TEXT PROVIDED BY MEDICAL SCHOOL):

Year One includes two semesters of Integrated Medical Sciences and Doctoring. Year Two consists of system-based pathophysiology with integrated pharmacology, pathology, physiology, and Doctoring. Students in the third and fourth years must complete 50 weeks of clinical clerkships and 30 weeks of electives.

FALL 2009 FACULTY PROFILE

Total teaching faculty: **710 (full-time), 0 (part-time)**

Of full-time faculty, those teaching in basic sciences: **27%**; in clinical programs: **73%**

Of part-time faculty, those teaching in basic sciences: **N/A**; in clinical programs: **N/A**

Full-time faculty/student ratio: **1.7**

SUPPORT SERVICES

The school offers students these services for dealing with stress: expanded-hour gym access, peer counseling, professional counseling, religious support, support groups.

RESIDENCY PROFILE

Most popular residency and specialty programs chosen by the 2008 and 2009 M.D. graduating classes: emergency medicine, family practice, internal medicine, obstetrics and gynecology, pathology–anatomic and clinical, pediatrics, psychiatry, radiology–diagnostic, surgery–general, internal medicine/pediatrics.

WHERE GRADS GO

37.3%

Proportion of 2007-2008 graduates who entered primary care specialties

14.9%

Proportion of 2008-2009 graduates who accepted in-state residencies

Case Western Reserve University

- 10900 Euclid Avenue, Cleveland, OH 44106
- Private
- Year Founded: 1843
- Tuition, 2009-2010: $47,290
- Enrollment 2009-2010 academic year: 817
- Website: http://casemed.case.edu/
- Specialty ranking: family medicine: 15, pediatrics: 16

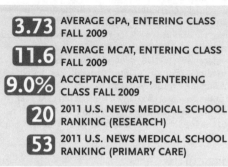

3.73	AVERAGE GPA, ENTERING CLASS FALL 2009
11.6	AVERAGE MCAT, ENTERING CLASS FALL 2009
9.0%	ACCEPTANCE RATE, ENTERING CLASS FALL 2009
20	2011 U.S. NEWS MEDICAL SCHOOL RANKING (RESEARCH)
53	2011 U.S. NEWS MEDICAL SCHOOL RANKING (PRIMARY CARE)

ADMISSIONS

Admissions phone number: **(216) 368-3450**
Admissions email address: **casemed-admissions@case.edu**
Application web site: **N/A**
Acceptance rate: **9.0%**
In-state acceptance rate: **8.7%**
Out-of-state acceptance rate: **9.0%**
Minority acceptance rate: **9.7%**
International acceptance rate: **7.5%**

Fall 2009 applications and acceptees

Type	Applied	Interviewed	Accepted	Enrolled
Total:	5,556	1,192	500	199
In-state:	738	176	64	30
Out-of-state:	4,818	1,016	436	169

Profile of admitted students

Average undergraduate grade point average: **3.73**
MCAT averages (scale: 1-15; writing test: J-T):
Composite score: **11.6**
Verbal reasoning score: **10.7**, Physical sciences score: **11.9**,
  Biological score: **12.1**, Writing score: **Q**
Proportion with undergraduate majors in: Biological
  sciences: **32%**, Physical sciences: **32%**, Non-sciences:
  8%, Other health professions: **2%**, Mixed disciplines and
  other: **26%**
Percentage of students not coming directly from college
  after graduation: **53%**

Dates and details

The American Medical College Application Service
  (AMCAS) application is accepted.
School asks for a second, school-specific application as part
  of the admissions process.
Oldest MCAT considered for Fall 2011 entry: **2008**
Earliest application date for the 2011-2012 first-year class:
  06/01
Latest application date: **11/01**
Acceptance dates for regular application for the class
  entering in Fall 2011.
Earliest: **15-OCT-11**

Latest: **01-NOV-11**
Applicants have 4 weeks to respond to admissions offer.
The school does consider requests for deferred entrance.
Starting month for the class of 2011–2012: **July**
The school doesn't have an Early Decision Plan (EDP).
A personal interview is required for admission.

Undergraduate coursework required

Medical school requires undergraduate work in these subjects: biology/zoology, English, organic chemistry, inorganic
(general) chemistry, physics, biochemistry, calculus.

ADMISSIONS POLICY
(TEXT PROVIDED BY SCHOOL):

The Admissions Committee selects students without
regard to age, national origin, race, religion, sex, or sexual
orientation. Although admitted students demonstrate exceptional academic strength; the candidate's written statements,
extracurricular activities, and letters of recommendation also
weigh heavily in the decision to extend an interview. The
School seeks a diverse student body.

FINANCIAL AID

Financial aid phone number: **(216) 368-3666**
Tuition, 2009-2010 academic year: **$47,290**
Room and board: **$17,890**
Percentage of students receiving financial aid in 2009-10:
  85%
Percentage of students receiving: Loans: **80%**,
  Grants/scholarships: **61%**, Work-study aid: **0%**
Average medical school debt for the class of 2008:
  $137,342

STUDENT BODY

Fall 2009 full-time enrollment: **817**
Men: **55%**, Women: **45%**, In-state: **29%**, Minorities: **41%**,
  American Indian: **0.5%**, Asian-American: **27.7%**,
  African-American: **7.7%**, Hispanic-American: **2.8%**,
  White: **49.9%**, International: **5.0%**, Unknown: **6.4%**

ACADEMIC PROGRAMS

The school's curriculum frequently give first-year students substantial contact with patients.

There are opportunities for first- or second-year students to work in community health clinics.

Program areas: AIDS, drug/alcohol abuse, family medicine, geriatrics, internal medicine, pediatrics, rural medicine, women's health

Joint degrees awarded: M.D./Ph.D., M.D./M.B.A., M.D./M.P.H., M.D./J.D., M.D./M.S., M.D./M.A.

Total National Institutes of Health (NIH) grants awarded to the medical school and affiliated hospitals: **$329.2 million**

CURRICULUM

(TEXT PROVIDED BY MEDICAL SCHOOL):

4-year University program develops physician scholars & leaders in science, patient care, health care policy. 5-year College program develops physician investigators by integrating research training across 5 years. Both programs focus on scholarship, student-centered small group learning, early patient experiences, research opportunities. See http://casemed.case.edu/admissions/education/chart.cfm

FALL 2009 FACULTY PROFILE

Total teaching faculty: **2,069 (full-time)**, **1,998 (part-time)**
Of full-time faculty, those teaching in basic sciences: **19%**; in clinical programs: **81%**

Of part-time faculty, those teaching in basic sciences: **10%**; in clinical programs: **90%**
Full-time faculty/student ratio: **2.5**

SUPPORT SERVICES

The school offers students these services for dealing with stress: expanded-hour gym access, peer counseling, professional counseling, religious support, support groups.

RESIDENCY PROFILE

Most popular residency and specialty programs chosen by the 2008 and 2009 M.D. graduating classes: anesthesiology, emergency medicine, family practice, internal medicine, obstetrics and gynecology, orthopaedic surgery, pediatrics, radiology–diagnostic, surgery–general.

WHERE GRADS GO

31.0%

Proportion of 2007-2008 graduates who entered primary care specialties

25.0%

Proportion of 2008-2009 graduates who accepted in-state residencies

Columbia University

- 630 W. 168th Street, New York, NY 10032
- Private
- **Year Founded:** 1767
- **Tuition, 2009-2010:** $49,347
- **Enrollment 2009-2010 academic year:** 638
- **Website:** http://www.cumc.columbia.edu/dept/ps
- **Specialty ranking:** AIDS: 6, drug/alcohol abuse: 4, internal medicine: 9, pediatrics: 12, women's health: 7

3.80 AVERAGE GPA, ENTERING CLASS FALL 2009

11.9 AVERAGE MCAT, ENTERING CLASS FALL 2009

4.3% ACCEPTANCE RATE, ENTERING CLASS FALL 2009

10 2011 U.S. NEWS MEDICAL SCHOOL RANKING (RESEARCH)

62 2011 U.S. NEWS MEDICAL SCHOOL RANKING (PRIMARY CARE)

ADMISSIONS

Admissions phone number: **(212) 305-3595**
Admissions email address: **psadmissions@columbia.edu**
Application web site:
http://www.cumc.columbia.edu/dept/ps
Acceptance rate: **4.3%**
In-state acceptance rate: **N/A**
Out-of-state acceptance rate: **N/A**
Minority acceptance rate: **N/A**
International acceptance rate: **N/A**

Fall 2009 applications and acceptees

Type	Applied	Interviewed	Accepted	Enrolled
Total:	7,052	1,096	301	154
In-state:	N/A	200	59	38
Out-of-state:	N/A	896	242	116

Profile of admitted students

Average undergraduate grade point average: **3.80**
MCAT averages (scale: 1-15; writing test: J-T):
Composite score: **11.9**
Verbal reasoning score: **11.2**, Physical sciences score: **12.1**, Biological score: **12.4**, Writing score: **Q**
Proportion with undergraduate majors in: Biological sciences: **44%**, Physical sciences: **30%**, Non-sciences: **14%**, Other health professions: **0%**, Mixed disciplines and other: **12%**
Percentage of students not coming directly from college after graduation: **46%**

Dates and details

The American Medical College Application Service (AMCAS) application is accepted.
School asks for a second, school-specific application as part of the admissions process.
Oldest MCAT considered for Fall 2011 entry: **2007**
Earliest application date for the 2011-2012 first-year class: **06/01**
Latest application date: **10/15**
Acceptance dates for regular application for the class entering in Fall 2011.

Earliest: **02-MAR-11**
Latest: **22-AUG-11**
Applicants have 3 weeks to respond to admissions offer.
The school does consider requests for deferred entrance.
Starting month for the class of 2011–2012: **August**
The school doesn't have an Early Decision Plan (EDP).
A personal interview is required for admission.

Undergraduate coursework required

Medical school requires undergraduate work in these subjects: biology, English, organic chemistry, physics, general chemistry.

ADMISSIONS POLICY

(TEXT PROVIDED BY SCHOOL):

For recent classes the mean GPA has been 3.79, and the mean total MCAT score between 35 and 36. Breadth of interests, leadership potential, and participation in extracurricular activities are also looked for. We seek diversity of background, geographical and otherwise. No preference is given to state of residence. Members of underrepresented minority groups are encouraged to apply.

FINANCIAL AID

Financial aid phone number: **(212) 305-4100**
Tuition, 2009-2010 academic year: **$49,347**
Room and board: **$14,652**
Percentage of students receiving financial aid in 2009-10: **82%**
Percentage of students receiving: Loans: **69%**, Grants/scholarships: **58%**, Work-study aid: **10%**
Average medical school debt for the class of 2008: **$113,146**

STUDENT BODY

Fall 2009 full-time enrollment: **638**
Men: **52%**, Women: **48%**, In-state: **34%**, Minorities: **38%**, American Indian: **0.3%**, Asian-American: **16.5%**, African-American: **10.0%**, Hispanic-American: **7.8%**, White: **57.7%**, International: **4.4%**, Unknown: **3.3%**

ACADEMIC PROGRAMS

The school's curriculum very frequently give first-year students substantial contact with patients.

There are opportunities for first- or second-year students to work in community health clinics.

Program areas: AIDS, drug/alcohol abuse, family medicine, geriatrics, internal medicine, pediatrics, rural medicine, women's health

Joint degrees awarded: M.D./Ph.D., M.D./M.B.A., M.D./M.P.H., M.D./M.S.

Total National Institutes of Health (NIH) grants awarded to the medical school and affiliated hospitals: **$468.3 million**

CURRICULUM
(TEXT PROVIDED BY MEDICAL SCHOOL):

The first two years at P&S combine basic sciences, introductory clinical experiences, skill-building, and physical diagnosis. The curriculum's depth and strength become evident in year 3, when students complete clinical clerkships in wide-ranging disciplines in inner city, suburban, or rural settings. Fourth-year courses re-emphasize the foundation of medical knowledge and critical data appraisal.

FALL 2009 FACULTY PROFILE

Total teaching faculty: **1,914 (full-time)**, **2,509 (part-time)**
Of full-time faculty, those teaching in basic sciences: **10%**; in clinical programs: **90%**

Of part-time faculty, those teaching in basic sciences: **3%**; in clinical programs: **97%**
Full-time faculty/student ratio: **3.0**

SUPPORT SERVICES

The school offers students these services for dealing with stress: expanded-hour gym access, peer counseling, professional counseling, religious support, support groups.

RESIDENCY PROFILE

Most popular residency and specialty programs chosen by the 2008 and 2009 M.D. graduating classes: anesthesiology, emergency medicine, internal medicine, neurological surgery, obstetrics and gynecology, orthopaedic surgery, pediatrics, psychiatry, radiology–diagnostic, surgery–general.

WHERE GRADS GO

28.0%

Proportion of 2007-2008 graduates who entered primary care specialties

47.0%

Proportion of 2008-2009 graduates who accepted in-state residencies

Cornell University
Weill

- 525 E. 68th Street, New York, NY 10065
- Private
- **Year Founded:** 1898
- **Tuition, 2009-2010:** $47,455
- **Enrollment 2009-2010 academic year:** 406
- **Website:** http://www.weill.cornell.edu
- **Specialty ranking:** AIDS: 14, internal medicine: 21

3.75 AVERAGE GPA, ENTERING CLASS FALL 2009

11.5 AVERAGE MCAT, ENTERING CLASS FALL 2009

4.5% ACCEPTANCE RATE, ENTERING CLASS FALL 2009

16 2011 U.S. NEWS MEDICAL SCHOOL RANKING (RESEARCH)

Unranked 2011 U.S. NEWS MEDICAL SCHOOL RANKING (PRIMARY CARE)

ADMISSIONS
Admissions phone number: **(212) 746-1067**
Admissions email address: **wcmc-admissions@med.cornell.edu**
Application web site:
http://www.weill.cornell.edu/education/admissions
Acceptance rate: **4.5%**
In-state acceptance rate: **5.6%**
Out-of-state acceptance rate: **4.2%**
Minority acceptance rate: **5.4%**
International acceptance rate: **2.1%**

Fall 2009 applications and acceptees

Type	Applied	Interviewed	Accepted	Enrolled
Total:	5,580	652	252	101
In-state:	1,138	143	64	33
Out-of-state:	4,442	509	188	68

Profile of admitted students
Average undergraduate grade point average: **3.75**
MCAT averages (scale: 1-15; writing test: J-T):
Composite score: **11.5**
Verbal reasoning score: **10.6**, Physical sciences score: **11.7**,
  Biological score: **12.1**, Writing score: **Q**
Proportion with undergraduate majors in: Biological
  sciences: **41%**, Physical sciences: **26%**, Non-sciences:
  16%, Other health professions: **2%**, Mixed disciplines
  and other: **15%**
Percentage of students not coming directly from college
  after graduation: **34%**

Dates and details
The American Medical College Application Service
  (AMCAS) application is accepted.
School asks for a second, school-specific application as part
  of the admissions process.
Oldest MCAT considered for Fall 2011 entry: **2008**
Earliest application date for the 2011-2012 first-year class:
  06/01
Latest application date: **10/15**

Acceptance dates for regular application for the class
  entering in Fall 2011.
Earliest: **15-DEC-10**
Latest: **15-AUG-11**
Applicants have 2 weeks to respond to admissions offer.
The school does consider requests for deferred entrance.
Starting month for the class of 2011–2012: **August**
The school does have an Early Decision Plan (EDP).
A personal interview is required for admission.

Undergraduate coursework required
Medical school requires undergraduate work in these subjects: biology, English, organic chemistry, inorganic (general) chemistry, physics, demonstration of writing skills.

ADMISSIONS POLICY
(TEXT PROVIDED BY SCHOOL):
  Admissions Web Page:
http://weill.cornell.edu/education/admissions/app.html

FINANCIAL AID
Financial aid phone number: **(212) 746-1066**
Tuition, 2009-2010 academic year: **$47,455**
Room and board: **$11,460**
Percentage of students receiving financial aid in 2009-10:
  81%
Percentage of students receiving: Loans: **72%**,
  Grants/scholarships: **65%**, Work-study aid: **19%**
Average medical school debt for the class of 2008:
  $116,024

STUDENT BODY
Fall 2009 full-time enrollment: **406**
Men: **53%**, Women: **47%**, In-state: **45%**, Minorities: **43%**,
  American Indian: **1.7%**, Asian-American: **19.5%**,
  African-American: **10.6%**, Hispanic-American: **11.1%**,
  White: **52.7%**, International: **1.5%**, Unknown: **3.0%**

ACADEMIC PROGRAMS
The school's curriculum very frequently give first-year
  students substantial contact with patients.

There are opportunities for first- or second-year students to work in community health clinics.

Program areas: AIDS, drug/alcohol abuse, family medicine, geriatrics, internal medicine, pediatrics, women's health

Joint degrees awarded: M.D./Ph.D., M.D./M.B.A.

Total National Institutes of Health (NIH) grants awarded to the medical school and affiliated hospitals: **$275.2 million**

CURRICULUM
(TEXT PROVIDED BY MEDICAL SCHOOL):
Curriculum Web Page with links for more detail: http://weill.cornell.edu/education/admissions/curr.html

FALL 2009 FACULTY PROFILE
Total teaching faculty: **1,823 (full-time), 2,684 (part-time)**
Of full-time faculty, those teaching in basic sciences: **11%**; in clinical programs: **89%**
Of part-time faculty, those teaching in basic sciences: **4%**; in clinical programs: **96%**
Full-time faculty/student ratio: **4.5**

SUPPORT SERVICES
The school offers students these services for dealing with stress: peer counseling, professional counseling, religious support, support groups.

RESIDENCY PROFILE
Most popular residency and specialty programs chosen by the 2008 and 2009 M.D. graduating classes: anesthesiology, emergency medicine, internal medicine, ophthalmology, orthopaedic surgery, pediatrics, psychiatry, radiology–diagnostic, surgery–general, transitional year.

WHERE GRADS GO

30.0%
Proportion of 2007-2008 graduates who entered primary care specialties

45.0%
Proportion of 2008-2009 graduates who accepted in-state residencies

Creighton University

- 2500 California Plaza, Omaha, NE 68178
- Private
- **Year Founded:** 1878
- **Tuition, 2009-2010:** $46,086
- **Enrollment 2009-2010 academic year:** 495
- **Website:** http://medicine.creighton.edu
- **Specialty ranking:** N/A

3.72	AVERAGE GPA, ENTERING CLASS FALL 2009
10.0	AVERAGE MCAT, ENTERING CLASS FALL 2009
6.0%	ACCEPTANCE RATE, ENTERING CLASS FALL 2009
Unranked	2011 U.S. NEWS MEDICAL SCHOOL RANKING (RESEARCH)
62	2011 U.S. NEWS MEDICAL SCHOOL RANKING (PRIMARY CARE)

ADMISSIONS

Admissions phone number: **(402) 280-2799**
Admissions email address: **medschadm@creighton.edu**
Application web site:
http://www2.creighton.edu/medschool/medicine/oma/index.php
Acceptance rate: **6.0%**
In-state acceptance rate: **4.4%**
Out-of-state acceptance rate: **6.1%**
Minority acceptance rate: **4.7%**
International acceptance rate: **0.0%**

Fall 2009 applications and acceptees

Type	Applied	Interviewed	Accepted	Enrolled
Total:	5,398	666	322	126
In-state:	540	52	24	14
Out-of-state:	4,858	614	298	112

Profile of admitted students

Average undergraduate grade point average: **3.72**
MCAT averages (scale: 1-15; writing test: J-T):
Composite score: **10.0**
Verbal reasoning score: **9.6**, Physical sciences score: **9.7**,
Biological score: **10.3**, Writing score: **P**
Proportion with undergraduate majors in: Biological
sciences: **52%**, Physical sciences: **22%**, Non-sciences:
26%, Other health professions: **0%**, Mixed disciplines
and other: **0%**
Percentage of students not coming directly from college
after graduation: **56%**

Dates and details

The American Medical College Application Service
(AMCAS) application is accepted.
School asks for a second, school-specific application as part
of the admissions process.
Oldest MCAT considered for Fall 2011 entry: **2008**
Earliest application date for the 2011-2012 first-year class:
06/01
Latest application date: **11/01**

Acceptance dates for regular application for the class
entering in Fall 2011.
Earliest: **15-OCT-10**
Latest: **N/A**
Applicants have 2 weeks to respond to admissions offer.
The school does consider requests for deferred entrance.
Starting month for the class of 2011–2012: **August**
The school does have an Early Decision Plan (EDP).
A personal interview is required for admission.

Undergraduate coursework required

Medical school requires undergraduate work in these subjects: biology, English, organic chemistry, inorganic (general) chemistry, physics.

ADMISSIONS POLICY
(TEXT PROVIDED BY SCHOOL):

Mandatory MCAT & 3 yrs accredited college work.
Preference to baccalaureate degree holders. Up to 27 semester hrs credit under CLEP or advanced placement.
Consideration given to significant humanity service, medical
experience, intellectual ability, emotional maturity, honesty
and motivation. Letters of recommendation important. No
restrictions on race, religion, sex, age, disability, ethnicity.

FINANCIAL AID

Financial aid phone number: **(402) 280-2666**
Tuition, 2009-2010 academic year: **$46,086**
Room and board: **$13,500**
Percentage of students receiving financial aid in 2009-10:
94%
Percentage of students receiving: Loans: **92%**,
Grants/scholarships: **59%**, Work-study aid: **0%**
Average medical school debt for the class of 2008:
$194,548

STUDENT BODY

Fall 2009 full-time enrollment: **495**
Men: **52%**, Women: **48%**, In-state: **11%**, Minorities: **19%**,
American Indian: **1.0%**, Asian-American: **13.7%**,

African-American: 3.2%, Hispanic-American: 0.8%, White: 73.7%, International: 0.4%, Unknown: 7.1%

ACADEMIC PROGRAMS

The school's curriculum occasionally give first-year students substantial contact with patients.

There are opportunities for first- or second-year students to work in community health clinics.

Program areas: drug/alcohol abuse, family medicine, geriatrics, internal medicine, pediatrics, rural medicine, women's health

Joint degrees awarded: M.D./Ph.D.

Total National Institutes of Health (NIH) grants awarded to the medical school and affiliated hospitals: **$12.2 million**

CURRICULUM

(TEXT PROVIDED BY MEDICAL SCHOOL):

Integrated curriculum that incorporates basic, clinical science with clinical experience a prominent piece. Curriculum integrates ethical and societal issues. Instructional and methodology utilizes case-based, small-group sessions and computer assisted instruction. A close faculty/student relationship. Competency-based evaluation used in all components. Students graded on pass/fail/honors system.

FALL 2009 FACULTY PROFILE

Total teaching faculty: **268 (full-time)**, **25 (part-time)**

Of full-time faculty, those teaching in basic sciences: **25%**; in clinical programs: **75%**

Of part-time faculty, those teaching in basic sciences: **20%**; in clinical programs: **80%**

Full-time faculty/student ratio: **0.5**

SUPPORT SERVICES

The school offers students these services for dealing with stress: expanded-hour gym access, peer counseling, professional counseling, religious support, support groups.

RESIDENCY PROFILE

Most popular residency and specialty programs chosen by the 2008 and 2009 M.D. graduating classes: anesthesiology, emergency medicine, family practice, internal medicine, obstetrics and gynecology, orthopaedic surgery, pathology–anatomic and clinical, pediatrics, radiology–diagnostic, surgery–general.

WHERE GRADS GO

44.0%

Proportion of 2007-2008 graduates who entered primary care specialties

19.0%

Proportion of 2008-2009 graduates who accepted in-state residencies

Dartmouth Medical School

- 1 Rope Ferry Road, Hanover, NH 03755-1404
- Private
- **Year Founded:** 1797
- **Tuition, 2009-2010:** $44,285
- **Enrollment 2009-2010 academic year:** 343
- **Website:** http://dms.dartmouth.edu
- **Specialty ranking:** family medicine: 15

3.73 AVERAGE GPA, ENTERING CLASS FALL 2009

11.1 AVERAGE MCAT, ENTERING CLASS FALL 2009

6.2% ACCEPTANCE RATE, ENTERING CLASS FALL 2009

34 2011 U.S. NEWS MEDICAL SCHOOL RANKING (RESEARCH)

39 2011 U.S. NEWS MEDICAL SCHOOL RANKING (PRIMARY CARE)

ADMISSIONS
Admissions phone number: **(603) 650-1505**
Admissions email address:
dms.admissions@dartmouth.edu
Application web site:
http://dms.dartmouth.edu/admissions/instructions
Acceptance rate: **6.2%**
In-state acceptance rate: **12.3%**
Out-of-state acceptance rate: **6.1%**
Minority acceptance rate: **5.6%**
International acceptance rate: **N/A**

Fall 2009 applications and acceptees

Type	Applied	Interviewed	Accepted	Enrolled
Total:	4,359	639	269	84
In-state:	73	31	9	5
Out-of-state:	4,286	608	260	79

Profile of admitted students
Average undergraduate grade point average: **3.73**
MCAT averages (scale: 1-15; writing test: J-T):
Composite score: **11.1**
Verbal reasoning score: **10.6**, Physical sciences score: **11.3**,
   Biological score: **11.5**, Writing score: **Q**
Proportion with undergraduate majors in: Biological
   sciences: **40%**, Physical sciences: **25%**, Non-sciences:
   19%, Other health professions: **1%**, Mixed disciplines
   and other: **15%**
Percentage of students not coming directly from college
   after graduation: **31%**

Dates and details
The American Medical College Application Service
   (AMCAS) application is accepted.
School asks for a second, school-specific application as part
   of the admissions process.
Oldest MCAT considered for Fall 2011 entry: **2008**
Earliest application date for the 2011-2012 first-year class:
   06/01
Latest application date: **11/01**

Acceptance dates for regular application for the class
   entering in Fall 2011.
Earliest: **15-OCT-10**
Latest: **15-AUG-11**
Applicants have 2 weeks to respond to admissions offer.
The school does consider requests for deferred entrance.
Starting month for the class of 2011-2012: **August**
The school doesn't have an Early Decision Plan (EDP).
A personal interview is required for admission.

Undergraduate coursework required
Medical school requires undergraduate work in these subjects: biology, organic chemistry, physics, calculus, general
chemistry.

ADMISSIONS POLICY
(TEXT PROVIDED BY SCHOOL):
   Admission requirements include: One year (8 semester
hours) each of general chemistry, organic chemistry, biology, and physics. A half-year of calculus. Facility in written
and spoken English. Equivalent of at least three years' college work at an American or Canadian post-secondary institution. A semester of biochemistry is encouraged, but not
required. Submission of MCAT scores is preferred.

FINANCIAL AID
Financial aid phone number: **(603) 650-1919**
Tuition, 2009-2010 academic year: **$44,285**
Room and board: **$10,250**
Percentage of students receiving financial aid in 2009-10:
   85%
Percentage of students receiving: Loans: **85%**,
   Grants/scholarships: **50%**, Work-study aid: **0%**
Average medical school debt for the class of 2008:
   $109,688

STUDENT BODY
Fall 2009 full-time enrollment: **343**
Men: **50%**, Women: **50%**, In-state: **9%**, Minorities: **25%**,
   American Indian: **0.9%**, Asian-American: **18.7%**,

African-American: 1.5%, Hispanic-American: 4.1%,
White: 57.1%, International: 11.7%, Unknown: 6.1%

ACADEMIC PROGRAMS

The school's curriculum frequently give first-year students
substantial contact with patients.

There are opportunities for first- or second-year students to
work in community health clinics.

Program areas: AIDS, drug/alcohol abuse, family
medicine, geriatrics, internal medicine, pediatrics, rural
medicine, women's health

Joint degrees awarded: M.D./Ph.D., M.D./M.B.A.,
M.D./M.P.H.

Total National Institutes of Health (NIH) grants awarded
to the medical school and affiliated hospitals: $83.4
million

CURRICULUM

(TEXT PROVIDED BY MEDICAL SCHOOL):

Yr 1: Intro. basic biomedical sciences, work with community clinicians to develop clinical skills. Yr 2:
Interdisciplinary pathophysiology program, cont. clinical
training. Yr 3: Required 7-week clerkships in 6 major clinical
disciplines. Yr 4: Two required 4-week clerkships, an
advanced 4-week sub-internship in field of choice,12-24
weeks of electives & 4 short courses on adv. clinical subjects.

FALL 2009 FACULTY PROFILE

Total teaching faculty: 884 (full-time), 1,055 (part-time)
Of full-time faculty, those teaching in basic sciences: 9%;
in clinical programs: 91%
Of part-time faculty, those teaching in basic sciences: 5%;
in clinical programs: 95%
Full-time faculty/student ratio: 2.6

SUPPORT SERVICES

The school offers students these services for dealing with
stress: expanded-hour gym access, peer counseling, professional counseling, support groups.

RESIDENCY PROFILE

Most popular residency and specialty programs chosen by
the 2008 and 2009 M.D. graduating classes: anesthesiology, emergency medicine, family practice, internal medicine, obstetrics and gynecology, ophthalmology, pediatrics,
psychiatry, radiology–diagnostic, surgery–general.

WHERE GRADS GO

32.6%

*Proportion of 2007-2008 graduates who entered primary
care specialties*

9.5%

*Proportion of 2008-2009 graduates who accepted in-state
residencies*

Drexel University

2900 Queen Lane, Philadelphia, PA 19129
- Private
- Year Founded: 1848
- Tuition, 2009-2010: $45,440
- Enrollment 2009-2010 academic year: 1,087
- Website: http://www.drexelmed.edu
- Specialty ranking: N/A

3.54 AVERAGE GPA, ENTERING CLASS FALL 2009

10.2 AVERAGE MCAT, ENTERING CLASS FALL 2009

7.6% ACCEPTANCE RATE, ENTERING CLASS FALL 2009

Unranked 2011 U.S. NEWS MEDICAL SCHOOL RANKING (RESEARCH)

Unranked 2011 U.S. NEWS MEDICAL SCHOOL RANKING (PRIMARY CARE)

ADMISSIONS
Admissions phone number: **(215) 991-8202**
Admissions email address: **Medadmis@drexel.edu**
Application web site:
   http://www.aamc.org/students/start.htm
Acceptance rate: **7.6%**
In-state acceptance rate: **22.0%**
Out-of-state acceptance rate: **6.1%**
Minority acceptance rate: **7.2%**
International acceptance rate: **N/A**

Fall 2009 applications and acceptees

Type	Applied	Interviewed	Accepted	Enrolled
Total:	8,757	1,339	666	260
In-state:	835	315	184	75
Out-of-state:	7,922	1,024	482	185

Profile of admitted students
Average undergraduate grade point average: **3.54**
MCAT averages (scale: 1-15; writing test: J-T):
Composite score: **10.2**
Verbal reasoning score: **9.6**, Physical sciences score: **10.3**,
   Biological score: **10.8**, Writing score: **O**
Proportion with undergraduate majors in: Biological
   sciences: **N/A**, Physical sciences: **N/A**, Non-sciences:
   N/A, Other health professions: **N/A**, Mixed disciplines
   and other: **N/A**
Percentage of students not coming directly from college
   after graduation: **12%**

Dates and details
The American Medical College Application Service
   (AMCAS) application is accepted.
School asks for a second, school-specific application as part
   of the admissions process.
Oldest MCAT considered for Fall 2011 entry: **2008**
Earliest application date for the 2011-2012 first-year class:
   06/01
Latest application date: **12/15**
Acceptance dates for regular application for the class
   entering in Fall 2011.

Earliest: **15-OCT-11**
Latest: **15-AUG-12**
Applicants have 3 weeks to respond to admissions offer.
The school does consider requests for deferred entrance.
Starting month for the class of 2011-2012: **August**
The school does have an Early Decision Plan (EDP).
A personal interview is required for admission.

Undergraduate coursework required
Medical school requires undergraduate work in these subjects: biology, English, organic chemistry, inorganic (general) chemistry, physics, general chemistry.

ADMISSIONS POLICY
(TEXT PROVIDED BY SCHOOL):
   Drexel University College of Medicine seeks highly qualified and motivated students who demonstrate the desire, intelligence, integrity, and emotional maturity to become excellent physicians. Because of the school's unique background, we encourage nontraditional applicants and are committed to a diverse student body.

FINANCIAL AID
Financial aid phone number: **(215) 991-8210**
Tuition, 2009-2010 academic year: **$45,440**
Room and board: **$15,888**
Percentage of students receiving financial aid in 2009-10:
   85%
Percentage of students receiving: Loans: **84%**,
   Grants/scholarships: **42%**, Work-study aid: **15%**
Average medical school debt for the class of 2008:
   $182,921

STUDENT BODY
Fall 2009 full-time enrollment: **1,087**
Men: **51%**, Women: **49%**, In-state: **29%**, Minorities: **44%**,
   American Indian: **0.6%**, Asian-American: **34.8%**,
   African-American: **4.7%**, Hispanic-American: **4.0%**,
   White: **49.4%**, International: **0.0%**, Unknown: **6.4%**

ACADEMIC PROGRAMS

The school's curriculum frequently give first-year students substantial contact with patients.

There are opportunities for first- or second-year students to work in community health clinics.

Program areas: AIDS, drug/alcohol abuse, family medicine, geriatrics, internal medicine, pediatrics, rural medicine, women's health

Joint degrees awarded: M.D./Ph.D., M.D./M.B.A., M.D./M.P.H.

Total National Institutes of Health (NIH) grants awarded to the medical school and affiliated hospitals: **N/A**

CURRICULUM

(TEXT PROVIDED BY MEDICAL SCHOOL):

Medical students are trained to consider each patient's case and needs in a comprehensive integrated manner, taking into account many more factors than the presenting physiological condition. The medical college is dedicated to preparing Physician Healers—doctors who practice the art, science and skill of medicine.

FALL 2009 FACULTY PROFILE

Total teaching faculty: **596 (full-time)**, **55 (part-time)**

Of full-time faculty, those teaching in basic sciences: **18%**; in clinical programs: **82%**

Of part-time faculty, those teaching in basic sciences: **15%**; in clinical programs: **85%**

Full-time faculty/student ratio: **0.5**

SUPPORT SERVICES

The school offers students these services for dealing with stress: expanded-hour gym access, peer counseling, professional counseling, religious support, support groups.

RESIDENCY PROFILE

Most popular residency and specialty programs chosen by the 2008 and 2009 M.D. graduating classes: anesthesiology, emergency medicine, family practice, internal medicine, obstetrics and gynecology, pediatrics, psychiatry, radiology–diagnostic, surgery–general.

WHERE GRADS GO

36.3%

Proportion of 2007-2008 graduates who entered primary care specialties

35.0%

Proportion of 2008-2009 graduates who accepted in-state residencies

Duke University

- **DUMC 3710, Durham, NC 27710**
- **Private**
- **Year Founded:** 1930
- **Tuition, 2009-2010:** $45,992
- **Enrollment 2009-2010 academic year:** 421
- **Website:** http://dukemed.duke.edu
- **Specialty ranking:** AIDS: 5, drug/alcohol abuse: 17, family medicine: 8, geriatrics: 4, internal medicine: 5, pediatrics: 9, women's health: 6

3.72 AVERAGE GPA, ENTERING CLASS FALL 2009

11.4 AVERAGE MCAT, ENTERING CLASS FALL 2009

4.3% ACCEPTANCE RATE, ENTERING CLASS FALL 2009

6 2011 U.S. NEWS MEDICAL SCHOOL RANKING (RESEARCH)

42 2011 U.S. NEWS MEDICAL SCHOOL RANKING (PRIMARY CARE)

ADMISSIONS

Admissions phone number: **(919) 684-2985**
Admissions email address: **medadm@mc.duke.edu**
Application web site:
  http://dukemed.duke.edu/AdmissionsFinancialAid/index.cfm
Acceptance rate: **4.3%**
In-state acceptance rate: **12.2%**
Out-of-state acceptance rate: **3.7%**
Minority acceptance rate: **5.1%**
International acceptance rate: **1.5%**

Fall 2009 applications and acceptees

Type	Applied	Interviewed	Accepted	Enrolled
Total:	4,966	1,010	216	100
In-state:	384	110	47	12
Out-of-state:	4,582	900	169	88

Profile of admitted students

Average undergraduate grade point average: **3.72**
MCAT averages (scale: 1-15; writing test: J-T):
Composite score: **11.4**
Verbal reasoning score: **10.3**, Physical sciences score: **11.9**, Biological score: **12.0**, Writing score: **P**
Proportion with undergraduate majors in: Biological sciences: **45%**, Physical sciences: **27%**, Non-sciences: **11%**, Other health professions: **15%**, Mixed disciplines and other: **2%**
Percentage of students not coming directly from college after graduation: **43%**

Dates and details

The American Medical College Application Service (AMCAS) application is accepted.
School asks for a second, school-specific application as part of the admissions process.
Oldest MCAT considered for Fall 2011 entry: **2006**
Earliest application date for the 2011-2012 first-year class: **06/15**
Latest application date: **11/01**

Acceptance dates for regular application for the class entering in Fall 2011.
Earliest: **01-MAR-10**
Latest: **01-JUN-10**
Applicants have 2 weeks to respond to admissions offer. The school does consider requests for deferred entrance. Starting month for the class of 2011–2012: **August** The school doesn't have an Early Decision Plan (EDP). A personal interview is required for admission.

Undergraduate coursework required

Medical school requires undergraduate work in these subjects: biology, English, organic chemistry, inorganic (general) chemistry, physics, mathematics, demonstration of writing skills, calculus, general chemistry.

ADMISSIONS POLICY
(TEXT PROVIDED BY SCHOOL):

Maturity, strong study habits, intelligence, character, integrity, and professionalism are essential qualifications for admission. Beyond these, premedical students should strive for an education that develops abilities to observe critically, think analytically, and work independently.

FINANCIAL AID

Financial aid phone number: **(919) 684-6649**
Tuition, 2009-2010 academic year: **$45,992**
Room and board: **$13,740**
Percentage of students receiving financial aid in 2009-10: **91%**
Percentage of students receiving: Loans: **65%**, Grants/scholarships: **68%**, Work-study aid: **0%**
Average medical school debt for the class of 2008: **$103,403**

STUDENT BODY

Fall 2009 full-time enrollment: **421**
Men: **51%**, Women: **49%**, In-state: **11%**, Minorities: **48%**, American Indian: **1.4%**, Asian-American: **22.1%**, African-American: **18.5%**, Hispanic-American: **2.6%**, White: **44.9%**, International: **3.8%**, Unknown: **6.7%**

ACADEMIC PROGRAMS

The school's curriculum frequently give first-year students substantial contact with patients.

There are opportunities for first- or second-year students to work in community health clinics.

Program areas: AIDS, drug/alcohol abuse, family medicine, geriatrics, internal medicine, pediatrics, rural medicine, women's health

Joint degrees awarded: M.D./Ph.D., M.D./M.B.A., M.D./M.P.H., M.D./J.D., M.D./M.S., M.D./M.A.

Total National Institutes of Health (NIH) grants awarded to the medical school and affiliated hospitals: **$398.8 million**

CURRICULUM

(TEXT PROVIDED BY MEDICAL SCHOOL):

Duke University School of Medicine offers an educational program unlike any other in the country. The basic sciences are taught in one year. The core clerkships are completed in the second year. The third year is devoted to scholarly investigation through one-on-one mentored research or the pursuit of a Masters or PhD degree. Elective clinical rotations are fulfilled in the fourth year.

FALL 2009 FACULTY PROFILE

Total teaching faculty: **1,427 (full-time), 0 (part-time)**
Of full-time faculty, those teaching in basic sciences: **14%**;
in clinical programs: **86%**

Of part-time faculty, those teaching in basic sciences: **N/A**; in clinical programs: **N/A**
Full-time faculty/student ratio: **3.4**

SUPPORT SERVICES

The school offers students these services for dealing with stress: expanded-hour gym access, peer counseling, professional counseling, religious support, support groups.

RESIDENCY PROFILE

Most popular residency and specialty programs chosen by the 2008 and 2009 M.D. graduating classes: anesthesiology, dermatology, emergency medicine, internal medicine, internal medicine–pediatrics, ophthalmology, orthopaedic surgery, pediatrics, radiology–diagnostic, surgery–general.

WHERE GRADS GO

33.0%
Proportion of 2007-2008 graduates who entered primary care specialties

32.0%
Proportion of 2008-2009 graduates who accepted in-state residencies

East Carolina University
Brody

■ 600 Moye Boulevard, Greenville, NC 27834
■ Public
■ Year Founded: 1975
■ Tuition, 2009-2010: In-state: $10,193; Out-of-State: $35,183
■ Enrollment 2009-2010 academic year: 306
■ Website: http://www.ecu.edu/bsomadmissions
■ Specialty ranking: family medicine: 22

3.60 AVERAGE GPA, ENTERING CLASS FALL 2009

9.3 AVERAGE MCAT, ENTERING CLASS FALL 2009

14.0% ACCEPTANCE RATE, ENTERING CLASS FALL 2009

Unranked 2011 U.S. NEWS MEDICAL SCHOOL RANKING (RESEARCH)

28 2011 U.S. NEWS MEDICAL SCHOOL RANKING (PRIMARY CARE)

ADMISSIONS

Admissions phone number: (252) 744-2202
Admissions email address: **somadmissions@ecu.edu**
Application web site: **N/A**
Acceptance rate: **14.0%**
In-state acceptance rate: **14.0%**
Out-of-state acceptance rate: **N/A**
Minority acceptance rate: **11.5%**
International acceptance rate: **N/A**

Fall 2009 applications and acceptees

Type	Applied	Interviewed	Accepted	Enrolled
Total:	879	505	123	78
In-state:	879	505	123	78
Out-of-state:	0	N/A	N/A	N/A

Profile of admitted students

Average undergraduate grade point average: **3.60**
MCAT averages (scale: 1-15; writing test: J-T):
Composite score: **9.3**
Verbal reasoning score: **9.0**, Physical sciences score: **9.0**,
   Biological score: **10.0**, Writing score: **P**
Proportion with undergraduate majors in: Biological
   sciences: **45%**, Physical sciences: **40%**, Non-sciences:
   4%, Other health professions: **2%**, Mixed disciplines and
   other: **9%**
Percentage of students not coming directly from college
   after graduation: **59%**

Dates and details

The American Medical College Application Service
   (AMCAS) application is accepted.
School asks for a second, school-specific application as part
   of the admissions process.
Oldest MCAT considered for Fall 2011 entry: **2007**
Earliest application date for the 2011-2012 first-year class:
   06/01
Latest application date: **11/15**
Acceptance dates for regular application for the class
   entering in Fall 2011.
Earliest: **15-OCT-10**

Latest: **10-AUG-11**
Applicants have 3 weeks to respond to admissions offer.
The school does consider requests for deferred entrance.
Starting month for the class of 2011–2012: **August**
The school does have an Early Decision Plan (EDP).
A personal interview is required for admission.

Undergraduate coursework required

Medical school requires undergraduate work in these subjects: biology, biology/zoology, English, organic chemistry,
inorganic (general) chemistry, physics.

ADMISSIONS POLICY
(TEXT PROVIDED BY SCHOOL):

   Factors encompass the intellectual, personal, and social
development of applicants. A variety of data is used (grades;
MCAT performance or other standardized tests; the personal and professional experiences; evaluations from faculty
members, etc; interviews, etc.). The BSOM is a state-sup-
ported school; very strong preference is given to qualified
residents of North Carolina.

FINANCIAL AID

Financial aid phone number: (252) 744-2278
Tuition, 2009-2010 academic year: **In-state: $10,193; Out-
   of-State: $35,183**
Room and board: **$11,162**
Percentage of students receiving financial aid in 2009-10:
   90%
Percentage of students receiving: Loans: **83%**,
   Grants/scholarships: **50%**, Work-study aid: **0%**
Average medical school debt for the class of 2008: **$85,177**

STUDENT BODY

Fall 2009 full-time enrollment: **306**
Men: **50%**, Women: **50%**, In-state: **100%**, Minorities: **33%**,
   American Indian: **1.3%**, Asian-American: **10.8%**,
   African-American: **14.1%**, Hispanic-American: **3.6%**,
   White: **66.7%**, International: **0.0%**, Unknown: **3.6%**

ACADEMIC PROGRAMS

The school's curriculum very frequently give first-year students substantial contact with patients.

There are opportunities for first or second year students to work in community health clinics.

Program areas: drug/alcohol abuse, family medicine, geriatrics, internal medicine, pediatrics, rural medicine, women's health

Joint degrees awarded: M.D./Ph.D., M.D./M.B.A., M.D./M.P.H.

Total National Institutes of Health (NIH) grants awarded to the medical school and affiliated hospitals: **$6.0 million**

CURRICULUM
(TEXT PROVIDED BY MEDICAL SCHOOL):

The curriculum provides a logical integration of basic science and clinical science knowledge over the four year span. Early experience in the patient care settings is achieved through preceptorships throughout the state and through contact with both standardized and clinical patients in the first two years. Innovative teaching methods are employed.

FALL 2009 FACULTY PROFILE

Total teaching faculty: **392 (full-time)**, **59 (part-time)**

Of full-time faculty, those teaching in basic sciences: **20%**; in clinical programs: **80%**

Of part-time faculty, those teaching in basic sciences: **20%**; in clinical programs: **80%**

Full-time faculty/student ratio: **1.3**

SUPPORT SERVICES

The school offers students these services for dealing with stress: expanded-hour gym access, peer counseling, professional counseling, religious support, support groups.

RESIDENCY PROFILE

Most popular residency and specialty programs chosen by the 2008 and 2009 M.D. graduating classes: anesthesiology, emergency medicine, family practice, internal medicine, obstetrics and gynecology, pathology–anatomic and clinical, pediatrics, pediatrics–adolescent medicine, surgery–general, internal medicine/pediatrics.

WHERE GRADS GO

52.3%

Proportion of 2007-2008 graduates who entered primary care specialties

36.0%

Proportion of 2008-2009 graduates who accepted in-state residencies

Eastern Virginia Medical School

■ 721 Fairfax Avenue, PO Box 1980, Norfolk, VA 23501-1980
■ Public
■ Year Founded: 1973
■ Tuition, 2009-2010: In-state: $27,620; Out-of-State: $50,380
■ Enrollment 2009-2010 academic year: 448
■ Website: http://www.evms.edu
■ Specialty ranking: N/A

3.46 AVERAGE GPA, ENTERING CLASS FALL 2009

10.3 AVERAGE MCAT, ENTERING CLASS FALL 2009

5.6% ACCEPTANCE RATE, ENTERING CLASS FALL 2009

Unranked 2011 U.S. NEWS MEDICAL SCHOOL RANKING (RESEARCH)

Unranked 2011 U.S. NEWS MEDICAL SCHOOL RANKING (PRIMARY CARE)

ADMISSIONS
Admissions phone number: **(757) 446-5812**
Admissions email address: **mclendm@evms.edu**
Application web site: **http://www.evms.edu/prospective-students-home/prospective-students-homepage.html**
Acceptance rate: **5.6%**
In-state acceptance rate: **19.1%**
Out-of-state acceptance rate: **3.0%**
Minority acceptance rate: **N/A**
International acceptance rate: **N/A**

Fall 2009 applications and acceptees

Type	Applied	Interviewed	Accepted	Enrolled
Total:	5,169	682	292	118
In-state:	848	371	162	71
Out-of-state:	4,321	311	130	47

Profile of admitted students
Average undergraduate grade point average: **3.46**
MCAT averages (scale: 1-15; writing test: J-T):
Composite score: **10.3**
Verbal reasoning score: **10.0**, Physical sciences score: **10.0**, Biological score: **11.0**, Writing score: **N/A**
Proportion with undergraduate majors in: Biological sciences: **35%**, Physical sciences: **14%**, Non-sciences: **7%**, Other health professions: **23%**, Mixed disciplines and other: **21%**
Percentage of students not coming directly from college after graduation: **70%**

Dates and details
The American Medical College Application Service (AMCAS) application is accepted.
School asks for a second, school-specific application as part of the admissions process.
Oldest MCAT considered for Fall 2011 entry: **2008**
Earliest application date for the 2011-2012 first-year class: **01/06**
Latest application date: **11/15**
Acceptance dates for regular application for the class entering in Fall 2011.

Earliest: **15-OCT-10**
Latest: **22-AUG-11**
Applicants have 2 weeks to respond to admissions offer. The school does consider requests for deferred entrance. Starting month for the class of 2011-2012: **August**
The school does have an Early Decision Plan (EDP).
A personal interview is required for admission.

Undergraduate coursework required
Medical school requires undergraduate work in these subjects: biology, organic chemistry, inorganic (general) chemistry, physics.

ADMISSIONS POLICY
(TEXT PROVIDED BY SCHOOL):
   EVMS requires academic excellence of those students admitted to the medical school. Academic ability is gauged by performance in undergraduate courses and scores on the MCAT. Applicants must demonstrate an understanding of the role of the physician, and an appreciation for the interactive and caring nature of the practitioner. Preference to applicants from Virginia, especially Hampton Roads.

FINANCIAL AID
Financial aid phone number: **(757) 446-5814**
Tuition, 2009-2010 academic year: **In-state: $27,620; Out-of-State: $50,380**
Room and board: **$12,285**
Percentage of students receiving financial aid in 2009-10: **76%**
Percentage of students receiving: Loans: **76%**, Grants/scholarships: **43%**, Work-study aid: **0%**
Average medical school debt for the class of 2008: **$143,605**

STUDENT BODY
Fall 2009 full-time enrollment: **448**
Men: **55%**, Women: **45%**, In-state: **63%**, Minorities: **23%**, American Indian: **N/A**, Asian-American: **N/A**, African-American: **N/A**, Hispanic-American: **N/A**, White: **N/A**, International: **N/A**, Unknown: **N/A**

ACADEMIC PROGRAMS

The school's curriculum frequently give first-year students substantial contact with patients.

There are opportunities for first- or second-year students to work in community health clinics.

Program areas: AIDS, drug/alcohol abuse, family medicine, geriatrics, internal medicine, pediatrics, rural medicine

Joint degrees awarded: M.D./M.P.H.

Total National Institutes of Health (NIH) grants awarded to the medical school and affiliated hospitals: N/A

CURRICULUM

(TEXT PROVIDED BY MEDICAL SCHOOL):

Provide a firm foundation in medical sciences and clinical skills; teach medical problem solving using the best available evidence; cultivate independent life-long learning and scholarship; develop an appreciation for the social and economic responsibilities of the medical profession; encourage self-awareness and communication skills; emphasize human values in the practice of medicine.

FALL 2009 FACULTY PROFILE

Total teaching faculty: 365 (full-time), 29 (part-time)

Of full-time faculty, those teaching in basic sciences: 13%; in clinical programs: 87%

Of part-time faculty, those teaching in basic sciences: 3%; in clinical programs: 97%

Full-time faculty/student ratio: 0.8

SUPPORT SERVICES

The school offers students these services for dealing with stress: expanded-hour gym access, peer counseling, professional counseling, religious support.

RESIDENCY PROFILE

Most popular residency and specialty programs chosen by the 2008 and 2009 M.D. graduating classes: anesthesiology, emergency medicine, family practice, internal medicine, obstetrics and gynecology, pediatrics, surgery–general.

WHERE GRADS GO

47.0%

Proportion of 2007-2008 graduates who entered primary care specialties

33.0%

Proportion of 2008-2009 graduates who accepted in-state residencies

East Tennessee State University
Quillen

- PO Box 70694, Johnson City, TN 37614
- Public
- Year Founded: 1974
- Tuition, 2009-2010: In-state: $24,457; Out-of-State: $48,215
- Enrollment 2009-2010 academic year: 253
- Website: http://com.etsu.edu
- Specialty ranking: family medicine: 20, rural medicine: 6

3.68 AVERAGE GPA, ENTERING CLASS FALL 2009

9.1 AVERAGE MCAT, ENTERING CLASS FALL 2009

8.8% ACCEPTANCE RATE, ENTERING CLASS FALL 2009

Unranked 2011 U.S. NEWS MEDICAL SCHOOL RANKING (RESEARCH)

46 2011 U.S. NEWS MEDICAL SCHOOL RANKING (PRIMARY CARE)

ADMISSIONS

Admissions phone number: **(423) 439-2033**
Admissions email address: **sacom@etsu.edu**
Application web site: **http://www.aamc.org**
Acceptance rate: **8.8%**
In-state acceptance rate: **22.4%**
Out-of-state acceptance rate: **1.4%**
Minority acceptance rate: **5.9%**
International acceptance rate: **N/A**

Fall 2009 applications and acceptees

Type	Applied	Interviewed	Accepted	Enrolled
Total:	1,445	233	127	66
In-state:	508	186	114	60
Out-of-state:	937	47	13	6

Profile of admitted students

Average undergraduate grade point average: **3.68**
MCAT averages (scale: 1-15; writing test: J-T):
Composite score: **9.1**
Verbal reasoning score: **9.1**, Physical sciences score: **8.7**, Biological score: **9.4**, Writing score: **O**
Proportion with undergraduate majors in: Biological sciences: **53%**, Physical sciences: **21%**, Non-sciences: **15%**, Other health professions: **9%**, Mixed disciplines and other: **2%**
Percentage of students not coming directly from college after graduation: **N/A**

Dates and details

The American Medical College Application Service (AMCAS) application is accepted.
School asks for a second, school-specific application as part of the admissions process.
Oldest MCAT considered for Fall 2011 entry: **2008**
Earliest application date for the 2011-2012 first-year class: **06/01**
Latest application date: **11/15**
Acceptance dates for regular application for the class entering in Fall 2011.
Earliest: **15-OCT-10**

Latest: **12-AUG-11**
Applicants have 2 weeks to respond to admissions offer.
The school does consider requests for deferred entrance.
Starting month for the class of 2011–2012: **August**
The school does have an Early Decision Plan (EDP).
A personal interview is required for admission.

Undergraduate coursework required

Medical school requires undergraduate work in these subjects: biology/zoology, English, organic chemistry, inorganic (general) chemistry, physics.

ADMISSIONS POLICY
(TEXT PROVIDED BY SCHOOL):

Quillen COM evaluates applicants on the basis of demonstrated academic achievement, MCAT scores, letters of recommendation, pertinent extracurricular work and research experience, non-scholastic accomplishment, motivation for the study and practice of medicine, and interest in a primary care practice in a rural or under served area. For more information, access web site http://com.etsu.edu.

FINANCIAL AID

Financial aid phone number: **(423) 439-2035**
Tuition, 2009-2010 academic year: **In-state: $24,457; Out-of-State: $48,215**
Room and board: **$12,621**
Percentage of students receiving financial aid in 2009-10: **N/A**
Percentage of students receiving: Loans: **N/A**, Grants/scholarships: **N/A**, Work-study aid: **N/A**
Average medical school debt for the class of 2008: **$115,594**

STUDENT BODY

Fall 2009 full-time enrollment: **253**
Men: **53%**, Women: **47%**, In-state: **92%**, Minorities: **14%**, American Indian: **N/A**, Asian-American: **8.7%**, African-American: **5.1%**, Hispanic-American: **0.4%**, White: **85.8%**, International: **N/A**, Unknown: **N/A**

ACADEMIC PROGRAMS

The school's curriculum frequently give first-year students substantial contact with patients.

There are opportunities for first- or second-year students to work in community health clinics.

Program areas: AIDS, drug/alcohol abuse, family medicine, geriatrics, internal medicine, pediatrics, rural medicine, women's health

Joint degrees awarded: N/A

Total National Institutes of Health (NIH) grants awarded to the medical school and affiliated hospitals: **N/A**

CURRICULUM
(TEXT PROVIDED BY MEDICAL SCHOOL):

The College of Medicine curriculum is designed to assist students in gaining the fundamental knowledge, attitude, skills, and practice principles required to enter residency training while encouraging the acquisition of lifelong habits of intellectual activity, independent thought, critical evaluation, and professionalism. For more information, access the Quillen web site at http://com.etsu.edu.

FALL 2009 FACULTY PROFILE

Total teaching faculty: **225 (full-time), 55 (part-time)**

Of full-time faculty, those teaching in basic sciences: **21%**; in clinical programs: **79%**

Of part-time faculty, those teaching in basic sciences: **2%**; in clinical programs: **98%**

Full-time faculty/student ratio: **0.9**

SUPPORT SERVICES

The school offers students these services for dealing with stress: expanded-hour gym access, peer counseling, professional counseling, religious support.

RESIDENCY PROFILE

Most popular residency and specialty programs chosen by the 2008 and 2009 M.D. graduating classes: emergency medicine, family practice, internal medicine, obstetrics and gynecology, pediatrics, psychiatry, surgery–general.

WHERE GRADS GO

50.9%

Proportion of 2007-2008 graduates who entered primary care specialties

31.6%

Proportion of 2008-2009 graduates who accepted in-state residencies

Emory University

- 1648 Pierce Drive, Atlanta, GA 30322-1053
- Private
- **Year Founded:** 1854
- **Tuition, 2009-2010:** $42,876
- **Enrollment 2009-2010 academic year:** 517
- **Website:** http://www.med.emory.edu
- **Specialty ranking:** AIDS: 21, internal medicine: 19

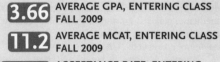

3.66	AVERAGE GPA, ENTERING CLASS FALL 2009
11.2	AVERAGE MCAT, ENTERING CLASS FALL 2009
8.0%	ACCEPTANCE RATE, ENTERING CLASS FALL 2009
20	2011 U.S. NEWS MEDICAL SCHOOL RANKING (RESEARCH)
25	2011 U.S. NEWS MEDICAL SCHOOL RANKING (PRIMARY CARE)

ADMISSIONS

Admissions phone number: **(404) 727-5660**
Admissions email address: **medadmiss@emory.edu**
Application web site: **N/A**
Acceptance rate: **8.0%**
In-state acceptance rate: **13.1%**
Out-of-state acceptance rate: **7.4%**
Minority acceptance rate: **8.3%**
International acceptance rate: **6.1%**

Fall 2009 applications and acceptees

Type	Applied	Interviewed	Accepted	Enrolled
Total:	3,971	659	319	138
In-state:	451	124	59	41
Out-of-state:	3,520	535	260	97

Profile of admitted students

Average undergraduate grade point average: **3.66**
MCAT averages (scale: 1-15; writing test: J-T):
Composite score: **11.2**
Verbal reasoning score: **10.8**, Physical sciences score: **11.3**, Biological score: **11.6**, Writing score: **P**
Proportion with undergraduate majors in: Biological sciences: **36%**, Physical sciences: **15%**, Non-sciences: **23%**, Other health professions: **0%**, Mixed disciplines and other: **26%**
Percentage of students not coming directly from college after graduation: **51%**

Dates and details

The American Medical College Application Service (AMCAS) application is accepted.
School asks for a second, school-specific application as part of the admissions process.
Oldest MCAT considered for Fall 2011 entry: **2007**
Earliest application date for the 2011-2012 first-year class: **06/01**
Latest application date: **10/15**
Acceptance dates for regular application for the class entering in Fall 2011.
Earliest: **01-NOV-10**

Latest: **15-MAR-11**
Applicants have 2 weeks to respond to admissions offer.
The school does consider requests for deferred entrance.
Starting month for the class of 2011–2012: **July**
The school doesn't have an Early Decision Plan (EDP).
A personal interview is required for admission.

Undergraduate coursework required

Medical school requires undergraduate work in these subjects: biology, English, organic chemistry, inorganic (general) chemistry, physics, humanities, behavioral science, demonstration of writing skills, general chemistry.

ADMISSIONS POLICY
(TEXT PROVIDED BY SCHOOL):

Students selected on the basis of scholastic achievement, extracurricular activities and personal qualities, without regard to race, sex, sexual orientation, age, disability, creed, veteran status, or national origin. Students apply via AMCAS, must have taken the MCAT within 4 years of matriculation, submit Emory supplemental application/fee, evaluation(s) and if invited, appear for an interview.

FINANCIAL AID

Financial aid phone number: **(404) 727-6039**
Tuition, 2009-2010 academic year: **$42,876**
Room and board: **$23,664**
Percentage of students receiving financial aid in 2009-10: **88%**
Percentage of students receiving: Loans: **77%**, Grants/scholarships: **73%**, Work-study aid: **0%**
Average medical school debt for the class of 2008: **$146,824**

STUDENT BODY

Fall 2009 full-time enrollment: **517**
Men: **47%**, Women: **53%**, In-state: **32%**, Minorities: **30%**, American Indian: **0.2%**, Asian-American: **17.6%**, African-American: **8.1%**, Hispanic-American: **3.7%**, White: **62.7%**, International: **2.5%**, Unknown: **5.2%**

ACADEMIC PROGRAMS

The school's curriculum frequently give first-year students substantial contact with patients.

There are opportunities for first- or second-year students to work in community health clinics.

Program areas: AIDS, drug/alcohol abuse, family medicine, geriatrics, internal medicine, pediatrics, women's health

Joint degrees awarded: M.D./Ph.D., M.D./M.P.H., M.D./M.S.

Total National Institutes of Health (NIH) grants awarded to the medical school and affiliated hospitals: **$282.6 million**

CURRICULUM

(TEXT PROVIDED BY MEDICAL SCHOOL):

The patient centered curriculum consists of 4 phases: Foundations, Applications (clerkships), Discovery (a supervised project), and Translation. Patient contact begins the first month; students enter the Applications phase in March of year 2. A society system provides for close student/faculty interaction over the entire 4 years, emphasizing professional development and life-long learning.

FALL 2009 FACULTY PROFILE

Total teaching faculty: **2,032 (full-time), 201 (part-time)**
Of full-time faculty, those teaching in basic sciences: **9%**; in clinical programs: **91%**

Of part-time faculty, those teaching in basic sciences: **2%**; in clinical programs: **98%**
Full-time faculty/student ratio: **3.9**

SUPPORT SERVICES

The school offers students these services for dealing with stress: expanded-hour gym access, peer counseling, professional counseling, religious support, support groups.

RESIDENCY PROFILE

Most popular residency and specialty programs chosen by the 2008 and 2009 M.D. graduating classes: anesthesiology, emergency medicine, family practice, internal medicine, neurology, ophthalmology, orthopaedic surgery, pediatrics, radiology–diagnostic, surgery–general.

WHERE GRADS GO

40.2%

Proportion of 2007-2008 graduates who entered primary care specialties

35.2%

Proportion of 2008-2009 graduates who accepted in-state residencies

Florida State University

■ 1115 W. Call Street, Tallahassee, FL 32306-4300
■ Public
■ Year Founded: 2000
■ Tuition, 2009-2010: In-state: $20,354; Out-of-State: $60,546
■ Enrollment 2009-2010 academic year: 455
■ Website: http://www.med.fsu.edu/
■ Specialty ranking: N/A

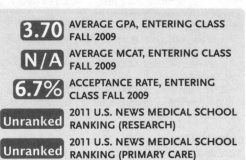

3.70 AVERAGE GPA, ENTERING CLASS FALL 2009

N/A AVERAGE MCAT, ENTERING CLASS FALL 2009

6.7% ACCEPTANCE RATE, ENTERING CLASS FALL 2009

Unranked 2011 U.S. NEWS MEDICAL SCHOOL RANKING (RESEARCH)

Unranked 2011 U.S. NEWS MEDICAL SCHOOL RANKING (PRIMARY CARE)

ADMISSIONS

Admissions phone number: **(850) 644-7904**
Admissions email address: **medadmissions@med.fsu.edu**
Application web site: **N/A**
Acceptance rate: **6.7%**
In-state acceptance rate: **11.5%**
Out-of-state acceptance rate: **0.4%**
Minority acceptance rate: **5.4%**
International acceptance rate: **N/A**

Fall 2009 applications and acceptees

Type	Applied	Interviewed	Accepted	Enrolled
Total:	3,280	370	221	119
In-state:	1,880	362	216	116
Out-of-state:	1,400	8	5	3

Profile of admitted students

Average undergraduate grade point average: **3.70**
MCAT averages (scale: 1-15; writing test: J-T):
Composite score: **N/A**
Verbal reasoning score: **9.1**, Physical sciences score: **9.2**, Biological score: **9.9**, Writing score: **O**
Proportion with undergraduate majors in: Biological sciences: **53%**, Physical sciences: **11%**, Non-sciences: **19%**, Other health professions: **4%**, Mixed disciplines and other: **14%**
Percentage of students not coming directly from college after graduation: **N/A**

Dates and details

The American Medical College Application Service (AMCAS) application is accepted.
School asks for a second, school-specific application as part of the admissions process.
Oldest MCAT considered for Fall 2011 entry: **2008**
Earliest application date for the 2011-2012 first-year class: **06/01**
Latest application date: **12/01**
Acceptance dates for regular application for the class entering in Fall 2011.
Earliest: **15-OCT-10**

Latest: **27-MAY-11**
Applicants have 2 weeks to respond to admissions offer.
The school does consider requests for deferred entrance.
Starting month for the class of 2011–2012: **June**
The school does have an Early Decision Plan (EDP).
A personal interview is required for admission.

Undergraduate coursework required

Medical school requires undergraduate work in these subjects: biology, English, organic chemistry, inorganic (general) chemistry, physics, biochemistry, mathematics, general chemistry.

ADMISSIONS POLICY
(TEXT PROVIDED BY SCHOOL):

We seek students who have demonstrated a commitment of service to others and we encourage applications from traditional and nontraditional students, as well as students from rural, inner city or other medically underserved areas. An applicant should have completed prerequisite courses in English, biology, chemistry, organic chemistry, physics, and biochemistry.

FINANCIAL AID

Financial aid phone number: **(850) 645-7270**
Tuition, 2009-2010 academic year: **In-state: $20,354; Out-of-State: $60,546**
Room and board: **$15,385**
Percentage of students receiving financial aid in 2009-10: **N/A**
Percentage of students receiving: Loans: **N/A**, Grants/scholarships: **N/A**, Work-study aid: **N/A**
Average medical school debt for the class of 2008: **$147,597**

STUDENT BODY

Fall 2009 full-time enrollment: **455**
Men: **43%**, Women: **57%**, In-state: **99%**, Minorities: **33%**, American Indian: **0.9%**, Asian-American: **13.2%**, African-American: **10.1%**, Hispanic-American: **8.8%**, White: **64.4%**, International: **0.0%**, Unknown: **2.6%**

ACADEMIC PROGRAMS

The school's curriculum very frequently give first-year students substantial contact with patients.

There are opportunities for first- or second-year students to work in community health clinics.

Program areas: AIDS, drug/alcohol abuse, family medicine, geriatrics, internal medicine, pediatrics, rural medicine, women's health

Joint degrees awarded: N/A

Total National Institutes of Health (NIH) grants awarded to the medical school and affiliated hospitals: **$4.7 million**

CURRICULUM
(TEXT PROVIDED BY MEDICAL SCHOOL):

In the faculty-scholar model highly skilled, innovative faculty members present a well-structured continuum of education in biomedical, behavioral and clinical sciences utilizing problem-based and small-group learning experiences. Community-based clinical education spans the four-year curriculum, providing access to more than 1,500 of the top physicians in Florida at locations across the state.

FALL 2009 FACULTY PROFILE

Total teaching faculty: **121 (full-time)**, **1,569 (part-time)**

Of full-time faculty, those teaching in basic sciences: **34%**; in clinical programs: **66%**

Of part-time faculty, those teaching in basic sciences: **4%**; in clinical programs: **96%**

Full-time faculty/student ratio: **0.3**

SUPPORT SERVICES

The school offers students these services for dealing with stress: expanded-hour gym access, professional counseling, support groups.

RESIDENCY PROFILE

Most popular residency and specialty programs chosen by the 2008 and 2009 M.D. graduating classes: anesthesiology, emergency medicine, family practice, internal medicine, neurology, obstetrics and gynecology, orthopaedic surgery, pediatrics, psychiatry, surgery–general.

WHERE GRADS GO

45.8%

Proportion of 2007-2008 graduates who entered primary care specialties

46.8%

Proportion of 2008-2009 graduates who accepted in-state residencies

Georgetown University

- 3900 Reservoir Road NW, Med-Dent Building, Washington, DC 20007
- Private
- **Year Founded:** 1851
- **Tuition, 2009-2010:** $46,177
- **Enrollment 2009-2010 academic year:** 804
- **Website:** http://som.georgetown.edu/
- **Specialty ranking:** N/A

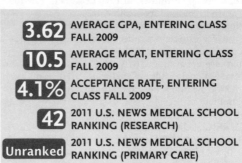

3.62	AVERAGE GPA, ENTERING CLASS FALL 2009
10.5	AVERAGE MCAT, ENTERING CLASS FALL 2009
4.1%	ACCEPTANCE RATE, ENTERING CLASS FALL 2009
42	2011 U.S. NEWS MEDICAL SCHOOL RANKING (RESEARCH)
Unranked	2011 U.S. NEWS MEDICAL SCHOOL RANKING (PRIMARY CARE)

ADMISSIONS

Admissions phone number: **(202) 687-1154**
Admissions email address:
medicaladmissions@georgetown.edu
Application web site:
http://som.georgetown.edu/prospectivestudents
Acceptance rate: **4.1%**
In-state acceptance rate: **9.6%**
Out-of-state acceptance rate: **4.0%**
Minority acceptance rate: **N/A**
International acceptance rate: **N/A**

Fall 2009 applications and acceptees

Type	Applied	Interviewed	Accepted	Enrolled
Total:	10,797	1,158	440	197
In-state:	52	10	5	4
Out-of-state:	10,745	1,148	435	193

Profile of admitted students

Average undergraduate grade point average: **3.62**
MCAT averages (scale: 1-15; writing test: J-T):
Composite score: **10.5**
Verbal reasoning score: **9.9**, Physical sciences score: **10.6**, Biological score: **11.0**, Writing score: **Q**
Proportion with undergraduate majors in: Biological sciences: **35%**, Physical sciences: **11%**, Non-sciences: **19%**, Other health professions: **7%**, Mixed disciplines and other: **28%**
Percentage of students not coming directly from college after graduation: **59%**

Dates and details

The American Medical College Application Service (AMCAS) application is accepted.
School asks for a second, school-specific application as part of the admissions process.
Oldest MCAT considered for Fall 2011 entry: **2008**
Earliest application date for the 2011-2012 first-year class: **05/01**
Latest application date: **10/31**

Acceptance dates for regular application for the class entering in Fall 2011.
Earliest: **16-OCT-10**
Latest: **03-AUG-11**
Applicants have 3 weeks to respond to admissions offer.
The school does consider requests for deferred entrance.
Starting month for the class of 2011–2012: **August**
The school doesn't have an Early Decision Plan (EDP).
A personal interview is required for admission.

Undergraduate coursework required

Medical school requires undergraduate work in these subjects: biology, English, organic chemistry, inorganic (general) chemistry, physics, mathematics.

ADMISSIONS POLICY
(TEXT PROVIDED BY SCHOOL):

Secondary Application requirements and procedures are emailed to each applicant. It requires a personal essay unique to Georgetown for consideration of admission. An applicant must not only present a strong academic profile, but must also demonstrate well-developed non-cognitive qualities. GU selects students on the basis of academic achievement, character, maturity, and motivation.

FINANCIAL AID

Financial aid phone number: **(202) 687-1693**
Tuition, 2009-2010 academic year: **$46,177**
Room and board: **$17,060**
Percentage of students receiving financial aid in 2009-10: **88%**
Percentage of students receiving: Loans: **86%**, Grants/scholarships: **48%**, Work-study aid: **1%**
Average medical school debt for the class of 2008: **$172,240**

STUDENT BODY

Fall 2009 full-time enrollment: **804**
Men: **51%**, Women: **49%**, In-state: **0%**, Minorities: **30%**, American Indian: **0.2%**, Asian-American: **17.8%**,

African-American: **7.1%**, Hispanic-American: **2.7%**, White: **62.8%**, International: **1.2%**, Unknown: **8.1%**

ACADEMIC PROGRAMS

The school's curriculum frequently give first-year students substantial contact with patients.

There are opportunities for first- or second-year students to work in community health clinics.

Program areas: AIDS, drug/alcohol abuse, family medicine, geriatrics, internal medicine, pediatrics, rural medicine, women's health

Joint degrees awarded: M.D./Ph.D., M.D./M.B.A., M.D./M.S., M.D./M.A.

Total National Institutes of Health (NIH) grants awarded to the medical school and affiliated hospitals: **$165.4 million**

CURRICULUM

(TEXT PROVIDED BY MEDICAL SCHOOL):

The first two years provide students with an early introduction to foundational science, the patient, as well as to the spiritual and ethical dimensions of medicine. In the third year the student serves clinical rotations conducted by departments at the Medical Center and its affiliates. The fourth year provides the student with supervised responsibility in the clinical management of patients.

FALL 2009 FACULTY PROFILE

Total teaching faculty: **1,833 (full-time)**, **289 (part-time)**

Of full-time faculty, those teaching in basic sciences: **12%**; in clinical programs: **88%**

Of part-time faculty, those teaching in basic sciences; **21%**; in clinical programs: **79%**

Full-time faculty/student ratio: **2.3**

SUPPORT SERVICES

The school offers students these services for dealing with stress: expanded-hour gym access, peer counseling, professional counseling, religious support, support groups.

RESIDENCY PROFILE

Most popular residency and specialty programs chosen by the 2008 and 2009 M.D. graduating classes: anesthesiology, emergency medicine, internal medicine, neurology, obstetrics and gynecology, ophthalmology, orthopaedic surgery, pediatrics, radiology–diagnostic, surgery–general.

WHERE GRADS GO

42.0%

Proportion of 2007-2008 graduates who entered primary care specialties

30.0%

Proportion of 2008-2009 graduates who accepted in-state residencies

George Washington University

■ 2300 Eye Street NW, Room 713W, Washington, DC 20037
■ Private
■ Year Founded: 1821
■ Tuition, 2009-2010: $47,644
■ Enrollment 2009-2010 academic year: 717
■ Website: http://www.gwumc.edu/
■ Specialty ranking: N/A

3.64 AVERAGE GPA, ENTERING CLASS FALL 2009

9.8 AVERAGE MCAT, ENTERING CLASS FALL 2009

3.2% ACCEPTANCE RATE, ENTERING CLASS FALL 2009

Unranked 2011 U.S. NEWS MEDICAL SCHOOL RANKING (RESEARCH)

Unranked 2011 U.S. NEWS MEDICAL SCHOOL RANKING (PRIMARY CARE)

ADMISSIONS

Admissions phone number: **(202) 994-3506**
Admissions email address: **medadmit@gwu.edu**
Application web site: **http://www.gwumc.edu/edu/admis/**
Acceptance rate: **3.2%**
In-state acceptance rate: **N/A**
Out-of-state acceptance rate: **N/A**
Minority acceptance rate: **N/A**
International acceptance rate: **N/A**

Fall 2009 applications and acceptees

Type	Applied	Interviewed	Accepted	Enrolled
Total:	10,557	1,107	334	177
In-state:	N/A	N/A	N/A	N/A
Out-of-state:	N/A	N/A	N/A	N/A

Profile of admitted students

Average undergraduate grade point average: **3.64**
MCAT averages (scale: 1-15; writing test: J-T):
Composite score: **9.8**
Verbal reasoning score: **9.6**, Physical sciences score: **9.6**,
Biological score: **10.2**, Writing score: **P**
Proportion with undergraduate majors in: Biological
sciences: **37%**, Physical sciences: **17%**, Non-sciences:
19%, Other health professions: **9%**, Mixed disciplines
and other: **19%**
Percentage of students not coming directly from college
after graduation: **59%**

Dates and details

The American Medical College Application Service
(AMCAS) application is accepted.
School asks for a second, school-specific application as part
of the admissions process.
Oldest MCAT considered for Fall 2011 entry: **2008**
Earliest application date for the 2011-2012 first-year class:
07/01
Latest application date: **12/01**
Acceptance dates for regular application for the class
entering in Fall 2011.
Earliest: **15-OCT-10**

Latest: **N/A**
Applicants have 3 weeks to respond to admissions offer.
The school does consider requests for deferred entrance.
Starting month for the class of 2011–2012: **August**
The school does have an Early Decision Plan (EDP).
A personal interview is required for admission.

Undergraduate coursework required

Medical school requires undergraduate work in these subjects: biology, biology/zoology, English, organic chemistry,
inorganic (general) chemistry, physics, humanities, general
chemistry.

ADMISSIONS POLICY

(TEXT PROVIDED BY SCHOOL):
     The Committee on Admissions uses data in AMCAS and
GW applications to review academic performance; MCAT
scores; experiences in leadership, health care, research, and
community service, personal comments and recommendation letters. Evidence of compassion, integrity, cooperation,
motivation, strength of character and interest in taking advantage of our unique program opportunities are important.

FINANCIAL AID

Financial aid phone number: **(202) 994-2960**
Tuition, 2009-2010 academic year: **$47,644**
Room and board: **$22,376**
Percentage of students receiving financial aid in 2009-10:
90%
Percentage of students receiving: Loans: **80%**,
Grants/scholarships: **39%**, Work-study aid: **0%**
Average medical school debt for the class of 2008:
$188,200

STUDENT BODY

Fall 2009 full-time enrollment: **717**
Men: **41%**, Women: **59%**, In-state: **0%**, Minorities: **37%**,
American Indian: **0.1%**, Asian-American: **24.0%**,
African-American: **11.9%**, Hispanic-American: **1.0%**,
White: **48.7%**, International: **2.5%**, Unknown: **11.9%**

ACADEMIC PROGRAMS

The school's curriculum very frequently give first-year students substantial contact with patients.

There are opportunities for first- or second-year students to work in community health clinics.

Program areas: AIDS, drug/alcohol abuse, family medicine, geriatrics, internal medicine, pediatrics, women's health

Joint degrees awarded: M.D./Ph.D., M.D./M.P.H.

Total National Institutes of Health (NIH) grants awarded to the medical school and affiliated hospitals: **$49.0 million**

CURRICULUM

(TEXT PROVIDED BY MEDICAL SCHOOL):

The GWU SMHS provides diverse learning opportunities. The first two years of instruction are taught in interdisciplinary or horizontally integrated courses. Required core clerkships comprise two thirds of the clinical curriculum. Training in interviewing, communication, physical diagnosis, and clinical decision making are completed in our state-of-the-art Clinical Learning/Simulation Center.

FALL 2009 FACULTY PROFILE

Total teaching faculty: **779 (full-time)**, **2,110 (part-time)**
Of full-time faculty, those teaching in basic sciences: **10%**; in clinical programs: **90%**

Of part-time faculty, those teaching in basic sciences: **4%**; in clinical programs: **96%**
Full-time faculty/student ratio: **1.1**

SUPPORT SERVICES

The school offers students these services for dealing with stress: professional counseling.

RESIDENCY PROFILE

Most popular residency and specialty programs chosen by the 2008 and 2009 M.D. graduating classes: anesthesiology, emergency medicine, family practice, internal medicine, obstetrics and gynecology, orthopaedic surgery, pediatrics, psychiatry, radiology–diagnostic, surgery–general.

WHERE GRADS GO

43.0%

Proportion of 2007-2008 graduates who entered primary care specialties

17.0%

Proportion of 2008-2009 graduates who accepted in-state residencies

Harvard University

- 25 Shattuck Street, Boston, MA 02115-6092
- Private
- Year Founded: 1782
- Tuition, 2009-2010: $45,833
- Enrollment 2009-2010 academic year: 705
- Website: http://hms.harvard.edu
- Specialty ranking: AIDS: 3, drug/alcohol abuse: 7, geriatrics: 7, internal medicine: 2, pediatrics: 1, women's health: 1

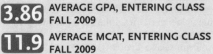

3.86 AVERAGE GPA, ENTERING CLASS FALL 2009

11.9 AVERAGE MCAT, ENTERING CLASS FALL 2009

4.5% ACCEPTANCE RATE, ENTERING CLASS FALL 2009

1 2011 U.S. NEWS MEDICAL SCHOOL RANKING (RESEARCH)

17 2011 U.S. NEWS MEDICAL SCHOOL RANKING (PRIMARY CARE)

ADMISSIONS

Admissions phone number: **(617) 432-1550**
Admissions email address:
admissions_office@hms.harvard.edu
Application web site:
http://hms.harvard.edu/admissions/default.asp?page=application
Acceptance rate: **4.5%**
In-state acceptance rate: **N/A**
Out-of-state acceptance rate: **N/A**
Minority acceptance rate: **5.0%**
International acceptance rate: **3.4%**

Fall 2009 applications and acceptees

Type	Applied	Interviewed	Accepted	Enrolled
Total:	5,031	830	224	165
In-state:	N/A	N/A	N/A	N/A
Out-of-state:	N/A	N/A	N/A	N/A

Profile of admitted students

Average undergraduate grade point average: **3.86**
MCAT averages (scale: 1-15; writing test: J-T):
Composite score: **11.9**
Verbal reasoning score: **10.8**, Physical sciences score: **12.5**, Biological score: **12.4**, Writing score: **R**
Proportion with undergraduate majors in: Biological sciences: **56%**, Physical sciences: **13%**, Non-sciences: **20%**, Other health professions: **N/A**, Mixed disciplines and other: **11%**
Percentage of students not coming directly from college after graduation: **20%**

Dates and details

The American Medical College Application Service (AMCAS) application is accepted.
School asks for a second, school-specific application as part of the admissions process.
Oldest MCAT considered for Fall 2011 entry: **N/A**
Earliest application date for the 2011-2012 first-year class: **01/06**
Latest application date: **12/31**

Acceptance dates for regular application for the class entering in Fall 2011.
Earliest: **03-OCT-10**
Latest: **31-DEC-10**
Applicants have 3 weeks to respond to admissions offer.
The school does consider requests for deferred entrance.
Starting month for the class of 2011–2012: **August**
The school doesn't have an Early Decision Plan (EDP).
A personal interview is required for admission.

Undergraduate coursework required

Medical school requires undergraduate work in these subjects: biology, English, organic chemistry, inorganic (general) chemistry, physics, molecular and cell biology, demonstration of writing skills, calculus.

ADMISSIONS POLICY
(TEXT PROVIDED BY SCHOOL):

Academic excellence is expected. Committee members consider the entire application, including the essay, extracurricular activities, life experiences, research, community work, and letters of recommendation. HMS looks for evidence of integrity, maturity, humanitarian concerns, leadership potential, and an aptitude for working with people. The 2009 entering class came from 59 different colleges.

FINANCIAL AID

Financial aid phone number: **(617) 432-0449**
Tuition, 2009-2010 academic year: **$45,833**
Room and board: **$12,520**
Percentage of students receiving financial aid in 2009-10: **81%**
Percentage of students receiving: Loans: **76%**, Grants/scholarships: **54%**, Work-study aid: **1%**
Average medical school debt for the class of 2008: **$103,663**

STUDENT BODY

Fall 2009 full-time enrollment: **705**
Men: **51%**, Women: **49%**, In-state: **N/A**, Minorities: **53%**, American Indian: **0.9%**, Asian-American: **29.8%**,

African-American: **10.1%**, Hispanic-American: **8.2%**,
White: **38.0%**, International: **6.4%**, Unknown: **6.7%**

ACADEMIC PROGRAMS
The school's curriculum frequently give first-year students
substantial contact with patients.
There are opportunities for first- or second-year students to
work in community health clinics.
Program areas: AIDS, drug/alcohol abuse, family
medicine, geriatrics, internal medicine, pediatrics, rural
medicine, women's health
Joint degrees awarded: M.D./Ph.D., M.D./M.B.A.,
M.D./M.P.H.
Total National Institutes of Health (NIH) grants awarded
to the medical school and affiliated hospitals: **$1,413.1
million**

CURRICULUM
(TEXT PROVIDED BY MEDICAL SCHOOL):
Harvard Medical School's Integrated Curriculum is
designed to prepare students for a career in medicine distinguished by a lifelong commitment to service, integrity,
excellence, and scholarship. The program integrates the biological, social, behavioral and clinical sciences throughout a
four-year period.

FALL 2009 FACULTY PROFILE
Total teaching faculty: **8,259 (full-time), 2,758 (part-time)**
Of full-time faculty, those teaching in basic sciences: **5%**;
in clinical programs: **95%**

Of part-time faculty, those teaching in basic sciences: **9%**;
in clinical programs: **91%**
Full-time faculty/student ratio: **11.7**

SUPPORT SERVICES
The school offers students these services for dealing with
stress: expanded-hour gym access, peer counseling, professional counseling, religious support, support groups.

RESIDENCY PROFILE
Most popular residency and specialty programs chosen by
the 2008 and 2009 M.D. graduating classes: anesthesiology, dermatology, emergency medicine, internal medicine,
neurological surgery, orthopaedic surgery, pediatrics, psychiatry, radiology–diagnostic, surgery–general.

WHERE GRADS GO

37.3%

*Proportion of 2007-2008 graduates who entered primary
care specialties*

45.0%

*Proportion of 2008-2009 graduates who accepted in-state
residencies*

Indiana University–Indianapolis

- 1120 South Drive, Indianapolis, IN 46202
- Public
- **Year Founded:** 1903
- **Tuition, 2009-2010:** In-state: $29,239; Out-of-State: $43,075
- **Enrollment 2009-2010 academic year:** 1,257
- **Website:** http://www.medicine.iu.edu
- **Specialty ranking:** rural medicine: 14

3.73 AVERAGE GPA, ENTERING CLASS FALL 2009

10.3 AVERAGE MCAT, ENTERING CLASS FALL 2009

14.8% ACCEPTANCE RATE, ENTERING CLASS FALL 2009

44 2011 U.S. NEWS MEDICAL SCHOOL RANKING (RESEARCH)

17 2011 U.S. NEWS MEDICAL SCHOOL RANKING (PRIMARY CARE)

ADMISSIONS

Admissions phone number: **(317) 274-3772**
Admissions email address: **inmedadm@iupui.edu**
Application web site:
  http://www.aamc.org/students/amcas
Acceptance rate: **14.8%**
In-state acceptance rate: **49.2%**
Out-of-state acceptance rate: **6.4%**
Minority acceptance rate: **N/A**
International acceptance rate: **5.8%**

Fall 2009 applications and acceptees

Type	Applied	Interviewed	Accepted	Enrolled
Total:	3,598	938	532	322
In-state:	703	580	346	268
Out-of-state:	2,895	358	186	54

Profile of admitted students

Average undergraduate grade point average: **3.73**
MCAT averages (scale: 1-15; writing test: J-T):
Composite score: **10.3**
Verbal reasoning score: **9.8**, Physical sciences score: **10.2**,
  Biological score: **10.7**, Writing score: **P**
Proportion with undergraduate majors in: Biological
  sciences: **43%**, Physical sciences: **24%**, Non-sciences:
  1%, Other health professions: **1%**, Mixed disciplines and
  other: **32%**
Percentage of students not coming directly from college
  after graduation: **19%**

Dates and details

The American Medical College Application Service
  (AMCAS) application is accepted.
School does not ask for a second, school-specific
  application as part of the admissions process.
Oldest MCAT considered for Fall 2011 entry: **2007**
Earliest application date for the 2011-2012 first-year class:
  06/01
Latest application date: **12/15**
Acceptance dates for regular application for the class
  entering in Fall 2011.

Earliest: **01-OCT-10**
Latest: **01-JUN-11**
Applicants have 3 weeks to respond to admissions offer.
The school does consider requests for deferred entrance.
Starting month for the class of 2011–2012: **August**
The school does have an Early Decision Plan (EDP).
A personal interview is required for admission.

Undergraduate coursework required

Medical school requires undergraduate work in these subjects: biology, organic chemistry, physics, general chemistry.

ADMISSIONS POLICY
(TEXT PROVIDED BY SCHOOL):

The IU School of Medicine admission requirements are
found at the school's website at medicine.iu.edu. The school
participates in AMCAS and the early decision program.
Preference is given to applicants who are Indiana residents.
A number of nonresidents are accepted each year; those
with significant ties to the state of Indiana may be given
greater consideration.

FINANCIAL AID

Financial aid phone number: **(317) 274-1967**
Tuition, 2009-2010 academic year: **In-state: $29,239; Out-
  of-State: $43,075**
Room and board: **$15,168**
Percentage of students receiving financial aid in 2009-10:
  94%
Percentage of students receiving: Loans: **91%**,
  Grants/scholarships: **34%**, Work-study aid: **0%**
Average medical school debt for the class of 2008:
  $162,964

STUDENT BODY

Fall 2009 full-time enrollment: **1,257**
Men: **57%**, Women: **43%**, In-state: **85%**, Minorities: **24%**,
  American Indian: **0.8%**, Asian-American: **11.9%**,
  African-American: **5.0%**, Hispanic-American: **4.7%**,
  White: **70.0%**, International: **1.8%**, Unknown: **5.9%**

ACADEMIC PROGRAMS

The school's curriculum frequently give first-year students substantial contact with patients.

There are opportunities for first- or second-year students to work in community health clinics.

Program areas: AIDS, drug/alcohol abuse, family medicine, geriatrics, internal medicine, pediatrics, rural medicine, women's health

Joint degrees awarded: M.D./Ph.D., M.D./M.B.A., M.D./M.P.H., M.D./M.S., M.D./M.A.

Total National Institutes of Health (NIH) grants awarded to the medical school and affiliated hospitals: **N/A**

CURRICULUM

(TEXT PROVIDED BY MEDICAL SCHOOL):

Indiana's only medical school, the IU School of Medicine is affiliated with Roudebush VA, Wishard and Clarian Health hospitals and Moi Univ. in Kenya. The 2nd largest U.S. medical school is hosted on 9 campuses in Indiana, it features a competency-based curriculum (meded.iusm.iu.edu) and a relationship-centered care program that fosters human interactions (meded.iusm.iu.edu/Resources/RCCIInfo.htm).

FALL 2009 FACULTY PROFILE

Total teaching faculty: 1,567 **(full-time)**, 117 **(part-time)**

Of full-time faculty, those teaching in basic sciences: **14%**; in clinical programs: **86%**

Of part-time faculty, those teaching in basic sciences: **7%**; in clinical programs: **93%**

Full-time faculty/student ratio: **1.2**

SUPPORT SERVICES

The school offers students these services for dealing with stress: expanded-hour gym access, peer counseling, professional counseling, religious support, support groups.

RESIDENCY PROFILE

Most popular residency and specialty programs chosen by the 2008 and 2009 M.D. graduating classes: anesthesiology, emergency medicine, family practice, internal medicine, obstetrics and gynecology, orthopaedic surgery, pediatrics, radiology–diagnostic, surgery–general, internal medicine/pediatrics.

WHERE GRADS GO

39.0%

Proportion of 2007-2008 graduates who entered primary care specialties

43.8%

Proportion of 2008-2009 graduates who accepted in-state residencies

Jefferson Medical College

- 1025 Walnut Street, Room 100, Philadelphia, PA 19107-5083
- Private
- Year Founded: 1824
- Tuition, 2009-2010: $44,547
- Enrollment 2009-2010 academic year: 1,018
- Website: http://www.tju.edu
- Specialty ranking: family medicine: 15, rural medicine: 17

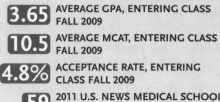

3.65 AVERAGE GPA, ENTERING CLASS FALL 2009

10.5 AVERAGE MCAT, ENTERING CLASS FALL 2009

4.8% ACCEPTANCE RATE, ENTERING CLASS FALL 2009

59 2011 U.S. NEWS MEDICAL SCHOOL RANKING (RESEARCH)

58 2011 U.S. NEWS MEDICAL SCHOOL RANKING (PRIMARY CARE)

ADMISSIONS

Admissions phone number: **(215) 955-6983**
Admissions email address: **jmc.admissions@jefferson.edu**
Application web site:
   http://www.jefferson.edu/jmc/admissions/
Acceptance rate: **4.8%**
In-state acceptance rate: **14.1%**
Out-of-state acceptance rate: **3.6%**
Minority acceptance rate: **4.9%**
International acceptance rate: **3.3%**

Fall 2009 applications and acceptees

Type	Applied	Interviewed	Accepted	Enrolled
Total:	9,713	803	464	255
In-state:	1,085	234	153	94
Out-of-state:	8,628	569	311	161

Profile of admitted students

Average undergraduate grade point average: **3.65**
MCAT averages (scale: 1-15; writing test: J-T):
Composite score: **10.5**
Verbal reasoning score: **10.2**, Physical sciences score: **10.6**,
   Biological score: **10.8**, Writing score: **Q**
Proportion with undergraduate majors in: Biological
   sciences: **33%**, Physical sciences: **14%**, Non-sciences:
   18%, Other health professions: **3%**, Mixed disciplines
   and other: **33%**
Percentage of students not coming directly from college
   after graduation: **55%**

Dates and details

The American Medical College Application Service
   (AMCAS) application is accepted.
School asks for a second, school-specific application as part
   of the admissions process.
Oldest MCAT considered for Fall 2011 entry: **2007**
Earliest application date for the 2011-2012 first-year class:
   06/01
Latest application date: **11/15**
Acceptance dates for regular application for the class
   entering in Fall 2011.

Earliest: **15-OCT-10**
Latest: **02-AUG-11**
Applicants have 2 weeks to respond to admissions offer.
The school does consider requests for deferred entrance.
Starting month for the class of 2011-2012: **August**
The school does have an Early Decision Plan (EDP).
A personal interview is required for admission.

Undergraduate coursework required

Medical school requires undergraduate work in these subjects: biology, organic chemistry, inorganic (general) chemistry, physics.

ADMISSIONS POLICY
(TEXT PROVIDED BY SCHOOL):

   Student selection is made after careful consideration of academic record, letters of recommendation, MCAT scores, performance in nonacademic areas including motivation, maturity, compassion, dedication, integrity and commitment. The MCAT is required, as is a bachelor's degree from a university in the US or Canada. Preference is given to Pennsylvania and Delaware residents.

FINANCIAL AID

Financial aid phone number: **(215) 955-2867**
Tuition, 2009-2010 academic year: **$44,547**
Room and board: **$16,005**
Percentage of students receiving financial aid in 2009-10:
   83%
Percentage of students receiving: Loans: **78%**,
   Grants/scholarships: **45%**, Work-study aid: **14%**
Average medical school debt for the class of 2008:
   $162,885

STUDENT BODY

Fall 2009 full-time enrollment: **1,018**
Men: **50%**, Women: **50%**, In-state: **49%**, Minorities: **36%**,
   American Indian: **0.2%**, Asian-American: **23.6%**,
   African-American: **2.1%**, Hispanic-American: **4.8%**,
   White: **63.9%**, International: **5.5%**, Unknown: **0.0%**

ACADEMIC PROGRAMS

The school's curriculum frequently give first-year students substantial contact with patients.

There are opportunities for first- or second-year students to work in community health clinics.

Program areas: AIDS, drug/alcohol abuse, family medicine, geriatrics, internal medicine, pediatrics, rural medicine, women's health

Joint degrees awarded: M.D./Ph.D., M.D./M.B.A., M.D./M.P.H., M.D./M.H.A.

Total National Institutes of Health (NIH) grants awarded to the medical school and affiliated hospitals: **$73.9 million**

CURRICULUM

(TEXT PROVIDED BY MEDICAL SCHOOL):

Jefferson's curriculum includes 2 years of basic science followed by 2 years of clinical instruction, including 3rd year rotations in family practice, obstetrics/gynecology, pediatrics, psychiatry, surgery and internal medicine. 4th year includes 16 weeks of electives; neurology/rehabilitation, 2 sub-internships; advanced basic science and ER/advanced clinical skills.

FALL 2009 FACULTY PROFILE

Total teaching faculty: 2,539 **(full-time)**, 51 **(part-time)**
Of full-time faculty, those teaching in basic sciences: **6%**; in clinical programs: **94%**

Of part-time faculty, those teaching in basic sciences: **2%**; in clinical programs: **98%**
Full-time faculty/student ratio: **2.5**

SUPPORT SERVICES

The school offers students these services for dealing with stress: expanded-hour gym access, peer counseling, professional counseling, religious support, support groups.

RESIDENCY PROFILE

Most popular residency and specialty programs chosen by the 2008 and 2009 M.D. graduating classes: anesthesiology, emergency medicine, family practice, internal medicine, obstetrics and gynecology, ophthalmology, orthopaedic surgery, pediatrics, radiology–diagnostic, surgery–general.

WHERE GRADS GO

38.3%

Proportion of 2007-2008 graduates who entered primary care specialties

37.5%

Proportion of 2008-2009 graduates who accepted in-state residencies

Johns Hopkins University

- 733 N. Broadway, Baltimore, MD 21205
- Private
- **Year Founded:** 1893
- **Tuition, 2009-2010:** $43,620
- **Enrollment 2009-2010 academic year:** 480
- **Website:** http://www.hopkinsmedicine.org
- **Specialty ranking:** AIDS: 2, drug/alcohol abuse: 1, geriatrics: 1, internal medicine: 1, pediatrics: 4, women's health: 4

3.87	AVERAGE GPA, ENTERING CLASS FALL 2009
11.9	AVERAGE MCAT, ENTERING CLASS FALL 2009
6.7%	ACCEPTANCE RATE, ENTERING CLASS FALL 2009
3	2011 U.S. NEWS MEDICAL SCHOOL RANKING (RESEARCH)
25	2011 U.S. NEWS MEDICAL SCHOOL RANKING (PRIMARY CARE)

ADMISSIONS

Admissions phone number: **(410) 955-3182**
Admissions email address: **somadmiss@jhmi.edu**
Application web site:
http://www.hopkinsmedicine.org/admissions
Acceptance rate: **6.7%**
In-state acceptance rate: **12.5%**
Out-of-state acceptance rate: **6.2%**
Minority acceptance rate: **7.5%**
International acceptance rate: **4.2%**

Fall 2009 applications and acceptees

Type	Applied	Interviewed	Accepted	Enrolled
Total:	3,655	759	244	120
In-state:	281	101	35	24
Out-of-state:	3,374	658	209	96

Profile of admitted students

Average undergraduate grade point average: **3.87**
MCAT averages (scale: 1-15; writing test: J-T):
Composite score: **11.9**
Verbal reasoning score: **10.9**, Physical sciences score: **12.3**, Biological score: **12.5**, Writing score: **R**
Proportion with undergraduate majors in: Biological sciences: **52%**, Physical sciences: **29%**, Non-sciences: **10%**, Other health professions: **0%**, Mixed disciplines and other: **9%**
Percentage of students not coming directly from college after graduation: **47%**

Dates and details

The American Medical College Application Service (AMCAS) application is accepted.
School asks for a second, school-specific application as part of the admissions process.
Oldest MCAT considered for Fall 2011 entry: **2007**
Earliest application date for the 2011-2012 first-year class: **07/01**
Latest application date: **10/15**
Acceptance dates for regular application for the class entering in Fall 2011.

Earliest: **15-OCT-11**
Latest: **01-AUG-10**
Applicants have 3 weeks to respond to admissions offer.
The school does consider requests for deferred entrance.
Starting month for the class of 2011-2012: **August**
The school does have an Early Decision Plan (EDP).
A personal interview is required for admission.

Undergraduate coursework required

Medical school requires undergraduate work in these subjects: biology, organic chemistry, inorganic (general) chemistry, physics, humanities, behavioral science, calculus, social sciences.

ADMISSIONS POLICY

(TEXT PROVIDED BY SCHOOL):
  Attendance at a fully accredited institution. If exclusively studied outside the U.S., academic course work must be supplemented by 1+ yr. course work at an accredited U.S. university; bachelor's (B.A. or B.S.) degree prior to matriculation. Fulfillment of the 7 prerequisites (refer to www.hopkinsmedicine.org/admissions for complete listing of all admissions requirements.) MCAT required.

FINANCIAL AID

Financial aid phone number: **(410) 955-1324**
Tuition, 2009-2010 academic year: **$43,620**
Room and board: **$17,736**
Percentage of students receiving financial aid in 2009-10: **80%**
Percentage of students receiving: Loans: **77%**, Grants/scholarships: **60%**, Work-study aid: **14%**
Average medical school debt for the class of 2008: **$94,717**

STUDENT BODY

Fall 2009 full-time enrollment: **480**
Men: **52%**, Women: **48%**, In-state: **27%**, Minorities: **46%**, American Indian: **0.6%**, Asian-American: **33.8%**, African-American: **7.9%**, Hispanic-American: **3.3%**, White: **51.0%**, International: **3.3%**, Unknown: **0.0%**

ACADEMIC PROGRAMS

The school's curriculum frequently give first-year students substantial contact with patients.

There are opportunities for first- or second-year students to work in community health clinics.

Program areas. AIDS, drug/alcohol abuse, family medicine, geriatrics, internal medicine, pediatrics, rural medicine, women's health

Joint degrees awarded: M.D./Ph.D.

Total National Institutes of Health (NIH) grants awarded to the medical school and affiliated hospitals: **$444.7 million**

CURRICULUM
(TEXT PROVIDED BY MEDICAL SCHOOL):

New curriculum implemented in 2009: Yr 1 clinical skills; Yr 1-2 longitudinal clerkship; emphasis on human variability/complex interaction of biology/systems in terms of disease; behavioral/social science taught in intersession weeks. Clinical curriculum includes 7 core & 3 advanced clerkships, intensive care & chronic care rotations; prominent use of simulations in Yr 2 transitional & Yr 4 capstone courses.

FALL 2009 FACULTY PROFILE

Total teaching faculty: **2,464 (full-time)**, **1,265 (part-time)**
Of full-time faculty, those teaching in basic sciences: **9%**; in clinical programs: **91%**

Of part-time faculty, those teaching in basic sciences: **2%**; in clinical programs: **98%**
Full-time faculty/student ratio: **5.1**

SUPPORT SERVICES

The school offers students these services for dealing with stress: expanded-hour gym access, peer counseling, professional counseling, support groups.

RESIDENCY PROFILE

Most popular residency and specialty programs chosen by the 2008 and 2009 M.D. graduating classes: anesthesiology, emergency medicine, internal medicine, neurological surgery, ophthalmology, pediatrics, psychiatry, radiology–diagnostic, surgery–general, transitional year.

WHERE GRADS GO

33.2%
Proportion of 2007-2008 graduates who entered primary care specialties

37.4%
Proportion of 2008-2009 graduates who accepted in-state residencies

Louisiana State University
Health Sciences Center–Shreveport

- PO Box 33932, 1501 Kings Highway, Shreveport, LA 71130-3932
- Public
- Year Founded: 1965
- Tuition, 2009-2010: In-state: $12,033; Out-of-State: $27,630
- Enrollment 2009-2010 academic year: 461
- Website: http://www.lsuhscshreveport.edu
- Specialty ranking: N/A

3.70 AVERAGE GPA, ENTERING CLASS FALL 2009

9.2 AVERAGE MCAT, ENTERING CLASS FALL 2009

41.4% ACCEPTANCE RATE, ENTERING CLASS FALL 2009

Unranked 2011 U.S. NEWS MEDICAL SCHOOL RANKING (RESEARCH)

Unranked 2011 U.S. NEWS MEDICAL SCHOOL RANKING (PRIMARY CARE)

ADMISSIONS

Admissions phone number: (318) 675-5190
Admissions email address: **shvadm@lsuhsc.edu**
Application web site:
   http://www.aamc.org/students/start.htm
Acceptance rate: **41.4%**
In-state acceptance rate: **41.4%**
Out-of-state acceptance rate: **N/A**
Minority acceptance rate: **25.0%**
International acceptance rate: **N/A**

Fall 2009 applications and acceptees

Type	Applied	Interviewed	Accepted	Enrolled
Total:	476	234	197	118
In-state:	476	234	197	118
Out-of-state:	0	0	0	0

Profile of admitted students

Average undergraduate grade point average: **3.70**
MCAT averages (scale: 1-15; writing test: J-T):
Composite score: **9.2**
Verbal reasoning score: **9.0**, Physical sciences score: **8.6**, Biological sciences score: **9.8**, Writing score: **P**
Proportion with undergraduate majors in: Biological sciences: **83%**, Physical sciences: **11%**, Non-sciences: **3%**, Other health professions: **0%**, Mixed disciplines and other: **3%**
Percentage of students not coming directly from college after graduation: **22%**

Dates and details

The American Medical College Application Service (AMCAS) application is accepted.
School asks for a second, school-specific application as part of the admissions process.
Oldest MCAT considered for Fall 2011 entry: **2008**
Earliest application date for the 2011-2012 first-year class: **06/01**
Latest application date: **11/01**
Acceptance dates for regular application for the class entering in Fall 2011.

Earliest: **01-SEP-10**
Latest: **29-JUL-11**
Applicants have 2 weeks to respond to admissions offer.
The school does consider requests for deferred entrance.
Starting month for the class of 2011-2012: **July**
The school does have an Early Decision Plan (EDP).
A personal interview is required for admission.

Undergraduate coursework required

Medical school requires undergraduate work in these subjects: biology, English, organic chemistry, physics, general chemistry.

ADMISSIONS POLICY
(TEXT PROVIDED BY SCHOOL):

A faculty-appointed committee is empowered to select applicants whom they deem to have the qualities most highly regarded as predicting success in med school and suitability for a future practice in medicine. Being a resident for LSU tuition purposes is required. While grades and MCAT score are very important, they are never sufficient. Selected applicants are invited to interview on-campus.

FINANCIAL AID

Financial aid phone number: (318) 675-5561
Tuition, 2009-2010 academic year: **In-state: $12,033; Out-of-State: $27,630**
Room and board: N/A
Percentage of students receiving financial aid in 2009-10: **83%**
Percentage of students receiving: Loans: **79%**, Grants/scholarships: **18%**, Work-study aid: **0%**
Average medical school debt for the class of 2008: **$119,207**

STUDENT BODY

Fall 2009 full-time enrollment: **461**
Men: **57%**, Women: **43%**, In-state: **100%**, Minorities: **12%**, American Indian: **0.2%**, Asian-American: **7.2%**, African-American: **3.9%**, Hispanic-American: **1.1%**, White: **86.8%**, International: **0.0%**, Unknown: **0.9%**

ACADEMIC PROGRAMS

The school's curriculum very frequently give first-year students substantial contact with patients.

There are opportunities for first- or second-year students to work in community health clinics.

Program areas: drug/alcohol abuse, family medicine, geriatrics, internal medicine, pediatrics, rural medicine, women's health

Joint degrees awarded: M.D./Ph.D.

Total National Institutes of Health (NIH) grants awarded to the medical school and affiliated hospitals: **$16.6 million**

CURRICULUM

(TEXT PROVIDED BY MEDICAL SCHOOL):

The goal of the M.D. curriculum is the shaping of students into competent, ethical, caring physicians, capable of providing high quality healthcare to persons & families, and active in supporting effective community health programs. The curriculum emphasizes person-oriented patient care, & the role of the physician as citizen, working for answers to societal problems in the community & the world.

FALL 2009 FACULTY PROFILE

Total teaching faculty: **367 (full-time)**, **89 (part-time)**

Of full-time faculty, those teaching in basic sciences: **19%**; in clinical programs: **81%**

Of part-time faculty, those teaching in basic sciences: **3%**; in clinical programs: **97%**

Full-time faculty/student ratio: **0.8**

SUPPORT SERVICES

The school offers students these services for dealing with stress: expanded-hour gym access, professional counseling, support groups.

RESIDENCY PROFILE

Most popular residency and specialty programs chosen by the 2008 and 2009 M.D. graduating classes: anesthesiology, family practice, internal medicine, obstetrics and gynecology, orthopaedic surgery, otolaryngology, pediatrics, radiology–diagnostic, surgery–general, urology.

WHERE GRADS GO

38.2%

Proportion of 2007-2008 graduates who entered primary care specialties

43.5%

Proportion of 2008-2009 graduates who accepted in-state residencies

Loyola University Chicago
Stritch

- 2160 S. First Avenue, Building 120, Maywood, IL 60153
- Private
- Year Founded: 1909
- Tuition, 2009-2010: $42,755
- Enrollment 2009-2010 academic year: 574
- Website: http://www.meddean.lumc.edu
- Specialty ranking: N/A

3.59 AVERAGE GPA, ENTERING CLASS FALL 2009

10.5 AVERAGE MCAT, ENTERING CLASS FALL 2009

6.6% ACCEPTANCE RATE, ENTERING CLASS FALL 2009

Unranked 2011 U.S. NEWS MEDICAL SCHOOL RANKING (RESEARCH)

Unranked 2011 U.S. NEWS MEDICAL SCHOOL RANKING (PRIMARY CARE)

ADMISSIONS
Admissions phone number: (708) 216-3229
Admissions email address: N/A
Application web site: N/A
Acceptance rate: 6.6%
In-state acceptance rate: 14.2%
Out-of-state acceptance rate: 5.1%
Minority acceptance rate: 4.8%
International acceptance rate: N/A

Fall 2009 applications and acceptees

Type	Applied	Interviewed	Accepted	Enrolled
Total:	5,493	515	362	145
In-state:	906	188	129	65
Out-of-state:	4,587	327	233	80

Profile of admitted students
Average undergraduate grade point average: 3.59
MCAT averages (scale: 1-15; writing test: J-T):
Composite score: 10.5
Verbal reasoning score: 10.2, Physical sciences score: 10.3, Biological score: 10.9, Writing score: N/A
Proportion with undergraduate majors in: Biological sciences: N/A, Physical sciences: N/A, Non-sciences: N/A, Other health professions: N/A, Mixed disciplines and other: N/A
Percentage of students not coming directly from college after graduation: N/A

Dates and details
The American Medical College Application Service (AMCAS) application is accepted.
School asks for a second, school-specific application as part of the admissions process.
Oldest MCAT considered for Fall 2011 entry: 2007
Earliest application date for the 2011-2012 first-year class: 06/01
Latest application date: 11/15
Acceptance dates for regular application for the class entering in Fall 2011.
Earliest: 15-OCT-10

Latest: 22-JUL-11
Applicants have 2 weeks to respond to admissions offer.
The school does consider requests for deferred entrance.
Starting month for the class of 2011–2012: July
The school doesn't have an Early Decision Plan (EDP).
A personal interview is required for admission.

Undergraduate coursework required
Medical school requires undergraduate work in these subjects: biology/zoology, organic chemistry, inorganic (general) chemistry, physics.

ADMISSIONS POLICY
(TEXT PROVIDED BY SCHOOL):
Applicants capable of succeeding in the rigors of medical education are evaluated on the personal qualifications they can bring to the medical profession. Essential characteristics include interest in lifelong learning, integrity, compassion, ability to assume responsibility, exploration of the medical field, nature of motivation to enter medicine, and involvement in extracurricular activities.

FINANCIAL AID
Financial aid phone number: (708) 216-3227
Tuition, 2009-2010 academic year: $42,755
Room and board: $17,679
Percentage of students receiving financial aid in 2009-10: 94%
Percentage of students receiving: Loans: 85%, Grants/scholarships: 73%, Work-study aid: 0%
Average medical school debt for the class of 2008: $161,976

STUDENT BODY
Fall 2009 full-time enrollment: 574
Men: 48%, Women: 52%, In-state: 45%, Minorities: 22%, American Indian: 0.0%, Asian-American: 12.2%, African-American: 4.5%, Hispanic-American: 4.9%, White: 75.1%, International: 0.0%, Unknown: 3.3%

ACADEMIC PROGRAMS

The school's curriculum very frequently give first-year students substantial contact with patients.

There are opportunities for first- or second-year students to work in community health clinics.

Program areas. AIDS, drug/alcohol abuse, family medicine, geriatrics, internal medicine, pediatrics, women's health

Joint degrees awarded: M.D./Ph.D., M.D./M.P.H., M.D./M.A.

Total National Institutes of Health (NIH) grants awarded to the medical school and affiliated hospitals: **$19.4 million**

CURRICULUM

(TEXT PROVIDED BY MEDICAL SCHOOL):

Years 1/2 provide instruction in the basic sciences and in developing skills in communicating with patients, taking a history, and performing a physical examination. Years 3/4 include required clerkships (medicine, surgery, family medicine, obstetrics/gynecology, pediatrics, psychiatry) and electives. Clerkships combine inpatient experience with extensive time in the ambulatory setting.

FALL 2009 FACULTY PROFILE

Total teaching faculty: **N/A (full-time)**, **N/A (part-time)**
Of full-time faculty, those teaching in basic sciences: **N/A**; in clinical programs: **N/A**

Of part-time faculty, those teaching in basic sciences: **N/A**; in clinical programs: **N/A**
Full-time faculty/student ratio: **N/A**

SUPPORT SERVICES

The school offers students these services for dealing with stress: expanded-hour gym access, peer counseling, professional counseling, religious support, support groups.

RESIDENCY PROFILE

Most popular residency and specialty programs chosen by the 2008 and 2009 M.D. graduating classes: anesthesiology–pediatric anesthesiology, emergency medicine, family practice, internal medicine, obstetrics and gynecology, orthopaedic surgery, otolaryngology, pediatrics, surgery–general, urology.

WHERE GRADS GO

42.0%

Proportion of 2007-2008 graduates who entered primary care specialties

N/A

Proportion of 2008-2009 graduates who accepted in-state residencies

Medical College of Wisconsin

- 8701 Watertown Plank Road, Milwaukee, WI 53226
- Private
- Year Founded: 1893
- Tuition, 2009-2010: $34,558
- Enrollment 2009-2010 academic year: 817
- Website: http://www.mcw.edu/acad/admission
- Specialty ranking: N/A

3.74 AVERAGE GPA, ENTERING CLASS FALL 2009

10.2 AVERAGE MCAT, ENTERING CLASS FALL 2009

6.6% ACCEPTANCE RATE, ENTERING CLASS FALL 2009

51 2011 U.S. NEWS MEDICAL SCHOOL RANKING (RESEARCH)

53 2011 U.S. NEWS MEDICAL SCHOOL RANKING (PRIMARY CARE)

ADMISSIONS

Admissions phone number: **(414) 456-8246**
Admissions email address: **medschool@mcw.edu**
Application web site:
http://www.mcw.edu/medicalschool/AppInfo.htm
Acceptance rate: **6.6%**
In-state acceptance rate: **20.5%**
Out-of-state acceptance rate: **5.1%**
Minority acceptance rate: **N/A**
International acceptance rate: **1.7%**

Fall 2009 applications and acceptees

Type	Applied	Interviewed	Accepted	Enrolled
Total:	6,373	651	420	204
In-state:	624	173	128	92
Out-of-state:	5,749	478	292	112

Profile of admitted students

Average undergraduate grade point average: **3.74**
MCAT averages (scale: 1-15; writing test: J-T):
Composite score: **10.2**
Verbal reasoning score: **9.6**, Physical sciences score: **10.0**,
  Biological score: **10.6**, Writing score: **P**
Proportion with undergraduate majors in: Biological
  sciences: **52%**, Physical sciences: **18%**, Non-sciences:
  17%, Other health professions: **8%**, Mixed disciplines
  and other: **5%**
Percentage of students not coming directly from college
  after graduation: **64%**

Dates and details

The American Medical College Application Service
  (AMCAS) application is accepted.
School asks for a second, school-specific application as part
  of the admissions process.
Oldest MCAT considered for Fall 2011 entry: **2008**
Earliest application date for the 2011-2012 first-year class:
  06/07
Latest application date: **11/01**
Acceptance dates for regular application for the class
  entering in Fall 2011.

Earliest: **15-OCT-10**
Latest: **01-AUG-11**
Applicants have 4 weeks to respond to admissions offer.
The school does consider requests for deferred entrance.
Starting month for the class of 2011-2012: **August**
The school does have an Early Decision Plan (EDP).
A personal interview is required for admission.

Undergraduate coursework required

Medical school requires undergraduate work in these subjects: biology, English, organic chemistry, inorganic (general) chemistry, physics, mathematics.

ADMISSIONS POLICY

(TEXT PROVIDED BY SCHOOL):
  The Admissions Committee bases its decisions on a
thoughtful appraisal of each candidate's suitability for the
profession of medicine—scholastic record, MCAT scores,
recommendations and involvement in college and community activities. The personal interview and qualities of personality, character/integrity and maturity are highly valued,
evaluated and are integral to the Committee's decisions.

FINANCIAL AID

Financial aid phone number: **(414) 456-8208**
Tuition, 2009-2010 academic year: **$34,558**
Room and board: **$9,000**
Percentage of students receiving financial aid in 2009-10:
  96%
Percentage of students receiving: Loans: **85%**,
  Grants/scholarships: **63%**, Work-study aid: **0%**
Average medical school debt for the class of 2008:
  $155,390

STUDENT BODY

Fall 2009 full-time enrollment: **817**
Men: **52%**, Women: **48%**, In-state: **42%**, Minorities: **27%**,
  American Indian: **0.7%**, Asian-American: **17.1%**,
  African-American: **4.5%**, Hispanic-American: **4.8%**,
  White: **65.5%**, International: **0.6%**, Unknown: **6.7%**

ACADEMIC PROGRAMS

The school's curriculum occasionally give first-year students substantial contact with patients.

There are opportunities for first- or second-year students to work in community health clinics.

Program areas: family medicine, geriatrics, internal medicine, pediatrics, rural medicine, women's health

Joint degrees awarded: M.D./Ph.D.

Total National Institutes of Health (NIH) grants awarded to the medical school and affiliated hospitals: **$128.0 million**

CURRICULUM

(TEXT PROVIDED BY MEDICAL SCHOOL):

Basic science courses along with clinical exposure occur during M1/M2 years. Rotations through required clerkships/electives are scheduled in the M3 year. During M4 year, students rotate in two subinternships, ambulatory medicine, an Integrated Selective and five 1-month electives. Students pursue and strengthen their own interests by participation in one of five recently implemented Pathways.

FALL 2009 FACULTY PROFILE

Total teaching faculty: **1,245 (full-time)**, **203 (part-time)**

Of full-time faculty, those teaching in basic sciences: **9%**; in clinical programs: **91%**

Of part-time faculty, those teaching in basic sciences: **12%**; in clinical programs: **88%**

Full-time faculty/student ratio: **1.5**

SUPPORT SERVICES

The school offers students these services for dealing with stress: expanded-hour gym access, peer counseling, professional counseling, religious support, support groups.

RESIDENCY PROFILE

Most popular residency and specialty programs chosen by the 2008 and 2009 M.D. graduating classes: anesthesiology, emergency medicine, family practice, internal medicine, obstetrics and gynecology, orthopaedic surgery, pediatrics, radiology–diagnostic, surgery–general, internal medicine/pediatrics.

WHERE GRADS GO

34.0%

Proportion of 2007-2008 graduates who entered primary care specialties

33.0%

Proportion of 2008-2009 graduates who accepted in-state residencies

Medical University of South Carolina

- 171 Ashley Avenue, Charleston, SC 29425
- Public
- Year Founded: 1824
- Tuition, 2009-2010: In-state: $33,829; Out-of-State: $57,161
- Enrollment 2009-2010 academic year: 670
- Website: http://www.musc.edu/com1
- Specialty ranking: drug/alcohol abuse: 10

3.59 AVERAGE GPA, ENTERING CLASS FALL 2009

9.8 AVERAGE MCAT, ENTERING CLASS FALL 2009

13.6% ACCEPTANCE RATE, ENTERING CLASS FALL 2009

Unranked 2011 U.S. NEWS MEDICAL SCHOOL RANKING (RESEARCH)

58 2011 U.S. NEWS MEDICAL SCHOOL RANKING (PRIMARY CARE)

ADMISSIONS

Admissions phone number: **(843) 792-2055**
Admissions email address: **taylorwl@musc.edu**
Application web site:
 http://academicdepartments.musc.edu/com1/admissions/index.htm
Acceptance rate: **13.6%**
In-state acceptance rate: **31.5%**
Out-of-state acceptance rate: **4.8%**
Minority acceptance rate: **15.9%**
International acceptance rate: **0.0%**

Fall 2009 applications and acceptees

Type	Applied	Interviewed	Accepted	Enrolled
Total:	1,468	419	199	155
In-state:	482	350	152	131
Out-of-state:	986	69	47	24

Profile of admitted students

Average undergraduate grade point average: **3.59**
MCAT averages (scale: 1-15; writing test: J-T):
Composite score: **9.8**
Verbal reasoning score: **9.7**, Physical sciences score: **9.6**, Biological score: **10.1**, Writing score: **O**
Proportion with undergraduate majors in: Biological sciences: **44%**, Physical sciences: **22%**, Non-sciences: **11%**, Other health professions: **8%**, Mixed disciplines and other: **15%**
Percentage of students not coming directly from college after graduation: **N/A**

Dates and details

The American Medical College Application Service (AMCAS) application is accepted.
School asks for a second, school-specific application as part of the admissions process.
Oldest MCAT considered for Fall 2011 entry: **2008**
Earliest application date for the 2011-2012 first-year class: **06/01**
Latest application date: **12/01**

Acceptance dates for regular application for the class entering in Fall 2011.
Earliest: **01-NOV-10**
Latest: **31-MAR-11**
Applicants have 4 weeks to respond to admissions offer. The school does consider requests for deferred entrance. Starting month for the class of 2011-2012: **August**
The school does have an Early Decision Plan (EDP).
A personal interview is required for admission.

Undergraduate coursework required

Medical school requires undergraduate work in these subjects: N/A.

ADMISSIONS POLICY
(TEXT PROVIDED BY SCHOOL):

 MCAT scores and BS/BA degree are required. MCAT by spring/fall of year prior to admission. SC residency is admission consideration. Academic background assessed using GPA and MCAT scores. Those passing the cutoff are invited for interviews. Noncognitive skills are evaluated during interviews. Letters of recommendation, leadership, volunteering, and clinical exposure to medicine are important.

FINANCIAL AID

Financial aid phone number: **(843) 792-2536**
Tuition, 2009-2010 academic year: **In-state: $33,829; Out-of-State: $57,161**
Room and board: **$13,320**
Percentage of students receiving financial aid in 2009-10: **85%**
Percentage of students receiving: Loans: **83%**, Grants/scholarships: **16%**, Work-study aid: **0%**
Average medical school debt for the class of 2008: **$163,794**

STUDENT BODY

Fall 2009 full-time enrollment: **670**
Men: **58%**, Women: **42%**, In-state: **90%**, Minorities: **24%**, American Indian: **1.0%**, Asian-American: **7.2%**, African-

American: 13.3%, Hispanic-American: 2.7%, White: 70.0%, International: 1.0%, Unknown: 4.8%

ACADEMIC PROGRAMS
The school's curriculum occasionally give first-year students substantial contact with patients.
There are opportunities for first- or second-year students to work in community health clinics.
Program areas: AIDS, drug/alcohol abuse, family medicine, geriatrics, internal medicine, pediatrics, rural medicine, women's health
Joint degrees awarded: M.D./Ph.D., M.D./M.B.A., M.D./M.P.H., M.D./M.S., M.D./M.H.A.
Total National Institutes of Health (NIH) grants awarded to the medical school and affiliated hospitals: **$94.2 million**

CURRICULUM
(TEXT PROVIDED BY MEDICAL SCHOOL):
The curriculum in the first 2 years integrates basic science concepts with problem solving strategies and clinical skills. The 3rd year consists of 6 clinical core clerkships and 4 clinical selectives. The 4th year consists of 2 core clerkships, an externship and 5 electives.

FALL 2009 FACULTY PROFILE
Total teaching faculty: **1,089 (full-time)**, **151 (part-time)**
Of full-time faculty, those teaching in basic sciences: **13%**; in clinical programs. 87%

Of part-time faculty, those teaching in basic sciences: **9%**; in clinical programs: **91%**
Full-time faculty/student ratio: **1.6**

SUPPORT SERVICES
The school offers students these services for dealing with stress: expanded-hour gym access, peer counseling, professional counseling, religious support, support groups.

RESIDENCY PROFILE
Most popular residency and specialty programs chosen by the 2008 and 2009 M.D. graduating classes: anesthesiology, emergency medicine, family practice, internal medicine, obstetrics and gynecology, pathology–anatomic and clinical, pediatrics, psychiatry, radiology–diagnostic, surgery–general.

WHERE GRADS GO

40.1%
Proportion of 2007-2008 graduates who entered primary care specialties

38.3%
Proportion of 2008-2009 graduates who accepted in-state residencies

Mercer University

- 1550 College Street, Macon, GA 31207
- Private
- **Year Founded:** 1982
- **Tuition, 2009-2010:** $38,400
- **Enrollment 2009-2010 academic year:** 311
- **Website:** http://medicine.mercer.edu
- **Specialty ranking:** N/A

3.53 AVERAGE GPA, ENTERING CLASS FALL 2009

9.2 AVERAGE MCAT, ENTERING CLASS FALL 2009

15.8% ACCEPTANCE RATE, ENTERING CLASS FALL 2009

Unranked 2011 U.S. NEWS MEDICAL SCHOOL RANKING (RESEARCH)

Unranked 2011 U.S. NEWS MEDICAL SCHOOL RANKING (PRIMARY CARE)

ADMISSIONS
Admissions phone number: **(478) 301-2542**
Admissions email address: **admissions@med.mercer.edu**
Application web site: **N/A**
Acceptance rate: **15.8%**
In-state acceptance rate: **15.8%**
Out-of-state acceptance rate: **N/A**
Minority acceptance rate: **10.2%**
International acceptance rate: **N/A**

Fall 2009 applications and acceptees

Type	Applied	Interviewed	Accepted	Enrolled
Total:	804	315	127	92
In-state:	804	315	127	92
Out-of-state:	0	0	0	0

Profile of admitted students
Average undergraduate grade point average: **3.53**
MCAT averages (scale: 1-15; writing test: J-T):
Composite score: **9.2**
Verbal reasoning score: **9.1**, Physical sciences score: **8.9**, Biological score: **9.7**, Writing score: **N/A**
Proportion with undergraduate majors in: Biological sciences: **N/A**, Physical sciences: **N/A**, Non-sciences: **N/A**, Other health professions: **N/A**, Mixed disciplines and other: **N/A**
Percentage of students not coming directly from college after graduation: **N/A**

Dates and details
The American Medical College Application Service (AMCAS) application is accepted.
School asks for a second, school-specific application as part of the admissions process.
Oldest MCAT considered for Fall 2011 entry: **2008**
Earliest application date for the 2011-2012 first-year class: **06/01**
Latest application date: **11/01**
Acceptance dates for regular application for the class entering in Fall 2011.
Earliest: **01-NOV-10**

Latest: **08-AUG-11**
Applicants have 2 weeks to respond to admissions offer.
The school does consider requests for deferred entrance.
Starting month for the class of 2011–2012: **August**
The school does have an Early Decision Plan (EDP).
A personal interview is required for admission.

Undergraduate coursework required
Medical school requires undergraduate work in these subjects: biology, organic chemistry, inorganic (general) chemistry, physics.

ADMISSIONS POLICY
(TEXT PROVIDED BY SCHOOL):
   Georgia residency is a requirement for admission.

FINANCIAL AID
Financial aid phone number: **(478) 301-2853**
Tuition, 2009-2010 academic year: **$38,400**
Room and board: **$13,740**
Percentage of students receiving financial aid in 2009-10: **94%**
Percentage of students receiving: Loans: **89%**, Grants/scholarships: **54%**, Work-study aid: **0%**
Average medical school debt for the class of 2008: **$165,823**

STUDENT BODY
Fall 2009 full-time enrollment: **311**
Men: **54%**, Women: **46%**, In-state: **100%**, Minorities: **15%**, American Indian: **0.0%**, Asian-American: **10.6%**, African-American: **2.6%**, Hispanic-American: **1.0%**, White: **84.9%**, International: **0.0%**, Unknown: **1.0%**

ACADEMIC PROGRAMS
The school's curriculum frequently give first-year students substantial contact with patients.
There are opportunities for first- or second-year students to work in community health clinics.

Program areas: AIDS, drug/alcohol abuse, family medicine, geriatrics, internal medicine, pediatrics, rural medicine, women's health

Joint degrees awarded: N/A

Total National Institutes of Health (NIH) grants awarded to the medical school and affiliated hospitals. **32.3 million**

CURRICULUM
(TEXT PROVIDED BY MEDICAL SCHOOL):
Please see our website for complete information.

FALL 2009 FACULTY PROFILE
Total teaching faculty: **300 (full-time), 824 (part-time)**

Of full-time faculty, those teaching in basic sciences: **16%;** in clinical programs: **84%**

Of part-time faculty, those teaching in basic sciences: **4%;** in clinical programs: **96%**

Full-time faculty/student ratio: **1.0**

SUPPORT SERVICES
The school offers students these services for dealing with stress: expanded-hour gym access, peer counseling, professional counseling, religious support.

RESIDENCY PROFILE
Most popular residency and specialty programs chosen by the 2008 and 2009 M.D. graduating classes: family practice, internal medicine, obstetrics and gynecology, pediatrics, surgery–general, internal medicine/pediatrics.

WHERE GRADS GO

38.6%
Proportion of 2007-2008 graduates who entered primary care specialties

32.5%
Proportion of 2008-2009 graduates who accepted in-state residencies

Michigan State University

- A110 E. Fee Hall, East Lansing, MI 48824
- Public
- Year Founded: 1964
- Tuition, 2009-2010: In-state: $26,953; Out-of-State: $58,175
- Enrollment 2009-2010 academic year: 610
- Website: http://humanmedicine.msu.edu
- Specialty ranking: rural medicine: 14

3.54 AVERAGE GPA, ENTERING CLASS FALL 2009

9.6 AVERAGE MCAT, ENTERING CLASS FALL 2009

6.6% ACCEPTANCE RATE, ENTERING CLASS FALL 2009

Unranked 2011 U.S. NEWS MEDICAL SCHOOL RANKING (RESEARCH)

23 2011 U.S. NEWS MEDICAL SCHOOL RANKING (PRIMARY CARE)

ADMISSIONS

Admissions phone number: (517) 353-9620
Admissions email address: MDadmissions@msu.edu
Application web site:
   http://mdadmissions.msu.edu/main/currapp.htm
Acceptance rate: 6.6%
In-state acceptance rate: 18.0%
Out-of-state acceptance rate: 3.0%
Minority acceptance rate: 8.1%
International acceptance rate: 2.9%

Fall 2009 applications and acceptees

Type	Applied	Interviewed	Accepted	Enrolled
Total:	5,471	486	359	155
In-state:	1,289	310	232	117
Out-of-state:	4,182	176	127	38

Profile of admitted students

Average undergraduate grade point average: 3.54
MCAT averages (scale: 1-15; writing test: J-T):
Composite score: 9.6
Verbal reasoning score: 9.2, Physical sciences score: 9.3, Biological score: 10.2, Writing score: O
Proportion with undergraduate majors in: Biological sciences: 60%, Physical sciences: 14%, Non-sciences: 12%, Other health professions: 4%, Mixed disciplines and other: 10%
Percentage of students not coming directly from college after graduation: 25%

Dates and details

The American Medical College Application Service (AMCAS) application is accepted.
School asks for a second, school-specific application as part of the admissions process.
Oldest MCAT considered for Fall 2011 entry: 2007
Earliest application date for the 2011-2012 first-year class: 06/01
Latest application date: 11/15
Acceptance dates for regular application for the class entering in Fall 2011.

Earliest: 15-OCT-10
Latest: 15-JUN-11
Applicants have 2 weeks to respond to admissions offer. The school does consider requests for deferred entrance. Starting month for the class of 2011-2012: August
The school does have an Early Decision Plan (EDP).
A personal interview is required for admission.

Undergraduate coursework required

Medical school requires undergraduate work in these subjects: biology, English, organic chemistry, inorganic (general) chemistry, humanities, mathematics, social sciences.

ADMISSIONS POLICY
(TEXT PROVIDED BY SCHOOL):

The college seeks an academically competent class that is broadly diverse in personalities, life experiences and talents and is reflective of rural and urban Michigan. Non-academic factors are uniquely considered with strong emphasis on medical/clinical experience, problem-solving ability/research, and interpersonal skills. Disadvantaged students are welcome; Michigan residents receive preference.

FINANCIAL AID

Financial aid phone number: (517) 353-5940
Tuition, 2009-2010 academic year: In-state: $26,953; Out-of-State: $58,175
Room and board: $13,632
Percentage of students receiving financial aid in 2009-10: 91%
Percentage of students receiving: Loans: 88%, Grants/scholarships: 40%, Work-study aid: 0%
Average medical school debt for the class of 2008: $172,697

STUDENT BODY

Fall 2009 full-time enrollment: 610
Men: 49%, Women: 51%, In-state: 73%, Minorities: 32%, American Indian: 1.1%, Asian-American: 17.9%, African-American: 8.5%, Hispanic-American: 4.4%, White: 65.4%, International: 0.8%, Unknown: 1.8%

ACADEMIC PROGRAMS

The school's curriculum occasionally give first-year students substantial contact with patients.

There are opportunities for first- or second-year students to work in community health clinics.

Program areas: AIDS, drug/alcohol abuse, family medicine, geriatrics, internal medicine, pediatrics, rural medicine, women's health

Joint degrees awarded: M.D./Ph.D., M.D./M.P.H., M.D./M.S., M.D./M.A., M.D./M.H.A.

Total National Institutes of Health (NIH) grants awarded to the medical school and affiliated hospitals: **$20.9 million**

CURRICULUM

(TEXT PROVIDED BY MEDICAL SCHOOL):

Curriculum uses a developmental approach to integrate biological, behavioral, and social sciences; early clinical skills; basic science teaching balanced with problem-based learning and clinical correlations; and professionalism with a community-integrated approach to clinical training in one of our community campuses. Special clinical programs address rural and underserved/vulnerable interests.

FALL 2009 FACULTY PROFILE

Total teaching faculty: **611 (full-time), 23 (part-time)**
Of full-time faculty, those teaching in basic sciences: **19%**; in clinical programs: **81%**

Of part-time faculty, those teaching in basic sciences: **30%**; in clinical programs: **70%**
Full-time faculty/student ratio: **1.0**

SUPPORT SERVICES

The school offers students these services for dealing with stress: expanded-hour gym access, professional counseling, support groups.

RESIDENCY PROFILE

Most popular residency and specialty programs chosen by the 2008 and 2009 M.D. graduating classes: anesthesiology, emergency medicine, family practice, internal medicine, obstetrics and gynecology, pediatrics, psychiatry, radiology–diagnostic, surgery–general, internal medicine/pediatrics.

WHERE GRADS GO

41.4%

Proportion of 2007-2008 graduates who entered primary care specialties

37.7%

Proportion of 2008-2009 graduates who accepted in-state residencies

Morehouse School of Medicine

- 720 Westview Drive SW, Atlanta, GA 30310
- Private
- **Year Founded:** 1975
- **Tuition, 2009-2010:** $36,714
- **Enrollment 2009-2010 academic year:** 329
- **Website:** http://www.msm.edu
- **Specialty ranking:** N/A

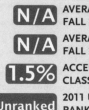

N/A AVERAGE GPA, ENTERING CLASS FALL 2009

N/A AVERAGE MCAT, ENTERING CLASS FALL 2009

1.5% ACCEPTANCE RATE, ENTERING CLASS FALL 2009

Unranked 2011 U.S. NEWS MEDICAL SCHOOL RANKING (RESEARCH)

30 2011 U.S. NEWS MEDICAL SCHOOL RANKING (PRIMARY CARE)

ADMISSIONS

Admissions phone number: **(404) 752-1650**
Admissions email address: **mdadmissions@msm.edu**
Application web site:
   http://www.msm.edu/Admissions.htm
Acceptance rate: **1.5%**
In-state acceptance rate: **N/A**
Out-of-state acceptance rate: **N/A**
Minority acceptance rate: **N/A**
International acceptance rate: **N/A**

Fall 2009 applications and acceptees

Type	Applied	Interviewed	Accepted	Enrolled
Total:	3,753	218	56	56
In-state:	443	N/A	N/A	N/A
Out-of-state:	3,310	N/A	N/A	N/A

Profile of admitted students

Average undergraduate grade point average: **N/A**
MCAT averages (scale: 1-15; writing test: J-T):
Composite score: **N/A**
Verbal reasoning score: **N/A**, Physical sciences score: **N/A**,
   Biological score: **N/A**, Writing score: **N/A**
Proportion with undergraduate majors in: Biological
   sciences: **73%**, Physical sciences: **5%**, Non-sciences: **N/A**,
   Other health professions: **N/A**, Mixed disciplines and
   other: **22%**
Percentage of students not coming directly from college
   after graduation: **N/A**

Dates and details

The American Medical College Application Service
   (AMCAS) application is accepted.
School asks for a second, school-specific application as part
   of the admissions process.
Oldest MCAT considered for Fall 2011 entry: **2008**
Earliest application date for the 2011-2012 first-year class:
   06/01
Latest application date: **12/01**
Acceptance dates for regular application for the class
   entering in Fall 2011.

Earliest: **15-JUL-20**
Latest: **08-JAN-11**
Applicants have N/A weeks to respond to admissions offer.
The school does consider requests for deferred entrance.
Starting month for the class of 2011–2012: **July**
The school does have an Early Decision Plan (EDP).
A personal interview is required for admission.

Undergraduate coursework required

Medical school requires undergraduate work in these subjects: biology, English, organic chemistry, physics, mathematics, general chemistry.

ADMISSIONS POLICY

(TEXT PROVIDED BY SCHOOL):
   Selection is based on MCAT scores, academic achievement and progress, difficulty and balance of academic program, extra-curricular activities. Committee also looks for
evidence that applicant will contribute to the advancement
of the practice of medicine. Data gathered include letters of
recommendation, academic record, supplemental application, and interview.

FINANCIAL AID

Financial aid phone number: **(404) 752-1655**
Tuition, 2009-2010 academic year: **$36,714**
Room and board: **N/A**
Percentage of students receiving financial aid in 2009-10:
   83%
Percentage of students receiving: Loans: **79%**,
   Grants/scholarships: **46%**, Work-study aid: **1%**
Average medical school debt for the class of 2008:
   $168,449

STUDENT BODY

Fall 2009 full-time enrollment: **329**
Men: **31%**, Women: **69%**, In-state: **N/A**, Minorities: **95%**,
   American Indian: **0.3%**, Asian-American: **14.6%**,
   African-American: **78.7%**, Hispanic-American: **1.5%**,
   White: **1.5%**, International: **2.7%**, Unknown: **0.6%**

ACADEMIC PROGRAMS

The school's curriculum rarely give first-year students substantial contact with patients.

There are opportunities for first- or second-year students to work in community health clinics.

Program areas: drug/alcohol abuse, family medicine, internal medicine, pediatrics, rural medicine, women's health

Joint degrees awarded: M.D./Ph.D.

Total National Institutes of Health (NIH) grants awarded to the medical school and affiliated hospitals: **$25.1 million**

CURRICULUM

(TEXT PROVIDED BY MEDICAL SCHOOL):

The MSM MD program focuses on primary healthcare. The curriculum includes clinical preceptorships, community service learning opportunities, clerkships in surgery, family medicine, maternal and child health, psychiatry, radiology, internal medicine, pediatrics, obstetrics/gynecology, rural primary care and ambulatory medicine, plus five electives.

FALL 2009 FACULTY PROFILE

Total teaching faculty: **212 (full-time), 47 (part-time)**

Of full-time faculty, those teaching in basic sciences: **26%**; in clinical programs: **74%**

Of part-time faculty, those teaching in basic sciences: **9%**; in clinical programs: **91%**

Full-time faculty/student ratio: **0.6**

SUPPORT SERVICES

The school offers students these services for dealing with stress: expanded-hour gym access, peer counseling, professional counseling, religious support, support groups.

RESIDENCY PROFILE

Most popular residency and specialty programs chosen by the 2008 and 2009 M.D. graduating classes: anesthesiology, emergency medicine, family practice, internal medicine, neurology, obstetrics and gynecology, pediatrics, psychiatry, radiology–diagnostic, surgery–general.

WHERE GRADS GO

65.0%

Proportion of 2007-2008 graduates who entered primary care specialties

30.0%

Proportion of 2008-2009 graduates who accepted in-state residencies

Mount Sinai School of Medicine

■ 1 Gustave L. Levy Place, PO Box 1217, New York, NY 10029
■ Private
■ Year Founded: 1963
■ Tuition, 2009-2010: $41,103
■ Enrollment 2009-2010 academic year: 534
■ Website: http://www.mssm.edu
■ Specialty ranking: AIDS: 14, geriatrics: 2

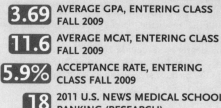

3.69	AVERAGE GPA, ENTERING CLASS FALL 2009
11.6	AVERAGE MCAT, ENTERING CLASS FALL 2009
5.9%	ACCEPTANCE RATE, ENTERING CLASS FALL 2009
18	2011 U.S. NEWS MEDICAL SCHOOL RANKING (RESEARCH)
62	2011 U.S. NEWS MEDICAL SCHOOL RANKING (PRIMARY CARE)

ADMISSIONS

Admissions phone number: **(212) 241-6696**
Admissions email address: **admissions@mssm.edu**
Application web site:
  http://www.aamc.org/students/amcas/start.htm
Acceptance rate: **5.9%**
In-state acceptance rate: **6.6%**
Out-of-state acceptance rate: **5.6%**
Minority acceptance rate: **6.4%**
International acceptance rate: **4.2%**

Fall 2009 applications and acceptees

Type	Applied	Interviewed	Accepted	Enrolled
Total:	6,572	855	385	140
In-state:	1,552	241	103	45
Out-of-state:	5,020	614	282	95

Profile of admitted students

Average undergraduate grade point average: **3.69**
MCAT averages (scale: 1-15; writing test: J-T):
Composite score: **11.6**
Verbal reasoning score: **10.9**, Physical sciences score: **12.0**,
  Biological score: **12.0**, Writing score: **Q**
Proportion with undergraduate majors in: Biological
  sciences: **30%**, Physical sciences: **21%**, Non-sciences:
  37%, Other health professions: **4%**, Mixed disciplines
  and other: **8%**
Percentage of students not coming directly from college
  after graduation: **57%**

Dates and details

The American Medical College Application Service
  (AMCAS) application is accepted.
School asks for a second, school-specific application as part
  of the admissions process.
Oldest MCAT considered for Fall 2011 entry: **2008**
Earliest application date for the 2011-2012 first-year class:
  06/01
Latest application date: **11/01**
Acceptance dates for regular application for the class
  entering in Fall 2011.

Earliest: **15-NOV-10**
Latest: **15-AUG-11**
Applicants have 2 weeks to respond to admissions offer.
The school does consider requests for deferred entrance.
Starting month for the class of 2011-2012: **August**
The school does have an Early Decision Plan (EDP).
A personal interview is required for admission.

Undergraduate coursework required

Medical school requires undergraduate work in these subjects: biology, English, organic chemistry, inorganic (general) chemistry, physics, mathematics.

ADMISSIONS POLICY

(TEXT PROVIDED BY SCHOOL):

  Applicants are considered based on qualifications including intellectual capability and academic achievement, motivation, potential for a career in medicine, service and
leadership, eagerness to shape one's own learning experience, maturity, and conformity to the School's standards of
character and health.

FINANCIAL AID

Financial aid phone number: **(212) 241-5245**
Tuition, 2009-2010 academic year: **$41,103**
Room and board: **$16,694**
Percentage of students receiving financial aid in 2009-10:
  77%
Percentage of students receiving: Loans: **65%**,
  Grants/scholarships: **37%**, Work-study aid: **9%**
Average medical school debt for the class of 2008:
  $133,186

STUDENT BODY

Fall 2009 full-time enrollment: **534**
Men: **48%**, Women: **52%**, In-state: **35%**, Minorities: **39%**,
  American Indian: **0.4%**, Asian-American: **24.3%**,
  African-American: **7.3%**, Hispanic-American: **9.4%**,
  White: **50.2%**, International: **4.5%**, Unknown: **3.9%**

ACADEMIC PROGRAMS

The school's curriculum very frequently give first-year students substantial contact with patients.

There are opportunities for first- or second-year students to work in community health clinics.

Program areas: AIDS, drug/alcohol abuse, family medicine, geriatrics, internal medicine, pediatrics, women's health

Joint degrees awarded: M.D./Ph.D., M.D./M.B.A., M.D./M.P.H., M.D./M.S.

Total National Institutes of Health (NIH) grants awarded to the medical school and affiliated hospitals: **$279.4 million**

CURRICULUM

(TEXT PROVIDED BY MEDICAL SCHOOL):

Mount Sinai School of Medicine offers an innovative curriculum that promotes early patient exposure during the first two years and integration of clinical medicine with the basic sciences throughout all four years. The clinical curriculum is designed to promote self-directed learning, clinical problem solving, and scientific inquiry through diverse and innovative educational offerings.

FALL 2009 FACULTY PROFILE

Total teaching faculty: **1,102 (full-time)**, **161 (part-time)**
Of full-time faculty, those teaching in basic sciences: **27%**; in clinical programs: **73%**

Of part-time faculty, those teaching in basic sciences: **7%**; in clinical programs: **93%**
Full-time faculty/student ratio: **2.1**

SUPPORT SERVICES

The school offers students these services for dealing with stress: expanded-hour gym access, peer counseling, professional counseling, religious support, support groups.

RESIDENCY PROFILE

Most popular residency and specialty programs chosen by the 2008 and 2009 M.D. graduating classes: anesthesiology, emergency medicine, internal medicine, obstetrics and gynecology, orthopaedic surgery, pathology–anatomic and clinical, psychiatry, surgery–general, transitional year.

WHERE GRADS GO

32.6%

Proportion of 2007-2008 graduates who entered primary care specialties

56.1%

Proportion of 2008-2009 graduates who accepted in-state residencies

New York Medical College

■ 40 Sunshine Cottage Road, Valhalla, NY 10595
■ Private
■ **Year Founded:** 1860
■ **Tuition, 2009-2010:** $47,790
■ **Enrollment 2009-2010 academic year:** 792
■ **Website:** http://www.nymc.edu
■ **Specialty ranking:** N/A

3.60 AVERAGE GPA, ENTERING CLASS FALL 2009

10.1 AVERAGE MCAT, ENTERING CLASS FALL 2009

8.2% ACCEPTANCE RATE, ENTERING CLASS FALL 2009

Unranked 2011 U.S. NEWS MEDICAL SCHOOL RANKING (RESEARCH)

Unranked 2011 U.S. NEWS MEDICAL SCHOOL RANKING (PRIMARY CARE)

ADMISSIONS

Admissions phone number: **(914) 594-4507**
Admissions email address: **mdadmit@nymc.edu**
Application web site:
  http://www.nymc.edu/Academics/SchoolOfMedicine/Admissions/index.html
Acceptance rate: **8.2%**
In-state acceptance rate: **11.9%**
Out-of-state acceptance rate: **7.3%**
Minority acceptance rate: **7.1%**
International acceptance rate: **1.4%**

Fall 2009 applications and acceptees

Type	Applied	Interviewed	Accepted	Enrolled
Total:	8,472	1,333	694	194
In-state:	1,584	328	188	64
Out-of-state:	6,888	1,005	506	130

Profile of admitted students

Average undergraduate grade point average: **3.60**
MCAT averages (scale: 1-15; writing test: J-T):
Composite score: **10.1**
Verbal reasoning score: **9.7**, Physical sciences score: **10.2**,
  Biological score: **10.6**, Writing score: **Q**
Proportion with undergraduate majors in: Biological
  sciences: **46%**, Physical sciences: **16%**, Non-sciences:
  12%, Other health professions: **4%**, Mixed disciplines
  and other: **22%**
Percentage of students not coming directly from college
  after graduation: **63%**

Dates and details

The American Medical College Application Service
  (AMCAS) application is accepted.
School asks for a second, school-specific application as part
  of the admissions process.
Oldest MCAT considered for Fall 2011 entry: **2008**
Earliest application date for the 2011-2012 first-year class:
  06/01
Latest application date: **12/15**

Acceptance dates for regular application for the class
  entering in Fall 2011.
Earliest: **15-NOV-10**
Latest: **01-AUG-11**
Applicants have 2 weeks to respond to admissions offer.
The school does consider requests for deferred entrance.
Starting month for the class of 2011–2012: **August**
The school does have an Early Decision Plan (EDP).
A personal interview is required for admission.

Undergraduate coursework required

Medical school requires undergraduate work in these subjects: biology, English, organic chemistry, inorganic (general) chemistry, physics.

ADMISSIONS POLICY
(TEXT PROVIDED BY SCHOOL):

  The College admits a diverse class respecting gender,
race and other factors. Students from historically underrepresented backgrounds are actively encouraged to apply. No
candidate will be denied admission based on race, color,
creed, religion, national or ethnic origin, age, sex, sexual orientation, or disability. See www.nymc.edu/Academics/
SchoolOfMedicine/Admissions/SelectionCriteria.html

FINANCIAL AID

Financial aid phone number: **(914) 594-4491**
Tuition, 2009-2010 academic year: **$47,790**
Room and board: **$19,484**
Percentage of students receiving financial aid in 2009-10:
  93%
Percentage of students receiving: Loans: **92%**,
  Grants/scholarships: **33%**, Work-study aid: **3%**
Average medical school debt for the class of 2008:
  $181,000

STUDENT BODY

Fall 2009 full-time enrollment: **792**
Men: **48%**, Women: **52%**, In-state: **29%**, Minorities: **37%**,
  American Indian: **0.1%**, Asian-American: **33.0%**,

African-American: **3.3%**, Hispanic-American: **1.0%**,
White: **53.3%**, International: **0.6%**, Unknown: **8.7%**

ACADEMIC PROGRAMS

The school's curriculum frequently give first-year students
substantial contact with patients.

There are opportunities for first- or second-year students to
work in community health clinics.

Program areas: AIDS, drug/alcohol abuse, family
medicine, geriatrics, internal medicine, pediatrics, rural
medicine, women's health

Joint degrees awarded: M.D./Ph.D., M.D./M.P.H.

Total National Institutes of Health (NIH) grants awarded
to the medical school and affiliated hospitals: **$19.4
million**

CURRICULUM

(TEXT PROVIDED BY MEDICAL SCHOOL):

For a description of the New York Medical College
School of Medicine curriculum, please visit
www.nymc.edu/Academics/SchoolOfMedicine/Undergrad
uateMedicalEducation/index.html

FALL 2009 FACULTY PROFILE

Total teaching faculty: **1,331 (full-time)**, **127 (part-time)**
Of full-time faculty, those teaching in basic sciences: **9%**;
in clinical programs: **91%**

Of part-time faculty, those teaching in basic sciences: **5%**;
in clinical programs: **95%**
Full-time faculty/student ratio: **1.7**

SUPPORT SERVICES

The school offers students these services for dealing with
stress: expanded-hour gym access, professional counseling,
religious support, support groups.

RESIDENCY PROFILE

Most popular residency and specialty programs chosen by
the 2008 and 2009 M.D. graduating classes: anesthesiology, emergency medicine, family practice, internal medicine, neurology, ophthalmology, pediatrics, physical
medicine and rehabilitation, radiology–diagnostic, surgery–general.

WHERE GRADS GO

37.9%

*Proportion of 2007-2008 graduates who entered primary
care specialties*

47.5%

*Proportion of 2008-2009 graduates who accepted in-state
residencies*

New York University

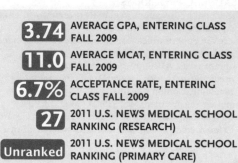

- 550 First Avenue, New York, NY 10016
- Private
- Year Founded: 1841
- Tuition, 2009-2010: $49,203
- Enrollment 2009-2010 academic year: 683
- Website: http://www.med.nyu.edu/education
- Specialty ranking: AIDS: 12, drug/alcohol abuse: 10

3.74 AVERAGE GPA, ENTERING CLASS FALL 2009

11.0 AVERAGE MCAT, ENTERING CLASS FALL 2009

6.7% ACCEPTANCE RATE, ENTERING CLASS FALL 2009

27 2011 U.S. NEWS MEDICAL SCHOOL RANKING (RESEARCH)

Unranked 2011 U.S. NEWS MEDICAL SCHOOL RANKING (PRIMARY CARE)

ADMISSIONS

Admissions phone number: **(212) 263-5290**
Admissions email address: **admissions@med.nyu.edu**
Application web site:
  http://www.med.nyu.edu/education/admissions.html
Acceptance rate: **6.7%**
In-state acceptance rate: **8.5%**
Out-of-state acceptance rate: **6.2%**
Minority acceptance rate: **8.2%**
International acceptance rate: **2.0%**

Fall 2009 applications and acceptees

Type	Applied	Interviewed	Accepted	Enrolled
Total:	**6,810**	**872**	**455**	**166**
In-state:	**1,404**	**230**	**119**	**67**
Out-of-state:	**5,406**	**642**	**336**	**99**

Profile of admitted students

Average undergraduate grade point average: **3.74**
MCAT averages (scale: 1-15; writing test: J-T):
Composite score: **11.0**
Verbal reasoning score: **10.3**, Physical sciences score: **11.3**,
  Biological score: **11.5**, Writing score: **Q**
Proportion with undergraduate majors in: Biological
  sciences: **43%**, Physical sciences: **30%**, Non-sciences:
  15%, Other health professions: **9%**, Mixed disciplines
  and other: **3%**
Percentage of students not coming directly from college
  after graduation: **38%**

Dates and details

The American Medical College Application Service
  (AMCAS) application is accepted.
School asks for a second, school-specific application as part
  of the admissions process.
Oldest MCAT considered for Fall 2011 entry: **2008**
Earliest application date for the 2011-2012 first-year class:
  06/01
Latest application date: **11/15**
Acceptance dates for regular application for the class
  entering in Fall 2011.

Earliest: **15-DEC-10**
Latest: **N/A**
Applicants have 2 weeks to respond to admissions offer.
The school does consider requests for deferred entrance.
Starting month for the class of 2011-2012: **August**
The school doesn't have an Early Decision Plan (EDP).
A personal interview is required for admission.

Undergraduate coursework required

Medical school requires undergraduate work in these subjects: biology/zoology, English, organic chemistry, inorganic
(general) chemistry, physics.

ADMISSIONS POLICY
(TEXT PROVIDED BY SCHOOL):

NYU participates in AMCAS. Applicants must have
attended an accredited college, completing 6 credits each in:
English, Inorganic Chemistry, Organic Chemistry, Physics,
and General Biology or Zoology. The MCAT and college faculty evaluations are required. Interviews are granted to those
who merit serious consideration. Those who were unsuccessful at another medical school are not eligible to apply.

FINANCIAL AID

Financial aid phone number: **(212) 263-5286**
Tuition, 2009-2010 academic year: **$49,203**
Room and board: **$13,500**
Percentage of students receiving financial aid in 2009-10:
  70%
Percentage of students receiving: Loans: **70%**,
  Grants/scholarships: **40%**, Work-study aid: **7%**
Average medical school debt for the class of 2008:
  $142,413

STUDENT BODY

Fall 2009 full-time enrollment: **683**
Men: **51%**, Women: **49%**, In-state: **45%**, Minorities: **37%**,
  American Indian: **0.6%**, Asian-American: **26.4%**,
  African-American: **3.1%**, Hispanic-American: **6.6%**,
  White: **57.4%**, International: **0.3%**, Unknown: **5.7%**

ACADEMIC PROGRAMS

The school's curriculum very frequently give first-year students substantial contact with patients.

There are opportunities for first- or second-year students to work in community health clinics.

Program areas: AIDS, drug/alcohol abuse, family medicine, geriatrics, internal medicine, pediatrics, rural medicine, women's health

Joint degrees awarded: M.D./Ph.D., M.D./M.P.H.

Total National Institutes of Health (NIH) grants awarded to the medical school and affiliated hospitals: **$183.7 million**

CURRICULUM

(TEXT PROVIDED BY MEDICAL SCHOOL):

NYU's program encourages self-directed learning. The pre-clinical curriculum is organized into thematic modules with small-group, case-based exercises. The clinical curriculum, with 9 core clerkships, stresses interactive, patient-based education; evidence-based problem solving; and spiral learning, building on a strong background in biomedical science and a rich, diverse clinical environment.

FALL 2009 FACULTY PROFILE

Total teaching faculty: **1,503 (full-time)**, **3,519 (part-time)**

Of full-time faculty, those teaching in basic sciences: **17%**; in clinical programs: **83%**

Of part-time faculty, those teaching in basic sciences: **7%**; in clinical programs: **93%**

Full-time faculty/student ratio: **2.2**

SUPPORT SERVICES

The school offers students these services for dealing with stress: expanded-hour gym access, peer counseling, professional counseling, religious support, support groups.

RESIDENCY PROFILE

Most popular residency and specialty programs chosen by the 2008 and 2009 M.D. graduating classes: anesthesiology, emergency medicine, internal medicine, neurology, orthopaedic surgery, pediatrics, psychiatry, radiology–diagnostic, surgery–general.

WHERE GRADS GO

39.3%

Proportion of 2007-2008 graduates who entered primary care specialties

55.3%

Proportion of 2008-2009 graduates who accepted in-state residencies

Northeastern Ohio Universities
College of Medicine

■ **4209 State Route 44, PO Box 95, Rootstown, OH 44272-0095**
■ **Public**
■ **Year Founded:** 1973
■ **Tuition, 2009-2010:** In-state: $30,599; Out-of-State: $59,212
■ **Enrollment 2009-2010 academic year:** 472
■ **Website:** http://www.neoucom.edu
■ **Specialty ranking:** N/A

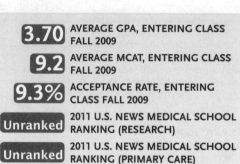

3.70	AVERAGE GPA, ENTERING CLASS FALL 2009
9.2	AVERAGE MCAT, ENTERING CLASS FALL 2009
9.3%	ACCEPTANCE RATE, ENTERING CLASS FALL 2009
Unranked	2011 U.S. NEWS MEDICAL SCHOOL RANKING (RESEARCH)
Unranked	2011 U.S. NEWS MEDICAL SCHOOL RANKING (PRIMARY CARE)

ADMISSIONS
Admissions phone number: **(330) 325-6270**
Admissions email address: **admission@neoucom.edu**
Application web site:
   http://www.neoucom.edu/audience/applicants/succeed/admi
Acceptance rate: **9.3%**
In-state acceptance rate: **20.2%**
Out-of-state acceptance rate: **0.7%**
Minority acceptance rate: **8.9%**
International acceptance rate: **0.0%**

Fall 2009 applications and acceptees

Type	Applied	Interviewed	Accepted	Enrolled
Total:	1,913	190	178	108
In-state:	848	181	171	102
Out-of-state:	1,065	9	7	6

Profile of admitted students
Average undergraduate grade point average: **3.70**
MCAT averages (scale: 1-15; writing test: J-T):
Composite score: **9.2**
Verbal reasoning score: **9.3**, Physical sciences score: **8.9**,
   Biological score: **9.3**, Writing score: **O**
Proportion with undergraduate majors in: Biological
   sciences: **62%**, Physical sciences: **8%**, Non-sciences: **4%**,
   Other health professions: **0%**, Mixed disciplines and
   other: **26%**
Percentage of students not coming directly from college
   after graduation: **33%**

Dates and details
The American Medical College Application Service
   (AMCAS) application is accepted.
School asks for a second, school-specific application as part
   of the admissions process.
Oldest MCAT considered for Fall 2011 entry: **2008**
Earliest application date for the 2011-2012 first-year class:
   06/01
Latest application date: **11/10**

Acceptance dates for regular application for the class
   entering in Fall 2011.
Earliest: **15-AUG-10**
Latest: **10-OCT-10**
Applicants have 2 weeks to respond to admissions offer.
The school doesn't consider requests for deferred entrance.
Starting month for the class of 2011–2012: **August**
The school does have an Early Decision Plan (EDP).
A personal interview is required for admission.

Undergraduate coursework required
Medical school requires undergraduate work in these subjects: organic chemistry, physics.

ADMISSIONS POLICY
(TEXT PROVIDED BY SCHOOL):
   Candidates must demonstrate the designated skills, abilities and attributes listed at www.neoucom.edu/Students/ADMI/Medical_Essential_Function.pdf. NEOUCOM is publicly chartered & funded in the state of Ohio and its charter mandates admission preference to Ohio residents as defined by the Board of Regents. Only U.S. citizens and permanent residents may be considered for admission.

FINANCIAL AID
Financial aid phone number: **(330) 325-6481**
Tuition, 2009-2010 academic year: **In-state: $30,599; Out-of-State: $59,212**
Room and board: **$10,500**
Percentage of students receiving financial aid in 2009-10:
   83%
Percentage of students receiving: Loans: **81%**,
   Grants/scholarships: **26%**, Work-study aid: **0%**
Average medical school debt for the class of 2008:
   $148,162

STUDENT BODY
Fall 2009 full-time enrollment: **472**
Men: **51%**, Women: **49%**, In-state: **95%**, Minorities: **39%**,
   American Indian: **0.0%**, Asian-American: **33.3%**,

African-American: 2.3%, Hispanic-American: 3.2%, White: 57.0%, International: 0.0%, Unknown: 4.2%

ACADEMIC PROGRAMS

The school's curriculum frequently give first-year students substantial contact with patients.

There are opportunities for first- or second-year students to work in community health clinics.

Program areas: AIDS, drug/alcohol abuse, family medicine, geriatrics, internal medicine, pediatrics, rural medicine, women's health

Joint degrees awarded: N/A

Total National Institutes of Health (NIH) grants awarded to the medical school and affiliated hospitals: **$3.0 million**

CURRICULUM

(TEXT PROVIDED BY MEDICAL SCHOOL):

The goal of NEOUCOM's curriculum is to develop and graduate students who demonstrate competence in the knowledge and practice of medicine, exhibit strong communication skills, display a caring attitude and exhibit professional character, all in the context of the community. These 5 C's guide the expected outcomes for students graduating from the College's program.

FALL 2009 FACULTY PROFILE

Total teaching faculty: 333 (full-time), 1,682 (part-time)
Of full-time faculty, those teaching in basic sciences: **13%**; in clinical programs: **87%**

Of part-time faculty, those teaching in basic sciences: **6%**; in clinical programs: **94%**
Full-time faculty/student ratio: **0.7**

SUPPORT SERVICES

The school offers students these services for dealing with stress: expanded-hour gym access, peer counseling, professional counseling, support groups.

RESIDENCY PROFILE

Most popular residency and specialty programs chosen by the 2008 and 2009 M.D. graduating classes: anesthesiology, emergency medicine, internal medicine, obstetrics and gynecology, pediatrics, radiology–diagnostic, surgery–general.

WHERE GRADS GO

 42.0%

Proportion of 2007-2008 graduates who entered primary care specialties

59.0%

Proportion of 2008-2009 graduates who accepted in-state residencies

Northwestern University
Feinberg

■ 420 E. Superior Street (Rubloff Building), 12th Floor, Chicago, IL 60611
■ Private
■ Year Founded: 1859
■ Tuition, 2009-2010: $45,737
■ Enrollment 2009-2010 academic year: 700
■ Website: http://www.feinberg.northwestern.edu
■ Specialty ranking: AIDS: 14, internal medicine: 17, pediatrics: 17, women's health: 12

3.74 AVERAGE GPA, ENTERING CLASS FALL 2009

11.5 AVERAGE MCAT, ENTERING CLASS FALL 2009

7.3% ACCEPTANCE RATE, ENTERING CLASS FALL 2009

18 2011 U.S. NEWS MEDICAL SCHOOL RANKING (RESEARCH)

49 2011 U.S. NEWS MEDICAL SCHOOL RANKING (PRIMARY CARE)

ADMISSIONS

Admissions phone number: (312) 503-8206
Admissions email address: med-admissions@northwestern.edu
Application web site: http://www.medschool.northwestern.edu/admissions/md/
Acceptance rate: 7.3%
In-state acceptance rate: 6.6%
Out-of-state acceptance rate: 7.4%
Minority acceptance rate: 8.4%
International acceptance rate: 1.7%

Fall 2009 applications and acceptees

Type	Applied	Interviewed	Accepted	Enrolled
Total:	6,750	639	491	164
In-state:	907	79	60	35
Out-of-state:	5,843	560	431	129

Profile of admitted students

Average undergraduate grade point average: 3.74
MCAT averages (scale: 1-15; writing test: J-T):
Composite score: 11.5
Verbal reasoning score: 10.5, Physical sciences score: 11.9, Biological score: 12.2, Writing score: Q
Proportion with undergraduate majors in: Biological sciences: 42%, Physical sciences: 25%, Non-sciences: 29%, Other health professions: 0%, Mixed disciplines and other: 4%
Percentage of students not coming directly from college after graduation: 14%

Dates and details

The American Medical College Application Service (AMCAS) application is accepted.
School asks for a second, school-specific application as part of the admissions process.
Oldest MCAT considered for Fall 2011 entry: 2008
Earliest application date for the 2011-2012 first-year class: 07/01
Latest application date: 10/15

Acceptance dates for regular application for the class entering in Fall 2011.
Earliest: 15-JAN-10
Latest: 01-APR-12
Applicants have 4 weeks to respond to admissions offer.
The school does consider requests for deferred entrance.
Starting month for the class of 2011–2012: August
The school doesn't have an Early Decision Plan (EDP).
A personal interview is required for admission.

Undergraduate coursework required

Medical school requires undergraduate work in these subjects: biology, organic chemistry, inorganic (general) chemistry, physics.

ADMISSIONS POLICY
(TEXT PROVIDED BY SCHOOL):

A full year each of modern biology, organic chemistry, inorganic chemistry, and general physics are recommended. The MCAT is required. No preference is given to residents of the State of Illinois. Applications from foreign nationals are welcome; all applicants are required to have completed at least 3 years of course work at an accredited US or Canadian college or university.

FINANCIAL AID

Financial aid phone number: (312) 503-8722
Tuition, 2009-2010 academic year: $45,737
Room and board: $14,958
Percentage of students receiving financial aid in 2009-10: 76%
Percentage of students receiving: Loans: 69%, Grants/scholarships: 47%, Work-study aid: 0%
Average medical school debt for the class of 2008: $151,978

STUDENT BODY

Fall 2009 full-time enrollment: 700
Men: 52%, Women: 48%, In-state: 27%, Minorities: 46%, American Indian: 0.9%, Asian-American: 34.6%,

African-American: **5.0%**, Hispanic-American: **5.9%**, White: **44.0%**, International: **3.7%**, Unknown: **6.0%**

ACADEMIC PROGRAMS

The school's curriculum frequently give first-year students substantial contact with patients.

There are opportunities for first- or second-year students to work in community health clinics.

Program areas: AIDS, drug/alcohol abuse, family medicine, geriatrics, internal medicine, pediatrics, rural medicine, women's health

Joint degrees awarded: M.D./Ph.D., M.D./M.P.H., M.D./M.A.

Total National Institutes of Health (NIH) grants awarded to the medical school and affiliated hospitals: **$232.6 million**

CURRICULUM

(TEXT PROVIDED BY MEDICAL SCHOOL):

The Feinberg curriculum cultivates leaders who will effect change in their communities and in the profession, and is designed for independent adult learners. There is one integrated basic science course in each of the first 2 years complemented by PBL sessions, labs, and tutorials. Clinical rotations are conducted within a consortium of affiliates, the McGaw Medical Center.

FALL 2009 FACULTY PROFILE

Total teaching faculty: **2,165 (full-time)**, **254 (part-time)**

Of full-time faculty, those teaching in basic sciences: **6%**; in clinical programs: **94%**

Of part-time faculty, those teaching in basic sciences: **2%**; in clinical programs: **98%**

Full-time faculty/student ratio: **3.1**

SUPPORT SERVICES

The school offers students these services for dealing with stress: professional counseling, religious support, support groups.

RESIDENCY PROFILE

Most popular residency and specialty programs chosen by the 2008 and 2009 M.D. graduating classes: anesthesiology, emergency medicine, internal medicine, obstetrics and gynecology, orthopaedic surgery, pediatrics, psychiatry, radiology–diagnostic, surgery–general, urology.

WHERE GRADS GO

36.2%

Proportion of 2007-2008 graduates who entered primary care specialties

43.5%

Proportion of 2008-2009 graduates who accepted in state residencies

Ohio State University

- 200 Meiling Hall, 370 W. Ninth Avenue, Columbus, OH 43210-1238
- **Public**
- **Year Founded:** 1834
- **Tuition, 2009-2010:** In-state: $29,423; Out-of-State: $33,301
- **Enrollment 2009-2010 academic year:** 855
- **Website:** http://medicine.osu.edu
- **Specialty ranking:** internal medicine: 26, pediatrics: 19, women's health: 18

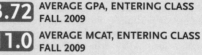

3.72	AVERAGE GPA, ENTERING CLASS FALL 2009
11.0	AVERAGE MCAT, ENTERING CLASS FALL 2009
11.0%	ACCEPTANCE RATE, ENTERING CLASS FALL 2009
27	2011 U.S. NEWS MEDICAL SCHOOL RANKING (RESEARCH)
39	2011 U.S. NEWS MEDICAL SCHOOL RANKING (PRIMARY CARE)

ADMISSIONS

Admissions phone number: **(614) 292-7137**
Admissions email address: **medicine@osu.edu**
Application web site: **http://www.aamc.org**
Acceptance rate: **11.0%**
In-state acceptance rate: **19.1%**
Out-of-state acceptance rate: **8.3%**
Minority acceptance rate: **9.5%**
International acceptance rate: **N/A**

Fall 2009 applications and acceptees

Type	Applied	Interviewed	Accepted	Enrolled
Total:	4,185	689	461	220
In-state:	1,043	279	199	129
Out-of-state:	3,142	410	262	91

Profile of admitted students

Average undergraduate grade point average: **3.72**
MCAT averages (scale: 1-15; writing test: J-T):
Composite score: **11.0**
Verbal reasoning score: **10.5**, Physical sciences score: **11.0**, Biological score: **11.5**, Writing score: **P**
Proportion with undergraduate majors in: Biological sciences: **46%**, Physical sciences: **14%**, Non-sciences: **9%**, Other health professions: **4%**, Mixed disciplines and other: **27%**
Percentage of students not coming directly from college after graduation: **40%**

Dates and details

The American Medical College Application Service (AMCAS) application is accepted.
School asks for a second, school-specific application as part of the admissions process.
Oldest MCAT considered for Fall 2011 entry: **2007**
Earliest application date for the 2011-2012 first-year class: **06/01**
Latest application date: **11/01**
Acceptance dates for regular application for the class entering in Fall 2011.
Earliest: **16-OCT-10**

Latest: **10-AUG-11**
Applicants have 2 weeks to respond to admissions offer.
The school does consider requests for deferred entrance.
Starting month for the class of 2011–2012: **August**
The school does have an Early Decision Plan (EDP).
A personal interview is required for admission.

Undergraduate coursework required

Medical school requires undergraduate work in these subjects: biology, biology/zoology, organic chemistry, inorganic (general) chemistry, physics, biochemistry, general chemistry.

ADMISSIONS POLICY
(TEXT PROVIDED BY SCHOOL):

Applicants are evaluated on: undergrad academic performance/MCAT/participation in health-related experiences/research/faculty references/personal interview. Competitive apps demonstrate skills in: independent thinking/decision-making/active involvement in community/leadership roles. The College seeks self-motivated compassionate apps that embody high ethical standards, honesty, concern for others.

FINANCIAL AID

Financial aid phone number: **(614) 688-4955**
Tuition, 2009-2010 academic year: **In-state: $29,423; Out-of-State: $33,301**
Room and board: **$9,080**
Percentage of students receiving financial aid in 2009-10: **92%**
Percentage of students receiving: Loans: **85%**, Grants/scholarships: **54%**, Work-study aid: **0%**
Average medical school debt for the class of 2008: **$140,772**

STUDENT BODY

Fall 2009 full-time enrollment: **855**
Men: **57%**, Women: **43%**, In-state: **85%**, Minorities: **31%**, American Indian: **0.0%**, Asian-American: **18.2%**,

African-American: **6.3%**, Hispanic-American: **5.0%**, White: **69.0%**, International: **0.1%**, Unknown: **1.3%**

ACADEMIC PROGRAMS

The school's curriculum frequently give first-year students substantial contact with patients.

There are opportunities for first- or second-year students to work in community health clinics.

Program areas: AIDS, drug/alcohol abuse, family medicine, geriatrics, internal medicine, pediatrics, rural medicine, women's health

Joint degrees awarded: M.D./Ph.D., M.D./M.B.A., M.D./M.P.H., M.D./J.D., M.D./M.H.A.

Total National Institutes of Health (NIH) grants awarded to the medical school and affiliated hospitals: **$198.8 million**

CURRICULUM

(TEXT PROVIDED BY MEDICAL SCHOOL):

The curriculum prepares students to provide high quality, patient centered, evidence based care with opportunities in research, medical education, and administration. Professionalism, ethical decision making, effective communication, and leadership are priorities. There are two parallel pathways to accommodate different learning styles. Clinical experiences in all specialties are available.

FALL 2009 FACULTY PROFILE

Total teaching faculty: **2,765 (full-time)**, **1,083 (part-time)**

Of full-time faculty, those teaching in basic sciences: **14%**; in clinical programs: **86%**

Of part-time faculty, those teaching in basic sciences: **15%**; in clinical programs: **85%**

Full-time faculty/student ratio: **3.2**

SUPPORT SERVICES

The school offers students these services for dealing with stress: expanded-hour gym access, professional counseling, support groups.

RESIDENCY PROFILE

Most popular residency and specialty programs chosen by the 2008 and 2009 M.D. graduating classes: anesthesiology, family practice, internal medicine, obstetrics and gynecology, ophthalmology, orthopaedic surgery, pediatrics, radiology–diagnostic, transitional year.

WHERE GRADS GO

40.0%

Proportion of 2007-2008 graduates who entered primary care specialties

42.0%

Proportion of 2008-2009 graduates who accepted in-state residencies

Oregon Health and Science University

- 3181 S.W. Sam Jackson Park Road, L102, Portland, OR 97239-3098
- Public
- **Year Founded:** 1887
- **Tuition, 2009-2010:** In-state: $38,689; Out-of-State: $51,845
- **Enrollment 2009-2010 academic year:** 523
- **Website:** http://www.ohsu.edu/xd
- **Specialty ranking:** family medicine: 2, rural medicine: 4, women's health: 16

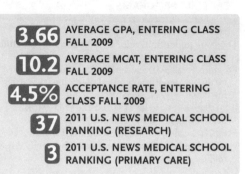

3.66 AVERAGE GPA, ENTERING CLASS FALL 2009

10.2 AVERAGE MCAT, ENTERING CLASS FALL 2009

4.5% ACCEPTANCE RATE, ENTERING CLASS FALL 2009

37 2011 U.S. NEWS MEDICAL SCHOOL RANKING (RESEARCH)

3 2011 U.S. NEWS MEDICAL SCHOOL RANKING (PRIMARY CARE)

ADMISSIONS

Admissions phone number: **(503) 494-2998**
Admissions email address: **N/A**
Application web site:
http://www.ohsu.edu/xd/education/schools/school-of-medicine/academic-programs/md-program/admissions
Acceptance rate: **4.5%**
In-state acceptance rate: **24.4%**
Out-of-state acceptance rate: **2.6%**
Minority acceptance rate: **3.5%**
International acceptance rate: **N/A**

Fall 2009 applications and acceptees

Type	Applied	Interviewed	Accepted	Enrolled
Total:	4,578	555	204	120
In-state:	398	228	97	88
Out-of-state:	4,180	327	107	32

Profile of admitted students

Average undergraduate grade point average: 3.66
MCAT averages (scale: 1-15; writing test: J-T):
Composite score: 10.2
Verbal reasoning score: 9.9, Physical sciences score: 9.8, Biological score: 10.8, Writing score: P
Proportion with undergraduate majors in: Biological sciences: 38%, Physical sciences: 15%, Non-sciences: 13%, Other health professions: 7%, Mixed disciplines and other: 27%
Percentage of students not coming directly from college after graduation: 75%

Dates and details

The American Medical College Application Service (AMCAS) application is accepted.
School asks for a second, school-specific application as part of the admissions process.
Oldest MCAT considered for Fall 2011 entry: 2008
Earliest application date for the 2011-2012 first-year class: 06/01
Latest application date: 10/15

Acceptance dates for regular application for the class entering in Fall 2011.
Earliest: **01-NOV-10**
Latest: **15-AUG-11**
Applicants have 2 weeks to respond to admissions offer.
The school doesn't consider requests for deferred entrance.
Starting month for the class of 2011–2012: **August**
The school doesn't have an Early Decision Plan (EDP).
A personal interview is required for admission.

Undergraduate coursework required

Medical school requires undergraduate work in these subjects: biology, English, organic chemistry, inorganic (general) chemistry, physics, biochemistry, humanities, mathematics, demonstration of writing skills, calculus, social sciences, general chemistry.

ADMISSIONS POLICY
(TEXT PROVIDED BY SCHOOL):

We seek students who demonstrate academic excellence and readiness for medicine and will contribute to the diversity necessary to enhance the medical education of all students. Applicants are selected on the basis of demonstrated motivation for medicine, humanistic attitudes, and a realistic understanding of the role of the physician in providing health care to all communities.

FINANCIAL AID

Financial aid phone number: **(503) 494-7800**
Tuition, 2009-2010 academic year: **In-state: $38,689; Out-of-State: $51,845**
Room and board: **$18,000**
Percentage of students receiving financial aid in 2009-10: 93%
Percentage of students receiving: Loans: **89%**, Grants/scholarships: **79%**, Work-study aid: **1%**
Average medical school debt for the class of 2008: **$170,000**

STUDENT BODY

Fall 2009 full-time enrollment: 523

Men: 47%, Women: 53%, In-state: 64%, Minorities: 23%,
  American Indian: 1.7%, Asian-American: 18.9%,
  African-American: 1.5%, Hispanic-American: 1.1%,
  White: 76.7%, International: 0.0%, Unknown: 0.0%

ACADEMIC PROGRAMS
The school's curriculum very frequently give first-year
  students substantial contact with patients.
There are opportunities for first- or second-year students to
  work in community health clinics.
Program areas: AIDS, drug/alcohol abuse, family
  medicine, geriatrics, internal medicine, pediatrics, rural
  medicine, women's health
Joint degrees awarded: M.D./Ph.D., M.D./M.P.H.
Total National Institutes of Health (NIH) grants awarded
  to the medical school and affiliated hospitals: $193.7
  million

CURRICULUM
(TEXT PROVIDED BY MEDICAL SCHOOL):
  Highlights: integrated and multi-disciplinary courses
with clinical relevance; lecture and non-lecture learning balanced in half-day sessions; early and longitudinal clinical
preceptorship; experience in a rural/or underserved area;
performance-based assessment of students utilizing standardized patients.

FALL 2009 FACULTY PROFILE
Total teaching faculty: 1,745 (full-time), 296 (part-time)
Of full-time faculty, those teaching in basic sciences: 11%;
  in clinical programs: 89%

Of part-time faculty, those teaching in basic sciences: 15%;
  in clinical programs: 85%
Full-time faculty/student ratio: 3.3

SUPPORT SERVICES
The school offers students these services for dealing with
stress: expanded-hour gym access, peer counseling, professional counseling, religious support, support groups.

RESIDENCY PROFILE
Most popular residency and specialty programs chosen by
the 2008 and 2009 M.D. graduating classes: anesthesiology, emergency medicine, family practice, internal medicine, obstetrics and gynecology, orthopaedic surgery,
pathology–anatomic and clinical, pediatrics, radiology–diagnostic, surgery–general.

WHERE GRADS GO

46.6%

*Proportion of 2007-2008 graduates who entered primary
care specialties*

34.0%

*Proportion of 2008-2009 graduates who accepted in-state
residencies*

Rush University

■ 600 S. Paulina Street, Chicago, IL 60612
■ Private
■ Year Founded: 1837
■ Tuition, 2009-2010: $46,272
■ Enrollment 2009-2010 academic year: 547
■ Website: http://www.rushu.rush.edu/medcol/
■ Specialty ranking: N/A

3.60 AVERAGE GPA, ENTERING CLASS FALL 2009

10.2 AVERAGE MCAT, ENTERING CLASS FALL 2009

4.1% ACCEPTANCE RATE, ENTERING CLASS FALL 2009

Unranked 2011 U.S. NEWS MEDICAL SCHOOL RANKING (RESEARCH)

Unranked 2011 U.S. NEWS MEDICAL SCHOOL RANKING (PRIMARY CARE)

ADMISSIONS
Admissions phone number: N/A
Admissions email address: RMC_Admissions@rush.edu
Application web site: http://www.aamc.org
Acceptance rate: 4.1%
In-state acceptance rate: 13.3%
Out-of-state acceptance rate: 1.5%
Minority acceptance rate: 4.0%
International acceptance rate: N/A

Fall 2009 applications and acceptees

Type	Applied	Interviewed	Accepted	Enrolled
Total:	6,480	364	267	138
In-state:	1,435	268	191	113
Out-of-state:	5,045	96	76	25

Profile of admitted students
Average undergraduate grade point average: 3.60
MCAT averages (scale: 1-15; writing test: J-T):
Composite score: 10.2
Verbal reasoning score: 9.9, Physical sciences score: 10.0,
    Biological score: 10.5, Writing score: Q
Proportion with undergraduate majors in: Biological
    sciences: 44%, Physical sciences: 20%, Non-sciences:
    30%, Other health professions: 3%, Mixed disciplines
    and other: 3%
Percentage of students not coming directly from college
    after graduation: N/A

Dates and details
The American Medical College Application Service
    (AMCAS) application is accepted.
School asks for a second, school-specific application as part
    of the admissions process.
Oldest MCAT considered for Fall 2011 entry: 2009
Earliest application date for the 2011-2012 first-year class:
    06/30
Latest application date: 11/01
Acceptance dates for regular application for the class
    entering in Fall 2011.
Earliest: 01-DEC-10

Latest: 31-AUG-11
Applicants have 2 weeks to respond to admissions offer.
The school does consider requests for deferred entrance.
Starting month for the class of 2011–2012: September
The school doesn't have an Early Decision Plan (EDP).
A personal interview is required for admission.

Undergraduate coursework required
Medical school requires undergraduate work in these subjects: biology, organic chemistry, inorganic (general) chemistry, physics.

ADMISSIONS POLICY
(TEXT PROVIDED BY SCHOOL):
    Admission Requirements: US citizen or permanent resi-
dency (preference given to Illinois residents); 90 semester
hours undergraduate study prior to matriculation, including
8 hours biology, inorganic chemistry, organic chemistry (or
4 hours of biochemistry) & physics; survey courses in the
sciences do not qualify; the MCAT exam must be taken by
the end of the year preceding the entering class year.

FINANCIAL AID
Financial aid phone number: (312) 942-6256
Tuition, 2009-2010 academic year: $46,272
Room and board: $10,100
Percentage of students receiving financial aid in 2009-10:
    90%
Percentage of students receiving: Loans: 88%,
    Grants/scholarships: 57%, Work-study aid: 6%
Average medical school debt for the class of 2008:
    $163,472

STUDENT BODY
Fall 2009 full-time enrollment: 547
Men: 50%, Women: 50%, In-state: 79%, Minorities: 30%,
    American Indian: 0.7%, Asian-American: 23.0%,
    African-American: 2.9%, Hispanic-American: 3.3%,
    White: 68.9%, International: 0.0%, Unknown: 1.1%

ACADEMIC PROGRAMS

The school's curriculum frequently give first-year students substantial contact with patients.

There are opportunities for first- or second-year students to work in community health clinics.

Program areas: AIDS, drug/alcohol abuse, family medicine, geriatrics, internal medicine, pediatrics, rural medicine, women's health

Joint degrees awarded: M.D./Ph.D.

Total National Institutes of Health (NIH) grants awarded to the medical school and affiliated hospitals: **$44.2 million**

CURRICULUM

(TEXT PROVIDED BY MEDICAL SCHOOL):

The M1, M2 yrs offer a balanced basic science curriculum, with a preceptorship experience & courses in physical diagnosis and communication skills. Students are paired with primary care physicians in outpatient settings throughout the Chicago area. The M3, M4 years focus on clinical skills, diagnosis and patient management in core specialty areas plus offers extensive elective experiences.

FALL 2009 FACULTY PROFILE

Total teaching faculty: **497 (full-time)**, **206 (part-time)**
Of full-time faculty, those teaching in basic sciences: **24%**; in clinical programs: **76%**

Of part-time faculty, those teaching in basic sciences: **9%**; in clinical programs: **91%**
Full-time faculty/student ratio: **0.9**

SUPPORT SERVICES

The school offers students these services for dealing with stress: expanded-hour gym access, professional counseling, support groups.

RESIDENCY PROFILE

Most popular residency and specialty programs chosen by the 2008 and 2009 M.D. graduating classes: anesthesiology, emergency medicine, family practice, internal medicine, neurology, obstetrics and gynecology, ophthalmology, pediatrics, radiology–diagnostic, surgery–general.

WHERE GRADS GO

41.0%
Proportion of 2007-2008 graduates who entered primary care specialties

46.0%
Proportion of 2008-2009 graduates who accepted in-state residencies

Southern Illinois University–Springfield

- 801 N. Rutledge, PO Box 19620, Springfield, IL 62794-9620
- Public
- **Year Founded:** 1970
- **Tuition, 2009-2010:** In-state: $27,262; Out-of-State: $75,238
- **Enrollment 2009-2010 academic year:** 293
- **Website:** http://www.siumed.edu/
- **Specialty ranking:** N/A

3.55 AVERAGE GPA, ENTERING CLASS FALL 2009

9.4 AVERAGE MCAT, ENTERING CLASS FALL 2009

13.4% ACCEPTANCE RATE, ENTERING CLASS FALL 2009

Unranked 2011 U.S. NEWS MEDICAL SCHOOL RANKING (RESEARCH)

Unranked 2011 U.S. NEWS MEDICAL SCHOOL RANKING (PRIMARY CARE)

ADMISSIONS

Admissions phone number: **(217) 545-6013**
Admissions email address: **admissions@siumed.edu**
Application web site: **N/A**
Acceptance rate: **13.4%**
In-state acceptance rate: **14.5%**
Out-of-state acceptance rate: **1.0%**
Minority acceptance rate: **N/A**
International acceptance rate: **N/A**

Fall 2009 applications and acceptees

Type	Applied	Interviewed	Accepted	Enrolled
Total:	1,190	304	160	72
In-state:	1,093	303	159	72
Out-of-state:	97	1	1	0

Profile of admitted students

Average undergraduate grade point average: **3.55**
MCAT averages (scale: 1-15; writing test: J-T):
Composite score: **9.4**
Verbal reasoning score: **9.4**, Physical sciences score: **9.0**, Biological score: **9.8**, Writing score: **O**
Proportion with undergraduate majors in: Biological sciences: **52%**, Physical sciences: **16%**, Non-sciences: **12%**, Other health professions: **6%**, Mixed disciplines and other: **14%**
Percentage of students not coming directly from college after graduation: **53%**

Dates and details

The American Medical College Application Service (AMCAS) application is accepted.
School asks for a second, school-specific application as part of the admissions process.
Oldest MCAT considered for Fall 2011 entry: **2008**
Earliest application date for the 2011-2012 first-year class: **06/01**
Latest application date: **11/15**
Acceptance dates for regular application for the class entering in Fall 2011.
Earliest: **01-DEC-10**

Latest: **12-AUG-11**
Applicants have 2 weeks to respond to admissions offer.
The school does consider requests for deferred entrance.
Starting month for the class of 2011–2012: **August**
The school doesn't have an Early Decision Plan (EDP).
A personal interview is required for admission.

Undergraduate coursework required

Medical school requires undergraduate work in these subjects: N/A.

ADMISSIONS POLICY

(TEXT PROVIDED BY SCHOOL):

Applicants need a good foundation in natural and social sciences and humanities; evidence of maturity, integrity, social awareness, compassion, service and good interpersonal skills, and identification with SIU's mission, to help central and southern Illinois meet its health care needs. Accepted students are from Illinois with preference to residents of downstate and other underserved areas.

FINANCIAL AID

Financial aid phone number: **(217) 545-2224**
Tuition, 2009-2010 academic year: **In-state: $27,262; Out-of-State: $75,238**
Room and board: **$9,450**
Percentage of students receiving financial aid in 2009-10: **93%**
Percentage of students receiving: Loans: **87%**, Grants/scholarships: **37%**, Work-study aid: **0%**
Average medical school debt for the class of 2008: **$126,472**

STUDENT BODY

Fall 2009 full-time enrollment: **293**
Men: **50%**, Women: **50%**, In-state: **100%**, Minorities: **27%**, American Indian: **1.0%**, Asian-American: **9.6%**, African-American: **13.3%**, Hispanic-American: **3.4%**, White: **72.7%**, International: **0.0%**, Unknown: **0.0%**

ACADEMIC PROGRAMS

The school's curriculum frequently give first-year students substantial contact with patients.

There are opportunities for first- or second-year students to work in community health clinics.

Program areas: AIDS, drug/alcohol abuse, family medicine, geriatrics, internal medicine, pediatrics, rural medicine, women's health

Joint degrees awarded: M.D./J.D.

Total National Institutes of Health (NIH) grants awarded to the medical school and affiliated hospitals: N/A

CURRICULUM

(TEXT PROVIDED BY MEDICAL SCHOOL):

SIU is recognized for innovative teaching and testing techniques with a competency-base curriculum emphasizing self-directed learning in small groups. It includes standardized patients, extensive clinical activities and study in medical humanities. Our goal is for SIU graduates to become humanistic and competent physicians who are lifelong learners. Its last LCME accreditation had no citations.

FALL 2009 FACULTY PROFILE

Total teaching faculty: 348 (full-time), 877 (part-time)

Of full-time faculty, those teaching in basic sciences: 34%; in clinical programs: 66%

Of part-time faculty, those teaching in basic sciences: 13%; in clinical programs: 87%

Full-time faculty/student ratio: 1.2

SUPPORT SERVICES

The school offers students these services for dealing with stress: peer counseling, professional counseling, support groups.

RESIDENCY PROFILE

Most popular residency and specialty programs chosen by the 2008 and 2009 M.D. graduating classes: anesthesiology, emergency medicine, family practice, internal medicine, obstetrics and gynecology, orthopaedic surgery, pediatrics, radiology–diagnostic, surgery–general.

WHERE GRADS GO

37.6%

Proportion of 2007-2008 graduates who entered primary care specialties

34.2%

Proportion of 2008-2009 graduates who accepted in-state residencies

Stanford University

- 300 Pasteur Drive, Suite M121, Stanford, CA 94305
- Private
- **Year Founded:** 1858
- **Tuition, 2009-2010:** $45,639
- **Enrollment 2009-2010 academic year:** 470
- **Website:** http://med.stanford.edu
- **Specialty ranking:** AIDS: 18, internal medicine: 11, pediatrics: 6, women's health: 12

3.75	AVERAGE GPA, ENTERING CLASS FALL 2009
11.3	AVERAGE MCAT, ENTERING CLASS FALL 2009
3.5%	ACCEPTANCE RATE, ENTERING CLASS FALL 2009
11	2011 U.S. NEWS MEDICAL SCHOOL RANKING (RESEARCH)
Unranked	2011 U.S. NEWS MEDICAL SCHOOL RANKING (PRIMARY CARE)

ADMISSIONS

Admissions phone number: **(650) 723-6861**
Admissions email address: **mdadmissions@stanford.edu**
Application web site: **http://www.aamc.org**
Acceptance rate: **3.5%**
In-state acceptance rate: **3.1%**
Out-of-state acceptance rate: **3.8%**
Minority acceptance rate: **4.0%**
International acceptance rate: **4.3%**

Fall 2009 applications and acceptees

Type	Applied	Interviewed	Accepted	Enrolled
Total:	5,820	450	206	86
In-state:	2,265	157	71	36
Out-of-state:	3,555	293	135	50

Profile of admitted students

Average undergraduate grade point average: **3.75**
MCAT averages (scale: 1-15; writing test: J-T):
Composite score: **11.3**
Verbal reasoning score: **10.5**, Physical sciences score: **11.7**, Biological score: **11.9**, Writing score: **Q**
Proportion with undergraduate majors in: Biological sciences: **45%**, Physical sciences: **24%**, Non-sciences: **13%**, Other health professions: **0%**, Mixed disciplines and other: **18%**
Percentage of students not coming directly from college after graduation: **52%**

Dates and details

The American Medical College Application Service (AMCAS) application is accepted.
School asks for a second, school-specific application as part of the admissions process.
Oldest MCAT considered for Fall 2011 entry: **2007**
Earliest application date for the 2011-2012 first-year class: **06/01**
Latest application date: **10/15**
Acceptance dates for regular application for the class entering in Fall 2011.
Earliest: **09-DEC-10**

Latest: **15-MAY-11**
Applicants have 2 weeks to respond to admissions offer.
The school does consider requests for deferred entrance.
Starting month for the class of 2011-2012: **August**
The school does have an Early Decision Plan (EDP).
A personal interview is required for admission.

Undergraduate coursework required

Medical school requires undergraduate work in these subjects: biology, organic chemistry, inorganic (general) chemistry, physics.

ADMISSIONS POLICY

(TEXT PROVIDED BY SCHOOL):

We are interested in students whose accomplishments reflect originality, creativity, and independent critical thinking; a strong humanitarian commitment; and enthusiasm for the basic sciences and humanities. We look at the nature and extent of community service caring experiences and academic commitments beyond required coursework. Evidence of originality and leadership skills are most valued.

FINANCIAL AID

Financial aid phone number: **(650) 723-6958**
Tuition, 2009-2010 academic year: **$45,639**
Room and board: **$23,097**
Percentage of students receiving financial aid in 2009-10: **85%**
Percentage of students receiving: Loans: **60%**, Grants/scholarships: **82%**, Work-study aid: **11%**
Average medical school debt for the class of 2008: **$86,137**

STUDENT BODY

Fall 2009 full-time enrollment: **470**
Men: **54%**, Women: **46%**, In-state: **39%**, Minorities: **57%**, American Indian: **0.9%**, Asian-American: **36.0%**, African-American: **3.6%**, Hispanic-American: **13.2%**, White: **41.9%**, International: **4.5%**, Unknown: **0.0%**

ACADEMIC PROGRAMS

The school's curriculum frequently give first-year students substantial contact with patients.

There are opportunities for first- or second-year students to work in community health clinics.

Program areas: AIDS, drug/alcohol abuse, family medicine, geriatrics, internal medicine, pediatrics, rural medicine, women's health

Joint degrees awarded: M.D./Ph.D., M.D./M.B.A., M.D./M.P.H., M.D./M.S.

Total National Institutes of Health (NIH) grants awarded to the medical school and affiliated hospitals: **N/A**

CURRICULUM
(TEXT PROVIDED BY MEDICAL SCHOOL):

The curriculum integrates basic science principles and clinical skills: Clinical skills instruction is led by 15 faculty who provide longitudinal mentorship; Scholarly Concentration projects provide students a mentored opportunity to gain familiarity with emerging areas of scholarship; Translating Discoveries curriculum exposes students to medical advances, with focus on the patient's perspective.

FALL 2009 FACULTY PROFILE

Total teaching faculty: **824 (full-time), 26 (part-time)**
Of full-time faculty, those teaching in basic sciences: **14%**; in clinical programs: **86%**

Of part-time faculty, those teaching in basic sciences: **42%**; in clinical programs: **58%**
Full-time faculty/student ratio: **1.8**

SUPPORT SERVICES

The school offers students these services for dealing with stress: expanded-hour gym access, peer counseling, professional counseling, religious support, support groups.

RESIDENCY PROFILE

Most popular residency and specialty programs chosen by the 2008 and 2009 M.D. graduating classes: anesthesiology, dermatology, emergency medicine, internal medicine, orthopaedic surgery, pediatrics, psychiatry, radiology–diagnostic, radiation oncology, surgery–general.

WHERE GRADS GO

30.6%
Proportion of 2007-2008 graduates who entered primary care specialties

60.0%
Proportion of 2008-2009 graduates who accepted in-state residencies

St. Louis University

- 1402 S. Grand Boulevard, St. Louis, MO 63104
- Private
- Year Founded: 1836
- Tuition, 2009-2010: $45,315
- Enrollment 2009-2010 academic year: 712
- Website: http://medschool.slu.edu
- Specialty ranking: geriatrics: 13

3.73 AVERAGE GPA, ENTERING CLASS FALL 2009

10.9 AVERAGE MCAT, ENTERING CLASS FALL 2009

8.7% ACCEPTANCE RATE, ENTERING CLASS FALL 2009

Unranked 2011 U.S. NEWS MEDICAL SCHOOL RANKING (RESEARCH)

Unranked 2011 U.S. NEWS MEDICAL SCHOOL RANKING (PRIMARY CARE)

ADMISSIONS

Admissions phone number: (314) 977-9870
Admissions email address: **slumd@slu.edu**
Application web site:
  http://medschool.slu.edu/admissions/
Acceptance rate: **8.7%**
In-state acceptance rate: **25.8%**
Out-of-state acceptance rate: **7.4%**
Minority acceptance rate: **8.0%**
International acceptance rate: **24.0%**

Fall 2009 applications and acceptees

Type	Applied	Interviewed	Accepted	Enrolled
Total:	6,249	951	543	177
In-state:	442	122	114	75
Out-of-state:	5,807	829	429	102

Profile of admitted students

Average undergraduate grade point average: **3.73**
MCAT averages (scale: 1-15; writing test: J-T):
Composite score: **10.9**
Verbal reasoning score: **10.5**, Physical sciences score: **11.1**,
  Biological score: **10.1**, Writing score: **P**
Proportion with undergraduate majors in: Biological
  sciences: **48%**, Physical sciences: **22%**, Non-sciences:
  15%, Other health professions: **0%**, Mixed disciplines
  and other: **16%**
Percentage of students not coming directly from college
  after graduation: **41%**

Dates and details

The American Medical College Application Service
  (AMCAS) application is accepted.
School asks for a second, school-specific application as part
  of the admissions process.
Oldest MCAT considered for Fall 2011 entry: **2007**
Earliest application date for the 2011-2012 first-year class:
  05/15
Latest application date: **12/15**
Acceptance dates for regular application for the class
  entering in Fall 2011.

Earliest: **15-OCT-10**
Latest: **03-AUG-11**
Applicants have 2 weeks to respond to admissions offer.
The school does consider requests for deferred entrance.
Starting month for the class of 2011–2012: **August**
The school does have an Early Decision Plan (EDP).
A personal interview is required for admission.

Undergraduate coursework required

Medical school requires undergraduate work in these subjects: biology/zoology, English, organic chemistry, inorganic (general) chemistry, physics, humanities, behavioral science.

ADMISSIONS POLICY
(TEXT PROVIDED BY SCHOOL):

Saint Louis University School of Medicine is a private institution that considers national and international applicants. Applicants are encouraged to have achieved a high level of academic performance and to manifest in their personal lives human qualities compatible with a career of service to society. The School strives to recruit, admit, retain and graduate a diverse student body.

FINANCIAL AID

Financial aid phone number: (314) 977-9840
Tuition, 2009-2010 academic year: **$45,315**
Room and board: **$11,988**
Percentage of students receiving financial aid in 2009-10:
  85%
Percentage of students receiving: Loans: **81%**,
  Grants/scholarships: **65%**, Work-study aid: **0%**
Average medical school debt for the class of 2008:
  $173,346

STUDENT BODY

Fall 2009 full-time enrollment: **712**
Men: **60%**, Women: **40%**, In-state: **52%**, Minorities: **31%**,
  American Indian: **0.1%**, Asian-American: **25.3%**,
  African-American: **2.8%**, Hispanic-American: **1.5%**,
  White: **60.8%**, International: **2.1%**, Unknown: **7.3%**

ACADEMIC PROGRAMS

The school's curriculum frequently give first-year students substantial contact with patients.

There are opportunities for first- or second-year students to work in community health clinics.

Program areas: AIDS, drug/alcohol abuse, family medicine, geriatrics, internal medicine, pediatrics, rural medicine, women's health

Joint degrees awarded: M.D./Ph.D., M.D./M.B.A., M.D./M.P.H.

Total National Institutes of Health (NIH) grants awarded to the medical school and affiliated hospitals: **$20.6 million**

CURRICULUM

(TEXT PROVIDED BY MEDICAL SCHOOL):

Beyond the essential objective of training competent physicians who are scholars of human biology, the medical school strives to graduate physicians who manifest in their personal and professional lives an appreciation for ethical and professional attitudes that reflect the Jesuit spirit and values, and affect the physicians' interactions with patients, colleagues, and society.

FALL 2009 FACULTY PROFILE

Total teaching faculty: **546 (full-time)**, **1,216 (part-time)**
Of full-time faculty, those teaching in basic sciences: **15%**; in clinical programs: **85%**

Of part-time faculty, those teaching in basic sciences: **1%**; in clinical programs: **99%**
Full-time faculty/student ratio: **0.8**

SUPPORT SERVICES

The school offers students these services for dealing with stress: expanded-hour gym access, professional counseling, religious support, support groups.

RESIDENCY PROFILE

Most popular residency and specialty programs chosen by the 2008 and 2009 M.D. graduating classes: anesthesiology, emergency medicine, family practice, internal medicine, obstetrics and gynecology, orthopaedic surgery, pediatrics, psychiatry, radiology–diagnostic, surgery–general.

WHERE GRADS GO

40.7%

Proportion of 2007-2008 graduates who entered primary care specialties

27.3%

Proportion of 2008-2009 graduates who accepted in-state residencies

Stony Brook University

- **Office of Admissions, Health Science Center, L4, Stony Brook, NY 11794-8434**
- **Public**
- **Year Founded:** 1971
- **Tuition, 2009-2010:** In-state: $24,049; Out-of-State: $41,889
- **Enrollment 2009-2010 academic year:** 492
- **Website:** http://www.stonybrookmedicalcenter.org/som/
- **Specialty ranking:** N/A

3.60	AVERAGE GPA, ENTERING CLASS FALL 2009
10.7	AVERAGE MCAT, ENTERING CLASS FALL 2009
7.9%	ACCEPTANCE RATE, ENTERING CLASS FALL 2009
55	2011 U.S. NEWS MEDICAL SCHOOL RANKING (RESEARCH)
58	2011 U.S. NEWS MEDICAL SCHOOL RANKING (PRIMARY CARE)

ADMISSIONS

Admissions phone number: **(631) 444-2113**
Admissions email address:
    somadmissions@stonybrook.edu
Application web site:
    http://www.stonybrookmedicalcenter.org/som/admissions
Acceptance rate: **7.9%**
In-state acceptance rate: **11.4%**
Out-of-state acceptance rate: **3.7%**
Minority acceptance rate: **6.3%**
International acceptance rate: **0.0%**

Fall 2009 applications and acceptees

Type	Applied	Interviewed	Accepted	Enrolled
Total:	3,853	630	304	124
In-state:	2,089	491	239	105
Out-of-state:	1,764	139	65	19

Profile of admitted students

Average undergraduate grade point average: **3.60**
MCAT averages (scale: 1-15; writing test: J-T):
Composite score: **10.7**
Verbal reasoning score: **10.0**, Physical sciences score: **11.0**, Biological score: **11.0**, Writing score: **P**
Proportion with undergraduate majors in: Biological sciences: **48%**, Physical sciences: **17%**, Non-sciences: **28%**, Other health professions: **0%**, Mixed disciplines and other: **7%**
Percentage of students not coming directly from college after graduation: **68%**

Dates and details

The American Medical College Application Service (AMCAS) application is accepted.
School asks for a second, school-specific application as part of the admissions process.
Oldest MCAT considered for Fall 2011 entry: **2006**
Earliest application date for the 2011-2012 first-year class: **06/01**
Latest application date: **12/15**

Acceptance dates for regular application for the class entering in Fall 2011.
Earliest: **15-OCT-10**
Latest: **12-AUG-11**
Applicants have 2 weeks to respond to admissions offer.
The school does consider requests for deferred entrance.
Starting month for the class of 2011–2012: **August**
The school does have an Early Decision Plan (EDP).
A personal interview is required for admission.

Undergraduate coursework required

Medical school requires undergraduate work in these subjects: biology, English, organic chemistry, inorganic (general) chemistry, physics.

ADMISSIONS POLICY

(TEXT PROVIDED BY SCHOOL):
    www.stonybrookmedicalcenter.org/som/admissions

FINANCIAL AID

Financial aid phone number: **(631) 444-2341**
Tuition, 2009-2010 academic year: **In-state: $24,049; Out-of-State: $41,889**
Room and board: **$10,855**
Percentage of students receiving financial aid in 2009-10: **87%**
Percentage of students receiving: Loans: **86%**, Grants/scholarships: **25%**, Work-study aid: **4%**
Average medical school debt for the class of 2008: **$142,323**

STUDENT BODY

Fall 2009 full-time enrollment: **492**
Men: **53%**, Women: **47%**, In-state: **95%**, Minorities: **46%**, American Indian: **0.8%**, Asian-American: **31.5%**, African-American: **7.7%**, Hispanic-American: **5.5%**, White: **54.1%**, International: **0.4%**, Unknown: **0.0%**

ACADEMIC PROGRAMS

The school's curriculum occasionally give first-year students substantial contact with patients.

There are opportunities for first- or second-year students to work in community health clinics.

Program areas: AIDS, drug/alcohol abuse, family medicine, geriatrics, internal medicine, pediatrics, women's health

Joint degrees awarded: M.D./Ph.D., M.D./M.B.A., M.D./M.P.H.

Total National Institutes of Health (NIH) grants awarded to the medical school and affiliated hospitals: **$68.1 million**

CURRICULUM
(TEXT PROVIDED BY MEDICAL SCHOOL):

www.stonybrookmedicalcenter.org/som/admissions

FALL 2009 FACULTY PROFILE
Total teaching faculty: **559 (full-time)**, **95 (part-time)**
Of full-time faculty, those teaching in basic sciences: **19%**; in clinical programs: **81%**
Of part-time faculty, those teaching in basic sciences: **2%**; in clinical programs: **98%**
Full-time faculty/student ratio: **1.1**

SUPPORT SERVICES
The school offers students these services for dealing with stress: expanded-hour gym access, peer counseling, professional counseling, religious support, support groups.

RESIDENCY PROFILE
Most popular residency and specialty programs chosen by the 2008 and 2009 M.D. graduating classes: anesthesiology, emergency medicine, internal medicine, obstetrics and gynecology, orthopaedic surgery, pediatrics, psychiatry, radiology–diagnostic, surgery–general.

WHERE GRADS GO

43.0%
Proportion of 2007-2008 graduates who entered primary care specialties

65.0%
Proportion of 2008-2009 graduates who accepted in-state residencies

SUNY–Syracuse

- 766 Irving Avenue, Syracuse, NY 13210
- Public
- Year Founded: 1834
- Tuition, 2009-2010: In-state: $24,112; Out-of-State: $41,952
- Enrollment 2009-2010 academic year: 633
- Website: http://www.upstate.edu/
- Specialty ranking: N/A

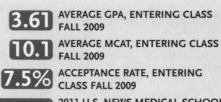

3.61	AVERAGE GPA, ENTERING CLASS FALL 2009
10.1	AVERAGE MCAT, ENTERING CLASS FALL 2009
7.5%	ACCEPTANCE RATE, ENTERING CLASS FALL 2009
Unranked	2011 U.S. NEWS MEDICAL SCHOOL RANKING (RESEARCH)
Unranked	2011 U.S. NEWS MEDICAL SCHOOL RANKING (PRIMARY CARE)

ADMISSIONS

Admissions phone number: **(315) 464-4570**
Admissions email address: **admiss@upstate.edu**
Application web site:
   http://www.aamc.org/audienceamcas.htm
Acceptance rate: **7.5%**
In-state acceptance rate: **15.8%**
Out-of-state acceptance rate: **2.5%**
Minority acceptance rate: **7.0%**
International acceptance rate: **N/A**

Fall 2009 applications and acceptees

Type	Applied	Interviewed	Accepted	Enrolled
Total:	5,008	800	377	152
In-state:	1,900	603	300	130
Out-of-state:	3,108	197	77	22

Profile of admitted students

Average undergraduate grade point average: **3.61**
MCAT averages (scale: 1-15; writing test: J-T):
Composite score: **10.1**
Verbal reasoning score: **9.4**, Physical sciences score: **10.5**,
   Biological score: **10.6**, Writing score: **P**
Proportion with undergraduate majors in: Biological
   sciences: **N/A**, Physical sciences: **N/A**, Non-sciences:
   N/A, Other health professions: **N/A**, Mixed disciplines
   and other: **N/A**
Percentage of students not coming directly from college
   after graduation: **N/A**

Dates and details

The American Medical College Application Service
   (AMCAS) application is accepted.
School asks for a second, school-specific application as part
   of the admissions process.
Oldest MCAT considered for Fall 2011 entry: **2007**
Earliest application date for the 2011-2012 first-year class:
   06/01
Latest application date: **10/15**
Acceptance dates for regular application for the class
   entering in Fall 2011.

Earliest: **15-OCT-10**
Latest: **N/A**
Applicants have 2 weeks to respond to admissions offer.
The school does consider requests for deferred entrance.
Starting month for the class of 2011–2012: **August**
The school does have an Early Decision Plan (EDP).
A personal interview is required for admission.

Undergraduate coursework required

Medical school requires undergraduate work in these subjects: biology, biology/zoology, English, organic chemistry,
inorganic (general) chemistry, physics, general chemistry.

ADMISSIONS POLICY
(TEXT PROVIDED BY SCHOOL):

   The Admissions Committee considers the following factors when selecting applicants: academic achievement in
the sciences, academic achievement in the humanities and
social sciences, volunteer and clinical experience, communication skills, meaningful experiences dealing with and relat-
ing to people, character, and motivation for selecting a
career in medicine.

FINANCIAL AID

Financial aid phone number: **(315) 464-4329**
Tuition, 2009-2010 academic year: **In-state: $24,112; Out-
   of-State: $41,952**
Room and board: **$17,631**
Percentage of students receiving financial aid in 2009-10:
   85%
Percentage of students receiving: Loans: **80%**,
   Grants/scholarships: **32%**, Work-study aid: **10%**
Average medical school debt for the class of 2008:
   $130,894

STUDENT BODY

Fall 2009 full-time enrollment: **633**
Men: **50%**, Women: **50%**, In-state: **N/A**, Minorities: **33%**,
   American Indian: **0.3%**, Asian-American: **18.9%**,
   African-American: **12.5%**, Hispanic-American: **0.8%**,
   White: **61.1%**, International: **6.3%**, Unknown: **0.0%**

ACADEMIC PROGRAMS

The school's curriculum occasionally give first-year students substantial contact with patients.

There are opportunities for first- or second-year students to work in community health clinics.

Program areas: AIDS, drug/alcohol abuse, family medicine, geriatrics, internal medicine, pediatrics, rural medicine, women's health

Joint degrees awarded: M.D./Ph.D., M.D./M.P.H.

Total National Institutes of Health (NIH) grants awarded to the medical school and affiliated hospitals: **$24.2 million**

CURRICULUM
(TEXT PROVIDED BY MEDICAL SCHOOL):

The organ-based curriculum integrates the basic and clinical sciences–with basic science courses teaching the clinical implications of the material–and provides clinical experience starting in the first semester. The organ systems approach enables an efficient, in-depth study of major concepts.

FALL 2009 FACULTY PROFILE

Total teaching faculty: **471 (full-time)**, **209 (part-time)**

Of full-time faculty, those teaching in basic sciences: **13%**; in clinical programs: **87%**

Of part-time faculty, those teaching in basic sciences: **4%**; in clinical programs: **96%**

Full-time faculty/student ratio: **0.7**

SUPPORT SERVICES

The school offers students these services for dealing with stress: peer counseling, professional counseling, religious support, support groups.

RESIDENCY PROFILE

Most popular residency and specialty programs chosen by the 2008 and 2009 M.D. graduating classes: anesthesiology, emergency medicine, internal medicine, orthopaedic surgery, pediatrics, radiology–diagnostic, surgery–general.

WHERE GRADS GO

35.0%

Proportion of 2007-2008 graduates who entered primary care specialties

54.0%

Proportion of 2008-2009 graduates who accepted in-state residencies

Temple University

- 3500 N. Broad Street, MERB 1140, Philadelphia, PA 19140
- Private
- Year Founded: 1901
- Tuition, 2009-2010: $41,936
- Enrollment 2009-2010 academic year: 741
- Website: http://www.temple.edu/medicine
- Specialty ranking: N/A

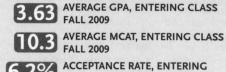

3.63 AVERAGE GPA, ENTERING CLASS FALL 2009

10.3 AVERAGE MCAT, ENTERING CLASS FALL 2009

6.2% ACCEPTANCE RATE, ENTERING CLASS FALL 2009

52 2011 U.S. NEWS MEDICAL SCHOOL RANKING (RESEARCH)

Unranked 2011 U.S. NEWS MEDICAL SCHOOL RANKING (PRIMARY CARE)

ADMISSIONS

Admissions phone number: (215) 707-3656
Admissions email address: **medadmissions@temple.edu**
Application web site: **http://www.aamc.org**
Acceptance rate: **6.2%**
In-state acceptance rate: **18.1%**
Out-of-state acceptance rate: **4.5%**
Minority acceptance rate: **6.0%**
International acceptance rate: **0.0%**

Fall 2009 applications and acceptees

Type	Applied	Interviewed	Accepted	Enrolled
Total:	9,179	861	565	196
In-state:	1,136	276	206	95
Out-of-state:	8,043	585	359	101

Profile of admitted students

Average undergraduate grade point average: **3.63**
MCAT averages (scale: 1-15; writing test: J-T):
Composite score: **10.3**
Verbal reasoning score: **9.8**, Physical sciences score: **10.3**,
  Biological score: **10.7**, Writing score: **Q**
Proportion with undergraduate majors in: Biological
  sciences: **71%**, Physical sciences: **0%**, Non-sciences:
  18%, Other health professions: **0%**, Mixed disciplines
  and other: **11%**
Percentage of students not coming directly from college
  after graduation: **58%**

Dates and details

The American Medical College Application Service
  (AMCAS) application is accepted.
School asks for a second, school-specific application as part
  of the admissions process.
Oldest MCAT considered for Fall 2011 entry: **2008**
Earliest application date for the 2011-2012 first-year class:
  06/01
Latest application date: **12/15**
Acceptance dates for regular application for the class
  entering in Fall 2011.
Earliest: **15-OCT-10**

Latest: **01-AUG-11**
Applicants have 2 weeks to respond to admissions offer.
The school does consider requests for deferred entrance.
Starting month for the class of 2011–2012: **August**
The school does have an Early Decision Plan (EDP).
A personal interview is required for admission.

Undergraduate coursework required

Medical school requires undergraduate work in these subjects: biology, organic chemistry, inorganic (general) chemistry, physics, humanities.

ADMISSIONS POLICY
(TEXT PROVIDED BY SCHOOL):

50% of the matriculants are PA residents; non-residents
with a particular interest in Temple and strong credentials
are encouraged to apply. The medical school recruits the
most qualified applicants while maintaining its long-stand-
ing commitment to matriculate students from a wide variety of ethnic, cultural, and religious backgrounds.

FINANCIAL AID

Financial aid phone number: **(215) 707-2667**
Tuition, 2009-2010 academic year: **$41,936**
Room and board: **$11,220**
Percentage of students receiving financial aid in 2009-10:
  92%
Percentage of students receiving: Loans: **85%**,
  Grants/scholarships: **42%**, Work-study aid: **8%**
Average medical school debt for the class of 2008:
  $176,184

STUDENT BODY

Fall 2009 full-time enrollment: **741**
Men: **53%**, Women: **47%**, In-state: **50%**, Minorities: **37%**,
  American Indian: **0.9%**, Asian-American: **20.5%**,
  African-American: **7.3%**, Hispanic-American: **8.6%**,
  White: **54.9%**, International: **0.0%**, Unknown: **7.7%**

ACADEMIC PROGRAMS

The school's curriculum frequently give first-year students substantial contact with patients.

There are opportunities for first- or second-year students to work in community health clinics.

Program areas: AIDS, drug/alcohol abuse, family medicine, geriatrics, internal medicine, pediatrics, rural medicine, women's health

Joint degrees awarded: M.D./Ph.D., M.D./M.B.A., M.D./M.P.H.

Total National Institutes of Health (NIH) grants awarded to the medical school and affiliated hospitals: **$108.2 million**

CURRICULUM
(TEXT PROVIDED BY MEDICAL SCHOOL):

The MD curriculum includes: Basic sciences in an integrated hybrid organ systems approach; Doctoring utilizing real and simulated patients; required clinical clerkships in family medicine, internal medicine, neurology, obstetrics/gynecology, pediatrics, psychiatry, surgery, emergency medicine, radiology, critical care/anesthesiology; a subinternship; and 20 weeks of clinical electives.

FALL 2009 FACULTY PROFILE

Total teaching faculty: **464 (full-time), 57 (part-time)**
Of full-time faculty, those teaching in basic sciences: **28%**; in clinical programs: **72%**

Of part-time faculty, those teaching in basic sciences: **16%**; in clinical programs: **84%**
Full-time faculty/student ratio: **0.6**

SUPPORT SERVICES

The school offers students these services for dealing with stress: expanded-hour gym access, peer counseling, professional counseling, support groups.

RESIDENCY PROFILE

Most popular residency and specialty programs chosen by the 2008 and 2009 M.D. graduating classes: anesthesiology, emergency medicine, family practice, internal medicine, neurology, obstetrics and gynecology, pediatrics, psychiatry, radiology–diagnostic, surgery–general.

WHERE GRADS GO

41.0%

Proportion of 2007-2008 graduates who entered primary care specialties

45.0%

Proportion of 2008-2009 graduates who accepted in-state residencies

Texas A&M Health Science Center

■ 147 Joe H. Reynolds Medical Building, College Station, TX 77843-1114
■ Public
■ Year Founded: 1971
■ Tuition, 2009-2010: In-state: $11,394; Out-of-State: $24,494
■ Enrollment 2009-2010 academic year: 481
■ Website: http://medicine.tamhsc.edu
■ Specialty ranking: N/A

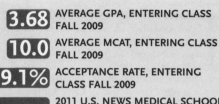

3.68 AVERAGE GPA, ENTERING CLASS FALL 2009

10.0 AVERAGE MCAT, ENTERING CLASS FALL 2009

19.1% ACCEPTANCE RATE, ENTERING CLASS FALL 2009

Unranked 2011 U.S. NEWS MEDICAL SCHOOL RANKING (RESEARCH)

Unranked 2011 U.S. NEWS MEDICAL SCHOOL RANKING (PRIMARY CARE)

ADMISSIONS
Admissions phone number: (979) 845-7743
Admissions email address:
admissions@medicine.tamhsc.edu
Application web site: **http://www.utsystem.edu/tmdsas/**
Acceptance rate: 19.1%
In-state acceptance rate: 21.3%
Out-of-state acceptance rate: 4.7%
Minority acceptance rate: 20.1%
International acceptance rate: 5.0%

Fall 2009 applications and acceptees

Type	Applied	Interviewed	Accepted	Enrolled
Total:	1,980	799	379	150
In-state:	1,722	736	367	138
Out-of-state:	258	63	12	12

Profile of admitted students
Average undergraduate grade point average: 3.68
MCAT averages (scale: 1-15; writing test: J-T):
Composite score: 10.0
Verbal reasoning score: 10.0, Physical sciences score: 10.0, Biological score: 10.0, Writing score: Q
Proportion with undergraduate majors in: Biological sciences: 52%, Physical sciences: 17%, Non-sciences: 19%, Other health professions: 2%, Mixed disciplines and other: 10%
Percentage of students not coming directly from college after graduation: 15%

Dates and details
The American Medical College Application Service (AMCAS) application is accepted.
School asks for a second, school-specific application as part of the admissions process.
Oldest MCAT considered for Fall 2011 entry: 2005
Earliest application date for the 2011-2012 first-year class: 05/01
Latest application date: 10/01
Acceptance dates for regular application for the class entering in Fall 2011.

Earliest: 15-NOV-10
Latest: 15-JUL-11
Applicants have 2 weeks to respond to admissions offer.
The school does consider requests for deferred entrance.
Starting month for the class of 2011–2012: July
The school doesn't have an Early Decision Plan (EDP).
A personal interview is required for admission.

Undergraduate coursework required
Medical school requires undergraduate work in these subjects: biology, English, organic chemistry, inorganic (general) chemistry, physics, calculus.

ADMISSIONS POLICY
(TEXT PROVIDED BY SCHOOL):
The College of Medicine considers for enrollment individuals who have completed at least 90 credit hours of undergraduate course work. 90% of the class must be comprised of Texas residents. Applicants are screened for interview on academic performance and intellectual capacity, dedication to service, capacity for effective interactions, special life circumstances, and other compelling factors.

FINANCIAL AID
Financial aid phone number: (979) 845-8854
Tuition, 2009-2010 academic year: **In-state: $11,394; Out-of-State: $24,494**
Room and board: $13,200
Percentage of students receiving financial aid in 2009-10: 85%
Percentage of students receiving: Loans: 82%, Grants/scholarships: 45%, Work-study aid: 0%
Average medical school debt for the class of 2008: $105,144

STUDENT BODY
Fall 2009 full-time enrollment: 481
Men: 53%, Women: 47%, In-state: 94%, Minorities: 48%, American Indian: 0.6%, Asian-American: 32.0%, African-American: 4.0%, Hispanic-American: 11.4%, White: 48.6%, International: 1.0%, Unknown: 2.3%

ACADEMIC PROGRAMS

The school's curriculum occasionally give first-year students substantial contact with patients.

There are opportunities for first- or second-year students to work in community health clinics.

Program areas: AIDS, drug/alcohol abuse, family medicine, geriatrics, internal medicine, pediatrics, rural medicine, women's health

Joint degrees awarded: M.D./Ph.D., M.D./M.B.A., M.D./M.P.H.

Total National Institutes of Health (NIH) grants awarded to the medical school and affiliated hospitals: **$10.4 million**

CURRICULUM

(TEXT PROVIDED BY MEDICAL SCHOOL):

The College of Medicine has implemented a new integrated systems-based curriculum. Students will have early clinical experiences and increased opportunities for translational research. The curriculum will introduce basic science concepts, followed by application of those concepts in health and disease, core clinical experiences, interdisciplinary experiences, and electives across all four years.

FALL 2009 FACULTY PROFILE

Total teaching faculty: **971 (full-time)**, **325 (part-time)**

Of full-time faculty, those teaching in basic sciences: **9%**; in clinical programs: **91%**

Of part-time faculty, those teaching in basic sciences: **8%**; in clinical programs: **92%**

Full-time faculty/student ratio: **2.0**

SUPPORT SERVICES

The school offers students these services for dealing with stress: expanded-hour gym access, peer counseling, professional counseling, religious support, support groups.

RESIDENCY PROFILE

Most popular residency and specialty programs chosen by the 2008 and 2009 M.D. graduating classes: emergency medicine, family practice, internal medicine, obstetrics and gynecology, orthopaedic surgery, pediatrics, radiology–diagnostic, surgery–general.

WHERE GRADS GO

44.0%

Proportion of 2007-2008 graduates who entered primary care specialties

52.9%

Proportion of 2008-2009 graduates who accepted in-state residencies

Texas Tech University
Health Sciences Center

- 3601 Fourth Street, Lubbock, TX 79430
- Public
- **Year Founded:** 1969
- **Tuition, 2009-2010:** In-state: $13,461; Out-of-State: $26,561
- **Enrollment 2009-2010 academic year:** 581
- **Website:** http://www.ttuhsc.edu/SOM/
- **Specialty ranking:** N/A

3.68	AVERAGE GPA, ENTERING CLASS FALL 2009
9.7	AVERAGE MCAT, ENTERING CLASS FALL 2009
10.3%	ACCEPTANCE RATE, ENTERING CLASS FALL 2009
Unranked	2011 U.S. NEWS MEDICAL SCHOOL RANKING (RESEARCH)
62	2011 U.S. NEWS MEDICAL SCHOOL RANKING (PRIMARY CARE)

ADMISSIONS

Admissions phone number: **(806) 743-2297**
Admissions email address: **somadm@ttuhsc.edu**
Application web site: **http://www.utsystem.edu/tmdsas/**
Acceptance rate: **10.3%**
In-state acceptance rate: **11.0%**
Out-of-state acceptance rate: **5.7%**
Minority acceptance rate: **9.5%**
International acceptance rate: **0.0%**

Fall 2009 applications and acceptees

Type	Applied	Interviewed	Accepted	Enrolled
Total:	2,943	640	304	140
In-state:	2,576	615	283	132
Out-of-state:	367	25	21	8

Profile of admitted students

Average undergraduate grade point average: **3.68**
MCAT averages (scale: 1-15; writing test: J-T):
Composite score: **9.7**
Verbal reasoning score: **9.5**, Physical sciences score: **9.5**,
  Biological score: **10.2**, Writing score: **R**
Proportion with undergraduate majors in: Biological
  sciences: **44%**, Physical sciences: **19%**, Non-sciences:
  16%, Other health professions: **4%**, Mixed disciplines
  and other: **17%**
Percentage of students not coming directly from college
  after graduation: **51%**

Dates and details

The American Medical College Application Service
  (AMCAS) application is not accepted.
School asks for a second, school-specific application as part
  of the admissions process.
Oldest MCAT considered for Fall 2011 entry: **2005**
Earliest application date for the 2011-2012 first-year class:
  N/A
Latest application date: **N/A**
Acceptance dates for regular application for the class
  entering in Fall 2011.
Earliest: **15-NOV-10**

Latest: **01-FEB-11**
Applicants have 2 weeks to respond to admissions offer.
The school does consider requests for deferred entrance.
Starting month for the class of 2011–2012: **August**
The school does have an Early Decision Plan (EDP).
A personal interview is required for admission.

Undergraduate coursework required

Medical school requires undergraduate work in these subjects: biology, biology/zoology, English, organic chemistry,
inorganic (general) chemistry, physics, mathematics, calculus, general chemistry.

ADMISSIONS POLICY
(TEXT PROVIDED BY SCHOOL):

3 years of study (90 semester hours) in a U.S. or
Canadian accredited college or university are required
including prerequisite courses. A baccalaureate degree is
highly desirable. The MCAT is a requirement of admission.
Applicants who have high intellectual ability, strong academics, compassion, motivation, the ability to communicate, maturity, and personal integrity are highly considered.

FINANCIAL AID

Financial aid phone number: **(806) 743-3025**
Tuition, 2009-2010 academic year: **In-state: $13,461; Out-
of-State: $26,561**
Room and board: **$13,269**
Percentage of students receiving financial aid in 2009-10:
  90%
Percentage of students receiving: Loans: **81%**,
  Grants/scholarships: **67%**, Work-study aid: **0%**
Average medical school debt for the class of 2008:
  $125,883

STUDENT BODY

Fall 2009 full-time enrollment: **581**
Men: **57%**, Women: **43%**, In-state: **97%**, Minorities: **38%**,
  American Indian: **0.9%**, Asian-American: **25.1%**,
  African-American: **2.6%**, Hispanic-American: **9.6%**,
  White: **58.2%**, International: **0.0%**, Unknown: **3.6%**

ACADEMIC PROGRAMS

The school's curriculum very frequently give first-year students substantial contact with patients.

There are opportunities for first- or second-year students to work in community health clinics.

Program areas: AIDS, drug/alcohol abuse, family medicine, geriatrics, internal medicine, pediatrics, rural medicine, women's health

Joint degrees awarded: M.D./Ph.D., M.D./M.B.A., M.D./J.D.

Total National Institutes of Health (NIH) grants awarded to the medical school and affiliated hospitals: **$7.2 million**

CURRICULUM

(TEXT PROVIDED BY MEDICAL SCHOOL):

Years 1 & 2 contain 4 interdisciplinary blocks and a year-long Early Clinical Experience where students learn patient care requirements with Master Clinical Teachers and community preceptors. Year 3 has 6 8-week clerkships a longitudinal Continuity Clinic and Integration Seminar; Year 4 has rotations in Neurology, Geriatrics, 3 selective rotations, and 4 elective months.

FALL 2009 FACULTY PROFILE

Total teaching faculty: **595 (full-time), 44 (part-time)**
Of full-time faculty, those teaching in basic sciences: **11%**; in clinical programs: **89%**

Of part-time faculty, those teaching in basic sciences: **2%**; in clinical programs: **98%**
Full-time faculty/student ratio: **1.0**

SUPPORT SERVICES

The school offers students these services for dealing with stress: expanded-hour gym access, peer counseling, professional counseling, support groups.

RESIDENCY PROFILE

Most popular residency and specialty programs chosen by the 2008 and 2009 M.D. graduating classes: anesthesiology, emergency medicine, family practice, internal medicine, obstetrics and gynecology, pediatrics, radiology–diagnostic.

WHERE GRADS GO

50.3%

Proportion of 2007-2008 graduates who entered primary care specialties

60.0%

Proportion of 2008-2009 graduates who accepted in-state residencies

Tufts University

- 136 Harrison Avenue, Boston, MA 02111
- Private
- Year Founded: 1893
- Tuition, 2009-2010: $50,968
- Enrollment 2009-2010 academic year: 748
- Website: http://www.tufts.edu/med
- Specialty ranking: N/A

3.60 AVERAGE GPA, ENTERING CLASS FALL 2009

10.6 AVERAGE MCAT, ENTERING CLASS FALL 2009

7.5% ACCEPTANCE RATE, ENTERING CLASS FALL 2009

44 2011 U.S. NEWS MEDICAL SCHOOL RANKING (RESEARCH)

33 2011 U.S. NEWS MEDICAL SCHOOL RANKING (PRIMARY CARE)

ADMISSIONS

Admissions phone number: **(617) 636-6571**
Admissions email address: **med-admissions@tufts.edu**
Application web site:
  http://www.tufts.edu/med/admissions/index.html
Acceptance rate: **7.5%**
In-state acceptance rate: **16.8%**
Out-of-state acceptance rate: **6.6%**
Minority acceptance rate: **6.7%**
International acceptance rate: **0.0%**

Fall 2009 applications and acceptees

Type	Applied	Interviewed	Accepted	Enrolled
Total:	7,361	917	555	200
In-state:	659	188	111	55
Out-of-state:	6,702	729	444	145

Profile of admitted students

Average undergraduate grade point average: **3.60**
MCAT averages (scale: 1-15; writing test: J-T):
Composite score: **10.6**
Verbal reasoning score: **10.1**, Physical sciences score: **10.7**,
  Biological score: **11.0**, Writing score: **P**
Proportion with undergraduate majors in: Biological
  sciences: **54%**, Physical sciences: **9%**, Non-sciences:
  31%, Other health professions: **4%**, Mixed disciplines
  and other: **2%**
Percentage of students not coming directly from college
  after graduation: **73%**

Dates and details

The American Medical College Application Service
  (AMCAS) application is accepted.
School asks for a second, school-specific application as part
  of the admissions process.
Oldest MCAT considered for Fall 2011 entry: **2006**
Earliest application date for the 2011-2012 first-year class:
  06/01
Latest application date: **11/01**
Acceptance dates for regular application for the class
  entering in Fall 2011.

Earliest: **15-OCT-10**
Latest: **17-AUG-11**
Applicants have 2 weeks to respond to admissions offer.
The school does consider requests for deferred entrance.
Starting month for the class of 2011–2012: **August**
The school does have an Early Decision Plan (EDP).
A personal interview is required for admission.

Undergraduate coursework required

Medical school requires undergraduate work in these subjects: biology, organic chemistry, inorganic (general) chemistry, physics.

ADMISSIONS POLICY
(TEXT PROVIDED BY SCHOOL):

Applicants who apply via the national application service (AMCAS) are requested to complete a school-specific secondary application. All applicants who complete a secondary application are considered for a personal interview based on the qualifications presented on their application. The Admissions Committee meets monthly and admits selected applicants on a rolling basis.

FINANCIAL AID

Financial aid phone number: **(617) 636-6574**
Tuition, 2009-2010 academic year: **$50,968**
Room and board: **$11,844**
Percentage of students receiving financial aid in 2009-10:
  79%
Percentage of students receiving: Loans: **74%**,
  Grants/scholarships: **27%**, Work-study aid: **10%**
Average medical school debt for the class of 2008:
  $192,162

STUDENT BODY

Fall 2009 full-time enrollment: **748**
Men: **55%**, Women: **45%**, In-state: **36%**, Minorities: **32%**,
  American Indian: **0.1%**, Asian-American: **23.9%**,
  African-American: **3.3%**, Hispanic-American: **4.8%**,
  White: **62.8%**, International: **0.7%**, Unknown: **4.3%**

ACADEMIC PROGRAMS

The school's curriculum frequently give first-year students substantial contact with patients.

There are opportunities for first- or second-year students to work in community health clinics.

Program areas: AIDS, drug/alcohol abuse, family medicine, geriatrics, internal medicine, pediatrics, rural medicine, women's health

Joint degrees awarded: M.D./Ph.D., M.D./M.B.A., M.D./M.P.H., M.D./M.A.

Total National Institutes of Health (NIH) grants awarded to the medical school and affiliated hospitals: **$101.5 million**

CURRICULUM
(TEXT PROVIDED BY MEDICAL SCHOOL):

Tufts University School of Medicine (TUSM), Boston MA, a leader in curricular innovation, provides a vibrant, student-centered community for educating physicians to enter any field of medicine. TUSM balances science with the art of medicine, and humanistic professional attitudes needed to competently face the rapid changes in the 21st century.

FALL 2009 FACULTY PROFILE

Total teaching faculty: **1,882 (full-time), 2,448 (part-time)**
Of full-time faculty, those teaching in basic sciences: **6%**; in clinical programs: **94%**

Of part-time faculty, those teaching in basic sciences: **6%**; in clinical programs: **94%**
Full-time faculty/student ratio: **2.5**

SUPPORT SERVICES

The school offers students these services for dealing with stress: expanded-hour gym access, peer counseling, professional counseling, religious support, support groups.

RESIDENCY PROFILE

Most popular residency and specialty programs chosen by the 2008 and 2009 M.D. graduating classes: anesthesiology, emergency medicine, family practice, internal medicine, obstetrics and gynecology, pediatrics, radiology–diagnostic, surgery–general.

WHERE GRADS GO

45.0%

Proportion of 2007-2008 graduates who entered primary care specialties

31.3%

Proportion of 2008-2009 graduates who accepted in-state residencies

Uniformed Services University
of the Health Sciences (Hebert)

- 4301 Jones Bridge Road, Bethesda, MD 20814
- Public
- Year Founded: 1972
- Tuition, 2009-2010: N/A
- Enrollment 2009-2010 academic year: 681
- Website: http://www.usuhs.mil
- Specialty ranking: N/A

3.51 AVERAGE GPA, ENTERING CLASS FALL 2009

10.1 AVERAGE MCAT, ENTERING CLASS FALL 2009

12.2% ACCEPTANCE RATE, ENTERING CLASS FALL 2009

Unranked 2011 U.S. NEWS MEDICAL SCHOOL RANKING (RESEARCH)

Unranked 2011 U.S. NEWS MEDICAL SCHOOL RANKING (PRIMARY CARE)

ADMISSIONS
Admissions phone number: **(800) 772-1743**
Admissions email address: **admissions@usuhs.mil**
Application web site: **N/A**
Acceptance rate: **12.2%**
In-state acceptance rate: **17.5%**
Out-of-state acceptance rate: **11.9%**
Minority acceptance rate: **7.4%**
International acceptance rate: **N/A**

Fall 2009 applications and acceptees

Type	Applied	Interviewed	Accepted	Enrolled
Total:	2,343	566	285	171
In-state:	126	34	22	12
Out-of-state:	2,217	532	263	159

Profile of admitted students
Average undergraduate grade point average: **3.51**
MCAT averages (scale: 1-15; writing test: J-T):
Composite score: **10.1**
Verbal reasoning score: **9.9**, Physical sciences score: **10.0**,
   Biological score: **10.4**, Writing score: **P**
Proportion with undergraduate majors in: Biological
   sciences: **43%**, Physical sciences: **21%**, Non-sciences:
   9%, Other health professions: **1%**, Mixed disciplines and
   other: **26%**
Percentage of students not coming directly from college
   after graduation: **61%**

Dates and details
The American Medical College Application Service
   (AMCAS) application is accepted.
School asks for a second, school-specific application as part
   of the admissions process.
Oldest MCAT considered for Fall 2011 entry: **2008**
Earliest application date for the 2011-2012 first-year class:
   06/01
Latest application date: **11/15**
Acceptance dates for regular application for the class
   entering in Fall 2011.
Earliest: **16-OCT-10**

Latest: **15-JUN-11**
Applicants have 2 weeks to respond to admissions offer.
The school does consider requests for deferred entrance.
Starting month for the class of 2011-2012: **June**
The school doesn't have an Early Decision Plan (EDP).
A personal interview is required for admission.

Undergraduate coursework required
Medical school requires undergraduate work in these subjects: biology, English, organic chemistry, inorganic (general) chemistry, physics, calculus.

ADMISSIONS POLICY
(TEXT PROVIDED BY SCHOOL):
   The SOM is a federal institution which does not give any
preference to in-state residents. The Admissions Committee
evaluates grades, MCATs, clinical work, extracurricular
activities, work experience, motivation for military medicine
and interviews. Interviewed applicants must pass a medical
examination and security clearance to be eligible to attend
the SOM as a commissioned officer.

FINANCIAL AID
Financial aid phone number: **N/A**
Tuition, 2009-2010 academic year: **N/A**
Room and board: **$0**
Percentage of students receiving financial aid in 2009-10:
   0%
Percentage of students receiving: Loans: **0%**,
   Grants/scholarships: **0%**, Work-study aid: **0%**
Average medical school debt for the class of 2008: **$0**

STUDENT BODY
Fall 2009 full-time enrollment: **681**
Men: **71%**, Women: **29%**, In-state: **5%**, Minorities: **19%**,
   American Indian: **0.7%**, Asian-American: **11.9%**,
   African-American: **1.5%**, Hispanic-American: **5.0%**,
   White: **73.7%**, International: **0.0%**, Unknown: **7.2%**

ACADEMIC PROGRAMS

The school's curriculum frequently give first-year students substantial contact with patients.

There are opportunities for first- or second-year students to work in community health clinics.

Program areas: AIDS, drug/alcohol abuse, family medicine, geriatrics, internal medicine, pediatrics, women's health

Joint degrees awarded: M.D./Ph.D.

Total National Institutes of Health (NIH) grants awarded to the medical school and affiliated hospitals: **$38.3 million**

CURRICULUM

(TEXT PROVIDED BY MEDICAL SCHOOL):

The School of Medicine's (SOM) curriculum is designed to graduate competent, compassionate, dedicated physicians to serve beneficiaries of the military and the public health service. The SOM places emphasis in areas critical to the uniformed physician: Trauma and Emergency Medicine, Infectious Disease and Parasitology, Humanities and Behavioral Sciences and Principles of Leadership and Teamwork.

FALL 2009 FACULTY PROFILE

Total teaching faculty: **315 (full-time), 2,444 (part-time)**

Of full-time faculty, those teaching in basic sciences: **33%**; in clinical programs: **67%**

Of part-time faculty, those teaching in basic sciences: **2%**; in clinical programs: **98%**

Full-time faculty/student ratio: **0.5**

SUPPORT SERVICES

The school offers students these services for dealing with stress: expanded-hour gym access, professional counseling, religious support, support groups.

RESIDENCY PROFILE

Most popular residency and specialty programs chosen by the 2008 and 2009 M.D. graduating classes: emergency medicine, family practice, internal medicine, obstetrics and gynecology, orthopaedic surgery, pediatrics, psychiatry, surgery–general, transitional year, internal medicine/psychiatry.

WHERE GRADS GO

30.0%

Proportion of 2007-2008 graduates who entered primary care specialties

13.0%

Proportion of 2008-2009 graduates who accepted in-state residencies

University at Buffalo–SUNY

- 155 Biomedical Education Building, Buffalo, NY 14214
- Public
- **Year Founded:** 1846
- **Tuition, 2009-2010:** In-state: $22,940; Out-of-State: $42,110
- **Enrollment 2009-2010 academic year:** 565
- **Website:** http://www.smbs.buffalo.edu/ome
- **Specialty ranking:** N/A

3.65	AVERAGE GPA, ENTERING CLASS FALL 2009
10.2	AVERAGE MCAT, ENTERING CLASS FALL 2009
10.2%	ACCEPTANCE RATE, ENTERING CLASS FALL 2009
59	2011 U.S. NEWS MEDICAL SCHOOL RANKING (RESEARCH)
Unranked	2011 U.S. NEWS MEDICAL SCHOOL RANKING (PRIMARY CARE)

ADMISSIONS
Admissions phone number: **(716) 829-3466**
Admissions email address: **jjrosso@buffalo.edu**
Application web site: **http://www.aamc.org**
Acceptance rate: **10.2%**
In-state acceptance rate: **14.7%**
Out-of-state acceptance rate: **6.4%**
Minority acceptance rate: **N/A**
International acceptance rate: **N/A**

Fall 2009 applications and acceptees

Type	Applied	Interviewed	Accepted	Enrolled
Total:	3,824	589	389	140
In-state:	1,744	354	256	100
Out-of-state:	2,080	235	133	40

Profile of admitted students
Average undergraduate grade point average: **3.65**
MCAT averages (scale: 1-15; writing test: J-T):
Composite score: **10.2**
Verbal reasoning score: **9.5**, Physical sciences score: **10.2**,
  Biological score: **10.9**, Writing score: **P**
Proportion with undergraduate majors in: Biological
  sciences: **26%**, Physical sciences: **23%**, Non-sciences:
  35%, Other health professions: **11%**, Mixed disciplines
  and other: **5%**
Percentage of students not coming directly from college
  after graduation: **N/A**

Dates and details
The American Medical College Application Service
  (AMCAS) application is accepted.
School asks for a second, school-specific application as part
  of the admissions process.
Oldest MCAT considered for Fall 2011 entry: **2007**
Earliest application date for the 2011-2012 first-year class:
  06/01
Latest application date: **11/15**
Acceptance dates for regular application for the class
  entering in Fall 2011.
Earliest: **15-OCT-10**

Latest: **15-AUG-11**
Applicants have 2 weeks to respond to admissions offer.
The school does consider requests for deferred entrance.
Starting month for the class of 2011–2012: **August**
The school does have an Early Decision Plan (EDP).
A personal interview is required for admission.

Undergraduate coursework required
Medical school requires undergraduate work in these subjects: biology, English, organic chemistry, inorganic (general) chemistry, physics.

ADMISSIONS POLICY
(TEXT PROVIDED BY SCHOOL):
Selection is based on scholastic achievement, aptitude,
personal qualifications, motivation. College record, MCAT,
letters of reference, personal interview provide information.
All applicants must be U.S. citizens or permanent residents. Minorities and disadvantaged students are encouraged to apply. In-state residency is not required but is
looked upon favorably.

FINANCIAL AID
Financial aid phone number: **(716) 645-2450**
Tuition, 2009-2010 academic year: **In-state: $22,940; Out-
  of-State: $42,110**
Room and board: **$12,423**
Percentage of students receiving financial aid in 2009-10:
  96%
Percentage of students receiving: Loans: **77%**,
  Grants/scholarships: **25%**, Work-study aid: **0%**
Average medical school debt for the class of 2008:
  $147,563

STUDENT BODY
Fall 2009 full-time enrollment: **565**
Men: **50%**, Women: **50%**, In-state: **100%**, Minorities: **34%**,
  American Indian: **0.7%**, Asian-American: **27.3%**,
  African-American: **3.2%**, Hispanic-American: **0.4%**,
  White: **66.0%**, International: **0.0%**, Unknown: **2.5%**

ACADEMIC PROGRAMS

The school's curriculum frequently give first-year students substantial contact with patients.

There are opportunities for first- or second-year students to work in community health clinics.

Program areas: AIDS, drug/alcohol abuse, family medicine, geriatrics, internal medicine, pediatrics, rural medicine

Joint degrees awarded: M.D./Ph.D., M.D./M.B.A., M.D./M.P.H.

Total National Institutes of Health (NIH) grants awarded to the medical school and affiliated hospitals: **$65.4 million**

CURRICULUM

(TEXT PROVIDED BY MEDICAL SCHOOL):

Years 1 and 2 of the medical curriculum begin with an organ-based interdisciplinary core curriculum. Modular lecture sections focus on organs of interest and their diseases. Students also attend small-group problem-based learning sessions. Students get practical experience in the Clinical Practice of Medicine course. In years 3 and 4, students rotate in the specialty clinical areas.

FALL 2009 FACULTY PROFILE

Total teaching faculty: **410 (full-time)**, **25 (part-time)**

Of full-time faculty, those teaching in basic sciences: **26%**; in clinical programs: **74%**

Of part-time faculty, those teaching in basic sciences: **60%**; in clinical programs: **40%**

Full-time faculty/student ratio: **0.7**

SUPPORT SERVICES

The school offers students these services for dealing with stress: professional counseling, religious support.

RESIDENCY PROFILE

Most popular residency and specialty programs chosen by the 2008 and 2009 M.D. graduating classes: emergency medicine, internal medicine, neurology, ophthalmology, otolaryngology, pediatrics, psychiatry, radiology–diagnostic, surgery–general, pediatrics/psychiatry/child adolescent psychiatry.

WHERE GRADS GO

28.4%

Proportion of 2007-2008 graduates who entered primary care specialties

51.6%

Proportion of 2008-2009 graduates who accepted in-state residencies

University of Alabama–Birmingham

■ **Medical Student Services, VH Suite 100, Birmingham, AL**
   35294-0019
■ **Public**
■ **Year Founded:** 1859
■ **Tuition, 2009-2010:** In-state: $21,053; Out-of-State: $54,307
■ **Enrollment 2009-2010 academic year:** 747
■ **Website:** http://www.medicine.uab.edu/admissions
■ **Specialty ranking:** AIDS: 9, geriatrics: 15, internal medicine:
   16, rural medicine: 14

3.74 AVERAGE GPA, ENTERING CLASS FALL 2009

10.1 AVERAGE MCAT, ENTERING CLASS FALL 2009

12.2% ACCEPTANCE RATE, ENTERING CLASS FALL 2009

26 2011 U.S. NEWS MEDICAL SCHOOL RANKING (RESEARCH)

23 2011 U.S. NEWS MEDICAL SCHOOL RANKING (PRIMARY CARE)

ADMISSIONS
Admissions phone number: **(205) 934-2433**
Admissions email address: **medschool@uab.edu**
Application web site: **N/A**
Acceptance rate: **12.2%**
In-state acceptance rate: **43.5%**
Out-of-state acceptance rate: **4.8%**
Minority acceptance rate: **9.9%**
International acceptance rate: **N/A**

Fall 2009 applications and acceptees

Type	Applied	Interviewed	Accepted	Enrolled
Total:	2,261	405	275	175
In-state:	432	252	188	150
Out-of-state:	1,829	153	87	25

Profile of admitted students
Average undergraduate grade point average: **3.74**
MCAT averages (scale: 1-15; writing test: J-T):
Composite score: **10.1**
Verbal reasoning score: **9.9**, Physical sciences score: **9.9**,
   Biological score: **10.5**, Writing score: **P**
Proportion with undergraduate majors in: Biological
   sciences: **43%**, Physical sciences: **30%**, Non-sciences:
   9%, Other health professions: **1%**, Mixed disciplines and
   other: **17%**
Percentage of students not coming directly from college
   after graduation: **N/A**

Dates and details
The American Medical College Application Service
   (AMCAS) application is accepted.
School asks for a second, school-specific application as part
   of the admissions process.
Oldest MCAT considered for Fall 2011 entry: **2008**
Earliest application date for the 2011-2012 first-year class:
   06/01
Latest application date: **11/01**
Acceptance dates for regular application for the class
   entering in Fall 2011.
Earliest: **06-OCT-10**

Latest: **N/A**
Applicants have 2 weeks to respond to admissions offer.
The school does consider requests for deferred entrance.
Starting month for the class of 2011–2012: **August**
The school does have an Early Decision Plan (EDP).
A personal interview is required for admission.

Undergraduate coursework required
Medical school requires undergraduate work in these subjects: biology, English, organic chemistry, inorganic (general) chemistry, physics, mathematics, general chemistry.

ADMISSIONS POLICY
(TEXT PROVIDED BY SCHOOL):
   The UASOM Admissions Committee is committed to
selecting applicants who possess the intelligence, skills, atti-
tudes, and other personal attributes to become excellent
physicians and to meet the health care needs of Alabama.
Other requirements are outlined in our Guidelines for the
Admissions Cycle at www.medicine.uab.edu/admissions.

FINANCIAL AID
Financial aid phone number: **(205) 934-8223**
Tuition, 2009-2010 academic year: **In-state: $21,053; Out-
of-State: $54,307**
Room and board: **$18,444**
Percentage of students receiving financial aid in 2009-10:
   77%
Percentage of students receiving: Loans: **70%**,
   Grants/scholarships: **30%**, Work-study aid: **0%**
Average medical school debt for the class of 2008:
   $101,682

STUDENT BODY
Fall 2009 full-time enrollment: **747**
Men: **59%**, Women: **41%**, In-state: **86%**, Minorities: **23%**,
   American Indian: **0.8%**, Asian-American: **13.9%**,
   African-American: **6.8%**, Hispanic-American: **1.2%**,
   White: **76.2%**, International: **0.0%**, Unknown: **1.1%**

ACADEMIC PROGRAMS

The school's curriculum frequently give first-year students substantial contact with patients.

There are opportunities for first- or second-year students to work in community health clinics.

Program areas: AIDS, drug/alcohol abuse, family medicine, geriatrics, internal medicine, pediatrics, rural medicine, women's health

Joint degrees awarded: M.D./Ph.D., M.D./M.P.H., M.D./M.S.

Total National Institutes of Health (NIH) grants awarded to the medical school and affiliated hospitals: **$195.1 million**

CURRICULUM

(TEXT PROVIDED BY MEDICAL SCHOOL):

UASOM has an integrated curriculum where basic science and clinical principles are taught in unison. In the first 2 years, students participate in fundamental basic science and organ-based modules along with intro to clinical medicine. In the last 2 years, students complete 6 core clerkships and then 3 acting internships and elective rotations. Students must complete a defined scholarly activity.

FALL 2009 FACULTY PROFILE

Total teaching faculty: **1,163 (full-time), 38 (part-time)**

Of full-time faculty, those teaching in basic sciences: **20%**; in clinical programs: **80%**

Of part-time faculty, those teaching in basic sciences: **11%**; in clinical programs: **89%**

Full-time faculty/student ratio: **1.6**

SUPPORT SERVICES

The school offers students these services for dealing with stress: expanded-hour gym access, peer counseling, professional counseling, religious support, support groups.

RESIDENCY PROFILE

Most popular residency and specialty programs chosen by the 2008 and 2009 M.D. graduating classes: anesthesiology, emergency medicine, family practice, internal medicine, obstetrics and gynecology, orthopaedic surgery, pediatrics, radiology–diagnostic, surgery–general.

WHERE GRADS GO

39.1%

Proportion of 2007-2008 graduates who entered primary care specialties

44.5%

Proportion of 2008-2009 graduates who accepted in-state residencies

University of Arizona

■ 1501 N. Campbell Avenue, Tucson, AZ 85724
■ Public
■ Year Founded: 1967
■ Tuition, 2009-2010: $22,699
■ Enrollment 2009-2010 academic year: 577
■ Website: http://www.medicine.arizona.edu/
■ Specialty ranking: N/A

3.68 AVERAGE GPA, ENTERING CLASS FALL 2009

9.8 AVERAGE MCAT, ENTERING CLASS FALL 2009

25.7% ACCEPTANCE RATE, ENTERING CLASS FALL 2009

Unranked 2011 U.S. NEWS MEDICAL SCHOOL RANKING (RESEARCH)

Unranked 2011 U.S. NEWS MEDICAL SCHOOL RANKING (PRIMARY CARE)

ADMISSIONS
Admissions phone number: **(520) 626-6214**
Admissions email address:
   admissions@medicine.arizona.edu
Application web site:
   http://www.admissions.medicine.arizona.edu/applicatio nProcedure.cfm
Acceptance rate: **25.7%**
In-state acceptance rate: **34.1%**
Out-of-state acceptance rate: **3.5%**
Minority acceptance rate: **N/A**
International acceptance rate: **N/A**

Fall 2009 applications and acceptees

Type	Applied	Interviewed	Accepted	Enrolled
Total:	826	494	212	163
In-state:	599	476	204	160
Out-of-state:	227	18	8	3

Profile of admitted students
Average undergraduate grade point average: **3.68**
MCAT averages (scale: 1-15; writing test: J-T):
Composite score: **9.8**
Verbal reasoning score: **9.6**, Physical sciences score: **9.6**, Biological score: **10.1**, Writing score: **Q**
Proportion with undergraduate majors in: Biological sciences: **44%**, Physical sciences: **18%**, Non-sciences: **19%**, Other health professions: **2%**, Mixed disciplines and other: **17%**
Percentage of students not coming directly from college after graduation: **61%**

Dates and details
The American Medical College Application Service (AMCAS) application is accepted.
School asks for a second, school-specific application as part of the admissions process.
Oldest MCAT considered for Fall 2011 entry: **2007**
Earliest application date for the 2011-2012 first-year class: **06/01**
Latest application date: **11/01**

Acceptance dates for regular application for the class entering in Fall 2011.
Earliest: **01-DEC-10**
Latest: **01-JUL-10**
Applicants have 2 weeks to respond to admissions offer.
The school does consider requests for deferred entrance.
Starting month for the class of 2011–2012: **August**
The school doesn't have an Early Decision Plan (EDP).
A personal interview is required for admission.

Undergraduate coursework required
Medical school requires undergraduate work in these subjects: biology/zoology, English, organic chemistry, inorganic (general) chemistry, physics.

ADMISSIONS POLICY
(TEXT PROVIDED BY SCHOOL):
   We consider only Arizona residents and WICHE students. We consider many factors including the entire academic record, performance on the MCAT, the applicant's personal statement, interviews and letters of recommendation. Applicants are chosen on the basis of their career goals, motivation, academic ability, integrity, maturity, altruism, communication skills and leadership abilities.

FINANCIAL AID
Financial aid phone number: **(520) 626-7145**
Tuition, 2009-2010 academic year: **$22,699**
Room and board: **$11,540**
Percentage of students receiving financial aid in 2009-10: **95%**
Percentage of students receiving: Loans: **85%**, Grants/scholarships: **71%**, Work-study aid: **4%**
Average medical school debt for the class of 2008: **$111,894**

STUDENT BODY
Fall 2009 full-time enrollment: **577**
Men: **44%**, Women: **56%**, In-state: **99%**, Minorities: **32%**, American Indian: **1.2%**, Asian-American: **17.7%**,

African-American: **2.8%**, Hispanic-American: **10.1%**, White: **68.3%**, International: **0.0%**, Unknown: **0.0%**

ACADEMIC PROGRAMS

The school's curriculum very frequently give first-year students substantial contact with patients.

There are opportunities for first- or second-year students to work in community health clinics.

Program areas: AIDS, drug/alcohol abuse, family medicine, geriatrics, internal medicine, pediatrics, rural medicine, women's health

Joint degrees awarded: M.D./Ph.D., M.D./M.B.A., M.D./M.P.H.

Total National Institutes of Health (NIH) grants awarded to the medical school and affiliated hospitals: **$65.1 million**

CURRICULUM
(TEXT PROVIDED BY MEDICAL SCHOOL):

The University of Arizona College of Medicine has two full, four-year campuses: the original campus in Tucson and our new campus in Phoenix in partnership with Arizona State University. Both provide state-of-the-art, fully integrated, organ-system-based curricula in the first two years and a unified, modern clinical curriculum in the third and fourth years.

FALL 2009 FACULTY PROFILE

Total teaching faculty: **1,033 (full-time)**, **50 (part-time)**
Of full-time faculty, those teaching in basic sciences: **11%**; in clinical programs: **89%**
Of part-time faculty, those teaching in basic sciences: **18%**; in clinical programs: **80%**
Full-time faculty/student ratio: **1.8**

SUPPORT SERVICES

The school offers students these services for dealing with stress: expanded-hour gym access, peer counseling, professional counseling, religious support, support groups.

RESIDENCY PROFILE

Most popular residency and specialty programs chosen by the 2008 and 2009 M.D. graduating classes: anesthesiology, dermatology, emergency medicine, family practice, internal medicine, obstetrics and gynecology, pediatrics, radiology–diagnostic, surgery–general, pediatrics/emergency medicine.

WHERE GRADS GO

41.0%

Proportion of 2007-2008 graduates who entered primary care specialties

40.0%

Proportion of 2008-2009 graduates who accepted in-state residencies

University of Arkansas
for Medical Sciences

■ 4301 W. Markham Street, Slot 551, Little Rock, AR 72205
■ Public
■ Year Founded: 1879
■ Tuition, 2009-2010: In-state: $18,032; Out-of-State: $35,156
■ Enrollment 2009-2010 academic year: 618
■ Website: http://www.uams.edu
■ Specialty ranking: geriatrics: 11

3.64 AVERAGE GPA, ENTERING CLASS FALL 2009

9.5 AVERAGE MCAT, ENTERING CLASS FALL 2009

25.6% ACCEPTANCE RATE, ENTERING CLASS FALL 2009

Unranked 2011 U.S. NEWS MEDICAL SCHOOL RANKING (RESEARCH)

33 2011 U.S. NEWS MEDICAL SCHOOL RANKING (PRIMARY CARE)

ADMISSIONS

Admissions phone number: **(501) 686-5354**
Admissions email address: **southtomg@uams.edu**
Application web site: **N/A**
Acceptance rate: **25.6%**
In-state acceptance rate: **N/A**
Out-of-state acceptance rate: **N/A**
Minority acceptance rate: **N/A**
International acceptance rate: **N/A**

Fall 2009 applications and acceptees

Type	Applied	Interviewed	Accepted	Enrolled
Total:	878	N/A	225	N/A
In-state:	N/A	N/A	N/A	N/A
Out-of-state:	N/A	N/A	N/A	N/A

Profile of admitted students

Average undergraduate grade point average: **3.64**
MCAT averages (scale: 1-15; writing test: J-T):
Composite score: **9.5**
Verbal reasoning score: **9.6**, Physical sciences score: **9.0**, Biological score: **9.9**, Writing score: **O**
Proportion with undergraduate majors in: Biological sciences: **55%**, Physical sciences: **25%**, Non-sciences: **10%**, Other health professions: **3%**, Mixed disciplines and other: **7%**
Percentage of students not coming directly from college after graduation: **15%**

Dates and details

The American Medical College Application Service (AMCAS) application is accepted.
School asks for a second, school-specific application as part of the admissions process.
Oldest MCAT considered for Fall 2011 entry: **2008**
Earliest application date for the 2011-2012 first-year class: **07/01**
Latest application date: **11/01**
Acceptance dates for regular application for the class entering in Fall 2011.
Earliest: **15-DEC-10**

Latest: **06-AUG-10**
Applicants have 2 weeks to respond to admissions offer.
The school does consider requests for deferred entrance.
Starting month for the class of 2011–2012: **N/A**
The school doesn't have an Early Decision Plan (EDP).
A personal interview is required for admission.

Undergraduate coursework required

Medical school requires undergraduate work in these subjects: biology, biology/zoology, English, organic chemistry, inorganic (general) chemistry, physics, mathematics, demonstration of writing skills, calculus, general chemistry.

ADMISSIONS POLICY
(TEXT PROVIDED BY SCHOOL):
N/A

FINANCIAL AID

Financial aid phone number: **(501) 686-5813**
Tuition, 2009-2010 academic year: **In-state: $18,032; Out-of-State: $35,156**
Room and board: **N/A**
Percentage of students receiving financial aid in 2009-10: **91%**
Percentage of students receiving: Loans: **88%**, Grants/scholarships: **45%**, Work-study aid: **0%**
Average medical school debt for the class of 2008: **$124,841**

STUDENT BODY

Fall 2009 full-time enrollment: **618**
Men: **59%**, Women: **41%**, In-state: **88%**, Minorities: **19%**, American Indian: **0.2%**, Asian-American: **11.5%**, African-American: **5.5%**, Hispanic-American: **2.3%**, White: **80.6%**, International: **0.0%**, Unknown: **0.0%**

ACADEMIC PROGRAMS

The school's curriculum frequently give first-year students substantial contact with patients.
There are opportunities for first- or second-year students to work in community health clinics.

Program areas: AIDS, drug/alcohol abuse, family
medicine, geriatrics, internal medicine, pediatrics, rural
medicine, women's health
Joint degrees awarded: M.D./Ph.D., M.D./M.B.A.,
M.D./M.P.H., M.D./J.D.
Total National Institutes of Health (NIH) grants awarded
to the medical school and affiliated hospitals: **$62.1
million**

CURRICULUM
(TEXT PROVIDED BY MEDICAL SCHOOL):
   N/A

FALL 2009 FACULTY PROFILE
Total teaching faculty: **1,031 (full-time)**, **138 (part-time)**
Of full-time faculty, those teaching in basic sciences: **11%**;
   in clinical programs: **89%**
Of part-time faculty, those teaching in basic sciences: **2%**;
   in clinical programs: **98%**
Full-time faculty/student ratio: **1.7**

SUPPORT SERVICES
The school offers students these services for dealing with
stress: expanded-hour gym access, peer counseling, professional counseling, religious support, support groups.

RESIDENCY PROFILE
Most popular residency and specialty programs chosen by
the 2008 and 2009 M.D. graduating classes: anesthesiology, emergency medicine, family practice, internal medicine, internal medicine–pediatrics, obstetrics and
gynecology, pediatrics, psychiatry, radiology–diagnostic, surgery–general.

WHERE GRADS GO

50.3%
*Proportion of 2007-2008 graduates who entered primary
care specialties*

53.5%
*Proportion of 2008-2009 graduates who accepted in-state
residencies*

University of California–Davis

- 4610 X Street, Sacramento, CA 95817
- Public
- **Year Founded:** 1966
- **Tuition, 2009-2010:** In-state: $30,256; Out-of-State: $42,501
- **Enrollment 2009-2010 academic year:** 407
- **Website:** http://www.ucdmc.ucdavis.edu
- **Specialty ranking:** rural medicine: 22

3.57 AVERAGE GPA, ENTERING CLASS FALL 2009

10.6 AVERAGE MCAT, ENTERING CLASS FALL 2009

 4.1% ACCEPTANCE RATE, ENTERING CLASS FALL 2009

 47 2011 U.S. NEWS MEDICAL SCHOOL RANKING (RESEARCH)

20 2011 U.S. NEWS MEDICAL SCHOOL RANKING (PRIMARY CARE)

ADMISSIONS
Admissions phone number: **(916) 734-4800**
Admissions email address: **medadmsinfo@ucdavis.edu**
Application web site:
> **http://www.ucdmc.ucdavis.edu/ome/admissions/require ments.html**

Acceptance rate: **4.1%**
In-state acceptance rate: **5.2%**
Out-of-state acceptance rate: **0.4%**
Minority acceptance rate: **4.2%**
International acceptance rate: **N/A**

Fall 2009 applications and acceptees

Type	Applied	Interviewed	Accepted	Enrolled
Total:	4,607	604	188	93
In-state:	3,540	572	184	91
Out-of-state:	1,067	32	4	2

Profile of admitted students
Average undergraduate grade point average: **3.57**
MCAT averages (scale: 1-15; writing test: J-T):
Composite score: **10.6**
Verbal reasoning score: **9.9**, Physical sciences score: **10.7**, Biological score: **11.2**, Writing score: **Q**
Proportion with undergraduate majors in: Biological sciences: **29%**, Physical sciences: **17%**, Non-sciences: **26%**, Other health professions: **2%**, Mixed disciplines and other: **26%**
Percentage of students not coming directly from college after graduation: **10%**

Dates and details
The American Medical College Application Service (AMCAS) application is accepted.
School asks for a second, school-specific application as part of the admissions process.
Oldest MCAT considered for Fall 2011 entry: **2007**
Earliest application date for the 2011-2012 first-year class: **06/04**
Latest application date: **10/01**

Acceptance dates for regular application for the class entering in Fall 2011.
Earliest: **15-OCT-10**
Latest: **01-JUL-11**
Applicants have 2 weeks to respond to admissions offer.
The school does consider requests for deferred entrance.
Starting month for the class of 2011–2012: **N/A**
The school doesn't have an Early Decision Plan (EDP).
A personal interview is required for admission.

Undergraduate coursework required
Medical school requires undergraduate work in these subjects: biology, English, organic chemistry, inorganic (general) chemistry, physics, molecular and cell biology, biochemistry, mathematics, demonstration of writing skills, calculus, general chemistry.

ADMISSIONS POLICY
(TEXT PROVIDED BY SCHOOL):
Receive an average of 4,500+ applications annually. Matriculate a class of 105 students with a variety of backgrounds. Candidates assessed on GPA and MCAT scores, voluntary activities, leadership, personal statement, letters of recommendation, and other criteria. Interviews are offered annually to 400-500 applicants. Faculty and students serve on the Admissions Committees and conduct interviews.

FINANCIAL AID
Financial aid phone number: **(916) 734-4120**
Tuition, 2009-2010 academic year: **In-state: $30,256; Out-of-State: $42,501**
Room and board: **$14,355**
Percentage of students receiving financial aid in 2009-10: **93%**
Percentage of students receiving: Loans: **84%**, Grants/scholarships: **93%**, Work-study aid: **0%**
Average medical school debt for the class of 2008: **$118,826**

STUDENT BODY

Fall 2009 full-time enrollment: **407**
Men: **41%**, Women: **59%**, In-state: **100%**, Minorities: **56%**,
   American Indian: **0.2%**, Asian-American: **38.3%**,
   African-American: **4.2%**, Hispanic-American: **10.6%**,
   White. **46.4%**, International. **0.0%**, Unknown. **0.2%**

ACADEMIC PROGRAMS

The school's curriculum very frequently give first-year
   students substantial contact with patients.
There are opportunities for first- or second-year students to
   work in community health clinics.
Program areas: AIDS, drug/alcohol abuse, family
   medicine, geriatrics, internal medicine, pediatrics, rural
   medicine, women's health
Joint degrees awarded: M.D./Ph.D., M.D./M.B.A.,
   M.D./M.P.H., M.D./M.S.
Total National Institutes of Health (NIH) grants awarded
   to the medical school and affiliated hospitals: **$94.9
   million**

CURRICULUM

(TEXT PROVIDED BY MEDICAL SCHOOL):
   A 4 yr. curriculum leading to an MD degree. The first 2
yrs. comprise 5 integrated blocks covering normal struc-
ture/function and pathophysiology. The 3rd yr. is composed
of 6 clinical clerkships. A longitudinal 3 yr. Doctoring
course focuses on clinical skills and professionalism. A flexible 4th yr. allows for electives and community service.
Pursuit of research/other degrees is encouraged.

FALL 2009 FACULTY PROFILE

Total teaching faculty: **659 (full-time)**, **123 (part-time)**
Of full-time faculty, those teaching in basic sciences: **8%**;
   in clinical programs: **92%**
Of part-time faculty, those teaching in basic sciences: **16%**;
   in clinical programs: **84%**
Full-time faculty/student ratio: **1.6**

SUPPORT SERVICES

The school offers students these services for dealing with
stress: expanded-hour gym access, peer counseling, professional counseling, religious support, support groups.

RESIDENCY PROFILE

Most popular residency and specialty programs chosen by
the 2008 and 2009 M.D. graduating classes: anesthesiology, emergency medicine, family practice, internal medicine, obstetrics and gynecology, orthopaedic surgery,
pediatrics, psychiatry, radiology–diagnostic, transitional
year.

WHERE GRADS GO

43.9%

*Proportion of 2007-2008 graduates who entered primary
care specialties*

77.8%

*Proportion of 2008-2009 graduates who accepted in-state
residencies*

University of California–Irvine

- 252 Irvine Hall, Irvine, CA 92697-3950
- Public
- Year Founded: 1967
- Tuition, 2009-2010: In-state: $27,336; Out-of-State: $39,581
- Enrollment 2009-2010 academic year: 420
- Website: http://www.ucihs.uci.edu
- Specialty ranking: N/A

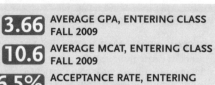

3.66	AVERAGE GPA, ENTERING CLASS FALL 2009
10.6	AVERAGE MCAT, ENTERING CLASS FALL 2009
6.5%	ACCEPTANCE RATE, ENTERING CLASS FALL 2009
47	2011 U.S. NEWS MEDICAL SCHOOL RANKING (RESEARCH)
Unranked	2011 U.S. NEWS MEDICAL SCHOOL RANKING (PRIMARY CARE)

ADMISSIONS

Admissions phone number: **(949) 824-5388**
Admissions email address: **medadmit@uci.edu**
Application web site: **N/A**
Acceptance rate: 6.5%
In-state acceptance rate: 7.8%
Out-of-state acceptance rate: 0.7%
Minority acceptance rate: 6.2%
International acceptance rate: 0.0%

Fall 2009 applications and acceptees

Type	Applied	Interviewed	Accepted	Enrolled
Total:	4,603	511	297	104
In-state:	3,709	494	291	103
Out-of-state:	894	17	6	1

Profile of admitted students

Average undergraduate grade point average: **3.66**
MCAT averages (scale: 1-15; writing test: J-T):
Composite score: **10.6**
Verbal reasoning score: **9.7**, Physical sciences score: **10.8**,
  Biological score: **11.3**, Writing score: **Q**
Proportion with undergraduate majors in: Biological
  sciences: **58%**, Physical sciences: **17%**, Non-sciences:
  25%, Other health professions: **0%**, Mixed disciplines
  and other: **N/A**
Percentage of students not coming directly from college
  after graduation: **40%**

Dates and details

The American Medical College Application Service
  (AMCAS) application is accepted.
School asks for a second, school-specific application as part
  of the admissions process.
Oldest MCAT considered for Fall 2011 entry: **2008**
Earliest application date for the 2011-2012 first-year class:
  06/01
Latest application date: **11/01**
Acceptance dates for regular application for the class
  entering in Fall 2011.
Earliest: **01-NOV-10**

Latest: **04-AUG-11**
Applicants have 2 weeks to respond to admissions offer.
The school does consider requests for deferred entrance.
Starting month for the class of 2011–2012: **August**
The school doesn't have an Early Decision Plan (EDP).
A personal interview is required for admission.

Undergraduate coursework required

Medical school requires undergraduate work in these subjects: biology, English, organic chemistry, inorganic (general) chemistry, physics, biochemistry, mathematics,
calculus, general chemistry.

ADMISSIONS POLICY
(TEXT PROVIDED BY SCHOOL):

The Admissions Committee screens for applicants
whose academic records indicate that they will be able to
handle the medical school curriculum. In addition, attributes deemed desirable in prospective students include leadership and participation in extracurricular activities.
Preference is given to California residents and applicants
who are either U.S. citizens or Permanent Residents.

FINANCIAL AID

Financial aid phone number: **(949) 824-6476**
Tuition, 2009-2010 academic year: **In-state: $27,336; Out-
of-State: $39,581**
Room and board: **$14,527**
Percentage of students receiving financial aid in 2009-10:
  92%
Percentage of students receiving: Loans: **78%**,
  Grants/scholarships: **74%**, Work-study aid: **0%**
Average medical school debt for the class of 2008:
  $112,793

STUDENT BODY

Fall 2009 full-time enrollment: 420
Men: 52%, Women: 48%, In-state: 100%, Minorities: 51%,
  American Indian: 0.2%, Asian-American: 36.2%,
  African-American: 2.1%, Hispanic-American: 12.6%,
  White: 47.4%, International: 0.0%, Unknown: 1.4%

ACADEMIC PROGRAMS

The school's curriculum frequently give first-year students substantial contact with patients.

There are opportunities for first- or second-year students to work in community health clinics.

Program areas: drug/alcohol abuse, family medicine, geriatrics, internal medicine, pediatrics, rural medicine, women's health

Joint degrees awarded: M.D./Ph.D., M.D./M.B.A., M.D./M.P.H., M.D./M.S.

Total National Institutes of Health (NIH) grants awarded to the medical school and affiliated hospitals: **$91.9 million**

CURRICULUM

(TEXT PROVIDED BY MEDICAL SCHOOL):

Students begin with instruction in the life and social sciences fundamental to medicine and instruction in the areas of interpersonal communication, physical assessment of patients, and professional conduct. Students then rotate through a series of core clinical clerkships, receive training in advanced clinical experiences, and complete a series of elective rotations tailored to their interests.

FALL 2009 FACULTY PROFILE

Total teaching faculty: **479 (full-time)**, **74 (part-time)**
Of full-time faculty, those teaching in basic sciences: **14%**; in clinical programs: **86%**

Of part-time faculty, those teaching in basic sciences: **1%**; in clinical programs: **99%**
Full-time faculty/student ratio: **1.1**

SUPPORT SERVICES

The school offers students these services for dealing with stress: expanded-hour gym access, peer counseling, professional counseling, religious support, support groups.

RESIDENCY PROFILE

Most popular residency and specialty programs chosen by the 2008 and 2009 M.D. graduating classes: anesthesiology, dermatology, emergency medicine, family practice, internal medicine, obstetrics and gynecology, orthopaedic surgery, pediatrics, psychiatry, radiology–diagnostic.

WHERE GRADS GO

38.0%

Proportion of 2007-2008 graduates who entered primary care specialties

72.0%

Proportion of 2008-2009 graduates who accepted in-state residencies

University of California–Los Angeles
Geffen

■ 12-138 CHS, 10833 Le Conte Avenue, Los Angeles, CA 90095-1720
■ **Public**
■ **Year Founded:** 1951
■ **Tuition, 2009-2010:** In-state: $26,114; Out-of-State: $38,359
■ **Enrollment 2009-2010 academic year:** 726
■ **Website:** http://www.medsch.ucla.edu
■ **Specialty ranking:** AIDS: 6, drug/alcohol abuse: 6, geriatrics: 3, internal medicine: 13, pediatrics: 18, women's health: 15

 3.81 AVERAGE GPA, ENTERING CLASS FALL 2009

 11.6 AVERAGE MCAT, ENTERING CLASS FALL 2009

4.1% ACCEPTANCE RATE, ENTERING CLASS FALL 2009

11 2011 U.S. NEWS MEDICAL SCHOOL RANKING (RESEARCH)

14 2011 U.S. NEWS MEDICAL SCHOOL RANKING (PRIMARY CARE)

ADMISSIONS

Admissions phone number: **(310) 825-6081**
Admissions email address: **somadmiss@mednet.ucla.edu**
Application web site:
   http://www.medstudent.ucla.edu/admiss
Acceptance rate: **4.1%**
In-state acceptance rate: **5.1%**
Out-of-state acceptance rate: **2.5%**
Minority acceptance rate: **7.8%**
International acceptance rate: **0.0%**

Fall 2009 applications and acceptees

Type	Applied	Interviewed	Accepted	Enrolled
Total:	5,678	821	231	121
In-state:	3,451	645	175	103
Out-of-state:	2,227	176	56	18

Profile of admitted students

Average undergraduate grade point average: **3.81**
MCAT averages (scale: 1-15; writing test: J-T):
Composite score: **11.6**
Verbal reasoning score: **10.6**, Physical sciences score: **11.9**, Biological score: **12.2**, Writing score: **Q**
Proportion with undergraduate majors in: Biological sciences: **60%**, Physical sciences: **25%**, Non-sciences: **5%**, Other health professions: **1%**, Mixed disciplines and other: **9%**
Percentage of students not coming directly from college after graduation: **N/A**

Dates and details

The American Medical College Application Service (AMCAS) application is accepted.
School asks for a second, school-specific application as part of the admissions process.
Oldest MCAT considered for Fall 2011 entry: **2008**
Earliest application date for the 2011-2012 first-year class: **06/15**
Latest application date: **11/01**
Acceptance dates for regular application for the class entering in Fall 2011.

Earliest: **01-DEC-10**
Latest: **01-AUG-11**
Applicants have 2 weeks to respond to admissions offer. The school does consider requests for deferred entrance. Starting month for the class of 2011–2012: **August**
The school doesn't have an Early Decision Plan (EDP). A personal interview is required for admission.

Undergraduate coursework required

Medical school requires undergraduate work in these subjects: biology, English, organic chemistry, inorganic (general) chemistry, physics, mathematics, calculus, general chemistry.

ADMISSIONS POLICY
(TEXT PROVIDED BY SCHOOL):

   We seek future leaders and those who will have distinguished careers in clinical practice, teaching, research, and public service. Preference is given to those who have shown broad training and high achievement and possess, to the greatest degree, those traits of personality and character essential to the success in medicine and the provision of quality, professional and humane medical care.

FINANCIAL AID

Financial aid phone number: **(310) 825-4181**
Tuition, 2009-2010 academic year: **In-state: $26,114; Out-of-State: $38,359**
Room and board: **$14,600**
Percentage of students receiving financial aid in 2009-10: **98%**
Percentage of students receiving: Loans: **92%**, Grants/scholarships: **97%**, Work-study aid: **0%**
Average medical school debt for the class of 2008: **$107,081**

STUDENT BODY

Fall 2009 full-time enrollment: **726**
Men: **52%**, Women: **48%**, In-state: **96%**, Minorities: **59%**, American Indian: **0.7%**, Asian-American: **33.9%**,

African-American: **9.5%**, Hispanic-American: **14.7%**,
White: **32.1%**, International: **0.1%**, Unknown: **9.0%**

ACADEMIC PROGRAMS

The school's curriculum frequently give first-year students
substantial contact with patients.

There are opportunities for first- or second-year students to
work in community health clinics.

Program areas: AIDS, drug/alcohol abuse, family
medicine, geriatrics, internal medicine, pediatrics,
women's health

Joint degrees awarded: M.D./Ph.D., M.D./M.B.A.,
M.D./M.P.H., M.D./M.S.

Total National Institutes of Health (NIH) grants awarded
to the medical school and affiliated hospitals: **$468.7
million**

CURRICULUM

(TEXT PROVIDED BY MEDICAL SCHOOL):

First 2 years there is an integration of basic, clinical, and
social sciences. Year 3 clerkships: Inpatient Medicine,
Family Medicine, Ambulatory Internal Med, OB/GYN,
Pediatrics, Psychiatry/Neurology, and Surgery and 3 longitudinal courses, Radiology, Doctoring and Longitudinal
Preceptorship. The senior year there are colleges, with mul-
tidisciplinary groups of faculty and students.

FALL 2009 FACULTY PROFILE

Total teaching faculty: 2,494 **(full-time)**, 282 **(part-time)**
Of full-time faculty, those teaching in basic sciences: **19%**;
in clinical programs: **81%**

Of part-time faculty, those teaching in basic sciences: **31%**;
in clinical programs: **69%**
Full-time faculty/student ratio: **3.4**

SUPPORT SERVICES

The school offers students these services for dealing with
stress: expanded-hour gym access, professional counseling,
religious support, support groups.

RESIDENCY PROFILE

Most popular residency and specialty programs chosen by
the 2008 and 2009 M.D. graduating classes: anesthesiology, emergency medicine, family practice, internal medicine, obstetrics and gynecology, ophthalmology, pediatrics,
psychiatry, radiology–diagnostic, surgery–general.

WHERE GRADS GO

40.0%

*Proportion of 2007-2008 graduates who entered primary
care specialties*

75.0%

*Proportion of 2008-2009 graduates who accepted in-state
residencies*

University of California–San Diego

- 9500 Gilman Drive, La Jolla, CA 92093-0602
- Public
- **Year Founded:** 1965
- **Tuition, 2009-2010:** In-state: $26,969; Out-of-State: $39,214
- **Enrollment 2009-2010 academic year:** 498
- **Website:** http://meded.ucsd.edu/
- **Specialty ranking:** AIDS: 10, drug/alcohol abuse: 8, family medicine: 11

3.76 AVERAGE GPA, ENTERING CLASS FALL 2009

11.0 AVERAGE MCAT, ENTERING CLASS FALL 2009

6.1% ACCEPTANCE RATE, ENTERING CLASS FALL 2009

16 2011 U.S. NEWS MEDICAL SCHOOL RANKING (RESEARCH)

28 2011 U.S. NEWS MEDICAL SCHOOL RANKING (PRIMARY CARE)

ADMISSIONS

Admissions phone number: **(858) 534-3880**
Admissions email address: **somadmissions@ucsd.edu**
Application web site:
  http://meded.ucsd.edu/asa/admissions
Acceptance rate: **6.1%**
In-state acceptance rate: **7.8%**
Out-of-state acceptance rate: **2.6%**
Minority acceptance rate: **5.4%**
International acceptance rate: **0.0%**

Fall 2009 applications and acceptees

Type	Applied	Interviewed	Accepted	Enrolled
Total:	5,092	694	310	125
In-state:	3,425	580	266	113
Out-of-state:	1,667	114	44	12

Profile of admitted students

Average undergraduate grade point average: **3.76**
MCAT averages (scale: 1-15; writing test: J-T):
Composite score: **11.0**
Verbal reasoning score: **10.1**, Physical sciences score: **11.4**, Biological score: **11.6**, Writing score: **Q**
Proportion with undergraduate majors in: Biological sciences: **52%**, Physical sciences: **10%**, Non-sciences: **17%**, Other health professions: **0%**, Mixed disciplines and other: **21%**
Percentage of students not coming directly from college after graduation: **61%**

Dates and details

The American Medical College Application Service (AMCAS) application is accepted.
School asks for a second, school-specific application as part of the admissions process.
Oldest MCAT considered for Fall 2011 entry: **2008**
Earliest application date for the 2011-2012 first-year class: **06/01**
Latest application date: **11/01**
Acceptance dates for regular application for the class entering in Fall 2011.

Earliest: **15-OCT-10**
Latest: **26-AUG-11**
Applicants have 2 weeks to respond to admissions offer.
The school does consider requests for deferred entrance.
Starting month for the class of 2011–2012: **August**
The school doesn't have an Early Decision Plan (EDP).
A personal interview is required for admission.

Undergraduate coursework required

Medical school requires undergraduate work in these subjects: biology, organic chemistry, inorganic (general) chemistry, physics, mathematics, general chemistry.

ADMISSIONS POLICY

(TEXT PROVIDED BY SCHOOL):
  Please refer to our catalog:
http://meded.ucsd.edu/asa/admissions/index.cfm

FINANCIAL AID

Financial aid phone number: **(858) 534-4664**
Tuition, 2009-2010 academic year: **In-state: $26,969; Out-of-State: $39,214**
Room and board: **$12,028**
Percentage of students receiving financial aid in 2009-10: **89%**
Percentage of students receiving: Loans: **80%**, Grants/scholarships: **53%**, Work-study aid: **1%**
Average medical school debt for the class of 2008: **$98,773**

STUDENT BODY

Fall 2009 full-time enrollment: **498**
Men: **52%**, Women: **48%**, In-state: **98%**, Minorities: **45%**, American Indian: **1.6%**, Asian-American: **34.5%**, African-American: **1.6%**, Hispanic-American: **7.2%**, White: **43.6%**, International: **0.0%**, Unknown: **11.4%**

ACADEMIC PROGRAMS

The school's curriculum frequently give first-year students substantial contact with patients.
There are opportunities for first- or second-year students to work in community health clinics.

Program areas: AIDS, drug/alcohol abuse, family medicine, geriatrics, internal medicine, pediatrics, rural medicine, women's health

Joint degrees awarded: M.D./Ph.D., M.D./M.P.H., M.D./M.S.

Total National Institutes of Health (NIH) grants awarded to the medical school and affiliated hospitals: **$301.1 million**

CURRICULUM
(TEXT PROVIDED BY MEDICAL SCHOOL):
    Please refer to our website:
http://meded.ucsd.edu/ugme/curriculum_requirements/
curriculum_overview

FALL 2009 FACULTY PROFILE
Total teaching faculty: **1,035 (full-time)**, **28 (part-time)**
Of full-time faculty, those teaching in basic sciences: **27%**; in clinical programs: **73%**
Of part-time faculty, those teaching in basic sciences: **29%**; in clinical programs: **71%**
Full-time faculty/student ratio: **2.1**

SUPPORT SERVICES
The school offers students these services for dealing with stress: expanded-hour gym access, peer counseling, professional counseling, religious support, support groups.

RESIDENCY PROFILE
Most popular residency and specialty programs chosen by the 2008 and 2009 M.D. graduating classes: anesthesiology, emergency medicine, family practice, internal medicine, obstetrics and gynecology, orthopaedic surgery, pediatrics, psychiatry, radiology–diagnostic, surgery–general.

WHERE GRADS GO

42.0%
Proportion of 2007-2008 graduates who entered primary care specialties

75.2%
Proportion of 2008-2009 graduates who accepted in-state residencies

University of California–San Francisco

- 513 Parnassus Avenue, Room S224, San Francisco, CA 94143-0410
- Public
- Year Founded: 1864
- Tuition, 2009-2010: In-state: $27,708; Out-of-State: $39,953
- Enrollment 2009-2010 academic year: 631
- Website: http://medschool.ucsf.edu/
- Specialty ranking: AIDS: 1, drug/alcohol abuse: 1, family medicine: 6, geriatrics: 10, internal medicine: 3, pediatrics: 7, women's health: 2

3.74 AVERAGE GPA, ENTERING CLASS FALL 2009

11.3 AVERAGE MCAT, ENTERING CLASS FALL 2009

4.5% ACCEPTANCE RATE, ENTERING CLASS FALL 2009

4 2011 U.S. NEWS MEDICAL SCHOOL RANKING (RESEARCH)

5 2011 U.S. NEWS MEDICAL SCHOOL RANKING (PRIMARY CARE)

ADMISSIONS

Admissions phone number: **(415) 476-4044**
Admissions email address: **admissions@medsch.ucsf.edu**
Application web site:
  http://medschool.ucsf.edu/admissions/
Acceptance rate: **4.5%**
In-state acceptance rate: **5.7%**
Out-of-state acceptance rate: **3.2%**
Minority acceptance rate: **N/A**
International acceptance rate: **N/A**

Fall 2009 applications and acceptees

Type	Applied	Interviewed	Accepted	Enrolled
Total:	5,991	502	270	149
In-state:	3,101	320	178	115
Out-of-state:	2,890	182	92	34

Profile of admitted students

Average undergraduate grade point average: **3.74**
MCAT averages (scale: 1-15; writing test: J-T):
Composite score: **11.3**
Verbal reasoning score: **10.5**, Physical sciences score: **11.5**, Biological score: **11.9**, Writing score: **R**
Proportion with undergraduate majors in: Biological sciences: **53%**, Physical sciences: **9%**, Non-sciences: **19%**, Other health professions: **2%**, Mixed disciplines and other: **17%**
Percentage of students not coming directly from college after graduation: **74%**

Dates and details

The American Medical College Application Service (AMCAS) application is accepted.
School asks for a second, school-specific application as part of the admissions process.
Oldest MCAT considered for Fall 2011 entry: **2008**
Earliest application date for the 2011-2012 first-year class: **06/01**
Latest application date: **10/15**
Acceptance dates for regular application for the class entering in Fall 2011.

Earliest: **15-DEC-10**
Latest: **01-SEP-11**
Applicants have 2 weeks to respond to admissions offer.
The school does consider requests for deferred entrance.
Starting month for the class of 2011-2012: **September**
The school doesn't have an Early Decision Plan (EDP).
A personal interview is required for admission.

Undergraduate coursework required

Medical school requires undergraduate work in these subjects: biology/zoology, organic chemistry, inorganic (general) chemistry, physics.

ADMISSIONS POLICY

(TEXT PROVIDED BY SCHOOL):
  Please refer to the UCSF School of Medicine Admissions web site for specific details regarding policies, preferences, criteria, selection factors, and procedures:
http://medschool.ucsf.edu/admissions

FINANCIAL AID

Financial aid phone number: **(415) 476-4181**
Tuition, 2009-2010 academic year: **In-state: $27,708; Out-of-State: $39,953**
Room and board: **$19,636**
Percentage of students receiving financial aid in 2009-10: **90%**
Percentage of students receiving: Loans: **82%**, Grants/scholarships: **90%**, Work-study aid: **1%**
Average medical school debt for the class of 2008: **$101,333**

STUDENT BODY

Fall 2009 full-time enrollment: **631**
Men: **45%**, Women: **55%**, In-state: **94%**, Minorities: **55%**, American Indian: **2.1%**, Asian-American: **29.6%**, African-American: **7.9%**, Hispanic-American: **15.2%**, White: **36.3%**, International: **0.0%**, Unknown: **8.9%**

ACADEMIC PROGRAMS

The school's curriculum frequently give first-year students substantial contact with patients.

There are opportunities for first- or second-year students to work in community health clinics.

Program areas: AIDS, drug/alcohol abuse, family medicine, geriatrics, internal medicine, pediatrics, rural medicine, women's health

Joint degrees awarded: M.D./Ph.D., M.D./M.P.H., M.D./M.S.

Total National Institutes of Health (NIH) grants awarded to the medical school and affiliated hospitals: **$471.2 million**

CURRICULUM
(TEXT PROVIDED BY MEDICAL SCHOOL):
Please refer to the UCSF School of Medicine website on Education for specific details about our curriculum, http://medschool.ucsf.edu/education

FALL 2009 FACULTY PROFILE
Total teaching faculty: **1,890 (full-time), 54 (part-time)**
Of full-time faculty, those teaching in basic sciences: **8%**; in clinical programs: **92%**
Of part-time faculty, those teaching in basic sciences: **13%**; in clinical programs: **87%**
Full-time faculty/student ratio: **3.0**

SUPPORT SERVICES
The school offers students these services for dealing with stress: peer counseling, professional counseling, support groups.

RESIDENCY PROFILE
Most popular residency and specialty programs chosen by the 2008 and 2009 M.D. graduating classes: anesthesiology, emergency medicine, family practice, internal medicine, obstetrics and gynecology, ophthalmology, pediatrics, psychiatry, radiology–diagnostic, surgery–general.

WHERE GRADS GO

39.1%
Proportion of 2007-2008 graduates who entered primary care specialties

64.8%
Proportion of 2008-2009 graduates who accepted in-state residencies

University of Chicago
Pritzker

- 5841 S. Maryland Avenue, MC 1000, Chicago, IL 60637-5416
- Private
- Year Founded: 1927
- Tuition, 2009-2010: $42,349
- Enrollment 2009-2010 academic year: 430
- Website: http://pritzker.bsd.uchicago.edu
- Specialty ranking: internal medicine: 22

 3.82 AVERAGE GPA, ENTERING CLASS FALL 2009

 **11.9** AVERAGE MCAT, ENTERING CLASS FALL 2009

3.7% ACCEPTANCE RATE, ENTERING CLASS FALL 2009

13 2011 U.S. NEWS MEDICAL SCHOOL RANKING (RESEARCH)

30 2011 U.S. NEWS MEDICAL SCHOOL RANKING (PRIMARY CARE)

ADMISSIONS

Admissions phone number: (773) 702-1937
Admissions email address:
  pritzkeradmissions@bsd.uchicago.edu
Application web site: N/A
Acceptance rate: 3.7%
In-state acceptance rate: 5.3%
Out-of-state acceptance rate: 3.4%
Minority acceptance rate: 5.1%
International acceptance rate: 0.8%

Fall 2009 applications and acceptees

Type	Applied	Interviewed	Accepted	Enrolled
Total:	6,439	507	237	88
In-state:	852	91	45	28
Out-of-state:	5,587	416	192	60

Profile of admitted students

Average undergraduate grade point average: 3.82
MCAT averages (scale: 1-15; writing test: J-T):
Composite score: 11.9
Verbal reasoning score: 11.1, Physical sciences score: 12.3,
  Biological score: 12.3, Writing score: Q
Proportion with undergraduate majors in: Biological
  sciences: 39%, Physical sciences: 30%, Non-sciences:
  26%, Other health professions: 0%, Mixed disciplines
  and other: 5%
Percentage of students not coming directly from college
  after graduation: 49%

Dates and details

The American Medical College Application Service
  (AMCAS) application is accepted.
School asks for a second, school-specific application as part
  of the admissions process.
Oldest MCAT considered for Fall 2011 entry: 2008
Earliest application date for the 2011-2012 first-year class:
  N/A
Latest application date: 10/15
Acceptance dates for regular application for the class
  entering in Fall 2011.

Earliest: 15-OCT-10
Latest: N/A
Applicants have 30 weeks to respond to admissions offer.
The school does consider requests for deferred entrance.
Starting month for the class of 2011–2012: **August**
The school does have an Early Decision Plan (EDP).
A personal interview is required for admission.

Undergraduate coursework required

Medical school requires undergraduate work in these subjects: biology, organic chemistry, inorganic (general) chemistry, physics.

ADMISSIONS POLICY
(TEXT PROVIDED BY SCHOOL):

The Pritzker School of Medicine seeks to attract diverse
students of exceptional promise who will become leaders
and innovators in science and medicine for the betterment
of humanity. To that end, over the past 4 years we have sub-
stantially increased the scholarship dollars available to our
students. Candidates who interview with us spend the day
on campus meeting with students, staff and faculty.

FINANCIAL AID

Financial aid phone number: (773) 702-1938
Tuition, 2009-2010 academic year: **$42,349**
Room and board: **$17,000**
Percentage of students receiving financial aid in 2009-10:
  95%
Percentage of students receiving: Loans: **74%**,
  Grants/scholarships: **86%**, Work-study aid: **0%**
Average medical school debt for the class of 2008:
  $175,809

STUDENT BODY

Fall 2009 full-time enrollment: **430**
Men: **51%**, Women: **49%**, In-state: **30%**, Minorities: **37%**,
  American Indian: **0.5%**, Asian-American: **21.4%**,
  African-American: **8.6%**, Hispanic-American: **6.3%**,
  White: **50.7%**, International: **3.0%**, Unknown: **9.5%**

ACADEMIC PROGRAMS

The school's curriculum frequently give first-year students substantial contact with patients.

There are opportunities for first- or second-year students to work in community health clinics.

Program areas: AIDS, drug/alcohol abuse, family medicine, geriatrics, internal medicine, pediatrics, women's health

Joint degrees awarded: M.D./Ph.D., M.D./M.B.A., M.D./J.D., M.D./M.S.W., M.D./M.S., M.D./M.A., M.D./M.H.A.

Total National Institutes of Health (NIH) grants awarded to the medical school and affiliated hospitals: **$261.1 million**

CURRICULUM

(TEXT PROVIDED BY MEDICAL SCHOOL):

Leveraging our formidable strengths in biomedical research and therapy development, the Chicago curriculum assures that our graduates are prepared for the medicine of today and tomorrow. Close contact with our world-renowned faculty via extensive small group interactions provides the guidance and insights required for successful careers as leading clinicians, researchers and educators.

FALL 2009 FACULTY PROFILE

Total teaching faculty: **883 (full-time), 105 (part-time)**

Of full-time faculty, those teaching in basic sciences: **16%**; in clinical programs: **84%**

Of part-time faculty, those teaching in basic sciences: **0%**; in clinical programs: **100%**

Full-time faculty/student ratio: **2.1**

SUPPORT SERVICES

The school offers students these services for dealing with stress: expanded-hour gym access, peer counseling, professional counseling, religious support, support groups.

RESIDENCY PROFILE

Most popular residency and specialty programs chosen by the 2008 and 2009 M.D. graduating classes: anesthesiology, emergency medicine, internal medicine, obstetrics and gynecology, orthopaedic surgery, pathology–anatomic and clinical, pediatrics, psychiatry, surgery–general, urology.

WHERE GRADS GO

43.0%
Proportion of 2007-2008 graduates who entered primary care specialties

37.0%
Proportion of 2008-2009 graduates who accepted in-state residencies

University of Cincinnati

- 231 Albert Sabin Way, Cincinnati, OH 45267-0552
- Public
- Year Founded: 1819
- Tuition, 2009-2010: In-state: $29,385; Out-of-State: $45,135
- Enrollment 2009-2010 academic year: 637
- Website: http://www.med.uc.edu
- Specialty ranking: pediatrics: 3

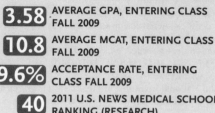

3.58 AVERAGE GPA, ENTERING CLASS FALL 2009

10.8 AVERAGE MCAT, ENTERING CLASS FALL 2009

9.6% ACCEPTANCE RATE, ENTERING CLASS FALL 2009

40 2011 U.S. NEWS MEDICAL SCHOOL RANKING (RESEARCH)

58 2011 U.S. NEWS MEDICAL SCHOOL RANKING (PRIMARY CARE)

ADMISSIONS

Admissions phone number: **(513) 558-7314**
Admissions email address: **comadmis@ucmail.uc.edu**
Application web site:
   http://comdows.uc.edu/MedOneStop/
Acceptance rate: **9.6%**
In-state acceptance rate: **19.0%**
Out-of-state acceptance rate: **5.4%**
Minority acceptance rate: **N/A**
International acceptance rate: **0.0%**

Fall 2009 applications and acceptees

Type	Applied	Interviewed	Accepted	Enrolled
Total:	3,684	642	352	166
In-state:	1,122	366	213	109
Out-of-state:	2,562	276	139	57

Profile of admitted students

Average undergraduate grade point average: **3.58**
MCAT averages (scale: 1-15; writing test: J-T):
Composite score: **10.8**
Verbal reasoning score: **10.3**, Physical sciences score: **10.9**,
   Biological score: **11.2**, Writing score: **O**
Proportion with undergraduate majors in: Biological
   sciences: **56%**, Physical sciences: **21%**, Non-sciences:
   14%, Other health professions: **1%**, Mixed disciplines
   and other: **8%**
Percentage of students not coming directly from college
   after graduation: **52%**

Dates and details

The American Medical College Application Service
   (AMCAS) application is accepted.
School asks for a second, school-specific application as part
   of the admissions process.
Oldest MCAT considered for Fall 2011 entry: **2008**
Earliest application date for the 2011-2012 first-year class:
   06/01
Latest application date: **11/15**
Acceptance dates for regular application for the class
   entering in Fall 2011.

Earliest: **15-OCT-10**
Latest: **05-AUG-11**
Applicants have 2 weeks to respond to admissions offer.
The school does consider requests for deferred entrance.
Starting month for the class of 2011-2012: **August**
The school does have an Early Decision Plan (EDP).
A personal interview is required for admission.

Undergraduate coursework required

Medical school requires undergraduate work in these subjects: N/A.

ADMISSIONS POLICY

(TEXT PROVIDED BY SCHOOL):
   UCCOM requires the AMCAS application, an online
supplementary and letters of recommendation. Applicants
are evaluated on a rolling basis for an interview and acceptance using a holistic evaluation of the applicants' academic,
extra-curricular activities, leadership and other personal
qualities. Each applicant can obtain information about their
progress in the admissions process on our Web site.

FINANCIAL AID

Financial aid phone number: **(513) 558-6797**
Tuition, 2009-2010 academic year: **In-state: $29,385; Out-
of-State: $45,135**
Room and board: **$19,188**
Percentage of students receiving financial aid in 2009-10:
   87%
Percentage of students receiving: Loans: **86%**,
   Grants/scholarships: **40%**, Work-study aid: **2%**
Average medical school debt for the class of 2008:
   $140,174

STUDENT BODY

Fall 2009 full-time enrollment: **637**
Men: **59%**, Women: **41%**, In-state: **91%**, Minorities: **32%**,
   American Indian: **0.0%**, Asian-American: **23.7%**,
   African-American: **6.4%**, Hispanic-American: **1.9%**,
   White: **68.0%**, International: **0.0%**, Unknown: **0.0%**

ACADEMIC PROGRAMS

The school's curriculum frequently give first-year students substantial contact with patients.

There are opportunities for first- or second-year students to work in community health clinics.

Program areas: AIDS, drug/alcohol abuse, family medicine, geriatrics, internal medicine, pediatrics, rural medicine, women's health

Joint degrees awarded: M.D./Ph.D., M.D./M.B.A.

Total National Institutes of Health (NIH) grants awarded to the medical school and affiliated hospitals: **$191.4 million**

CURRICULUM

(TEXT PROVIDED BY MEDICAL SCHOOL):

The primary educational mission at the University of Cincinnati College of Medicine (UCCOM) is to provide a stimulating learning environment intended to create the undifferentiated MD who is ready to excel in his or her chosen residency and who will provide excellent patient care. Refer to http://www.med.uc.edu/ for more detailed information on the curriculum.

FALL 2009 FACULTY PROFILE

Total teaching faculty: **1,498 (full-time)**, **131 (part-time)**
Of full-time faculty, those teaching in basic sciences: **7%**; in clinical programs: **93%**

Of part-time faculty, those teaching in basic sciences: **6%**; in clinical programs: **94%**
Full-time faculty/student ratio: **2.4**

SUPPORT SERVICES

The school offers students these services for dealing with stress: expanded hour gym access, peer counseling, professional counseling, support groups.

RESIDENCY PROFILE

Most popular residency and specialty programs chosen by the 2008 and 2009 M.D. graduating classes: anesthesiology, emergency medicine, family practice, internal medicine, obstetrics and gynecology, orthopaedic surgery, pediatrics, psychiatry, radiology–diagnostic, surgery–general.

WHERE GRADS GO

36.3%

Proportion of 2007-2008 graduates who entered primary care specialties

46.0%

Proportion of 2008-2009 graduates who accepted in-state residencies

University of Colorado—Denver

- 13001 E. 17th Place, MS C290, Aurora, CO 80045
- Public
- Year Founded: 1883
- Tuition, 2009-2010: In-state: $28,151; Out-of-State: $52,977
- Enrollment 2009-2010 academic year: 614
- Website: http://www.uchsc.edu/som/admissions
- Specialty ranking: family medicine: 9, internal medicine: 22, pediatrics: 9

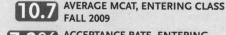

3.69 AVERAGE GPA, ENTERING CLASS FALL 2009

10.7 AVERAGE MCAT, ENTERING CLASS FALL 2009

7.3% ACCEPTANCE RATE, ENTERING CLASS FALL 2009

27 2011 U.S. NEWS MEDICAL SCHOOL RANKING (RESEARCH)

5 2011 U.S. NEWS MEDICAL SCHOOL RANKING (PRIMARY CARE)

ADMISSIONS

Admissions phone number: **(303) 724-8025**
Admissions email address: **somadmin@ucdenver.edu**
Application web site: **http://www.aamc.org**
Acceptance rate: **7.3%**
In-state acceptance rate: **25.5%**
Out-of-state acceptance rate: **3.9%**
Minority acceptance rate: **5.6%**
International acceptance rate: **3.1%**

Fall 2009 applications and acceptees

Type	Applied	Interviewed	Accepted	Enrolled
Total:	3,660	638	269	160
In-state:	584	310	149	120
Out-of-state:	3,076	328	120	40

Profile of admitted students

Average undergraduate grade point average: **3.69**
MCAT averages (scale: 1-15; writing test: J-T):
Composite score: **10.7**
Verbal reasoning score: **10.4**, Physical sciences score: **10.6**, Biological score: **11.2**, Writing score: **P**
Proportion with undergraduate majors in: Biological sciences: **32%**, Physical sciences: **25%**, Non-sciences: **23%**, Other health professions: **0%**, Mixed disciplines and other: **20%**
Percentage of students not coming directly from college after graduation: **72%**

Dates and details

The American Medical College Application Service (AMCAS) application is accepted.
School asks for a second, school-specific application as part of the admissions process.
Oldest MCAT considered for Fall 2011 entry: **2008**
Earliest application date for the 2011-2012 first-year class: **06/07**
Latest application date: **11/01**
Acceptance dates for regular application for the class entering in Fall 2011.
Earliest: **16-OCT-10**

Latest: **23-AUG-10**
Applicants have 2 weeks to respond to admissions offer.
The school does consider requests for deferred entrance.
Starting month for the class of 2011–2012: **August**
The school doesn't have an Early Decision Plan (EDP).
A personal interview is required for admission.

Undergraduate coursework required

Medical school requires undergraduate work in these subjects: biology, English, organic chemistry, inorganic (general) chemistry, physics, mathematics, general chemistry.

ADMISSIONS POLICY

(TEXT PROVIDED BY SCHOOL):

Places are offered through a holistic admissions process. Personal interviews and letters of recommendation are central. Important qualities include academic excellence, strength of character, motivation and maturity. Colorado is committed to selecting a diverse class from a wide variety of ethnic, social and educational backgrounds. Of the 160 places in the class the majority are from Colorado.

FINANCIAL AID

Financial aid phone number: **(303) 556-2886**
Tuition, 2009-2010 academic year: **In-state: $28,151; Out-of-State: $52,977**
Room and board: **$16,200**
Percentage of students receiving financial aid in 2009-10: **96%**
Percentage of students receiving: Loans: **91%**, Grants/scholarships: **76%**, Work-study aid: **5%**
Average medical school debt for the class of 2008: **$138,352**

STUDENT BODY

Fall 2009 full-time enrollment: **614**
Men: **52%**, Women: **48%**, In-state: **81%**, Minorities: **18%**, American Indian: **1.0%**, Asian-American: **9.3%**, African-American: **1.8%**, Hispanic-American: **5.2%**, White: **79.3%**, International: **0.3%**, Unknown: **3.1%**

ACADEMIC PROGRAMS

The school's curriculum frequently give first-year students substantial contact with patients.

There are opportunities for first- or second-year students to work in community health clinics.

Program areas: drug/alcohol abuse, family medicine, internal medicine, pediatrics, rural medicine, women's health

Joint degrees awarded: M.D./Ph.D.

Total National Institutes of Health (NIH) grants awarded to the medical school and affiliated hospitals: **$200.8 million**

CURRICULUM

(TEXT PROVIDED BY MEDICAL SCHOOL):

The University of Colorado Denver School of Medicine has an innovative curriculum comprised of sequential interdisciplinary blocks integrating clinical and basic science materials across all 4 years. Rural health, global health, and advocacy tracks are available. A mentored scholarly project is required of all students, in preparation for lifelong learning. http://www.uchsc.edu/som/educa.htm

FALL 2009 FACULTY PROFILE

Total teaching faculty: 2,290 **(full-time)**, 208 **(part-time)**
Of full-time faculty, those teaching in basic sciences: **8%**; in clinical programs: **92%**

Of part-time faculty, those teaching in basic sciences: **4%**; in clinical programs: **96%**
Full-time faculty/student ratio: **3.7**

SUPPORT SERVICES

The school offers students these services for dealing with stress: peer counseling, professional counseling.

RESIDENCY PROFILE

Most popular residency and specialty programs chosen by the 2008 and 2009 M.D. graduating classes: anesthesiology, emergency medicine, family practice, internal medicine, pediatrics, surgery–general.

WHERE GRADS GO

44.0%

Proportion of 2007-2008 graduates who entered primary care specialties

41.5%

Proportion of 2008-2009 graduates who accepted in-state residencies

University of Connecticut

- 263 Farmington Avenue, Farmington, CT 06030-1905
- Public
- Year Founded: 1961
- Tuition, 2009-2010: In-state: $29,576; Out-of-State: $52,621
- Enrollment 2009-2010 academic year: 346
- Website: http://medicine.uchc.edu
- Specialty ranking: N/A

3.71 AVERAGE GPA, ENTERING CLASS FALL 2009

10.5 AVERAGE MCAT, ENTERING CLASS FALL 2009

7.1% ACCEPTANCE RATE, ENTERING CLASS FALL 2009

55 2011 U.S. NEWS MEDICAL SCHOOL RANKING (RESEARCH)

42 2011 U.S. NEWS MEDICAL SCHOOL RANKING (PRIMARY CARE)

ADMISSIONS

Admissions phone number: **(860) 679-3874**
Admissions email address: **sanford@ns01.uchc.edu**
Application web site: **N/A**
Acceptance rate: **7.1%**
In-state acceptance rate: **29.3%**
Out-of-state acceptance rate: **3.0%**
Minority acceptance rate: **6.0%**
International acceptance rate: **1.3%**

Fall 2009 applications and acceptees

Type	Applied	Interviewed	Accepted	Enrolled
Total:	2,760	392	195	85
In-state:	427	239	125	68
Out-of-state:	2,333	153	70	17

Profile of admitted students

Average undergraduate grade point average: **3.71**
MCAT averages (scale: 1-15; writing test: J-T):
Composite score: **10.5**
Verbal reasoning score: **9.9**, Physical sciences score: **10.3**, Biological score: **11.2**, Writing score: **Q**
Proportion with undergraduate majors in: Biological sciences: **60%**, Physical sciences: **20%**, Non-sciences: **12%**, Other health professions: **6%**, Mixed disciplines and other: **2%**
Percentage of students not coming directly from college after graduation: **52%**

Dates and details

The American Medical College Application Service (AMCAS) application is accepted.
School asks for a second, school-specific application as part of the admissions process.
Oldest MCAT considered for Fall 2011 entry: **2007**
Earliest application date for the 2011-2012 first-year class: **06/01**
Latest application date: **12/15**
Acceptance dates for regular application for the class entering in Fall 2011.
Earliest: **15-OCT-10**

Latest: **19-AUG-11**
Applicants have 2 weeks to respond to admissions offer.
The school does consider requests for deferred entrance.
Starting month for the class of 2011–2012: **August**
The school does have an Early Decision Plan (EDP).
A personal interview is required for admission.

Undergraduate coursework required

Medical school requires undergraduate work in these subjects: biology, biology/zoology, English, organic chemistry, inorganic (general) chemistry, physics, general chemistry.

ADMISSIONS POLICY

(TEXT PROVIDED BY SCHOOL):

The Committee considers the applicant's achievements, ability, motivation, and character. The Committee carefully considers the applicant's academic history, MCAT scores, and full range of research, clinical, community service, and extracurricular activities. The SoM has a strong tradition of seeking a very diverse entering class.

FINANCIAL AID

Financial aid phone number: **(860) 679-3574**
Tuition, 2009-2010 academic year: **In-state: $29,576; Out-of-State: $52,621**
Room and board: **N/A**
Percentage of students receiving financial aid in 2009-10: **87%**
Percentage of students receiving: Loans: **82%**, Grants/scholarships: **58%**, Work-study aid: **0%**
Average medical school debt for the class of 2008: **$117,410**

STUDENT BODY

Fall 2009 full-time enrollment: **346**
Men: **44%**, Women: **56%**, In-state: **91%**, Minorities: **32%**, American Indian: **1.2%**, Asian-American: **15.0%**, African-American: **11.3%**, Hispanic-American: **4.9%**, White: **63.9%**, International: **1.4%**, Unknown: **2.3%**

ACADEMIC PROGRAMS

The school's curriculum very frequently give first-year students substantial contact with patients.

There are opportunities for first- or second-year students to work in community health clinics.

Program areas: AIDS, drug/alcohol abuse, family medicine, geriatrics, internal medicine, pediatrics, rural medicine, women's health

Joint degrees awarded: M.D./Ph.D., M.D./M.B.A., M.D./M.P.H., M.D./M.S., M.D./M.A.

Total National Institutes of Health (NIH) grants awarded to the medical school and affiliated hospitals: **$54.8 million**

CURRICULUM

(TEXT PROVIDED BY MEDICAL SCHOOL):

The curriculum consists of four years of instruction divided into three phases. Phase 1 (first two years) covers the core basic science instruction and the foundations of clinical medicine. Phase 2 (year 3) provides the core clinical experiences required of all students. Phase 3 (year 4) builds upon the clinical foundation of phase 2.

FALL 2009 FACULTY PROFILE

Total teaching faculty: **897 (full-time)**, **114 (part-time)**
Of full-time faculty, those teaching in basic sciences: **14%**; in clinical programs: **86%**

Of part-time faculty, those teaching in basic sciences: **27%**; in clinical programs: **73%**
Full-time faculty/student ratio: **2.6**

SUPPORT SERVICES

The school offers students these services for dealing with stress: peer counseling, professional counseling, support groups.

RESIDENCY PROFILE

Most popular residency and specialty programs chosen by the 2008 and 2009 M.D. graduating classes: emergency medicine, family practice, neurology, obstetrics and gynecology, orthopaedic surgery, pediatrics, psychiatry, radiology–diagnostic, surgery–general.

WHERE GRADS GO

45.0%

Proportion of 2007-2008 graduates who entered primary care specialties

44.0%

Proportion of 2008-2009 graduates who accepted in-state residencies

University of Florida

- Box 100215 UFHSC, Gainesville, FL 32610-0215
- Public
- Year Founded: 1956
- Tuition, 2009-2010: In-state: $28,652; Out-of-State: $56,500
- Enrollment 2009-2010 academic year: 527
- Website: http://www.med.ufl.edu
- Specialty ranking: N/A

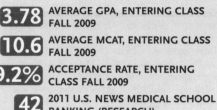

3.78 AVERAGE GPA, ENTERING CLASS FALL 2009

10.6 AVERAGE MCAT, ENTERING CLASS FALL 2009

9.2% ACCEPTANCE RATE, ENTERING CLASS FALL 2009

42 2011 U.S. NEWS MEDICAL SCHOOL RANKING (RESEARCH)

Unranked 2011 U.S. NEWS MEDICAL SCHOOL RANKING (PRIMARY CARE)

ADMISSIONS

Admissions phone number: **(352) 273-7990**
Admissions email address: **med-admissions@ufl.edu**
Application web site: **http://www.aamc.org/amcas**
Acceptance rate: **9.2%**
In-state acceptance rate: **14.2%**
Out-of-state acceptance rate: **1.2%**
Minority acceptance rate: **7.3%**
International acceptance rate: **0.0%**

Fall 2009 applications and acceptees

Type	Applied	Interviewed	Accepted	Enrolled
Total:	2,624	347	241	128
In-state:	1,618	328	229	123
Out-of-state:	1,006	19	12	5

Profile of admitted students

Average undergraduate grade point average: **3.78**
MCAT averages (scale: 1-15; writing test: J-T):
Composite score: **10.6**
Verbal reasoning score: **9.9**, Physical sciences score: **10.8**,
  Biological score: **11.0**, Writing score: **Q**
Proportion with undergraduate majors in: Biological
  sciences: **37%**, Physical sciences: **19%**, Non-sciences:
  14%, Other health professions: **2%**, Mixed disciplines
  and other: **28%**
Percentage of students not coming directly from college
  after graduation: **26%**

Dates and details

The American Medical College Application Service
  (AMCAS) application is accepted.
School asks for a second, school-specific application as part
  of the admissions process.
Oldest MCAT considered for Fall 2011 entry: **2008**
Earliest application date for the 2011-2012 first-year class:
  06/01
Latest application date: **12/01**
Acceptance dates for regular application for the class
  entering in Fall 2011.
Earliest: **16-OCT-10**

Latest: **09-AUG-10**
Applicants have 3 weeks to respond to admissions offer.
The school does consider requests for deferred entrance.
Starting month for the class of 2011–2012: **August**
The school doesn't have an Early Decision Plan (EDP).
A personal interview is required for admission.

Undergraduate coursework required

Medical school requires undergraduate work in these subjects: biology, organic chemistry, physics, biochemistry, general chemistry.

ADMISSIONS POLICY
(TEXT PROVIDED BY SCHOOL):

  Initial selection: GPA, MCAT, no cut-offs. Pre-med
course quality, GPA progress, activities affect request for
secondary. FL residents favored. Interview: selection based
on academics, motivation, grasp of profession, recommendations; evaluates personal strengths, service, research.
Admit bright, dedicated, interesting people evidencing
integrity, conscientiousness, love of learning, compassion.

FINANCIAL AID

Financial aid phone number: **(352) 273-7939**
Tuition, 2009-2010 academic year: **In-state: $28,652; Out-of-State: $56,500**
Room and board: **$9,465**
Percentage of students receiving financial aid in 2009-10: **84%**
Percentage of students receiving: Loans: **76%**,
  Grants/scholarships: **63%**, Work-study aid: **0%**
Average medical school debt for the class of 2008:
  $107,589

STUDENT BODY

Fall 2009 full-time enrollment: **527**
Men: **52%**, Women: **48%**, In-state: **99%**, Minorities: **32%**,
  American Indian: **0.9%**, Asian-American: **19.7%**,
  African-American: **4.6%**, Hispanic-American: **7.2%**,
  White: **63.0%**, International: **0.0%**, Unknown: **4.6%**

ACADEMIC PROGRAMS

The school's curriculum very frequently give first-year students substantial contact with patients.

There are opportunities for first- or second-year students to work in community health clinics.

Program areas: AIDS, drug/alcohol abuse, family medicine, geriatrics, internal medicine, pediatrics, rural medicine, women's health

Joint degrees awarded: M.D./Ph.D., M.D./M.B.A., M.D./M.P.H., M.D./J.D., M.D./M.S., M.D./M.A.

Total National Institutes of Health (NIH) grants awarded to the medical school and affiliated hospitals: **$81.4 million**

CURRICULUM

(TEXT PROVIDED BY MEDICAL SCHOOL):

Competency-based curriculum emphasizes early development of clinical skills, professionalism, access to high-quality research track. Competencies provide a set of knowledge, skills and behaviors that all students must master to graduate. Clinical training strengthened by the involvement of our urban hospital in Jacksonville, providing students with broad exposure to different types of patients.

FALL 2009 FACULTY PROFILE

Total teaching faculty: **1,230 (full-time)**, **134 (part-time)**
Of full-time faculty, those teaching in basic sciences: **13%**; in clinical programs: **87%**

Of part-time faculty, those teaching in basic sciences: **4%**; in clinical programs: **96%**
Full-time faculty/student ratio: **2.3**

SUPPORT SERVICES

The school offers students these services for dealing with stress: expanded-hour gym access, peer counseling, professional counseling, religious support, support groups.

RESIDENCY PROFILE

Most popular residency and specialty programs chosen by the 2008 and 2009 M.D. graduating classes: anesthesiology, emergency medicine, family practice, internal medicine, obstetrics and gynecology, pediatrics, psychiatry, radiology–diagnostic, surgery–general.

WHERE GRADS GO

35.0%

Proportion of 2007-2008 graduates who entered primary care specialties

25.3%

Proportion of 2008-2009 graduates who accepted in-state residencies

University of Hawaii–Manoa
Burns

- 651 Ilalo Street, Honolulu, HI 96813
- Public
- Year Founded: 1967
- Tuition, 2009-2010: In-state: $25,215; Out-of-State: $51,303
- Enrollment 2009-2010 academic year: 254
- Website: http://jabsom.hawaii.edu
- Specialty ranking: geriatrics: 18, rural medicine: 22

3.62 AVERAGE GPA, ENTERING CLASS FALL 2009

9.6 AVERAGE MCAT, ENTERING CLASS FALL 2009

6.9% ACCEPTANCE RATE, ENTERING CLASS FALL 2009

Unranked 2011 U.S. NEWS MEDICAL SCHOOL RANKING (RESEARCH)

49 2011 U.S. NEWS MEDICAL SCHOOL RANKING (PRIMARY CARE)

ADMISSIONS
Admissions phone number: **(808) 692-1000**
Admissions email address: **medadmin@hawaii.edu**
Application web site:
   http://jabsom.hawaii.edu/jabsom/admissions/mdprogram.php
Acceptance rate: **6.9%**
In-state acceptance rate: **35.4%**
Out-of-state acceptance rate: **2.6%**
Minority acceptance rate: **13.5%**
International acceptance rate: **3.1%**

Fall 2009 applications and acceptees

Type	Applied	Interviewed	Accepted	Enrolled
Total:	1,700	215	118	62
In-state:	223	151	79	55
Out-of-state:	1,477	64	39	7

Profile of admitted students
Average undergraduate grade point average: **3.62**
MCAT averages (scale: 1-15; writing test: J-T):
Composite score: **9.6**
Verbal reasoning score: **9.0**, Physical sciences score: **10.0**,
   Biological score: **10.0**, Writing score: **P**
Proportion with undergraduate majors in: Biological
   sciences: **61%**, Physical sciences: **19%**, Non-sciences:
   15%, Other health professions: **2%**, Mixed disciplines
   and other: **3%**
Percentage of students not coming directly from college
   after graduation: **73%**

Dates and details
The American Medical College Application Service
   (AMCAS) application is accepted.
School asks for a second, school-specific application as part
   of the admissions process.
Oldest MCAT considered for Fall 2011 entry: **2008**
Earliest application date for the 2011-2012 first-year class:
   06/01
Latest application date: **11/01**

Acceptance dates for regular application for the class
   entering in Fall 2011.
Earliest: **10-OCT-10**
Latest: **N/A**
Applicants have 2 weeks to respond to admissions offer.
The school does consider requests for deferred entrance.
Starting month for the class of 2011–2012: **July**
The school does have an Early Decision Plan (EDP).
A personal interview is required for admission.

Undergraduate coursework required
Medical school requires undergraduate work in these subjects: biology, organic chemistry, physics, molecular and cell biology, biochemistry, general chemistry.

ADMISSIONS POLICY
(TEXT PROVIDED BY SCHOOL):
   JABSOM trains outstanding physicians & scientists for Hawaii & the Pacific, to conduct research & community service. We expect academic potential, personal attributes (commitment, community awareness, leadership & interpersonal skills, compassion, emotional and physical stamina to be a physician) & ties to serve people of Hawaii. Our students mirror the rich diversity of our state's population.

FINANCIAL AID
Financial aid phone number: **(808) 956-7251**
Tuition, 2009-2010 academic year: **In-state: $25,215; Out-of-State: $51,303**
Room and board: **N/A**
Percentage of students receiving financial aid in 2009-10: **82%**
Percentage of students receiving: Loans: **70%**,
   Grants/scholarships: **53%**, Work-study aid: **0%**
Average medical school debt for the class of 2008: **$79,872**

STUDENT BODY
Fall 2009 full-time enrollment: **254**
Men: **47%**, Women: **53%**, In-state: **87%**, Minorities: **71%**,
   American Indian: **0.8%**, Asian-American: **83.5%**,

African-American: 0.0%, Hispanic-American: 0.4%, White: 13.8%, International: 1.6%, Unknown: 0.0%

ACADEMIC PROGRAMS

The school's curriculum very frequently give first-year students substantial contact with patients.

There are opportunities for first- or second-year students to work in community health clinics.

Program areas: AIDS, drug/alcohol abuse, family medicine, geriatrics, internal medicine, pediatrics, rural medicine, women's health

Joint degrees awarded: N/A

Total National Institutes of Health (NIH) grants awarded to the medical school and affiliated hospitals: **$31.2 million**

CURRICULUM

(TEXT PROVIDED BY MEDICAL SCHOOL):

Preclinical curriculum is Problem Based Learning, which allows students to learn basic & clinical science underlying health/illness thru case based small group, self directed learning. Clinical yrs are based in community hospitals and practices & includes rural medicine. We emphasize evidenced based medicine, compassionate communication & clinical skills. Research opportunities are available.

FALL 2009 FACULTY PROFILE

Total teaching faculty: **244 (full-time), 152 (part-time)**

Of full-time faculty, those teaching in basic sciences: **36%**; in clinical programs: **64%**

Of part-time faculty, those teaching in basic sciences: **10%**; in clinical programs: **90%**

Full-time faculty/student ratio: 1.8

SUPPORT SERVICES

The school offers students these services for dealing with stress: professional counseling, support groups.

RESIDENCY PROFILE

Most popular residency and specialty programs chosen by the 2008 and 2009 M.D. graduating classes: emergency medicine, family practice, internal medicine, obstetrics and gynecology, orthopaedic surgery, pediatrics, surgery–general.

WHERE GRADS GO

50.0%

Proportion of 2007-2008 graduates who entered primary care specialties

31.0%

Proportion of 2008-2009 graduates who accepted in-state residencies

University of Iowa
Carver

- 200 CMAB, Iowa City, IA 52242-1101
- Public
- Year Founded: 1847
- Tuition, 2009-2010: In-state: $28,248; Out-of-State: $44,062
- Enrollment 2009-2010 academic year: 576
- Website: http://www.medicine.uiowa.edu
- Specialty ranking: internal medicine: 20, rural medicine: 13, women's health: 18

 3.70 AVERAGE GPA, ENTERING CLASS FALL 2009

10.4 AVERAGE MCAT, ENTERING CLASS FALL 2009

 9.7% ACCEPTANCE RATE, ENTERING CLASS FALL 2009

27 2011 U.S. NEWS MEDICAL SCHOOL RANKING (RESEARCH)

10 2011 U.S. NEWS MEDICAL SCHOOL RANKING (PRIMARY CARE)

ADMISSIONS

Admissions phone number: **(319) 335-8052**
Admissions email address: **medical-admissions@uiowa.edu**
Application web site:
   http://www.medicine.uiowa.edu/osac/admissions
Acceptance rate: **9.7%**
In-state acceptance rate: **39.9%**
Out-of-state acceptance rate: **5.7%**
Minority acceptance rate: **11.4%**
International acceptance rate: **N/A**

Fall 2009 applications and acceptees

Type	Applied	Interviewed	Accepted	Enrolled
Total:	2,763	673	268	148
In-state:	321	265	128	97
Out-of-state:	2,442	408	140	51

Profile of admitted students

Average undergraduate grade point average: **3.70**
MCAT averages (scale: 1-15; writing test: J-T):
Composite score: **10.4**
Verbal reasoning score: **10.0**, Physical sciences score: **10.3**, Biological score: **10.8**, Writing score: **P**
Proportion with undergraduate majors in: Biological sciences: **53%**, Physical sciences: **9%**, Non-sciences: **17%**, Other health professions: **1%**, Mixed disciplines and other: **20%**
Percentage of students not coming directly from college after graduation: **20%**

Dates and details

The American Medical College Application Service (AMCAS) application is accepted.
School asks for a second, school-specific application as part of the admissions process.
Oldest MCAT considered for Fall 2011 entry: **2005**
Earliest application date for the 2011-2012 first-year class: **06/01**
Latest application date: **11/01**

Acceptance dates for regular application for the class entering in Fall 2011.
Earliest: **15-OCT-10**
Latest: **17-AUG-11**
Applicants have 2 weeks to respond to admissions offer. The school does consider requests for deferred entrance. Starting month for the class of 2011–2012: **August**
The school does have an Early Decision Plan (EDP). A personal interview is required for admission.

Undergraduate coursework required

Medical school requires undergraduate work in these subjects: biology, English, organic chemistry, inorganic (general) chemistry, physics, humanities, mathematics, behavioral science, demonstration of writing skills, social sciences, general chemistry.

ADMISSIONS POLICY
(TEXT PROVIDED BY SCHOOL):

The College is committed to the recruitment, selection and retention of a highly-qualified and diverse student body. Applicants must attain at least a 2.5 GPA; a bachelor's degree; US citizenship, permanent residency or asylum. Factors considered: overall academic record; science GPA; MCAT; service commitment; personal qualities; on-site interview. 70% of admitted students are Iowa residents.

FINANCIAL AID

Financial aid phone number: **(319) 335-8059**
Tuition, 2009-2010 academic year: **In-state: $28,248; Out-of-State: $44,062**
Room and board: **$9,900**
Percentage of students receiving financial aid in 2009-10: **95%**
Percentage of students receiving: Loans: **90%**, Grants/scholarships: **65%**, Work-study aid: **0%**
Average medical school debt for the class of 2008: **$124,440**

STUDENT BODY

Fall 2009 full-time enrollment: **576**

Men: 50%, Women: 50%, In-state: 68%, Minorities: 20%,
American Indian: 0.7%, Asian-American: 10.6%,
African-American: 4.9%, Hispanic-American: 4.7%,
White: 78.8%, International: 0.0%, Unknown: 0.3%

ACADEMIC PROGRAMS

The school's curriculum occasionally give first-year
students substantial contact with patients.

There are opportunities for first- or second-year students to
work in community health clinics.

Program areas: AIDS, drug/alcohol abuse, family
medicine, geriatrics, internal medicine, pediatrics, rural
medicine, women's health

Joint degrees awarded: M.D./Ph.D., M.D./M.B.A.,
M.D./M.P.H., M.D./J.D.

Total National Institutes of Health (NIH) grants awarded
to the medical school and affiliated hospitals: **$166.0
million**

CURRICULUM
(TEXT PROVIDED BY MEDICAL SCHOOL):

Case-based and small-group learning, clinical correlation
and integration of material are emphasized. Year 1: normal
structure/function; Year 2: abnormal structure/function.
Medical history-taking, physical diagnosis, patient contact
are offered in the first two years through Foundations of
Clinical Practice. The clinical years provide a broad base of
knowledge and skills required for residency.

FALL 2009 FACULTY PROFILE

Total teaching faculty: **832 (full-time), 99 (part-time)**

Of full-time faculty, those teaching in basic sciences: **10%**;
in clinical programs: **90%**

Of part-time faculty, those teaching in basic sciences: **5%**;
in clinical programs: **95%**

Full-time faculty/student ratio: 1.4

SUPPORT SERVICES

The school offers students these services for dealing with
stress: peer counseling, professional counseling, support
groups.

RESIDENCY PROFILE

Most popular residency and specialty programs chosen by
the 2008 and 2009 M.D. graduating classes: anesthesiology, emergency medicine, family practice, internal medicine, pediatrics, radiology–diagnostic.

WHERE GRADS GO

41.0%

*Proportion of 2007-2008 graduates who entered primary
care specialties*

25.0%

*Proportion of 2008-2009 graduates who accepted in-state
residencies*

University of Kansas Medical Center

- 3901 Rainbow Boulevard, Kansas City, KS 66160
- Public
- **Year Founded:** 1905
- **Tuition, 2009-2010:** In-state: $28,178; Out-of-State: $47,626
- **Enrollment 2009-2010 academic year:** 723
- **Website:** http://www.kumc.edu/som/som.html
- **Specialty ranking:** N/A

3.65	AVERAGE GPA, ENTERING CLASS FALL 2009
9.5	AVERAGE MCAT, ENTERING CLASS FALL 2009
9.5%	ACCEPTANCE RATE, ENTERING CLASS FALL 2009
Unranked	2011 U.S. NEWS MEDICAL SCHOOL RANKING (RESEARCH)
53	2011 U.S. NEWS MEDICAL SCHOOL RANKING (PRIMARY CARE)

ADMISSIONS

Admissions phone number: **(913) 588-5245**
Admissions email address: **premedinfo@kumc.edu**
Application web site: **N/A**
Acceptance rate: **9.5%**
In-state acceptance rate: **40.5%**
Out-of-state acceptance rate: **2.0%**
Minority acceptance rate: **5.0%**
International acceptance rate: **0.0%**

Fall 2009 applications and acceptees

Type	Applied	Interviewed	Accepted	Enrolled
Total:	2,263	458	216	175
In-state:	444	353	180	153
Out-of-state:	1,819	105	36	22

Profile of admitted students

Average undergraduate grade point average: **3.65**
MCAT averages (scale: 1-15; writing test: J-T):
Composite score: **9.5**
Verbal reasoning score: **9.5**, Physical sciences score: **9.0**, Biological score: **10.0**, Writing score: **Q**
Proportion with undergraduate majors in: Biological sciences: **52%**, Physical sciences: **16%**, Non-sciences: **15%**, Other health professions: **1%**, Mixed disciplines and other: **18%**
Percentage of students not coming directly from college after graduation: **46%**

Dates and details

The American Medical College Application Service (AMCAS) application is accepted.
School asks for a second, school-specific application as part of the admissions process.
Oldest MCAT considered for Fall 2011 entry: **2007**
Earliest application date for the 2011-2012 first-year class: **06/07**
Latest application date: **10/15**
Acceptance dates for regular application for the class entering in Fall 2011.
Earliest: **01-NOV-10**

Latest: **20-JUL-11**
Applicants have 2 weeks to respond to admissions offer.
The school does consider requests for deferred entrance.
Starting month for the class of 2011-2012: **July**
The school does have an Early Decision Plan (EDP).
A personal interview is required for admission.

Undergraduate coursework required

Medical school requires undergraduate work in these subjects: biology, English, organic chemistry, inorganic (general) chemistry, physics, mathematics, general chemistry.

ADMISSIONS POLICY
(TEXT PROVIDED BY SCHOOL):

Qualified Kansas residents receive strong admissions preference; successful nonresident applicants have significant Kansas ties and/or add breadth to the class. Academic performance, personal qualities, motivation for medicine, and commitment to service are assessed through the use of AMCAS and secondary applications, letters of recommendation, and interviews.

FINANCIAL AID

Financial aid phone number: **(913) 588-5170**
Tuition, 2009-2010 academic year: **In-state: $28,178; Out-of-State: $47,626**
Room and board: **$11,106**
Percentage of students receiving financial aid in 2009-10: **95%**
Percentage of students receiving: Loans: **82%**, Grants/scholarships: **90%**, Work-study aid: **0%**
Average medical school debt for the class of 2008: **$123,309**

STUDENT BODY

Fall 2009 full-time enrollment: **723**
Men: **50%**, Women: **50%**, In-state: **87%**, Minorities: **20%**, American Indian: **1.0%**, Asian-American: **9.7%**, African-American: **5.1%**, Hispanic-American: **4.0%**, White: **63.3%**, International: **0.0%**, Unknown: **16.9%**

ACADEMIC PROGRAMS

The school's curriculum occasionally give first-year students substantial contact with patients.

There are opportunities for first- or second-year students to work in community health clinics.

Program areas: AIDS, drug/alcohol abuse, family medicine, geriatrics, internal medicine, pediatrics, rural medicine, women's health

Joint degrees awarded: M.D./Ph.D., M.D./M.P.H., M.D./M.H.A.

Total National Institutes of Health (NIH) grants awarded to the medical school and affiliated hospitals: **$63.8 million**

CURRICULUM

(TEXT PROVIDED BY MEDICAL SCHOOL):

The first two years at KUMC consist of required modules integrating core basic science disciplines as well as basic skills and biopsychosocial topics relevant to clinical practice. Years three and four consist of required clerkships in core clinical disciplines and electives. The curriculum integrates large and small group learning and laboratory exercises, and makes extensive use of technology.

FALL 2009 FACULTY PROFILE

Total teaching faculty: **663 (full-time)**, **140 (part-time)**

Of full-time faculty, those teaching in basic sciences: **22%**; in clinical programs: **78%**

Of part-time faculty, those teaching in basic sciences: **16%**; in clinical programs: **84%**

Full-time faculty/student ratio: **0.9**

SUPPORT SERVICES

The school offers students these services for dealing with stress: peer counseling, professional counseling

RESIDENCY PROFILE

Most popular residency and specialty programs chosen by the 2008 and 2009 M.D. graduating classes: anesthesiology, emergency medicine, family practice, internal medicine, obstetrics and gynecology, orthopaedic surgery, pediatrics, radiology–diagnostic, surgery–general.

WHERE GRADS GO

42.4%

Proportion of 2007-2008 graduates who entered primary care specialties

32.7%

Proportion of 2008-2009 graduates who accepted in-state residencies

University of Kentucky

- 138 Leader Avenue, Lexington, KY 40506-9983
- Public
- Year Founded: 1956
- Tuition, 2009-2010: In-state: $29,341; Out-of-State: $53,747
- Enrollment 2009-2010 academic year: 439
- Website: http://www.mc.uky.edu/medicine/
- Specialty ranking: drug/alcohol abuse: 15, family medicine: 22

3.68 AVERAGE GPA, ENTERING CLASS FALL 2009

10.3 AVERAGE MCAT, ENTERING CLASS FALL 2009

9.1% ACCEPTANCE RATE, ENTERING CLASS FALL 2009

59 2011 U.S. NEWS MEDICAL SCHOOL RANKING (RESEARCH)

56 2011 U.S. NEWS MEDICAL SCHOOL RANKING (PRIMARY CARE)

ADMISSIONS

Admissions phone number: **(859) 323-6161**
Admissions email address: **kymedap@uky.edu**
Application web site:
http://www.aamc.org/students/amcas/start.htm
Acceptance rate: **9.1%**
In-state acceptance rate: **27.7%**
Out-of-state acceptance rate: **4.6%**
Minority acceptance rate: **N/A**
International acceptance rate: **N/A**

Fall 2009 applications and acceptees

Type	Applied	Interviewed	Accepted	Enrolled
Total:	2,099	378	191	115
In-state:	412	226	114	78
Out-of-state:	1,687	152	77	37

Profile of admitted students

Average undergraduate grade point average: **3.68**
MCAT averages (scale: 1-15; writing test: J-T):
Composite score: **10.3**
Verbal reasoning score: **9.8**, Physical sciences score: **10.2**, Biological score: **11.0**, Writing score: **O**
Proportion with undergraduate majors in: Biological sciences: **63%**, Physical sciences: **19%**, Non-sciences: **8%**, Other health professions: **0%**, Mixed disciplines and other: **10%**
Percentage of students not coming directly from college after graduation: **30%**

Dates and details

The American Medical College Application Service (AMCAS) application is accepted.
School asks for a second, school-specific application as part of the admissions process.
Oldest MCAT considered for Fall 2011 entry: **2008**
Earliest application date for the 2011-2012 first-year class: **06/01**
Latest application date: **11/01**
Acceptance dates for regular application for the class entering in Fall 2011.

Earliest: **15-OCT-09**
Latest: **01-AUG-10**
Applicants have 2 weeks to respond to admissions offer.
The school does consider requests for deferred entrance.
Starting month for the class of 2011–2012: **August**
The school does have an Early Decision Plan (EDP).
A personal interview is required for admission.

Undergraduate coursework required

Medical school requires undergraduate work in these subjects: biology, English, organic chemistry, inorganic (general) chemistry, physics.

ADMISSIONS POLICY

(TEXT PROVIDED BY SCHOOL):
Preference is given to Kentucky residents. Non-residents are encouraged to apply. Competitive non-resident applicants should have overall records which compare favorably with average matriculants.

FINANCIAL AID

Financial aid phone number: **(859) 257-1652**
Tuition, 2009-2010 academic year: **In-state: $29,341; Out-of-State: $53,747**
Room and board: **$14,850**
Percentage of students receiving financial aid in 2009-10: **92%**
Percentage of students receiving: Loans: **82%**, Grants/scholarships: **48%**, Work-study aid: **16%**
Average medical school debt for the class of 2008: **$135,835**

STUDENT BODY

Fall 2009 full-time enrollment: **439**
Men: **59%**, Women: **41%**, In-state: **78%**, Minorities: **18%**, American Indian: **0.0%**, Asian-American: **10.9%**, African-American: **4.1%**, Hispanic-American: **0.5%**, White: **75.9%**, International: **3.6%**, Unknown: **5.0%**

ACADEMIC PROGRAMS

The school's curriculum very frequently give first-year students substantial contact with patients.

There are opportunities for first- or second-year students to work in community health clinics.

Program areas: AIDS, drug/alcohol abuse, family medicine, geriatrics, internal medicine, pediatrics, rural medicine, women's health

Joint degrees awarded: M.D./Ph.D., M.D./M.B.A., M.D./M.P.H.

Total National Institutes of Health (NIH) grants awarded to the medical school and affiliated hospitals: $65.0 million

CURRICULUM
(TEXT PROVIDED BY MEDICAL SCHOOL):

The curriculum emphasizes early clinical experiences, integration of the basic and clinical sciences, teaching in ambulatory clinic settings, and primary care. We believe that this curriculum will result in a generation of physicians who will be lifelong learners. The curriculum uses many learning methods, including standardized patients and human patient simulators.

FALL 2009 FACULTY PROFILE
Total teaching faculty: 802 (full-time), 203 (part-time)
Of full-time faculty, those teaching in basic sciences: 25%; in clinical programs: 75%

Of part-time faculty, those teaching in basic sciences: 8%; in clinical programs: 92%
Full-time faculty/student ratio: 1.8

SUPPORT SERVICES
The school offers students these services for dealing with stress: expanded-hour gym access, professional counseling, support groups.

RESIDENCY PROFILE
Most popular residency and specialty programs chosen by the 2008 and 2009 M.D. graduating classes: emergency medicine, family practice, internal medicine, neurology, obstetrics and gynecology, orthopaedic surgery, pediatrics, psychiatry, radiology–diagnostic, internal medicine/pediatrics.

WHERE GRADS GO

43.0%

Proportion of 2007-2008 graduates who entered primary care specialties

36.5%

Proportion of 2008-2009 graduates who accepted in-state residencies

University of Louisville

■ Abell Administration Center, H.S.C., Louisville, KY 40202
■ Public
■ Year Founded: 1837
■ Tuition, 2009-2010: In-state: $26,329; Out-of-State: $43,425
■ Enrollment 2009-2010 academic year: 610
■ Website: http://www.louisville.edu
■ Specialty ranking: N/A

3.63 AVERAGE GPA, ENTERING CLASS FALL 2009

9.8 AVERAGE MCAT, ENTERING CLASS FALL 2009

10.2% ACCEPTANCE RATE, ENTERING CLASS FALL 2009

Unranked 2011 U.S. NEWS MEDICAL SCHOOL RANKING (RESEARCH)

Unranked 2011 U.S. NEWS MEDICAL SCHOOL RANKING (PRIMARY CARE)

ADMISSIONS

Admissions phone number: **(502) 852-5193**
Admissions email address: **medadm@louisville.edu**
Application web site: **http://www.aamc.org**
Acceptance rate: **10.2%**
In-state acceptance rate: **44.5%**
Out-of-state acceptance rate: **3.7%**
Minority acceptance rate: **7.0%**
International acceptance rate: **13.3%**

Fall 2009 applications and acceptees

Type	Applied	Interviewed	Accepted	Enrolled
Total:	2,492	384	253	160
In-state:	393	250	175	120
Out-of-state:	2,099	134	78	40

Profile of admitted students

Average undergraduate grade point average: **3.63**
MCAT averages (scale: 1-15; writing test: J-T):
Composite score: **9.8**
Verbal reasoning score: **9.6**, Physical sciences score: **9.5**,
  Biological score: **10.2**, Writing score: **N**
Proportion with undergraduate majors in: Biological
  sciences: **48%**, Physical sciences: **26%**, Non-sciences:
  8%, Other health professions: **0%**, Mixed disciplines and
  other: **18%**
Percentage of students not coming directly from college
  after graduation: **11%**

Dates and details

The American Medical College Application Service
  (AMCAS) application is accepted.
School asks for a second, school-specific application as part
  of the admissions process.
Oldest MCAT considered for Fall 2011 entry: **2008**
Earliest application date for the 2011-2012 first-year class:
  06/01
Latest application date: **10/15**
Acceptance dates for regular application for the class
  entering in Fall 2011.
Earliest: **15-OCT-10**

Latest: **11-AUG-10**
Applicants have 2 weeks to respond to admissions offer.
The school does consider requests for deferred entrance.
Starting month for the class of 2011–2012: **August**
The school does have an Early Decision Plan (EDP).
A personal interview is required for admission.

Undergraduate coursework required

Medical school requires undergraduate work in these subjects: biology, English, organic chemistry, inorganic (general) chemistry, physics, mathematics, calculus, general
chemistry.

ADMISSIONS POLICY
(TEXT PROVIDED BY SCHOOL):

  Because we are a state institution, we give preference to
qualified residents of KY. Applicants are selected on the
basis of their individual merits without bias to sex, race,
creed, national origin, age or handicap. They are chosen on
the basis of intellect, integrity, maturity, and demonstrated
sensitivity toward others. Significant weight is given to
interview scores, which are held at the SOM.

FINANCIAL AID

Financial aid phone number: **(502) 852-5187**
Tuition, 2009-2010 academic year: **In-state: $26,329; Out-
of-State: $43,425**
Room and board: **$8,494**
Percentage of students receiving financial aid in 2009-10:
  94%
Percentage of students receiving: Loans: **90%**,
  Grants/scholarships: **35%**, Work-study aid: **0%**
Average medical school debt for the class of 2008:
  $144,399

STUDENT BODY

Fall 2009 full-time enrollment: **610**
Men: **56%**, Women: **44%**, In-state: **79%**, Minorities: **19%**,
  American Indian: **0.2%**, Asian-American: **10.5%**,
  African-American: **7.2%**, Hispanic-American: **1.1%**,
  White: **76.6%**, International: **0.0%**, Unknown: **4.4%**

ACADEMIC PROGRAMS

The school's curriculum occasionally give first-year students substantial contact with patients.

There are opportunities for first- or second-year students to work in community health clinics.

Program areas: family medicine, geriatrics, internal medicine, pediatrics, rural medicine, women's health

Joint degrees awarded: M.D./Ph.D., M.D./M.B.A., M.D./M.P.H., M.D./M.S., M.D./M.A.

Total National Institutes of Health (NIH) grants awarded to the medical school and affiliated hospitals: **$41.7 million**

CURRICULUM

(TEXT PROVIDED BY MEDICAL SCHOOL):

The educational program has been developed to provide an efficiently organized, penetrating presentation of the general topics considered essential for all physicians, yet has sufficient flexibility to allow effective development of the student's individual abilities and interests. The two major components of this program are the core curriculum and the preclinical/clinical elective program.

FALL 2009 FACULTY PROFILE

Total teaching faculty: **722 (full-time), 66 (part-time)**
Of full-time faculty, those teaching in basic sciences: **14%**; in clinical programs: **86%**

Of part-time faculty, those teaching in basic sciences: **6%**; in clinical programs: **94%**
Full-time faculty/student ratio: **1.2**

SUPPORT SERVICES

The school offers students these services for dealing with stress: expanded-hour gym access, peer counseling, professional counseling, support groups.

RESIDENCY PROFILE

Most popular residency and specialty programs chosen by the 2008 and 2009 M.D. graduating classes: anesthesiology, emergency medicine, family practice, internal medicine, obstetrics and gynecology, orthopaedic surgery, pediatrics, psychiatry, radiology–diagnostic, surgery–general.

WHERE GRADS GO

41.3%
Proportion of 2007-2008 graduates who entered primary care specialties

38.7%
Proportion of 2008-2009 graduates who accepted in-state residencies

University of Maryland

- 655 W. Baltimore Street, Room 14-029, Baltimore, MD 21201-1559
- Public
- **Year Founded:** 1807
- **Tuition, 2009-2010:** In-state: $25,604; Out-of-State: $45,648
- **Enrollment 2009-2010 academic year:** 645
- **Website:** http://medschool.umaryland.edu
- **Specialty ranking:** AIDS: 18

3.71 AVERAGE GPA, ENTERING CLASS FALL 2009

10.3 AVERAGE MCAT, ENTERING CLASS FALL 2009

7.5% ACCEPTANCE RATE, ENTERING CLASS FALL 2009

40 2011 U.S. NEWS MEDICAL SCHOOL RANKING (RESEARCH)

46 2011 U.S. NEWS MEDICAL SCHOOL RANKING (PRIMARY CARE)

ADMISSIONS

Admissions phone number: **(410) 706-7478**
Admissions email address: **mfoxwell@som.umaryland.edu**
Application web site: **N/A**
Acceptance rate: **7.5%**
In-state acceptance rate: **25.3%**
Out-of-state acceptance rate: **3.6%**
Minority acceptance rate: **6.1%**
International acceptance rate: **4.5%**

Fall 2009 applications and acceptees

Type	Applied	Interviewed	Accepted	Enrolled
Total:	4,570	594	344	160
In-state:	821	310	208	123
Out-of-state:	3,749	284	136	37

Profile of admitted students

Average undergraduate grade point average: **3.71**
MCAT averages (scale: 1-15; writing test: J-T):
Composite score: **10.3**
Verbal reasoning score: **10.0**, Physical sciences score: **10.2**, Biological score: **10.6**, Writing score: **P**
Proportion with undergraduate majors in: Biological sciences: **48%**, Physical sciences: **22%**, Non-sciences: **20%**, Other health professions: **4%**, Mixed disciplines and other: **6%**
Percentage of students not coming directly from college after graduation: **50%**

Dates and details

The American Medical College Application Service (AMCAS) application is accepted.
School asks for a second, school-specific application as part of the admissions process.
Oldest MCAT considered for Fall 2011 entry: **2007**
Earliest application date for the 2011-2012 first-year class: **06/01**
Latest application date: **11/01**
Acceptance dates for regular application for the class entering in Fall 2011.
Earliest: **15-OCT-10**

Latest: **N/A**
Applicants have 3 weeks to respond to admissions offer.
The school does consider requests for deferred entrance.
Starting month for the class of 2011–2012: **August**
The school does have an Early Decision Plan (EDP).
A personal interview is required for admission.

Undergraduate coursework required

Medical school requires undergraduate work in these subjects: biology/zoology, English, organic chemistry, inorganic (general) chemistry, physics.

ADMISSIONS POLICY

(TEXT PROVIDED BY SCHOOL):

We admit those who possess the ability to successfully complete the academically rigorous curriculum and have personal characteristics that one desires in a personal physician. Close attention is paid to extracurricular activities, life experiences and letters of recommendation for evidence of maturity, stability, judgment, empathy, intellectual curiosity, leadership and commitment to excellence.

FINANCIAL AID

Financial aid phone number: **(410) 706-7347**
Tuition, 2009-2010 academic year: **In-state: $25,604; Out-of-State: $45,648**
Room and board: **$21,500**
Percentage of students receiving financial aid in 2009-10: **90%**
Percentage of students receiving: Loans: **85%**, Grants/scholarships: **81%**, Work-study aid: **0%**
Average medical school debt for the class of 2008: **$138,252**

STUDENT BODY

Fall 2009 full-time enrollment: **645**
Men: **42%**, Women: **58%**, In-state: **82%**, Minorities: **36%**, American Indian: **0.0%**, Asian-American: **22.6%**, African-American: **11.2%**, Hispanic-American: **2.5%**, White: **55.8%**, International: **0.2%**, Unknown: **7.8%**

ACADEMIC PROGRAMS

The school's curriculum frequently give first-year students substantial contact with patients.

There are opportunities for first- or second-year students to work in community health clinics.

Program areas: AIDS, drug/alcohol abuse, family medicine, geriatrics, internal medicine, pediatrics, rural medicine, women's health

Joint degrees awarded: M.D./Ph.D., M.D./M.B.A., M.D./M.P.H., M.D./M.H.I., M.D./M.S., M.D./M.H.A.

Total National Institutes of Health (NIH) grants awarded to the medical school and affiliated hospitals: **N/A**

CURRICULUM
(TEXT PROVIDED BY MEDICAL SCHOOL):

The curriculum at the University of Maryland School of Medicine is designed to prepare individuals for academic success during medical school, and to help students develop skills and attitudes to be life-long learners throughout their careers in medicine. Laptops are required for study, lab exercises and exams. A curriculum description is available on a school-based Website.

FALL 2009 FACULTY PROFILE

Total teaching faculty: **1,207 (full-time)**, **224 (part-time)**
Of full-time faculty, those teaching in basic sciences: **19%**; in clinical programs: **81%**

Of part-time faculty, those teaching in basic sciences: **11%**; in clinical programs: **89%**
Full-time faculty/student ratio: **1.9**

SUPPORT SERVICES

The school offers students these services for dealing with stress: expanded-hour gym access, peer counseling, professional counseling, support groups.

RESIDENCY PROFILE

Most popular residency and specialty programs chosen by the 2008 and 2009 M.D. graduating classes: emergency medicine, family practice, internal medicine, radiology–diagnostic.

WHERE GRADS GO

39.4%

Proportion of 2007-2008 graduates who entered primary care specialties

33.3%

Proportion of 2008-2009 graduates who accepted in-state residencies

University of Massachusetts–Worcester

- 55 Lake Avenue N, Worcester, MA 01655
- Public
- Year Founded: 1970
- Tuition, 2009-2010: $15,738
- Enrollment 2009-2010 academic year: 469
- Website: http://www.umassmed.edu
- Specialty ranking: family medicine: 20

3.67 AVERAGE GPA, ENTERING CLASS FALL 2009

10.8 AVERAGE MCAT, ENTERING CLASS FALL 2009

22.2% ACCEPTANCE RATE, ENTERING CLASS FALL 2009

47 2011 U.S. NEWS MEDICAL SCHOOL RANKING (RESEARCH)

9 2011 U.S. NEWS MEDICAL SCHOOL RANKING (PRIMARY CARE)

ADMISSIONS

Admissions phone number: **(508) 856-2323**
Admissions email address: **admissions@umassmed.edu**
Application web site:
  http://www.aamc.org/students/amcas/start.htm
Acceptance rate: **22.2%**
In-state acceptance rate: **23.3%**
Out-of-state acceptance rate: **12.9%**
Minority acceptance rate: **N/A**
International acceptance rate: **N/A**

Fall 2009 applications and acceptees

Type	Applied	Interviewed	Accepted	Enrolled
Total:	865	512	192	125
In-state:	772	486	180	120
Out-of-state:	93	26	12	5

Profile of admitted students

Average undergraduate grade point average: **3.67**
MCAT averages (scale: 1-15; writing test: J-T):
Composite score: **10.8**
Verbal reasoning score: **10.3**, Physical sciences score: **10.8**,
  Biological score: **11.3**, Writing score: **Q**
Proportion with undergraduate majors in: Biological
  sciences: **35%**, Physical sciences: **31%**, Non-sciences:
  26%, Other health professions: **2%**, Mixed disciplines
  and other: **6%**
Percentage of students not coming directly from college
  after graduation: **74%**

Dates and details

The American Medical College Application Service
  (AMCAS) application is accepted.
School asks for a second, school-specific application as part
  of the admissions process.
Oldest MCAT considered for Fall 2011 entry: **2007**
Earliest application date for the 2011-2012 first-year class:
  06/01
Latest application date: **11/01**
Acceptance dates for regular application for the class
  entering in Fall 2011.

Earliest: **16-OCT-10**
Latest: **15-AUG-11**
Applicants have 2 weeks to respond to admissions offer.
The school does consider requests for deferred entrance.
Starting month for the class of 2011–2012: **August**
The school does have an Early Decision Plan (EDP).
A personal interview is required for admission.

Undergraduate coursework required

Medical school requires undergraduate work in these subjects: biology, biology/zoology, English, organic chemistry,
inorganic (general) chemistry, physics.

ADMISSIONS POLICY

(TEXT PROVIDED BY SCHOOL):

Factors include in-state residency with the exception of
Ph.D./M.D. Program; content and breadth of scholastic
preparation; service/avocation with people in a helping role;
diversity (prior educational/professional experience, social
or cultural background); communication/interpersonal
skills; professional attributes (altruism, compassion); commitment to primary care and service to Massachusetts.

FINANCIAL AID

Financial aid phone number: **(508) 856-2265**
Tuition, 2009-2010 academic year: **$15,738**
Room and board: **$12,554**
Percentage of students receiving financial aid in 2009-10:
  93%
Percentage of students receiving: Loans: **90%**,
  Grants/scholarships: **31%**, Work-study aid: **0%**
Average medical school debt for the class of 2008: **$117,332**

STUDENT BODY

Fall 2009 full-time enrollment: **469**
Men: **45%**, Women: **55%**, In-state: **98%**, Minorities: **22%**,
  American Indian: **0.0%**, Asian-American: **14.7%**,
  African-American: **4.9%**, Hispanic-American: **1.9%**,
  White: **78.5%**, International: **0.0%**, Unknown: **0.0%**

ACADEMIC PROGRAMS

The school's curriculum very frequently give first-year students substantial contact with patients.

There are opportunities for first- or second-year students to work in community health clinics.

Program areas: AIDS, drug/alcohol abuse, family medicine, geriatrics, internal medicine, pediatrics, rural medicine, women's health

Joint degrees awarded: M.D./Ph.D.

Total National Institutes of Health (NIH) grants awarded to the medical school and affiliated hospitals: **N/A**

CURRICULUM

(TEXT PROVIDED BY MEDICAL SCHOOL):

Reflecting our educational goal of "training physicians in the full range of medical disciplines with emphasis on practice in the primary care specialties, in the public sector, and in underserved areas of Massachusetts," our curriculum teaches "core" knowledge, skills, attitudes, and values as the foundation for training the "undifferentiated" physician.

FALL 2009 FACULTY PROFILE

Total teaching faculty: **1,068 (full-time), 203 (part-time)**

Of full-time faculty, those teaching in basic sciences: **22%**; in clinical programs: **78%**

Of part-time faculty, those teaching in basic sciences: **7%**; in clinical programs: **93%**

Full-time faculty/student ratio: **2.3**

SUPPORT SERVICES

The school offers students these services for dealing with stress: expanded-hour gym access, peer counseling, professional counseling, religious support, support groups.

RESIDENCY PROFILE

Most popular residency and specialty programs chosen by the 2008 and 2009 M.D. graduating classes: anesthesiology, emergency medicine, family practice, internal medicine, internal medicine–pediatrics, neurology, obstetrics and gynecology, pediatrics, radiology–diagnostic, surgery–general.

WHERE GRADS GO

54.9%

Proportion of 2007-2008 graduates who entered primary care specialties

55.8%

Proportion of 2008-2009 graduates who accepted in-state residencies

Univ. of Med. and Dent. of New Jersey
New Brunswick (Johnson)

■ 125 Paterson Street, New Brunswick, NJ 08903-0019
■ Public
■ Year Founded: 1961
■ Tuition, 2009-2010: In-state: $29,688; Out-of-State: $44,500
■ Enrollment 2009-2010 academic year: 700
■ Website: http://rwjms.umdnj.edu
■ Specialty ranking: N/A

3.64	AVERAGE GPA, ENTERING CLASS FALL 2009
10.4	AVERAGE MCAT, ENTERING CLASS FALL 2009
9.8%	ACCEPTANCE RATE, ENTERING CLASS FALL 2009
Unranked	2011 U.S. NEWS MEDICAL SCHOOL RANKING (RESEARCH)
Unranked	2011 U.S. NEWS MEDICAL SCHOOL RANKING (PRIMARY CARE)

ADMISSIONS

Admissions phone number: **(732) 235-4576**
Admissions email address: **rwjapadm@umdnj.edu**
Application web site: **http://www.aamc.org**
Acceptance rate: **9.8%**
In-state acceptance rate: **24.5%**
Out-of-state acceptance rate: **1.8%**
Minority acceptance rate: **9.0%**
International acceptance rate: **0.0%**

Fall 2009 applications and acceptees

Type	Applied	Interviewed	Accepted	Enrolled
Total:	3,341	500	328	163
In-state:	1,174	419	288	155
Out-of-state:	2,167	81	40	8

Profile of admitted students

Average undergraduate grade point average: **3.64**
MCAT averages (scale: 1-15; writing test: J-T):
Composite score: **10.4**
Verbal reasoning score: **9.9**, Physical sciences score: **10.5**,
  Biological score: **10.9**, Writing score: **P**
Proportion with undergraduate majors in: Biological
  sciences: **43%**, Physical sciences: **19%**, Non-sciences:
  23%, Other health professions: **3%**, Mixed disciplines
  and other: **12%**
Percentage of students not coming directly from college
  after graduation: **52%**

Dates and details

The American Medical College Application Service
  (AMCAS) application is accepted.
School does not ask for a second, school-specific
  application as part of the admissions process.
Oldest MCAT considered for Fall 2011 entry: **2008**
Earliest application date for the 2011-2012 first-year class:
  06/01
Latest application date: **12/15**
Acceptance dates for regular application for the class
  entering in Fall 2011.
Earliest: **15-OCT-10**

Latest: **05-AUG-11**
Applicants have 2 weeks to respond to admissions offer.
The school does consider requests for deferred entrance.
Starting month for the class of 2011-2012: **August**
The school does have an Early Decision Plan (EDP).
A personal interview is required for admission.

Undergraduate coursework required

Medical school requires undergraduate work in these subjects: biology/zoology, English, organic chemistry, inorganic
(general) chemistry, physics, mathematics.

ADMISSIONS POLICY
(TEXT PROVIDED BY SCHOOL):

  Preference given to NJ residents, out of state applicants
with outstanding credentials are encouraged to apply.
Selection criteria include academic achievement, MCAT
and non-academic factors: extracurriculars, motivation,
character, humanism, commitment to service, sensitivity to
diversity, and personal interviews. Interviews by invitation.

FINANCIAL AID

Financial aid phone number: **(732) 235-4689**
Tuition, 2009-2010 academic year: **In-state: $29,688; Out-
  of-State: $44,500**
Room and board: **$13,660**
Percentage of students receiving financial aid in 2009-10:
  82%
Percentage of students receiving: Loans: **81%**,
  Grants/scholarships: **23%**, Work-study aid: **5%**
Average medical school debt for the class of 2008: **$132,911**

STUDENT BODY

Fall 2009 full-time enrollment: **700**
Men: **45%**, Women: **55%**, In-state: **99%**, Minorities: **44%**,
  American Indian: **0.1%**, Asian-American: **30.7%**,
  African-American: **8.7%**, Hispanic-American: **4.0%**,
  White: **46.6%**, International: **0.0%**, Unknown: **9.9%**

ACADEMIC PROGRAMS

The school's curriculum frequently give first-year students substantial contact with patients.

There are opportunities for first- or second-year students to work in community health clinics.

Program areas: AIDS, drug/alcohol abuse, family medicine, geriatrics, internal medicine, pediatrics, rural medicine, women's health

Joint degrees awarded: M.D./Ph.D., M.D./M.B.A., M.D./M.P.H., M.D./J.D., M.D./M.S.

Total National Institutes of Health (NIH) grants awarded to the medical school and affiliated hospitals: **$44.8 million**

CURRICULUM

(TEXT PROVIDED BY MEDICAL SCHOOL):

The curriculum fosters graduates who provide ethical and culturally sensitive care; it encompasses 6 core competencies: Patient Care, Medical Knowledge, Practice-Based Learning and Improvement, Interpersonal and Communication Skills, Professionalism, and Systems-Based Practice. Clinical experiences are begun early and enhanced with standardized patients, individual observation and feedback.

FALL 2009 FACULTY PROFILE

Total teaching faculty: **949 (full-time), 200 (part-time)**

Of full-time faculty, those teaching in basic sciences: **7%**; in clinical programs: **93%**

Of part-time faculty, those teaching in basic sciences: **12%**; in clinical programs: **88%**

Full-time faculty/student ratio: **1.4**

SUPPORT SERVICES

The school offers students these services for dealing with stress: peer counseling, professional counseling, support groups.

RESIDENCY PROFILE

Most popular residency and specialty programs chosen by the 2008 and 2009 M.D. graduating classes: anesthesiology, emergency medicine, family practice, internal medicine, ophthalmology, orthopaedic surgery, pediatrics, psychiatry, radiology–diagnostic, surgery–general.

WHERE GRADS GO

42.3%

Proportion of 2007-2008 graduates who entered primary care specialties

27.4%

Proportion of 2008-2009 graduates who accepted in-state residencies

University of Miami
Miller

- 1600 N.W. 10th Avenue, Miami, FL 33136
- Private
- Year Founded: 1952
- Tuition, 2009-2010: $30,188
- Enrollment 2009-2010 academic year: 733
- Website: http://www.miami.edu/medical-admissions
- Specialty ranking: AIDS: 14

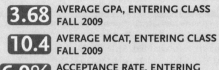

3.68 AVERAGE GPA, ENTERING CLASS FALL 2009

10.4 AVERAGE MCAT, ENTERING CLASS FALL 2009

6.9% ACCEPTANCE RATE, ENTERING CLASS FALL 2009

47 2011 U.S. NEWS MEDICAL SCHOOL RANKING (RESEARCH)

Unranked 2011 U.S. NEWS MEDICAL SCHOOL RANKING (PRIMARY CARE)

ADMISSIONS

Admissions phone number: **(305) 243-3234**
Admissions email address: **med.admissions@miami.edu**
Application web site: **N/A**
Acceptance rate: **6.9%**
In-state acceptance rate: **13.9%**
Out-of-state acceptance rate: **3.5%**
Minority acceptance rate: **7.5%**
International acceptance rate: **N/A**

Fall 2009 applications and acceptees

Type	Applied	Interviewed	Accepted	Enrolled
Total:	4,922	449	342	195
In-state:	1,640	283	228	144
Out-of-state:	3,282	166	114	51

Profile of admitted students

Average undergraduate grade point average: **3.68**
MCAT averages (scale: 1-15; writing test: J-T):
Composite score: **10.4**
Verbal reasoning score: **10.0**, Physical sciences score: **10.3**, Biological score: **10.8**, Writing score: **P**
Proportion with undergraduate majors in: Biological sciences: **41%**, Physical sciences: **8%**, Non-sciences: **5%**, Other health professions: **1%**, Mixed disciplines and other: **45%**
Percentage of students not coming directly from college after graduation: **12%**

Dates and details

The American Medical College Application Service (AMCAS) application is accepted.
School asks for a second, school-specific application as part of the admissions process.
Oldest MCAT considered for Fall 2011 entry: **2007**
Earliest application date for the 2011-2012 first-year class: **06/15**
Latest application date: **01/31**
Acceptance dates for regular application for the class entering in Fall 2011.
Earliest: **15-OCT-10**

Latest: **01-AUG-11**
Applicants have 4 weeks to respond to admissions offer.
The school does consider requests for deferred entrance.
Starting month for the class of 2011–2012: **August**
The school doesn't have an Early Decision Plan (EDP).
A personal interview is required for admission.

Undergraduate coursework required

Medical school requires undergraduate work in these subjects: biology/zoology, English, organic chemistry, inorganic (general) chemistry, physics.

ADMISSIONS POLICY
(TEXT PROVIDED BY SCHOOL):

The UM Miller School of Medicine participates in AMCAS and accepts applications only from U.S. citizens and permanent U.S. residents. Although Florida residents are given preference, since 2001 UM has been recruiting and enrolling non-Floridians in each first year class. For more information on the application process visit http://www.miami.edu/medical-admissions and click on M.D. Program.

FINANCIAL AID

Financial aid phone number: **(305) 243-6211**
Tuition, 2009-2010 academic year: **$30,188**
Room and board: **$24,655**
Percentage of students receiving financial aid in 2009-10: **77%**
Percentage of students receiving: Loans: **77%**, Grants/scholarships: **42%**, Work-study aid: **0%**
Average medical school debt for the class of 2008: **$155,420**

STUDENT BODY

Fall 2009 full-time enrollment: **733**
Men: **55%**, Women: **45%**, In-state: **69%**, Minorities: **41%**, American Indian: **0.3%**, Asian-American: **21.0%**, African-American: **7.2%**, Hispanic-American: **12.7%**, White: **51.3%**, International: **0.0%**, Unknown: **7.6%**

ACADEMIC PROGRAMS

The school's curriculum frequently give first-year students substantial contact with patients.

There are opportunities for first- or second-year students to work in community health clinics.

Program areas: AIDS, drug/alcohol abuse, family medicine, geriatrics, internal medicine, pediatrics, rural medicine, women's health

Joint degrees awarded: M.D./Ph.D., M.D./M.B.A., M.D./M.P.H.

Total National Institutes of Health (NIH) grants awarded to the medical school and affiliated hospitals: **$122.8 million**

CURRICULUM

(TEXT PROVIDED BY MEDICAL SCHOOL):

The curriculum at the University of Miami Miller School of Medicine is designed to develop broadly educated, responsible physicians equipped with the knowledge base, clinical skills, and professional attitudes to provide the very best in patient care. For more information on the curriculum, visit http://www.miami.edu/medical-admissions and click on M.D. Program.

FALL 2009 FACULTY PROFILE

Total teaching faculty: **1,428 (full-time), 29 (part-time)**
Of full-time faculty, those teaching in basic sciences: **9%**; in clinical programs: **91%**

Of part-time faculty, those teaching in basic sciences: **0%**; in clinical programs: **100%**
Full-time faculty/student ratio: **1.9**

SUPPORT SERVICES

The school offers students these services for dealing with stress: expanded-hour gym access, professional counseling.

RESIDENCY PROFILE

Most popular residency and specialty programs chosen by the 2008 and 2009 M.D. graduating classes: anesthesiology, dermatology, emergency medicine, family practice, internal medicine, obstetrics and gynecology, ophthalmology, pediatrics, radiology–diagnostic, surgery–general.

WHERE GRADS GO

37.7%

Proportion of 2007-2008 graduates who entered primary care specialties

37.4%

Proportion of 2008-2009 graduates who accepted in-state residencies

University of Michigan–Ann Arbor

- 1301 Catherine Road, Ann Arbor, MI 48109-0624
- Public
- **Year Founded:** 1848
- **Tuition, 2009-2010:** In-state: $27,473; Out-of-State: $43,827
- **Enrollment 2009-2010 academic year:** 670
- **Website:** http://www.med.umich.edu/medschool/
- **Specialty ranking:** AIDS: 23, drug/alcohol abuse: 15, family medicine: 4, geriatrics: 4, internal medicine: 7, pediatrics: 14, women's health: 10

3.75 AVERAGE GPA, ENTERING CLASS FALL 2009

11.8 AVERAGE MCAT, ENTERING CLASS FALL 2009

8.4% ACCEPTANCE RATE, ENTERING CLASS FALL 2009

6 2011 U.S. NEWS MEDICAL SCHOOL RANKING (RESEARCH)

14 2011 U.S. NEWS MEDICAL SCHOOL RANKING (PRIMARY CARE)

ADMISSIONS

Admissions phone number: **(734) 764-6317**
Admissions email address: **umichmedadmiss@umich.edu**
Application web site:
   http://www.aamc.org/students/amcas/start.htm
Acceptance rate: **8.4%**
In-state acceptance rate: **10.9%**
Out-of-state acceptance rate: **7.8%**
Minority acceptance rate: **N/A**
International acceptance rate: **N/A**

Fall 2009 applications and acceptees

Type	Applied	Interviewed	Accepted	Enrolled
Total:	5,134	695	430	170
In-state:	1,009	179	110	81
Out-of-state:	4,125	516	320	89

Profile of admitted students

Average undergraduate grade point average: **3.75**
MCAT averages (scale: 1-15; writing test: J-T):
Composite score: **11.8**
Verbal reasoning score: **11.0**, Physical sciences score: **11.9**, Biological score: **12.4**, Writing score: **Q**
Proportion with undergraduate majors in: Biological sciences: **38%**, Physical sciences: **26%**, Non-sciences: **8%**, Other health professions: **13%**, Mixed disciplines and other: **15%**
Percentage of students not coming directly from college after graduation: **26%**

Dates and details

The American Medical College Application Service (AMCAS) application is accepted.
School asks for a second, school-specific application as part of the admissions process.
Oldest MCAT considered for Fall 2011 entry: **2005**
Earliest application date for the 2011-2012 first-year class: **N/A**
Latest application date: **N/A**
Acceptance dates for regular application for the class entering in Fall 2011.
Earliest: **N/A**
Latest: **N/A**
Applicants have 28 weeks to respond to admissions offer. The school does consider requests for deferred entrance. Starting month for the class of 2011–2012: **August**
The school doesn't have an Early Decision Plan (EDP).
A personal interview is required for admission.

Undergraduate coursework required

Medical school requires undergraduate work in these subjects: biology, English, organic chemistry, inorganic (general) chemistry, physics, biochemistry, humanities.

ADMISSIONS POLICY

(TEXT PROVIDED BY SCHOOL):
   Each applicant will be considered in the pool of the entire group of applicants, and will be assessed on essential attributes and their unique potential to contribute to the educational experience at the Medical School and to the profession of medicine. For detailed information about our admissions process, please visit: www.med.umich.edu/medschool/admissions/process/

FINANCIAL AID

Financial aid phone number: **(734) 763-4147**
Tuition, 2009-2010 academic year: **In-state: $27,473**; Out-of-State: **$43,827**
Room and board: **$21,477**
Percentage of students receiving financial aid in 2009-10: **89%**
Percentage of students receiving: Loans: **81%**, Grants/scholarships: **65%**, Work-study aid: **0%**
Average medical school debt for the class of 2008: **$111,139**

STUDENT BODY

Fall 2009 full-time enrollment: **670**
Men: **48%**, Women: **52%**, In-state: **43%**, Minorities: **37%**, American Indian: **0.7%**, Asian-American: **25.1%**, African-American: **5.4%**, Hispanic-American: **5.4%**, White: **55.8%**, International: **0.0%**, Unknown: **7.6%**

ACADEMIC PROGRAMS

The school's curriculum frequently give first-year students substantial contact with patients.

There are opportunities for first- or second-year students to work in community health clinics.

Program areas: AIDS, drug/alcohol abuse, family medicine, geriatrics, internal medicine, pediatrics, rural medicine, women's health

Joint degrees awarded: M.D./Ph.D., M.D./M.B.A., M.D./M.P.H., M.D./J.D., M.D./M.S.W., M.D./M.S., M.D./M.A., M.D./M.H.A.

Total National Institutes of Health (NIH) grants awarded to the medical school and affiliated hospitals: **$443.4 million**

CURRICULUM

(TEXT PROVIDED BY MEDICAL SCHOOL):

At the University of Michigan Medical School, medical education begins and ends with patient care. While students will learn about cells, tissues, organ systems and disease through lectures, labs and textbooks, it all comes to life through patient interaction. For detailed information about our innovative curriculum, please visit: www.med.umich.edu/medschool/admissions/curriculum/

FALL 2009 FACULTY PROFILE

Total teaching faculty: **1,775 (full-time)**, **449 (part-time)**
Of full-time faculty, those teaching in basic sciences: **9%**; in clinical programs: **91%**

Of part-time faculty, those teaching in basic sciences: **10%**; in clinical programs: **90%**
Full-time faculty/student ratio: **2.6**

SUPPORT SERVICES

The school offers students these services for dealing with stress: expanded-hour gym access, peer counseling, professional counseling, support groups.

RESIDENCY PROFILE

Most popular residency and specialty programs chosen by the 2008 and 2009 M.D. graduating classes: anesthesiology, emergency medicine, internal medicine, obstetrics and gynecology, ophthalmology, otolaryngology, pediatrics, psychiatry, radiology–diagnostic, surgery–general.

WHERE GRADS GO

35.2%

Proportion of 2007-2008 graduates who entered primary care specialties

35.5%

Proportion of 2008-2009 graduates who accepted in-state residencies

University of Minnesota

- 420 Delaware Street SE, MMC 293, Minneapolis, MN 55455
- Public
- Year Founded: 1851
- Tuition, 2009-2010: In-state: $36,136; Out-of-State: $44,044
- Enrollment 2009-2010 academic year: 984
- Website: http://www.med.umn.edu
- Specialty ranking: family medicine: 11, rural medicine: 3

3.71 AVERAGE GPA, ENTERING CLASS FALL 2009

10.4 AVERAGE MCAT, ENTERING CLASS FALL 2009

8.7% ACCEPTANCE RATE, ENTERING CLASS FALL 2009

38 2011 U.S. NEWS MEDICAL SCHOOL RANKING (RESEARCH)

11 2011 U.S. NEWS MEDICAL SCHOOL RANKING (PRIMARY CARE)

ADMISSIONS

Admissions phone number: **(612) 625-7977**
Admissions email address: **meded@umn.edu**
Application web site: **N/A**
Acceptance rate: **8.7%**
In-state acceptance rate: **22.4%**
Out-of-state acceptance rate: **4.1%**
Minority acceptance rate: **6.7%**
International acceptance rate: **4.0%**

Fall 2009 applications and acceptees

Type	Applied	Interviewed	Accepted	Enrolled
Total:	4,611	582	402	229
In-state:	1,154	366	259	175
Out-of-state:	3,457	216	143	54

Profile of admitted students

Average undergraduate grade point average: **3.71**
MCAT averages (scale: 1-15; writing test: J-T):
Composite score: **10.4**
Verbal reasoning score: **10.0**, Physical sciences score: **10.3**, Biological score: **10.9**, Writing score: **P**
Proportion with undergraduate majors in: Biological sciences: **47%**, Physical sciences: **23%**, Non-sciences: **9%**, Other health professions: **1%**, Mixed disciplines and other: **20%**
Percentage of students not coming directly from college after graduation: **63%**

Dates and details

The American Medical College Application Service (AMCAS) application is accepted.
School asks for a second, school-specific application as part of the admissions process.
Oldest MCAT considered for Fall 2011 entry: **2007**
Earliest application date for the 2011-2012 first-year class: **06/01**
Latest application date: **11/15**
Acceptance dates for regular application for the class entering in Fall 2011.
Earliest: **15-OCT-10**

Latest: **15-MAY-11**
Applicants have 2 weeks to respond to admissions offer.
The school does consider requests for deferred entrance.
Starting month for the class of 2011–2012: **August**
The school does have an Early Decision Plan (EDP).
A personal interview is required for admission.

Undergraduate coursework required

Medical school requires undergraduate work in these subjects: biology, inorganic (general) chemistry, humanities, social sciences.

ADMISSIONS POLICY
(TEXT PROVIDED BY SCHOOL):

We welcome to our competency-based curriculum applicants who demonstrate essential qualities of a physician and experience in medicine. Our applicants may hold any bachelor's degree but must perform well on the MCAT. We offer several dual-degree programs on the Twin Cities campus, while the 2-year program at Duluth focuses on preparing students to serve rural and American Indian communities.

FINANCIAL AID

Financial aid phone number: **(612) 625-4998**
Tuition, 2009-2010 academic year: **In-state: $36,136; Out-of-State: $44,044**
Room and board: **$12,015**
Percentage of students receiving financial aid in 2009-10: **92%**
Percentage of students receiving: Loans: **83%**, Grants/scholarships: **73%**, Work-study aid: **1%**
Average medical school debt for the class of 2008: **$174,964**

STUDENT BODY

Fall 2009 full-time enrollment: **984**
Men: **51%**, Women: **49%**, In-state: **84%**, Minorities: **21%**, American Indian: **4.2%**, Asian-American: **9.5%**, African-American: **2.3%**, Hispanic-American: **3.5%**, White: **78.9%**, International: **1.7%**, Unknown: **N/A**

ACADEMIC PROGRAMS

The school's curriculum occasionally give first-year students substantial contact with patients.

There are opportunities for first- or second-year students to work in community health clinics.

Program areas: AIDS, drug/alcohol abuse, family medicine, geriatrics, internal medicine, pediatrics, rural medicine, women's health

Joint degrees awarded: M.D./Ph.D., M.D./M.B.A., M.D./M.P.H., M.D./M.H.I., M.D./J.D., M.D./M.S.

Total National Institutes of Health (NIH) grants awarded to the medical school and affiliated hospitals: **$153.8 million**

CURRICULUM

(TEXT PROVIDED BY MEDICAL SCHOOL):

In our new integrated curriculum (www.meded.umn.edu/admissions/curriculum.php), student progress is based on achieving and documenting competencies. The program emphasizes science, progressive development of clinical skills, critical thinking, independent learning time, and advisor-guided flexibility in structure and scheduling. Students may pursue a wide range of clinical/academic interests.

FALL 2009 FACULTY PROFILE

Total teaching faculty: **1,637 (full-time)**, **115 (part-time)**
Of full-time faculty, those teaching in basic sciences: **11%**; in clinical programs: **89%**

Of part-time faculty, those teaching in basic sciences: **9%**; in clinical programs: **91%**
Full-time faculty/student ratio: **1.7**

SUPPORT SERVICES

The school offers students these services for dealing with stress: peer counseling, professional counseling, support groups.

RESIDENCY PROFILE

Most popular residency and specialty programs chosen by the 2008 and 2009 M.D. graduating classes: anesthesiology, emergency medicine, family practice, internal medicine, obstetrics and gynecology, orthopaedic surgery, pediatrics, psychiatry, radiology–diagnostic, surgery–general.

WHERE GRADS GO

42.0%
Proportion of 2007-2008 graduates who entered primary care specialties

48.2%
Proportion of 2008-2009 graduates who accepted in-state residencies

University of Missouri

- ■ 1 Hospital Drive, Columbia, MO 65212
- ■ Public
- ■ Year Founded: 1872
- ■ Tuition, 2009-2010: In-state: $24,856; Out-of-State: $48,367
- ■ Enrollment 2009-2010 academic year: 387
- ■ Website: http://som.missouri.edu/
- ■ Specialty ranking: family medicine: 7

3.77 AVERAGE GPA, ENTERING CLASS FALL 2009

10.1 AVERAGE MCAT, ENTERING CLASS FALL 2009

11.2% ACCEPTANCE RATE, ENTERING CLASS FALL 2009

Unranked 2011 U.S. NEWS MEDICAL SCHOOL RANKING (RESEARCH)

33 2011 U.S. NEWS MEDICAL SCHOOL RANKING (PRIMARY CARE)

ADMISSIONS

Admissions phone number: **(573) 882-9219**
Admissions email address: **MizzouMed@missouri.edu**
Application web site:
http://som.missouri.edu/process.shtml
Acceptance rate: **11.2%**
In-state acceptance rate: **27.2%**
Out-of-state acceptance rate: **2.3%**
Minority acceptance rate: **6.1%**
International acceptance rate: **33.3%**

Fall 2009 applications and acceptees

Type	Applied	Interviewed	Accepted	Enrolled
Total:	1,281	292	144	95
In-state:	459	237	125	84
Out-of-state:	822	55	19	11

Profile of admitted students

Average undergraduate grade point average: **3.77**
MCAT averages (scale: 1-15; writing test: J-T):
Composite score: **10.1**
Verbal reasoning score: **9.9**, Physical sciences score: **9.8**, Biological score: **10.4**, Writing score: **P**
Proportion with undergraduate majors in: Biological sciences: **50%**, Physical sciences: **19%**, Non-sciences: **9%**, Other health professions: **2%**, Mixed disciplines and other: **20%**
Percentage of students not coming directly from college after graduation: **26%**

Dates and details

The American Medical College Application Service (AMCAS) application is accepted.
School asks for a second, school-specific application as part of the admissions process.
Oldest MCAT considered for Fall 2011 entry: **2007**
Earliest application date for the 2011-2012 first-year class: **06/01**
Latest application date: **11/01**
Acceptance dates for regular application for the class entering in Fall 2011.

Earliest: **30-NOV-10**
Latest: **15-JUL-11**
Applicants have 4 weeks to respond to admissions offer. The school does consider requests for deferred entrance. Starting month for the class of 2011–2012: **July**
The school does have an Early Decision Plan (EDP). A personal interview is required for admission.

Undergraduate coursework required

Medical school requires undergraduate work in these subjects: biology, English, organic chemistry, inorganic (general) chemistry, physics, mathematics, demonstration of writing skills, general chemistry.

ADMISSIONS POLICY
(TEXT PROVIDED BY SCHOOL):

Personal interviews are required. Strong preference is given to Missouri residents. Interview selection is based on academic performance; personal qualities, social concern and integrity; and tested motivation for medicine. Required coursework includes: English/writing intensive courses; general chemistry w/ lab; organic chemistry w/ lab; biology w/ lab; and physics w/ lab. The MCAT is required.

FINANCIAL AID

Financial aid phone number: **(573) 882-2923**
Tuition, 2009-2010 academic year: **In-state: $24,856; Out-of-State: $48,367**
Room and board: **$9,380**
Percentage of students receiving financial aid in 2009-10: **94%**
Percentage of students receiving: Loans: **88%**, Grants/scholarships: **70%**, Work-study aid: **0%**
Average medical school debt for the class of 2008: **$131,948**

STUDENT BODY

Fall 2009 full-time enrollment: **387**
Men: **50%**, Women: **50%**, In-state: **88%**, Minorities: **18%**, American Indian: **1.3%**, Asian-American: **11.1%**,

African-American: **4.4%**, Hispanic-American: **1.3%**, White: **77.3%**, International: **0.0%**, Unknown: **4.7%**

ACADEMIC PROGRAMS

The school's curriculum frequently give first-year students substantial contact with patients.

There are opportunities for first- or second-year students to work in community health clinics.

Program areas: AIDS, drug/alcohol abuse, family medicine, geriatrics, internal medicine, pediatrics, rural medicine, women's health

Joint degrees awarded: M.D./Ph.D., M.D./M.S.

Total National Institutes of Health (NIH) grants awarded to the medical school and affiliated hospitals: **$24.6 million**

CURRICULUM

(TEXT PROVIDED BY MEDICAL SCHOOL):

The MU School of Medicine is a leader in problem-based learning, a method of teaching that combines independent learning in small groups with early exposure to patient care. As part of an academic medical center, the school is devoted to improving patient care, education and research.

FALL 2009 FACULTY PROFILE

Total teaching faculty: **557 (full-time), 130 (part-time)**

Of full-time faculty, those teaching in basic sciences: **20%**; in clinical programs: **80%**

Of part-time faculty, those teaching in basic sciences: **14%**; in clinical programs: **86%**

Full-time faculty/student ratio: **1.4**

SUPPORT SERVICES

The school offers students these services for dealing with stress: expanded-hour gym access, peer counseling, professional counseling, religious support, support groups.

RESIDENCY PROFILE

Most popular residency and specialty programs chosen by the 2008 and 2009 M.D. graduating classes: anesthesiology, emergency medicine, family practice, internal medicine, obstetrics and gynecology, pathology–anatomic and clinical, pediatrics, radiology–diagnostic, surgery–general, internal medicine/pediatrics.

WHERE GRADS GO

46.3%

Proportion of 2007-2008 graduates who entered primary care specialties

43.6%

Proportion of 2008-2009 graduates who accepted in-state residencies

University of Nebraska Medical Center

- 985527 Nebraska Medical Center, Omaha, NE 68198-5527
- Public
- Year Founded: 1880
- Tuition, 2009-2010: In-state: $26,650; Out-of-State: $59,250
- Enrollment 2009-2010 academic year: 488
- Website: http://www.unmc.edu/com/admissions.htm
- Specialty ranking: rural medicine: 17

3.70	AVERAGE GPA, ENTERING CLASS FALL 2009
9.7	AVERAGE MCAT, ENTERING CLASS FALL 2009
11.8%	ACCEPTANCE RATE, ENTERING CLASS FALL 2009
Unranked	2011 U.S. NEWS MEDICAL SCHOOL RANKING (RESEARCH)
14	2011 U.S. NEWS MEDICAL SCHOOL RANKING (PRIMARY CARE)

ADMISSIONS

Admissions phone number: **(402) 559-2259**
Admissions email address: **grrogers@unmc.edu**
Application web site: **N/A**
Acceptance rate: **11.8%**
In-state acceptance rate: **42.7%**
Out-of-state acceptance rate: **3.6%**
Minority acceptance rate: **6.2%**
International acceptance rate: **0.0%**

Fall 2009 applications and acceptees

Type	Applied	Interviewed	Accepted	Enrolled
Total:	1,402	343	166	125
In-state:	295	206	126	109
Out-of-state:	1,107	137	40	16

Profile of admitted students

Average undergraduate grade point average: **3.70**
MCAT averages (scale: 1-15; writing test: J-T):
Composite score: **9.7**
Verbal reasoning score: **9.5**, Physical sciences score: **9.4**,
  Biological score: **10.2**, Writing score: **P**
Proportion with undergraduate majors in: Biological
  sciences: **40%**, Physical sciences: **34%**, Non-sciences:
  14%, Other health professions: **4%**, Mixed disciplines
  and other: **8%**
Percentage of students not coming directly from college
  after graduation: **49%**

Dates and details

The American Medical College Application Service
  (AMCAS) application is accepted.
School asks for a second, school-specific application as part
  of the admissions process.
Oldest MCAT considered for Fall 2011 entry: **2008**
Earliest application date for the 2011-2012 first-year class:
  06/01
Latest application date: **11/01**
Acceptance dates for regular application for the class
  entering in Fall 2011.
Earliest: **01-DEC-10**

Latest: **15-MAR-11**
Applicants have 2 weeks to respond to admissions offer.
The school doesn't consider requests for deferred entrance.
Starting month for the class of 2011–2012: **August**
The school does have an Early Decision Plan (EDP).
A personal interview is required for admission.

Undergraduate coursework required

Medical school requires undergraduate work in these subjects: biology, English, organic chemistry, inorganic (general) chemistry, physics, biochemistry, humanities,
demonstration of writing skills, calculus, general chemistry.

ADMISSIONS POLICY

(TEXT PROVIDED BY SCHOOL):
  Selection is based on a total assessment of each candidate's motivation, interest, character, demonstrated intellectual ability, previous academic record including its trends,
personal interviews, scores on the MCAT and general fitness and promise for a career in medicine. Although preference is given to residents of Nebraska, students from other
states are considered for admission.

FINANCIAL AID

Financial aid phone number: **(402) 559-4199**
Tuition, 2009-2010 academic year: **In-state: $26,650; Out-
of-State: $59,250**
Room and board: **$14,400**
Percentage of students receiving financial aid in 2009-10:
  99%
Percentage of students receiving: Loans: **91%**,
  Grants/scholarships: **62%**, Work-study aid: **0%**
Average medical school debt for the class of 2008:
  $128,337

STUDENT BODY

Fall 2009 full-time enrollment: **488**
Men: **58%**, Women: **42%**, In-state: **89%**, Minorities: **11%**,
  American Indian: **0.4%**, Asian-American: **4.9%**,
  African-American: **2.5%**, Hispanic-American: **0.4%**,
  White: **91.6%**, International: **0.2%**, Unknown: **0.0%**

ACADEMIC PROGRAMS

The school's curriculum frequently give first-year students substantial contact with patients.

There are opportunities for first- or second-year students to work in community health clinics.

Program areas: AIDS, drug/alcohol abuse, family medicine, geriatrics, internal medicine, pediatrics, rural medicine, women's health

Joint degrees awarded: M.D./Ph.D., M.D./M.P.H.

Total National Institutes of Health (NIH) grants awarded to the medical school and affiliated hospitals: **N/A**

CURRICULUM

(TEXT PROVIDED BY MEDICAL SCHOOL):

The College aims to provide a sound basis for support of career choices in medical practice, teaching, research or administration by stimulating students to obtain a background of basic information, a command of the language of biomedical science, a mastery of the skills necessary for clinical problem-solving, a habit of self-education and a sympathetic understanding of the behavior of people.

FALL 2009 FACULTY PROFILE

Total teaching faculty: **639 (full-time)**, **103 (part-time)**

Of full-time faculty, those teaching in basic sciences: **12%**; in clinical programs: **88%**

Of part-time faculty, those teaching in basic sciences: **6%**; in clinical programs: **94%**

Full-time faculty/student ratio: **1.3**

SUPPORT SERVICES

The school offers students these services for dealing with stress: expanded-hour gym access, professional counseling, religious support, support groups.

RESIDENCY PROFILE

Most popular residency and specialty programs chosen by the 2008 and 2009 M.D. graduating classes: anesthesiology, emergency medicine, family practice, internal medicine, obstetrics and gynecology, pediatrics, psychiatry, surgery–general.

WHERE GRADS GO

60.0%

Proportion of 2007-2008 graduates who entered primary care specialties

40.0%

Proportion of 2008-2009 graduates who accepted in-state residencies

University of Nevada–Reno

- Pennington Building, Mailstop 357, Reno, NV 89557-0357
- Public
- **Year Founded:** 1969
- **Tuition, 2009-2010:** In-state: $17,656; Out-of-State: $39,038
- **Enrollment 2009-2010 academic year:** 245
- **Website:** http://www.medicine.nevada.edu
- **Specialty ranking:** N/A

3.65	AVERAGE GPA, ENTERING CLASS FALL 2009
10.5	AVERAGE MCAT, ENTERING CLASS FALL 2009
30.1%	ACCEPTANCE RATE, ENTERING CLASS FALL 2009
Unranked	2011 U.S. NEWS MEDICAL SCHOOL RANKING (RESEARCH)
Unranked	2011 U.S. NEWS MEDICAL SCHOOL RANKING (PRIMARY CARE)

ADMISSIONS

Admissions phone number: **(775) 784-6063**
Admissions email address: **asa@med.unr.edu**
Application web site: **N/A**
Acceptance rate: **30.1%**
In-state acceptance rate: **39.1%**
Out-of-state acceptance rate: **19.2%**
Minority acceptance rate: **N/A**
International acceptance rate: **N/A**

Fall 2009 applications and acceptees

Type	Applied	Interviewed	Accepted	Enrolled
Total:	286	196	86	62
In-state:	156	156	61	54
Out-of-state:	130	40	25	8

Profile of admitted students

Average undergraduate grade point average: **3.65**
MCAT averages (scale: 1-15; writing test: J-T):
Composite score: **10.5**
Verbal reasoning score: **9.9**, Physical sciences score: **9.7**, Biological score: **10.4**, Writing score: **Q**
Proportion with undergraduate majors in: Biological sciences: **58%**, Physical sciences: **34%**, Non-sciences: **7%**, Other health professions: **N/A**, Mixed disciplines and other: **1%**
Percentage of students not coming directly from college after graduation: **10%**

Dates and details

The American Medical College Application Service (AMCAS) application is accepted.
School asks for a second, school-specific application as part of the admissions process.
Oldest MCAT considered for Fall 2011 entry: **N/A**
Earliest application date for the 2011-2012 first-year class: **N/A**
Latest application date: **N/A**
Acceptance dates for regular application for the class entering in Fall 2011.
Earliest: **15-JAN-11**

Latest: **15-APR-11**
Applicants have 2 weeks to respond to admissions offer.
The school does consider requests for deferred entrance.
Starting month for the class of 2011–2012: **August**
The school does have an Early Decision Plan (EDP).
A personal interview is required for admission.

Undergraduate coursework required

Medical school requires undergraduate work in these subjects: biology, organic chemistry, inorganic (general) chemistry, physics, behavioral science.

ADMISSIONS POLICY

(TEXT PROVIDED BY SCHOOL):

Evaluation is based on: academic performance; MCAT results; nature/depth of scholarly, extracurricular, health-care related activities; letters of evaluation; and personal interview. First priority is given to residents of Nevada; applicants from Alaska, Idaho, Montana and Wyoming are also considered. We are committed to the recruitment, selection, and retention of underrepresented minorities.

FINANCIAL AID

Financial aid phone number: **(775) 784-4666**
Tuition, 2009-2010 academic year: **In-state: $17,656; Out-of-State: $39,038**
Room and board: **$13,590**
Percentage of students receiving financial aid in 2009-10: **90%**
Percentage of students receiving: Loans: **90%**, Grants/scholarships: **80%**, Work-study aid: **0%**
Average medical school debt for the class of 2008: **$108,224**

STUDENT BODY

Fall 2009 full-time enrollment: **245**
Men: **51%**, Women: **49%**, In-state: **92%**, Minorities: **31%**, American Indian: **N/A**, Asian-American: **N/A**, African-American: **N/A**, Hispanic-American: **N/A**, White: **N/A**, International: **N/A**, Unknown: **N/A**

ACADEMIC PROGRAMS

The school's curriculum occasionally give first-year
students substantial contact with patients.

There are opportunities for first- or second-year students to
work in community health clinics.

Program areas: drug/alcohol abuse, family medicine,
geriatrics, internal medicine, pediatrics, rural medicine,
women's health

Joint degrees awarded: M.D./Ph.D., M.D./M.P.H.

Total National Institutes of Health (NIH) grants awarded
to the medical school and affiliated hospitals: **N/A**

CURRICULUM

(TEXT PROVIDED BY MEDICAL SCHOOL):

Curriculum blends traditional coursework with early clinical learning experiences. Patient Care intro. (2-year course)
exposes students to patient history taking, physical exam
and clinical diagnosis. Clinical Problem Solving (Years 1-2)
and Clinical Reasoning in Medicine (Year 3) extends this
process through patient case mgmt. 4-week Advanced
Clinical Experience in Rural Health Care is required.

FALL 2009 FACULTY PROFILE

Total teaching faculty: **242 (full-time)**, **67 (part-time)**

Of full-time faculty, those teaching in basic sciences: **36%**;
in clinical programs: **64%**

Of part-time faculty, those teaching in basic sciences: **10%**;
in clinical programs: **90%**

Full-time faculty/student ratio: **1.0**

SUPPORT SERVICES

The school offers students these services for dealing with
stress: peer counseling, professional counseling, support
groups.

RESIDENCY PROFILE

Most popular residency and specialty programs chosen by
the 2008 and 2009 M.D. graduating classes: anesthesiology, emergency medicine, family practice, internal medicine, surgery–general.

WHERE GRADS GO

19.3%

*Proportion of 2007-2008 graduates who entered primary
care specialties*

9.0%

*Proportion of 2008-2009 graduates who accepted in-state
residencies*

University of New Mexico

- Basic Medical Sciences Building, Room 107, Albuquerque, NM 87131
- Public
- Year Founded: 1964
- Tuition, 2009-2010: In-state: $18,365; Out-of-State: $47,105
- Enrollment 2009-2010 academic year: 323
- Website: http://hsc.unm.edu/som/
- Specialty ranking: family medicine: 10, rural medicine: 2

3.57 AVERAGE GPA, ENTERING CLASS FALL 2009

9.4 AVERAGE MCAT, ENTERING CLASS FALL 2009

16.2% ACCEPTANCE RATE, ENTERING CLASS FALL 2009

Unranked 2011 U.S. NEWS MEDICAL SCHOOL RANKING (RESEARCH)

33 2011 U.S. NEWS MEDICAL SCHOOL RANKING (PRIMARY CARE)

ADMISSIONS

Admissions phone number: (505) 272-4766
Admissions email address:
somadmissions@salud.unm.edu
Application web site: **http://hsc.unm.edu/som/admissions**
Acceptance rate: **16.2%**
In-state acceptance rate: **43.5%**
Out-of-state acceptance rate: **2.0%**
Minority acceptance rate: **17.4%**
International acceptance rate: **N/A**

Fall 2009 applications and acceptees

Type	Applied	Interviewed	Accepted	Enrolled
Total:	604	206	98	77
In-state:	207	188	90	73
Out-of-state:	397	18	8	4

Profile of admitted students

Average undergraduate grade point average: **3.57**
MCAT averages (scale: 1-15; writing test: J-T):
Composite score: **9.4**
Verbal reasoning score: **9.3**, Physical sciences score: **8.8**, Biological score: **10.2**, Writing score: **N/A**
Proportion with undergraduate majors in: Biological sciences: **35%**, Physical sciences: **30%**, Non-sciences: **12%**, Other health professions: **5%**, Mixed disciplines and other: **18%**
Percentage of students not coming directly from college after graduation: **57%**

Dates and details

The American Medical College Application Service (AMCAS) application is accepted.
School asks for a second, school-specific application as part of the admissions process.
Oldest MCAT considered for Fall 2011 entry: **2005**
Earliest application date for the 2011-2012 first-year class: **06/01**
Latest application date: **11/15**
Acceptance dates for regular application for the class entering in Fall 2011.

Earliest: **15-MAR-11**
Latest: **N/A**
Applicants have 2 weeks to respond to admissions offer.
The school does consider requests for deferred entrance.
Starting month for the class of 2011–2012: **July**
The school does have an Early Decision Plan (EDP).
A personal interview is required for admission.

Undergraduate coursework required

Medical school requires undergraduate work in these subjects: biology, organic chemistry, inorganic (general) chemistry, physics, biochemistry, general chemistry.

ADMISSIONS POLICY
(TEXT PROVIDED BY SCHOOL):

Selection is based on academic achievement, motivation for medicine, problem-solving ability, self-appraisal, ability to relate to people, maturity, breadth of interests and achievement, professional goals, and likelihood of serving the health care needs of the State following postgraduate training. As a state-funded institution we primarily accept students from the State of New Mexico.

FINANCIAL AID

Financial aid phone number: (505) 272-8008
Tuition, 2009-2010 academic year: **In-state: $18,365; Out-of-State: $47,105**
Room and board: **$11,254**
Percentage of students receiving financial aid in 2009-10: **91%**
Percentage of students receiving: Loans: **86%**, Grants/scholarships: **66%**, Work-study aid: **0%**
Average medical school debt for the class of 2008: **$119,564**

STUDENT BODY

Fall 2009 full-time enrollment: **323**
Men: **44%**, Women: **56%**, In-state: **100%**, Minorities: **39%**, American Indian: **4.6%**, Asian-American: **5.0%**, African-American: **1.5%**, Hispanic-American: **27.6%**, White: **53.6%**, International: **0.0%**, Unknown: **7.7%**

ACADEMIC PROGRAMS

The school's curriculum very frequently give first-year students substantial contact with patients.

There are opportunities for first- or second-year students to work in community health clinics.

Program areas: AIDS, drug/alcohol abuse, family medicine, geriatrics, internal medicine, pediatrics, rural medicine, women's health

Joint degrees awarded: M.D./Ph.D., M.D./M.P.H.

Total National Institutes of Health (NIH) grants awarded to the medical school and affiliated hospitals: **$56.6 million**

CURRICULUM

(TEXT PROVIDED BY MEDICAL SCHOOL):

UNM includes PBL, TBL & community-based learning. Phase I includes PBL, TBL, lectures, labs, & clinical experiences. Phase II has experiences in FM, IM, Neuro, Ob-Gyn, Peds, Psychiatry, & Surgery. Phase III: One month is spent in a community site, a one-month ICU rotation, one-month sub-internship, one-month interdisciplinary ambulatory care rotation, and various electives chosen by the student.

FALL 2009 FACULTY PROFILE

Total teaching faculty: **748 (full-time)**, **183 (part-time)**

Of full-time faculty, those teaching in basic sciences: **9%**; in clinical programs: **91%**

Of part-time faculty, those teaching in basic sciences: **5%**; in clinical programs: **95%**

Full-time faculty/student ratio: **2.3**

SUPPORT SERVICES

The school offers students these services for dealing with stress: expanded-hour gym access, peer counseling, professional counseling, support groups.

RESIDENCY PROFILE

Most popular residency and specialty programs chosen by the 2008 and 2009 M.D. graduating classes: anesthesiology, emergency medicine, family practice, internal medicine, obstetrics and gynecology, pathology–anatomic and clinical, pediatrics, psychiatry, surgery–general.

WHERE GRADS GO

40.9%

Proportion of 2007-2008 graduates who entered primary care specialties

49.3%

Proportion of 2008-2009 graduates who accepted in-state residencies

University of North Carolina—Chapel Hill

- **CB #7000, 4030 Bondurant Hall, Chapel Hill, NC 27599-7000**
- **Public**
- **Year Founded:** 1879
- **Tuition, 2009-2010:** In-state: $13,360; Out-of-State: $37,426
- **Enrollment 2009-2010 academic year:** 734
- **Website:** http://www.med.unc.edu/admit/
- **Specialty ranking:** AIDS: 8, family medicine: 3, geriatrics: 14, internal medicine: 22, rural medicine: 7, women's health: 10

3.64	AVERAGE GPA, ENTERING CLASS FALL 2009
10.7	AVERAGE MCAT, ENTERING CLASS FALL 2009
5.1%	ACCEPTANCE RATE, ENTERING CLASS FALL 2009
20	2011 U.S. NEWS MEDICAL SCHOOL RANKING (RESEARCH)
2	2011 U.S. NEWS MEDICAL SCHOOL RANKING (PRIMARY CARE)

ADMISSIONS

Admissions phone number: **(919) 962-8331**
Admissions email address: **admissions@med.unc.edu**
Application web site: **N/A**
Acceptance rate: **5.1%**
In-state acceptance rate: **17.8%**
Out-of-state acceptance rate: **1.5%**
Minority acceptance rate: **4.4%**
International acceptance rate: **5.1%**

Fall 2009 applications and acceptees

Type	Applied	Interviewed	Accepted	Enrolled
Total:	4,116	639	211	160
In-state:	914	517	163	139
Out-of-state:	3,202	122	48	21

Profile of admitted students

Average undergraduate grade point average: **3.64**
MCAT averages (scale: 1-15; writing test: J-T):
Composite score: **10.7**
Verbal reasoning score: **10.4**, Physical sciences score: **10.7**, Biological score: **11.0**, Writing score: **P**
Proportion with undergraduate majors in: Biological sciences: **47%**, Physical sciences: **18%**, Non-sciences: **10%**, Other health professions: **4%**, Mixed disciplines and other: **21%**
Percentage of students not coming directly from college after graduation: **56%**

Dates and details

The American Medical College Application Service (AMCAS) application is accepted.
School asks for a second, school-specific application as part of the admissions process.
Oldest MCAT considered for Fall 2011 entry: **2006**
Earliest application date for the 2011-2012 first-year class: **06/01**
Latest application date: **11/15**
Acceptance dates for regular application for the class entering in Fall 2011.
Earliest: **15-OCT-10**

Latest: **08-AUG-11**
Applicants have 3 weeks to respond to admissions offer.
The school does consider requests for deferred entrance.
Starting month for the class of 2011–2012: **August**
The school doesn't have an Early Decision Plan (EDP).
A personal interview is required for admission.

Undergraduate coursework required

Medical school requires undergraduate work in these subjects: biology, English, organic chemistry, inorganic (general) chemistry, physics, general chemistry.

ADMISSIONS POLICY

(TEXT PROVIDED BY SCHOOL):

The Committee on Admissions evaluates the qualifications of applicants to select those with the greatest potential in the medical field. Preference is given to North Carolina residents. Consideration is given to each candidate's motivation, maturity, leadership, integrity, and personal accomplishments, in addition to the scholastic record.
Reapplications are compared to those previously submitted.

FINANCIAL AID

Financial aid phone number: **(919) 962-6117**
Tuition, 2009-2010 academic year: **In-state: $13,360; Out-of-State: $37,426**
Room and board: **$27,426**
Percentage of students receiving financial aid in 2009-10: **89%**
Percentage of students receiving: Loans: **79%**, Grants/scholarships: **80%**, Work-study aid: **0%**
Average medical school debt for the class of 2008: **$100,090**

STUDENT BODY

Fall 2009 full-time enrollment: **734**
Men: **49%**, Women: **51%**, In-state: **74%**, Minorities: **27%**, American Indian: **N/A**, Asian-American: **N/A**, African-American: **N/A**, Hispanic-American: **N/A**, White: **N/A**, International: **N/A**, Unknown: **N/A**

ACADEMIC PROGRAMS

The school's curriculum frequently give first-year students substantial contact with patients.

There are opportunities for first- or second-year students to work in community health clinics.

Program areas: AIDS, drug/alcohol abuse, family medicine, geriatrics, internal medicine, pediatrics, rural medicine, women's health

Joint degrees awarded: M.D./Ph.D.

Total National Institutes of Health (NIH) grants awarded to the medical school and affiliated hospitals: **$237.0 million**

CURRICULUM

(TEXT PROVIDED BY MEDICAL SCHOOL):

UNC School of Medicine is committed to graduating a diverse body of physicians dedicated to public service and leadership in research and patient care. A new curriculum provides an integrated, self-directed approach to learning, with opportunities to explore areas of professional interest, community service, and research. 97% of our senior graduates were matched in 2009.

FALL 2009 FACULTY PROFILE

Total teaching faculty: **1,379 (full-time)**, **155 (part-time)**
Of full-time faculty, those teaching in basic sciences: **18%**; in clinical programs: **82%**

Of part-time faculty, those teaching in basic sciences: **9%**; in clinical programs: **91%**
Full-time faculty/student ratio: **1.9**

SUPPORT SERVICES

The school offers students these services for dealing with stress: peer counseling, professional counseling, support groups.

RESIDENCY PROFILE

Most popular residency and specialty programs chosen by the 2008 and 2009 M.D. graduating classes: anesthesiology, emergency medicine, family practice, internal medicine, obstetrics and gynecology, pathology–anatomic and clinical, pediatrics, psychiatry, radiology–diagnostic, surgery–general.

WHERE GRADS GO

51.3%

Proportion of 2007-2008 graduates who entered primary care specialties

41.7%

Proportion of 2008-2009 graduates who accepted in-state residencies

University of North Dakota

- 501 N. Columbia Road, Stop 9037, Grand Forks, ND 58202-9037
- Public
- Year Founded: 1905
- Tuition, 2009-2010: In-state: $24,893; Out-of-State: $44,724
- Enrollment 2009-2010 academic year: 241
- Website: http://www.med.und.nodak.edu
- Specialty ranking: rural medicine: 5

3.71 AVERAGE GPA, ENTERING CLASS FALL 2009

9.1 AVERAGE MCAT, ENTERING CLASS FALL 2009

30.2% ACCEPTANCE RATE, ENTERING CLASS FALL 2009

Unranked 2011 U.S. NEWS MEDICAL SCHOOL RANKING (RESEARCH)

Unranked 2011 U.S. NEWS MEDICAL SCHOOL RANKING (PRIMARY CARE)

ADMISSIONS

Admissions phone number: **(701) 777-4221**
Admissions email address: **jdheit@medicine.nodak.edu**
Application web site:
   http://www.med.und.nodak.edu/admissions.html
Acceptance rate: **30.2%**
In-state acceptance rate: **46.0%**
Out-of-state acceptance rate: **17.5%**
Minority acceptance rate: **33.3%**
International acceptance rate: **N/A**

Fall 2009 applications and acceptees

Type	Applied	Interviewed	Accepted	Enrolled
Total:	308	151	93	66
In-state:	137	106	63	48
Out-of-state:	171	45	30	18

Profile of admitted students

Average undergraduate grade point average: **3.71**
MCAT averages (scale: 1-15; writing test: J-T):
Composite score: **9.1**
Verbal reasoning score: **9.1**, Physical sciences score: **8.7**,
   Biological score: **9.6**, Writing score: **N**
Proportion with undergraduate majors in: Biological
   sciences: **53%**, Physical sciences: **19%**, Non-sciences:
   18%, Other health professions: **1%**, Mixed disciplines
   and other: **10%**
Percentage of students not coming directly from college
   after graduation: **24%**

Dates and details

The American Medical College Application Service
   (AMCAS) application is not accepted.
School does not ask for a second, school-specific
   application as part of the admissions process.
Oldest MCAT considered for Fall 2011 entry: **2007**
Earliest application date for the 2011-2012 first-year class:
   01/07
Latest application date: **01/11**
Acceptance dates for regular application for the class
   entering in Fall 2011.

Earliest: **31-DEC-69**
Latest: **08-JAN-11**
Applicants have 4 weeks to respond to admissions offer.
The school does consider requests for deferred entrance.
Starting month for the class of 2011–2012: **August**
The school doesn't have an Early Decision Plan (EDP).
A personal interview is required for admission.

Undergraduate coursework required

Medical school requires undergraduate work in these subjects: biology/zoology, English, organic chemistry, inorganic (general) chemistry, physics, mathematics, behavioral science, general chemistry.

ADMISSIONS POLICY
(TEXT PROVIDED BY SCHOOL):

   North Dakota residents and applicants certified by WICHE receive preference. Residents of Minnesota and others with a ND connection also are considered. Enrolled members of federally recognized tribes, regardless of state of residency, may apply through the INMED Program. Applicants who have completed an undergraduate degree and are broadly educated in the sciences and humanities are preferred.

FINANCIAL AID

Financial aid phone number: **(701) 777-2849**
Tuition, 2009-2010 academic year: **In-state: $24,893; Out-of-State: $44,724**
Room and board: **$9,104**
Percentage of students receiving financial aid in 2009-10:
   97%
Percentage of students receiving: Loans: **90%**,
   Grants/scholarships: **59%**, Work-study aid: **0%**
Average medical school debt for the class of 2008:
   $138,054

STUDENT BODY

Fall 2009 full-time enrollment: **241**
Men: **47%**, Women: **53%**, In-state: **85%**, Minorities: **13%**,
   American Indian: **9.5%**, Asian-American: **2.9%**, African-

American: 0.0%, Hispanic-American: 0.8%, White: 86.7%, International: 0.0%, Unknown: 0.0%

ACADEMIC PROGRAMS

The school's curriculum frequently give first-year students substantial contact with patients.

There aren't opportunities for first- or second-year students to work in community health clinics.

Program areas: AIDS, drug/alcohol abuse, family medicine, geriatrics, internal medicine, pediatrics, rural medicine, women's health

Joint degrees awarded: M.D./Ph.D., M.D./M.P.H., M.D./M.S.

Total National Institutes of Health (NIH) grants awarded to the medical school and affiliated hospitals: **$5.6 million**

CURRICULUM

(TEXT PROVIDED BY MEDICAL SCHOOL):

UNDSMHS is a university-based, community-integrated medical education program. The curriculum for Years 01/02 is organized in eight ten-week blocks, using an inter-disciplinary case-based and organ systems approach. Years 03/04 consists of core clerkships, acting internships and electives. A limited number of students may complete 28 weeks of Year 03 in a rural community through the ROME Program.

FALL 2009 FACULTY PROFILE

Total teaching faculty: **142 (full-time)**, **1,315 (part-time)**

Of full-time faculty, those teaching in basic sciences: **63%**; in clinical programs: **37%**

Of part-time faculty, those teaching in basic sciences: **28%**; in clinical programs: **72%**

Full-time faculty/student ratio: **0.6**

SUPPORT SERVICES

The school offers students these services for dealing with stress: expanded-hour gym access, peer counseling, professional counseling, religious support, support groups.

RESIDENCY PROFILE

Most popular residency and specialty programs chosen by the 2008 and 2009 M.D. graduating classes: anesthesiology, emergency medicine, family practice, internal medicine, neurology, obstetrics and gynecology, pediatrics, psychiatry, radiology–diagnostic, surgery–general.

WHERE GRADS GO

41.7%

Proportion of 2007-2008 graduates who entered primary care specialties

23.3%

Proportion of 2008-2009 graduates who accepted in-state residencies

University of Oklahoma

- PO Box 26901, BMSB 357, Oklahoma City, OK 73190
- Public
- **Year Founded:** 1900
- **Tuition, 2009-2010:** In-state: $20,648; Out-of-State: $44,766
- **Enrollment 2009-2010 academic year:** 653
- **Website:** http://www.medicine.ouhsc.edu
- **Specialty ranking:** N/A

3.72 AVERAGE GPA, ENTERING CLASS FALL 2009

9.7 AVERAGE MCAT, ENTERING CLASS FALL 2009

13.5% ACCEPTANCE RATE, ENTERING CLASS FALL 2009

Unranked 2011 U.S. NEWS MEDICAL SCHOOL RANKING (RESEARCH)

Unranked 2011 U.S. NEWS MEDICAL SCHOOL RANKING (PRIMARY CARE)

ADMISSIONS

Admissions phone number: **(405) 271-2331**
Admissions email address: **adminmed@ouhsc.edu**
Application web site: **http://www.aamc.org**
Acceptance rate: **13.5%**
In-state acceptance rate: **49.3%**
Out-of-state acceptance rate: **3.0%**
Minority acceptance rate: **9.6%**
International acceptance rate: **N/A**

Fall 2009 applications and acceptees

Type	Applied	Interviewed	Accepted	Enrolled
Total:	1,567	285	211	162
In-state:	353	243	174	150
Out-of-state:	1,214	42	37	12

Profile of admitted students

Average undergraduate grade point average: **3.72**
MCAT averages (scale: 1-15; writing test: J-T):
Composite score: **9.7**
Verbal reasoning score: **9.9**, Physical sciences score: **9.3**, Biological score: **10.0**, Writing score: **Q**
Proportion with undergraduate majors in: Biological sciences: **44%**, Physical sciences: **32%**, Non-sciences: **11%**, Other health professions: **4%**, Mixed disciplines and other: **9%**
Percentage of students not coming directly from college after graduation: **36%**

Dates and details

The American Medical College Application Service (AMCAS) application is accepted.
School asks for a second, school-specific application as part of the admissions process.
Oldest MCAT considered for Fall 2011 entry: **2007**
Earliest application date for the 2011-2012 first-year class: **06/01**
Latest application date: **10/15**
Acceptance dates for regular application for the class entering in Fall 2011.
Earliest: **01-NOV-10**

Latest: **N/A**
Applicants have 2 weeks to respond to admissions offer.
The school does consider requests for deferred entrance.
Starting month for the class of 2011-2012: **August**
The school doesn't have an Early Decision Plan (EDP).
A personal interview is required for admission.

Undergraduate coursework required

Medical school requires undergraduate work in these subjects: biology/zoology, English, organic chemistry, inorganic (general) chemistry, physics, molecular and cell biology, humanities, social sciences.

ADMISSIONS POLICY
(TEXT PROVIDED BY SCHOOL):

Acceptance is based on GPA, MCAT, letters of evaluation, and personal interview. Emphasis is placed on self-awareness, self-discipline, empathy, personal competence, social competence, and over-all evaluation of character. Non-residents can occupy 15% of class. The University of Oklahoma College of Medicine does not discriminate on the basis of race, sex, creed, national origin, age, or handicap.

FINANCIAL AID

Financial aid phone number: **(405) 271-2118**
Tuition, 2009-2010 academic year: **In-state: $20,648; Out-of-State: $44,766**
Room and board: **N/A**
Percentage of students receiving financial aid in 2009-10: **89%**
Percentage of students receiving: Loans: **87%**, Grants/scholarships: **33%**, Work-study aid: **0%**
Average medical school debt for the class of 2008: **$137,543**

STUDENT BODY

Fall 2009 full-time enrollment: **653**
Men: **61%**, Women: **39%**, In-state: **92%**, Minorities: **20%**, American Indian: **6.1%**, Asian-American: **12.7%**, African-American: **0.9%**, Hispanic-American: **0.2%**, White: **59.3%**, International: **0.0%**, Unknown: **20.8%**

ACADEMIC PROGRAMS

The school's curriculum frequently give first-year students substantial contact with patients.

There are opportunities for first- or second-year students to work in community health clinics.

Program areas: family medicine, geriatrics, internal medicine, pediatrics, rural medicine, women's health

Joint degrees awarded: M.D./Ph.D., M.D./M.P.H., M.D./M.S., M.D./M.H.A.

Total National Institutes of Health (NIH) grants awarded to the medical school and affiliated hospitals: **N/A**

CURRICULUM

(TEXT PROVIDED BY MEDICAL SCHOOL):

The curriculum consists of 2 years of basic sciences and 2 in clinical sciences. The first 2 years are complemented by a Web-based curriculum. First year courses provide a strong basic science foundation, and second-year classes form a bridge leading into the clinical portion of the curriculum. The curriculum provides early exposure to patients. The clinical program provides training at two sites.

FALL 2009 FACULTY PROFILE

Total teaching faculty: **800 (full-time), 224 (part-time)**

Of full-time faculty, those teaching in basic sciences: **11%**; in clinical programs: **89%**

Of part-time faculty, those teaching in basic sciences: **2%**; in clinical programs: **98%**

Full-time faculty/student ratio: **1.2**

SUPPORT SERVICES

The school offers students these services for dealing with stress: expanded hour gym access, professional counseling, support groups.

RESIDENCY PROFILE

Most popular residency and specialty programs chosen by the 2008 and 2009 M.D. graduating classes: anesthesiology, emergency medicine, family practice, internal medicine, neurology, obstetrics and gynecology, pediatrics, psychiatry, radiology–diagnostic, surgery–general.

WHERE GRADS GO

38.5%

Proportion of 2007-2008 graduates who entered primary care specialties

39.8%

Proportion of 2008-2009 graduates who accepted in-state residencies

University of Pennsylvania

- 237 John Morgan Building, 3620 Hamilton Walk, Philadelphia, PA 19104-6055
- Private
- **Year Founded:** 1765
- **Tuition, 2009-2010:** $45,546
- **Enrollment 2009-2010 academic year:** 622
- **Website:** http://www.med.upenn.edu
- **Specialty ranking:** AIDS: 11, drug/alcohol abuse: 4, geriatrics: 12, internal medicine: 4, pediatrics: 2, women's health: 3

3.81 AVERAGE GPA, ENTERING CLASS FALL 2009

11.9 AVERAGE MCAT, ENTERING CLASS FALL 2009

4.8% ACCEPTANCE RATE, ENTERING CLASS FALL 2009

2 2011 U.S. NEWS MEDICAL SCHOOL RANKING (RESEARCH)

7 2011 U.S. NEWS MEDICAL SCHOOL RANKING (PRIMARY CARE)

ADMISSIONS

Admissions phone number: **(215) 898-8001**
Admissions email address: **admiss@mail.med.upenn.edu**
Application web site:
   http://www.med.upenn.edu/admiss/applications.html
Acceptance rate: **4.8%**
In-state acceptance rate: **9.5%**
Out-of-state acceptance rate: **4.2%**
Minority acceptance rate: **4.8%**
International acceptance rate: **1.3%**

Fall 2009 applications and acceptees

Type	Applied	Interviewed	Accepted	Enrolled
Total:	5,532	852	265	161
In-state:	566	120	54	38
Out-of-state:	4,966	732	211	123

Profile of admitted students

Average undergraduate grade point average: **3.81**
MCAT averages (scale: 1-15; writing test: J-T):
Composite score: **11.9**
Verbal reasoning score: **11.1**, Physical sciences score: **12.3**, Biological score: **12.4**, Writing score: **Q**
Proportion with undergraduate majors in: Biological sciences: **36%**, Physical sciences: **22%**, Non-sciences: **34%**, Other health professions: **0%**, Mixed disciplines and other: **8%**
Percentage of students not coming directly from college after graduation: **61%**

Dates and details

The American Medical College Application Service (AMCAS) application is accepted.
School asks for a second, school-specific application as part of the admissions process.
Oldest MCAT considered for Fall 2011 entry: **2007**
Earliest application date for the 2011-2012 first-year class: **06/01**
Latest application date: **10/15**
Acceptance dates for regular application for the class entering in Fall 2011.

Earliest: **01-MAR-11**
Latest: **01-AUG-11**
Applicants have 8 weeks to respond to admissions offer.
The school does consider requests for deferred entrance.
Starting month for the class of 2011-2012: **August**
The school does have an Early Decision Plan (EDP).
A personal interview is required for admission.

Undergraduate coursework required

Medical school requires undergraduate work in these subjects: biology, English, organic chemistry, physics, mathematics, general chemistry.

ADMISSIONS POLICY

(TEXT PROVIDED BY SCHOOL):
   Selection factors include academic excellence, out of class activities, & life experience. Community service, research, letters of recommendation & leadership are valued.
Personal qualities of maturity, integrity, ability to work with others, & humanitarian concerns are sought. Diversity is a part of the school mission. Further information can be obtained at the website: www.med.upenn.edu/admiss

FINANCIAL AID

Financial aid phone number: **(215) 573-3423**
Tuition, 2009-2010 academic year: **$45,546**
Room and board: **$18,410**
Percentage of students receiving financial aid in 2009-10: **85%**
Percentage of students receiving: Loans: **64%**, Grants/scholarships: **70%**, Work-study aid: **2%**
Average medical school debt for the class of 2008: **$121,389**

STUDENT BODY

Fall 2009 full-time enrollment: **622**
Men: **51%**, Women: **49%**, In-state: **38%**, Minorities: **32%**, American Indian: **0.6%**, Asian-American: **16.4%**, African-American: **7.6%**, Hispanic-American: **7.6%**, White: **59.0%**, International: **1.1%**, Unknown: **7.7%**

ACADEMIC PROGRAMS

The school's curriculum frequently give first-year students substantial contact with patients.

There are opportunities for first- or second-year students to work in community health clinics.

Program areas: AIDS, drug/alcohol abuse, family medicine, geriatrics, internal medicine, pediatrics, rural medicine, women's health

Joint degrees awarded: M.D./Ph.D., M.D./M.B.A., M.D./M.P.H., M.D./J.D., M.D./M.S.

Total National Institutes of Health (NIH) grants awarded to the medical school and affiliated hospitals: **$641.6 million**

CURRICULUM

(TEXT PROVIDED BY MEDICAL SCHOOL):

Curriculum 2000, www.med.upenn.edu/admiss/curriculum.html

Module 1 Core Principles, Aug, Yr1–Dec, Yr1

Module 2 Integrative Systems & Diseases, Jan, Yr1–Dec, Yr2

Module 3 Technology & Practice of Medicine, Aug, Yr1–Dec, Yr2

Module 4 Required clinical clerkships, Jan, Yr2–Dec, Yr3

Module 5 Electives & scholarly pursuit, Jan,Yr3–May, Yr4

Module 6 Professionalism & Humanism, Aug, Yr1–May, Yr4

FALL 2009 FACULTY PROFILE

Total teaching faculty: **2,398 (full-time)**, **1,012 (part-time)**

Of full-time faculty, those teaching in basic sciences: **9%**; in clinical programs: **91%**

Of part-time faculty, those teaching in basic sciences: **6%**; in clinical programs: **94%**

Full-time faculty/student ratio: **3.9**

SUPPORT SERVICES

The school offers students these services for dealing with stress: peer counseling, professional counseling, support groups.

RESIDENCY PROFILE

Most popular residency and specialty programs chosen by the 2008 and 2009 M.D. graduating classes: anesthesiology, dermatology, emergency medicine, internal medicine, ophthalmology, otolaryngology, pediatrics, psychiatry, radiology–diagnostic, surgery–general.

WHERE GRADS GO

42.0%

Proportion of 2007-2008 graduates who entered primary care specialties

38.0%

Proportion of 2008-2009 graduates who accepted in-state residencies

University of Pittsburgh

- 401 Scaife Hall, Pittsburgh, PA 15261
- Public
- Year Founded: 1886
- Tuition, 2009-2010: In-state: $37,486; Out-of-State: $41,506
- Enrollment 2009-2010 academic year: 569
- Website: http://www.medschool.pitt.edu
- Specialty ranking: drug/alcohol abuse: 8, geriatrics: 8, internal medicine: 14, pediatrics: 13, women's health: 4

3.74 AVERAGE GPA, ENTERING CLASS FALL 2009

11.7 AVERAGE MCAT, ENTERING CLASS FALL 2009

7.8% ACCEPTANCE RATE, ENTERING CLASS FALL 2009

14 2011 U.S. NEWS MEDICAL SCHOOL RANKING (RESEARCH)

12 2011 U.S. NEWS MEDICAL SCHOOL RANKING (PRIMARY CARE)

ADMISSIONS

Admissions phone number: (412) 648-9891
Admissions email address:
  admissions@medschool.pitt.edu
Application web site:
  https://admissions.medschool.pitt.edu
Acceptance rate: **7.8%**
In-state acceptance rate: **10.4%**
Out-of-state acceptance rate: **7.3%**
Minority acceptance rate: **8.3%**
International acceptance rate: **0.0%**

Fall 2009 applications and acceptees

Type	Applied	Interviewed	Accepted	Enrolled
Total:	5,202	975	404	148
In-state:	800	169	83	41
Out-of-state:	4,402	806	321	107

Profile of admitted students

Average undergraduate grade point average: **3.74**
MCAT averages (scale: 1-15; writing test: J-T):
Composite score: **11.7**
Verbal reasoning score: **10.8**, Physical sciences score: **12.0**,
  Biological score: **12.2**, Writing score: **P**
Proportion with undergraduate majors in: Biological
  sciences: **37%**, Physical sciences: **18%**, Non-sciences:
  11%, Other health professions: **3%**, Mixed disciplines
  and other: **31%**
Percentage of students not coming directly from college
  after graduation: **53%**

Dates and details

The American Medical College Application Service
  (AMCAS) application is accepted.
School asks for a second, school-specific application as part
  of the admissions process.
Oldest MCAT considered for Fall 2011 entry: **2007**
Earliest application date for the 2011-2012 first-year class:
  06/01
Latest application date: **11/01**

Acceptance dates for regular application for the class
  entering in Fall 2011.
Earliest: **15-NOV-10**
Latest: **08-AUG-11**
Applicants have 2 weeks to respond to admissions offer.
The school does consider requests for deferred entrance.
Starting month for the class of 2011–2012: **August**
The school doesn't have an Early Decision Plan (EDP).
A personal interview is required for admission.

Undergraduate coursework required

Medical school requires undergraduate work in these subjects: biology, English, organic chemistry, inorganic (general) chemistry, physics, general chemistry.

ADMISSIONS POLICY

(TEXT PROVIDED BY SCHOOL):
  All applicants are invited to complete a secondary application. We admit on a rolling basis. Our committee seeks to
admit diverse, intellectually talented, creative and compassionate students. Applicants should have medical exposure
and extracurricular activities. Applicants interview with students and faculty. These interviews are important in the
final decision.

FINANCIAL AID

Financial aid phone number: (412) 648-9891
Tuition, 2009-2010 academic year: **In-state: $37,486; Out-
of-State: $41,506**
Room and board: **$15,110**
Percentage of students receiving financial aid in 2009-10:
  92%
Percentage of students receiving: Loans: **81%**,
  Grants/scholarships: **66%**, Work-study aid: **0%**
Average medical school debt for the class of 2008:
  $141,018

STUDENT BODY

Fall 2009 full-time enrollment: **569**
Men: **55%**, Women: **45%**, In-state: **31%**, Minorities: **43%**,
  American Indian: **0.0%**, Asian-American: **27.4%**,

African-American: **8.6%**, Hispanic-American: **5.3%**,
White: **53.1%**, International: **0.0%**, Unknown: **5.6%**

ACADEMIC PROGRAMS

The school's curriculum frequently give first-year students
substantial contact with patients.

There are opportunities for first or second year students to
work in community health clinics.

Program areas: AIDS, drug/alcohol abuse, family
medicine, geriatrics, internal medicine, pediatrics, rural
medicine, women's health

Joint degrees awarded: M.D./Ph.D., M.D./M.P.H.,
M.D./M.S., M.D./M.A.

Total National Institutes of Health (NIH) grants awarded
to the medical school and affiliated hospitals: **$410.2
million**

CURRICULUM

(TEXT PROVIDED BY MEDICAL SCHOOL):

We seek to train tomorrow's physician-scientists, academic leaders, and finest practicing physicians. To accom-
plish these goals, the curriculum combines a strong
foundation in basic science with early introduction to
patients, small-group learning, and an emphasis on critical
thinking and problem solving. Each student participates in
a mentored scholarly project.

FALL 2009 FACULTY PROFILE

Total teaching faculty: **2,092 (full-time)**, **76 (part-time)**
Of full-time faculty, those teaching in basic sciences: **10%**;
in clinical programs: **90%**

Of part-time faculty, those teaching in basic sciences: **7%**;
in clinical programs: **93%**
Full-time faculty/student ratio: **3.7**

SUPPORT SERVICES

The school offers students these services for dealing with
stress: expanded hour gym access, peer counseling, professional counseling, support groups.

RESIDENCY PROFILE

Most popular residency and specialty programs chosen by
the 2008 and 2009 M.D. graduating classes: anesthesiology, emergency medicine, family practice, internal medicine, obstetrics and gynecology, orthopaedic surgery,
pediatrics, psychiatry, radiology–diagnostic.

WHERE GRADS GO

38.5%

*Proportion of 2007-2008 graduates who entered primary
care specialties*

35.2%

*Proportion of 2008-2009 graduates who accepted in-state
residencies*

University of Rochester

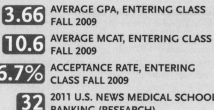

- 601 Elmwood Avenue, Box 706, Rochester, NY 14642
- Private
- **Year Founded:** 1925
- **Tuition, 2009-2010:** $43,410
- **Enrollment 2009-2010 academic year:** 440
- **Website:**
  http://www.urmc.rochester.edu/education/md/admissions
- **Specialty ranking:** family medicine: 22, internal medicine: 25

3.66	AVERAGE GPA, ENTERING CLASS FALL 2009
10.6	AVERAGE MCAT, ENTERING CLASS FALL 2009
6.7%	ACCEPTANCE RATE, ENTERING CLASS FALL 2009
32	2011 U.S. NEWS MEDICAL SCHOOL RANKING (RESEARCH)
20	2011 U.S. NEWS MEDICAL SCHOOL RANKING (PRIMARY CARE)

ADMISSIONS
Admissions phone number: **(585) 275-4542**
Admissions email address:
  mdadmish@urmc.rochester.edu
Application web site:
  https://admissions.urmc.rochester.edu/studentlogin.cfm
Acceptance rate: **6.7%**
In-state acceptance rate: **9.4%**
Out-of-state acceptance rate: **5.7%**
Minority acceptance rate: **5.3%**
International acceptance rate: **N/A**

Fall 2009 applications and acceptees

Type	Applied	Interviewed	Accepted	Enrolled
Total:	4,208	675	281	104
In-state:	1,099	242	103	50
Out-of-state:	3,109	433	178	54

Profile of admitted students
Average undergraduate grade point average: **3.66**
MCAT averages (scale: 1-15; writing test: J-T):
Composite score: **10.6**
Verbal reasoning score: **10.1**, Physical sciences score: **10.6**, Biological score: **11.1**, Writing score: **Q**
Proportion with undergraduate majors in: Biological sciences: **35%**, Physical sciences: **25%**, Non-sciences: **17%**, Other health professions: **0%**, Mixed disciplines and other: **23%**
Percentage of students not coming directly from college after graduation: **52%**

Dates and details
The American Medical College Application Service (AMCAS) application is accepted.
School asks for a second, school-specific application as part of the admissions process.
Oldest MCAT considered for Fall 2011 entry: **2007**
Earliest application date for the 2011-2012 first-year class: **05/01**
Latest application date: **10/15**

Acceptance dates for regular application for the class entering in Fall 2011.
Earliest: **16-OCT-10**
Latest: **09-AUG-11**
Applicants have 2 weeks to respond to admissions offer.
The school does consider requests for deferred entrance.
Starting month for the class of 2011–2012: **August**
The school doesn't have an Early Decision Plan (EDP).
A personal interview is required for admission.

Undergraduate coursework required
Medical school requires undergraduate work in these subjects: biology, biology/zoology, English, organic chemistry, inorganic (general) chemistry, physics, humanities, demonstration of writing skills, social sciences, general chemistry.

ADMISSIONS POLICY
(TEXT PROVIDED BY SCHOOL):
A strong academic record and good scores on the MCAT are a necessary but not sufficient criteria for admission. In addition, the Admissions Committee looks for evidence of scholarship, leadership, community service, integrity, maturity and excellent interpersonal skills. Rochester seeks students who value human diversity, exhibit a love of learning and appreciate the science and art of medicine.

FINANCIAL AID
Financial aid phone number: **(585) 275-4523**
Tuition, 2009-2010 academic year: **$43,410**
Room and board: **$16,000**
Percentage of students receiving financial aid in 2009-10: **89%**
Percentage of students receiving: Loans: **79%**, Grants/scholarships: **55%**, Work-study aid: **18%**
Average medical school debt for the class of 2008: **$142,554**

STUDENT BODY
Fall 2009 full-time enrollment: **440**
Men: **51%**, Women: **49%**, In-state: **48%**, Minorities: **35%**, American Indian: **0.5%**, Asian-American: **19.1%**,

African-American: **10.9%**, Hispanic-American: **4.3%**,
White: **65.2%**, International: **0.0%**, Unknown: **0.0%**

ACADEMIC PROGRAMS
The school's curriculum frequently give first-year students
   substantial contact with patients.
There are opportunities for first or second year students to
   work in community health clinics.
Program areas: AIDS, drug/alcohol abuse, family
   medicine, geriatrics, internal medicine, pediatrics, rural
   medicine, women's health
Joint degrees awarded: M.D./Ph.D., M.D./M.B.A.
Total National Institutes of Health (NIH) grants awarded
   to the medical school and affiliated hospitals: **$161.3
   million**

CURRICULUM
(TEXT PROVIDED BY MEDICAL SCHOOL):
   The SMD Double Helix Curriculum weaves together
basic science and clinical strands of medical education
through all four years, with enhanced teaching of the scientific principles of biomedical, clinical and translational
research, of information management and data analytic
skills, and of the psychosocial aspects of health and illness.

FALL 2009 FACULTY PROFILE
Total teaching faculty: **1,465 (full-time)**, **160 (part-time)**
Of full-time faculty, those teaching in basic sciences: **20%**;
   in clinical programs: **80%**

Of part-time faculty, those teaching in basic sciences: **10%**;
   in clinical programs: **90%**
Full-time faculty/student ratio: **3.3**

SUPPORT SERVICES
The school offers students these services for dealing with
stress: expanded hour gym access, peer counseling, professional counseling, religious support, support groups.

RESIDENCY PROFILE
Most popular residency and specialty programs chosen by
the 2008 and 2009 M.D. graduating classes: anesthesiology, emergency medicine, family practice, internal medicine, neurology–child neurology, pediatrics, psychiatry,
surgery–general.

WHERE GRADS GO

35.5%

*Proportion of 2007-2008 graduates who entered primary
care specialties*

27.7%

*Proportion of 2008-2009 graduates who accepted in-state
residencies*

University of South Carolina

- 6311 Garners Ferry Road, Columbia, SC 29208
- Public
- **Year Founded:** 1974
- **Tuition, 2009-2010:** In-state: $28,278; Out-of-State: $61,912
- **Enrollment 2009-2010 academic year:** 329
- **Website:** http://www.med.sc.edu
- **Specialty ranking:** N/A

3.68 AVERAGE GPA, ENTERING CLASS FALL 2009

9.4 AVERAGE MCAT, ENTERING CLASS FALL 2009

7.0% ACCEPTANCE RATE, ENTERING CLASS FALL 2009

Unranked 2011 U.S. NEWS MEDICAL SCHOOL RANKING (RESEARCH)

Unranked 2011 U.S. NEWS MEDICAL SCHOOL RANKING (PRIMARY CARE)

ADMISSIONS

Admissions phone number: **(803) 733-3325**
Admissions email address: **jeanette.ford@uscmed.sc.edu**
Application web site: **N/A**
Acceptance rate: **7.0%**
In-state acceptance rate: **26.5%**
Out-of-state acceptance rate: **1.8%**
Minority acceptance rate: **4.5%**
International acceptance rate: **N/A**

Fall 2009 applications and acceptees

Type	Applied	Interviewed	Accepted	Enrolled
Total:	2,119	349	148	79
In-state:	445	281	118	65
Out-of-state:	1,674	68	30	14

Profile of admitted students

Average undergraduate grade point average: **3.68**
MCAT averages (scale: 1-15; writing test: J-T):
Composite score: **9.4**
Verbal reasoning score: **9.6**, Physical sciences score: **8.9**,
  Biological score: **9.6**, Writing score: **O**
Proportion with undergraduate majors in: Biological
  sciences: **53%**, Physical sciences: **24%**, Non-sciences:
  14%, Other health professions: **6%**, Mixed disciplines
  and other: **3%**
Percentage of students not coming directly from college
  after graduation: **21%**

Dates and details

The American Medical College Application Service
  (AMCAS) application is accepted.
School asks for a second, school-specific application as part
  of the admissions process.
Oldest MCAT considered for Fall 2011 entry: **2005**
Earliest application date for the 2011-2012 first-year class:
  06/01
Latest application date: **12/01**
Acceptance dates for regular application for the class
  entering in Fall 2011.
Earliest: **15-OCT-10**

Latest: **02-AUG-10**
Applicants have 2 weeks to respond to admissions offer.
The school does consider requests for deferred entrance.
Starting month for the class of 2011–2012: **August**
The school does have an Early Decision Plan (EDP).
A personal interview is required for admission.

Undergraduate coursework required

Medical school requires undergraduate work in these subjects: biology, English, organic chemistry, inorganic (general) chemistry.

ADMISSIONS POLICY
(TEXT PROVIDED BY SCHOOL):

The Admissions Committee is composed of School of
Medicine basic science and clinical faculty, alumni, and
medical students. All aspects of an application are considered. The selection criteria include: academic perform-
ance/MCAT, personal essay, letters of recommendation,
work/volunteer experiences, and interviews/personal attributes. Preference is given to SC residents for admission.

FINANCIAL AID

Financial aid phone number: **(803) 733-3135**
Tuition, 2009-2010 academic year: **In-state: $28,278; Out-
of-State: $61,912**
Room and board: **$12,613**
Percentage of students receiving financial aid in 2009-10:
  95%
Percentage of students receiving: Loans: **88%**,
  Grants/scholarships: **40%**, Work-study aid: **0%**
Average medical school debt for the class of 2008:
  $125,232

STUDENT BODY

Fall 2009 full-time enrollment: **329**
Men: **53%**, Women: **47%**, In-state: **95%**, Minorities: **19%**,
  American Indian: **0.3%**, Asian-American: **11.9%**,
  African-American: **5.2%**, Hispanic-American: **1.2%**,
  White: **81.5%**, International: **0.0%**, Unknown: **0.0%**

ACADEMIC PROGRAMS

The school's curriculum occasionally give first-year
students substantial contact with patients.

There are opportunities for first- or second-year students to
work in community health clinics.

Program areas: family medicine, geriatrics, internal
medicine, pediatrics, rural medicine, women's health

Joint degrees awarded: M.D./Ph.D., M.D./M.P.H.

Total National Institutes of Health (NIH) grants awarded
to the medical school and affiliated hospitals: **$11.3
million**

CURRICULUM

(TEXT PROVIDED BY MEDICAL SCHOOL):

The 1st and 2nd year curriculum focuses on normal
structure and function as well as pathology and general
therapeutic principles. 3rd year includes 8 weeks in medicine, surgery, and pediatrics; 6 weeks in family medicine,
obstetrics/gynecology, and psychiatry; 2 weeks in neurology
and 4 weeks of electives. 4th year includes required 4-week
rotations in medicine, surgery, and an acting internship.

FALL 2009 FACULTY PROFILE

Total teaching faculty: **241 (full-time)**, **40 (part-time)**

Of full-time faculty, those teaching in basic sciences: **28%**;
in clinical programs: **72%**

Of part-time faculty, those teaching in basic sciences: **10%**;
in clinical programs: **90%**

Full-time faculty/student ratio: **0.7**

SUPPORT SERVICES

The school offers students these services for dealing with
stress: expanded-hour gym access, peer counseling, professional counseling.

RESIDENCY PROFILE

Most popular residency and specialty programs chosen by
the 2008 and 2009 M.D. graduating classes: anesthesiology, emergency medicine, family practice, internal medicine, obstetrics and gynecology, pathology–anatomic and
clinical, pediatrics, psychiatry, radiology–diagnostic, surgery–general.

WHERE GRADS GO

40.2%

*Proportion of 2007-2008 graduates who entered primary
care specialties*

39.2%

*Proportion of 2008-2009 graduates who accepted in-state
residencies*

University of South Dakota
Sanford

- 1400 W. 22nd Street, Sioux Falls, SD 57105
- Public
- **Year Founded:** 1907
- **Tuition, 2009-2010:** In-state: $21,099; Out-of-State: $43,274
- **Enrollment 2009-2010 academic year:** 214
- **Website:** http://www.usd.edu/med/md
- **Specialty ranking:** family medicine: 22, rural medicine: 10

3.62 AVERAGE GPA, ENTERING CLASS FALL 2009

9.8 AVERAGE MCAT, ENTERING CLASS FALL 2009

18.5% ACCEPTANCE RATE, ENTERING CLASS FALL 2009

Unranked 2011 U.S. NEWS MEDICAL SCHOOL RANKING (RESEARCH)

Unranked 2011 U.S. NEWS MEDICAL SCHOOL RANKING (PRIMARY CARE)

ADMISSIONS

Admissions phone number: **(605) 677-6886**
Admissions email address: **md@usd.edu**
Application web site: **http://www.usd.edu/medical-school/medical-doctor-program/application-procedures.cfm**
Acceptance rate: **18.5%**
In-state acceptance rate: **48.0%**
Out-of-state acceptance rate: **5.7%**
Minority acceptance rate: **7.7%**
International acceptance rate: **0.0%**

Fall 2009 applications and acceptees

Type	Applied	Interviewed	Accepted	Enrolled
Total:	405	153	75	54
In-state:	123	113	59	46
Out-of-state:	282	40	16	8

Profile of admitted students

Average undergraduate grade point average: **3.62**
MCAT averages (scale: 1-15; writing test: J-T):
Composite score: **9.8**
Verbal reasoning score: **9.4**, Physical sciences score: **9.7**, Biological score: **10.4**, Writing score: **O**
Proportion with undergraduate majors in: Biological sciences: **38%**, Physical sciences: **22%**, Non-sciences: **18%**, Other health professions: **0%**, Mixed disciplines and other: **22%**
Percentage of students not coming directly from college after graduation: **44%**

Dates and details

The American Medical College Application Service (AMCAS) application is accepted.
School asks for a second, school-specific application as part of the admissions process.
Oldest MCAT considered for Fall 2011 entry: **2008**
Earliest application date for the 2011-2012 first-year class: **06/01**
Latest application date: **11/15**

Acceptance dates for regular application for the class entering in Fall 2011.
Earliest: **15-NOV-10**
Latest: **31-MAR-11**
Applicants have 2 weeks to respond to admissions offer.
The school does consider requests for deferred entrance.
Starting month for the class of 2011-2012: **August**
The school doesn't have an Early Decision Plan (EDP).
A personal interview is required for admission.

Undergraduate coursework required

Medical school requires undergraduate work in these subjects: biology, organic chemistry, inorganic (general) chemistry, physics, mathematics.

ADMISSIONS POLICY
(TEXT PROVIDED BY SCHOOL):

All accepted applicants are either residents of SD or have very strong ties to the state. All SD resident applicants are granted an interview. Factors considered are academic strength, interest in primary care, interest in practice in SD, motivation, interpersonal skills, a record of service to others and/or leadership experiences, and a demonstrated beginning understanding of the career.

FINANCIAL AID

Financial aid phone number: **(605) 677-5112**
Tuition, 2009-2010 academic year: **In-state: $21,099; Out-of-State: $43,274**
Room and board: **$21,940**
Percentage of students receiving financial aid in 2009-10: **97%**
Percentage of students receiving: Loans: **90%**, Grants/scholarships: **88%**, Work-study aid: **0%**
Average medical school debt for the class of 2008: **$127,554**

STUDENT BODY

Fall 2009 full-time enrollment: **214**
Men: **54%**, Women: **46%**, In-state: **94%**, Minorities: **3%**, American Indian: **2.8%**, Asian-American: **2.8%**,

African-American: 0.5%, Hispanic-American: 0.5%, White: 93.0%, International: 0.0%, Unknown: 0.5%

ACADEMIC PROGRAMS

The school's curriculum occasionally give first-year students substantial contact with patients.

There are opportunities for first- or second-year students to work in community health clinics.

Program areas: drug/alcohol abuse, family medicine, geriatrics, internal medicine, pediatrics, rural medicine, women's health

Joint degrees awarded: M.D./Ph.D.

Total National Institutes of Health (NIH) grants awarded to the medical school and affiliated hospitals: **$11.2 million**

CURRICULUM

(TEXT PROVIDED BY MEDICAL SCHOOL):

First 2 years are a blended curriculum of traditional subjects and problem/case based learning. The third year on 2 campuses is in block form with 48 weeks in major rotations and 3 weeks of clinical colloquium. The third campus is based in a multi-specialty clinic with students taking all 6 major rotations all year. The fourth year has 16 required weeks, 22 elective weeks and 6 flex weeks.

FALL 2009 FACULTY PROFILE

Total teaching faculty: **301 (full-time)**, **774 (part-time)**
Of full-time faculty, those teaching in basic sciences: **12%**; in clinical programs: **88%**
Of part-time faculty, those teaching in basic sciences: **1%**; in clinical programs: **99%**
Full-time faculty/student ratio: **1.4**

SUPPORT SERVICES

The school offers students these services for dealing with stress: professional counseling.

RESIDENCY PROFILE

Most popular residency and specialty programs chosen by the 2008 and 2009 M.D. graduating classes: anesthesiology, emergency medicine, family practice, internal medicine, obstetrics and gynecology, pathology–anatomic and clinical, pediatrics, psychiatry, radiology–diagnostic, surgery–general.

WHERE GRADS GO

36.9%
Proportion of 2007-2008 graduates who entered primary care specialties

23.5%
Proportion of 2008-2009 graduates who accepted in-state residencies

University of Southern California
Keck

- 1975 Zonal Avenue, KAM 500, Los Angeles, CA 90033
- Private
- **Year Founded:** 1895
- **Tuition, 2009-2010:** $49,268
- **Enrollment 2009-2010 academic year:** 670
- **Website:** http://www.usc.edu/keck
- **Specialty ranking:** N/A

3.62	AVERAGE GPA, ENTERING CLASS FALL 2009
10.8	AVERAGE MCAT, ENTERING CLASS FALL 2009
5.5%	ACCEPTANCE RATE, ENTERING CLASS FALL 2009
34	2011 U.S. NEWS MEDICAL SCHOOL RANKING (RESEARCH)
Unranked	2011 U.S. NEWS MEDICAL SCHOOL RANKING (PRIMARY CARE)

ADMISSIONS

Admissions phone number: **(323) 442-2552**
Admissions email address: **medadmit@usc.edu**
Application web site: **http://www.usc.edu/keck**
Acceptance rate: **5.5%**
In-state acceptance rate: **6.7%**
Out-of-state acceptance rate: **4.2%**
Minority acceptance rate: **4.9%**
International acceptance rate: **1.4%**

Fall 2009 applications and acceptees

Type	Applied	Interviewed	Accepted	Enrolled
Total:	6,308	543	348	166
In-state:	3,401	349	227	117
Out-of-state:	2,907	194	121	49

Profile of admitted students

Average undergraduate grade point average: **3.62**
MCAT averages (scale: 1-15; writing test: J-T):
Composite score: **10.8**
Verbal reasoning score: **9.9**, Physical sciences score: **11.0**,
 Biological score: **11.5**, Writing score: **Q**
Proportion with undergraduate majors in: Biological
 sciences: **48%**, Physical sciences: **17%**, Non-sciences:
 17%, Other health professions: **1%**, Mixed disciplines
 and other: **17%**
Percentage of students not coming directly from college
 after graduation: **40%**

Dates and details

The American Medical College Application Service
 (AMCAS) application is accepted.
School asks for a second, school-specific application as part
 of the admissions process.
Oldest MCAT considered for Fall 2011 entry: **2008**
Earliest application date for the 2011-2012 first-year class:
 06/01
Latest application date: **11/01**
Acceptance dates for regular application for the class
 entering in Fall 2011.
Earliest: **01-NOV-10**

Latest: **01-AUG-11**
Applicants have 2 weeks to respond to admissions offer.
The school does consider requests for deferred entrance.
Starting month for the class of 2011–2012: **August**
The school does have an Early Decision Plan (EDP).
A personal interview is required for admission.

Undergraduate coursework required

Medical school requires undergraduate work in these subjects: biology, English, organic chemistry, inorganic (general) chemistry, physics, molecular and cell biology,
humanities, social sciences, general chemistry.

ADMISSIONS POLICY
(TEXT PROVIDED BY SCHOOL):

The Keck School of Medicine Admissions Committee
views the attributes of each applicant holistically, considering the following: Performance in college; GPA; MCAT;
personal characteristics such as communication skills, compassion, empathy, history of leadership, civic service and a
commitment to social justice; interest in teaching, research
or providing patient care to underserved populations.

FINANCIAL AID

Financial aid phone number: **(213) 740-5462**
Tuition, 2009-2010 academic year: **$49,268**
Room and board: **$15,842**
Percentage of students receiving financial aid in 2009-10:
 88%
Percentage of students receiving: Loans: **83%**,
 Grants/scholarships: **52%**, Work-study aid: **0%**
Average medical school debt for the class of 2008:
 $170,870

STUDENT BODY

Fall 2009 full-time enrollment: **670**
Men: **52%**, Women: **48%**, In-state: **73%**, Minorities: **41%**,
 American Indian: **0.6%**, Asian-American: **23.9%**,
 African-American: **4.0%**, Hispanic-American: **12.8%**,
 White: **47.2%**, International: **1.9%**, Unknown: **9.6%**

ACADEMIC PROGRAMS

The school's curriculum very frequently give first-year students substantial contact with patients.

There are opportunities for first- or second-year students to work in community health clinics.

Program areas: AIDS, drug/alcohol abuse, family medicine, geriatrics, internal medicine, pediatrics, rural medicine, women's health

Joint degrees awarded: M.D./Ph.D., M.D./M.B.A., M.D./M.P.H., M.D./M.S.

Total National Institutes of Health (NIH) grants awarded to the medical school and affiliated hospitals: **$177.5 million**

CURRICULUM

(TEXT PROVIDED BY MEDICAL SCHOOL):

Students experience unparalleled patient interactions throughout the four-year continuum and utilize the world-renowned Los Angeles County + USC Medical Center. The integrated curriculum incorporates the basic sciences in clinical case studies. Education is structured around organ systems and clerkships emphasizing small-group learning, professionalism, ethics and cultural competence.

FALL 2009 FACULTY PROFILE

Total teaching faculty: **1,232 (full-time), 111 (part-time)**
Of full-time faculty, those teaching in basic sciences: **13%**; in clinical programs: **87%**

Of part-time faculty, those teaching in basic sciences: **9%**; in clinical programs: **91%**
Full-time faculty/student ratio: **1.8**

SUPPORT SERVICES

The school offers students these services for dealing with stress: expanded hour gym access, peer counseling, professional counseling, religious support, support groups.

RESIDENCY PROFILE

Most popular residency and specialty programs chosen by the 2008 and 2009 M.D. graduating classes: anesthesiology, emergency medicine, family practice, internal medicine, orthopaedic surgery, pediatrics, psychiatry, radiology–diagnostic, surgery–general, transitional year.

WHERE GRADS GO

31.0%

Proportion of 2007-2008 graduates who entered primary care specialties

69.0%

Proportion of 2008-2009 graduates who accepted in-state residencies

University of South Florida

■ 12901 Bruce B. Downs Boulevard, MDC 2, Tampa, FL 33612
■ Public
■ Year Founded: 1965
■ Tuition, 2009-2010: In-state: $26,833; Out-of-State: $54,044
■ Enrollment 2009-2010 academic year: 482
■ Website: http://www.health.usf.edu/medicine/home.html
■ Specialty ranking: N/A

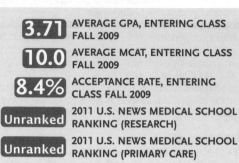

3.71 AVERAGE GPA, ENTERING CLASS FALL 2009

10.0 AVERAGE MCAT, ENTERING CLASS FALL 2009

8.4% ACCEPTANCE RATE, ENTERING CLASS FALL 2009

Unranked 2011 U.S. NEWS MEDICAL SCHOOL RANKING (RESEARCH)

Unranked 2011 U.S. NEWS MEDICAL SCHOOL RANKING (PRIMARY CARE)

ADMISSIONS
Admissions phone number: **(813) 974-2229**
Admissions email address: **md-admissions@health.usf.edu**
Application web site: **N/A**
Acceptance rate: **8.4%**
In-state acceptance rate: **12.0%**
Out-of-state acceptance rate: **2.6%**
Minority acceptance rate: **12.5%**
International acceptance rate: **N/A**

Fall 2009 applications and acceptees

Type	Applied	Interviewed	Accepted	Enrolled
Total:	2,991	400	252	120
In-state:	1,844	332	222	112
Out-of-state:	1,147	68	30	8

Profile of admitted students
Average undergraduate grade point average: **3.71**
MCAT averages (scale: 1-15; writing test: J-T):
Composite score: **10.0**
Verbal reasoning score: **10.0**, Physical sciences score: **10.0**,
  Biological score: **11.0**, Writing score: **P**
Proportion with undergraduate majors in: Biological
  sciences: **50%**, Physical sciences: **8%**, Non-sciences: **4%**,
  Other health professions: **3%**, Mixed disciplines and
  other: **35%**
Percentage of students not coming directly from college
  after graduation: **59%**

Dates and details
The American Medical College Application Service
  (AMCAS) application is accepted.
School asks for a second, school-specific application as part
  of the admissions process.
Oldest MCAT considered for Fall 2011 entry: **2007**
Earliest application date for the 2011-2012 first-year class:
  06/01
Latest application date: **12/01**
Acceptance dates for regular application for the class
  entering in Fall 2011.
Earliest: **15-OCT-10**

Latest: **09-AUG-11**
Applicants have 4 weeks to respond to admissions offer.
The school does consider requests for deferred entrance.
Starting month for the class of 2011–2012: **August**
The school does have an Early Decision Plan (EDP).
A personal interview is required for admission.

Undergraduate coursework required
Medical school requires undergraduate work in these subjects: biology, English, organic chemistry, inorganic (general) chemistry, physics, mathematics, general chemistry.

ADMISSIONS POLICY
(TEXT PROVIDED BY SCHOOL):
   Traditionally accepts Florida students only, but now able to take limited, superior, out-of-state applicants. Preference is given to individuals demonstrating outstanding scholarship, leadership skills, and exemplary humanism.

FINANCIAL AID
Financial aid phone number: **(813) 974-2068**
Tuition, 2009-2010 academic year: **In-state: $26,833; Out-of-State: $54,044**
Room and board: **$11,000**
Percentage of students receiving financial aid in 2009-10: **88%**
Percentage of students receiving: Loans: **85%**,
  Grants/scholarships: **40%**, Work-study aid: **0%**
Average medical school debt for the class of 2008: **$119,020**

STUDENT BODY
Fall 2009 full-time enrollment: **482**
Men: **49%**, Women: **51%**, In-state: **99%**, Minorities: **41%**,
  American Indian: **0.6%**, Asian-American: **24.5%**,
  African-American: **5.6%**, Hispanic-American: **10.2%**,
  White: **54.8%**, International: **0.0%**, Unknown: **4.4%**

ACADEMIC PROGRAMS
The school's curriculum very frequently give first-year students substantial contact with patients.

There are opportunities for first- or second-year students to work in community health clinics.

Program areas: AIDS, drug/alcohol abuse, family medicine, geriatrics, internal medicine, pediatrics, rural medicine, women's health

Joint degrees awarded: M.D./Ph.D., M.D./M.B.A., M.D./M.P.H., M.D./J.D.

Total National Institutes of Health (NIH) grants awarded to the medical school and affiliated hospitals: **$113.6 million**

CURRICULUM

(TEXT PROVIDED BY MEDICAL SCHOOL):

Highly integrated with clinical care, skills testing, and medical professionalism—use integrated courses at all levels.

FALL 2009 FACULTY PROFILE

Total teaching faculty: **954 (full-time), 33 (part-time)**

Of full-time faculty, those teaching in basic sciences: **10%**; in clinical programs: **90%**

Of part-time faculty, those teaching in basic sciences: **21%**; in clinical programs: **79%**

Full-time faculty/student ratio: **2.0**

SUPPORT SERVICES

The school offers students these services for dealing with stress: expanded-hour gym access, peer counseling, professional counseling, religious support, support groups.

RESIDENCY PROFILE

Most popular residency and specialty programs chosen by the 2008 and 2009 M.D. graduating classes: anesthesiology, emergency medicine, family practice, internal medicine, neurology, obstetrics and gynecology, pediatrics, psychiatry, radiology–diagnostic, surgery–general.

WHERE GRADS GO

36.0%

Proportion of 2007-2008 graduates who entered primary care specialties

48.5%

Proportion of 2008-2009 graduates who accepted in-state residencies

University of Tennessee
Health Science Center

- 910 Madison Avenue, Suite 1002, Memphis, TN 38163
- Public
- Year Founded: 1911
- Tuition, 2009-2010: In-state: $24,219; Out-of-State: $45,129
- Enrollment 2009-2010 academic year: 620
- Website: http://www.uthsc.edu/Medicine/
- Specialty ranking: N/A

3.63 AVERAGE GPA, ENTERING CLASS FALL 2009

10.0 AVERAGE MCAT, ENTERING CLASS FALL 2009

18.6% ACCEPTANCE RATE, ENTERING CLASS FALL 2009

Unranked 2011 U.S. NEWS MEDICAL SCHOOL RANKING (RESEARCH)

Unranked 2011 U.S. NEWS MEDICAL SCHOOL RANKING (PRIMARY CARE)

ADMISSIONS

Admissions phone number: **(901) 448-5559**
Admissions email address: **diharris@uthsc.edu**
Application web site:
   http://www.uthsc.edu/Medicine/Admissions/
Acceptance rate: **18.6%**
In-state acceptance rate: **35.3%**
Out-of-state acceptance rate: **4.5%**
Minority acceptance rate: **15.4%**
International acceptance rate: **0.0%**

Fall 2009 applications and acceptees

Type	Applied	Interviewed	Accepted	Enrolled
Total:	1,353	468	251	165
In-state:	617	414	218	157
Out-of-state:	736	54	33	8

Profile of admitted students

Average undergraduate grade point average: **3.63**
MCAT averages (scale: 1-15; writing test: J-T):
Composite score: **10.0**
Verbal reasoning score: **10.0**, Physical sciences score: **10.0**,
   Biological score: **10.0**, Writing score: **O**
Proportion with undergraduate majors in: Biological
   sciences: **41%**, Physical sciences: **24%**, Non-sciences:
   17%, Other health professions: **1%**, Mixed disciplines
   and other: **18%**
Percentage of students not coming directly from college
   after graduation: **59%**

Dates and details

The American Medical College Application Service
   (AMCAS) application is accepted.
School asks for a second, school-specific application as part
   of the admissions process.
Oldest MCAT considered for Fall 2011 entry: **2005**
Earliest application date for the 2011-2012 first-year class:
   06/01
Latest application date: **11/15**
Acceptance dates for regular application for the class
   entering in Fall 2011.

Earliest: **15-OCT-10**
Latest: **15-APR-11**
Applicants have 2 weeks to respond to admissions offer.
The school does consider requests for deferred entrance.
Starting month for the class of 2011–2012: **August**
The school doesn't have an Early Decision Plan (EDP).
A personal interview is required for admission.

Undergraduate coursework required

Medical school requires undergraduate work in these subjects: biology, English, organic chemistry, inorganic (general) chemistry, physics.

ADMISSIONS POLICY
(TEXT PROVIDED BY SCHOOL):

The criteria the Committee on Admissions uses in the
selection process are the academic record, MCAT scores,
preprofessional evaluations, and personal interviews. After
review of the AMCAS application, a supplemental application will be sent to applicants considered competitive for
further review. Both cognitive and non-cognitive aspects are
considered in applicant evaluation.

FINANCIAL AID

Financial aid phone number: **(901) 448-5568**
Tuition, 2009-2010 academic year: **In-state: $24,219; Out-
   of-State: $45,129**
Room and board: **$17,226**
Percentage of students receiving financial aid in 2009-10:
   89%
Percentage of students receiving: Loans: **84%**,
   Grants/scholarships: **45%**, Work-study aid: **0%**
Average medical school debt for the class of 2008:
   $110,041

STUDENT BODY

Fall 2009 full-time enrollment: **620**
Men: **60%**, Women: **40%**, In-state: **96%**, Minorities: **22%**,
   American Indian: **0.2%**, Asian-American: **10.0%**,
   African-American: **10.2%**, Hispanic-American: **1.8%**,
   White: **69.7%**, International: **0.0%**, Unknown: **8.2%**

ACADEMIC PROGRAMS

The school's curriculum occasionally give first-year students substantial contact with patients.

There are opportunities for first- or second-year students to work in community health clinics.

Program areas: family medicine, geriatrics, internal medicine, pediatrics, women's health

Joint degrees awarded: M.D./Ph.D., M.D./M.S.

Total National Institutes of Health (NIH) grants awarded to the medical school and affiliated hospitals: **N/A**

CURRICULUM

(TEXT PROVIDED BY MEDICAL SCHOOL):

The biomedical sciences are taught in an integrated way. Clinical exposure begins in the first semester. The third-year clerkships begin in early May featuring patient problem-solving and an increasing level of responsibility. The fourth year consists of six clerkships and four electives. Seniors are required to evaluate health care delivery focusing on patient safety and quality improvement.

FALL 2009 FACULTY PROFILE

Total teaching faculty: **745 (full-time)**, **142 (part-time)**

Of full-time faculty, those teaching in basic sciences: **17%**; in clinical programs: **83%**

Of part-time faculty, those teaching in basic sciences: **7%**; in clinical programs: **93%**

Full-time faculty/student ratio: **1.2**

SUPPORT SERVICES

The school offers students these services for dealing with stress: expanded-hour gym access, peer counseling, professional counseling, religious support, support groups.

RESIDENCY PROFILE

Most popular residency and specialty programs chosen by the 2008 and 2009 M.D. graduating classes: anesthesiology, emergency medicine, family practice, internal medicine, obstetrics and gynecology, orthopaedic surgery, pediatrics, radiology–diagnostic, surgery–general, urology.

WHERE GRADS GO

39.0%

Proportion of 2007-2008 graduates who entered primary care specialties

42.7%

Proportion of 2008-2009 graduates who accepted in-state residencies

University of Texas
Health Science Center–Houston

- 6431 Fannin Street, MSB G.420, Houston, TX 77030
- Public
- Year Founded: 1969
- Tuition, 2009-2010: In-state: $12,159; Out-of-State: $24,384
- Enrollment 2009-2010 academic year: 944
- Website: http://www.med.uth.tmc.edu
- Specialty ranking: N/A

3.70 AVERAGE GPA, ENTERING CLASS FALL 2009

10.5 AVERAGE MCAT, ENTERING CLASS FALL 2009

11.3% ACCEPTANCE RATE, ENTERING CLASS FALL 2009

52 2011 U.S. NEWS MEDICAL SCHOOL RANKING (RESEARCH)

Unranked 2011 U.S. NEWS MEDICAL SCHOOL RANKING (PRIMARY CARE)

ADMISSIONS

Admissions phone number: **(713) 500-5116**
Admissions email address: **msadmissions@uth.tmc.edu**
Application web site: **http://www.utsystem.edu/tmdsas**
Acceptance rate: **11.3%**
In-state acceptance rate: **12.4%**
Out-of-state acceptance rate: **6.1%**
Minority acceptance rate: **9.6%**
International acceptance rate: **2.3%**

Fall 2009 applications and acceptees

Type	Applied	Interviewed	Accepted	Enrolled
Total:	3,668	981	413	230
In-state:	3,014	894	373	211
Out-of-state:	654	87	40	19

Profile of admitted students

Average undergraduate grade point average: **3.70**
MCAT averages (scale: 1-15; writing test: J-T):
Composite score: **10.5**
Verbal reasoning score: **10.1**, Physical sciences score: **10.5**,
  Biological score: **11.0**, Writing score: **P**
Proportion with undergraduate majors in: Biological
  sciences: **50%**, Physical sciences: **15%**, Non-sciences:
  13%, Other health professions: **1%**, Mixed disciplines
  and other: **21%**
Percentage of students not coming directly from college
  after graduation: **25%**

Dates and details

The American Medical College Application Service
  (AMCAS) application is not accepted.
School does not ask for a second, school-specific
  application as part of the admissions process.
Oldest MCAT considered for Fall 2011 entry: **N/A**
Earliest application date for the 2011-2012 first-year class:
  N/A
Latest application date: **N/A**
Acceptance dates for regular application for the class
  entering in Fall 2011.
Earliest: **15-OCT-10**

Latest: **01-AUG-11**
Applicants have 2 weeks to respond to admissions offer.
The school doesn't consider requests for deferred entrance.
Starting month for the class of 2011–2012: **August**
The school doesn't have an Early Decision Plan (EDP).
A personal interview is required for admission.

Undergraduate coursework required

Medical school requires undergraduate work in these subjects: biology, English, organic chemistry, inorganic (general) chemistry, physics.

ADMISSIONS POLICY
(TEXT PROVIDED BY SCHOOL):

Applicants are selected with an emphasis on motivation
and potential for service, especially in the state of Texas.
Emphasis is given to students who have a broad education
and who display intellectual diversity. The applicant's academic record is evaluated with special attention to the subjects taken and the demonstration of a broadly based
comprehensive educational experience.

FINANCIAL AID

Financial aid phone number: **(713) 500-3860**
Tuition, 2009-2010 academic year: **In-state: $12,159; Out-
of-State: $24,384**
Room and board: **$15,070**
Percentage of students receiving financial aid in 2009-10:
  78%
Percentage of students receiving: Loans: **77%**,
  Grants/scholarships: **26%**, Work-study aid: **0%**
Average medical school debt for the class of 2008:
  $116,197

STUDENT BODY

Fall 2009 full-time enrollment: **944**
Men: **58%**, Women: **42%**, In-state: **95%**, Minorities: **32%**,
  American Indian: **0.3%**, Asian-American: **12.6%**,
  African-American: **5.0%**, Hispanic-American: **14.1%**,
  White: **64.1%**, International: **0.3%**, Unknown: **3.6%**

ACADEMIC PROGRAMS

The school's curriculum very frequently give first-year students substantial contact with patients.

There are opportunities for first- or second-year students to work in community health clinics.

Program areas: AIDS, drug/alcohol abuse, family medicine, geriatrics, internal medicine, pediatrics, rural medicine, women's health

Joint degrees awarded: M.D./Ph.D., M.D./M.P.H.

Total National Institutes of Health (NIH) grants awarded to the medical school and affiliated hospitals: **N/A**

CURRICULUM

(TEXT PROVIDED BY MEDICAL SCHOOL):

The first two academic years are divided into four semesters which are devoted to preparing the student for clerkship experiences in the clinical years. The student progresses through a series of clinical clerkships in the major disciplines for the next 12 months. In the remaining year, there are four months of required clerkships and five to seven months of electives.

FALL 2009 FACULTY PROFILE

Total teaching faculty: **878 (full-time), 94 (part-time)**
Of full-time faculty, those teaching in basic sciences: **13%**; in clinical programs: **87%**

Of part-time faculty, those teaching in basic sciences: **5%**; in clinical programs: **95%**
Full-time faculty/student ratio: **0.9**

SUPPORT SERVICES

The school offers students these services for dealing with stress: expanded-hour gym access, peer counseling, professional counseling, support groups.

RESIDENCY PROFILE

Most popular residency and specialty programs chosen by the 2008 and 2009 M.D. graduating classes: anesthesiology, emergency medicine, family practice, internal medicine, neurology, obstetrics and gynecology, pediatrics, radiology–diagnostic, surgery–general.

WHERE GRADS GO

30.0%

Proportion of 2007-2008 graduates who entered primary care specialties

58.0%

Proportion of 2008-2009 graduates who accepted in-state residencies

University of Texas
Health Science Center–San Antonio

- 7703 Floyd Curl Drive, San Antonio, TX 78229-3900
- Public
- **Year Founded:** 1968
- **Tuition, 2009-2010:** In-state: $15,170; Out-of-State: $28,270
- **Enrollment 2009-2010 academic year:** 900
- **Website:** http://som.uthscsa.edu
- **Specialty ranking:** N/A

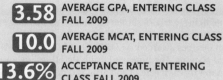

3.58 AVERAGE GPA, ENTERING CLASS FALL 2009

10.0 AVERAGE MCAT, ENTERING CLASS FALL 2009

13.6% ACCEPTANCE RATE, ENTERING CLASS FALL 2009

55 2011 U.S. NEWS MEDICAL SCHOOL RANKING (RESEARCH)

42 2011 U.S. NEWS MEDICAL SCHOOL RANKING (PRIMARY CARE)

ADMISSIONS

Admissions phone number: **(210) 567-6080**
Admissions email address: **msprospect@uthscsa.edu**
Application web site: **http://www.utsystem.edu/tmdsas**
Acceptance rate: **13.6%**
In-state acceptance rate: **15.1%**
Out-of-state acceptance rate: **6.7%**
Minority acceptance rate: **14.8%**
International acceptance rate: **0.0%**

Fall 2009 applications and acceptees

Type	Applied	Interviewed	Accepted	Enrolled
Total:	3,568	969	487	217
In-state:	2,969	864	447	203
Out-of-state:	599	105	40	14

Profile of admitted students

Average undergraduate grade point average: **3.58**
MCAT averages (scale: 1-15; writing test: J-T):
Composite score: **10.0**
Verbal reasoning score: **10.0**, Physical sciences score: **10.0**,
   Biological score: **11.0**, Writing score: **Q**
Proportion with undergraduate majors in: Biological
   sciences: **29%**, Physical sciences: **11%**, Non-sciences:
   14%, Other health professions: **0%**, Mixed disciplines
   and other: **47%**
Percentage of students not coming directly from college
   after graduation: **30%**

Dates and details

The American Medical College Application Service
   (AMCAS) application is not accepted.
School does not ask for a second, school-specific
   application as part of the admissions process.
Oldest MCAT considered for Fall 2011 entry: **2004**
Earliest application date for the 2011-2012 first-year class:
   05/01
Latest application date: **10/01**
Acceptance dates for regular application for the class
   entering in Fall 2011.
Earliest: **15-OCT-10**

Latest: **16-JUL-11**
Applicants have 2 weeks to respond to admissions offer.
The school does consider requests for deferred entrance.
Starting month for the class of 2011–2012: **July**
The school doesn't have an Early Decision Plan (EDP).
A personal interview is required for admission.

Undergraduate coursework required

Medical school requires undergraduate work in these subjects: biology, English, organic chemistry, inorganic (general) chemistry, physics, biochemistry, calculus.

ADMISSIONS POLICY
(TEXT PROVIDED BY SCHOOL):

   Applicants are evaluated on academic performance in
undergraduate school with special emphasis on the sciences
and personal achievements which prepare them to be a
physician. Knowledge of the profession of medicine gained
through observing or volunteering in a practice or hospital
is essential as is service for the underserved in the community. Up to 10% of the class may be non-residents.

FINANCIAL AID

Financial aid phone number: **(210) 567-2635**
Tuition, 2009-2010 academic year: **In-state: $15,170; Out-
   of-State: $28,270**
Room and board: **$16,463**
Percentage of students receiving financial aid in 2009-10:
   87%
Percentage of students receiving: Loans: **86%**,
   Grants/scholarships: **63%**, Work-study aid: **0%**
Average medical school debt for the class of 2008: **$118,321**

STUDENT BODY

Fall 2009 full-time enrollment: **900**
Men: **48%**, Women: **52%**, In-state: **92%**, Minorities: **40%**,
   American Indian: **0.4%**, Asian-American: **16.9%**,
   African-American: **5.1%**, Hispanic-American: **17.6%**,
   White: **55.2%**, International: **0.1%**, Unknown: **4.7%**

ACADEMIC PROGRAMS

The school's curriculum occasionally give first-year students substantial contact with patients.

There are opportunities for first- or second-year students to work in community health clinics.

Program areas: AIDS, drug/alcohol abuse, family medicine, geriatrics, internal medicine, pediatrics, rural medicine, women's health

Joint degrees awarded: M.D./Ph.D., M.D./M.P.H.

Total National Institutes of Health (NIH) grants awarded to the medical school and affiliated hospitals: **$99.3 million**

CURRICULUM

(TEXT PROVIDED BY MEDICAL SCHOOL):

The MS1/MS2 courses are coordinated in organ-system modules. Learning experiences in patient communication and physical exam skills begin with standardized patients in a state-of-the-art clinical skills center and continues with actual patients. MS3 consists of six different clerkships with choices of multiple clinical sites. MS4 is 24 weeks of electives/selectives and 5 weeks of capstone courses.

FALL 2009 FACULTY PROFILE

Total teaching faculty: 1,035 **(full-time)**, 133 **(part-time)**

Of full-time faculty, those teaching in basic sciences: **21%**; in clinical programs: **79%**

Of part-time faculty, those teaching in basic sciences: **31%**; in clinical programs: **69%**

Full-time faculty/student ratio: **1.2**

SUPPORT SERVICES

The school offers students these services for dealing with stress: expanded hour gym access, peer counseling, professional counseling, support groups.

RESIDENCY PROFILE

Most popular residency and specialty programs chosen by the 2008 and 2009 M.D. graduating classes: anesthesiology, emergency medicine, family practice, internal medicine, obstetrics and gynecology, orthopaedic surgery, pediatrics, psychiatry, radiology–diagnostic, surgery–general.

WHERE GRADS GO

47.0%

Proportion of 2007-2008 graduates who entered primary care specialties

46.0%

Proportion of 2008-2009 graduates who accepted in-state residencies

University of Texas
Medical Branch—Galveston

- **301 University Boulevard, Galveston, TX 77555-0133**
- **Public**
- **Year Founded:** 1891
- **Tuition, 2009-2010:** In-state: $14,270; Out-of-State: $27,370
- **Enrollment 2009-2010 academic year:** 920
- **Website:** http://www.utmb.edu/somstudentaffairs
- **Specialty ranking:** N/A

3.76 AVERAGE GPA, ENTERING CLASS FALL 2009

10.0 AVERAGE MCAT, ENTERING CLASS FALL 2009

18.5% ACCEPTANCE RATE, ENTERING CLASS FALL 2009

59 2011 U.S. NEWS MEDICAL SCHOOL RANKING (RESEARCH)

Unranked 2011 U.S. NEWS MEDICAL SCHOOL RANKING (PRIMARY CARE)

ADMISSIONS
Admissions phone number: **(409) 772-6958**
Admissions email address: **tsilva@utmb.edu**
Application web site: **https://www.utsystem.edu/tmdsas**
Acceptance rate: **18.5%**
In-state acceptance rate: **20.0%**
Out-of-state acceptance rate: **11.1%**
Minority acceptance rate: **33.3%**
International acceptance rate: **10.0%**

Fall 2009 applications and acceptees

Type	Applied	Interviewed	Accepted	Enrolled
Total:	3,587	929	663	229
In-state:	2,990	869	597	211
Out-of-state:	597	60	66	18

Profile of admitted students
Average undergraduate grade point average: **3.76**
MCAT averages (scale: 1-15; writing test: J-T):
Composite score: **10.0**
Verbal reasoning score: **9.2**, Physical sciences score: **9.4**, Biological score: **9.4**, Writing score: **P**
Proportion with undergraduate majors in: Biological sciences: **65%**, Physical sciences: **10%**, Non-sciences: **9%**, Other health professions: **1%**, Mixed disciplines and other: **15%**
Percentage of students not coming directly from college after graduation: **55%**

Dates and details
The American Medical College Application Service (AMCAS) application is not accepted.
School does not ask for a second, school-specific application as part of the admissions process.
Oldest MCAT considered for Fall 2011 entry: **2006**
Earliest application date for the 2011-2012 first-year class: **05/17**
Latest application date: **10/01**
Acceptance dates for regular application for the class entering in Fall 2011.
Earliest: **15-NOV-10**

Latest: **31-DEC-10**
Applicants have 2 weeks to respond to admissions offer.
The school does consider requests for deferred entrance.
Starting month for the class of 2011–2012: **August**
The school doesn't have an Early Decision Plan (EDP).
A personal interview is required for admission.

Undergraduate coursework required
Medical school requires undergraduate work in these subjects: biology, English, organic chemistry, inorganic (general) chemistry, physics, calculus, general chemistry.

ADMISSIONS POLICY
(TEXT PROVIDED BY SCHOOL):
  UTMB receives applications from the Texas Medical Dental Application Services where they are computer screened and then screened by the Admissions Committee. Each applicant is interviewed separately by faculty members with the evaluations placed in the file. Ranking is by a secret ballot. The names with the highest ranks are submitted for the matching.

FINANCIAL AID
Financial aid phone number: **(409) 772-4955**
Tuition, 2009-2010 academic year: **In-state: $14,270; Out-of-State: $27,370**
Room and board: **N/A**
Percentage of students receiving financial aid in 2009-10: **N/A**
Percentage of students receiving: Loans: **N/A**, Grants/scholarships: **N/A**, Work-study aid: **N/A**
Average medical school debt for the class of 2008: **$122,556**

STUDENT BODY
Fall 2009 full-time enrollment: **920**
Men: **54%**, Women: **46%**, In-state: **94%**, Minorities: **43%**, American Indian: **0.5%**, Asian-American: **15.9%**, African-American: **10.0%**, Hispanic-American: **16.6%**, White: **52.2%**, International: **0.8%**, Unknown: **4.0%**

ACADEMIC PROGRAMS

The school's curriculum very frequently give first-year students substantial contact with patients.

There are opportunities for first- or second-year students to work in community health clinics.

Program areas: AIDS, family medicine, geriatrics, internal medicine, pediatrics, rural medicine, women's health

Joint degrees awarded: M.D./Ph.D., M.D./M.B.A., M.D./M.P.H., M.D./M.S., M.D./M.H.A.

Total National Institutes of Health (NIH) grants awarded to the medical school and affiliated hospitals: **$117.5 million**

CURRICULUM

(TEXT PROVIDED BY MEDICAL SCHOOL):

The student-centered curriculum at UTMB emphasizes application of basic science to clinical problems, clinical decision making, lifelong learning, and professionalism. It features year 1 clinical experiences, a year 3 elective, and heavy use of standardized patients and simulators. Interested students can receive specialized experiences in global health, bilingual medicine, or aerospace medicine.

FALL 2009 FACULTY PROFILE

Total teaching faculty: **1,015 (full-time)**, **54 (part-time)**
Of full-time faculty, those teaching in basic sciences: 23%; in clinical programs: 77%

Of part-time faculty, those teaching in basic sciences: 9%; in clinical programs: 91%
Full-time faculty/student ratio: 1.1

SUPPORT SERVICES

The school offers students these services for dealing with stress: expanded hour gym access, professional counseling, religious support, support groups.

RESIDENCY PROFILE

Most popular residency and specialty programs chosen by the 2008 and 2009 M.D. graduating classes: anesthesiology, emergency medicine, family practice, internal medicine, obstetrics and gynecology, pathology–anatomic and clinical, pediatrics, psychiatry, radiology–diagnostic, surgery–general.

WHERE GRADS GO

37.8%
Proportion of 2007-2008 graduates who entered primary care specialties

53.5%
Proportion of 2008-2009 graduates who accepted in-state residencies

University of Texas
Southwestern Medical Center–Dallas

- 5323 Harry Hines Boulevard, Dallas, TX 75390
- Public
- **Year Founded:** 1943
- **Tuition, 2009-2010:** In-state: $14,640; Out-of-State: $27,740
- **Enrollment 2009-2010 academic year:** 896
- **Website:** http://www.utsouthwestern.edu/
- **Specialty ranking:** internal medicine: 15

 3.80 AVERAGE GPA, ENTERING CLASS FALL 2009

 11.2 AVERAGE MCAT, ENTERING CLASS FALL 2009

 12.3% ACCEPTANCE RATE, ENTERING CLASS FALL 2009

20 2011 U.S. NEWS MEDICAL SCHOOL RANKING (RESEARCH)

20 2011 U.S. NEWS MEDICAL SCHOOL RANKING (PRIMARY CARE)

ADMISSIONS
Admissions phone number: **(214) 648-5617**
Admissions email address:
admissions@utsouthwestern.edu
Application web site:
http://www.utsouthwestern.edu/medapp
Acceptance rate: **12.3%**
In-state acceptance rate: **12.1%**
Out-of-state acceptance rate: **13.3%**
Minority acceptance rate: **12.1%**
International acceptance rate: **4.9%**

Fall 2009 applications and acceptees

Type	Applied	Interviewed	Accepted	Enrolled
Total:	3,334	774	409	228
In-state:	2,762	689	333	193
Out-of-state:	572	85	76	35

Profile of admitted students
Average undergraduate grade point average: **3.80**
MCAT averages (scale: 1-15; writing test: J-T):
Composite score: **11.2**
Verbal reasoning score: **10.5**, Physical sciences score: **11.4**,
Biological score: **11.8**, Writing score: **Q**
Proportion with undergraduate majors in: Biological
sciences: **33%**, Physical sciences: **39%**, Non-sciences:
11%, Other health professions: **N/A**, Mixed disciplines
and other: **13%**
Percentage of students not coming directly from college
after graduation: **36%**

Dates and details
The American Medical College Application Service
(AMCAS) application is not accepted.
School asks for a second, school-specific application as part
of the admissions process.
Oldest MCAT considered for Fall 2011 entry: **2006**
Earliest application date for the 2011-2012 first-year class:
05/15
Latest application date: **10/01**

Acceptance dates for regular application for the class
entering in Fall 2011.
Earliest: **15-NOV-10**
Latest: **13-AUG-11**
Applicants have 3 weeks to respond to admissions offer.
The school does consider requests for deferred entrance.
Starting month for the class of 2011–2012: **August**
The school doesn't have an Early Decision Plan (EDP).
A personal interview is required for admission.

Undergraduate coursework required
Medical school requires undergraduate work in these subjects: biology, biology/zoology, English, organic chemistry,
inorganic (general) chemistry, physics, calculus.

ADMISSIONS POLICY
(TEXT PROVIDED BY SCHOOL):
Consideration is given to academic performance, curriculum, MCAT scores, recommendations, research, extracurricular activities, socioeconomic background, ethnicity,
personal integrity and compassion, English communication,
personal qualities, & motivation. Applicants evaluated with
regard to the school's mission. Personal interview required.
By state law ninety percent must be Texas residents.

FINANCIAL AID
Financial aid phone number: **(214) 648-3611**
Tuition, 2009-2010 academic year: **In-state: $14,640; Out-
of-State: $27,740**
Room and board: **$17,529**
Percentage of students receiving financial aid in 2009-10:
87%
Percentage of students receiving: Loans: **79%**,
Grants/scholarships: **66%**, Work-study aid: **4%**
Average medical school debt for the class of 2008:
$94,000

STUDENT BODY
Fall 2009 full-time enrollment: **896**
Men: **54%**, Women: **46%**, In-state: **88%**, Minorities: **53%**,
American Indian: **0.1%**, Asian-American: **32.7%**,

African-American: 5.5%, Hispanic-American: 14.1%,
White: 40.4%, International: 1.0%, Unknown: 6.3%

ACADEMIC PROGRAMS

The school's curriculum occasionally give first-year
students substantial contact with patients.

There are opportunities for first- or second-year students to
work in community health clinics.

Program areas: AIDS, drug/alcohol abuse, family
medicine, geriatrics, internal medicine, pediatrics, rural
medicine, women's health

Joint degrees awarded: M.D./Ph.D., M.D./M.P.H.,
M.D./M.S.

Total National Institutes of Health (NIH) grants awarded
to the medical school and affiliated hospitals: **$191.2
million**

CURRICULUM

(TEXT PROVIDED BY MEDICAL SCHOOL):

First year begins with a study of the human body and
processes at molecular and cellular levels. Second year
offers opportunity to begin study of disease processes and
therapeutics. Third and fourth years offer direct patient care
experiences. Core clerkships, acute and ambulatory rotations, and Sub-Internship required. Curriculum changes
with accreditation requirements.
http://medschool.swmed.edu

FALL 2009 FACULTY PROFILE

Total teaching faculty: **1,822 (full-time)**, **249 (part-time)**

Of full-time faculty, those teaching in basic sciences: **15%**;
in clinical programs: **85%**

Of part-time faculty, those teaching in basic sciences: **4%**;
in clinical programs: **96%**

Full-time faculty/student ratio: **2.0**

SUPPORT SERVICES

The school offers students these services for dealing with
stress: expanded-hour gym access, professional counseling,
support groups.

RESIDENCY PROFILE

Most popular residency and specialty programs chosen by
the 2008 and 2009 M.D. graduating classes: anesthesiology, emergency medicine, family practice, internal medicine, obstetrics and gynecology, pathology–anatomic and
clinical, pediatrics, radiology–diagnostic, surgery–general.

WHERE GRADS GO

41.0%

*Proportion of 2007-2008 graduates who entered primary
care specialties*

52.0%

*Proportion of 2008-2009 graduates who accepted in-state
residencies*

University of Toledo

- 3000 Arlington Avenue, Toledo, OH 43614
- Public
- Year Founded: 1969
- Tuition, 2009-2010: In-state: $27,428; Out-of-State: $56,234
- Enrollment 2009-2010 academic year: 666
- Website: http://hsc.utoledo.edu
- Specialty ranking: N/A

3.62	AVERAGE GPA, ENTERING CLASS FALL 2009
10.0	AVERAGE MCAT, ENTERING CLASS FALL 2009
8.9%	ACCEPTANCE RATE, ENTERING CLASS FALL 2009
Unranked	2011 U.S. NEWS MEDICAL SCHOOL RANKING (RESEARCH)
Unranked	2011 U.S. NEWS MEDICAL SCHOOL RANKING (PRIMARY CARE)

ADMISSIONS

Admissions phone number: **(419) 383-4229**
Admissions email address: **medadmissions@utoledo.edu**
Application web site:
http://www.utoledo.edu/med/md/admissions/secondary.html
Acceptance rate: **8.9%**
In-state acceptance rate: **21.9%**
Out-of-state acceptance rate: **4.2%**
Minority acceptance rate: **N/A**
International acceptance rate: **N/A**

Fall 2009 applications and acceptees

Type	Applied	Interviewed	Accepted	Enrolled
Total:	3,951	503	350	175
In-state:	1,047	279	229	117
Out-of-state:	2,904	224	121	58

Profile of admitted students

Average undergraduate grade point average: **3.62**
MCAT averages (scale: 1-15; writing test: J-T):
Composite score: **10.0**
Verbal reasoning score: **10.0**, Physical sciences score: **10.0**, Biological score: **10.0**, Writing score: **P**
Proportion with undergraduate majors in: Biological sciences: **61%**, Physical sciences: **14%**, Non-sciences: **15%**, Other health professions: **7%**, Mixed disciplines and other: **3%**
Percentage of students not coming directly from college after graduation: **35%**

Dates and details

The American Medical College Application Service (AMCAS) application is accepted.
School asks for a second, school-specific application as part of the admissions process.
Oldest MCAT considered for Fall 2011 entry: **2008**
Earliest application date for the 2011-2012 first-year class: **06/01**
Latest application date: **11/01**

Acceptance dates for regular application for the class entering in Fall 2011.
Earliest: **15-OCT-10**
Latest: **15-JUL-11**
Applicants have 2 weeks to respond to admissions offer.
The school does consider requests for deferred entrance.
Starting month for the class of 2011–2012: **August**
The school does have an Early Decision Plan (EDP).
A personal interview is required for admission.

Undergraduate coursework required

Medical school requires undergraduate work in these subjects: biology, English, organic chemistry, inorganic (general) chemistry, physics, mathematics.

ADMISSIONS POLICY
(TEXT PROVIDED BY SCHOOL):

Categories used to assess each candidate include: evaluation of communication and interpersonal skills, commitment to caring for others, community service and leadership, diversity and social awareness, and professionalism. Requirements include MCAT, bachelor's degree and a comprehensive command and understanding of English.

FINANCIAL AID

Financial aid phone number: **(419) 383-4232**
Tuition, 2009-2010 academic year: **In-state: $27,428; Out-of-State: $56,234**
Room and board: **N/A**
Percentage of students receiving financial aid in 2009-10: **87%**
Percentage of students receiving: Loans: **73%**, Grants/scholarships: **30%**, Work-study aid: **7%**
Average medical school debt for the class of 2008: **$141,250**

STUDENT BODY

Fall 2009 full-time enrollment: **666**
Men: **56%**, Women: **44%**, In-state: **90%**, Minorities: **27%**, American Indian: **0.5%**, Asian-American: **19.7%**,

African-American: **4.7%**, Hispanic-American: **2.0%**, White: **64.7%**, International: **0.2%**, Unknown: **8.4%**

ACADEMIC PROGRAMS
The school's curriculum rarely give first-year students substantial contact with patients.

There are opportunities for first or second year students to work in community health clinics.

Program areas: family medicine, geriatrics, internal medicine, pediatrics, rural medicine, women's health

Joint degrees awarded: M.D./Ph.D., M.D./M.B.A., M.D./M.P.H., M.D./M.S.

Total National Institutes of Health (NIH) grants awarded to the medical school and affiliated hospitals: **$11.3 million**

CURRICULUM
(TEXT PROVIDED BY MEDICAL SCHOOL):

The curriculum is composed of an integrated basic science/clinical science four-year approach to medical education with emphasis on clinically oriented objectives and problem-based learning. Years 3 & 4 include mandatory clerkships in internal medicine, pediatrics, surgery, obstetrics/gynecology, neurology psychiatry and family medicine.

FALL 2009 FACULTY PROFILE
Total teaching faculty: **287 (full-time)**, **45 (part-time)**
Of full-time faculty, those teaching in basic sciences: **25%**; in clinical programs: **75%**

Of part-time faculty, those teaching in basic sciences: **16%**; in clinical programs: **84%**
Full-time faculty/student ratio: **0.4**

SUPPORT SERVICES
The school offers students these services for dealing with stress: expanded hour gym access, peer counseling, professional counseling, support groups.

RESIDENCY PROFILE
Most popular residency and specialty programs chosen by the 2008 and 2009 M.D. graduating classes: anesthesiology, emergency medicine, family practice, internal medicine, obstetrics and gynecology, pathology–anatomic and clinical, pediatrics, psychiatry, radiology–diagnostic, surgery–general.

WHERE GRADS GO

37.2%
Proportion of 2007-2008 graduates who entered primary care specialties

33.2%
Proportion of 2008-2009 graduates who accepted in-state residencies

University of Utah

■ 30 N. 1900 E, Salt Lake City, UT 84132-2101
■ Public
■ Year Founded: 1941
■ Tuition, 2009-2010: In-state: $25,139; Out-of-State: $46,882
■ Enrollment 2009-2010 academic year: 396
■ Website: http://medicine.utah.edu
■ Specialty ranking: family medicine: 19, rural medicine: 17, women's health: 18

3.64 AVERAGE GPA, ENTERING CLASS FALL 2009

9.5 AVERAGE MCAT, ENTERING CLASS FALL 2009

9.1% ACCEPTANCE RATE, ENTERING CLASS FALL 2009

52 2011 U.S. NEWS MEDICAL SCHOOL RANKING (RESEARCH)

25 2011 U.S. NEWS MEDICAL SCHOOL RANKING (PRIMARY CARE)

ADMISSIONS

Admissions phone number: (801) 581-7498
Admissions email address:
   deans.admissions@hsc.utah.edu
Application web site: **http://medicine.utah.edu/admissions**
Acceptance rate: **9.1%**
In-state acceptance rate: **17.4%**
Out-of-state acceptance rate: **4.6%**
Minority acceptance rate: **7.8%**
International acceptance rate: **5.6%**

Fall 2009 applications and acceptees

Type	Applied	Interviewed	Accepted	Enrolled
Total:	1,241	517	113	82
In-state:	437	321	76	61
Out-of-state:	804	196	37	21

Profile of admitted students

Average undergraduate grade point average: **3.64**
MCAT averages (scale: 1-15; writing test: J-T):
Composite score: **9.5**
Verbal reasoning score: **9.2**, Physical sciences score: **9.2**, Biological score: **10.2**, Writing score: **N/A**
Proportion with undergraduate majors in: Biological sciences: **39%**, Physical sciences: **22%**, Non-sciences: **10%**, Other health professions: **13%**, Mixed disciplines and other: **16%**
Percentage of students not coming directly from college after graduation: **37%**

Dates and details

The American Medical College Application Service (AMCAS) application is accepted.
School asks for a second, school-specific application as part of the admissions process.
Oldest MCAT considered for Fall 2011 entry: **2008**
Earliest application date for the 2011-2012 first-year class: **06/01**
Latest application date: **11/01**
Acceptance dates for regular application for the class entering in Fall 2011.

Earliest: **15-OCT-10**
Latest: **N/A**
Applicants have 2 weeks to respond to admissions offer.
The school does consider requests for deferred entrance.
Starting month for the class of 2011–2012: **August**
The school doesn't have an Early Decision Plan (EDP).
A personal interview is required for admission.

Undergraduate coursework required

Medical school requires undergraduate work in these subjects: biology, organic chemistry, inorganic (general) chemistry, physics, molecular and cell biology, biochemistry, humanities, demonstration of writing skills, social sciences.

ADMISSIONS POLICY
(TEXT PROVIDED BY SCHOOL):

We select the most capable students to have a balanced but heterogeneous group that will excel in art and science of medicine. We recognize a diverse student body promotes an atmosphere of creativity, experimentation and discussion that is conducive to learning. Exposure to various perspectives and experiences prepares students to care for all patients.75% of positions are offered to Utah residents.

FINANCIAL AID

Financial aid phone number: (801) 581-6474
Tuition, 2009-2010 academic year: **In-state: $25,139; Out-of-State: $46,882**
Room and board: **$9,360**
Percentage of students receiving financial aid in 2009-10: **95%**
Percentage of students receiving: Loans: **90%**, Grants/scholarships: **52%**, Work-study aid: **0%**
Average medical school debt for the class of 2008: **$137,289**

STUDENT BODY

Fall 2009 full-time enrollment: 396
Men: **66%**, Women: **34%**, In-state: **94%**, Minorities: **21%**, American Indian: **0.3%**, Asian-American: **14.9%**,

African-American: **0.8%**, Hispanic-American: **4.8%**,
White: **74.7%**, International: **0.0%**, Unknown: **4.5%**

ACADEMIC PROGRAMS

The school's curriculum frequently give first-year students
substantial contact with patients.

There are opportunities for first or second year students to
work in community health clinics.

Program areas: family medicine, geriatrics, internal
medicine, pediatrics, rural medicine, women's health

Joint degrees awarded: M.D./Ph.D., M.D./M.P.H.

Total National Institutes of Health (NIH) grants awarded
to the medical school and affiliated hospitals: **$84.4
million**

CURRICULUM

(TEXT PROVIDED BY MEDICAL SCHOOL):

First two years include anatomy, biochemistry, physiology, microbiology, genetics, pharmacology, pathology,
organ systems, clinical medicine and behavioral science.
The third year has clerkships in Medicine, Pediatrics,
Surgery, Ob/gyn, Psychiatry, and Family Medicine. The
fourth year has courses in ethics, health care delivery, public health, clinical neurology, a sub-internship, and electives.

FALL 2009 FACULTY PROFILE

Total teaching faculty: **1,203 (full-time)**, **325 (part-time)**

Of full-time faculty, those teaching in basic sciences: **8%**;
in clinical programs: **92%**

Of part-time faculty, those teaching in basic sciences: **5%**;
in clinical programs: **95%**

Full-time faculty/student ratio: **3.0**

SUPPORT SERVICES

The school offers students these services for dealing with
stress: peer counseling, professional counseling, support
groups.

RESIDENCY PROFILE

Most popular residency and specialty programs chosen by
the 2008 and 2009 M.D. graduating classes: anesthesiology, emergency medicine, family practice, internal medicine, obstetrics and gynecology, ophthalmology, orthopaedic
surgery, pediatrics, physical medicine and rehabilitation,
surgery–general.

WHERE GRADS GO

41.6%

*Proportion of 2007-2008 graduates who entered primary
care specialties*

25.2%

*Proportion of 2008-2009 graduates who accepted in-state
residencies*

University of Vermont

- E-126 Given Building, 89 Beaumont Avenue, Burlington, VT 05405
- Public
- Year Founded: 1822
- Tuition, 2009-2010: In-state: $29,583; Out-of-State: $50,403
- Enrollment 2009-2010 academic year: 458
- Website: https://www.med.uvm.edu/admissions
- Specialty ranking: family medicine: 15, rural medicine: 8

3.70 AVERAGE GPA, ENTERING CLASS FALL 2009

10.0 AVERAGE MCAT, ENTERING CLASS FALL 2009

3.9% ACCEPTANCE RATE, ENTERING CLASS FALL 2009

55 2011 U.S. NEWS MEDICAL SCHOOL RANKING (RESEARCH)

4 2011 U.S. NEWS MEDICAL SCHOOL RANKING (PRIMARY CARE)

ADMISSIONS
Admissions phone number: **(802) 656-2154**
Admissions email address: **medadmissions@uvm.edu**
Application web site:
http://www.med.uvm.edu/admissions/TB1+BL+I+C.asp? SiteAreaID=552
Acceptance rate: **3.9%**
In-state acceptance rate: **50.6%**
Out-of-state acceptance rate: **3.3%**
Minority acceptance rate: **3.4%**
International acceptance rate: **1.6%**

Fall 2009 applications and acceptees

Type	Applied	Interviewed	Accepted	Enrolled
Total:	5,797	585	226	115
In-state:	77	55	39	24
Out-of-state:	5,720	530	187	91

Profile of admitted students
Average undergraduate grade point average: **3.70**
MCAT averages (scale: 1-15; writing test: J-T):
Composite score: **10.0**
Verbal reasoning score: **10.0**, Physical sciences score: **10.0**, Biological score: **10.0**, Writing score: **Q**
Proportion with undergraduate majors in: Biological sciences: **34%**, Physical sciences: **15%**, Non-sciences: **16%**, Other health professions: **8%**, Mixed disciplines and other: **27%**
Percentage of students not coming directly from college after graduation: **69%**

Dates and details
The American Medical College Application Service (AMCAS) application is accepted.
School asks for a second, school-specific application as part of the admissions process.
Oldest MCAT considered for Fall 2011 entry: **2007**
Earliest application date for the 2011-2012 first-year class: **06/01**
Latest application date: **11/01**

Acceptance dates for regular application for the class entering in Fall 2011.
Earliest: **15-OCT-10**
Latest: **08-AUG-11**
Applicants have 2 weeks to respond to admissions offer. The school does consider requests for deferred entrance.
Starting month for the class of 2011-2012: **August**
The school does have an Early Decision Plan (EDP).
A personal interview is required for admission.

Undergraduate coursework required
Medical school requires undergraduate work in these subjects: biology, organic chemistry, inorganic (general) chemistry, physics, general chemistry.

ADMISSIONS POLICY
(TEXT PROVIDED BY SCHOOL):
We encourage students with a broad and balanced educational background during their undergraduate years. Work must demonstrate intellectual drive, independent thinking, curiosity, and self-discipline. We seek in applicants the same humanistic qualities and attitudes we consider essential in a physician: integrity, a respect for others choices and rights, compassion, empathy, and personal insight.

FINANCIAL AID
Financial aid phone number: **(802) 656-5700**
Tuition, 2009-2010 academic year: **In-state: $29,583; Out-of-State: $50,403**
Room and board: **$10,923**
Percentage of students receiving financial aid in 2009-10: **89%**
Percentage of students receiving: Loans: **83%**, Grants/scholarships: **48%**, Work-study aid: **0%**
Average medical school debt for the class of 2008: **$158,313**

STUDENT BODY
Fall 2009 full-time enrollment: **458**
Men: **46%**, Women: **54%**, In-state: **30%**, Minorities: **24%**, American Indian: **0.0%**, Asian-American: **14.2%**,

African-American: **1.7%**, Hispanic-American: **6.3%**, White: **72.9%**, International: **2.6%**, Unknown: **2.2%**

ACADEMIC PROGRAMS

The school's curriculum frequently give first-year students substantial contact with patients.

There are opportunities for first- or second-year students to work in community health clinics.

Program areas: AIDS, drug/alcohol abuse, family medicine, geriatrics, internal medicine, pediatrics, rural medicine, women's health

Joint degrees awarded: M.D./Ph.D.

Total National Institutes of Health (NIH) grants awarded to the medical school and affiliated hospitals: **N/A**

CURRICULUM

(TEXT PROVIDED BY MEDICAL SCHOOL):

Our curriculum is designed to integrate expanding medical knowledge with a desire for life-long learning. Courses are designed from well-defined learning objectives and students are measured to ensure their competency in mastering these objectives. Principles of professionalism and humanism are also integrated throughout all four years.

FALL 2009 FACULTY PROFILE

Total teaching faculty: **555 (full-time)**, **1,512 (part-time)**
Of full-time faculty, those teaching in basic sciences: **13%**; in clinical programs: **87%**

Of part-time faculty, those teaching in basic sciences: **1%**; in clinical programs: **99%**
Full-time faculty/student ratio: **1.2**

SUPPORT SERVICES

The school offers students these services for dealing with stress: expanded-hour gym access, peer counseling, professional counseling, religious support, support groups.

RESIDENCY PROFILE

Most popular residency and specialty programs chosen by the 2008 and 2009 M.D. graduating classes: anesthesiology, emergency medicine, family practice, internal medicine, obstetrics and gynecology, orthopaedic surgery, pediatrics, psychiatry, surgery–general.

WHERE GRADS GO

58.0%

Proportion of 2007-2008 graduates who entered primary care specialties

19.0%

Proportion of 2008-2009 graduates who accepted in-state residencies

University of Virginia

- PO Box 800793, McKim Hall, Charlottesville, VA 22908-0793
- Public
- Year Founded: 1819
- Tuition, 2009-2010: In-state: $35,150; Out-of-State: $44,708
- Enrollment 2009-2010 academic year: 571
- Website:
  http://www.healthsystem.virginia.edu/internet/admissions
- Specialty ranking: family medicine: 22, geriatrics: 20

 3.75 AVERAGE GPA, ENTERING CLASS FALL 2009

 11.3 AVERAGE MCAT, ENTERING CLASS FALL 2009

 14.0% ACCEPTANCE RATE, ENTERING CLASS FALL 2009

 25 2011 U.S. NEWS MEDICAL SCHOOL RANKING (RESEARCH)

39 2011 U.S. NEWS MEDICAL SCHOOL RANKING (PRIMARY CARE)

ADMISSIONS

Admissions phone number: **(434) 924-5571**
Admissions email address: **medsch-adm@virginia.edu**
Application web site: **http://www.aamc.org**
Acceptance rate: **14.0%**
In-state acceptance rate: **22.9%**
Out-of-state acceptance rate: **11.7%**
Minority acceptance rate: **16.4%**
International acceptance rate: **11.6%**

Fall 2009 applications and acceptees

Type	Applied	Interviewed	Accepted	Enrolled
Total:	2,702	545	377	143
In-state:	545	153	125	81
Out-of-state:	2,157	392	252	62

Profile of admitted students

Average undergraduate grade point average: **3.75**
MCAT averages (scale: 1-15; writing test: J-T):
Composite score: **11.3**
Verbal reasoning score: **10.5**, Physical sciences score: **11.6**, Biological score: **11.7**, Writing score: **P**
Proportion with undergraduate majors in: Biological sciences: **36%**, Physical sciences: **20%**, Non-sciences: **15%**, Other health professions: **1%**, Mixed disciplines and other: **28%**
Percentage of students not coming directly from college after graduation: **50%**

Dates and details

The American Medical College Application Service (AMCAS) application is accepted.
School asks for a second, school-specific application as part of the admissions process.
Oldest MCAT considered for Fall 2011 entry: **2008**
Earliest application date for the 2011-2012 first-year class: **05/01**
Latest application date: **11/01**
Acceptance dates for regular application for the class entering in Fall 2011.
Earliest: **16-OCT-10**

Latest: **01-AUG-11**
Applicants have 3 weeks to respond to admissions offer.
The school does consider requests for deferred entrance.
Starting month for the class of 2011-2012: **August**
The school doesn't have an Early Decision Plan (EDP).
A personal interview is required for admission.

Undergraduate coursework required

Medical school requires undergraduate work in these subjects: biology, organic chemistry, inorganic (general) chemistry, physics.

ADMISSIONS POLICY

(TEXT PROVIDED BY SCHOOL):

The Admissions Committee seeks to admit applicants who will make contributions in clinical care, medical research, or education, and takes into account academics, MCATs, and evidence of a commitment to medicine. Final decisions are based on personal interviews and an overall assessment of the applicant's academic and personal qualities. Approximately 57% of the class comes from Virginia.

FINANCIAL AID

Financial aid phone number: **(434) 924-0033**
Tuition, 2009-2010 academic year: **In-state: $35,150; Out-of-State: $44,708**
Room and board: **$19,818**
Percentage of students receiving financial aid in 2009-10: **91%**
Percentage of students receiving: Loans: **81%**, Grants/scholarships: **68%**, Work-study aid: **0%**
Average medical school debt for the class of 2008: **$122,369**

STUDENT BODY

Fall 2009 full-time enrollment: **571**
Men: **53%**, Women: **47%**, In-state: **58%**, Minorities: **31%**, American Indian: **N/A**, Asian-American: **N/A**, African-American: **N/A**, Hispanic-American: **N/A**, White: **N/A**, International: **N/A**, Unknown: **N/A**

ACADEMIC PROGRAMS

The school's curriculum frequently give first-year students substantial contact with patients.

There are opportunities for first- or second-year students to work in community health clinics.

Program areas: AIDS, drug/alcohol abuse, family medicine, geriatrics, internal medicine, pediatrics, rural medicine, women's health

Joint degrees awarded: M.D./Ph.D., M.D./M.B.A., M.D./M.P.H., M.D./M.S., M.D./M.A.

Total National Institutes of Health (NIH) grants awarded to the medical school and affiliated hospitals: **$145.8 million**

CURRICULUM
(TEXT PROVIDED BY MEDICAL SCHOOL):

The system-based Cells to Society Curriculum combines the practice and science of medicine. Clinical performance development is integrated with foundations and organ systems courses. Clerkships are followed by an array of selectives/electives. Students enjoy experiential activities, patient cases, self-directed and team-based learning, lectures, and hospital/community-based clinical experiences.

FALL 2009 FACULTY PROFILE

Total teaching faculty: **941 (full-time)**, **89 (part-time)**
Of full-time faculty, those teaching in basic sciences: **21%**; in clinical programs: **79%**

Of part-time faculty, those teaching in basic sciences: **11%**; in clinical programs: **89%**
Full-time faculty/student ratio: **1.6**

SUPPORT SERVICES

The school offers students these services for dealing with stress: expanded-hour gym access, peer counseling, professional counseling, religious support, support groups.

RESIDENCY PROFILE

Most popular residency and specialty programs chosen by the 2008 and 2009 M.D. graduating classes: anesthesiology, emergency medicine, family practice, internal medicine, obstetrics and gynecology, orthopaedic surgery, pediatrics, radiology–diagnostic, surgery–general.

WHERE GRADS GO

35.0%

Proportion of 2007-2008 graduates who entered primary care specialties

16.0%

Proportion of 2008-2009 graduates who accepted in-state residencies

University of Washington

■ PO Box 356340, Seattle, WA 98195
■ Public
■ Year Founded: 1946
■ Tuition, 2009-2010: In-state: $21,472; Out-of-State: $50,512
■ Enrollment 2009-2010 academic year: 901
■ Website: http://www.uwmedicine.org
■ Specialty ranking: AIDS: 4, drug/alcohol abuse: 12, family medicine: 1, geriatrics: 6, internal medicine: 6, pediatrics: 8, rural medicine: 1, women's health: 9

3.67 AVERAGE GPA, ENTERING CLASS FALL 2009

10.3 AVERAGE MCAT, ENTERING CLASS FALL 2009

6.2% ACCEPTANCE RATE, ENTERING CLASS FALL 2009

6 2011 U.S. NEWS MEDICAL SCHOOL RANKING (RESEARCH)

1 2011 U.S. NEWS MEDICAL SCHOOL RANKING (PRIMARY CARE)

ADMISSIONS

Admissions phone number: (206) 543-7212
Admissions email address: askuwsom@u.washington.edu
Application web site:
   http://depts.washington.edu/mdadmit/secondary
Acceptance rate: 6.2%
In-state acceptance rate: 21.4%
Out-of-state acceptance rate: 1.1%
Minority acceptance rate: 4.2%
International acceptance rate: 0.0%

Fall 2009 applications and acceptees

Type	Applied	Interviewed	Accepted	Enrolled
Total:	4,266	683	266	216
In-state:	1,075	604	230	202
Out-of-state:	3,191	79	36	14

Profile of admitted students

Average undergraduate grade point average: 3.67
MCAT averages (scale: 1-15; writing test: J-T):
Composite score: 10.3
Verbal reasoning score: 10.1, Physical sciences score: 10.0, Biological score: 10.9, Writing score: Q
Proportion with undergraduate majors in: Biological sciences: 53%, Physical sciences: 17%, Non-sciences: 23%, Other health professions: 1%, Mixed disciplines and other: 6%
Percentage of students not coming directly from college after graduation: 38%

Dates and details

The American Medical College Application Service (AMCAS) application is accepted.
School asks for a second, school-specific application as part of the admissions process.
Oldest MCAT considered for Fall 2011 entry: 2008
Earliest application date for the 2011-2012 first-year class: 06/01
Latest application date: 11/01
Acceptance dates for regular application for the class entering in Fall 2011.

Earliest: 01-NOV-10
Latest: 01-AUG-11
Applicants have 2 weeks to respond to admissions offer. The school does consider requests for deferred entrance. Starting month for the class of 2011-2012: August
The school doesn't have an Early Decision Plan (EDP). A personal interview is required for admission.

Undergraduate coursework required

Medical school requires undergraduate work in these subjects: biology, inorganic (general) chemistry, physics, humanities, social sciences, general chemistry.

ADMISSIONS POLICY

(TEXT PROVIDED BY SCHOOL):

Criteria: motivation, maturity, integrity, academic performance, humanitarian qualities, service, communication skills, health issues knowledge, analytical thinking skill, & intellectual curiosity. 40 hours MD shadowing required. Preference for WWAMI state residents. Only U.S. citizens or permanent residents. Secondary application required. Criminal background check required. Limit 3 applications.

FINANCIAL AID

Financial aid phone number: (206) 685-9229
Tuition, 2009-2010 academic year: **In-state: $21,472; Out-of-State: $50,512**
Room and board: $15,141
Percentage of students receiving financial aid in 2009-10: 91%
Percentage of students receiving: Loans: 85%, Grants/scholarships: 68%, Work-study aid: 0%
Average medical school debt for the class of 2008: $112,530

STUDENT BODY

Fall 2009 full-time enrollment: 901
Men: 46%, Women: 54%, In-state: 78%, Minorities: 24%, American Indian: 1.6%, Asian-American: 15.8%, African-American: 2.4%, Hispanic-American: 3.8%, White: 66.4%, International: 0.0%, Unknown: 10.1%

ACADEMIC PROGRAMS

The school's curriculum frequently give first-year students substantial contact with patients.

There are opportunities for first- or second-year students to work in community health clinics.

Program areas: AIDS, drug/alcohol abuse, family medicine, geriatrics, internal medicine, pediatrics, rural medicine, women's health

Joint degrees awarded: M.D./Ph.D., M.D./M.P.H., M.D./M.H.A.

Total National Institutes of Health (NIH) grants awarded to the medical school and affiliated hospitals: **$713.2 million**

CURRICULUM

(TEXT PROVIDED BY MEDICAL SCHOOL):

1st & 2nd year curriculum: discipline-based & organ-system approaches–lecture and small group teaching. Intro to Clinical Medicine spans years 1 & 2. 3rd & 4th year: required & elective clinical clerkships in the WWAMI (Washington, Wyoming, Alaska, Montana, Idaho) region. Assignment to small colleges with clinical mentor; community service pathways; and a required research experience.

FALL 2009 FACULTY PROFILE

Total teaching faculty: **2,309 (full-time), 407 (part-time)**
Of full-time faculty, those teaching in basic sciences: **17%**; in clinical programs: **83%**

Of part-time faculty, those teaching in basic sciences: **11%**; in clinical programs: **89%**
Full-time faculty/student ratio: **2.6**

SUPPORT SERVICES

The school offers students these services for dealing with stress: expanded hour gym access, peer counseling, professional counseling, support groups.

RESIDENCY PROFILE

Most popular residency and specialty programs chosen by the 2008 and 2009 M.D. graduating classes: anesthesiology, emergency medicine, family practice, internal medicine, obstetrics and gynecology, orthopaedic surgery, pediatrics, psychiatry, surgery–general, transitional year.

WHERE GRADS GO

46.0%
Proportion of 2007-2008 graduates who entered primary care specialties

36.0%
Proportion of 2008-2009 graduates who accepted in-state residencies

University of Wisconsin–Madison

- 750 Highland Avenue, Madison, WI 53705-2221
- Public
- Year Founded: 1848
- Tuition, 2009-2010: In-state: $24,616; Out-of-State: $35,740
- Enrollment 2009-2010 academic year: 635
- Website: http://www.med.wisc.edu/education
- Specialty ranking: family medicine: 5, internal medicine: 26, rural medicine: 8

 **3.72** AVERAGE GPA, ENTERING CLASS FALL 2009

 10.4 AVERAGE MCAT, ENTERING CLASS FALL 2009

 8.8% ACCEPTANCE RATE, ENTERING CLASS FALL 2009

27 2011 U.S. NEWS MEDICAL SCHOOL RANKING (RESEARCH)

12 2011 U.S. NEWS MEDICAL SCHOOL RANKING (PRIMARY CARE)

ADMISSIONS
Admissions phone number: **(608) 265-6344**
Admissions email address: **eamenzer@wisc.edu**
Application web site:
http://www.med.wisc.edu/Education/md/admissions/main/102
Acceptance rate: **8.8%**
In-state acceptance rate: **26.6%**
Out-of-state acceptance rate: **4.2%**
Minority acceptance rate: **7.4%**
International acceptance rate: **N/A**

Fall 2009 applications and acceptees

Type	Applied	Interviewed	Accepted	Enrolled
Total:	3,151	496	277	168
In-state:	650	366	173	132
Out-of-state:	2,501	130	104	36

Profile of admitted students
Average undergraduate grade point average: **3.72**
MCAT averages (scale: 1-15; writing test: J-T):
Composite score: **10.4**
Verbal reasoning score: **9.9**, Physical sciences score: **10.3**, Biological score: **10.9**, Writing score: **P**
Proportion with undergraduate majors in: Biological sciences: **63%**, Physical sciences: **10%**, Non-sciences: **7%**, Other health professions: **1%**, Mixed disciplines and other: **19%**
Percentage of students not coming directly from college after graduation: **60%**

Dates and details
The American Medical College Application Service (AMCAS) application is accepted.
School asks for a second, school-specific application as part of the admissions process.
Oldest MCAT considered for Fall 2011 entry: **2006**
Earliest application date for the 2011-2012 first-year class: **06/01**
Latest application date: **11/01**

Acceptance dates for regular application for the class entering in Fall 2011.
Earliest: **15-OCT-10**
Latest: **15-AUG-11**
Applicants have 2 weeks to respond to admissions offer.
The school does consider requests for deferred entrance.
Starting month for the class of 2011–2012: **August**
The school does have an Early Decision Plan (EDP).
A personal interview is required for admission.

Undergraduate coursework required
Medical school requires undergraduate work in these subjects: biology, biology/zoology, organic chemistry, inorganic (general) chemistry, physics, biochemistry, mathematics, general chemistry.

ADMISSIONS POLICY
(TEXT PROVIDED BY SCHOOL):
Consider applicant's undergraduate & graduate academic performance, MCAT scores, extracurricular activities, exposure to medicine, patient care, community service, employment record, personal, educational, and socio-economic background, response to challenges, character (honesty, integrity, empathy, maturity, leadership, self-discipline) and emotional stability. Preference is given to residents.

FINANCIAL AID
Financial aid phone number: **(608) 262-3060**
Tuition, 2009-2010 academic year: **In-state: $24,616; Out-of-State: $35,740**
Room and board: **$17,115**
Percentage of students receiving financial aid in 2009-10: **95%**
Percentage of students receiving: Loans: **92%**, Grants/scholarships: **18%**, Work-study aid: **0%**
Average medical school debt for the class of 2008: **$130,507**

STUDENT BODY
Fall 2009 full-time enrollment: **635**

Men: **47%**, Women: **53%**, In-state: **80%**, Minorities: **25%**,
American Indian: **0.0%**, Asian-American: **17.0%**,
African-American: **4.9%**, Hispanic-American: **2.8%**,
White: **75.3%**, International: **0.0%**, Unknown: **0.0%**

ACADEMIC PROGRAMS

The school's curriculum frequently give first year students
substantial contact with patients.

There are opportunities for first- or second-year students to
work in community health clinics.

Program areas: AIDS, drug/alcohol abuse, family
medicine, geriatrics, internal medicine, pediatrics, rural
medicine, women's health

Joint degrees awarded: M.D./Ph.D., M.D./M.P.H.

Total National Institutes of Health (NIH) grants awarded
to the medical school and affiliated hospitals: **$187.7
million**

CURRICULUM
(TEXT PROVIDED BY MEDICAL SCHOOL):

The first-year core curriculum builds a firm base in the
sciences fundamental to clinical medicine. In the second
year, the courses emphasize organ systems, mechanisms of
disease and abnormalities, and therapeutic intervention.
Beginning in the third year, clerkships expose students to a
wide variety of clinical settings, including outpatient, inpatient, community-based, rural and inner city.

FALL 2009 FACULTY PROFILE

Total teaching faculty: **1,084 (full-time)**, **316 (part-time)**

Of full-time faculty, those teaching in basic sciences: **16%**;
in clinical programs: **84%**

Of part-time faculty, those teaching in basic sciences: **1%**;
in clinical programs: **99%**

Full time faculty/student ratio: **1.7**

SUPPORT SERVICES

The school offers students these services for dealing with
stress: expanded-hour gym access, professional counseling,
support groups.

RESIDENCY PROFILE

Most popular residency and specialty programs chosen by
the 2008 and 2009 M.D. graduating classes: anesthesiology, emergency medicine, family practice, internal medicine, obstetrics and gynecology, ophthalmology,
pathology–anatomic and clinical, pediatrics, radiology–diagnostic, surgery–general.

WHERE GRADS GO

38.4%

*Proportion of 2007-2008 graduates who entered primary
care specialties*

33.1%

*Proportion of 2008-2009 graduates who accepted in-state
residencies*

Vanderbilt University

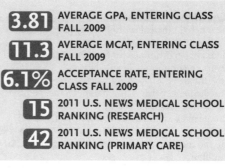

- **21st Avenue S and Garland Avenue, Nashville, TN 37232-2104**
- **Private**
- **Year Founded:** 1875
- **Tuition, 2009-2010:** $42,352
- **Enrollment 2009-2010 academic year:** 451
- **Website:** http://www.mc.vanderbilt.edu/medschool/
- **Specialty ranking:** AIDS: 18, internal medicine: 12, pediatrics: 20

3.81 AVERAGE GPA, ENTERING CLASS FALL 2009

11.3 AVERAGE MCAT, ENTERING CLASS FALL 2009

6.1% ACCEPTANCE RATE, ENTERING CLASS FALL 2009

15 2011 U.S. NEWS MEDICAL SCHOOL RANKING (RESEARCH)

42 2011 U.S. NEWS MEDICAL SCHOOL RANKING (PRIMARY CARE)

ADMISSIONS
Admissions phone number: **(615) 322-2145**
Admissions email address: **N/A**
Application web site:
   http://www.mc.vanderbilt.edu/medschool/admissions/online_app.php
Acceptance rate: **6.1%**
In-state acceptance rate: **7.2%**
Out-of-state acceptance rate: **6.1%**
Minority acceptance rate: **7.3%**
International acceptance rate: **6.9%**

Fall 2009 applications and acceptees

Type	Applied	Interviewed	Accepted	Enrolled
Total:	4,892	1,014	300	111
In-state:	318	54	23	19
Out-of-state:	4,574	960	277	92

Profile of admitted students
Average undergraduate grade point average: **3.81**
MCAT averages (scale: 1-15; writing test: J-T):
Composite score: **11.3**
Verbal reasoning score: **10.4**, Physical sciences score: **11.5**, Biological score: **11.8**, Writing score: **Q**
Proportion with undergraduate majors in: Biological sciences: **37%**, Physical sciences: **23%**, Non-sciences: **11%**, Other health professions: **2%**, Mixed disciplines and other: **27%**
Percentage of students not coming directly from college after graduation: **11%**

Dates and details
The American Medical College Application Service (AMCAS) application is accepted.
School asks for a second, school-specific application as part of the admissions process.
Oldest MCAT considered for Fall 2011 entry: **2007**
Earliest application date for the 2011-2012 first-year class: **06/01**
Latest application date: **11/15**

Acceptance dates for regular application for the class entering in Fall 2011.
Earliest: **16-OCT-10**
Latest: **29-JUL-10**
Applicants have 2 weeks to respond to admissions offer.
The school does consider requests for deferred entrance.
Starting month for the class of 2011–2012: **August**
The school does have an Early Decision Plan (EDP).
A personal interview is required for admission.

Undergraduate coursework required
Medical school requires undergraduate work in these subjects: biology, English, organic chemistry, inorganic (general) chemistry, physics.

ADMISSIONS POLICY
(TEXT PROVIDED BY SCHOOL):
   VUSM seeks to admit a diverse group of academically exceptional students whose attributes and accomplishments suggest they will become leaders and scholars in medicine. After initial review of AMCAS data, 21% of applicants are invited to interview and provide secondary essays and recommendations. A faculty-student committee reviews all data in a holistic manner and offers rolling admissions.

FINANCIAL AID
Financial aid phone number: **(615) 343-6310**
Tuition, 2009-2010 academic year: **$42,352**
Room and board: **$10,800**
Percentage of students receiving financial aid in 2009-10: **100%**
Percentage of students receiving: Loans: **68%**, Grants/scholarships: **100%**, Work-study aid: **0%**
Average medical school debt for the class of 2008: **$120,000**

STUDENT BODY
Fall 2009 full-time enrollment: **451**
Men: **53%**, Women: **47%**, In-state: **18%**, Minorities: **27%**, American Indian: **0.4%**, Asian-American: **17.1%**,

African-American: **8.9%**, Hispanic-American: **0.7%**, White: **57.0%**, International: **6.4%**, Unknown: **9.5%**

ACADEMIC PROGRAMS

The school's curriculum frequently give first-year students substantial contact with patients.

There are opportunities for first- or second-year students to work in community health clinics.

Program areas: AIDS, drug/alcohol abuse, family medicine, geriatrics, internal medicine, pediatrics, women's health

Joint degrees awarded: M.D./Ph.D., M.D./M.B.A., M.D./M.P.H., M.D./J.D., M.D./M.S., M.D./M.A.

Total National Institutes of Health (NIH) grants awarded to the medical school and affiliated hospitals: **$315.1 million**

CURRICULUM

(TEXT PROVIDED BY MEDICAL SCHOOL):

Vanderbilt's curriculum provides students with the knowledge, skills and attitudes to become leaders and scholars in medicine. Students build a strong foundation in the biomedical and social sciences while developing clinical competence and a sustainable professional identity. A mentored scholarly project is required and electives throughout the program allow exploration of individual interests.

FALL 2009 FACULTY PROFILE

Total teaching faculty: **2,034 (full-time)**, **87 (part-time)**
Of full-time faculty, those teaching in basic sciences: **21%**; in clinical programs: **79%**

Of part-time faculty, those teaching in basic sciences: **3%**; in clinical programs: **97%**
Full-time faculty/student ratio: **4.5**

SUPPORT SERVICES

The school offers students these services for dealing with stress: expanded-hour gym access, peer counseling, professional counseling, religious support, support groups.

RESIDENCY PROFILE

Most popular residency and specialty programs chosen by the 2008 and 2009 M.D. graduating classes: anesthesiology, emergency medicine, internal medicine, obstetrics and gynecology, orthopaedic surgery, pediatrics, radiology–diagnostic, surgery–general, internal medicine/pediatrics.

WHERE GRADS GO

30.7%
Proportion of 2007-2008 graduates who entered primary care specialties

28.5%
Proportion of 2008-2009 graduates who accepted in-state residencies

Virginia Commonwealth University

- PO Box 980565, Richmond, VA 23298-0565
- Public
- Year Founded: 1838
- Tuition, 2009-2010: In-state: $28,566; Out-of-State: $42,612
- Enrollment 2009-2010 academic year: 760
- Website: http://www.medschool.vcu.edu
- Specialty ranking: N/A

3.62 AVERAGE GPA, ENTERING CLASS FALL 2009

9.8 AVERAGE MCAT, ENTERING CLASS FALL 2009

7.1% ACCEPTANCE RATE, ENTERING CLASS FALL 2009

Unranked 2011 U.S. NEWS MEDICAL SCHOOL RANKING (RESEARCH)

Unranked 2011 U.S. NEWS MEDICAL SCHOOL RANKING (PRIMARY CARE)

ADMISSIONS

Admissions phone number: **(804) 828-9629**
Admissions email address: **somume@hsc.vcu.edu**
Application web site:
https://www.apps.som.vcu.edu/app_web/login/login.aspx
Acceptance rate: **7.1%**
In-state acceptance rate: **24.0%**
Out-of-state acceptance rate: **4.4%**
Minority acceptance rate: **7.6%**
International acceptance rate: **N/A**

Fall 2009 applications and acceptees

Type	Applied	Interviewed	Accepted	Enrolled
Total:	6,222	901	443	200
In-state:	875	431	210	111
Out-of-state:	5,347	470	233	89

Profile of admitted students

Average undergraduate grade point average: **3.62**
MCAT averages (scale: 1-15; writing test: J-T):
Composite score: **9.8**
Verbal reasoning score: **9.3**, Physical sciences score: **9.7**, Biological score: **10.3**, Writing score: **P**
Proportion with undergraduate majors in: Biological sciences: **43%**, Physical sciences: **16%**, Non-sciences: **15%**, Other health professions: **0%**, Mixed disciplines and other: **26%**
Percentage of students not coming directly from college after graduation: **64%**

Dates and details

The American Medical College Application Service (AMCAS) application is accepted.
School asks for a second, school-specific application as part of the admissions process.
Oldest MCAT considered for Fall 2011 entry: **2008**
Earliest application date for the 2011-2012 first-year class: **06/01**
Latest application date: **10/15**

Acceptance dates for regular application for the class entering in Fall 2011.
Earliest: **16-OCT-10**
Latest: **08-AUG-11**
Applicants have 2 weeks to respond to admissions offer.
The school does consider requests for deferred entrance.
Starting month for the class of 2011-2012: **August**
The school does have an Early Decision Plan (EDP).
A personal interview is required for admission.

Undergraduate coursework required

Medical school requires undergraduate work in these subjects: biology, biology/zoology, English, organic chemistry, inorganic (general) chemistry, physics, mathematics, demonstration of writing skills, general chemistry.

ADMISSIONS POLICY
(TEXT PROVIDED BY SCHOOL):

Applicants are selected on the basis of their professionalism and academic skills. Medically related experiences, academic performance and the interview are all important. The school gives preference to residents of Virginia and does not discriminate on the basis of age, race, sex, creed, national origin, or handicap. Applicants must be citizens or permanent residents of the United States or Canada.

FINANCIAL AID

Financial aid phone number: **(804) 828-4006**
Tuition, 2009-2010 academic year: **In-state: $28,566; Out-of-State: $42,612**
Room and board: **$13,400**
Percentage of students receiving financial aid in 2009-10: **96%**
Percentage of students receiving: Loans: **91%**, Grants/scholarships: **51%**, Work-study aid: **0%**
Average medical school debt for the class of 2008: **$153,147**

STUDENT BODY

Fall 2009 full-time enrollment: **760**
Men: **53%**, Women: **47%**, In-state: **58%**, Minorities: **41%**, American Indian: **0.9%**, Asian-American: **31.4%**,

African-American: **5.9%**, Hispanic-American: **2.4%**, White: **57.6%**, International: **0.4%**, Unknown: **1.3%**

ACADEMIC PROGRAMS

The school's curriculum very frequently give first-year students substantial contact with patients.

There are opportunities for first or second year students to work in community health clinics.

Program areas: AIDS, drug/alcohol abuse, family medicine, geriatrics, internal medicine, pediatrics, rural medicine, women's health

Joint degrees awarded: M.D./Ph.D., M.D./M.P.H., M.D./M.S., M.D./M.H.A.

Total National Institutes of Health (NIH) grants awarded to the medical school and affiliated hospitals: **$84.7 million**

CURRICULUM
(TEXT PROVIDED BY MEDICAL SCHOOL):

The first year focuses on structure and function, and the second year covers pathologic displays in treatment of disease. An M1/M2 longitudinal course provides clinical experience with physicians and small group instruction on basic clinical medicine. M3 students receive clinical training, rotating through various hospitals and ambulatory services. M4 students choose from a variety of electives.

FALL 2009 FACULTY PROFILE

Total teaching faculty: **1,245 (full-time)**, **103 (part-time)**

Of full-time faculty, those teaching in basic sciences: **18%**; in clinical programs: **82%**

Of part-time faculty, those teaching in basic sciences: **16%**; in clinical programs: **84%**

Full-time faculty/student ratio: **1.6**

SUPPORT SERVICES

The school offers students these services for dealing with stress: expanded-hour gym access, peer counseling, professional counseling, religious support, support groups.

RESIDENCY PROFILE

Most popular residency and specialty programs chosen by the 2008 and 2009 M.D. graduating classes: anesthesiology, emergency medicine, family practice, internal medicine, obstetrics and gynecology, orthopaedic surgery, pediatrics, radiology–diagnostic, surgery–general, transitional year.

WHERE GRADS GO

36.4%

Proportion of 2007-2008 graduates who entered primary care specialties

30.5%

Proportion of 2008-2009 graduates who accepted in-state residencies

Wake Forest University

- Medical Center Boulevard, Winston-Salem, NC 27157
- Private
- Year Founded: 1941
- Tuition, 2009-2010: $39,395
- Enrollment 2009-2010 academic year: 475
- Website: http://www.wfubmc.edu
- Specialty ranking: geriatrics: 15

3.60 AVERAGE GPA, ENTERING CLASS FALL 2009

10.2 AVERAGE MCAT, ENTERING CLASS FALL 2009

4.1% ACCEPTANCE RATE, ENTERING CLASS FALL 2009

44 2011 U.S. NEWS MEDICAL SCHOOL RANKING (RESEARCH)

33 2011 U.S. NEWS MEDICAL SCHOOL RANKING (PRIMARY CARE)

ADMISSIONS
Admissions phone number: **(336) 716-4264**
Admissions email address: **medadmit@wfubmc.edu**
Application web site: **N/A**
Acceptance rate: **4.1%**
In-state acceptance rate: **12.4%**
Out-of-state acceptance rate: **3.2%**
Minority acceptance rate: **N/A**
International acceptance rate: **N/A**

Fall 2009 applications and acceptees

Type	Applied	Interviewed	Accepted	Enrolled
Total:	7,102	584	292	120
In-state:	731	150	91	47
Out-of-state:	6,371	434	201	73

Profile of admitted students
Average undergraduate grade point average: **3.60**
MCAT averages (scale: 1-15; writing test: J-T):
Composite score: **10.2**
Verbal reasoning score: **10.1**, Physical sciences score: **10.0**,
  Biological score: **10.5**, Writing score: **Q**
Proportion with undergraduate majors in: Biological
  sciences: **44%**, Physical sciences: **15%**, Non-sciences:
  26%, Other health professions: **0%**, Mixed disciplines
  and other: **15%**
Percentage of students not coming directly from college
  after graduation: **50%**

Dates and details
The American Medical College Application Service
  (AMCAS) application is accepted.
School asks for a second, school-specific application as part
  of the admissions process.
Oldest MCAT considered for Fall 2011 entry: **2007**
Earliest application date for the 2011-2012 first-year class:
  06/01
Latest application date: **11/01**
Acceptance dates for regular application for the class
  entering in Fall 2011.
Earliest: **01-OCT-10**

Latest: **21-JUL-11**
Applicants have 2 weeks to respond to admissions offer.
The school does consider requests for deferred entrance.
Starting month for the class of 2011-2012: **July**
The school does have an Early Decision Plan (EDP).
A personal interview is required for admission.

Undergraduate coursework required
Medical school requires undergraduate work in these subjects: biology, biology/zoology, organic chemistry, inorganic (general) chemistry, physics, general chemistry.

ADMISSIONS POLICY
(TEXT PROVIDED BY SCHOOL):
  The MCAT, GPA, personal qualities assessed in the personal interviews. A national pool is considered, thus state of residence is inconsequential.

FINANCIAL AID
Financial aid phone number: **(336) 716-2889**
Tuition, 2009-2010 academic year: **$39,395**
Room and board: **$20,780**
Percentage of students receiving financial aid in 2009-10:
  94%
Percentage of students receiving: Loans: **90%**,
  Grants/scholarships: **70%**, Work-study aid: **0%**
Average medical school debt for the class of 2008:
  $149,793

STUDENT BODY
Fall 2009 full-time enrollment: **475**
Men: **54%**, Women: **46%**, In-state: **37%**, Minorities: **28%**,
  American Indian: **1.1%**, Asian-American: **13.5%**, African-
  American: **10.1%**, Hispanic-American: **2.9%**, White:
  58.9%, International: **4.2%**, Unknown: **9.3%**

ACADEMIC PROGRAMS
The school's curriculum frequently give first-year students
  substantial contact with patients.
There are opportunities for first- or second-year students to
  work in community health clinics.

Program areas: AIDS, drug/alcohol abuse, family
medicine, geriatrics, internal medicine, pediatrics, rural
medicine, women's health
Joint degrees awarded: M.D./Ph.D., M.D./M.B.A.,
M.D./M.S., M.D./M.A.
Total National Institutes of Health (NIH) grants awarded
to the medical school and affiliated hospitals: N/A

CURRICULUM
(TEXT PROVIDED BY MEDICAL SCHOOL):

The curriculum is organized to meet the seven goals of
the undergraduate medical education program: the development of proficiency in self-directed and lifelong learning
skills, the acquisition of appropriate core biomedical science
knowledge, clinical, problem solving/clinical reasoning,
interviewing & communication skills, information management skills, and professional attitudes and behavior.

FALL 2009 FACULTY PROFILE
Total teaching faculty: **945 (full-time)**, **516 (part-time)**
Of full-time faculty, those teaching in basic sciences: **24%**;
in clinical programs: **76%**
Of part-time faculty, those teaching in basic sciences: **19%**;
in clinical programs: **81%**
Full-time faculty/student ratio: **2.0**

SUPPORT SERVICES
The school offers students these services for dealing with
stress: expanded-hour gym access, professional counseling,
religious support.

RESIDENCY PROFILE
Most popular residency and specialty programs chosen by
the 2008 and 2009 M.D. graduating classes: anesthesiology, emergency medicine, family practice, internal medicine, neurology, obstetrics and gynecology, orthopaedic
surgery, pediatrics, psychiatry, surgery–general.

WHERE GRADS GO

46.0%

*Proportion of 2007-2008 graduates who entered primary
care specialties*

34.0%

*Proportion of 2008-2009 graduates who accepted in-state
residencies*

Washington University in St. Louis

- 660 S. Euclid Avenue, St. Louis, MO 63110
- Private
- Year Founded: 1891
- Tuition, 2009-2010: $47,150
- Enrollment 2009-2010 academic year: 475
- Website: http://medschool.wustl.edu
- Specialty ranking: AIDS: 21, drug/alcohol abuse: 12, internal medicine: 8, pediatrics: 9, women's health: 12

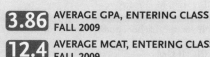

3.86 AVERAGE GPA, ENTERING CLASS FALL 2009

12.4 AVERAGE MCAT, ENTERING CLASS FALL 2009

11.0% ACCEPTANCE RATE, ENTERING CLASS FALL 2009

4 2011 U.S. NEWS MEDICAL SCHOOL RANKING (RESEARCH)

30 2011 U.S. NEWS MEDICAL SCHOOL RANKING (PRIMARY CARE)

ADMISSIONS

Admissions phone number: (314) 362-6858
Admissions email address: **wumscoa@wustl.edu**
Application web site:
  http://medschool.wustl.edu/admissions/
Acceptance rate: **11.0%**
In-state acceptance rate: **11.0%**
Out-of-state acceptance rate: **11.0%**
Minority acceptance rate: **9.2%**
International acceptance rate: **17.2%**

Fall 2009 applications and acceptees

Type	Applied	Interviewed	Accepted	Enrolled
Total:	3,035	1,196	335	121
In-state:	163	54	18	10
Out-of-state:	2,872	1,142	317	111

Profile of admitted students

Average undergraduate grade point average: **3.86**
MCAT averages (scale: 1-15; writing test: J-T):
Composite score: **12.4**
Verbal reasoning score: **11.4**, Physical sciences score: **12.8**, Biological score: **12.9**, Writing score: **Q**
Proportion with undergraduate majors in: Biological sciences: **33%**, Physical sciences: **26%**, Non-sciences: **15%**, Other health professions: **0%**, Mixed disciplines and other: **26%**
Percentage of students not coming directly from college after graduation: **31%**

Dates and details

The American Medical College Application Service (AMCAS) application is accepted.
School asks for a second, school-specific application as part of the admissions process.
Oldest MCAT considered for Fall 2011 entry: **2008**
Earliest application date for the 2011-2012 first-year class: **06/15**
Latest application date: **12/01**
Acceptance dates for regular application for the class entering in Fall 2011.

Earliest: **01-NOV-10**
Latest: **15-AUG-11**
Applicants have 2 weeks to respond to admissions offer.
The school does consider requests for deferred entrance.
Starting month for the class of 2011-2012: **August**
The school doesn't have an Early Decision Plan (EDP).
A personal interview is required for admission.

Undergraduate coursework required

Medical school requires undergraduate work in these subjects: biology, organic chemistry, inorganic (general) chemistry, physics, mathematics, calculus, general chemistry.

ADMISSIONS POLICY
(TEXT PROVIDED BY SCHOOL):

WUSM seeks to enroll bright, energetic, compassionate students who want to learn to practice medicine at the edge of what is known. The recruitment and selection process seeks to identify people who are personally and academically accomplished and who are energized by interacting with and improving the well being of others. For more information, please go to http://medicine.wustl.edu/admissions/

FINANCIAL AID

Financial aid phone number: (314) 362-6862
Tuition, 2009-2010 academic year: **$47,150**
Room and board: **$10,139**
Percentage of students receiving financial aid in 2009-10: **88%**
Percentage of students receiving: Loans: **52%**, Grants/scholarships: **73%**, Work-study aid: **0%**
Average medical school debt for the class of 2008: **$101,191**

STUDENT BODY

Fall 2009 full-time enrollment: **475**
Men: **51%**, Women: **49%**, In-state: **8%**, Minorities: **39%**, American Indian: **0.6%**, Asian-American: **28.4%**, African-American: **5.5%**, Hispanic-American: **4.4%**, White: **49.1%**, International: **1.5%**, Unknown: **10.5%**

ACADEMIC PROGRAMS

The school's curriculum frequently give first-year students substantial contact with patients.

There are opportunities for first- or second-year students to work in community health clinics.

Program areas: AIDS, drug/alcohol abuse, family medicine, geriatrics, internal medicine, pediatrics, rural medicine

Joint degrees awarded: M.D./Ph.D., M.D./M.P.H., M.D./M.S., M.D./M.A.

Total National Institutes of Health (NIH) grants awarded to the medical school and affiliated hospitals: **$348.0 million**

CURRICULUM

(TEXT PROVIDED BY MEDICAL SCHOOL):

The Washington University School of Medicine curriculum offers a core experience that presents the principles, methods of investigation, problems and opportunities in each of the major disciplines of medical science and medical practice. The required elective program helps students decide where major interests lie. For more information, go to http://medschool.wustl.edu/admissions/

FALL 2009 FACULTY PROFILE

Total teaching faculty: 1,657 (full-time), 130 (part-time)

Of full-time faculty, those teaching in basic sciences: 9%; in clinical programs: 91%

Of part-time faculty, those teaching in basic sciences: 5%; in clinical programs: 95%

Full-time faculty/student ratio: 3.5

SUPPORT SERVICES

The school offers students these services for dealing with stress: expanded-hour gym access, peer counseling, professional counseling, religious support, support groups.

RESIDENCY PROFILE

Most popular residency and specialty programs chosen by the 2008 and 2009 M.D. graduating classes: anesthesiology, dermatology, emergency medicine, internal medicine, ophthalmology, orthopaedic surgery, pediatrics, radiology–diagnostic, surgery–general.

WHERE GRADS GO

33.3%

Proportion of 2007-2008 graduates who entered primary care specialties

27.5%

Proportion of 2008-2009 graduates who accepted in-state residencies

Wayne State University

- 540 E. Canfield, Detroit, MI 48201
- Public
- Year Founded: 1868
- Tuition, 2009-2010: In-state: $29,275; Out-of-State: $59,275
- Enrollment 2009-2010 academic year: 1,287
- Website: http://www.med.wayne.edu/Admissions
- Specialty ranking: N/A

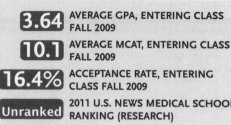

3.64 AVERAGE GPA, ENTERING CLASS FALL 2009

10.1 AVERAGE MCAT, ENTERING CLASS FALL 2009

16.4% ACCEPTANCE RATE, ENTERING CLASS FALL 2009

Unranked 2011 U.S. NEWS MEDICAL SCHOOL RANKING (RESEARCH)

Unranked 2011 U.S. NEWS MEDICAL SCHOOL RANKING (PRIMARY CARE)

ADMISSIONS

Admissions phone number: **(313) 577-1466**
Admissions email address: **admissions@med.wayne.edu**
Application web site: **N/A**
Acceptance rate: **16.4%**
In-state acceptance rate: **29.5%**
Out-of-state acceptance rate: **8.8%**
Minority acceptance rate: **14.5%**
International acceptance rate: **8.0%**

Fall 2009 applications and acceptees

Type	Applied	Interviewed	Accepted	Enrolled
Total:	3,809	1,007	624	290
In-state:	1,400	558	413	222
Out-of-state:	2,409	449	211	68

Profile of admitted students

Average undergraduate grade point average: **3.64**
MCAT averages (scale: 1-15; writing test: J-T):
Composite score: **10.1**
Verbal reasoning score: **9.3**, Physical sciences score: **10.3**,
  Biological score: **10.6**, Writing score: **P**
Proportion with undergraduate majors in: Biological
  sciences: **53%**, Physical sciences: **20%**, Non-sciences:
  11%, Other health professions: **1%**, Mixed disciplines and
  other: **15%**
Percentage of students not coming directly from college
  after graduation: **13%**

Dates and details

The American Medical College Application Service
  (AMCAS) application is accepted.
School asks for a second, school-specific application as part
  of the admissions process.
Oldest MCAT considered for Fall 2011 entry: **2007**
Earliest application date for the 2011-2012 first-year class:
  06/01
Latest application date: **12/15**
Acceptance dates for regular application for the class
  entering in Fall 2011.
Earliest: **21-OCT-10**

Latest: **15-JUL-11**
Applicants have 3 weeks to respond to admissions offer.
The school does consider requests for deferred entrance.
Starting month for the class of 2011–2012: **August**
The school does have an Early Decision Plan (EDP).
A personal interview is required for admission.

Undergraduate coursework required

Medical school requires undergraduate work in these subjects: biology, English, organic chemistry, inorganic (general) chemistry, physics.

ADMISSIONS POLICY
(TEXT PROVIDED BY SCHOOL):

We consider the entire record, GPA, MCAT, recommendations, interview, disadvantages overcome, and service to underserved populations; extracurricular activities and health-patient care activities are highly valued. Research is valued, but not required. Competitive applicants complete a secondary application and are considered for interview. Only U.S. and Canadian citizens are eligible.

FINANCIAL AID

Financial aid phone number: **(313) 577-1039**
Tuition, 2009-2010 academic year: **In-state: $29,275; Out-of-State: $59,275**
Room and board: **$13,250**
Percentage of students receiving financial aid in 2009-10:
  85%
Percentage of students receiving: Loans: **83%**,
  Grants/scholarships: **37%**, Work-study aid: **2%**
Average medical school debt for the class of 2008:
  $141,556

STUDENT BODY

Fall 2009 full-time enrollment: **1,287**
Men: **53%**, Women: **47%**, In-state: **85%**, Minorities: **30%**,
  American Indian: **0.3%**, Asian-American: **18.8%**,
  African-American: **9.7%**, Hispanic-American: **1.6%**,
  White: **55.8%**, International: **3.8%**, Unknown: **9.9%**

ACADEMIC PROGRAMS

The school's curriculum frequently give first-year students substantial contact with patients.

There are opportunities for first- or second-year students to work in community health clinics.

Program areas: AIDS, drug/alcohol abuse, family medicine, geriatrics, internal medicine, pediatrics, rural medicine, women's health

Joint degrees awarded: M.D./Ph.D., M.D./M.S.

Total National Institutes of Health (NIH) grants awarded to the medical school and affiliated hospitals: **N/A**

CURRICULUM

(TEXT PROVIDED BY MEDICAL SCHOOL):

The four-year Wayne State Medical School program has 158 weeks of basic and clinical science. The Year 1 and 2 curriculum focuses on normal and abnormal structure and function of the human body. The Clinical Science curriculum in Years 3 includes eight required clerkships, while the Year 4 curriculum has three required courses and five electives.

FALL 2009 FACULTY PROFILE

Total teaching faculty: **1,084 (full-time)**, **34 (part-time)**
Of full-time faculty, those teaching in basic sciences: **21%**; in clinical programs: **79%**

Of part-time faculty, those teaching in basic sciences: **26%**; in clinical programs: **74%**
Full-time faculty/student ratio: **0.8**

SUPPORT SERVICES

The school offers students these services for dealing with stress: expanded hour gym access, peer counseling, professional counseling, support groups.

RESIDENCY PROFILE

Most popular residency and specialty programs chosen by the 2008 and 2009 M.D. graduating classes: N/A.

WHERE GRADS GO

32.0%

Proportion of 2007-2008 graduates who entered primary care specialties

60.0%

Proportion of 2008-2009 graduates who accepted in-state residencies

West Virginia University

- 1 Medical Center Drive , Morgantown, WV 26506-9111
- Public
- Year Founded: 1903
- Tuition, 2009-2010: In-state: $21,270; Out-of-State: $46,018
- Enrollment 2009-2010 academic year: 432
- Website: http://www.hsc.wvu.edu/som/students
- Specialty ranking: rural medicine: 10

3.73 AVERAGE GPA, ENTERING CLASS FALL 2009

9.7 AVERAGE MCAT, ENTERING CLASS FALL 2009

6.3% ACCEPTANCE RATE, ENTERING CLASS FALL 2009

Unranked 2011 U.S. NEWS MEDICAL SCHOOL RANKING (RESEARCH)

49 2011 U.S. NEWS MEDICAL SCHOOL RANKING (PRIMARY CARE)

ADMISSIONS

Admissions phone number: **(304) 293-2408**
Admissions email address: **medadmissions@hsc.wvu.edu**
Application web site: **http://www.aamc.org**
Acceptance rate: **6.3%**
In-state acceptance rate: **37.7%**
Out-of-state acceptance rate: **3.5%**
Minority acceptance rate: **6.0%**
International acceptance rate: **N/A**

Fall 2009 applications and acceptees

Type	Applied	Interviewed	Accepted	Enrolled
Total:	2,577	369	163	110
In-state:	212	113	80	69
Out-of-state:	2,365	256	83	41

Profile of admitted students

Average undergraduate grade point average: **3.73**
MCAT averages (scale: 1-15; writing test: J-T):
Composite score: **9.7**
Verbal reasoning score: **9.5**, Physical sciences score: **9.5**, Biological score: **10.0**, Writing score: **O**
Proportion with undergraduate majors in: Biological sciences: **47%**, Physical sciences: **35%**, Non-sciences: **14%**, Other health professions: **4%**, Mixed disciplines and other: **0%**
Percentage of students not coming directly from college after graduation: **7%**

Dates and details

The American Medical College Application Service (AMCAS) application is accepted.
School asks for a second, school-specific application as part of the admissions process.
Oldest MCAT considered for Fall 2011 entry: **2009**
Earliest application date for the 2011-2012 first-year class: **06/01**
Latest application date: **11/01**
Acceptance dates for regular application for the class entering in Fall 2011.
Earliest: **15-OCT-10**

Latest: **01-AUG-11**
Applicants have 2 weeks to respond to admissions offer.
The school does consider requests for deferred entrance.
Starting month for the class of 2011–2012: **August**
The school does have an Early Decision Plan (EDP).
A personal interview is required for admission.

Undergraduate coursework required

Medical school requires undergraduate work in these subjects: biology/zoology, English, organic chemistry, inorganic (general) chemistry, physics, behavioral science, social sciences, general chemistry.

ADMISSIONS POLICY

(TEXT PROVIDED BY SCHOOL):
   Entrance requirements: AMCAS application and on site interview. MCAT (1/09 or later); 3 yrs. US/Can college; > 90 hrs with at least C grade; 8 hrs each (with lab) Biol/Zool, Inorg Chem, Org Chem. Physics; 6 hr each Engl, Behav Sci/Soc Sci; Biochem and Cell/Molec Biol highly recommended. Community service, medical shadowing are strongly considered. Required US citizenship.

FINANCIAL AID

Financial aid phone number: **(304) 293-3706**
Tuition, 2009-2010 academic year: **In-state: $21,270; Out-of-State: $46,018**
Room and board: **$7,857**
Percentage of students receiving financial aid in 2009-10: **94%**
Percentage of students receiving: Loans: **85%**, Grants/scholarships: **50%**, Work-study aid: **0%**
Average medical school debt for the class of 2008: **$141,825**

STUDENT BODY

Fall 2009 full-time enrollment: **432**
Men: **61%**, Women: **39%**, In-state: **68%**, Minorities: **16%**, American Indian: **0.0%**, Asian-American: **14.1%**, African-American: **0.7%**, Hispanic-American: **1.4%**, White: **83.8%**, International: **0.0%**, Unknown: **0.0%**

ACADEMIC PROGRAMS

The school's curriculum occasionally give first-year students substantial contact with patients.

There are opportunities for first- or second-year students to work in community health clinics.

Program areas: AIDS, drug/alcohol abuse, family medicine, geriatrics, internal medicine, pediatrics, rural medicine, women's health

Joint degrees awarded: M.D./Ph.D., M.D./M.P.H.

Total National Institutes of Health (NIH) grants awarded to the medical school and affiliated hospitals: **$17.8 million**

CURRICULUM

(TEXT PROVIDED BY MEDICAL SCHOOL):

Competency-based preparation. Basic science courses blocked & integrated. Summer clinical & research externships. Required laptop program. 3rd year requirements in medicine, surgery, family medicine, pediatrics, OB/GYN, psychiatry/neurology. Required selective/elective 4th-year. Requirements: Passage of USMLE Steps 1&2, WVU SOM CPX, 100-hours community service, 3-months rural primary care.

FALL 2009 FACULTY PROFILE

Total teaching faculty: **644 (full-time)**, **120 (part-time)**

Of full-time faculty, those teaching in basic sciences: **12%**; in clinical programs: **88%**

Of part-time faculty, those teaching in basic sciences: **3%**; in clinical programs: **98%**

Full-time faculty/student ratio: **1.5**

SUPPORT SERVICES

The school offers students these services for dealing with stress: expanded hour gym access, peer counseling, professional counseling, support groups.

RESIDENCY PROFILE

Most popular residency and specialty programs chosen by the 2008 and 2009 M.D. graduating classes: anesthesiology, emergency medicine, family practice, internal medicine, obstetrics and gynecology, orthopaedic surgery, pediatrics, surgery–general, transitional year, internal medicine/pediatrics.

WHERE GRADS GO

50.0%

Proportion of 2007-2008 graduates who entered primary care specialties

40.0%

Proportion of 2008-2009 graduates who accepted in-state residencies

Wright State University
Boonshoft

- PO Box 1751, Dayton, OH 45401-1751
- Public
- **Year Founded:** 1974
- **Tuition, 2009-2010:** In-state: $28,867; Out-of-State: $43,867
- **Enrollment 2009-2010 academic year:** 417
- **Website:** http://www.med.wright.edu
- **Specialty ranking:** N/A

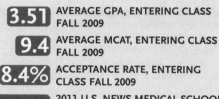

3.51 AVERAGE GPA, ENTERING CLASS FALL 2009

9.4 AVERAGE MCAT, ENTERING CLASS FALL 2009

8.4% ACCEPTANCE RATE, ENTERING CLASS FALL 2009

Unranked 2011 U.S. NEWS MEDICAL SCHOOL RANKING (RESEARCH)

Unranked 2011 U.S. NEWS MEDICAL SCHOOL RANKING (PRIMARY CARE)

ADMISSIONS

Admissions phone number: **(937) 775-2934**
Admissions email address: som_saa@wright.edu
Application web site:
 http://www.med.wright.edu/admiss/index.html#
Acceptance rate: **8.4%**
In-state acceptance rate: **19.3%**
Out-of-state acceptance rate: **2.2%**
Minority acceptance rate: **N/A**
International acceptance rate: **N/A**

Fall 2009 applications and acceptees

Type	Applied	Interviewed	Accepted	Enrolled
Total:	2,832	453	238	100
In-state:	1,024	364	198	91
Out-of-state:	1,808	89	40	9

Profile of admitted students

Average undergraduate grade point average: **3.51**
MCAT averages (scale: 1-15; writing test: J-T):
Composite score: **9.4**
Verbal reasoning score: **9.1**, Physical sciences score: **9.3**,
 Biological score: **9.9**, Writing score: **P**
Proportion with undergraduate majors in: Biological
 sciences: **72%**, Physical sciences: **8%**, Non-sciences: **13%**,
 Other health professions: **6%**, Mixed disciplines and
 other: **1%**
Percentage of students not coming directly from college
 after graduation: **23%**

Dates and details

The American Medical College Application Service
 (AMCAS) application is accepted.
School asks for a second, school-specific application as part
 of the admissions process.
Oldest MCAT considered for Fall 2011 entry: **2007**
Earliest application date for the 2011-2012 first-year class:
 06/01
Latest application date: **10/15**
Acceptance dates for regular application for the class
 entering in Fall 2011.

Earliest: **15-OCT-10**
Latest: **01-AUG-11**
Applicants have 2 weeks to respond to admissions offer.
The school does consider requests for deferred entrance.
Starting month for the class of 2011–2012: **August**
The school does have an Early Decision Plan (EDP).
A personal interview is required for admission.

Undergraduate coursework required

Medical school requires undergraduate work in these subjects: biology, English, organic chemistry, inorganic (general) chemistry, physics, mathematics, general chemistry.

ADMISSIONS POLICY
(TEXT PROVIDED BY SCHOOL):

 The School seeks a student body of diverse social, ethnic,
and educational backgrounds. Intellectual ability, dedication
to human concerns, altruism, compassion, communication
skills, maturity, motivation, leadership, and potential for
medical service in an under-served area of Ohio are considered. Non residents of Ohio are encouraged to apply.

FINANCIAL AID

Financial aid phone number: **(937) 775-2934**
Tuition, 2009-2010 academic year: **In-state: $28,867; Out-
 of-State: $43,867**
Room and board: **$11,946**
Percentage of students receiving financial aid in 2009-10:
 95%
Percentage of students receiving: Loans: **86%**,
 Grants/scholarships: **52%**, Work-study aid: **3%**
Average medical school debt for the class of 2008:
 $160,750

STUDENT BODY

Fall 2009 full-time enrollment: **417**
Men: **46%**, Women: **54%**, In-state: **98%**, Minorities: **27%**,
 American Indian: **0.2%**, Asian-American: **16.1%**,
 African-American: **7.0%**, Hispanic-American: **1.4%**,
 White: **72.7%**, International: **0.0%**, Unknown: **2.6%**

ACADEMIC PROGRAMS

The school's curriculum very frequently give first-year students substantial contact with patients.

There are opportunities for first- or second-year students to work in community health clinics.

Program areas: AIDS, drug/alcohol abuse, family medicine, geriatrics, internal medicine, pediatrics, rural medicine, women's health

Joint degrees awarded: M.D./Ph.D., M.D./M.B.A., M.D./M.P.H.

Total National Institutes of Health (NIH) grants awarded to the medical school and affiliated hospitals: $7.9 million

CURRICULUM
(TEXT PROVIDED BY MEDICAL SCHOOL):

During the first two years, students are taught in an interdisciplinary fashion. Students have patient contact in the first week. In the second year, 8 organ systems are taught. Clinically based enrichment electives are offered as immersion experiences in the first two years. In the third year, students are exposed to the basic disciplines of medicine. The fourth year includes mostly electives.

FALL 2009 FACULTY PROFILE

Total teaching faculty: 372 (full-time), 1,262 (part-time)
Of full-time faculty, those teaching in basic sciences: 13%; in clinical programs: 87%

Of part-time faculty, those teaching in basic sciences: 3%; in clinical programs: 97%

Full-time faculty/student ratio: 0.9

SUPPORT SERVICES

The school offers students these services for dealing with stress: peer counseling, professional counseling, support groups.

RESIDENCY PROFILE

Most popular residency and specialty programs chosen by the 2008 and 2009 M.D. graduating classes: anesthesiology, emergency medicine, family practice, internal medicine, obstetrics and gynecology, orthopaedic surgery, pediatrics, psychiatry, radiology–diagnostic, surgery–general.

WHERE GRADS GO

46.0%
Proportion of 2007-2008 graduates who entered primary care specialties

49.0%
Proportion of 2008-2009 graduates who accepted in-state residencies

Yale University

- 333 Cedar Street, PO Box 208055, New Haven, CT 06520-8055
- Private
- **Year Founded:** 1810
- **Tuition, 2009-2010:** $44,350
- **Enrollment 2009-2010 academic year:** 414
- **Website:** http://info.med.yale.edu/ysm
- **Specialty ranking:** AIDS: 13, drug/alcohol abuse: 1, geriatrics: 8, internal medicine: 10, pediatrics: 14, women's health: 7

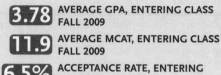

3.78 AVERAGE GPA, ENTERING CLASS FALL 2009

11.9 AVERAGE MCAT, ENTERING CLASS FALL 2009

6.5% ACCEPTANCE RATE, ENTERING CLASS FALL 2009

6 2011 U.S. NEWS MEDICAL SCHOOL RANKING (RESEARCH)

Unranked 2011 U.S. NEWS MEDICAL SCHOOL RANKING (PRIMARY CARE)

ADMISSIONS

Admissions phone number: **(203) 785-2643**
Admissions email address: **medical.admissions@yale.edu**
Application web site:
   http://info.med.yale.edu/education/admissions
Acceptance rate: **6.5%**
In-state acceptance rate: **13.1%**
Out-of-state acceptance rate: **6.2%**
Minority acceptance rate: **7.6%**
International acceptance rate: **4.8%**

Fall 2009 applications and acceptees

Type	Applied	Interviewed	Accepted	Enrolled
Total:	4,081	806	265	99
In-state:	183	53	24	17
Out-of-state:	3,898	753	241	82

Profile of admitted students

Average undergraduate grade point average: **3.78**
MCAT averages (scale: 1-15; writing test: J-T):
Composite score: **11.9**
Verbal reasoning score: **10.9**, Physical sciences score: **12.2**, Biological score: **12.6**, Writing score: **R**
Proportion with undergraduate majors in: Biological sciences: **59%**, Physical sciences: **29%**, Non-sciences: **8%**, Other health professions: **0%**, Mixed disciplines and other: **4%**
Percentage of students not coming directly from college after graduation: **57%**

Dates and details

The American Medical College Application Service (AMCAS) application is accepted.
School asks for a second, school-specific application as part of the admissions process.
Oldest MCAT considered for Fall 2011 entry: **2007**
Earliest application date for the 2011-2012 first-year class: **06/01**
Latest application date: **10/15**
Acceptance dates for regular application for the class entering in Fall 2011.

Earliest: **15-MAR-11**
Latest: **30-AUG-11**
Applicants have 3 weeks to respond to admissions offer.
The school does consider requests for deferred entrance.
Starting month for the class of 2011–2012: **August**
The school does have an Early Decision Plan (EDP).
A personal interview is required for admission.

Undergraduate coursework required

Medical school requires undergraduate work in these subjects: biology/zoology, organic chemistry, inorganic (general) chemistry, physics.

ADMISSIONS POLICY
(TEXT PROVIDED BY SCHOOL):

   Yale seeks a diverse class of exceptional students who aspire to careers of leadership in the practice of medicine and the biomedical sciences. No rigid cut-offs are used in evaluating candidates. University grades, MCAT scores, medical and research experience, extracurricular activities, and personal qualities are all considered. State of residence and citizenship are not factors.

FINANCIAL AID

Financial aid phone number: **(203) 785-2645**
Tuition, 2009-2010 academic year: **$44,350**
Room and board: **$11,310**
Percentage of students receiving financial aid in 2009-10: **84%**
Percentage of students receiving: Loans: **69%**, Grants/scholarships: **64%**, Work-study aid: **4%**
Average medical school debt for the class of 2008: **$124,135**

STUDENT BODY

Fall 2009 full-time enrollment: **414**
Men: **51%**, Women: **49%**, In-state: **10%**, Minorities: **44%**, American Indian: **0.7%**, Asian-American: **26.8%**, African-American: **9.4%**, Hispanic-American: **6.8%**, White: **43.7%**, International: **9.4%**, Unknown: **3.1%**

ACADEMIC PROGRAMS

The school's curriculum very frequently give first-year students substantial contact with patients.

There are opportunities for first- or second-year students to work in community health clinics.

Program areas: AIDS, drug/alcohol abuse, family medicine, geriatrics, internal medicine, pediatrics, rural medicine, women's health

Joint degrees awarded: M.D./Ph.D., M.D./M.B.A., M.D./M.P.H., M.D./J.D., M.D./M.S.

Total National Institutes of Health (NIH) grants awarded to the medical school and affiliated hospitals: **$353.9 million**

CURRICULUM

(TEXT PROVIDED BY MEDICAL SCHOOL):

The core curriculum is divided into preclinical and clinical years. In the preclinical years the scientific basis of health and disease is presented. In the clinical years students rotate through clerkships followed by an Integrative Clinical Medicine course. Complementing the core curriculum are opportunities to explore the leading edge of scientific discovery and learn scientific reasoning.

FALL 2009 FACULTY PROFILE

Total teaching faculty: **1,139 (full-time)**, **57 (part-time)**

Of full-time faculty, those teaching in basic sciences: **18%**; in clinical programs: **82%**

Of part-time faculty, those teaching in basic sciences: **4%**; in clinical programs: **96%**

Full-time faculty/student ratio: **2.8**

SUPPORT SERVICES

The school offers students these services for dealing with stress: expanded-hour gym access, peer counselling, professional counseling, religious support, support groups.

RESIDENCY PROFILE

Most popular residency and specialty programs chosen by the 2008 and 2009 M.D. graduating classes: anesthesiology, dermatology, emergency medicine, internal medicine, obstetrics and gynecology, orthopaedic surgery, pediatrics, psychiatry, radiology–diagnostic, surgery–general.

WHERE GRADS GO

21.7%

Proportion of 2007-2008 graduates who entered primary care specialties

19.6%

Proportion of 2008-2009 graduates who accepted in-state residencies

Yeshiva University
Einstein

- 1300 Morris Park Avenue, Bronx, NY 10461
- Private
- **Year Founded:** 1955
- **Tuition, 2009-2010:** $45,227
- **Enrollment 2009-2010 academic year:** 780
- **Website:** http://www.einstein.yu.edu
- **Specialty ranking:** N/A

3.72 AVERAGE GPA, ENTERING CLASS FALL 2009

10.6 AVERAGE MCAT, ENTERING CLASS FALL 2009

6.9% ACCEPTANCE RATE, ENTERING CLASS FALL 2009

38 2011 U.S. NEWS MEDICAL SCHOOL RANKING (RESEARCH)

46 2011 U.S. NEWS MEDICAL SCHOOL RANKING (PRIMARY CARE)

ADMISSIONS

Admissions phone number: **(718) 430-2106**
Admissions email address: **admissions@einstein.yu.edu**
Application web site:
  http://www.einstein.yu.edu/home/admissions/Default.htm
Acceptance rate: **6.9%**
In-state acceptance rate: **10.2%**
Out-of-state acceptance rate: **6.0%**
Minority acceptance rate: **7.3%**
International acceptance rate: **2.2%**

Fall 2009 applications and acceptees

Type	Applied	Interviewed	Accepted	Enrolled
Total:	7,149	1,399	493	183
In-state:	1,543	403	157	85
Out-of-state:	5,606	996	336	98

Profile of admitted students

Average undergraduate grade point average: **3.72**
MCAT averages (scale: 1-15; writing test: J-T):
Composite score: **10.6**
Verbal reasoning score: **9.9**, Physical sciences score: **10.8**, Biological score: **11.1**, Writing score: **P**
Proportion with undergraduate majors in: Biological sciences: **54%**, Physical sciences: **16%**, Non-sciences: **26%**, Other health professions: **0%**, Mixed disciplines and other: **4%**
Percentage of students not coming directly from college after graduation: **25%**

Dates and details

The American Medical College Application Service (AMCAS) application is accepted.
School asks for a second, school-specific application as part of the admissions process.
Oldest MCAT considered for Fall 2011 entry: **2006**
Earliest application date for the 2011-2012 first-year class: **06/01**
Latest application date: **11/01**

Acceptance dates for regular application for the class entering in Fall 2011.
Earliest: **15-JAN-11**
Latest: **17-AUG-11**
Applicants have 2 weeks to respond to admissions offer.
The school does consider requests for deferred entrance.
Starting month for the class of 2011–2012: **August**
The school does have an Early Decision Plan (EDP).
A personal interview is required for admission.

Undergraduate coursework required

Medical school requires undergraduate work in these subjects: biology, English, organic chemistry, inorganic (general) chemistry, physics, mathematics.

ADMISSIONS POLICY

(TEXT PROVIDED BY SCHOOL):
  N/A

FINANCIAL AID

Financial aid phone number: **(718) 430-2336**
Tuition, 2009-2010 academic year: **$45,227**
Room and board: **$15,000**
Percentage of students receiving financial aid in 2009-10: **79%**
Percentage of students receiving: Loans: **75%**, Grants/scholarships: **53%**, Work-study aid: **0%**
Average medical school debt for the class of 2008: **$135,350**

STUDENT BODY

Fall 2009 full-time enrollment: **780**
Men: **49%**, Women: **51%**, In-state: **43%**, Minorities: **24%**, American Indian: **0.1%**, Asian-American: **15.4%**, African-American: **3.8%**, Hispanic-American: **3.1%**, White: **40.1%**, International: **2.2%**, Unknown: **35.3%**

ACADEMIC PROGRAMS

The school's curriculum frequently give first-year students substantial contact with patients.
There are opportunities for first- or second-year students to work in community health clinics.

Program areas: AIDS, drug/alcohol abuse, family
medicine, geriatrics, internal medicine, pediatrics, rural
medicine, women's health
Joint degrees awarded: M.D./Ph.D., M.D./M.P.H.,
M.D./M.S.
Total National Institutes of Health (NIH) grants awarded
to the medical school and affiliated hospitals: $214.1
million

CURRICULUM
(TEXT PROVIDED BY MEDICAL SCHOOL):

Years 1 and 2 are interdisciplinary courses (case-based
learning in small groups) and Introduction to Clinical
Medicine. Year 3 consists of clerkship rotations. Year 4
includes ambulatory care, Neurology and a hospital-based
sub-internship. Fourth year electives include global health
fellowships, and research.

FALL 2009 FACULTY PROFILE
Total teaching faculty: **2,775 (full-time), 321 (part-time)**
Of full-time faculty, those teaching in basic sciences: **13%;**
in clinical programs: **87%**
Of part-time faculty, those teaching in basic sciences: **5%;**
in clinical programs: **95%**
Full-time faculty/student ratio: **3.6**

SUPPORT SERVICES
The school offers students these services for dealing with
stress: expanded-hour gym access, peer counseling, professional counseling, religious support, support groups.

RESIDENCY PROFILE
Most popular residency and specialty programs chosen by
the 2008 and 2009 M.D. graduating classes: anesthesiology, emergency medicine, family practice, internal medicine, obstetrics and gynecology, ophthalmology, orthopaedic
surgery, pediatrics, psychiatry, radiology–diagnostic.

WHERE GRADS GO

45.0%

*Proportion of 2007-2008 graduates who entered primary
care specialties*

56.0%

*Proportion of 2008-2009 graduates who accepted in-state
residencies*

A.T. Still University of Health Sciences
Kirksville

- 800 W. Jefferson Street, Kirksville, MO 63501
- Private
- Year Founded: 1892
- Tuition, 2009-2010: $41,070
- Enrollment 2009-2010 academic year: 698
- Website: http://www.atsu.edu
- Specialty ranking: N/A

3.47 AVERAGE GPA, ENTERING CLASS FALL 2009

8.7 AVERAGE MCAT, ENTERING CLASS FALL 2009

10.9% ACCEPTANCE RATE, ENTERING CLASS FALL 2009

Unranked 2011 U.S. NEWS MEDICAL SCHOOL RANKING (RESEARCH)

Unranked 2011 U.S. NEWS MEDICAL SCHOOL RANKING (PRIMARY CARE)

ADMISSIONS

Admissions phone number: **(866) 626-2878**
Admissions email address: **admissions@atsu.edu**
Application web site: **http://aacomas.aacom.org**
Acceptance rate: **10.9%**
In-state acceptance rate: **23.4%**
Out-of-state acceptance rate: **10.0%**
Minority acceptance rate: **7.6%**
International acceptance rate: **19.4%**

Fall 2009 applications and acceptees

Type	Applied	Interviewed	Accepted	Enrolled
Total:	3,234	513	353	172
In-state:	209	78	49	39
Out-of-state:	3,025	435	304	133

Profile of admitted students

Average undergraduate grade point average: **3.47**
MCAT averages (scale: 1-15; writing test: J-T):
Composite score: **8.7**
Verbal reasoning score: **8.7**, Physical sciences score: **8.1**,
   Biological score: **9.2**, Writing score: **O**
Proportion with undergraduate majors in: Biological
   sciences: **52%**, Physical sciences: **10%**, Non-sciences:
   10%, Other health professions: **10%**, Mixed disciplines
   and other: **18%**
Percentage of students not coming directly from college
   after graduation: **N/A**

Dates and details

The American Medical College Application Service
   (AMCAS) application is not accepted.
School asks for a second, school-specific application as part
   of the admissions process.
Oldest MCAT considered for Fall 2011 entry: **2007**
Earliest application date for the 2011-2012 first-year class:
   05/01
Latest application date: **02/01**
Acceptance dates for regular application for the class
   entering in Fall 2011.
Earliest: **01-OCT-10**

Latest: **22-AUG-11**
Applicants have **4** weeks to respond to admissions offer.
The school does consider requests for deferred entrance.
Starting month for the class of 2011–2012: **August**
The school does have an Early Decision Plan (EDP).
A personal interview is required for admission.

Undergraduate coursework required

Medical school requires undergraduate work in these subjects: biology, English, organic chemistry, inorganic (general) chemistry, physics.

ADMISSIONS POLICY
(TEXT PROVIDED BY SCHOOL):

   Admissions Committee screens applicants for academic
achievement, clinical involvement, interpersonal relations,
leadership and service, maturity, motivation, and osteopathic awareness. Those selected are interviewed prior to
acceptance. Applicants are notified as soon as the
Committee decides on their status. A signed admission
agreement along with a non-refundable acceptance fee is
required.

FINANCIAL AID

Financial aid phone number: **(660) 626-2529**
Tuition, 2009-2010 academic year: **$41,070**
Room and board: **$10,912**
Percentage of students receiving financial aid in 2009-10:
   94%
Percentage of students receiving: Loans: **94%**,
   Grants/scholarships: **19%**, Work-study aid: **18%**
Average medical school debt for the class of 2008:
   $176,958

STUDENT BODY

Fall 2009 full-time enrollment: **698**
Men: **61%**, Women: **39%**, In-state: **27%**, Minorities: **15%**,
   American Indian: **0.0%**, Asian-American: **10.2%**,
   African-American: **1.3%**, Hispanic-American: **2.0%**,
   White: **79.2%**, International: **1.6%**, Unknown: **5.7%**

ACADEMIC PROGRAMS

The school's curriculum very frequently give first-year students substantial contact with patients.

There are opportunities for first- or second-year students to work in community health clinics.

Program areas: AIDS, drug/alcohol abuse, family medicine, geriatrics, internal medicine, pediatrics, rural medicine, women's health

Joint degrees awarded: D.O./M.P.H., D.O./M.S., D.O./M.H.A.

Total National Institutes of Health (NIH) grants awarded to the medical school and affiliated hospitals: **$.4 million**

CURRICULUM

(TEXT PROVIDED BY MEDICAL SCHOOL):

The Kirksville College of Osteopathic Medicine, has a 4 year curriculum that is predominately disciplined-based. The first and second year provide primarily Basic Science courses and a longitudinal course, designed to teach doctoring skills. Included are communication skills, physical exam skills, history taking skills, documentation, HIPPA, ethics, epidemiology, community medicine & geriatrics.

FALL 2009 FACULTY PROFILE

Total teaching faculty: **57 (full-time)**, **34 (part-time)**

Of full-time faculty, those teaching in basic sciences: **39%**; in clinical programs: **61%**

Of part-time faculty, those teaching in basic sciences: **12%**; in clinical programs: **88%**

Full-time faculty/student ratio: **0.1**

SUPPORT SERVICES

The school offers students these services for dealing with stress: expanded-hour gym access, peer counseling, professional counseling, religious support, support groups.

RESIDENCY PROFILE

Most popular residency and specialty programs chosen by the 2008 and 2009 M.D. graduating classes: emergency medicine, family practice, internal medicine, obstetrics and gynecology, pediatrics.

WHERE GRADS GO

51.0%

Proportion of 2007-2008 graduates who entered primary care specialties

20.0%

Proportion of 2008-2009 graduates who accepted in-state residencies

Des Moines University

- 3200 Grand Avenue, Des Moines, IA 50312
- Private
- Year Founded: 1898
- Tuition, 2009-2010: $35,840
- Enrollment 2009-2010 academic year: 869
- Website: http://www.dmu.edu
- Specialty ranking: N/A

3.70 AVERAGE GPA, ENTERING CLASS FALL 2009

9.0 AVERAGE MCAT, ENTERING CLASS FALL 2009

14.6% ACCEPTANCE RATE, ENTERING CLASS FALL 2009

Unranked 2011 U.S. NEWS MEDICAL SCHOOL RANKING (RESEARCH)

Unranked 2011 U.S. NEWS MEDICAL SCHOOL RANKING (PRIMARY CARE)

ADMISSIONS
Admissions phone number: **(515) 271-1450**
Admissions email address: **doadmit@dmu.edu**
Application web site: **N/A**
Acceptance rate: **14.6%**
In-state acceptance rate: **40.3%**
Out-of-state acceptance rate: **12.8%**
Minority acceptance rate: **9.1%**
International acceptance rate: **7.6%**

Fall 2009 applications and acceptees

Type	Applied	Interviewed	Accepted	Enrolled
Total:	3,204	665	467	221
In-state:	206	119	83	58
Out-of-state:	2,998	546	384	163

Profile of admitted students
Average undergraduate grade point average: **3.70**
MCAT averages (scale: 1-15; writing test: J-T):
Composite score: **9.0**
Verbal reasoning score: **8.9**, Physical sciences score: **8.6**, Biological score: **9.6**, Writing score: **O**
Proportion with undergraduate majors in: Biological sciences: **56%**, Physical sciences: **21%**, Non-sciences: **9%**, Other health professions: **2%**, Mixed disciplines and other: **12%**
Percentage of students not coming directly from college after graduation: **66%**

Dates and details
The American Medical College Application Service (AMCAS) application is not accepted.
School asks for a second, school-specific application as part of the admissions process.
Oldest MCAT considered for Fall 2011 entry: **2007**
Earliest application date for the 2011-2012 first-year class: **05/01**
Latest application date: **02/01**
Acceptance dates for regular application for the class entering in Fall 2011.
Earliest: **15-SEP-10**
Latest: **30-APR-11**
Applicants have 12 weeks to respond to admissions offer. The school does consider requests for deferred entrance. Starting month for the class of 2011–2012: **August** The school doesn't have an Early Decision Plan (EDP). A personal interview is required for admission.

Undergraduate coursework required
Medical school requires undergraduate work in these subjects: biology/zoology, English, organic chemistry, inorganic (general) chemistry, physics, biochemistry.

ADMISSIONS POLICY
(TEXT PROVIDED BY SCHOOL):
   The admission policies define acceptable premedical education and designate admission procedures. The practice of osteopathic medicine requires good communication skills, an understanding of individuals within their social environment, logical and quantitative thinking and a solid background in the sciences. Students are encouraged to complete a diversified undergraduate program.

FINANCIAL AID
Financial aid phone number: **(515) 271-1470**
Tuition, 2009-2010 academic year: **$35,840**
Room and board: **$14,040**
Percentage of students receiving financial aid in 2009-10: **95%**
Percentage of students receiving: Loans: **89%**, Grants/scholarships: **37%**, Work-study aid: **N/A**
Average medical school debt for the class of 2008: **$165,220**

STUDENT BODY
Fall 2009 full-time enrollment: **869**
Men: **52%**, Women: **48%**, In-state: **25%**, Minorities: **10%**, American Indian: **0.1%**, Asian-American: **8.6%**, African-American: **0.5%**, Hispanic-American: **1.8%**, White: **81.1%**, International: **1.8%**, Unknown: **6.0%**

ACADEMIC PROGRAMS

The school's curriculum occasionally give first-year students substantial contact with patients.

There are opportunities for first- or second-year students to work in community health clinics.

Program areas: family medicine, geriatrics, internal medicine, pediatrics, rural medicine, women's health

Joint degrees awarded: D.O./M.P.H., D.O./M.S., D.O./M.H.A.

Total National Institutes of Health (NIH) grants awarded to the medical school and affiliated hospitals: **$.1 million**

CURRICULUM

(TEXT PROVIDED BY MEDICAL SCHOOL):

The 1st year is focused on fundamental scientific principles that support the study of medicine. The 2nd year utilizes an organ system approach. The curriculum uses a combination of lectures, small group discussion, standardized patient & simulation experiences, & laboratory exercises. The 3rd & 4th years are spent in a clinical setting. International rotations are available.

FALL 2009 FACULTY PROFILE

Total teaching faculty: **48 (full-time)**, **885 (part-time)**

Of full-time faculty, those teaching in basic sciences: **56%**; in clinical programs: **44%**

Of part-time faculty, those teaching in basic sciences: **1%**; in clinical programs: **99%**

Full-time faculty/student ratio: **0.1**

SUPPORT SERVICES

The school offers students these services for dealing with stress: expanded-hour gym access, professional counseling.

RESIDENCY PROFILE

Most popular residency and specialty programs chosen by the 2008 and 2009 M.D. graduating classes: anesthesiology, emergency medicine, family practice, internal medicine, obstetrics and gynecology, orthopaedic surgery, pediatrics, physical medicine and rehabilitation, psychiatry, transitional year.

WHERE GRADS GO

48.0%

Proportion of 2007-2008 graduates who entered primary care specialties

16.0%

Proportion of 2008-2009 graduates who accepted in-state residencies

Edward Via Virginia
College of Osteopathic Medicine

- 2265 Kraft Drive, Blacksburg, VA 24060
- Private
- Year Founded: 2003
- Tuition, 2009-2010: $34,386
- Enrollment 2009-2010 academic year: 689
- Website: http://www.vcom.vt.edu
- Specialty ranking: N/A

3.53 AVERAGE GPA, ENTERING CLASS FALL 2009

8.3 AVERAGE MCAT, ENTERING CLASS FALL 2009

10.1% ACCEPTANCE RATE, ENTERING CLASS FALL 2009

Unranked 2011 U.S. NEWS MEDICAL SCHOOL RANKING (RESEARCH)

Unranked 2011 U.S. NEWS MEDICAL SCHOOL RANKING (PRIMARY CARE)

ADMISSIONS

Admissions phone number: **(540) 231-6138**
Admissions email address: **mprice@vcom.vt.edu**
Application web site: **http://www.aacom.org**
Acceptance rate: **10.1%**
In-state acceptance rate: **36.3%**
Out-of-state acceptance rate: **7.6%**
Minority acceptance rate: **6.2%**
International acceptance rate: **0.0%**

Fall 2009 applications and acceptees

Type	Applied	Interviewed	Accepted	Enrolled
Total:	3,150	449	317	189
In-state:	270	135	98	69
Out-of-state:	2,880	314	219	120

Profile of admitted students

Average undergraduate grade point average: **3.53**
MCAT averages (scale: 1-15; writing test: J-T):
Composite score: **8.3**
Verbal reasoning score: **8.0**, Physical sciences score: **8.0**,
   Biological score: **9.0**, Writing score: **Q**
Proportion with undergraduate majors in: Biological
   sciences: **57%**, Physical sciences: **14%**, Non-sciences:
   10%, Other health professions: **11%**, Mixed disciplines
   and other: **8%**
Percentage of students not coming directly from college
   after graduation: **50%**

Dates and details

The American Medical College Application Service
   (AMCAS) application is not accepted.
School asks for a second, school-specific application as part
   of the admissions process.
Oldest MCAT considered for Fall 2011 entry: **2007**
Earliest application date for the 2011-2012 first-year class:
   06/01
Latest application date: **02/01**
Acceptance dates for regular application for the class
   entering in Fall 2011.
Earliest: **01-OCT-10**

Latest: **04-APR-11**
Applicants have 3 weeks to respond to admissions offer.
The school does consider requests for deferred entrance.
Starting month for the class of 2011-2012: **August**
The school does have an Early Decision Plan (EDP).
A personal interview is required for admission.

Undergraduate coursework required

Medical school requires undergraduate work in these subjects: biology, English, organic chemistry, physics, demonstration of writing skills, general chemistry.

ADMISSIONS POLICY
(TEXT PROVIDED BY SCHOOL):

   Basic Requirements: Undergraduate degree including 8
hours Biology, General Chemistry, and Organic Chemistry,
6 hours Physics, English, and additional Science with minimum GPA of 2.75 and a recent MCAT score no earlier than
April 2007. Preference is given to competitive candidates
who are likely to fulfill our mission to prepare globally-
minded, community-focused physicians.

FINANCIAL AID

Financial aid phone number: **(540) 231-6021**
Tuition, 2009-2010 academic year: **$34,386**
Room and board: **$26,472**
Percentage of students receiving financial aid in 2009-10:
   94%
Percentage of students receiving: Loans: **87%**,
   Grants/scholarships: **52%**, Work-study aid: **0%**
Average medical school debt for the class of 2008:
   $165,833

STUDENT BODY

Fall 2009 full-time enrollment: **689**
Men: **49%**, Women: **51%**, In-state: **35%**, Minorities: **26%**,
   American Indian: **1.2%**, Asian-American: **11.9%**, African-
   American: **8.1%**, Hispanic-American: **5.2%**, White:
   67.2%, International: **0.3%**, Unknown: **6.1%**

ACADEMIC PROGRAMS

The school's curriculum frequently give first-year students substantial contact with patients.

There are opportunities for first- or second-year students to work in community health clinics.

Program areas: drug/alcohol abuse, family medicine, geriatrics, internal medicine, pediatrics, rural medicine, women's health

Joint degrees awarded: D.O./Ph.D., D.O./M.B.A., D.O./M.P.H., D.O./M.S.

Total National Institutes of Health (NIH) grants awarded to the medical school and affiliated hospitals: **$.3 million**

CURRICULUM

(TEXT PROVIDED BY MEDICAL SCHOOL):

The curriculum at VCOM is innovative and modern. The faculty recognizes that students learn in a number of ways. Students generally assimilate a knowledge base through instruction, reading, and experience. VCOM developed a hybrid curriculum consisting of lectures, computerized case tutorials, laboratory experiences, clinical skills laboratories, and clinical experiences throughout the four years.

FALL 2009 FACULTY PROFILE

Total teaching faculty: **41 (full-time)**, **475 (part-time)**
Of full-time faculty, those teaching in basic sciences: **39%**; in clinical programs: **61%**

Of part-time faculty, those teaching in basic sciences: **0%**; in clinical programs: **100%**
Full-time faculty/student ratio: **0.1**

SUPPORT SERVICES

The school offers students these services for dealing with stress: expanded hour gym access, peer counseling, professional counseling, religious support, support groups.

RESIDENCY PROFILE

Most popular residency and specialty programs chosen by the 2008 and 2009 M.D. graduating classes: anesthesiology, emergency medicine, family practice, family practice–sports medicine, internal medicine, obstetrics and gynecology, orthopaedic surgery, pediatrics, psychiatry.

WHERE GRADS GO

55.0%

Proportion of 2007-2008 graduates who entered primary care specialties

18.0%

Proportion of 2008-2009 graduates who accepted in-state residencies

Lake Erie College of Osteopathic Med.

- 1858 W. Grandview Boulevard, Erie, PA 16509
- Private
- **Year Founded:** 1992
- **Tuition, 2009-2010:** $27,500
- **Enrollment 2009-2010 academic year:** 1,717
- **Website:** http://www.lecom.edu
- **Specialty ranking:** N/A

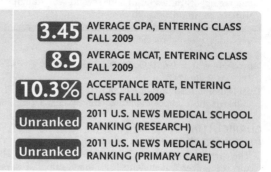

3.45 AVERAGE GPA, ENTERING CLASS FALL 2009

8.9 AVERAGE MCAT, ENTERING CLASS FALL 2009

10.3% ACCEPTANCE RATE, ENTERING CLASS FALL 2009

Unranked 2011 U.S. NEWS MEDICAL SCHOOL RANKING (RESEARCH)

Unranked 2011 U.S. NEWS MEDICAL SCHOOL RANKING (PRIMARY CARE)

ADMISSIONS

Admissions phone number: **(814) 866-6641**
Admissions email address: **admissions@lecom.edu**
Application web site: **http://www.aacom.org**
Acceptance rate: **10.3%**
In-state acceptance rate: **14.2%**
Out-of-state acceptance rate: **9.2%**
Minority acceptance rate: **18.5%**
International acceptance rate: **N/A**

Fall 2009 applications and acceptees

Type	Applied	Interviewed	Accepted	Enrolled
Total:	7,978	2,347	819	529
In-state:	1,743	983	247	201
Out-of-state:	6,235	1,364	572	328

Profile of admitted students

Average undergraduate grade point average: **3.45**
MCAT averages (scale: 1-15; writing test: J-T):
Composite score: **8.9**
Verbal reasoning score: **8.9**, Physical sciences score: **8.4**,
  Biological score: **9.4**, Writing score: **O**
Proportion with undergraduate majors in: Biological
  sciences: **63%**, Physical sciences: **15%**, Non-sciences:
  12%, Other health professions: **1%**, Mixed disciplines
  and other: **9%**
Percentage of students not coming directly from college
  after graduation: **21%**

Dates and details

The American Medical College Application Service
  (AMCAS) application is not accepted.
School asks for a second, school-specific application as part
  of the admissions process.
Oldest MCAT considered for Fall 2011 entry: **2008**
Earliest application date for the 2011-2012 first-year class:
  06/01
Latest application date: **04/01**
Acceptance dates for regular application for the class
  entering in Fall 2011.
Earliest: **01-SEP-09**

Latest: **26-JUL-10**
Applicants have 4 weeks to respond to admissions offer.
The school does consider requests for deferred entrance.
Starting month for the class of 2011–2012: **July**
The school doesn't have an Early Decision Plan (EDP).
A personal interview is required for admission.

Undergraduate coursework required

Medical school requires undergraduate work in these subjects: biology, English, organic chemistry, inorganic (general) chemistry, physics, molecular and cell biology,
humanities, mathematics, behavioral science, demonstration of writing skills, social sciences, general chemistry.

ADMISSIONS POLICY
(TEXT PROVIDED BY SCHOOL):

LECOM seeks students who will excel in academics, clinical care, research and community service. Successful candidates have GPAs of 3.3 or higher and MCATs of 24 or
higher. LECOM requires a D.O. recommendation showing
the applicant has awareness of osteopathic medicine.
Working with a physician prepares students for the
required interview. LECOM sets no limits on out-of-state
resident admissions.

FINANCIAL AID

Financial aid phone number: **(814) 866-6641**
Tuition, 2009-2010 academic year: **$27,500**
Room and board: **$11,550**
Percentage of students receiving financial aid in 2009-10:
  93%
Percentage of students receiving: Loans: **89%**,
  Grants/scholarships: **31%**, Work-study aid: **0%**
Average medical school debt for the class of 2008:
  $158,000

STUDENT BODY

Fall 2009 full-time enrollment: **1,717**
Men: **54%**, Women: **46%**, In-state: **29%**, Minorities: **26%**,
  American Indian: **0.5%**, Asian-American: **17.4%**,

African-American: **1.5%**, Hispanic-American: **3.4%**, White: **74.7%**, International: **0.1%**, Unknown: **2.5%**

ACADEMIC PROGRAMS

The school's curriculum occasionally give first-year students substantial contact with patients.

There are opportunities for first- or second-year students to work in community health clinics.

Program areas: AIDS, drug/alcohol abuse, family medicine, geriatrics, internal medicine, pediatrics, rural medicine, women's health

Joint degrees awarded: D.O./M.S.

Total National Institutes of Health (NIH) grants awarded to the medical school and affiliated hospitals: **$.0 million**

CURRICULUM

(TEXT PROVIDED BY MEDICAL SCHOOL):

LECOM offers student-centered learning pathways at three locations: Erie and Greensburg, Pennsylvania and Bradenton Florida. LECOM students also choose from traditional lecture-discussion, small group problem-based learning, and independent study curricula. The new Primary Care Scholars pathway provides a condensed three-year track to becoming a family physician.

FALL 2009 FACULTY PROFILE

Total teaching faculty: **568 (full-time)**, **1,484 (part-time)**

Of full-time faculty, those teaching in basic sciences: **9%**; in clinical programs: **91%**

Of part-time faculty, those teaching in basic sciences: **2%**; in clinical programs: **98%**

Full-time faculty/student ratio: **0.3**

SUPPORT SERVICES

The school offers students these services for dealing with stress: expanded-hour gym access, peer counseling, professional counseling, religious support, support groups.

RESIDENCY PROFILE

Most popular residency and specialty programs chosen by the 2008 and 2009 M.D. graduating classes: anesthesiology, emergency medicine, family practice, internal medicine, neurology, obstetrics and gynecology, physical medicine and rehabilitation, psychiatry, surgery–general.

WHERE GRADS GO

61.0%

Proportion of 2007-2008 graduates who entered primary care specialties

32.0%

Proportion of 2008-2009 graduates who accepted in-state residencies

Michigan State University

- A308 E. Fee Hall, East Lansing, MI 48824
- Public
- **Year Founded:** 1969
- **Tuition, 2009-2010:** In-state: $32,114; Out-of-State: $69,581
- **Enrollment 2009-2010 academic year:** 959
- **Website:** http://www.com.msu.edu
- **Specialty ranking:** N/A

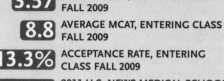

3.57	AVERAGE GPA, ENTERING CLASS FALL 2009
8.8	AVERAGE MCAT, ENTERING CLASS FALL 2009
13.3%	ACCEPTANCE RATE, ENTERING CLASS FALL 2009
Unranked	2011 U.S. NEWS MEDICAL SCHOOL RANKING (RESEARCH)
7	2011 U.S. NEWS MEDICAL SCHOOL RANKING (PRIMARY CARE)

ADMISSIONS

Admissions phone number: **(517) 353-7740**
Admissions email address: **com.admissions@hc.msu.edu**
Application web site: **http://com.msu.edu/admissions**
Acceptance rate: **13.3%**
In-state acceptance rate: **47.9%**
Out-of-state acceptance rate: **2.1%**
Minority acceptance rate: **7.6%**
International acceptance rate: **N/A**

Fall 2009 applications and acceptees

Type	Applied	Interviewed	Accepted	Enrolled
Total:	3,455	552	459	315
In-state:	841	494	403	292
Out-of-state:	2,614	58	56	23

Profile of admitted students

Average undergraduate grade point average: **3.57**
MCAT averages (scale: 1-15; writing test: J-T):
Composite score: **8.8**
Verbal reasoning score: **8.5**, Physical sciences score: **8.6**, Biological score: **9.4**, Writing score: **O**
Proportion with undergraduate majors in: Biological sciences: **60%**, Physical sciences: **4%**, Non-sciences: **14%**, Other health professions: **8%**, Mixed disciplines and other: **14%**
Percentage of students not coming directly from college after graduation: **15%**

Dates and details

The American Medical College Application Service (AMCAS) application is not accepted.
School asks for a second, school-specific application as part of the admissions process.
Oldest MCAT considered for Fall 2011 entry: **2007**
Earliest application date for the 2011-2012 first-year class: **06/10**
Latest application date: **12/01**
Acceptance dates for regular application for the class entering in Fall 2011.
Earliest: **09-SEP-10**

Latest: **17-JUN-11**
Applicants have 10 weeks to respond to admissions offer.
The school does consider requests for deferred entrance.
Starting month for the class of 2011–2012: **June**
The school doesn't have an Early Decision Plan (EDP).
A personal interview isn't required for admission.

Undergraduate coursework required

Medical school requires undergraduate work in these subjects: biology, biology/zoology, English, organic chemistry, inorganic (general) chemistry, physics, biochemistry, behavioral science, general chemistry.

ADMISSIONS POLICY

(TEXT PROVIDED BY SCHOOL):

Minimum to receive a secondary: 2.7 science and overall GPA, total MCAT score of 18 (min. 4 verbal, 5 phys sci, and 6 biologic sci). Application review is 60% academic and 40% nonacademic. Final eval: academic ability, level/type of coursework, MCAT scores, academic honors, commitment to service, breadth of experiences, communication, leadership, collaboration, problem solving, critical thinking.

FINANCIAL AID

Financial aid phone number: **(517) 353-5188**
Tuition, 2009-2010 academic year: **In-state: $32,114; Out-of-State: $69,581**
Room and board: **$15,792**
Percentage of students receiving financial aid in 2009-10: **92%**
Percentage of students receiving: Loans: **86%**, Grants/scholarships: **48%**, Work-study aid: **N/A**
Average medical school debt for the class of 2008: **$171,752**

STUDENT BODY

Fall 2009 full-time enrollment: **959**
Men: **54%**, Women: **46%**, In-state: **92%**, Minorities: **19%**, American Indian: **0.4%**, Asian-American: **13.7%**, African-American: **2.9%**, Hispanic-American: **2.0%**, White: **80.6%**, International: **0.4%**, Unknown: **0.0%**

ACADEMIC PROGRAMS

The school's curriculum occasionally give first-year students substantial contact with patients.

There are opportunities for first- or second-year students to work in community health clinics.

Program areas: AIDS, drug/alcohol abuse, family medicine, geriatrics, internal medicine, pediatrics, rural medicine, women's health

Joint degrees awarded: D.O./Ph.D., D.O./M.P.H., D.O./M.S.

Total National Institutes of Health (NIH) grants awarded to the medical school and affiliated hospitals: **$5.1 million**

CURRICULUM

(TEXT PROVIDED BY MEDICAL SCHOOL):

The college is dedicated to assist in meeting the ever-growing public demand for physicians who can provide comprehensive and continuing health care to all members of the family. While the educational program of MSUCOM is geared to the training of primary care physicians, the curricula are also designed to meet the continuing need for medical specialists and teacher-investigators.

FALL 2009 FACULTY PROFILE

Total teaching faculty: **212 (full-time), 34 (part-time)**
Of full-time faculty, those teaching in basic sciences: **32%**; in clinical programs: **68%**

Of part-time faculty, those teaching in basic sciences: **15%**; in clinical programs: **85%**
Full-time faculty/student ratio: **0.2**

SUPPORT SERVICES

The school offers students these services for dealing with stress: expanded-hour gym access, peer counseling, professional counseling, religious support, support groups.

RESIDENCY PROFILE

Most popular residency and specialty programs chosen by the 2008 and 2009 M.D. graduating classes: anesthesiology, emergency medicine, family practice, internal medicine, neurology, obstetrics and gynecology, orthopaedic surgery, pediatrics, surgery–general, transitional year.

WHERE GRADS GO

80.5%
Proportion of 2007-2008 graduates who entered primary care specialties

82.7%
Proportion of 2008-2009 graduates who accepted in-state residencies

Nova Southeastern University

- 3200 S. University Drive, Fort Lauderdale, FL 33328
- Private
- Year Founded: 1979
- Tuition, 2009-2010: $32,933
- Enrollment 2009-2010 academic year: 925
- Website: http://medicine.nova.edu
- Specialty ranking: N/A

3.44 AVERAGE GPA, ENTERING CLASS FALL 2009

9.6 AVERAGE MCAT, ENTERING CLASS FALL 2009

17.3% ACCEPTANCE RATE, ENTERING CLASS FALL 2009

Unranked 2011 U.S. NEWS MEDICAL SCHOOL RANKING (RESEARCH)

Unranked 2011 U.S. NEWS MEDICAL SCHOOL RANKING (PRIMARY CARE)

ADMISSIONS

Admissions phone number: **(954) 262-1101**
Admissions email address: **comreply@nova.edu**
Application web site: **http://hpd.nova.edu/**
Acceptance rate: **17.3%**
In-state acceptance rate: **22.4%**
Out-of-state acceptance rate: **15.6%**
Minority acceptance rate: **12.3%**
International acceptance rate: **N/A**

Fall 2009 applications and acceptees

Type	Applied	Interviewed	Accepted	Enrolled
Total:	2,651	508	458	235
In-state:	647	162	145	101
Out-of-state:	2,004	346	313	134

Profile of admitted students

Average undergraduate grade point average: **3.44**
MCAT averages (scale: 1-15; writing test: J-T):
Composite score: **9.6**
Verbal reasoning score: **9.4**, Physical sciences score: **9.4**,
 Biological score: **9.4**, Writing score: **M**
Proportion with undergraduate majors in: Biological
 sciences: **28%**, Physical sciences: **6%**, Non-sciences:
 17%, Other health professions: **4%**, Mixed disciplines
 and other: **45%**
Percentage of students not coming directly from college
 after graduation: **6%**

Dates and details

The American Medical College Application Service
 (AMCAS) application is not accepted.
School asks for a second, school-specific application as part
 of the admissions process.
Oldest MCAT considered for Fall 2011 entry: **2008**
Earliest application date for the 2011-2012 first-year class:
 05/15
Latest application date: **02/01**
Acceptance dates for regular application for the class
 entering in Fall 2011.
Earliest: **01-SEP-10**

Latest: **01-MAY-11**
Applicants have 4 weeks to respond to admissions offer.
The school does consider requests for deferred entrance.
Starting month for the class of 2011–2012: **August**
The school doesn't have an Early Decision Plan (EDP).
A personal interview is required for admission.

Undergraduate coursework required

Medical school requires undergraduate work in these subjects: biology, English, organic chemistry, inorganic (general) chemistry, physics, humanities, demonstration of
writing skills, general chemistry.

ADMISSIONS POLICY

(TEXT PROVIDED BY SCHOOL):
 Prefer bachelor's but at least 90 semester hours.
Prerequisites: biology, chemistry, organic chemistry,
physics–8 semester hours; English composition and literature–3 semester hours, MCATs; preprofessional committee
letter or a letter from 3 professors and 1 physician; personal
interview for invited applicants. Florida residents eligible for
reduced tuition.

FINANCIAL AID

Financial aid phone number: **(954) 262-3380**
Tuition, 2009-2010 academic year: **$32,933**
Room and board: **$18,260**
Percentage of students receiving financial aid in 2009-10:
 97%
Percentage of students receiving: Loans: **96%**,
 Grants/scholarships: **3%**, Work-study aid: **0%**
Average medical school debt for the class of 2008:
 $162,148

STUDENT BODY

Fall 2009 full-time enrollment: **925**
Men: **54%**, Women: **46%**, In-state: **49%**, Minorities: **36%**,
 American Indian: **0.4%**, Asian-American: **22.5%**,
 African-American: **3.2%**, Hispanic-American: **9.7%**,
 White: **57.7%**, International: **1.7%**, Unknown: **4.6%**

ACADEMIC PROGRAMS

The school's curriculum very frequently give first-year students substantial contact with patients.

There are opportunities for first- or second-year students to work in community health clinics.

Program areas: AIDS, drug/alcohol abuse, family medicine, geriatrics, internal medicine, pediatrics, rural medicine, women's health

Joint degrees awarded: D.O./M.B.A., D.O./M.P.H., D.O./M.H.I.

Total National Institutes of Health (NIH) grants awarded to the medical school and affiliated hospitals: **$.6 million**

CURRICULUM

(TEXT PROVIDED BY MEDICAL SCHOOL):

Curriculum emphasizes primary care and a holistic approach to patients with students in clinical settings in the 1st year. Clinical exposure continues in 2nd year with standardized patients and a systems approach to integrating didactic coursework. Years 3 and 4 involve 16 months of rotations featuring 3 months in rural medically underserved locations. There are also 5 months of electives.

FALL 2009 FACULTY PROFILE

Total teaching faculty: 111 (full-time), 950 (part-time)
Of full-time faculty, those teaching in basic sciences: 27%; in clinical programs: 73%

Of part-time faculty, those teaching in basic sciences: 0%; in clinical programs: 100%
Full-time faculty/student ratio: 0.1

SUPPORT SERVICES

The school offers students these services for dealing with stress: expanded hour gym access, peer counseling, professional counseling, religious support, support groups.

RESIDENCY PROFILE

Most popular residency and specialty programs chosen by the 2008 and 2009 M.D. graduating classes: anesthesiology, emergency medicine, family practice, internal medicine, pediatrics, surgery–general.

WHERE GRADS GO

50.0%
Proportion of 2007-2008 graduates who entered primary care specialties

22.0%
Proportion of 2008-2009 graduates who accepted in-state residencies

Ohio University

- **Grosvenor and Irvine Halls, Athens, OH 45701**
- **Public**
- **Year Founded:** 1975
- **Tuition, 2009-2010:** In-state: $27,744; Out-of-State: $39,210
- **Enrollment 2009-2010 academic year:** 461
- **Website:** http://www.oucom.ohiou.edu
- **Specialty ranking:** family medicine: 22

3.63	AVERAGE GPA, ENTERING CLASS FALL 2009
8.2	AVERAGE MCAT, ENTERING CLASS FALL 2009
5.2%	ACCEPTANCE RATE, ENTERING CLASS FALL 2009
Unranked	2011 U.S. NEWS MEDICAL SCHOOL RANKING (RESEARCH)
Unranked	2011 U.S. NEWS MEDICAL SCHOOL RANKING (PRIMARY CARE)

ADMISSIONS

Admissions phone number: **(740) 593-4313**
Admissions email address: **admissions@oucom.ohiou.edu**
Application web site: **http://www.aacom.org**
Acceptance rate: **5.2%**
In-state acceptance rate: **26.6%**
Out-of-state acceptance rate: **1.1%**
Minority acceptance rate: **4.1%**
International acceptance rate: **0.0%**

Fall 2009 applications and acceptees

Type	Applied	Interviewed	Accepted	Enrolled
Total:	3,379	213	177	120
In-state:	553	173	147	97
Out-of-state:	2,826	40	30	23

Profile of admitted students

Average undergraduate grade point average: **3.63**
MCAT averages (scale: 1-15; writing test: J-T):
Composite score: **8.2**
Verbal reasoning score: **7.9**, Physical sciences score: **7.9**,
  Biological score: **8.7**, Writing score: **P**
Proportion with undergraduate majors in: Biological
  sciences: **62%**, Physical sciences: **12%**, Non-sciences:
  5%, Other health professions: **12%**, Mixed disciplines
  and other: **9%**
Percentage of students not coming directly from college
  after graduation: **56%**

Dates and details

The American Medical College Application Service
  (AMCAS) application is not accepted.
School asks for a second, school-specific application as part
  of the admissions process.
Oldest MCAT considered for Fall 2011 entry: **2008**
Earliest application date for the 2011-2012 first-year class:
  N/A
Latest application date: **N/A**
Acceptance dates for regular application for the class
  entering in Fall 2011.
Earliest: **22-JUL-10**

Latest: **26-JUL-11**
Applicants have 2 weeks to respond to admissions offer.
The school does consider requests for deferred entrance.
Starting month for the class of 2011–2012: **July**
The school doesn't have an Early Decision Plan (EDP).
A personal interview is required for admission.

Undergraduate coursework required

Medical school requires undergraduate work in these subjects: biology, biology/zoology, English, organic chemistry,
inorganic (general) chemistry, physics, behavioral science,
social sciences, general chemistry.

ADMISSIONS POLICY
(TEXT PROVIDED BY SCHOOL):

Superior academic performance and strong MCATs, dedication to humane medical care delivery, motivation for
osteopathic medicine, excellent communication skills; 4-
year baccalaureate degree preferred; must be U.S. citizen or
hold permanent visa, present letters of recommendation,
and preference given to Ohio residents. Information available at www.oucom.ohiou.edu/Admissions/deadlines.htm.

FINANCIAL AID

Financial aid phone number: **(740) 593-2158**
Tuition, 2009-2010 academic year: **In-state: $27,744; Out-
  of-State: $39,210**
Room and board: **$12,992**
Percentage of students receiving financial aid in 2009-10:
  92%
Percentage of students receiving: Loans: **91%**,
  Grants/scholarships: **24%**, Work-study aid: **0%**
Average medical school debt for the class of 2008:
  $150,868

STUDENT BODY

Fall 2009 full-time enrollment: **461**
Men: **47%**, Women: **53%**, In-state: **95%**, Minorities: **25%**,
  American Indian: **1.3%**, Asian-American: **9.1%**, African-
  American: **10.6%**, Hispanic-American: **4.3%**, White:
  74.6%, International: **0.0%**, Unknown: **0.0%**

ACADEMIC PROGRAMS

The school's curriculum very frequently give first-year students substantial contact with patients.

There are opportunities for first- or second-year students to work in community health clinics.

Program areas: AIDS, drug/alcohol abuse, family medicine, geriatrics, internal medicine, pediatrics, rural medicine, women's health

Joint degrees awarded: D.O./Ph.D., D.O./M.B.A., D.O./M.P.H., D.O./M.S.W., D.O./M.S., D.O./M.A., D.O./M.H.A.

Total National Institutes of Health (NIH) grants awarded to the medical school and affiliated hospitals: **$.9 million**

CURRICULUM

(TEXT PROVIDED BY MEDICAL SCHOOL):

Student empowerment and clinical relevance form the basis of OUCOMs two tracks of study. Years 1 and 2 integrate clinical, biomedical & social medicine fundamentals and include patient interaction. Years 3 and 4 involve clinical rotations in our hospital system with didactic components in medicine, ethics and law. See http://www.oucom.ohiou.edu/Admissions/curricula.htm

FALL 2009 FACULTY PROFILE

Total teaching faculty: **96 (full-time)**, **1,822 (part-time)**

Of full-time faculty, those teaching in basic sciences: **56%**; in clinical programs: **44%**

Of part-time faculty, those teaching in basic sciences: **1%**; in clinical programs: **99%**

Full-time faculty/student ratio: **0.2**

SUPPORT SERVICES

The school offers students these services for dealing with stress: expanded-hour gym access, peer counseling, professional counseling, religious support, support groups.

RESIDENCY PROFILE

Most popular residency and specialty programs chosen by the 2008 and 2009 M.D. graduating classes: anesthesiology, emergency medicine, family practice, internal medicine, obstetrics and gynecology, orthopaedic surgery, pediatrics, psychiatry, surgery–general, transitional year.

WHERE GRADS GO

47.0%

Proportion of 2007-2008 graduates who entered primary care specialties

73.0%

Proportion of 2008-2009 graduates who accepted in-state residencies

Oklahoma State University

- 1111 W. 17th Street, Tulsa, OK 74107-1898
- Public
- Year Founded: 1972
- Tuition, 2009-2010: In-state: $20,065; Out-of-State: $37,987
- Enrollment 2009-2010 academic year: 357
- Website: http://healthsciences.okstate.edu
- Specialty ranking: N/A

3.59 AVERAGE GPA, ENTERING CLASS FALL 2009

8.4 AVERAGE MCAT, ENTERING CLASS FALL 2009

23.0% ACCEPTANCE RATE, ENTERING CLASS FALL 2009

Unranked 2011 U.S. NEWS MEDICAL SCHOOL RANKING (RESEARCH)

Unranked 2011 U.S. NEWS MEDICAL SCHOOL RANKING (PRIMARY CARE)

ADMISSIONS

Admissions phone number: **(918) 561-8421**
Admissions email address: **sarah.quinten@okstate.edu**
Application web site: **http://www.aacom.org**
Acceptance rate: **23.0%**
In-state acceptance rate: **48.1%**
Out-of-state acceptance rate: **7.4%**
Minority acceptance rate: **15.1%**
International acceptance rate: **N/A**

Fall 2009 applications and acceptees

Type	Applied	Interviewed	Accepted	Enrolled
Total:	614	210	141	92
In-state:	235	174	113	82
Out-of-state:	379	36	28	10

Profile of admitted students

Average undergraduate grade point average: **3.59**
MCAT averages (scale: 1-15; writing test: J-T):
Composite score: **8.4**
Verbal reasoning score: **8.4**, Physical sciences score: **7.9**, Biological score: **9.0**, Writing score: **N**
Proportion with undergraduate majors in: Biological sciences: **59%**, Physical sciences: **12%**, Non-sciences: **8%**, Other health professions: **6%**, Mixed disciplines and other: **15%**
Percentage of students not coming directly from college after graduation: **N/A**

Dates and details

The American Medical College Application Service (AMCAS) application is not accepted.
School asks for a second, school-specific application as part of the admissions process.
Oldest MCAT considered for Fall 2011 entry: **2007**
Earliest application date for the 2011-2012 first-year class: **06/01**
Latest application date: **02/01**
Acceptance dates for regular application for the class entering in Fall 2011.
Earliest: **01-OCT-11**

Latest: **08-AUG-11**
Applicants have 8 weeks to respond to admissions offer.
The school does consider requests for deferred entrance.
Starting month for the class of 2011–2012: **August**
The school doesn't have an Early Decision Plan (EDP).
A personal interview is required for admission.

Undergraduate coursework required

Medical school requires undergraduate work in these subjects: biology, biology/zoology, English, organic chemistry, inorganic (general) chemistry, physics, molecular and cell biology, biochemistry, general chemistry.

ADMISSIONS POLICY
(TEXT PROVIDED BY SCHOOL):

Scholarship, aptitude, and motivation, academic achievement, evaluations from pre-professional committees and osteopathic physicians, MCAT results, on-campus interview, motivation to be osteopathic physician are factors. Preference to Oklahoma applicants. Qualified minority students actively recruited.

FINANCIAL AID

Financial aid phone number: **(918) 561-1228**
Tuition, 2009-2010 academic year: **In-state: $20,065; Out-of-State: $37,987**
Room and board: **$7,200**
Percentage of students receiving financial aid in 2009-10: **95%**
Percentage of students receiving: Loans: **92%**, Grants/scholarships: **16%**, Work-study aid: **32%**
Average medical school debt for the class of 2008: **$146,359**

STUDENT BODY

Fall 2009 full-time enrollment: **357**
Men: **52%**, Women: **48%**, In-state: **85%**, Minorities: **27%**, American Indian: **9.5%**, Asian-American: **7.0%**, African-American: **4.8%**, Hispanic-American: **5.6%**, White: **71.7%**, International: **0.0%**, Unknown: **1.4%**

ACADEMIC PROGRAMS

The school's curriculum occasionally give first-year students substantial contact with patients.

There are opportunities for first- or second-year students to work in community health clinics.

Program areas: AIDS, drug/alcohol abuse, family medicine, geriatrics, internal medicine, pediatrics, rural medicine, women's health

Joint degrees awarded: D.O./Ph.D., D.O./M.B.A., D.O./M.S.

Total National Institutes of Health (NIH) grants awarded to the medical school and affiliated hospitals: **$.6 million**

CURRICULUM

(TEXT PROVIDED BY MEDICAL SCHOOL):

Curriculum is student-centered; hands-on experience, problem-based and small group learning. Training in all areas of medicine, also osteopathic manipulation. First year: biomedical sciences; second year: case-based learning and problem solving as it relates to conditions seen in primary care; third and fourth years: clinical rotations in hospitals in urban and rural areas.

FALL 2009 FACULTY PROFILE

Total teaching faculty: **94 (full-time)**, **643 (part-time)**

Of full-time faculty, those teaching in basic sciences: **39%**; in clinical programs: **61%**

Of part-time faculty, those teaching in basic sciences: **5%**; in clinical programs: **95%**

Full-time faculty/student ratio: **0.3**

SUPPORT SERVICES

The school offers students these services for dealing with stress: expanded hour gym access, peer counseling, professional counseling, religious support, support groups.

RESIDENCY PROFILE

Most popular residency and specialty programs chosen by the 2008 and 2009 M.D. graduating classes: anesthesiology, emergency medicine, family practice, internal medicine, obstetrics and gynecology, pediatrics, psychiatry, radiology–diagnostic, surgery–general.

WHERE GRADS GO

45.0%

Proportion of 2007-2008 graduates who entered primary care specialties

55.0%

Proportion of 2008-2009 graduates who accepted in-state residencies

Pikeville College

- 147 Sycamore Street, Pikeville, KY 41501
- Private
- **Year Founded:** 1997
- **Tuition, 2009-2010:** $33,450
- **Enrollment 2009-2010 academic year:** 302
- **Website:** http://www.pc.edu
- **Specialty ranking:** N/A

3.44 AVERAGE GPA, ENTERING CLASS FALL 2009

7.4 AVERAGE MCAT, ENTERING CLASS FALL 2009

5.1% ACCEPTANCE RATE, ENTERING CLASS FALL 2009

Unranked 2011 U.S. NEWS MEDICAL SCHOOL RANKING (RESEARCH)

Unranked 2011 U.S. NEWS MEDICAL SCHOOL RANKING (PRIMARY CARE)

ADMISSIONS

Admissions phone number: **(606) 218-5406**
Admissions email address: **ahamilto@pc.edu**
Application web site: **http://www.aacom.org**
Acceptance rate: **5.1%**
In-state acceptance rate: **41.7%**
Out-of-state acceptance rate: **3.2%**
Minority acceptance rate: **3.0%**
International acceptance rate: **0.0%**

Fall 2009 applications and acceptees

Type	Applied	Interviewed	Accepted	Enrolled
Total:	2,301	253	118	81
In-state:	115	70	48	32
Out-of-state:	2,186	183	70	49

Profile of admitted students

Average undergraduate grade point average: **3.44**
MCAT averages (scale: 1-15; writing test: J-T):
Composite score: **7.4**
Verbal reasoning score: **7.4**, Physical sciences score: **7.0**, Biological score: **7.9**, Writing score: **N**
Proportion with undergraduate majors in: Biological sciences: **70%**, Physical sciences: **15%**, Non-sciences: **14%**, Other health professions: **1%**, Mixed disciplines and other: **0%**
Percentage of students not coming directly from college after graduation: **49%**

Dates and details

The American Medical College Application Service (AMCAS) application is not accepted.
School asks for a second, school-specific application as part of the admissions process.
Oldest MCAT considered for Fall 2011 entry: **2008**
Earliest application date for the 2011-2012 first-year class: **05/01**
Latest application date: **02/01**
Acceptance dates for regular application for the class entering in Fall 2011.
Earliest: **01-NOV-10**

Latest: **01-AUG-11**
Applicants have 6 weeks to respond to admissions offer.
The school does consider requests for deferred entrance.
Starting month for the class of 2011-2012: **August**
The school doesn't have an Early Decision Plan (EDP).
A personal interview is required for admission.

Undergraduate coursework required

Medical school requires undergraduate work in these subjects: biology, biology/zoology, English, organic chemistry, inorganic (general) chemistry, physics, general chemistry.

ADMISSIONS POLICY
(TEXT PROVIDED BY SCHOOL):

Applicants to the college are considered on their intellectual ability, scholastic achievement, commitment, and suitability to succeed in the study of osteopathic medicine and their ability to help achieve the mission of the school.

FINANCIAL AID

Financial aid phone number: **(606) 218-5407**
Tuition, 2009-2010 academic year: **$33,450**
Room and board: **N/A**
Percentage of students receiving financial aid in 2009-10: **97%**
Percentage of students receiving: Loans: **93%**, Grants/scholarships: **42%**, Work-study aid: **N/A**
Average medical school debt for the class of 2008: **$158,470**

STUDENT BODY

Fall 2009 full-time enrollment: **302**
Men: **56%**, Women: **44%**, In-state: **50%**, Minorities: **6%**, American Indian: **0.3%**, Asian-American: **6.3%**, African-American: **2.3%**, Hispanic-American: **1.3%**, White: **85.8%**, International: **1.0%**, Unknown: **3.0%**

ACADEMIC PROGRAMS

The school's curriculum occasionally give first-year students substantial contact with patients.

There are opportunities for first- or second-year students to work in community health clinics.

Program areas: AIDS, drug/alcohol abuse, family medicine, geriatrics, internal medicine, pediatrics, rural medicine, women's health

Joint degrees awarded: N/A

Total National Institutes of Health (NIH) grants awarded to the medical school and affiliated hospitals: N/A

CURRICULUM

(TEXT PROVIDED BY MEDICAL SCHOOL):

First and second year: Didactic lecture and lab, problem-based learning, computer-based case studies, primary care office interactions, scientific paper review and presentation, essay production. Third and fourth year: clinical rotations, clinical conferences, computer-based case studies.

FALL 2009 FACULTY PROFILE

Total teaching faculty: **20 (full-time)**, **860 (part-time)**

Of full-time faculty, those teaching in basic sciences: **70%**; in clinical programs: **30%**

Of part-time faculty, those teaching in basic sciences: **0%**; in clinical programs: **100%**

Full-time faculty/student ratio: **0.1**

SUPPORT SERVICES

The school offers students these services for dealing with stress: peer counseling, professional counseling, religious support, support groups.

RESIDENCY PROFILE

Most popular residency and specialty programs chosen by the 2008 and 2009 M.D. graduating classes: emergency medicine, family practice, internal medicine, obstetrics and gynecology, pediatrics, surgery–general.

WHERE GRADS GO

64.0%

Proportion of 2007-2008 graduates who entered primary care specialties

15.0%

Proportion of 2008-2009 graduates who accepted in-state residencies

Touro University

- 1310 Johnson Lane, Vallejo, CA 94592
- Private
- Year Founded: 1997
- Tuition, 2009-2010: $39,000
- Enrollment 2009-2010 academic year: 540
- Website: http://www.tu.edu
- Specialty ranking: N/A

3.42 AVERAGE GPA, ENTERING CLASS FALL 2009

9.3 AVERAGE MCAT, ENTERING CLASS FALL 2009

6.0% ACCEPTANCE RATE, ENTERING CLASS FALL 2009

Unranked 2011 U.S. NEWS MEDICAL SCHOOL RANKING (RESEARCH)

Unranked 2011 U.S. NEWS MEDICAL SCHOOL RANKING (PRIMARY CARE)

ADMISSIONS

Admissions phone number: **(707) 638-5270**
Admissions email address: **donald.haight@tu.edu**
Application web site:
   http://www.tu.edu/departments.php?id=48&page=737
Acceptance rate: **6.0%**
In-state acceptance rate: **N/A**
Out-of-state acceptance rate: **N/A**
Minority acceptance rate: **N/A**
International acceptance rate: **N/A**

Fall 2009 applications and acceptees

Type	Applied	Interviewed	Accepted	Enrolled
Total:	3,653	425	219	135
In-state:	N/A	N/A	N/A	N/A
Out-of-state:	N/A	N/A	N/A	N/A

Profile of admitted students

Average undergraduate grade point average: **3.42**
MCAT averages (scale: 1-15; writing test: J-T):
Composite score: **9.3**
Verbal reasoning score: **8.5**, Physical sciences score: **8.9**,
   Biological score: **10.5**, Writing score: **P**
Proportion with undergraduate majors in: Biological
   sciences: **68%**, Physical sciences: **26%**, Non-sciences:
   5%, Other health professions: **1%**, Mixed disciplines and
   other: **0%**
Percentage of students not coming directly from college
   after graduation: **34%**

Dates and details

The American Medical College Application Service
   (AMCAS) application is not accepted.
School asks for a second, school-specific application as part
   of the admissions process.
Oldest MCAT considered for Fall 2011 entry: **2007**
Earliest application date for the 2011-2012 first-year class:
   N/A
Latest application date: **N/A**
Acceptance dates for regular application for the class
   entering in Fall 2011.

Earliest: **01-OCT-10**
Latest: **30-JUN-11**
Applicants have 2 weeks to respond to admissions offer.
The school does consider requests for deferred entrance.
Starting month for the class of 2011-2012: **August**
The school doesn't have an Early Decision Plan (EDP).
A personal interview is required for admission.

Undergraduate coursework required

Medical school requires undergraduate work in these subjects: biology, English, organic chemistry, inorganic (general) chemistry, physics, behavioral science.

ADMISSIONS POLICY
(TEXT PROVIDED BY SCHOOL):

   TUCOM-CA has no mandate to enroll particular percentages of in-State residents. Complete the primary application
with AACOMAS. TUCOM's code number is 618. Qualified
candidates will be instructed to complete the secondary
application process. TUCOM requires letters of recommendation from a pre-professional advisory committee or two
letters from science faculty and a physician letter.

FINANCIAL AID

Financial aid phone number: **(707) 638-5280**
Tuition, 2009-2010 academic year: **$39,000**
Room and board: **$14,798**
Percentage of students receiving financial aid in 2009-10:
   92%
Percentage of students receiving: Loans: **91%**,
   Grants/scholarships: **16%**, Work-study aid: **8%**
Average medical school debt for the class of 2008:
   $156,000

STUDENT BODY

Fall 2009 full-time enrollment: **540**
Men: **N/A**, Women: **N/A**, In-state: **N/A**, Minorities: **N/A**,
   American Indian: **N/A**, Asian-American: **N/A**, African-
   American: **N/A**, Hispanic-American: **N/A**, White: **N/A**,
   International: **N/A**, Unknown: **N/A**

ACADEMIC PROGRAMS

The school's curriculum occasionally give first-year students substantial contact with patients.

There are opportunities for first- or second-year students to work in community health clinics.

Program areas: AIDS, drug/alcohol abuse, family medicine, geriatrics, internal medicine, pediatrics, rural medicine

Joint degrees awarded: D.O./M.P.H.

Total National Institutes of Health (NIH) grants awarded to the medical school and affiliated hospitals: N/A

CURRICULUM
(TEXT PROVIDED BY MEDICAL SCHOOL):

TUCOM-CA students take courses in all subject areas one would expect any physician to master Our goal is to prepare students for the realities of medicine as it presently exists, as well as how it is likely to be in the future. Practice in problem-solving is part of the daily classroom clinical experience as we strive to deliver a curriculum consistent with emerging directions of healthcare.

FALL 2009 FACULTY PROFILE

Total teaching faculty: 70 (full-time), 6 (part-time)

Of full-time faculty, those teaching in basic sciences: 47%; in clinical programs: 53%

Of part-time faculty, those teaching in basic sciences: N/A; in clinical programs: 100%

Full-time faculty/student ratio: 0.1

SUPPORT SERVICES

The school offers students these services for dealing with stress: expanded-hour gym access, peer counseling, professional counseling, religious support, support groups.

RESIDENCY PROFILE

Most popular residency and specialty programs chosen by the 2008 and 2009 M.D. graduating classes: emergency medicine, family practice, internal medicine, obstetrics and gynecology, pediatrics.

WHERE GRADS GO

56.0%
Proportion of 2007-2008 graduates who entered primary care specialties

47.0%
Proportion of 2008-2009 graduates who accepted in-state residencies

Univ. of Med. and Dent. of New Jersey
Stratford

- 1 Medical Center Drive, Stratford, NJ 08084-1501
- Public
- Year Founded: 1977
- Tuition, 2009-2010: In-state: $29,178; Out-of-State: $43,990
- Enrollment 2009-2010 academic year: 463
- Website: http://som.umdnj.edu
- Specialty ranking: geriatrics: 20

3.54 AVERAGE GPA, ENTERING CLASS FALL 2009

9.0 AVERAGE MCAT, ENTERING CLASS FALL 2009

6.2% ACCEPTANCE RATE, ENTERING CLASS FALL 2009

Unranked 2011 U.S. NEWS MEDICAL SCHOOL RANKING (RESEARCH)

Unranked 2011 U.S. NEWS MEDICAL SCHOOL RANKING (PRIMARY CARE)

ADMISSIONS
Admissions phone number: (856) 566-7050
Admissions email address: somadm@umdnj.edu
Application web site: https://aacomas.aacom.org/
Acceptance rate: 6.2%
In-state acceptance rate: 31.9%
Out-of-state acceptance rate: 1.8%
Minority acceptance rate: 6.0%
International acceptance rate: N/A

Fall 2009 applications and acceptees

Type	Applied	Interviewed	Accepted	Enrolled
Total:	3,669	362	227	135
In-state:	536	275	171	111
Out-of-state:	3,133	87	56	24

Profile of admitted students
Average undergraduate grade point average: 3.54
MCAT averages (scale: 1-15; writing test: J-T):
Composite score: 9.0
Verbal reasoning score: 8.7, Physical sciences score: 8.8, Biological score: 9.5, Writing score: Q
Proportion with undergraduate majors in: Biological sciences: 48%, Physical sciences: 16%, Non-sciences: 8%, Other health professions: 9%, Mixed disciplines and other: 19%
Percentage of students not coming directly from college after graduation: 64%

Dates and details
The American Medical College Application Service (AMCAS) application is not accepted.
School asks for a second, school-specific application as part of the admissions process.
Oldest MCAT considered for Fall 2011 entry: 2006
Earliest application date for the 2011-2012 first-year class: 05/01
Latest application date: 02/01
Acceptance dates for regular application for the class entering in Fall 2011.
Earliest: 17-SEP-10

Latest: 29-APR-11
Applicants have 2 weeks to respond to admissions offer.
The school does consider requests for deferred entrance.
Starting month for the class of 2011–2012: August
The school doesn't have an Early Decision Plan (EDP).
A personal interview is required for admission.

Undergraduate coursework required
Medical school requires undergraduate work in these subjects: biology, English, organic chemistry, inorganic (general) chemistry, physics, mathematics, behavioral science.

ADMISSIONS POLICY
(TEXT PROVIDED BY SCHOOL):
Applicants must submit MCATs and premedical committee letter. Accepted students must have baccalaureate degree upon matriculation to UMDNJSOM. Applicants may complete online application through AACOMAS and must be submitted between 6/1 of that year and 2/1 of the year of desired admission. Must be U.S. citizen/permanent resident at time of application. Out-of-state students encouraged to apply.

FINANCIAL AID
Financial aid phone number: (856) 566-6008
Tuition, 2009-2010 academic year: In-state: $29,178; Out-of-State: $43,990
Room and board: $13,650
Percentage of students receiving financial aid in 2009-10: N/A
Percentage of students receiving: Loans: N/A, Grants/scholarships: N/A, Work-study aid: N/A
Average medical school debt for the class of 2008: $138,227

STUDENT BODY
Fall 2009 full-time enrollment: 463
Men: 44%, Women: 56%, In-state: 95%, Minorities: 51%, American Indian: 0.0%, Asian-American: 22.0%, African-American: 14.9%, Hispanic-American: 7.1%, White: 48.6%, International: 0.0%, Unknown: 7.3%

ACADEMIC PROGRAMS

The school's curriculum frequently give first-year students substantial contact with patients.

There are opportunities for first- or second-year students to work in community health clinics.

Program areas: AIDS, drug/alcohol abuse, family medicine, geriatrics, internal medicine, pediatrics, rural medicine, women's health

Joint degrees awarded: D.O./Ph.D., D.O./M.B.A., D.O./M.P.H., D.O./J.D., D.O./M.S.

Total National Institutes of Health (NIH) grants awarded to the medical school and affiliated hospitals: **$3.2 million**

CURRICULUM

(TEXT PROVIDED BY MEDICAL SCHOOL):

Curriculum combines case based learning, small groups, cultural competency, interdisciplinary training. Clinical Education Center used for interpersonal, communications, ethics, palliative care, physical diagnosis. Formative, summative assessment of learning. Students have regular input into curricular process. Osteopathic Manipulation integrated. Problem-based learning also offered.

FALL 2009 FACULTY PROFILE

Total teaching faculty: **192 (full-time), 34 (part-time)**

Of full-time faculty, those teaching in basic sciences: **18%**; in clinical programs: **82%**

Of part-time faculty, those teaching in basic sciences: **12%**; in clinical programs: **88%**

Full-time faculty/student ratio: **0.4**

SUPPORT SERVICES

The school offers students these services for dealing with stress: expanded-hour gym access, professional counseling

RESIDENCY PROFILE

Most popular residency and specialty programs chosen by the 2008 and 2009 M.D. graduating classes: anesthesiology, emergency medicine, family practice, internal medicine, obstetrics and gynecology, pediatrics, physical medicine and rehabilitation, psychiatry, radiology–diagnostic, internal medicine/emergency medicine.

WHERE GRADS GO

49.5%

Proportion of 2007-2008 graduates who entered primary care specialties

39.8%

Proportion of 2008-2009 graduates who accepted in-state residencies

University of New England

■ 11 Hills Beach Road, Biddeford, ME 04005
■ Private
■ Year Founded: 1978
■ Tuition, 2009-2010: $43,755
■ Enrollment 2009-2010 academic year: 495
■ Website: http://www.une.edu/com/
■ Specialty ranking: geriatrics: 20, rural medicine: 17

3.45 AVERAGE GPA, ENTERING CLASS FALL 2009

8.9 AVERAGE MCAT, ENTERING CLASS FALL 2009

6.3% ACCEPTANCE RATE, ENTERING CLASS FALL 2009

Unranked 2011 U.S. NEWS MEDICAL SCHOOL RANKING (RESEARCH)

Unranked 2011 U.S. NEWS MEDICAL SCHOOL RANKING (PRIMARY CARE)

ADMISSIONS

Admissions phone number: **(800) 477-4863**
Admissions email address: **unecomadmissions@une.edu**
Application web site: **https://aacomas.aacom.org**
Acceptance rate: **6.3%**
In-state acceptance rate: **43.1%**
Out-of-state acceptance rate: **5.6%**
Minority acceptance rate: **1.8%**
International acceptance rate: **N/A**

Fall 2009 applications and acceptees

Type	Applied	Interviewed	Accepted	Enrolled
Total:	3,385	284	213	124
In-state:	65	48	28	24
Out-of-state:	3,320	236	185	100

Profile of admitted students

Average undergraduate grade point average: **3.45**
MCAT averages (scale: 1-15; writing test: J-T):
Composite score: **8.9**
Verbal reasoning score: **9.1**, Physical sciences score: **8.5**,
  Biological score: **9.2**, Writing score: **Q**
Proportion with undergraduate majors in: Biological
  sciences: **45%**, Physical sciences: **23%**, Non-sciences:
  12%, Other health professions: **6%**, Mixed disciplines
  and other: **14%**
Percentage of students not coming directly from college
  after graduation: **68%**

Dates and details

The American Medical College Application Service
  (AMCAS) application is not accepted.
School asks for a second, school-specific application as part
  of the admissions process.
Oldest MCAT considered for Fall 2011 entry: **2008**
Earliest application date for the 2011-2012 first-year class:
  05/01
Latest application date: **02/01**
Acceptance dates for regular application for the class
  entering in Fall 2011.
Earliest: **01-SEP-10**

Latest: **10-AUG-11**
Applicants have 4 weeks to respond to admissions offer.
The school does consider requests for deferred entrance.
Starting month for the class of 2011–2012: **August**
The school doesn't have an Early Decision Plan (EDP).
A personal interview is required for admission.

Undergraduate coursework required

Medical school requires undergraduate work in these subjects: biology, biology/zoology, English, organic chemistry,
inorganic (general) chemistry, physics, biochemistry, general chemistry.

ADMISSIONS POLICY
(TEXT PROVIDED BY SCHOOL):

Academic record and scholastic ability; exposure to and
experience in health care and human services; leadership,
community service and/or research experience; interest in
practicing primary care, practicing in New England and/or
working in underserved communities; and the maturity and
desire to work collaboratively with classmates, faculty,
health care providers and patients.

FINANCIAL AID

Financial aid phone number: **(207) 283-0171**
Tuition, 2009-2010 academic year: **$43,755**
Room and board: **$12,000**
Percentage of students receiving financial aid in 2009-10:
  95%
Percentage of students receiving: Loans: **88%**,
  Grants/scholarships: **23%**, Work-study aid: **0%**
Average medical school debt for the class of 2008:
  $205,014

STUDENT BODY

Fall 2009 full-time enrollment: **495**
Men: **47%**, Women: **53%**, In-state: **19%**, Minorities: **8%**,
  American Indian: **0.0%**, Asian-American: **6.9%**,
  African-American: **0.8%**, Hispanic-American: **0.6%**,
  White: **80.6%**, International: **0.4%**, Unknown: **10.7%**

ACADEMIC PROGRAMS

The school's curriculum frequently give first-year students substantial contact with patients.

There are opportunities for first- or second-year students to work in community health clinics.

Program areas: AIDS, drug/alcohol abuse, family medicine, geriatrics, internal medicine, pediatrics, rural medicine, women's health

Joint degrees awarded: D.O./M.P.H., D.O./M.S.

Total National Institutes of Health (NIH) grants awarded to the medical school and affiliated hospitals: **$.0 million**

CURRICULUM

(TEXT PROVIDED BY MEDICAL SCHOOL):

Please see:

http://www.une.edu/com/curriculum/index.cfm and
http://www.une.edu/com/clinical/

FALL 2009 FACULTY PROFILE

Total teaching faculty: 58 **(full-time)**, 560 **(part-time)**

Of full-time faculty, those teaching in basic sciences: **31%**; in clinical programs: **69%**

Of part-time faculty, those teaching in basic sciences: **2%**; in clinical programs: **98%**

Full-time faculty/student ratio: **0.1**

SUPPORT SERVICES

The school offers students these services for dealing with stress: expanded-hour gym access, peer counseling, professional counseling.

RESIDENCY PROFILE

Most popular residency and specialty programs chosen by the 2008 and 2009 M.D. graduating classes: anesthesiology, emergency medicine, family practice, internal medicine, obstetrics and gynecology, pediatrics, physical medicine and rehabilitation, psychiatry, surgery–general.

WHERE GRADS GO

63.0%

Proportion of 2007-2008 graduates who entered primary care specialties

16.4%

Proportion of 2008-2009 graduates who accepted in-state residencies

University of North Texas
Health Science Center

- 3500 Camp Bowie Boulevard, Fort Worth, TX 76107-2699
- Public
- Year Founded: 1966
- Tuition, 2009-2010: In-state: $14,877; Out-of-State: $30,627
- Enrollment 2009-2010 academic year: 685
- Website: http://www.hsc.unt.edu
- Specialty ranking: family medicine: 11, geriatrics: 15, rural medicine: 22

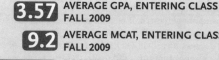

3.57	AVERAGE GPA, ENTERING CLASS FALL 2009
9.2	AVERAGE MCAT, ENTERING CLASS FALL 2009
20.4%	ACCEPTANCE RATE, ENTERING CLASS FALL 2009
Unranked	2011 U.S. NEWS MEDICAL SCHOOL RANKING (RESEARCH)
19	2011 U.S. NEWS MEDICAL SCHOOL RANKING (PRIMARY CARE)

ADMISSIONS

Admissions phone number: **(800) 535-8266**
Admissions email address:
TCOMAdmissions@hsc.unt.edu
Application web site:
http://www.hsc.unt.edu/education/tcom/Admissions.cfm
Acceptance rate: **20.4%**
In-state acceptance rate: **21.7%**
Out-of-state acceptance rate: **11.4%**
Minority acceptance rate: **19.0%**
International acceptance rate: **12.5%**

Fall 2009 applications and acceptees

Type	Applied	Interviewed	Accepted	Enrolled
Total:	2,045	640	418	186
In-state:	1,791	587	389	173
Out-of-state:	254	53	29	13

Profile of admitted students

Average undergraduate grade point average: **3.57**
MCAT averages (scale: 1-15; writing test: J-T):
Composite score: **9.2**
Verbal reasoning score: **9.0**, Physical sciences score: **8.9**, Biological score: **9.8**, Writing score: **P**
Proportion with undergraduate majors in: Biological sciences: **68%**, Physical sciences: **8%**, Non-sciences: **11%**, Other health professions: **10%**, Mixed disciplines and other: **3%**
Percentage of students not coming directly from college after graduation: **37%**

Dates and details

The American Medical College Application Service (AMCAS) application is not accepted.
School asks for a second, school-specific application as part of the admissions process.
Oldest MCAT considered for Fall 2011 entry: **2006**
Earliest application date for the 2011-2012 first-year class: **05/01**
Latest application date: **10/01**

Acceptance dates for regular application for the class entering in Fall 2011.
Earliest: **15-OCT-10**
Latest: **15-JUL-11**
Applicants have 2 weeks to respond to admissions offer.
The school does consider requests for deferred entrance.
Starting month for the class of 2011-2012: **July**
The school does have an Early Decision Plan (EDP).
A personal interview is required for admission.

Undergraduate coursework required

Medical school requires undergraduate work in these subjects: biology, biology/zoology, English, organic chemistry, inorganic (general) chemistry, physics, mathematics, demonstration of writing skills, calculus, general chemistry.

ADMISSIONS POLICY
(TEXT PROVIDED BY SCHOOL):

Applicants are evaluated on a variety of characteristics such as performance in course work, test scores, motivation, socioeconomic background, interview scores, letters of evaluation and ability to contribute to the diversity of the class. Only selected applicants are invited to campus for interviews. At least ninety-percent of the incoming class must be from the Texas resident applicant pool.

FINANCIAL AID

Financial aid phone number: **(800) 346-8266**
Tuition, 2009-2010 academic year: **In-state: $14,877; Out-of-State: $30,627**
Room and board: **$15,125**
Percentage of students receiving financial aid in 2009-10: **90%**
Percentage of students receiving: Loans: **88%**, Grants/scholarships: **53%**, Work-study aid: **2%**
Average medical school debt for the class of 2008: **$114,454**

STUDENT BODY

Fall 2009 full-time enrollment: **685**

Men: 54%, Women: 46%, In-state: 96%, Minorities: 45%, American Indian: 0.6%, Asian-American: 31.7%, African-American: 2.6%, Hispanic-American: 9.6%, White: 53.6%, International: 0.7%, Unknown: 1.2%

ACADEMIC PROGRAMS

The school's curriculum frequently give first-year students substantial contact with patients.

There are opportunities for first- or second-year students to work in community health clinics.

Program areas: AIDS, drug/alcohol abuse, family medicine, geriatrics, internal medicine, pediatrics, rural medicine, women's health

Joint degrees awarded: D.O./Ph.D., D.O./M.P.H., D.O./M.S.

Total National Institutes of Health (NIH) grants awarded to the medical school and affiliated hospitals: **$18.9 million**

CURRICULUM

(TEXT PROVIDED BY MEDICAL SCHOOL):

The TCOM curriculum is a hybrid model that includes early student clinical exposure and application based learning theory. Using interactive clinical learning sessions, students receive the best of case based, problem based, systems based, and traditional medical education curriculum.

FALL 2009 FACULTY PROFILE

Total teaching faculty: **410 (full-time)**, **54 (part-time)**

Of full-time faculty, those teaching in basic sciences: **17%**; in clinical programs: **83%**

Of part-time faculty, those teaching in basic sciences: **9%**; in clinical programs: **91%**

Full-time faculty/student ratio: **0.6**

SUPPORT SERVICES

The school offers students these services for dealing with stress: expanded-hour gym access, peer counseling, professional counseling, religious support, support groups.

RESIDENCY PROFILE

Most popular residency and specialty programs chosen by the 2008 and 2009 M.D. graduating classes: anesthesiology, emergency medicine, family practice, internal medicine, obstetrics and gynecology, pathology–anatomic and clinical, pediatrics, psychiatry, surgery–general, transitional year.

WHERE GRADS GO

68.6%

Proportion of 2007-2008 graduates who entered primary care specialties

61.1%

Proportion of 2008-2009 graduates who accepted in-state residencies

Western University of Health Sciences

- 309 E. Second Street, Pomona, CA 91766-1854
- Private
- Year Founded: 1977
- Tuition, 2009-2010: $43,340
- Enrollment 2009-2010 academic year: 874
- Website: http://prospective.westernu.edu/index.html
- Specialty ranking: N/A

3.56 AVERAGE GPA, ENTERING CLASS FALL 2009

9.3 AVERAGE MCAT, ENTERING CLASS FALL 2009

14.2% ACCEPTANCE RATE, ENTERING CLASS FALL 2009

Unranked 2011 U.S. NEWS MEDICAL SCHOOL RANKING (RESEARCH)

Unranked 2011 U.S. NEWS MEDICAL SCHOOL RANKING (PRIMARY CARE)

ADMISSIONS

Admissions phone number: **(909) 469-5335**
Admissions email address: **admissions@westernu.edu**
Application web site: **http://www.aacom.org**
Acceptance rate: **14.2%**
In-state acceptance rate: **22.9%**
Out-of-state acceptance rate: **10.5%**
Minority acceptance rate: **12.4%**
International acceptance rate: **100.0%**

Fall 2009 applications and acceptees

Type	Applied	Interviewed	Accepted	Enrolled
Total:	3,903	716	553	222
In-state:	1,161	360	266	151
Out-of-state:	2,742	356	287	71

Profile of admitted students

Average undergraduate grade point average: **3.56**
MCAT averages (scale: 1-15; writing test: J-T):
Composite score: **9.3**
Verbal reasoning score: **8.6**, Physical sciences score: **9.3**,
  Biological score: **9.9**, Writing score: **O**
Proportion with undergraduate majors in: Biological
  sciences: **58%**, Physical sciences: **7%**, Non-sciences: **15%**,
  Other health professions: **12%**, Mixed disciplines and
  other: **8%**
Percentage of students not coming directly from college
  after graduation: **N/A**

Dates and details

The American Medical College Application Service
  (AMCAS) application is not accepted.
School asks for a second, school-specific application as part
  of the admissions process.
Oldest MCAT considered for Fall 2011 entry: **N/A**
Earliest application date for the 2011-2012 first-year class:
  N/A
Latest application date: **N/A**
Acceptance dates for regular application for the class
  entering in Fall 2011.
Earliest: **31-DEC-69**

Latest: **31-DEC-69**
Applicants have 12 weeks to respond to admissions offer.
The school does consider requests for deferred entrance.
Starting month for the class of 2011-2012: **August**
The school doesn't have an Early Decision Plan (EDP).
A personal interview is required for admission.

Undergraduate coursework required

Medical school requires undergraduate work in these subjects: biology/zoology, English, organic chemistry, inorganic
(general) chemistry, physics, behavioral science.

ADMISSIONS POLICY
(TEXT PROVIDED BY SCHOOL):

COMP accepts applications from qualified candidates.
While grades and MCAT scores are important and suggest
future academic success, COMP recognizes that these do
not guarantee success as a physician. Non-academic criteria
are also important. COMP seeks a diverse and balanced student population. An on-campus interview is required.

FINANCIAL AID

Financial aid phone number: **(909) 469-5350**
Tuition, 2009-2010 academic year: **$43,340**
Room and board: **$12,942**
Percentage of students receiving financial aid in 2009-10:
  93%
Percentage of students receiving: Loans: **90%**,
  Grants/scholarships: **49%**, Work-study aid: **0%**
Average medical school debt for the class of 2008:
  $191,254

STUDENT BODY

Fall 2009 full-time enrollment: **874**
Men: **53%**, Women: **47%**, In-state: **61%**, Minorities: **45%**,
  American Indian: **0.2%**, Asian-American: **40.5%**,
  African-American: **0.7%**, Hispanic-American: **3.0%**,
  White: **46.2%**, International: **1.8%**, Unknown: **7.6%**

ACADEMIC PROGRAMS

The school's curriculum frequently give first-year students substantial contact with patients.

There are opportunities for first- or second-year students to work in community health clinics.

Program areas: AIDS, drug/alcohol abuse, family medicine, geriatrics, internal medicine, pediatrics, rural medicine, women's health

Joint degrees awarded: D.O./M.S.

Total National Institutes of Health (NIH) grants awarded to the medical school and affiliated hospitals: **$.7 million**

CURRICULUM
(TEXT PROVIDED BY MEDICAL SCHOOL):

The curriculum is divided into three phases: Introduction to the basic sciences; correlated system teaching, incorporating basic and clinical sciences in the study of the organ systems of the body; clinical experiences.

FALL 2009 FACULTY PROFILE

Total teaching faculty: **57 (full-time)**, **0 (part-time)**
Of full-time faculty, those teaching in basic sciences: **56%**; in clinical programs: **44%**

Of part-time faculty, those teaching in basic sciences: **N/A**; in clinical programs: **N/A**
Full-time faculty/student ratio: **0.1**

SUPPORT SERVICES

The school offers students these services for dealing with stress: expanded-hour gym access, peer counseling, professional counseling, religious support, support groups.

RESIDENCY PROFILE

Most popular residency and specialty programs chosen by the 2008 and 2009 M.D. graduating classes: anesthesiology, emergency medicine, family practice, internal medicine, obstetrics and gynecology, pediatrics, physical medicine and rehabilitation, psychiatry, radiology–diagnostic, surgery–general.

WHERE GRADS GO

50.0%

Proportion of 2007-2008 graduates who entered primary care specialties

42.0%

Proportion of 2008-2009 graduates who accepted in-state residencies

West Virginia
School of Osteopathic Medicine

- 400 N. Lee Street, Lewisburg, WV 24901
- Public
- **Year Founded:** 1972
- **Tuition, 2009-2010:** In-state: $20,150; Out-of-State: $50,150
- **Enrollment 2009-2010 academic year:** 778
- **Website:** http://www.wvsom.edu
- **Specialty ranking:** family medicine: 11, rural medicine: 10

3.44 AVERAGE GPA, ENTERING CLASS FALL 2009

8.0 AVERAGE MCAT, ENTERING CLASS FALL 2009

14.5% ACCEPTANCE RATE, ENTERING CLASS FALL 2009

Unranked 2011 U.S. NEWS MEDICAL SCHOOL RANKING (RESEARCH)

Unranked 2011 U.S. NEWS MEDICAL SCHOOL RANKING (PRIMARY CARE)

ADMISSIONS
Admissions phone number: **(800) 356-7836**
Admissions email address: **admissions@wvsom.edu**
Application web site: **http://www.aacom.org**
Acceptance rate: **14.5%**
In-state acceptance rate: **47.7%**
Out-of-state acceptance rate: **13.1%**
Minority acceptance rate: **N/A**
International acceptance rate: **N/A**

Fall 2009 applications and acceptees

Type	Applied	Interviewed	Accepted	Enrolled
Total:	3,297	588	477	193
In-state:	132	77	63	51
Out-of-state:	3,165	511	414	142

Profile of admitted students
Average undergraduate grade point average: **3.44**
MCAT averages (scale: 1-15; writing test: J-T):
Composite score: **8.0**
Verbal reasoning score: **8.0**, Physical sciences score: **7.6**,
   Biological score: **8.5**, Writing score: **M**
Proportion with undergraduate majors in: Biological
   sciences: **64%**, Physical sciences: **16%**, Non-sciences:
   6%, Other health professions: **3%**, Mixed disciplines and
   other: **11%**
Percentage of students not coming directly from college
   after graduation: **28%**

Dates and details
The American Medical College Application Service
   (AMCAS) application is not accepted.
School asks for a second, school-specific application as part
   of the admissions process.
Oldest MCAT considered for Fall 2011 entry: **2008**
Earliest application date for the 2011-2012 first-year class:
   06/01
Latest application date: **02/15**
Acceptance dates for regular application for the class
   entering in Fall 2011.
Earliest: **N/A**

Latest: **N/A**
Applicants have 14 weeks to respond to admissions offer.
The school does consider requests for deferred entrance.
Starting month for the class of 2011-2012: **August**
The school doesn't have an Early Decision Plan (EDP).
A personal interview is required for admission.

Undergraduate coursework required
Medical school requires undergraduate work in these subjects: biology/zoology, English, organic chemistry, inorganic
(general) chemistry, physics.

ADMISSIONS POLICY
(TEXT PROVIDED BY SCHOOL):
   Students are the key to WVSOM's commitment to
improving health care. The Admissions Committee strives
to fill each class with students motivated toward primary
care in rural communities; seeking students who share the
school's commitment to rural health care, as well as aptitude, maturity, ability to relate to people, motivation for
osteopathic medicine, personal conduct, and scholarship.

FINANCIAL AID
Financial aid phone number: **(800) 356-7836**
Tuition, 2009-2010 academic year: **In-state: $20,150; Out-
   of-State: $50,150**
Room and board: **$14,170**
Percentage of students receiving financial aid in 2009-10:
   98%
Percentage of students receiving: Loans: **96%**,
   Grants/scholarships: **18%**, Work-study aid: **7%**
Average medical school debt for the class of 2008:
   $180,630

STUDENT BODY
Fall 2009 full-time enrollment: **778**
Men: **53%**, Women: **47%**, In-state: **28%**, Minorities: **19%**,
   American Indian: **0.4%**, Asian-American: **14.1%**,
   African-American: **1.4%**, Hispanic-American: **3.1%**,
   White: **76.0%**, International: **0.0%**, Unknown: **5.0%**

ACADEMIC PROGRAMS

The school's curriculum frequently give first-year students substantial contact with patients.

There are opportunities for first- or second-year students to work in community health clinics.

Program areas: AIDS, drug/alcohol abuse, family medicine, geriatrics, internal medicine, pediatrics, rural medicine, women's health

Joint degrees awarded: N/A

Total National Institutes of Health (NIH) grants awarded to the medical school and affiliated hospitals: **$.0 million**

CURRICULUM
(TEXT PROVIDED BY MEDICAL SCHOOL):

WVSOM provides a system tract or problem based learning tract for students. Extensive clinical contact is available throughout the program. Objective Structured Clinical Evaluations and extensive use of robotics are components of both tracts. The clinical years are identical for both tracts and utilize clinician preceptors throughout the state as well as clinical settings outside of WV.

FALL 2009 FACULTY PROFILE

Total teaching faculty: **54 (full-time)**, **125 (part-time)**
Of full-time faculty, those teaching in basic sciences: **44%**; in clinical programs: **56%**

Of part-time faculty, those teaching in basic sciences: **0%**; in clinical programs: **100%**
Full-time faculty/student ratio: **0.1**

SUPPORT SERVICES

The school offers students these services for dealing with stress: expanded-hour gym access, peer counseling, professional counseling, religious support, support groups.

RESIDENCY PROFILE

Most popular residency and specialty programs chosen by the 2008 and 2009 M.D. graduating classes: anesthesiology, emergency medicine, family practice, internal medicine, obstetrics and gynecology, orthopaedic surgery, pediatrics, physical medicine and rehabilitation, surgery–general, transitional year.

WHERE GRADS GO

70.3%

Proportion of 2007-2008 graduates who entered primary care specialties

24.7%

Proportion of 2008-2009 graduates who accepted in-state residencies

Additional Schools

Basic contact information for those schools that did not respond to the U.S.News survey is provided below.

ALBANY MEDICAL COLLEGE
- 47 New Scotland Avenue, Albany, NY 12208
- Private
- Year Founded: 1839
- Website: http://www.amc.edu

HOWARD UNIVERSITY
- 520 W. Street NW, Washington, DC 20059
- Private
- Year Founded: 1868
- Website: http://medicine.howard.edu

LOMA LINDA UNIVERSITY
- Loma Linda, CA 92350
- Private
- Website: http://www.llu.edu/

LOUISIANA STATE UNIVERSITY HEALTH SCIENCES CENTER—NEW ORLEANS
- Admissions Office, 1901 Perdido Street, New Orleans, LA 70112-1393
- Public
- Year Founded: 1941
- Website: http://www.medschool.lsumc.edu

MARSHALL UNIVERSITY (EDWARDS)
- 1600 Medical Center Drive, Huntington, WV 25701-3655
- Public
- Year Founded: 1977
- Website: http://musom.marshall.edu

MAYO MEDICAL SCHOOL
- 200 First Street SW, Rochester, MN 55905
- Private
- Year Founded: 1972
- Website: http://www.mayo.edu/mms/

MEDICAL COLLEGE OF GEORGIA
- 1120 15th Street, Augusta, GA 30912-4750
- Public
- Year Founded: 1828
- Website: http://www.mcg.edu/som/index.html

MEHARRY MEDICAL COLLEGE
- 1005 D. B. Todd Jr. Boulevard, Nashville, TN, 37208
- Private
- Year Founded: 1876
- Website: http://www.mmc.edu

PENNSYLVANIA STATE UNIV. COLLEGE OF MED.
- 500 University Drive, Hershey, PA 17033
- Public
- Year Founded: 1967
- Website: http://www.hmc.psu.edu

ROSALIND FRANKLIN UNIVERSITY OF MEDICINE AND SCIENCE
- 3333 Green Bay Road, North Chicago, IL 60064
- Private
- Year Founded: 1912
- Website: http://www.rosalindfranklin.edu

SUNY DOWNSTATE MEDICAL CENTER
- 450 Clarkson Avenue, Box 60, Brooklyn, NY 11203
- Public
- Year Founded: 1860
- Website: http://www.hscbklyn.edu

TULANE UNIVERSITY
- 1430 Tulane Avenue, SL67, New Orleans, LA 70112-2699
- Private
- Year Founded: 1834
- Website: http://www.mcl.tulane.edu

UNIVERSITY OF ILLINOIS—CHICAGO
- 1853 W. Polk Street, M/C 784, Chicago, IL 60612
- Public
- Year Founded: 1881
- Website: http://www.uic.edu/depts/mcam

UNIVERSITY OF MEDICINE AND DENTISTRY OF NEW JERSEY—NEWARK
- 185 S. Orange Avenue, PO Box 1709, Newark, NJ 07101-1709
- Public
- Year Founded: 1954
- Website: http://www.njms.umdnj.edu

UNIVERSITY OF MISSISSIPPI
- 2500 N. State Street, Jackson, MS 39216-4505
- Public
- Year Founded: 1903
- Website: http://www.umc.edu

UNIVERSITY OF MISSOURI—KANSAS CITY
- 2411 Holmes, Kansas City, MO 64108
- Public
- Year Founded: 1971
- Website: http://www.med.umkc.edu

UNIVERSITY OF SOUTH ALABAMA

- 307 University Boulevard, 170 CSAB, Mobile, AL 36688
- Public
- Website: http://southmed.usouthal.edu/

KANSAS CITY UNIVERSITY OF MEDICINE AND BIOSCIENCES

- 1750 Independence Avenue, Kansas City, MO 64106-1453
- Private
- Year Founded: 1916
- Website: http://www.uhs.edu

MIDWESTERN UNIVERSITY–DOWNERS GROVE

- 555 31st Street, Downers Grove, IL 60515
- Private
- Year Founded: 1900
- Website: http://www.midwestern.edu

MIDWESTERN UNIVERSITY–GLENDALE

- 19555 N. 59th Avenue, Glendale, AZ 85308
- Private
- Year Founded: 1995
- Website: http://www.midwestern.edu

NEW YORK INSTITUTE OF TECHNOLOGY

- Old Westbury, Northern Blvd, Long Island, NY 11568
- Private
- Year Founded: 1977
- Website: http://www.nyit.edu

PHILADELPHIA COLLEGE OF OSTEOPATHIC MEDICINE

- 4170 City Avenue, Philadelphia, PA 19131
- Private
- Year Founded: 1899
- Website: http://www.pcom.edu

Resources for Late Starters

Postbaccalaureate programs for nonscientists

What if you come late to your decision to apply to med school and have little or no science background? Here are several highly regarded postbaccalaureate programs designed to help career-changers make their dreams come true. They offer all the science courses you'll need as well as advice and support when it comes time to apply to medical school; students who successfully complete the coursework are "sponsored" by the program, meaning the program vouches for their readiness to go on. (For a complete list of postbac premed programs, go to www.aamc.org.) Once you complete a program, it usually takes another year to apply to medical school, unless the program has "linkage" with one or more medical schools—an arrangement that allows qualified students to go directly to those med schools when they complete the postbac program.

BRYN MAWR COLLEGE

Canwyll House
101 North Merion Avenue
Bryn Mawr, PA 19010-2899
(610) 526-7350
Website: www.brynmawr.edu/postbac
Year started: 1972
Description: One-year program. Full-time, days only. Three courses per semester. Each usually has a laboratory. Classes are predominantly postbac classes although some are open to undergrads.
Enrollment: 87
Admissions requirements: Minimum undergraduate GPA of 3.3; standardized testing required. Interview required for competitive applicants.
Acceptance rate: 60%
Average MCAT score of those who apply to medical school: 31.5
Acceptance rate into medical school in 2009: 100% (over past 5 years: 98%)
Tuition: $3,635 per course; $3,510 summer
Financial aid: (610) 526-5267
Linkage with: Brown University School of Medicine, Dartmouth Medical College, Drexel University College of Medicine, George Washington University School of Medicine, Jefferson Medical College, SUNY at Downstate College of Medicine, SUNY Stony Brook School of Medicine, Health Sciences Center, Temple University School of Medicine, University of Rochester School of Medicine

COLUMBIA UNIVERSITY

Lewisohn Hall, Room 408
Mail Code 4101
2970 Broadway
New York, NY 10027
(212) 854-2772
Website: www.gs.columbia.edu/postbac/
Year started: 1955
Description: Two-year program. Full-time or part-time, days or evenings. General chemistry prerequisite for both bio and organic chemistry. Minimum 120 hours of clinical volunteer work; 18–20 hours research volunteer work required. Postbac students are mixed with undergrad premed students.
Enrollment: 400+

Admissions requirements: Minimum undergraduate GPA of 3.0; standardized testing, if taken, must be submitted. Interview not required.

Acceptance rate into program: 50–60%

Average MCAT score of those sponsored: 31

Acceptance rate into medical school of those sponsored in 2001 (last year available): 92%

Tuition: $1,270 per credit (need 20 credits to get certificate). Full program is 38 credits: $48,260.

Financial aid: (212) 854-5410

Linkage with: Ben Gurion University of the Negev; Brown University School of Medicine; Jefferson Medical College of Thomas Jefferson University; Drexel University College of Medicine; National University of Ireland, University College, Cork; New York Medical College; SUNY Brooklyn School of Medicine; SUNY Stony Brook School of Medicine; Temple University School of Medicine; Trinity College–Dublin; UMDNJ–New Jersey Medical School; UMDNJ–Robert Wood Johnson Medical School

GOUCHER COLLEGE

Postbaccalaureate Premedical Program
1021 Dulaney Valley Road
Baltimore, MD 21204-2794
(800) 414-3437

Website: www.goucher.edu/postbac

Year started: 1980

Description: One-year program. Full-time, days only. Classes separate from undergrads. Three courses per semester; intensive general chemistry over the summer. Volunteer work required.

Enrollment: 25–30

Admissions requirements: Standardized testing required. Interview required.

Acceptance rate into program: 20–30%

Average MCAT score of those sponsored: 32

Acceptance rate into medical school in 2009: 100%

Tuition: $750 per credit. The typical curriculum consists of 34 credits, bringing total tuition to $25,500.

Financial aid: (410) 337-6430

Linkage with: Brown Medical School, George Washington University School of Medicine, Drexel University School of Medicine, SUNY Stony Brook School of Medicine, Temple University School of Medicine, Tulane University School of Medicine, University of Pittsburgh School of Medicine

HARVARD UNIVERSITY

Health Careers Program
Harvard University Extension School
51 Brattle Street
Cambridge, MA 02138
(617) 495-2926

Website: www.extension.harvard.edu/hcp

Year started: 1980

Description: Two-year program, part-time evenings only. Postbac students are separated from undergrad premed students. Standard load is two courses per term. Students expected to find patient-contact work, either paid or volunteer.

Enrollment: 200+

Admissions requirements: Minimum undergraduate GPA of 3.0, no standardized test required. No interview required.

Acceptance rate into program: 90%

Average MCAT score of those sponsored: 32

Acceptance rate into medical school in 2009: 89%

Tuition: $200+ per credit

Financial aid: (617) 495-4293

JOHNS HOPKINS UNIVERSITY

3400 North Charles Street

Wyman Park Building, Suite G1

Baltimore, MD 21218

(410) 516-7748

Website: www.jhu.edu/postbac

Description: One-year program. Full-time, days only. Four or five courses with no more than two lab science courses each semester. Students participate in a "journal club" and "mini-medical school" to learn about and discuss contemporary medical/health care issues. Students engage in a wide choice of clinical activities, including medical tutorials with medical school faculty, structured hospital internships and volunteer programs, and volunteer work in the community. Postbac students are mixed in with undergrad premed students.

Enrollment: 25–30

Admissions requirements: Minimum undergraduate GPA of 3.0 plus; standardized testing (SAT, ACT, or GRE) required. Interview required.

Acceptance rate into program: 19%

Average MCAT Score of medical school applicants: approximately 31

Acceptance rate into medical school of applicants in 2009: 100%

Tuition: $29,364 ($630 per credit)

Financial aid: (410) 516-4688

Linkage with: George Washington University School of Medicine, UMDNJ–Robert Wood Johnson Medical School, and University of Rochester

MILLS COLLEGE

5000 MacArthur Boulevard

Oakland, CA 94613

(510) 430-2317

Website: www.mills.edu

Year started: 1979

Description: One- or two-year program. Full-time or part-time, days only. Students take two or three courses per semester. Volunteer work not required, but encouraged. Postbac students are separated from undergrad premed students.

Enrollment: 50-60

Admissions requirements: Minimum undergraduate GPA of 3.0; standardized testing required. No interview required.

Acceptance rate into program: Varies considerably from year to year; approximately 75%

Average MCAT score of those sponsored: 31

Acceptance rate into medical school for those sponsored in 2009: 87.5%

Tuition: $25,960 ($6,490 per credit)

Financial aid: Need to respond on application; Mills College will not discuss aid over the phone.

Linkage with: Tulane University Medical School

SCRIPPS COLLEGE W.M. KECK SCIENCE CENTER

925 N. Mills Avenue

Claremont, CA 91711

(909) 621-8764

Website:

www.scrippscollege.edu/academics/postbac

Year started: 1994

Description: One- or two-year program. Full-time or part-time, days only. Postbac students are mixed with undergrad premed students. Students in the one-year program take three or four courses per semester and two summer courses each summer. Students in the two-year program take two courses per semester and are required to work at least 20 hours a week. Internships and volunteer work required.

Enrollment: 12-15

Admissions requirements: Minimum undergraduate GPA of 3.0; standardized testing required. Interview required.

Acceptance rate into program: 27%

Average MCAT score of those sponsored: 31.2

Acceptance rate into medical school for those sponsored in 2009: 100%

Tuition: $20,000–$26,000 per year, depending on number of courses

Financial aid: (909) 621-8275

Linkage with: University of Pittsburgh School of Medicine, Drexel University School of Medicine, George Washington School of Medicine, Temple University School of Medicine, Western University School of Medicine, College of Osteopathic Medicine of the Pacific

TUFTS UNIVERSITY

419 Boston Ave. Dowling Hall

Medford, MA 02155

(617) 627-2321

Website: http://studentservices.tufts.edu/postbac

Year started: 1988

Description: 11 to 20 months depending on student. Full-time, days only. Two laboratory science courses per semester and other electives available. Volunteer or paid part-time work recommended. Postbac students are mixed in with undergrad premed students.

Enrollment: 40

Admissions requirements: Minimum undergraduate GPA of 3.0; standardized testing required. No interview required.

Acceptance rate into program: 30–40%

Average MCAT score of those sponsored: 30–31

Acceptance rate into medical school of those sponsored in 2009: 90%

Tuition: $25,250 (one-time fee)

Financial aid: Once admitted, students can discuss it with counselors.

Linkage with: Tufts University School of Medicine and University of New England College of Osteopathic Medicine

UNIVERSITY OF PENNSYLVANIA

3440 Market Street, Suite 100

College of General Studies

Philadelphia, PA 19104-3335

(215) 898-3110

Website: www.sas.upenn.edu/CGS/postbac/premed

Year started: 1977

Description: One- or two-year program. Full-time or part-time, days, or evenings. Postbac students are separated from undergrad premed students.

Enrollment: 50–70

Admissions requirements: Minimum undergraduate GPA of 3.0; standardized testing required. Interview required.

Acceptance rate into program: N/A

Average MCAT score of those sponsored: N/A

Acceptance rate into medical school of those sponsored in 2009: 100%

Tuition: $11,015 per academic year

Financial aid: www.sfs.upenn.edu/home

Linkage with: George Washington University School of Medicine, Jefferson Medical College, Drexel University College of Medicine, Temple University School of Medicine, UMDNJ–Robert Wood Johnson School of Medicine, University of Pittsburgh School of Medicine

Overseas Options
Foreign medical schools that welcome Americans

If you don't get into an American medical school, one possible alternate route is a foreign or "off-shore" school that accepts a significant number of U.S. applicants (see Chapter 6). Before you make a choice, be sure you know what you're getting into: Visit the school, find out what kind of program it offers and how many Americans attend, how students do on the United States Medical Licensing Examination (USMLE), and how many end up with residencies in the States. Below is a sampling of programs that accept Americans.

AMERICAN UNIVERSITY OF THE CARIBBEAN SCHOOL OF MEDICINE
Jordan Road
Cupecoy
St. Maarten, N.A.
Admissions: Medical Education Information Office
901 Ponce de Leon Boulevard, Suite 201
Coral Gables, Florida 33134
(866) 372-2282
Website: www.aucmed.edu
Year founded: 1978. AUC offers basic medical sciences in St. Maarten and clinical rotations at affiliated hospitals in the U.S., U.K., and Ireland. Graduates include more than 3,500 licensed physicians practicing in the U.S. Semesters begin in January, May, and September.
Enrollment: 380 in basic sciences; 235 in clinical sciences
Percentage of U.S. citizens (or permanent residents): 88.4
Admissions information: Average GPA: 3.1; average

MCAT: 22
Acceptance rate: 51%
Language: Courses taught in English
Pass rate on USMLE Step 1: N/A
Percentage of first-year residency placements in U.S.: 81.5% (110 of 135 graduates)
Tuition: $14,500 per semester (basic sciences); $16,100 per semester (clinical sciences)
Financial aid: (305) 446-0600, ext. 22 or 23

BEN-GURION UNIVERSITY OF THE NEGEV
Beer Sheva, Israel
M.D. Program in International Health and Medicine in collaboration with Columbia University Medical Center
Admissions: 630 W. 168th Street, PH15E-1512
New York, New York 10032
(212) 305-9587
Website: http://cpmcnet.columbia.edu/dept/bgcu-md
Year founded: 1996
Enrollment: Average entering class size is 30; currently 123 students in the four-year program.
Percentage of U.S. citizens: 66%
Admissions information: Average undergraduate GPA of 3.5 ; average MCAT score: 29. Interview is required.
Acceptance rate: 46%
Language: courses taught in English
Pass rate on USMLE Step 1: more than 95% for U.S. students
Percentage of first-year residency placements in U.S.: 100% in 2009
Tuition: $31,500

Financial aid: American students may use Stafford and alternative loans; and after the first semester, all students may apply for limited scholarships based on financial need.

ROSS UNIVERSITY SCHOOL OF MEDICINE

Dominica, West Indies

Admissions: 499 Thornall St, 10th Floor
Edison, NJ 08837
(732) 978-5300
Website: www.rossu.edu/medical-school/
Year founded: 1978
Enrollment: 2,500 plus
Percentage of U.S. citizens: 93%
Admissions information: Mean undergraduate GPA of 3.25; MCAT score: N/A (though now required). Interview is required.
Acceptance rate: Approximately 55%
Language: Courses taught in English
Pass rate on USMLE Step 1: 88% for first-time test takers; 94% for first- and second-time test takers.
Percentage of first-year residency placements in U.S.: 64.2% through the match; 16.3% prematch; 19.5% outside the match. Typically, 96% of eligible graduates achieve a residency position in the States.
Tuition: $14,665 per semester
Financial aid: (732) 978-5300

ST. GEORGE'S UNIVERSITY MEDICAL SCHOOL

Grenada, West Indies

Admissions: The North American Correspondent c/o University Services, Ltd.
1 East Main Street Bay Shore, NY 11706
(800) 899-6337, ext. 280 or (631) 665-8500
Website: www.sgu.edu
Year founded: 1976
Enrollment: 2,349
Percentage of U.S. citizens: 75%

Admissions information: average undergraduate GPA for the entering class of 3.3; MCAT Score: 24. Interview required
Language: Courses taught in English
Pass rate on USMLE Step 1: 90%
Percentage of first-year residency placements in U.S.: 99% of those eligible U.S. graduates who applied obtained residency positions in 650 hospitals throughout 50 states.
Tuition: $21,552 (Basic Sciences); $21,755 (Clinical)
Financial aid: 1-631-665-8500, ext. 232

TECHNION-ISRAEL INSTITUTE OF TECHNOLOGY

The Technion American Medical Students (TEAMS) Program
12th Efron St., P.O. Box 9649
Haifa, 31096, Israel
011-972-829-5248
Website: http://teams.technion.ac.il
Year founded: 1983
Enrollment: 60 Americans
Percentage of U.S. citizens: 100% in the TEAMS program (U.S. citizens make up 10–15% of Technion student body).
Admissions information: Average GPA of above 3.4 and average MCAT score of 24 are required Interview is required.
Acceptance rate into program: 70%
Language: Courses taught in English
Pass rate on USMLE Step 1: 98%
Percentage of first-year residency placements in U.S.: 100%
Tuition: $25,000
Financial aid: Federal and private
Attrition rate: Less than 1 percent

TEL AVIV UNIVERSITY SACKLER SCHOOL OF MEDICINE

New York State/American Program
Ramat Aviv Israel
Admissions: 17 E. 62nd Street
New York, NY 10021
(212) 688-8811
Website: www.tau.ac.il/medicine
Year founded: 1976
Enrollment: 300
Percentage of U.S. citizens: 100%
Admissions information: Minimum undergraduate GPA of 3.0. MCAT score: minimum of 8 on each section. Interview required.
Acceptance rate: 50%
Language: Courses are taught in English.
Pass rate on USMLE Step 1: 98%
Percentage of first-year residency placements in U.S.: 100%
Tuition: $22,000
Financial aid: Federal Stafford loan and several private loans

UNIVERSIDAD AUTÓNOMA DE GUADALAJARA

Av. Patria # 1201, Lomas del Valle, 3a. Sección
Guadalajara, Jalisco, México C.P. 44100
Admissions: 4715 Fredericksburg Road, Suite 300, San Antonio, TX 78229
(800) 531-5494
20 Corporate Woods Boulevard, Suite 205, Albany, NY 12211- 2370
(866) 434-7392
Website: www.uag.mx
Year founded: 1935
Enrollment: 4,000 plus
Percentage of U.S. citizens: 20%
Admissions information: Average GPA of 2.9; MCAT: 24. Interview required.
Acceptance rate: 33%
Language: Lectures and some labs taught in English for only the first two years, then Spanish.
Pass rate on USMLE Step 1: 82%
Percentage of first-year residency placements in U.S.: 92%
Tuition: $17,580
Financial aid: Yes

Alphabetical Index of Schools

A.T. Still University of Health
Sciences (Kirksville), 322
Albany Medical College, 352

Baylor College of Medicine, 112
Boston University, 114
Brown University (Alpert), 116

Case Western Reserve Univ., 118
Columbia University, 120
Cornell University (Weill), 122
Creighton University, 124

Dartmouth Medical School, 126
Des Moines University, 324
Drexel University, 128
Duke University, 130

East Carolina Univ. (Brody), 132
East Tennessee State University
(Quillen), 136
Eastern Virginia Med. School, 134
Edward Via Virginia College of
Osteopathic Medicine, 326
Emory University, 138

Florida State University, 140

George Washington Univ., 144
Georgetown University, 142

Harvard University, 146
Howard University, 352

Indiana Univ.–Indianapolis, 148

Jefferson Medical College, 150
Johns Hopkins University, 152

Kansas City University of
Medicine and Biosciences, 353

Lake Erie College of Osteopathic
Medicine, 328
Loma Linda University, 352

Louisiana State Univ. Health Sci.
Center–New Orleans, 352
Louisiana State Univ. Health Sci.
Center–Shreveport, 154
Loyola University Chicago
(Stritch), 156

Marshall Univ. (Edwards), 352
Mayo Medical School, 352
Medical College of Georgia, 352
Medical College of Wisconsin, 158
Medical University of South
Carolina, 160
Meharry Medical College, 352
Mercer University, 162
Michigan State University, 164
Michigan State University College
of Osetopathic Medicine, 330
Midwestern University, 353
Midwestern University, 353
Morehouse School of Med., 166
Mount Sinai School of Med., 168

New York Inst. of Technology, 353
New York Medical College, 170
New York University, 172
Northeastern Ohio Universities
College of Medicine, 174
Northwestern Univ. (Feinberg), 176
Nova Southeastern University, 332

Ohio State University, 178
Ohio University, 334
Oklahoma State University, 336
Oregon Health and Science
University, 180

Pennsylvania State University
College of Medicine, 352
Philadelphia College of
Osteopathic Medicine, 353
Pikeville College, 338

Rosalind Franklin University of
Medicine and Science, 352
Rush University, 182

Southern Illinois University–
Springfield, 184
St. Louis University, 188
Stanford University, 186
Stony Brook University, 190
SUNY Downstate Med. Center, 352
SUNY–Syracuse, 192

Temple University, 194
Texas A&M Health Science
Center, 196
Texas Tech University Health
Sciences Center, 198
Touro University, 340
Tufts University, 200
Tulane University, 352

Uniformed Services Univ. of the
Health Sciences (Hebert), 202
University at Buffalo–SUNY, 204
University of Alabama–
Birmingham, 206
University of Arizona, 208
University of Arkansas for
Medical Sciences, 210
Univ. of California–Davis, 212
Univ. of California–Irvine, 214
University of California–Los
Angeles (Geffen), 216
University of California–San
Diego, 218
University of California–San
Francisco, 220
Univ. of Chicago (Pritzker), 222
University of Cincinnati, 224
Univ. of Colorado–Denver, 226
University of Connecticut, 228
University of Florida, 230
University of Hawaii–Manoa
(Burns), 232
University of Illinois–Chicago, 352
University of Iowa (Carver), 234
University of Kansas Medical
Center, 236
University of Kentucky, 238
University of Louisville, 240

Index of Schools by State

Alabama
University of Alabama–
    Birmingham, 206
University of South Alabama, 353

Arizona
Midwestern University, 353
University of Arizona, 208

Arkansas
University of Arkansas for
    Medical Sciences, 210

California
Loma Linda University, 352
Stanford University, 186
Touro University, 340
Univ. of California–Davis, 212
Univ. of California–Irvine, 214
University of California–Los
    Angeles (Geffen), 216
University of California–San
    Diego, 218
University of California–San
    Francisco, 220
University of Southern California
    (Keck), 278
Western University of Health
    Sciences, 348

Colorado
Univ. of Colorado–Denver, 226

Connecticut
University of Connecticut, 228
Yale University, 318

District of Columbia
George Washington Univ., 144
Georgetown University, 142
Howard University, 352

Florida
Florida State University, 140
Nova Southeastern University, 332
University of Florida, 230

University of Miami (Miller), 248
University of South Florida, 280

Georgia
Emory University, 138
Medical College of Georgia, 352
Mercer University, 162
Morehouse School of Med., 166

Hawaii
University of Hawaii–Manoa
    (Burns), 232

Illinois
Loyola University Chicago
    (Stritch), 156
Midwestern University, 353
Northwestern University
    (Feinberg), 176
Rosalind Franklin University of
    Medicine and Science, 352
Rush University, 182
Southern Illinois University–
    Springfield, 184
Univ. of Chicago (Pritzker), 222
University of Illinois–Chicago, 352

Indiana
Indiana Univ.–Indianapolis, 148

Iowa
Des Moines University, 324
University of Iowa (Carver), 234

Kansas
University of Kansas Medical
    Center, 236

Kentucky
Pikeville College, 338
University of Kentucky, 238
University of Louisville, 240

Louisiana
Louisiana State Univ. Health Sci.
    Center–New Orleans, 352

Louisiana State Univ. Health Sci.
    Center–Shreveport, 154
Tulane University, 352

Maine
University of New England, 344

Maryland
Johns Hopkins University, 152
Uniformed Services Univ. of the
    Health Sciences (Hebert), 202
University of Maryland, 242

Massachusetts
Boston University, 114
Harvard University, 146
Tufts University, 200
University of Massachusetts–
    Worcester, 244

Michigan
Michigan State University, 164
Michigan State University College
    of Osetopathic Medicine, 330
University of Michigan–Ann
    Arbor, 250
Wayne State University, 312

Minnesota
Mayo Medical School, 352
University of Minnesota, 252

Mississippi
University of Mississippi, 352

Missouri
A.T. Still University of Health
    Sciences (Kirksville), 322
Kansas City University of
    Medicine and Biosciences, 353
St. Louis University, 188
University of Missouri, 254
University of Missouri–Kansas
    City, 352
Washington University in St.
    Louis, 310

Nebraska
Creighton University, 124
University of Nebraska Medical
Center, 256

Nevada
University of Nevada–Reno, 258

New Hampshire
Dartmouth Medical School, 126

New Jersey
Univ. of Med. and Dent. of NJ–
New Brunswick (Johnson), 246
Univ. of Med. and Dent. of NJ–
Newark, 352
Univ. of Med. and Dent. of NJ–
Stratford, 342

New Mexico
University of New Mexico, 260

New York
Albany Medical College, 352
Columbia University, 120
Cornell University (Weill), 122
Mount Sinai School of Med., 168
New York Inst. of Technology, 353
New York Medical College, 170
New York University, 172
Stony Brook University, 190
SUNY Downstate Med. Center, 352
SUNY–Syracuse, 192
University at Buffalo–SUNY, 204
University of Rochester, 272
Yeshiva University (Einstein), 320

North Carolina
Duke University, 130
East Carolina Univ. (Brody), 132
University of North Carolina–
Chapel Hill, 262
Wake Forest University, 308

North Dakota
University of North Dakota, 264

Ohio
Case Western Reserve Univ., 118

Northeastern Ohio Universities
College of Medicine, 174
Ohio State University, 178
Ohio University, 334
University of Cincinnati, 224
University of Toledo, 292
Wright State University
(Boonshoft), 316

Oklahoma
Oklahoma State University, 336
University of Oklahoma, 266

Oregon
Oregon Health and Science
University, 180

Pennsylvania
Drexel University, 128
Jefferson Medical College, 150
Lake Erie College of Osteopathic
Medicine, 328
Pennsylvania State University
College of Medicine, 352
Philadelphia College of
Osteopathic Medicine, 353
Temple University, 194
University of Pennsylvania, 268
University of Pittsburgh, 270

Rhode Island
Brown University (Alpert), 116

South Carolina
Medical University of South
Carolina, 160
University of South Carolina, 274

South Dakota
University of South Dakota
(Sanford), 276

Tennessee
East Tennessee State University
(Quillen), 136
Meharry Medical College, 352
University of Tennessee Health
Science Center, 282
Vanderbilt University, 304

Texas
Baylor College of Medicine, 112
Texas A&M Health Science
Center, 196
Texas Tech University Health
Sciences Center, 198
University of North Texas Health
Science Center, 346
University of Texas Health
Science Center–Houston, 284
University of Texas Health Sci.
Center–San Antonio, 286
University of Texas Medical
Branch–Galveston, 288
University of Texas Southwestern
Medical Center–Dallas, 290

Utah
University of Utah, 294

Vermont
University of Vermont, 296

Virginia
Eastern Virginia Med. School, 134
Edward Via Virginia College of
Osteopathic Medicine, 326
University of Virginia, 298
Virginia Commonwealth
University, 306

Washington
University of Washington, 300

West Virginia
Marshall Univ. (Edwards), 352
West Virginia School of
Osteopathic Medicine, 350
West Virginia University, 314

Wisconsin
Medical College of Wisconsin, 158
University of Wisconsin–
Madison, 302

About the Authors & Editors

Founded in 1933, Washington, D.C.–based *U.S.News & World Report* delivers a unique brand of weekly magazine journalism to its 12.2 million readers. In 1983, *U.S. News* began its exclusive annual rankings of American colleges and universities. The *U.S. News* education franchise is second to none, with its annual college and graduate school rankings among the most eagerly anticipated magazine issues in the country.

Josh Fischman, the book's lead writer and editor, covers health and science for *U.S. News & World Report*. Previously, he was editor-in-chief at *Earth*, deputy news editor at *Science*, and a senior editor at *Discover*. He has also cowritten the children's book *101 Things Every Kid Should Know about Dinosaurs*. He has won the Blakeslee Award for excellence in medical reporting from the American Heart Association.

Anne McGrath, editor, is a deputy editor at *U.S.News & World Report*, where she covers health. Previously, she was managing editor of "America's Best Colleges" and "America's Best Graduate Schools," the two *U.S. News* annual publications featuring rankings of the country's colleges and universities.

Robert Morse is the director of data research at *U.S.News & World Report*. He is in charge of the research, data collection, methodologies, and survey design for the annual "America's Best Colleges" rankings and the "America's Best Graduate Schools" rankings.

Brian Kelly is the executive editor of *U.S.News & World Report*. As the magazine's No. 2 editor, he oversees the weekly magazine, the website, and a series of newsstand books. He is a former editor at the *Washington Post* and the author of three books.

Other writers who contributed chapters or passages to the book are **Ulrich Boser**, **Kristin Davis**, **Justin Ewers**, **Helen Fields**, **Dan Gilgoff**, **Vicky Hallett**, **Cory Hatch**, **Bernadine Healy**, **Caroline Hsu**, **Katy Kelly**, **Carolyn Kleiner Butler**, **Samantha Levine**, **Marianne Szegedy-Maszak**, **Stacy Schultz**, **Nancy Shute**, **Rachel K. Sobel**, and **Amanda Spake**. The work involved in producing the directory and *U.S. News* Insider's Index was handled by **Sam Flanigan**. Thanks to **David Griffin** for his work in designing the book and to **Sara Sklaroff** for project editing. Thanks as well to **James Bock** for his copyediting assistance and to members of the **factchecking team** for making sure we got it right.

Notes

Notes

Notes